FEDERAL REORGANIZATION: THE EXECUTIVE BRANCH

PUBLIC DOCUMENTS SERIES

Series Editors: Tyrus G. Fain, with Katharine C. Plant and Ross Milloy

FEDERAL REORGANIZATION: THE EXECUTIVE BRANCH

Public Documents Series

Compiled and Edited by Tyrus G. Fain
in collaboration with
Katharine C. Plant and Ross Milloy

With a Foreword by
Bert Lance

R. R. BOWKER COMPANY
New York & London, 1977

Published by R. R. Bowker Company
1180 Avenue of the Americas, New York, N.Y. 10036
Copyright © 1977 by Xerox Corporation
All rights reserved
Printed and bound in the United States of America

Library of Congress Cataloging in Publication Data
Main entry under title:

Federal reorganization.

(Public documents series)
Bibliography: p.
Includes index.
1. United States—Executive departments—Addresses, essays, lectures. 2. Independent regulatory-commissions—United States—Addresses, essays, lectures. 3. Zero-base budgeting—United States—Addresses, essays, lectures. I. Fain, Tyrus G. II. Plant, Katharine C. III. Milloy, Ross. IV. Series.
JK421.F434   353   77-23444
ISBN 0-8352-0981-4

CONTENTS

PART II
REGULATORY REFORM

FOREWORD

As the public official responsible for directing reorganization efforts in the federal government, I might be discouraged by the experience of those who preceded me. The history of reorganization initiatives presented here is mixed. It is a record, in important part, of problems identified but not solved, of promises made but not kept.

The documents reproduced in this book were available to Governor Carter's advisers and research staff in 1975 and 1976, but they were not conveniently collected in a single volume. Their lesson was clear: reorganization of the federal government, although necessary and popular, has been the source of frustration and disillusionment.

Over the last several years, national pollsters have documented a public conviction that government is cumbersome, ineffective, and remote. Reform and reorganization of the way the federal government related to the American people became a central part of the president's mandate from the electorate.

This administration begins this difficult task with several advantages not shared by earlier reorganization efforts. One of these is the fact that public frustration with the size, complexity, cost, and wastefulness of government is higher today than it has been at least since the first Hoover Commission began its work at the end of World War II. At the same time the American people are more aware than they perhaps ever have been of the nature of limits on government action and of the need to carefully allocate public and private resources. Congress is sensitive to this frustration—and to the limits under which we must operate—and it is eager to join us in taking bold and imaginative action. We share a mandate for change.

Another very important advantage we have is the deep personal commitment of President Carter to the success of his reorganization program. We are led by a president who successfully revamped an antiquated government structure in Georgia with a streamlined organization which became a model widely copied by other states. Some 300 separate agencies were consolidated into fewer than 30 agencies. I was involved in that effort too and take pride in the fact that the Georgia Department of Transportation, which had more than 9,500 employees when I became its director, has only 7,000 today.

As governor, Jimmy Carter invested a major part of his energy, time, and political capital in pushing that reorganization to success. As president, he has committed himself to devoting a similar effort to management and organization issues.

A third advantage we have stems from the president's decision to give the reorganization project leverage and staying power by placing it in the Office of Management and Budget (OMB). One of my responsibilities, as director of OMB, is to exercise our budget review responsibility to support the reorganization objectives of the president.

And finally, to be quite candid, we have the advantage of the lessons that have been learned from the failures—and the successes—of so many recent reorganization initiatives. Many of these lessons are developed in the chapters that follow.

Our study of the reorganization efforts in the last three administrations has led us to pinpoint four critical factors in their frequent inability to deliver what they promised.

First, reorganization plans were too often developed in secret, in a political vacuum. Consultation with Congress, affected interest groups, agency personnel, state and local government officials, and the general public, was either superficial or after the fact of policy decision. Secrecy was not an end in itself, of course, but a tactic, to avoid giving the forces resistant to change an early opportunity to maneuver and mass their own defensive strength. The results demonstrate that this was often precisely the wrong tactic.

Second, the past reorganization proposals were typically superficial. The proposals failed to address the problems at the program level where government meets the people. Their focus was on organizational box-shuffling at the agency level where the government meets the cabinet and the president. Improvements in administrative management and intergovernmental cooperation that contribute to the quality of service delivery were often neglected. Consolidation and reorganization at the top is an important element in what we are about, but success must be measured—and proposals developed with the people at the receiving end clearly in mind.

Third, reorganization efforts have been conducted by study commissions, reporting to the Executive office, with no continuing institutional base of their own. There has typically been little connection between the formulators of reorganization policy and those who must implement it in the rest of government.

Fourth, partly as a result of the preceding factors of secrecy, superficiality, and dependence on outside commissions, reorganization has been conceived as sweeping, monumental change that takes place at a single point in time. The concept of reorganization as a continuing process, a series of adaptive modifications that improve organization gradually, has been given short shrift.

As this is written, the Carter Administration's reorganization program is just getting underway. But we have already identified a number of pathfinding principles to guide our efforts for the next four years. Careful readers of this volume will be able to identify many points of difference between our principles and those that have guided previous reorganization efforts. These are the principles we intend to follow:

1. *Broad Objectives.* We define the purpose of reorganization broadly: to make government work better—more efficiently, responsively, openly, and predictably—through substantial improvements in the organization and management of the Executive branch. The President's Reorganization Project will seek to achieve this overall goal by:

ensuring maximum efficiency and economy in government operations;

promoting more effective planning and consolidation of government activities;

simplifying government so average citizens can understand it;

making government more responsive to citizens' needs;

opening government's proceedings and documents to the public, subject only to the rights of citizens to privacy and genuine concerns of national security;

reducing fragmentation, overlap, and unnecessary paperwork;

demanding higher levels of performance by government officials by developing incentives for increased productivity;

giving managers the authority necessary to do the job and then holding them accountable;

increasing the predictability and consistency of government actions;

emphasizing those tasks government can do and limiting those it cannot; and

improving the relationships between federal, state, and local governments to ensure a balanced partnership and better coordination.

Secretary Joseph Califano, in announcing an early reorganization of the Department of Health, Education, and Welfare, emphasized the breadth of our vision. I agree with him that "the Carter Administration's emphasis on reorganization is not managerial fascination with box-shifting and linedrawing on an organization chart, but rather a profound dedication to government that is credible because it is humane *and* efficient."

2. *Step-by-Step Approach*. We will follow an incremental approach staged over a four-year period rather than develop a one-step grand design that would result in a total, comprehensive plan unveiled on a fixed date. Many improvements in management and organization will not require congressional approval and can be accomplished by administrative order. New programs and policies will be carefully related to and made consistent with the organizational goals of the administration.

History teaches that efforts to redesign the Executive branch in a single scheme or plan are not digestible by our political system. More importantly, such efforts are themselves difficult to comprehend. They ignore the underlying complexities of our government.

3. *Emphasis on Program Analysis from the Bottom Up*. We will follow a bottom-up rather than a top-down approach. Our investigations will begin with identification and analysis of policy failures at the program level. This is the opposite of structural reorganization from the top, guided by abstract management principles. Implicit in our approach is the active involvement of program officials not only in the federal government, but also in state and local government, where effective service delivery must be a cooperative process—and of the people who are the ultimate beneficiaries (or victims) of government action or inaction.

4. *Participation by Departments and Agencies*. We believe that officials charged with the implementation of reorganization proposals must be involved in their development. Department and agency staff will systematically provide input during the study process, and many of them will serve directly on project teams. Further, a review mechanism will be established to obtain departmental comments on draft recommendations before a final decision on them is made.

The president decided from the beginning to lodge a greater share of power and discretion in his cabinet. The secretaries were instructed in the first week of the Carter Administration to take the lead in developing internal reorganization initiatives.

5. *Close Working Relationship with Congress*. The Reorganization Act of 1977, signed into law by President Carter on April 6, 1977, was passed by margins of over ten-to-one in both the House and Senate. We look upon Congress as an ally in the reorganization process. Its members and its staff will be a primary source of information and advice.

It should be noted in this context that the reorganization plan authority renewed on April 6, 1977, is changed somewhat from the authority available to previous presidents. It permits the administration to have as many as three reorganization plans (instead of just one) pending before Congress at one time. It allows the president to amend a plan within 30 days after its initial submission to Congress; previously, a sound plan could have been rejected because no one had authority to make minor but critical changes once it was submitted. And finally, the 1977 Act permits a single member of either House to call for a full vote at an appropriate time in the consideration process. All of these changes have the effect of increasing the opportunities for cooperation between Congress and the Executive branch on reorganization matters.

6. *Public Involvement.* In sharp contrast to earlier reorganization efforts, the Carter Administration program will include a strong public awareness component to involve, inform, and win the support of citizen groups and the general public. We shall depend on public awareness and participation to help us pinpoint problems, to originate ideas and solutions, and to provide reactions to various options developed by reorganization study teams. The process will be an open one. In adopting this open approach, we are rejecting the argument that early disclosure will tip our hand and give time for opposition to mobilize for defeat of new initiatives. We feel, rather, that opposition is strengthened when Congress and interest groups are surprised by plans to which they have not contributed. The result of an open process should be wider and deeper support in the long run.

An important feature of the program will be the appointment of senior advisers—persons with a broad range of backgrounds and skills—who will assist the effort in their individual capacities to develop ideas and provide advice. Public participation and openness will be an essential feature of the reorganization process, just as it is an important objective of the reform and reorganization proposals we develop.

7. *Priority Planning.* Initial targets of reorganization have been selected to fulfill major compaign commitments and a number of projects are already underway as this is written. These include the creation of a Department of Energy, streamlining the Executive office of the president and civil rights enforcement activities, and consolidation of consumer advocacy functions. Later initiatives will be developed by functional area study teams which will comprehensively review government agencies and programs in five areas:

Energy, Environment and Natural Resources

National Security and International Affairs

Human Resources

Economic and Regional Development

General Government

The result of this review will be an agenda of projects for action throughout the first term of the Carter Administration.

Meanwhile, other initiatives cutting across functional areas will be proceeding parallel to structural reorganization. These will include zero-base budgeting, paperwork reduction, and civil service reform. We anticipate that many organizational issues will surface as program managers analyze and justify functions in zero-base budget development. The simplification of structure and elimination of unneeded and unproductive programs will be the end products of these coordinated activities.

BERT LANCE
Director, Office of Management and Budget
Executive Office of the President

PREFACE

This edited volume of government documents on the reorganization of the Executive branch is the second title in the Public Documents Series. The series addresses subjects of major and topical public policy concerns and seeks to make government documents more accessible to the public.

As our nation begins its third century, it is appropriate to reconsider our national purpose and direction. We are a nation that has been united in revolution and divided in civil war. We have reaffirmed our constitutional dedication to the principles of the "common defense" by engaging in world wars. We have expanded our boundaries to include masses of immigrants. Rural communities have been transformed into cities and with that has come urbanization. We have accomplished radical industrial and technological advances. But, has our government been responsive to these changing realities? What is the effect of government? Must we reexamine the legitimacy of its tasks, its efficiency, its organization? These have been the questions and concerns of twentieth-century presidents and their administrations. Today, in the aftermath of the Watergate scandal and the war in Vietnam, there is a high level of alienation and public distrust of government and its institutions, which has heavily influenced presidential and congressional efforts to reexamine governmental functions and to reorganize government—in particular, the Executive branch, the most diverse of the three branches of the federal bureaucracy.

In his campaign for presidency, Jimmy Carter pledged to reorganize and streamline the Executive branch. Throughout his campaign, he stressed his lack of association with the established bureaucracy and his intention to bring new faces to the reorganization job. On March 31, 1977, Congress gave the president the authority he had sought to reorganize—realizing the promise and the political momentum for reform. As the new administration and its party's leadership in Congress begin the task, there is a documented body of studies on which to build new proposals.

This documentary collection covers many of the subjects which the Carter administration and Congress will have to examine and contains some of the proposals which President Carter himself proposes to employ. Most of the documents have appeared in government publications and are either out of print or difficult to obtain. Many were released by the government without indexes or other bibliographic controls. The series' editors have made an effort to extract from this vast quantity of information the most significant material, the most concise summaries, and the illustrative facts, making them available in a single volume. This compilation is intended to provide a starting point for understanding and evaluating specific proposals on reorganization. It represents a baseline report on the status of Executive branch reorganization. Apart from its historical value, its usefulness will be enhanced by the reader's ability to keep abreast of other materials as they are generated and released.

The scope of the book encompasses documents released from 1971 (with the issuance of the Ash Council report) to 1976 (with the election of Jimmy Carter as president) and includes a variety of congressional hearings, reports, and statements, as well as Executive branch studies. Every facet of Executive branch reorganization is not dealt with in detail—only those areas in which major action appears imminent and in which proposals are pending. The focus of the text is on the consolidation of Executive departments and agencies (Ash and Nixon recommendations); regulatory reform (a body of proposals seemingly supported by everyone from Richard Nixon to Ralph Nader); and zero-base budgeting/sunset legislation (the Carter approach).

The volume is organized into three parts. Part I deals with the consolidation of Executive departments and agencies. The recommendations of the U.S. President's Advisory Council on Executive Organization (Ash Council), which was created by Richard Nixon and Roy Ash, echoed those of several earlier task forces on federal reorganization by calling for consolidation of a number of related functions into a smaller number of federal departments. The administrative rationale for this and the recommended form are set forth in reprinted documents. Part II examines regulatory reform. The many regulatory bodies or agencies which play a significant role in commerce, as well as protecting the health and well-being of the public, have become the scapegoat of federal reorganization and reform. Falling into a constitutional "no man's land," the dozen or so major bodies have been subjected to increasing criticism from a wide political spectrum. The Ash Council report provides the only recent and significant specific proposal for structural change of regulatory bodies and is reprinted in abridged form. The delayed actions, red tape, and mismanagement of regulatory agencies are recounted from congressional hearings, as are the views of past regulators and the views of some of those who have participated in the presidential appointment process from previous administrations. One recent piece of legislation addressed specifically to regulatory agencies, and one which received wide support, is the Percy-Byrd Regulatory Reform Act. This is described and portions from the hearings held on it are reprinted.

Part III examines two highly significant tools for regulatory reform, whose scope extends to all structures of government: sunset procedures and zero-base budgeting. Scarcely any documentary literature was generated at the federal level on these approaches to administrative management before 1977. The apparent success of the zero-base system in Georgia during and after the Carter years, not to mention the rise to the presidency of its champion, has made the adaptation of such a system at the federal level almost inevitable. Sunset laws, mandating the discontinuation of specific programs unless they are rejustified, are in force in several states and are attracting the same measure of attention as zero-base budgeting. A major initiative toward installation of such systems at the federal level, the Government Economy and Spending Reform Act of 1976, was introduced by Senator Edmund Muskie in the 94th Congress and received wide bipartisan support. Jimmy Carter and the Democratic platform endorsed the legislation during the presidential campaign, and it is likely that the 95th Congress will enact it into law. The proposals encompassed in Muskie's bill are reprinted, along with part of the testimony presented in the course of the hearings held on it by the Senate Committee on Government Operations. (The name of the Senate Committee on Government Operations was changed to the Committee on Governmental Affairs in February 1977.)

Other important developments related to federal reorganization which should be noted and which are dealt with in Appendix 2 of this volume are:

Passage of the Congressional Budget Act of 1974 and establishment of the Congressional Budget Office as a legislative counterpart of the Office of Management and Budget;

Debate and passage of legislation affecting the Postal Reorganization of 1971, operations of the Postal Commission, and the appropriation of funds to subsidize postal operations;

Consideration of financial systems' reform proposals affecting the regulatory bodies with responsibility for monetary and banking matters;

The emergence of a "federal energy establishment" with responsibility for shaping and implementing the Executive branch's energy policy and recent congressional staff proposals to reorganize and consolidate a variety of activities;

Consideration and debate on the Watergate Reorganization and Reform Act and other matters pertaining to malfeasance and ethical conduct by federal officials, the structure of Executive oversight, the Office of Special Prosecutor, and federal involvement in campaign practices.

The recommendations of the Commission on the Organization of the Government for the Conduct of Foreign Policy (Murphy Commission) and the President's Commission on CIA Activities within the United States (Rockefeller Commission), pertaining to organization and operation of U.S. foreign policy and the intelligence establishment, are treated in *The Intelligence Community*, the first title in the Public Documents Series.

The current organization and responsibilities of the federal departments, agencies, commissions, and other bodies are not explicitly stated in this text because of space limitations. However, some of the congressional hearings and staff studies included contain descriptions of the organization and operations of various departments and agencies. For further reference to the current organization of federal departments and agencies, the reader should consult *The U.S. Government Manual* ([5]), a standard reference work which is revised on a yearly basis.

The editors of the Public Documents Series follow a policy of not expressing personal views on the merits of specific proposals, but in this case we feel compelled to observe that the quality of government documentation and analysis bearing upon federal reorganization proposals is below that found in other areas of public policy. In the course of reviewing the documents for this volume, concern as to whether the most significant material had been tapped prompted the editors to examine unpublished presidential papers and to seek interviews with members of commissions and task forces to determine where more detailed documentation and thoughtful analysis might be found. The conclusion was that it did not exist in the public domain.

Acknowledgment and appreciation for contributions to this work must begin with recognition of the largely anonymous government authors who prepared the documents reprinted. By long-standing tradition, they are seldom identified—so this expression of gratitude is general—of necessity. Alice Keefer, a librarian with the Library of Congress and the Public Documents Series' staff librarian, directed the acquisition of the documents and assembled the bibliography. Her assistance was invaluable. Many others were helpful in locating and assessing the material and in providing ideas and orientation. Among those deserving special thanks are Roy Ash, Alan Wade, Nye Stevens, Peter Petkas, Paul Jensen, Tom Reston, Ed Wise, and Melbourne Spector. The staff of the Lyndon B. Johnson Library in Austin, Texas, was particularly kind in allowing access to some of the private papers of the former president. Kate Plant and Ross Milloy, as coeditors of this work, made outstanding contributions. They somehow preserve both professionalism and good humor, despite the onerous tasks assigned them. Finally, Nancy Volkman of the R. R. Bowker Company, must be thanked for her patient skill as editor and adviser. Without Nancy and her colleagues, Desmond Reaney and Judy Garodnick, this book would never have been realized.

TYRUS G. FAIN

GUIDE TO USE

The documents in this volume were edited and, at times, abridged; where abridgement occurs, it is because of space limitations or because the editors sought to reduce redundancy—in an attempt to offer the most apposite information. Like the sources from which the text was drawn, there are inevitably gaps and inconsistencies in the style and format of the book. The editors have provided explanatory bridging narrative to facilitate transition between the documents, to lend continuity, and to elucidate the material. This narrative is set apart from the documents by horizontal lines. The editors have also provided notes and references at the end of seven of the book's nine chapters, to give background on and perspective to the documents. The boldface numbers in the margin of the text (e.g., **N1, N2, N3**) refer to these notes and references.

The source of each document has been identified by the bracketed number appearing with the headings in chapters. The number, which is followed by the page numbers in the original source, refers to the numbered documents listed in the bibliography. Ellipses points have been inserted by the editors to indicate deletions of nonpertinent material from the original document. Because of these deletions, there are gaps in the numbering of the original documents' footnotes.

The volume concludes with a bibliography; appendixes containing a list of acronyms; congressional and Library of Congress reports and proposals; an index of included documents; and a subject and name index.

INTRODUCTION

The Constitution provides the structure and functions of the three branches of the federal government: the Legislative, the Judicial, and the Executive. The most complex and most diverse is the Executive branch and its organization has been challenged by presidents and Congress alike. The structure of the Executive branch has evolved from the ambiguity of its constitutional mandate. Article II, Section 1 provides that "The executive Power shall be vested in a President of the United States of America. He shall hold his Office during the Term of four Years . . . together with the Vice President, chosen for the same term. . . ." Section 2 says the president "may require the Opinion, in writing, of the principal Officer in each of the executive Departments, upon any Subject relating to the Duties of their respective Offices . . ." and specifies that officers shall be appointed by the president, with the "Advice and Consent of the Senate," except when "Congress may by law vest the Appointment of such inferior Officers, as they think proper, in the President alone, in the Courts of Law, or in the Heads of Departments." But the Constitution does not specify the manner in which the president shall organize or direct his Cabinet and/or the Executive agencies of government that may be established.

Over the years, a number of commissions, task forces, and study groups have addressed the problem of reorganizing the Executive branch. The documentation of their findings, included in this compilation, and as indicated in the Preface, serves as an introduction to the major issues of Executive branch reorganization. The material in this Introduction reflect contemporary thinking on the subject, tracing the progress of earlier reorganization attempts and summarizing the issues and initiatives under consideration. The two documents that follow are drawn from a Library of Congress, Congressional Research Service issue brief on "Executive Reorganization" ([43]) and a report of the House Committee on Government Operations, *Executive Reorganization: A Summary Analysis* ([23]). It should be noted that these documents were written before Congress gave President Carter reorganization authority on March 31, 1977.

THE CONGRESSIONAL PERSPECTIVE OF REORGANIZATION AT MID-DECADE ([43], pp. 1-3)

Issue Definition

The ever-increasing scope of Federal Government activities in this century has compelled political leaders, administrators, and academicians to focus their attention on the organizational structure and efficiency of the executive branch. Virtually every President since Theodore Roosevelt has established a committee or commission to study the organization of the executive branch and to recommend ways and

means to improve performance and accountability. Congress has conducted numerous oversight studies of its own and has cooperated with the
President in seeking a more responsive and responsible administration
of the laws.

Background and Policy Analysis

A review of the landmarks in Federal administrative development in
this century reveals that Congress has given the President and his department heads many new forms of authority and staff to discharge their
managerial tasks. Foremost among these managerial tools has been the
executive budget, the Executive Office of the President, and the power
to initiate reorganization plans, subject to legislative veto. While it
is true that these tools represent major innovative steps contributing
to central administrative control by the President over the bureaucracy,
it is also true that in recent years Congress has expanded its role in
overseeing the administration of the executive branch and thus, to some
degree, has diminished the President's role as Chief Administrator.

Notwithstanding evidence of improved management of the Executive
Branch, there is a widely held opinion today that the Federal government is both too big and too involved in economic and social regulation.
As a counter to this situation, considerable support has been given to
the concept of requiring mandatory terminal dates for programs or agencies, and often both. This type of legislation, discussed more fully
later, is collectively referred to as "sunset laws."

METHODS OF REORGANIZATION

There are essentially four methods by which agencies may be established, reorganized, or terminated.

1. Statutes. The Congress has the Constitutional power to establish,
reorganize, or abolish any agency of Government by statute. New executive departments have traditionally, with one exception, been established by statute. It is also common for agencies to be established as
part of more general programmatic legislation.

2. Presidential Directives. In his Constitutional capacity as Chief
Executive, Commander-in-Chief, or by delegation of authority by Congress,
the President has exercised broad authority to create or abolish agencies, or to delegate functions. His normal method of action is by
Executive Order; other procedures include Presidential Announcement,
Presidential Memorandums, and military orders. Congressional approval
is not necessary for actions initiated by these directives.

3. Reorganization Plans. The Reorganization Act of 1949, as amended,
authorized the President to prepare and submit reorganization plans for
realigning departments or agency authority, transferring administrative
units or functions from one department or agency to another, or abolishing old agencies and creating new ones to administer the transferred
functions. The reorganization plans were to lie for 60 days and take
effect if, within the 60-day period, a disapproving resolution was not
enacted by either the House or Senate. It should be noted that the
Presidential reorganization plan authority expired on Apr. 1, 1973, and
has not been renewed by Congress.

4. Internal Departmental Reorganizations. As the President can be delegated authority by Congress to create, abolish, or reorganize agencies, so can heads of departments (agencies) delegate such authority to heads of component units. Thus, internal reorganizations within departments and agencies do not require Congressional approval.

STATUTORY AUTHORITY FOR PRESIDENTIAL INITIATIVE

The 1949 Reorganization Act

The genesis of the Presidential reorganization authority is to be found in the economy measures of 1932 and 1933, when the concept of executive initiative and congressional review of reorganizations first was written into law. Subsequent enactments in 1939 and 1945 substituted the reorganization plan for the executive order and changed the procedures for congressional veto. The most recent legislation providing reorganization authority was the Reorganization Act of 1949 (63 Stat. 203; 5 U.S.C. 901-913), as amended, which expired on Apr. 1, 1973, was not renewed by Congress. On Apr. 9, 1975, President Ford submitted to Congress a proposal to re-establish the authority to submit reorganization plans for a 4-year period.

In the 24 years following the enactment of the 1949 law, some 93 reorganization plans were submitted by the President to Congress, which allowed 73 plans to take effect. Among the important agencies created by reorganization plans have been the Office of Management and Budget, Office of Telecommunications Policy, National Oceanic and Atmospheric Administration, ACTION, and Environmental Protection Agency. In one instance, and executive department was created by reorganization plan (Health, Education, and Welfare, in 1953). While this proposal was favored by Congress, a similar proposal to establish a Department of Urban Affairs and Housing in 1962 met resistance and eventuated in an amendment to the basic Reorganization Act barring the creation, consolidation, or abolition of executive departments by reorganization plans. Under the Presidential reorganization authority, President Nixon submitted eight reorganization plans between 1969 and 1973; none was disapproved by Congress.

The 1949 Act, as amended, authorized the President to submit to Congress plans for the reorganization of Federal Government agencies by means of transfer, consolidation, or abolition. If the Congress did not vote its disapproval within 60 days, the plan took effect. Once submitted, Congress could not amend the plan but had to either accept or reject it in toto.

Over the years a number of modifications were made to the original Act. Action in only one House, not both chambers, was made sufficient to defeat a plan. Also, the reorganization procedures could not be used to establish a new department. Only one plan could be submitted within a 30-day period, and it had to deal with only one logically consistent subject matter. Finally, a plan could not create new legal authority. This latter point was important to Congress as it prevented the reorganization procedure from being used to subvert congressional authority to legislate. The most recent extension of the reorganization authority occurred with the passage of P.L. 92-179 on Dec. 10, 1971, extending the authority until Apr. 1, 1973.

RECENT PRESIDENTIAL INITIATIVES ([23], pp. 16-18)

The development of reorganization proposals by study groups during the Kennedy and Johnson administrations has interest in this context. Unfortunately, the basic documents of the study groups have not been published, but the outlines of the recommendations are well-known and were discussed in part by witnesses at the subcommittee hearings.[48]

A reorganization study group, or task force as it was called, was started in the Kennedy administration. This group, chaired by Don K. Price, dean of what is now the John F. Kennedy School of Government, Harvard University, with staff support by the Bureau of the Budget, reported in 1964 after President Johnson took office. It recommended, among other things, the creation of five new executive departments: Transportation; Education; Natural Resources; Economic Development; and Housing and Community Development.

President Johnson set up another task force, chaired by Ben M. Heineman, president of Northwest Industries, Inc., which reexamined the work of the Price group and came up with recommendations for Departments of Natural Resources, Social Services, and Economic Development. By the time the Heineman task force reported in 1967, the Department of Transportation had been created by statute,[49] as recommended by the Price task force, and was not an issue. As for a separate Department of Education, Mr. Heineman testified that his group differed with the Price task force and decided against splitting up the Department of Health, Education, and Welfare into two departments, one for Education and the other for Health and Welfare.[50]

Having persuaded the Congress, at separate intervals, to enact the laws creating the Department of Housing and Urban Development and the Department of Transportation, President Johnson then moved to recommend a department concerned with economic development, which he termed a Department of Business and Labor. It contemplated the merger of the existing Departments of Commerce and Labor and the acquisition of numerous other governmental functions bearing on economic affairs. The proposal surfaced in President Johnson's state of the Union message of January 10, 1967, and was restated in his budget message of January 24 and his economic message of January 26, 1967.[51]

Again, in a special message to the Congress on the quality of American government, President Johnson reiterated his request for a Department of Business and Labor, stating, "I strongly believe that in the years ahead the new department will be a vital force for the progress and prosperity of a growing nation."[52] Mindful, however, that organized labor was cool if not antagonistic to the plan, President Johnson stated that he would call upon the President's Advisory Committee on Labor-Management Policy, which had been established by President Kennedy's executive order in 1961, to consider the proposal for a new department. He said that he would await the advice of the committee before taking further action. Thereafter, the proposal was dropped and nothing more was said about it.

---

[48] Hearings, pp. 234-6, 396, 402, 405.
[49] P.L. 98-670, approved Oct. 15, 1966, 80 Stat. 931.
[50] Hearings, p. 237.
[51] See H. Doc. No. 90-1, Cong. Rec., vol. 113, p. 36 (Jan. 10, 1967) ; H. Doc. No. 90-15, Cong. Rec., vol 113, p. 1297 (Jan. 24, 1967) ; H. Doc. No. 90-28, Cong. Rec., vol. 113, p. 1619 (Jan. 26, 1967).
[52] Cong. Rec., vol. 113, p. 7223 (Mar. 17, 1967).

According to Joseph A. Califano, Jr., who served as a presidential assistant and was intimately acquainted with the reorganization dialog inside the Johnson administration, if President Johnson had decided to run again and had won re-election, it is probable that new executive departments would have been proposed. Natural Resources and Human Resources were likely candidates.[53] Mr. Heineman similarly testified to President Johnson's intention to make reorganization a "No. 1 priority" in a second full term.[54]

President Nixon established his own study group, formally called the President's Advisory Council on Executive Organization, better known as the Ash Council after its chairman, Roy L. Ash, chairman of the board of Litton Industries.[55] Established on April 8, 1969, the Ash Council made a number of reorganization studies and submitted memoranda, with recommendations to President Nixon. Two of these memoranda, dealing with departmental reorganization,[56] were made public by the President after forming the basis for his recommendations to the Congress in his state of the Union message of January 22, 1971, and his separate message on reorganization of March 25, 1971.

CONVERGENCE OF RECOMMENDATIONS

Although there were some differences among the Price, Heineman, and Ash group studies, the basic thrust and concept of broad departmental divisions in Government organization were essentially the same. Each favored a department for economic affairs, however titled, involving a merger of the existing Departments of Labor and Commerce, and a broad range of economic-type functions. Each favored a Department of Natural Resources, based on the existing Department of Interior and related components or functions from the Department of Agriculture and the Corps of Engineers. Each favored a department which joined housing and community development, broader in scope than the existing housing department and drawing functions from other departments related to housing, home financing, highways, community water systems, and the like. A Department of Human Resources (or Social Services) was favored by the Ash and Heineman groups, based on the existing Department of Health, Education, and Welfare and manpower functions of the Department of Labor.

There were some notable differences in choice of organizational components. For example, the Price group, unlike the Ash group, favored inclusion of the Federal Home Loan Bank Board and the housing and loan guarantee functions of the Veterans' Administration in what it called the Department of Housing and Community Development. Again, the Price group, unlike the Heineman and Ash groups, favored a splitup of the Department of Health, Education, and Welfare and a separate Department of Education rather than a new and expanded Department of Human Resources.

President Nixon followed the Ash Council's recommendations with some modifications, the most important of which was the proposed

---

[53] Hearings, p. 401–2.
[54] Hearings, p. 252.
[55] Other members of the Advisory Council on Executive Organization were: George Baker, former dean of the Graduate School of Business Administration, Harvard University; John B. Connally, former Governor of Texas and now Secretary of the Treasury; Frederick R. Kappel, former chairman of the board, American Telephone & Telegraph Co.; Richard M. Paget, president of the New York management consultant firm of Cresap, McCormick & Paget. Walter N. Thayer, president of Whitney Communications Corp., served as a special consultant and also as a member of the Council by a later appointment.
[56] Memoranda for the President of the United States, "Establishment of a Department of Natural Resources, Organization for Social and Economic Programs," submitted by The President's Advisory Council on Executive Organization, Feb. 5, 1971.

dissolution of the Department of Transportation, barely 5 years old, and division of its major components between the Departments of Economic Affairs and Community Development.[57] The Ash Council sidestepped the immediate issue, suggesting in one of its memorandums that "certain programs of the Department of Transportation have a major impact on the economy and may be considered for incorporation [in the department dealing with economic affairs] at some future date."[58]

REORGANIZATION AUTHORITY PROPOSALS IN THE 93d CONGRESS ([43], pp. 3-18)

Two bills were introduced in the Senate during the 93d Congress to extend the authority of the President to submit Reorganization Plans. The primary bill, S. 2003, was introduced on June 14, 1973, by Senators Percy, Javits, and Ribicoff, and reflected the results of negotiations between Senator Percy and the Administration.

The principal change in the 1949 Act proposed in this bill was that henceforth the President would submit to the Senate and House, not less than 30 days prior to transmittal of a plan, notice of the proposed reorganization. The intent of this modification to the 1949 Act was to allow the House and Senate an opportunity to provide "input" to the White House since Congress would still not be permitted to make amendments to the plan after it was submitted. Also, this bill extended the authority for 4 years rather than the usual 2 years.

A second bill, S. 936, was introduced by Senator Robert Byrd (D-W.Va.) which contained an interesting feature. The wording of Section 5 of the bill was as follows, "...a reorganization plan is effective at the end of the first period of 60 calendar days of continuous session of Congress after the date on which the plan is transmitted to it if, between the date of transmittal and the end of the 60-day period, the two Houses pass a concurrent resolution stating in substance that the Congress favors the reorganization plan." What this provision sought to accomplish was to reverse the presumption of validity regarding the submittance of reorganization plans to one of invalidity. Congress would have to act positively within 60 days or the plan would be considered void.

The bill (H.R. 7882), introduced in the House by Representative Holifield, Chairman of the House Government Operations Committee, provided for a simple 2-year extension of the authority provided in the 1949 Act, as amended.

No hearings were held on any of the above bills during the 93d Congress.

REORGANIZATION AUTHORITY PROPOSALS IN THE 94th CONGRESS

President Ford submitted to Congress on Apr. 9, 1975, a proposal to re-establish for a 4-year period the authority of the President to submit reorganization plans. The proposed draft provides for a simple extension

[57] A comparison of the President's reorganization proposals with those of the Ash Council is contained in "Paper Relating to the President's Departmental Reorganization Program: A Reference Compilation," March 1971, pp. 34–38 (hereinafter cited as Ref. Comp.). As noted in the text, a revised compilation was reissued in February 1972.
[58] Id. at 113. The Ash Council used the name "Department of Economic Growth and Productivity," which the administration changed to "Department of Economic Affairs." See also Mr. Ash's testimony in hearings, pp. 202–203.

of the President's authority and for no alterations in the 1949 Reorganization Act, as amended, which had been in effect prior to Apr. 1, 1973.
No legislation to renew the President's authority to submit reorganization plans has been introduced in either house.

EXECUTIVE REORGANIZATION: AN ENDURING ISSUE

The subject of executive branch reorganization has an enduring quality. There is no neutral model for the perfect executive branch organization to which the protagonists can repair. Indeed, reorganization
appears to be one of the most fundamental of political tools through
which individuals and groups gain power and influence over others.
While there is no ideal executive organization, there has emerged
certain value guidelines which by their nature prompt people to take
sides on reorganization issues.

Virtually all reorganizations are justified on the grounds of increasing "economy and efficiency." Often, "accountability" is added
for good measure. The statutory specification of purposes for reorganization is to be found in title 5 of the U.S. Code, section 903.
There is no doubt that reorganizations may achieve some or all of the
formalistic objectives listed as justifications. Nonetheless, most
reorganizations are principally a product of political motivations,
rightly understood. A reorganization may be designed to upgrade or
downgrade an agency or one of its programs, or even, on occasion, an
individual associated with the agency. Frequently, it is easier to
promote, diminish, or eliminate a program through reorganization than
to act in a straightforward legislative manner. Sometimes, reorganizations are a method of by-passing Congressional or interest group
opposition. And finally, reorganizations give the appearance, if not
the reality, of "action," occasionally a worthwhile objective in itself.

Executive reorganization became popular as a concept and an activity
during what has been described as the Administrative Management period,
roughly from 1920 to 1970. The principal administrative goal of the
intellectual groups dominant during that period was to reinforce the in-
stitutionalized Presidency as the administrative chief of the executive
branch. The Presidency was to be strengthened by the unified executive
budget required under the Budget and Accounting Act of 1921, the establishment of the Executive Office of the President, and the passage of
legislation enabling the President to submit reorganization plans to
Congress, the latter two events occurring in 1939.

Executive reorganization can be considered from both a comprehensive
and a partial perspective. There have been several comprehensive reviews of the executive branch in the past, most notably the first and
second Hoover Commissions and the Ash Council. For the most part, however, the subject of executive reorganization has been studied on a
more limited scale, principally in terms of a particular policy field.

The two Hoover Commissions were unusual among the studies of the
Executive Branch in that they were Congressionally inspired -- although
with Presidential cooperation, comprehensive in coverage, bipartisan,
and guided by a certain philosophical unanimity as to the proper role
of the President in the administrative structure of the Government.
The members were disposed toward strengthening the President and departmental secretaries as administrative managers of the executive
branch. It is also noteworthy that during the period of the first

Hoover Commission, 1947-49, the executive branch still had a number of agencies originally created in the wake of depression, war, and demobilization. The executive branch, in a word, was considerably more fragmented than it is today.

There are four basic sources for studies of the Executive Branch organization and the making of recommendations for change; 1) national commissions; 2) Executive Branch task forces; 3) Congressional committees; and 4) private organizations. Each of these types of organizations has been utilized in recent years, and each has produced studies with recommendations for reorganization.

National Commissions. While there has been no commission established in recent years with a mandate as broad as that of the Hoover Commissions, several commissions have enjoyed rather expansive fields in which to roam. For example, a Commission on the Organization of the Government for the Conduct of Foreign Policy (known as the Murphy Commission after its Chairman, Robert Murphy) was established in 1973 to study and submit findings and recommendations as to methods of making the formulation and implementation of the Nation's foreign policy more effective. The Commission included members from Congress, officers of the executive branch, and public citizens. The Commission sent its report and recommendations to the President and Congress on June 27, 1975.

Another national commission with a mixed membership and a broad mandate is the National Commission on Supplies and Shortages established in 1974. This Commission is "expected" to recommend the establishment of a new government instrumentality or agency for coordinating and dealing with materials and commodity information-gathering in its final report to be submitted Dec. 31, 1976.

More typical of the national commissions are those with a relatively narrow focus and without a specific charge to recommend institutional reorganization. Examples of this latter type commission are the National Study Commission on Records and Documents of Federal Officials, established in 1974, and the Commission on Government Procurement, which submitted its report in 1972.

Executive Branch Task Forces. In recent years the executive branch has engaged in considerable self-study and encouraged internal reorganizations to facilitate its own adaptability to changing circumstances. There has been a wide range of groups or task forces charged with studying aspects of the executive branch organization, ranging from the extensive year-long efforts of the President's Advisory Council on Executive Organization (Ash Council) to small, ad-hoc interagency groups.

Presidents have differed in their approaches to reorganization. Possibly the most durable of the reorganization groups was the President's Advisory Committee on Government Organization (PACGO), which functioned between 1953 and 1961 with Nelson A. Rockefeller as Chairman during most of this period. The committee met almost daily during the first months of the Eisenhower Administration and was largely responsible, according to its Chairman, for the ten reorganization plans transmitted to Congress that became law in 1953.

President Kennedy did not have any Executive Branch advisory committees on reorganization, although he did solicit a report on regulatory commissions from James Landis which contained reorganization proposals. Lyndon Johnson established two task forces, chaired by Donald K. Price and Ben Heineman respectively, but the reports from the task forces to the President were never made public. President Nixon, as noted, established the Ash Council, which concluded its work with major proposals for changing the shape of the Executive Branch.

Thus far in his Administration, President Ford has not proposed a national commission on the scale of the Hoover Commissions, nor an Executive Branch study in the tradition of the Ash Council. The President did propose, however, on Oct. 8, 1974, that Congress pass legislation to establish a mixed national commission to examine Federal regulatory institutions and practices. Two Senate committees held hearings on this proposal, but the Congressional and committee leaderships determined that Congress should hold its own hearings and make its own studies under committee supervision.

The President, perceiving the prospect that Congress would not establish a national commission to study regulatory agencies, summoned all commissioners of the major regulatory commissions to a White House "summit meeting" on June 25, 1975. To assist the President in developing a legislative strategy with regards to economic regulation, the President established a Domestic Council Review Group for Regulatory Reform (DCRG). The DCRG has been developing the President's proposals to alter the organization and procedures of regulatory agencies. The Domestic Council and the Office of Management and Budget, both products of Ash Council recommendations, are involved in continuous review of executive organization, although the President's incentives and options in this field have been much reduced with the expiration of his authority to submit reorganization plans to Congress.

Congressional Committees. Congressional interest in the organization of the executive branch is long-standing. A review of administrative history reveals that following the Civil War, Congressional inquiries came in rapid succession, each studying some aspect of the bureaucracy it felt was not performing efficiently. While these efforts resulted in little improvement, it is interesting to note that throughout the latter half of the nineteenth century, much of the initiative shown to improve administrative performance came from Congress, not the President.

In the twentieth century, the Congress and the President have vied for preeminence in executive reorganization. While the President has, on balance, been the dominant force, the Congress has made major contributions in the field. Congressional strength in reorganization rests upon a constitutional base; namely, that Congress must establish all new departments, and that agencies cannot exist without appropriations approved by Congress.

Executive reorganization takes place each time Congress establishes a new department or agency. Occasionally Congress will establish an agency that the President does not want, even in his own Executive Office. Congress also provides impetus for reorganization through hearings and investigations. The executive intelligence community is cur-

rently being reorganized, largely in response to the hearings by the
Senate Select Committee on Intelligence Activities, popularly known as
the Church Committee. Also, Congressional committee inquiries into
various regulatory fields are likely to result in proposals for institutional reorganization.

The immediate future is likely to see more reorganization activity
by the Congress, relative to the President, because the President's
authority to submit reorganization plans to Congress has expired and
Congress has thus far chosen not to renew it. Hence, the legislative
process will have to be followed for most reorganizations of the
Executive Branch.

Private Organizations. There have been three major privately funded
commissions in recent decades which have taken a broad view of American
national policies and the Federal government. First, and also the most
comprehensive, was the Committee on Recent Social Trends, which was
established by President Hoover in 1929 and issued its massive report
in 1932. Much more modest was the 1960 Report by the President's Commission on National Goals, written in cooperation with the American
Assembly of Columbia University. In 1973, a Commission on Critical
Choices was created to be chaired by former Governor Rockefeller. The
Commission was to study social trends and their impact on the future.
Rockefeller resigned in 1975 and the scope of the work slated for the
Commission was reduced.

In addition to these rather architectonic reviews of America, other
private studies have been focused on American government. A notable
example of this type of report was an analysis of the Watergate Affair
in terms of governmental institutions prepared in 1974 by the National
Academy of Public Administration. This report, "Watergate: Its Implications for Responsible Government," recommended many organizational
changes in the executive branch.

TIME FOR A NEW HOOVER COMMISSION?

Over the years there have been numerous bills introduced to establish
a major commission patterned after the Hoover Commission. Proponents
argue that it is time for an overall review of the executive branch.
Incremental changes are fine, but since they affect only a part of the
whole, distortions are bound to emerge and a long-term study which includes participants from the Executive and Legislative Branches and the
private sector is needed.

The closest legislation has come to establishing a new Hoover Commission occurred in 1968 when the Senate passed S. 3640 to create an
eight-man commission to study the organization and management of the
executive branch. The Senate Government Operations Committee reported
a clean bill (S. 3640 -- S.Rept. 1451) after its Subcommittee on Executive Reorganization early in 1968 held seven days of hearings on five
related bills.

A major problem confronting any proposal for a new Hoover Commission
is how to avoid duplicating or overlapping the work of other commissions
and the on-going administrative oversight responsibilities of congres-

sional committees. Often there is little enthusiasm among members of Congress, particularly those on critical oversight committees, for what they consider to be "still another commission." A further obstacle for these proposals to overcome is the fact that there is no longer a working consensus as to what role the President ought to play as chief administrative officer of the Government. There is concern expressed as to what direction such a Commission might follow.

In the 94th Congress, several bills have been introduced to establish a Commission similar to that of the Hoover Commission. S. 61, introduced by Sen. Pearson, calls for a Commission to be established, conduct its study and make recommendations, then cease. Sen. Mondale has introduced legislation (S. 3888) to provide for an Executive Organization Review Commission that would be reconstituted every tenth year.

The great constant of the Executive Branch organizational structure is the need for change. The impetus for change is likely to be from all the sources previously described: national commissions, Presidential advisory units, congressional committees, and private organizations. Furthermore, there are serious proposals for deliberately reversing the presumption in favor of programs and organizations to a presumption in favor of their automatic demise unless Congress acts positively. All these forces for change will be at work in the near future and the executive branch will not escape the consequences.

REORGANIZATION THROUGH MANAGEMENT PROCESSES: SUNSET AND ZERO-BASE BUDGETING

Partly as a result of Watergate and partly because many have perceived that they are required to work and live under an increasing burden of regulations, there has emerged in recent years a bias against the enlargement of the Federal Government. At least some of this resentment may be traced to the literally hundereds of Federal programs, each with its own set of regulations and administrative overhead, which have been initiated over the past quarter-century. For the most part, these programs have been expensive, and the evidence suggests that they have not produced the intended results. Indeed, the net result appears to be negative, as studies indicate that regulation tends to decrease competition rather than increase it, and that the sheer volume of rules has diminished personal and corporate freedom in basic daily life decisions.

Congress has taken note of this concern and has begun an assessment of the role of regulations in the economic and social life of the Nation. This assessment has proceeded from various sources and from several perspectives.

One approach to the problem of multiple and regulations has become popularly known as "sunset laws." This term originated in Colorado where the State legislature in 1975 passed a law whereby the State's 40 boards and committees having regulatory authority would be terminated at the end of 7 years unless the legislature voted to continue them. Several other States shortly thereafter enacted similar legislation.

It should be noted that the term "sunset laws" is frequently used to apply to two related, but different, concepts. The most common usage refers to placing a time limit on the life of a government agency, re-

quiring thereafter an affirmative act by the legislature for it to continue in existence. It was this type of law, passed by the legislature
of Colorado, that attracted media attention.

The second usage of the term relates to programs and the imposition
of a reauthorization requirement every few years. It is this latter
approach that is reflected in three major pieces of legislation (S. 2925,
S. 2812 and S. 3428) currently under consideration in the Senate. While
the term "sunset law" is popularly used to cover both approaches, they
are different in their essentials and in their probable consequences.
It is considerably more traumatic, for example, to have an agency
cease to exist, while its programmatic responsibilities remain, than it
is for a program or set of regulations to cease while the agency continues to perform its other tasks.

The legislative proposals currently being considered differ also as
to their coverage. In some instances, virtually all agencies of government and their programs will be up for periodic review, evaluation,
modification, and possible termination. Other proposals are somewhat
more limited in their approach, focusing on economic regulatory agencies
and programs.

Two Senate bills upon which hearings have been held illustrate variations on the "sunset" concept. Sen. Muskie introduced S. 2925, the
Government Economy and Spending Reform Act, which would put all government programs and activities, with some exceptions, on a five-year reauthorization schedule. If not reauthorized, the program would be
terminated. This bill would further establish a schedule for authorization for programs and activities on the basis of groupings by budget
functions. A zero-based budgetary review would be instituted for each
program. The second bill, S. 2812, Regulatory Reform Act, introduced by
Sen. Percy and Sen. Byrd (W. Va.), is more limited in scope in that it
is concerned only with agencies and programs having an impact on the
economy. This bill provides that over a period of 5 years, from 1977
through 1981, the President would submit to Congress comprehensive plans
for "reforming" regulation in five specific areas of the economy, e.g.,
banking and finance. Each plan would include recommendations for increasing competition, and for procedural, organizational, and structural
changes -- including the merger, modification, establishment or abolition of Federal regulations, functions and agencies. The plans would
be referred to the appropriate Congressional committees. An "action-
forcing mechanism" is proposed whereby the President's plan would become law unless Congress acted by a certain date.

The bill submitted by the Administration (S. 3428), Agenda for Government Reform, is closer to the approach suggested in S. 2812 than that
of S. 2925 in that the President would limit mandatory review to regulatory agencies. The regulatory agencies would be categorized into four
sectors, with one sector being evaluated each year and the President
being required to submit recommendations for change and the Congress
being required to act, either affirmatively or negatively, on these
recommendations. The objective of these proposals, and others, is to
insure that programs and regulations are evaluated in a systemmatic
manner. One important element of this evaluation will be the publication of analyses as to the costs and benefits accruing from various regulatory efforts. The Senate Government Operations Committee has held
hearings on these bills and others during the Spring of 1976.

While there is little disagreement regarding the need for more evaluation of Federal programs, there is criticism of the "sunset" concept as it emerged in legislative proposals. Critics argue, for instance, that Congress need not indulge itself by passing a detailed bill with mandatory features, because Congress already has sufficient authority and need only to set about seriously performing its oversight functions to achieve the same results. Concern is also voiced over the sheer magnitude of the job Congress is imposing on the Executive Branch and itself. Some contend it would be better to recognize the current limitations of our evaluation capabilities and attempt to study a few selected programs, and then move on as our experience permits....

LANDMARK STUDIES OF THE EXECUTIVE BRANCH

Keep Commission. While there were several studies of various aspects of the Federal bureaucracy in the 19th century, the first overall effort to review the workings of the executive agencies was undertaken by the Commission on Department Methods (1905-1909), otherwise known as the Keep Commission. Although the Commission did not publish a complete report, its work and findings stimulated management improvements in many bureaus and in such varied fields as accounting and costing, archives and records administration, simplification of paperwork and improvements in personnel administration, procurement and supply, and contracting procedures.

Committee on Economy and Efficiency. President William Howard Taft appointed a Committee on Economy and Efficiency in 1910. Its report in 1913 not only asserted the continuing need for executive initiative in reorganizations, but pointed out the importance of managerial research by a competent survey staff before reorganization decisions were arrived at. The Committee proposed that this staff be part of a Bureau of the Budget which would report to the President. This latter recommendation languished for some years, finding fruition in the Budget and Accounting Act of 1921 (42 Stat. 20), which established the Bureau of the Budget.

Joint Committee on Reorganization. The Joint Committee on Reorganization was named in 1923 by Congress, with a Chairman appointed by President Harding. Solicited for its views, the Harding Administration recommended, among other things, the establishment of a Department of Education and Welfare and a Department of National Defense, and the placement of all independent agencies in executive departments except those which had quasi-judicial functions or acted as service agencies for all departments.

President's Committee on Administrative Management. President Franklin D. Roosevelt made executive reorganization a major item on the agenda of his second term and sent to Congress in January 1937 the Report of his Committee on Administrative Management (Brownlow Committee). This Report proposed, among other things, that some 100 independent agencies, administrations, boards, and commissions be placed within 12 executive departments. Of these departments, two -- Public Works and Social Welfare -- would be new additions to the Cabinet. Although these recommendations were not adopted, the work of the Brownlow Committee had a few notable results, particularly in strengthening the staff resources of the President and in preparing the way for the creation of several large executive agencies.

Another contribution of lasting importance was the Committee's affirmation of broad Presidential authority to initiate executive reorganization. Responsibility for administrative management was necessarily the President's; integral to that responsibility, it was pointed out, was control over reorganization. Up to this time the Congress had delegated substantial reorganization authority to the President only in emergency periods of war and depression. The President's Committee advanced the proposition that reorganization was essentially an executive function. Only the broad outlines of departmental design, it maintained, were to be determined by Congress. The continuing process of internal distribution of activities was a function of the Executive.

The Reorganization Act of 1939, which Congress vetoed, was not a product of the Brownlow Committee. The bill nonetheless conformed to the principles enunciated by the Committee two years previous. The device of the legislative veto, of course, provides a practical means for ultimate congressional control over plans submitted by the President.

Hoover Commission I (1947-1949). The Commission on Organization of the Executive Branch of the Government (Hoover Commission I) was established in part to bring into an integrated organization structure the numerous agencies left in the wake of war and demobilization. It was established by Congress, although it had the active cooperation of the President throughout its existence. The enabling statute of the first Hoover Commission required the Commission to be bipartisan and it was composed of six Democrats and six Republican members.

The major emphasis of the reports of the Hoover Commission I was on centralization of responsibility for policy-making and setting of standards, and on delegation and decentralization of operational decisions. The importance of equipping the President with effective staff arms for overall management was also reaffirmed.

In evaluating the results which followed the publication of the reports of the Hoover Commission I, Herbert Emmerich concluded:

> The record of results achieved after the commission submitted its recommendations was extraordinary. Substantially following the suggestings of the reports, the Congress established the General Services Administration and passed the Military Unification Act and the State Department Reorganization Act. In the Reorganization Act of 1949 the President was given continuing reorganization authority, although of a more restricted nature than had been recommended by the commission. Under the authority of this act, President Truman effected many of the commission's proposals -- strengthening the Executive Office, strengthening the positions of the chairmen of the Civil Service Commission and the Maritime Commission, reorganizing the Post Office Department, and transferring the Employment Service to the Department of Labor and the Public Roads Administration to the Department of Commerce. In the closing days of its first session, the Eighty-first Congress raised the Federal salary ceiling in the direction urged by the Commission. (Federal Organization and Administrative Management, pp. 95-96)

Hoover Commission II (1953-1955). In 1953, Congress established another Commission on the Organization of the Executive Branch of the

Government, otherwise known as Hoover Commission II. While the first
Hoover Commission had been principally interested in improving the
administrative management of the government, the second Hoover Commission was concerned with issues of policy and function.

The underlying premise of the Commission's work was that the Federal
government ought to reduce its functions, not only to save money and
reduce taxes, but primarily to eliminate competition with private enterprise. Because of the pressures of the depression and the war, numerous
agencies and programs had been established to regulate, supplement, and
assist the private sector, but many of these agencies and programs were
counterproductive. This Commission, therefore, was more concerned with
what the government should do rather than how it should be organized
and managed.

The very nature of the Commission's task and philosophy insured that
its results would not receive as favorable a reception as had its first
effort. Its terms of reference were too broad and ill-defined and the
political timing of its reports was miscalculated. Indeed, the mood of
the country appeared to have shifted towards greater government involvement in everyday life, not less. Notwithstanding the dated nature of
its report, however, the second Hoover Commission did raise important
questions of policy and operation, many of which are still under discussion today.

Advisory Council on Executive Organization (1969-1971). President
Richard Nixon appointed the Advisory Council on Executive Organization
(Ash Council) in 1969 and named 6 private citizens to the Council. The
concept underlying the work of the Ash Council was that the Federal
government's domestic programs should be administered by a small number of major purpose departments. The objective of this reorganization would be to increase the effectiveness of the management of federal
programs and agencies rather than merely saving money.

A "model" department would be one where the Secretary would be assisted by a small number of Secretarial officers having department-wide
responsibilities. Specifically provided were a Deputy Secretary who
would serve as an alter-ego and principal overseer of internal management for the Secretary, two Under Secretaries, a number of Assistant
Secretaries, and a General Counsel. These officers, with the exception
of the Deputy Secretary, would serve in a staff capacity.

To provide a means for a rational grouping of the large bureaus and
programs to be inherited by the proposed four new departments, the concept of the "Administration" was introduced as a first tier device for
program direction. These organizations, patterned after the operating
administrations in the Department of Transportation, were provided as
management centers -- each with a major segment of the department's
administrative program. These Administrations would be headed by
Administrators with a rank higher than the Assistant Secretaries.

The combined use of cross-cutting secretarial officers, concerned
with functions affecting all elements of the department, and program
administrators, charged with directing important segments of the
department's operating responsibilities, was expected to facilitate
decentralized management while simultaneously providing for effective
Secretarial control and department cohesion. The above changes, to be
made in the central office, would be accompanied by significant alteration in the field structure of the agencies. In most instances it was
anticipated that the regional directors would be comprehensive supervisors.

The President submitted his reorganization proposals to Congress on Mar. 25, 1971. The proposals would have abolished seven existing departments and created four new executive departments -- Human Resources; Community Development; Natural Resources; and Economic Affairs. Overview hearings were held on these proposals in general as well as hearings on the specific proposals for Departments of Community Development and Natural Resources. No legislation passed during the 92d Congress, and the bills were not re-introduced during the 93d Congress.

CHRONOLOGY OF EVENTS

This Congressional Research Service chronology was published in August 1976. In updating the chronology, the following items should be noted.

1/20/77   Jimmy Carter inaugurated as 39th president of the United States and pledges to undertake a major reorganization of the Executive branch.

10/1/76   94th Congress adjourns without taking action on any of several reorganization proposals or without extending the president's authority to submit reorganization plans.

05/13/76 -- President submits to Congress a legislative proposal (S. 3428) to require review of economic regulatory programs over a 4-year period. Presidential recommendations as to continuation or alterations in programs or agencies would become standing business of Congress, requiring action.

03/17/76 -- Senate Subcommittee on Intergovernmental Relations of the Government Operations Committee, chaired by Senator Muskie, held hearings on the Government Economy and Spending Act of 1976 (S. 2925). These hearings continued during the Spring months.

04/09/75 -- President Ford submitted to the Congress a draft of proposed legislation to re-establish for a 4-year period the authority of the President to submit reorganization plans to Congress.

06/14/73 -- Senator Percy introduced S. 2003, extending until Apr. 1, 1977, the President's authority to submit reorganization plans to Congress. (No action was taken during the 93d Congress.)

04/01/73 -- Presidential authority to submit reorganization plans under P.L. 92-179 expired.

12/10/71 -- Extension of President's authority to submit reorganization plans until Apr. 1, 1973, was enacted as P.L. 92-179.

11/19/70 -- Memorandum on Organization for Social and Economic Programs with recommendations, was submitted to the President by the President's Advisory Council on Executive Organization (Ash Council).

04/05/69 -- President's Advisory Council on Executive Organization was appointed.

07/10/53 -- Legislation was enacted (67 Stat. 142) establishing the
Commission on Organization of the Executive Branch of the
Government (Second Hoover Commission). (The Commission
ceased to exist on June 30, 1955.)

06/20/49 -- Reorganization Act of 1949 was enacted (63 Stat. 203;
5 U.S.C. 901-913).

07/07/47 -- Legislation was enacted (61 Stat. 246) establishing the
Commission on the Organization of the Executive Branch of
the Government (First Hoover Commission). [The Commission
ceased to exist on June 12, 1949.]

12/18/41 -- War Powers Act of 1941 was enacted (55 Stat. 561). Title I

06/20/32 -- Executive Reorganization Act of 1932 was enacted (47 Stat.
413). Title IV authorized the President to consolidate,
redistribute, and transfer various agencies and functions,
but did not permit him to abolish any executive departments
or agency created by statute, or to transfer or eliminate
its functions.

PART I

CONSOLIDATION OF EXECUTIVE DEPARTMENTS AND AGENCIES

Introduction

The need for reorganization of the Executive departments and agencies has been the subject of various study groups, commissions, and task forces over the past thirty years.[1] The recommendations of those investigative bodies state these recurrent themes: the number of agencies of government should be reduced; departments should be organized around broad goals; similar or related programs should be grouped together in one department to diminish the need for interagency coordination and to concentrate the decision-making tasks; in order to achieve a balance in national priorities, mechanisms are needed to control the parochial influences exerted on agency staff by expert advocates from the constituency they serve. These recommendations lead to the conclusion that a number of federal departments and agencies should be consolidated and that the President's relationship to them should be redefined.

The issue of consolidation seems to resurface with each new administration, but plans for consolidation invariably collide with political and administrative imperatives, usually to the detriment of any sweeping change. Meanwhile, the number of Executive departments has increased, functions become more dispersed, and departments and agencies are accused of serving special interests. After President Nixon disclosed plans to consolidate various functions into a few "super departments" in March 1971, it was announced that the Department of Agriculture (noted for being "owned" by its clientele) would be handled as a special case and kept as a single department. More recently, due to criticism in the press and in Congress over the proliferation of federal energy programs into 22 separate government agencies, there was pressure to consider establishing another new department concerned with energy and fuels ([5], p. 851).

As stated in the Introduction to this volume, the studies of Price and Heineman represent the reorganization efforts of the Kennedy and Johnson Administrations.[2] The 1964 Task Force on Government Organization, established by President Kennedy, was chaired by Don Price, dean of Harvard University's School of Government. The Price report indicated: ". . . it is not necessary to set up another Hoover Commission. In fact, that would be a mistake. . . . [Planning] should be done in close relation to the determination of your policy goals. This has to be . . . within the circle of your responsible advisers . . ." ([11]). The Price task force recommended the creation of five new departments: Transportation, Education, Natural Resources, Economic Development, and Housing and Community Development.

President Johnson set up the 1966 Task Force on Government Organization, chaired by the president of Northwest Industries, Inc., Ben Heineman. The Heineman task force suggested an organizational consolidation of all administrative functions of the federal government into six departments: Social Services, National Resources and Development, Economic Affairs, Science and Environmental Preservation, Foreign Affairs, and National Security Affairs. With few structural exceptions, these recommendations for reform closely parallel those subsequently generated by Nixon's Ash Council. In its "administratively confidential" memorandum to President Johnson, Heineman's task force observed: ". . . Presidential authority to carry through the measures he proposes is fragmented and circumscribed. The executive branch does not belong exclusively to him; its command and subordination structure is pluralistic in character; its unwieldy size too vast for personal surveillance. We firmly believe that organizational reform to steepen and 'presidentialize' the pyramid of top executives who support the President as Chief Executive is indispensable to give the President a fighting chance to perform his management tasks.'' ([12])

The President's Advisory Council on Executive Organization (the Ash Council) was commissioned by President Nixon and headed by Roy Ash, former director of Litton Industries and subsequent director of the Office of Management and Budget. The council was composed of prominent citizens, some of whom had extensive experience in government.[3] The Ash Council and the Price and Heineman task forces represent a coalescing of views on the role and organization of the Executive department heads directly responsible to the president, thereby assuring a more direct and efficient line of command between the president and cabinet members. Concurrently, this approach limits the possibility of special interest intrusion or domination of ''line subordinates who are forced by responsibilities to assume a more narrow perspective and to reflect parochial interest in their advice to the President'' ([103], p. 51). In March 1971, Nixon submitted to Congress his reorganization plans, which were based largely on the findings and recommendations of the Ash Council.[4] The Nixon plans called for the establishment of four new departments: Community Development, Human Resources, Natural Resources, and Economic Affairs. The general proposals underwent Congressional overview hearings, while only two of the specific proposals—Departments of Community Development and Natural Resources—were subjected to additional hearings. None of the Nixon administration proposals were approved in the 92nd Congress, and they were not reintroduced in subsequent Congresses. The Nixon proposal on the consolidation of Executive agencies is reprinted in this chapter as a point of departure for future examinations of the departments.

Whatever merits the Nixon/Ash consolidation plans may have (and they are remarkably similar to those presented to Kennedy and Johnson), there was little chance they could be implemented after Watergate and its deleterious effect on the Nixon Administration. Congress virtually ignored the recommendations, and the president's reorganization authority under the 1949 Act (63 Stat. 203: 5 U.S.C. 901–913) was allowed to expire in 1973.

Reorganization of the Executive branch was revived as an issue in the presidential campaign of 1976 by Jimmy Carter. Two weeks after Carter's election he asked the congressional leadership to reinstate the Reorganization Act of 1949. The reorganization plans of the Nixon Administration serve to provide a documentary base for comparison both for the Carter task forces, in examining alternatives, and for the Congress, in their examination of any forthcoming proposals. However, party politics does play a role in these matters and it is likely that the Carter proposals will not bear much identification with any Nixon plan. President Carter's aides have already expressed doubt that their efforts will be directed towards consolidation of agencies along the lines suggested by the Ash Council and earlier bodies. Jimmy Carter leans heavily towards the sunset/zero-base budgeting modes of reform, but these approaches are relatively untried, certainly on the scale of federal management. For that reason, as well as the president's desire to gain control of the bureaucracy, departmental consolidation cannot be eliminated as a viable alternative. It may be resurrected, in whole or in part, as the most economical and effective proposal for swift government reorganization.

1. The first overall review of the federal bureaucracy took place in 1905 by the Commission on Department Methods; no report was published. Presidents Taft and Harding also attempted to assess the need for reorganization, but the serious reorganization proposals (especially those dealing with consolidation of agencies) evolved in the administration of President Franklin D. Roosevelt. In 1937, he established the Committee on Administrative Management, known also as the Brownlow Commission.

2. The Price and Heineman reports are, as yet, unpublished; they are available, however, in the collection of the Lyndon B. Johnson Library in Austin, Texas.

3. Members of the Ash Council were: John Connally, secretary of the treasury under Nixon; George Baker, former dean of the Graduate School of Business Administration of Harvard University; Frederick Kappel, former chairman of the board, American Telephone and Telegraph Co.; Richard Paget, president of the New York management consultant firm of Cresap, McCormick & Paget; and Walter Thayer, president of Whitney Communications Corp., who served as a special consultant and also as a member of the council by a later appointment.

4. The Nixon plans differed somewhat from the Ash Council recommendations. Upon release of the Ash memoranda, Nixon explained: ''The differences will reflect conclusions I have reached as a result of my own experience in government, as well as proposals for Executive reorganization made earlier in this Administration and in previous administrations.'' Refer to [103].

Chapter 1
Scope and Purpose of
1971 Reorganization

INTRODUCTION ([23], pp. 1–5)

On November 11, 1971, President Nixon sent a message to Congress detailing the administration's recommendations on reorganization. It was referred to the Senate and House Committees on Government Operations for review (the name of the Senate Committee on Government Operations was changed to the Committee on Governmental Affairs in February 1977); those committees had jurisdiction over such matters and proceeded to hold hearings and conduct staff studies. The House Committee, chaired by Representative Chet Holifield, submitted its report to the Speaker of the House, with a request that it be printed and distributed in March of 1972. Portions of that report are reprinted in this chapter.

The House report is an analysis of Nixon's proposal for modifying the structure of cabinet-level departments, as well as the allocation of their functional responsibilities. The Nixon plan called for the most sweeping changes in this area to date. The fact that it was put forward by a politically discredited administration does not alter the significance of the recommendations nor their validity. Indeed, the proposal includes much of the research and conclusions of the preceding administrations of John Kennedy and Lyndon Johnson.

In his state of the Union message presented to a joint session of the 92d Congress on January 22, 1971, President Nixon proposed six "great goals" of his administration, of which one (the sixth) was "a complete reform of the Federal Government itself." He said: [1]

> Based on a long, intensive study with the aid of the best advice obtainable, I have concluded that a sweeping reorganization of the Executive Branch is needed if the Government is to keep up with the times and with the needs of the people.

The President's proposal, as put forth in the state of the Union message, would:

—leave four executive departments in being: State, Treasury, Defense, and Justice;

—abolish seven existing departments: Agriculture,[2] Interior, Commerce, Transportation, Labor, Health, Education, and Wel-

---

[1] H. Doc. No. 92–1, p. 7 (Jan. 22, 1971). The state of the Union message is printed in the Congressional Record of Jan. 22, 1971, daily edition, at pp. H92–H95. The five other goals enunciated by the President are welfare reform, improved health care, a stable economy, a better environment, and revenue sharing with State and local governments.

[2] On November 11, 1971, the President announced a revision in the reorganization program that would retain the Department of Agriculture, though somewhat reduced in size.

fare, and Housing and Urban Development; and
—create four new executive departments: Human Resources, Community Development, Natural Resources, and Economic Affairs.

The new organizations would comprise, in the President's words: [3]

—First, a department dealing with the concerns of people—as individuals, as members of a family—a department focused on human needs.

—Second, a department concerned with the community— rural communities and urban—and with all that it takes to make a community function as a community.

—Third, a department concerned with our physical environment, and with the preservation and balanced use of those great natural resources on which our nation depends.

—And fourth, a department concerned with our prosperity— with our jobs, our businesses, and those many activities that keep our economy running smoothly and well.

STATEMENT OF JUSTIFICATION

Subsequently, on March 25, 1971, President Nixon sent a special message on reorganization to the Congress. It presented, in forceful and eloquent terms, the administration's case for reorganization. In the President's view, the major cause of ineffectiveness in Government is not men or money but machinery. To restore the confidence of the people, there must be comprehensive, not piecemeal, reform.

A serious weakness is the fragmentation of functions and scattering of responsibilities in the Federal Government. The President cited these examples: [4]

Nine different Federal departments and 20 independent agencies are now involved in education matters. Seven departments and eight independent agencies are involved in health. In many major cities, there are at least 20 or 30 separate manpower programs, funded by a variety of Federal offices. Three departments help develop our water resources and four agencies in two departments are involved in the management of public lands. Federal recreation areas are administered by six different agencies in three departments of the Government. Seven agencies provide assistance for water and sewer systems. Six departments of the Government collect similar economic information—often from the same sources—and at least seven departments are concerned with international trade. While we cannot eliminate all of this diffusion we can do a great deal to bring similar functions under common commands.

This scattering of functions and responsibilities, according to the President's analysis, makes it difficult to develop a comprehensive

---

[3] H. Doc. No. 92–1, p. 7 (Jan. 22, 1971).
[4] H. Doc. No. 92–75 (Mar. 25, 1971) at 3–4.

strategy and launch a coordinated attack on complex problems. One department or agency may duplicate the work of another and all may be working at cross purposes. Departments with narrow missions tend to represent parochial interests, and the advice and support of department heads become less useful to the President. He finds himself overburdened by the need to resolve conflicts which the department heads would be better able to handle themselves if the executive branch were better organized.

Perhaps the most significant consequence of scattered responsibilities in the executive branch, the President said, is "the hobbling of elected leadership." "If the President or the Congress wants to launch a program or change a program or even find out how a program is working, it often becomes necessary to consult with a half dozen or more authorities, each of whom can blame the others when something goes wrong." [5]

In looking at the present organization of the Federal Government, the President found that "many of the existing units deal with methods and subjects rather than purposes and goals." Government, he concluded, should be organized around basic goals. This is necessary because "only when a department is set up to achieve a given set of purposes, can we effectively hold that department accountable for achieving them. Only when the responsibility for realizing basic objectives is clearly focused in a specific governmental unit, can we reasonably hope that these objectives will be realized." [6]

Thus, the President indicated the basic purpose of his reorganization: [7]

> Under the proposals which I am submitting, those in the Federal Government who deal with common or closely related problems would work together in the same organizational framework. Each department would be given a mission broad enough so that it could set comprehensive policy directions and resolve internally the policy conflicts which are most likely to arise. The responsibilities of each department would be defined in a way that minimizes parochialism and enables the President and the Congress to hold specific officials responsible for the achievement of specific goals.

Legislative Bills on Reorganization

President Nixon's message of March 25, 1971, was accompanied by drafts of legislative bills to create the four new executive departments. The message, the text of the bills, section-by-section analyses, and other background and supplementary materials were compiled by the Office of Management and Budget in a document entitled "Papers Relating to the President's Departmental Reorganization Program: A Reference Compilation," dated March 1971, commonly referred to as the "Gray Book." This publication recently was revised to reflect

---

[5] Id. at 6.
[6] Id. at 7–8.
[7] Id. at 8.

certain policy and technical changes in the reorganization proposals and the new edition, with a green cover, was issued shortly before the report.

N1

Chairman Holifield introduced, by request, the legislative bills, which are numbered H.R. 6959 (Department of Natural Resources); H.R. 6960 (Department of Economic Affairs): H.R. 6961 (Department of Human Resources); and H.R. 6962 (Department of Community Development).[8] The bills were referred to the Committee on Government Operations and, in turn, to the Subcommittee on Legislation and Military Operations, of which Mr. Holifield also is chairman.

OVERVIEW HEARINGS

Before deciding to take up the bills individually, the subcommittee held overview hearings on the whole reorganization package on June 2, 3, 7, 8, 14, and 16; July 7, 8, 22, and 27, 1971.[9] The purpose of these hearings, as Chairman Holifield explained in his opening statement, was to "get an overview of the reorganization proposals and to explore, in a preliminary way, some of their complex ramifications and possible consequences." He went on to say: [10]

> As chairman of the Committee on Government Operations and of this subcommittee, I want to make it clear that the President's reorganization proposals will be accorded full and fair hearings. We approach this subject with an open mind, recognizing, on the one hand, that Government organization must keep pace with changing needs, and on the other hand, that reorganization for its own sake is not necessarily justified.
>
> We will want to go behind the official rhetoric and take a hard look at the facts, and we will want to hear from critics as well as advocates. . . .

Administration witnesses in the first round of hearings were headed by the Honorable George P. Shultz, Director of the Office of Management and Budget, assisted by experts in his office. These included Arnold R. Weber, Associate Director; Dwight A. Ink, Assistant Director for Organization and Management Systems; and Alan Dean, Coordinator, President's Departmental Reorganization Program. Roy L. Ash, board chairman of Litton Industries, Inc., who conducted the basic reorganization study for the administration, also testified.

Prominent persons associated with preceding administrations who testified in support of the reorganization measures were: Ben W. Heineman, president of Northwest Industries, Inc., who had chaired a reorganization study for President Johnson; Charles L. Schultze, a former Director of the Bureau of the Budget; Joseph A. Califano, Jr., former Special Assistant to President Johnson; and Wilbur J. Cohen, former Secretary of the Department of Health, Education, and Welfare.

---

[8] Companion bills in the Senate, introduced by Senator Percy and others, were S. 1430, S. 1431, S. 1432 and S. 1433.

[9] The Senate Committee on Government Operations held overview hearings on May 25 and 26 and June 22, 1971.

[10] "Reorganization of Executive Departments (Part 1—Overview)," hearings before a subcommittee of the Committee on Government Operations, House of Representatives, on H.R. 6959, H.R. 6960, H.R. 6961, and H.R. 6962 on June 2, 3, 7, 8, 14, and 16; July 7, 8, 22, and 27, 1971, p. 142 (hereinafter cited as Hearings).

At the subcommittee's request, the National Academy of Public Administration assembled a panel of experts on Government organization, and a full day of the hearings was devoted to informed discussion and analysis of the reorganization proposals by this group with varied background experience in Federal, State, and local government, industry, and universities.[11]

Representatives of the U.S. Chamber of Commerce also testified.

Technical features of the reorganization bills relating to appropriations, contracting, personnel, and other matters were analyzed in testimony by representatives of the General Accounting Office, General Services Administration, and the Civil Service Commission. The emphasis in this part was not on basic policy or concepts, but on administrative provisions which required comparative analysis across the four bills and reconciliation with existing laws bearing on these subjects.

In preparing for the hearings, the subcommittee staff requested and received assistance in the form of special studies and analyses from the General Accounting Office, the Office of Management and Budget, and the Congressional Research Service of the Library of Congress.

After the overview hearings were completed, the subcommittee commenced hearings on H.R. 6962, the bill to establish a Department of Community Development....

SCOPE OF NIXON/ASH PROPOSALS ([23], pp. 19–51)

President Nixon's reorganization proposals, as originally stated, would abolish seven existing departments, along with designated agencies, and reassign all their functions to four new executive departments to be created by statute. Three of the four new departments each would retain an existing department as a core or base upon which to build. Community Development would absorb Housing and Urban Development; Natural Resources would absorb Interior; and Human Resources would absorb Health, Education, and Welfare.

The fourth Department—Economic Affairs—would not start with a single core department as a base, but would draw basic functions from Labor, Transportation, Commerce, and elsewhere. According to the original proposal, the bulk of agricultural functions also was to be transferred to Economic Affairs, but this feature of the reorganization was later abandoned by President Nixon, as described below.

Administration spokesmen emphasize that more is contemplated in the proposed reorganizations than merely a change of names and a shuffling around of a few functions. Each new department, even those building upon existing departmental bases, would have important new functions, expanded missions, streamlined authorities, and strengthened internal organization and management so that each may be regarded as an entirely new department. Even the Department of Agriculture, stripped down under the revised plan to administer functions

---

[11] Members of the National Academy of Public Administration panel were: Roy W. Crawley, Associate Executive Director, National Academy of Public Administration; William G. Colman, Consultant, Governmental Affairs and Federal-State Relations; John J. Corson, Chairman of the Board, Frey Consultants, Inc.; Frederick O.'R. Hayes, former Budget Director, city of New York; John P. Perkins, Director of the Public Administration program, Graduate School of Management, Northwestern University; and Harvey Sherman, Director, Organization and Procedures Department, Port of New York Authority.

more directly concerned with the agricultural economy, is described as a new department.[59]

COMPOSITION OF NEW DEPARTMENTS

The composition of the new departments, including the more important transfers, is briefly described below....

Department of Community Development

In addition to absorbing the Department of Housing and Urban Development (except college housing), DCD would acquire important components from Agriculture, Transportation, and several offices or agencies. Transfers from Agriculture include Rural Electrification Administration, Farmers Home Administration (functions relating to water waste disposal loans and rural housing), Rural Telephone Bank, and Rural Telephone Service. Transfers from Transportation comprise Federal Highway Administration programs (except motor carrier safety) and Urban Mass Transportation Administration. Additional transfers to the new Department include community action and special impact programs from Office of Economic Opportunity, planning and public works functions from Economic Development Administration of the Commerce Department, and disaster relief functions from Small Business Administration and Office of Emergency Preparedness.

Department of Natural Resources

In addition to absorbing the Department of the Interior, DNR would draw important component agencies or functions from Agriculture, Commerce, and Transportation, as well as from Army Corps of Engineers and Atomic Energy Commission. Among the transfers from Agriculture are Forest Service and Soil Conservation Service. Commerce would give up National Oceanic and Atmospheric Administration, and Transportation would give up its oil and gas pipeline safety programs. The new Department also would absorb the Water Resources Council, and planning and funding functions for civil works from the Corps of Engineers and for civilian reactor developments from the Atomic Energy Commission. Uranium enrichment and raw materials also would be transferred from the Commission to the new Department.

N2

Department of Human Resources

In addition to absorbing the Department of Health, Education, and Welfare, DHR would acquire important components or functions from Labor and Agriculture and minor functions from two other departments. Among the transfers from Labor would be Manpower Administration, Employment Service, and Women's Bureau. Transfers from Agriculture include inspection services relating primarily to meat, poultry, and egg products; and food and nutrition services. Commerce would give up its product safety program, and Housing and Urban Development its college housing functions, to the new department.

---

[59] Testimony of Hon. Earl L. Butz, Secretary of Agriculture, at hearings before a subcommittee of the Committee on Government Operations, House of Representatives on H.R. 6962 to create a Department of Community Development, Jan. 25, 1972, transcript p. 1375.

Department of Economic Affairs

As is noted above, Economic Affairs was to take major components and functions from Labor, Commerce, and Transportation and from other sources. Transfers from Labor would include Bureau of Labor Statistics, Employment Standards Administration (except Women's Bureau and Bureau of Employees' Compensation), Labor-Management Services Administration, and Occupational Health and Safety Administration. Transfers from Commerce would include Bureaus of Domestic and International Commerce, Bureau of the Census, Maritime Administration, Patent Office, and National Bureau of Standards (except product safety). Department of Transportation would give up Federal Aviation Administration, Federal Railroad Administration, U.S. Coast Guard, St. Lawrence Seaway Corporation, National Highway Traffic Safety Administration, and National Transportation Safety Board. Additionally, the new department would acquire National Institute of Occupational Health and Safety (from Department of Health, Education, and Welfare), Small Business Administration (except residential disaster loans), Federal Mediation and Conciliation Service, and nonregulatory functions of the National Mediation Board.

CHANGE IN PLANS

The bulk of agencies and functions now in the Department of Agriculture also was included in the reorganization proposal for the Department of Economic Affairs, but President Nixon announced on November 11, 1971, at the time of naming a new Secretary of Agriculture, a change in his reorganization scheme. Departmental status for Agriculture would be retained, comprising those functions initially assigned for transfer to Economic Affairs. Other functions of Agriculture assigned for transfer to Community Development, Natural Resources, and Human Resources would go according to plan.[60]

Among the agencies or functions originally designated for transfer to the Department of Economic Affairs, but now left in the Department of Agriculture, are the following:

Commodity Credit Corporation
Commodity Exchange Authority
Agricultural Stabilization and Conservation Service
Export Market Service
Federal Crop Insurance Corporation
Foreign Agricultural Service
Cooperative State Research Service
Agricultural Research Service (with certain exceptions)

Cooperative Extension Service
Packers and Stockyards Administration
Consumer and Marketing Service (except food inspection programs)
Farmers Cooperative Service
Farmers Home Administration loan functions relating to farm operations, ownership, and emergencies

The truncated Department of Agriculture would have about 28,000 employees instead of 85,600, and annual expenditures of $5.2 billion instead of $8.7 billion; it would approximate in size—number of employees—the new Department of Community Development.

[60] A fact sheet concerning the President's decision was submitted to Chairman Holifield by the Honorable George P. Shultz, Director of the Office of Management and Budget.

Excluded Agencies

The reorganization proposals, sweeping as they are, are not all inclusive. Major independent agencies such as the National Aeronautics and Space Administration, the Atomic Energy Commission, and the National Science Foundation, are left out—except that certain functions of NASA's Office of Technology Utilization would go to the Department of Economic Affairs, and certain AEC programs would go to the Department of Natural Resources. Conceivably, these three independent agencies could have formed the nucleus of a new department covering primarily scientific and technological affairs, but the reorganization proposals did not include such a department.

Another excluded agency is the Veterans' Administration. In terms of combining similar functions, a case could be made for transferring VA housing functions to the proposed Department of Community Development—as recommended by the Price task force—and VA health and medical services to the proposed Department of Human Resources. There may be, on the other hand, political and administrative logic in preserving the VA as a self-contained entity, particularly with the growing numbers of veterans of the Vietnam war. The VA, with a $6 billion yearly budget and more than 140,000 full-time employees, is larger than most executive departments and employs more persons than would any of the proposed new departments.

The reorganization scheme, in fact, did not attempt to sweep into a reconstituted departmental framework the scores of independent agencies, offices, boards, and commissions in the manner proposed by some previous Presidents. A number of independent units would be transferred in whole or in part, but the organizing principle was aimed more at establishing broad departmental missions than at eliminating the assortment of independent agencies.

The regulatory agencies, particularly, have presented a vexing problem to advocates of reorganization. From time to time, proposals have been made to assign the regulatory agencies—or at least their nonregulatory functions—to executive departments. The Ash Council, which made a separate study of certain regulatory agencies, did not favor their inclusion in the revised departmental structure. It recommended that the multimembership of designated regulatory agencies be replaced by single administrators; that the railway/motor, airline, and maritime regulatory commissions be combined into a new transportation regulatory agency; and that an administrative court be established to hear appeals from final decisions of regulatory agencies.[61].

Compromise Arrangements

The proposed reorganizations reflect two types of compromise arrangements: (1) Practical adjustments in developing the original blueprint, such as the exclusion of certain agencies or functions; and (2) changes dictated by events or situations which emerged after the reorganization blueprint was developed and publicized.

Illustrative of the adjustments in the first category are those affecting the Atomic Energy Commission and the Corps of Engineers. In

N3

[61] "A New Regulatory Framework," report on selected independent regulatory agencies by the President's Advisory Council on Executive Organization, January 1971.

each case, there is a split between policy and funding on the one side, and program execution on the other. Thus, policy and funding with regard to AEC's civilian power development would be transferred to the Department of Natural Resources, but the Commission would carry on and manage the actual technical work. Similarly, the Corps of Engineers would give up to the same department its planning, evaluation, and funding functions in the civil works area, but it would continue its dredging, dam-building, and other long-established services.

There are those who believe that such split responsibilities reduce the effectiveness of agency performance. Others see no real obstacle to having the policy and funding functions in one department and the execution of programs in a service-type agency located elsewhere.

Another example concerns the Bureau of Indian Affairs in the Interior Department. One of the five basic administrations in the proposed Department of Natural Resources would be concerned with Indian and territorial affairs and would conduct programs to improve the lot of Indians, Alaskan natives, and territorial people. Responsibilities along this line long have been held by the Bureau of Indian Affairs and other units in the Department of Interior, which functions are to be assimilated in the Department of Natural Resources. It could be argued that the Department of Human Resources is a much more suitable place for administering programs dealing with people, but for historical and practical reasons, including the preferences of Indian tribe spokesmen, the transfer was not made.[62]

The compromise regarding the Department of Agriculture falls in the second category; it was not built into the initial plan for departmental reorganization. It came at a time when farm prices were low, discontent in the farm belt was manifest, opposition to the breakup of the Department of Agriculture was heard in the Congress, and a new Secretary of Agriculture was about to be named.[63] As the appointee, the Honorable Earl L. Butz, indicated in subsequent testimony before the subcommittee, one would obviously not look forward to being the last Secretary of the Department.

Among other changes made after the reorganization proposals were announced were those relating to the Federal Cochairmen of the Appalachian Regional Commission and of the Regional Action Planning Commissions, authorized respectively by the Appalachian Regional Development Act and title V of the Public Works and Economic Development Act of 1965. Originally, their functions were to have been transferred to the Secretary of the proposed Department of Community Development, which possibly would have affected the balance of joint Federal-State agency relationships and disrupted the working of the Commissions. Protests from Governors, Members of Congress, and others in the affected States undoubtedly prompted these adjustments.

Whereas some reorganization decisions have been tempered by political or administrative necessities, others would make clean breaks

---

[62] Hearings, p. 161.
[63] According to the OMB fact sheet, "* * * it would reassure the farm community and help secure the support needed in Congress to get action on the reorganization proposals if a Department of Agriculture were to be retained as a separate executive department." See appendix 2, p. 71. For House floor statements opposing the disestablishment of the Department of Agriculture, see Cong. Rec., Oct. 6, 1971 (daily edition), pp. H 9282–9293.

with the past against the anticipated opposition of particular interest groups in and out of Government. For example, the Forest Service, now in the Department of Agriculture, and for many years a bone of contention in reorganization proposals, would be lodged in the Department of Natural Resources. The Rural Electrification Administration and certain functions of the Farmers Home Administration would end up in the Department of Community Development on the premise that traditional rural-urban distinctions are no longer valid for administrative purposes, and that the respective services of the transferred components are more community- than farm-oriented.

The Department of Agriculture, a century old and a symbol of the farmer's voice in Government, would have been disestablished, according to this rationale, except for the President's above-noted change in plans.

RATIONALE OF 1971 PROPOSED ORGANIZATION

It is important to understand what is old and new in the reorganization concept advanced by the President. For many years the accepted criterion for departmental organization in the executive branch was "major purpose." The theory was that functions scattered throughout the Government should be reassembled according to each department's major purpose (basic mission) and, if necessary, a new department or two would be added to assimilate appropriate functions. Similarity or likeness of function was the controlling consideration, so that overlapping and duplication (hence, waste) could be eliminated.

It did not follow necessarily that the departments would be large in size; the size depended on the mission and the functions to be sorted out and reassembled. Conceivably, some departments could be reduced in size, because it was contended that department heads should be relieved (by transfer out) of functions extraneous to their mission. They were said to be busy enough running their departments without being burdened by all kinds of extraneous responsibilities conferred upon them by the exigencies of time and circumstance. This rationale recently has been applied in the case of the Department of Agriculture after President Nixon decided not to abolish it.

The principle that the executive departments of the Federal Government should be organized according to major purpose dates back at least 50 years,[65] was written into law in 1932,[66] and was restated by the Hoover Commission in 1949.[67]

Herbert Hoover was fond of saying that related functions should be put together, "cheek by jowl." [68] President Nixon adheres to this

---

[65] President Taft said in a message to the Congress: "Only by grouping services according to their character can substantial progress be made in eliminating duplication * * *." Cong. Rec., vol. 48, p. 1027 (Jan. 17, 1912). The Joint Committee on Reorganization, created by the Congress in 1920, had the mission to study the redistribution of Government activities "so that each executive department shall embrace only services having close working relation with each other and ministering directly to the primary purpose for which the same are maintained and operated." In 1921, President Harding endorsed this principle. See Mansfield, op. cit., p. 470.

[66] 47 Stat. 413.

[67] "General Management of the Executive Branch," a report to the Congress by the Commission on Organization of the Executive Branch, February 1949, p. 34. The Commission recommended (No. 1): "The numerous agencies of the executive branch must be grouped into departments as nearly as possible by major purposes in order to give a coherent mission to each department."

[68] Mr. Hoover's characterization appears in the Commission's report as follows: "By placing related functions cheek-by-jowl the overlaps can be eliminated, and, of even greater importance, coordinated policies can be developed." Id.

idea when he says "* * * we can do a great deal to bring similar functions under common commands." [69]

Organizing Around Basic Goals

Mr. Nixon goes further, however, equating "major purpose" as an organizing principle to "basic goals" and "the great purposes of government in modern society." On the one hand he offers the reorganization proposals in a context of continuity with those of his predecessors ranging back to President Franklin D. Roosevelt. On the other hand, he states that Government has grown and changed, and a "new understanding" is required to reorganize the Government for effective performance. "The key to that new understanding," Mr. Nixon says, "is the concept that the executive branch of the Government should be organized around basic goals." [70]

Expanding the organizing principle from "major purpose" to "great purpose" or "basic goal" suggests that ends are emphasized more than means. Ends are few and general; means are specific and diverse. As Mr. Nixon put it, "* * * we often find ourselves using *a variety of means* to achieve a *single* set of goals." [71] (Emphasis in original.) The clear implication is that not only similar but dissimilar functions may be combined in one department, so long as they are regarded as contributing toward a basic goal.

Thus, the Department of Economic Affairs would encompass such disparate activities as mediation of labor disputes, census taking, promoting the merchant marine, helping small business, granting patents, investigating airline crashes, testing materials, doing telecommunications research, and promoting international travel and trade—on the premise that they all bear upon the economic health of the Nation. Under the original plan to transfer major components of the Department of Agriculture, the list of functions assembled in a single department would have been even lengthier and more diversified.

Transportation, according to the goal criteria, is no longer regarded as adequate for separate departmental status because it is considered to be a means to other ends rather than an end in itself. In Mr. Nixon's words: "* * * the Department of Transportation * * * is now organized around methods and not around purposes." [72] Consequently, the Department of Transportation, created in 1966, is to be dissolved and its components or function reassigned. The earlier rationale for unification of transportation functions, based on technology and economics, gives way to competing rationales for reintegrating transportation functions in departments concerned severally with community development and economic affairs.

It is not self-evident that Government can be effectively organized around basic goals. Such goals, characteristically, are broad, overlapping, and open-ended. Furthermore, they can be formulated in different ways, so that alternative or additional organizational patterns could be readily devised. It could be said, for example, that national security is a basic goal, and this would justify merging the Departments of Defense and State into a single Department of Na-

---

[69] H. Doc. No. 92–75, p. 4 (Mar. 25, 1971).
[70] Id., p. 7.
[71] Id.
[72] Id. at 10–11.

tional Security. Of course, there are many political and practical reasons why such a merger would not be made.

Similarly, it could be said that since everything that Government does affects the economy or the citizenry, conceivably all the domestic functions of Government could be brought within the confines of a single giant department. When the Ash Council called "for a department concerned with the whole economy," which it called a Department of Economic Growth and Productivity, it was suggesting a move far along toward this concept. In practice, of course, the functions of Government are and must be divided among a number of departments.

CREATION OF SUPER DEPARTMENTS

The assignment of departmental functions according to basic goals works toward fewer departments of larger size, or what have been termed "super departments." [74] This follows from the necessarily broad definitions of basic goals; it also reflects the administrative necessities of policymaking and power. If the Secretaries are to develop broad policies, resolve conflicts, and allocate resources in meaningful ways, they must have dominion over relatively large sectors of Government activity. In Mr. Nixon's words: "Each department would be given a mission broad enough so that it could set comprehensive policy directions and resolve internally the policy conflicts which are most likely to arise." [75]

As already suggested, if Government activities are brought together because they are associated with a basic goal, functional similarity may or may not be present. Resource allocation in pursuit of a goal, after all, is a problem of choice among functions which differ from, as well as resemble, each other. Organization by major purpose, according to conventional theory, seeks to weed out overlap and duplication of similar functions. Organization according to basic goal seeks to give the department head a broad enough command of competing resources so he can make intelligent choices in budget allocations. All such resources compete with each other, in the final analysis, whether they are functionally similar or different.

The broader the goal, the more likely that dissimilar or disparate functions will be embraced in the same departmental confines, giving the department the characteristics of a conglomerate. Conglomeration is inevitable when the organizing principle for departmental functions is raised to such high and broad purposes as the health of the economy, the welfare of people, community development, and conservation of resources. To the extent that existing departments, such as Health, Education, and Welfare, may be said to be organized around basic goals, the conglomerate aspects are evident, and they are bound to increase as the departments are expanded in size and scope of responsibilities, which the President proposes.

It has been suggested that the Ash Council, which drew up the basic blueprint for the President's proposed reorganization, was drawing upon the business experience of its chairman, and possibly other members, in building or directing corporate conglomerates. [76] The analogy

---

[74] John D. Millett, Chairman of the National Academy of Public Administration, in a memorandum to the subcommittee, described President Nixon's proposals for reorganizing the executive departments as embodying "a new concept in Federal Government administrative organization * * * that of the 'super executive department'." Hearings, p. 438.
[75] H. Doc. No. 92–75, p. 8 (Mar. 25, 1971).
[76] See hearings, pp. 217–219, 550–553.

of the corporate conglomerate is useful in the sense that the organizing principle for component business units or ventures in a conglomerate is not their functional similarity but their profitability. As long as a component contributes to the common goal of making money, it does not make any difference whether the firm manufactures cement, pork products, or semiconductors.

As explained above, however, the organizational patterns conceived by the Ash Council were not essentially different from those drawn up by study groups in the preceding administration. The difference is that the present administration has articulated a more systematic statement of basic goals as organizing criteria and has proposed wide-ranging reorganizations in a single package.

BIGNESS AND EFFICIENCY

Whatever the organizational ramifications, advocates of the goal-oriented departments before the subcommittee directed much of their commentary to dispelling the notion that bigness necessarily means inefficiency or lack of management control. It was pointed out that none of the proposed departments approaches the Department of Defense in size; and except for the proposed Department of Economic Affairs, none would be larger than some existing civil departments or agencies.[77] The testimony suggested that some relatively small departments had been poorly managed and some big ones well run,[78] though it must be recognized that evaluations of departmental performance tend to be subjective or impressionistic, vary over time, and may apply to one part of a department and not to another.

As an example, many persons believe that the Department of Health, Education, and Welfare is too large and unwieldy for effective management, and there are proposals to break it into smaller segments by creating separate Departments of Health and Education.[79] On the other hand, these proposals may reflect more the desires of professional groups for separate departmental expression in Government than management necessities. There are former Secretaries of the Department of Health, Education, and Welfare on both sides of the manageability question. And others point out that regardless of what judgments are made about the performance of the Department as a whole, the Social Security Administration, a major component with about 55,000 of the Department's 110,000 employees, is very well managed.[80]

The Department of Defense is another case in point. With its more than 1 million civilian employees, and its 2.5 million military personnel, the Department of Defense overshadows every other department of the Government. The judgment as to whether that Department is

[77] The Department of Economic Affairs, as initially proposed, would have about 160,000 employees. Human Resources 122,000, Natural Resources 111,000 and Community Development 30,000. According to the testimony of George P. Shultz, Director of the Office of Management and Budget, "Three of the new departments are not significantly larger than certain of the domestic departments which are being superseded." Hearings, p. 148.

[78] Hearings, pp. 156, 196, 259, 411 et passim.

[79] Among bills for departmental reorganization introduced in the 92d Congress are several to create a separate Department of Health and a separate Department of Education. The unpublished report of the Price task force recommended a separate Department of Education, leaving HEW as the Department of Health and Welfare. The National Education Association also favors a separate cabinet department for education. See also Rufus E. Miles, Jr., "The Case for a Federal Department of Education," Public Administration Review, vol. XXVII, No. 1, March 1967.

[80] According to the testimony of John J. Corson, about half of the 110,000 employees in the Department of HEW are in the Social Security Administration which is "generally recognized to be one of the best administered agencies in the Federal Government." Hearings, p. 496.

well or poorly managed depends on the time, the circumstance, the quality of leadership, the vantage point of the observer, and the particular issues involved. In some segments of Government activity under its charge, the Department of Defense is regarded as a model of efficiency; in others, a continuing example of inefficiency and waste.

The experience of New York City, which created super agencies for administration, is of collateral interest. According to testimony before the subcommittee, some 49 city departments were consolidated into nine super agencies or administrations, of which eight are still in being. In total employment, some of them are larger than Federal departments. As an example, the human resources agency in New York City has more employees than the Federal Department of Housing and Urban Development; this would still be true after a transition to a Federal Department of Community Development.[81]

Testimony by a former budget director of the city of New York indicated that many problems were encountered in consolidation, and there was an increase rather than a decrease in administrative overhead. He pointed out that "the reorganizations are not self-executing," but that time, money, and talent have to be expended before the benefits of reorganization are fully realized. At this point in time, after 5 years of experience, the benefits of New York City's change to super agencies are not conclusive; although on balance, the witness believed it was the right move to make.[82]

Administration officials believe that large departments in the Federal Government can be effectively managed. To make this belief a self-fulfilling prophecy, they have done more intensive work on the internal organization and management of the proposed new departments than has been done in any previous case of large-scale reorganization.

ELEMENTS OF ARBITRARINESS

The mix of functions, similar and dissimilar, which makes up a large department has elements of arbitrariness. Such arbitrariness is inevitable in all Government organizations because purposes cannot be that well defined, nor is it practicable to extract all similar functions from departments or agencies with diverse missions and bring them together in neat, orderly groupings. Arbitrariness is likely to increase, however, as the organizing principle is broadened.

The Department of Human Resources, for example, is to be concerned with the health and welfare of individuals and families. Housing also is vital to their health and welfare, but the Department of Community Development is to take care of housing. Not all housing would go to Community Development in the proposed reorganizations, however, because the basic goal concept of organization pulls college housing into Human Resources, while for political or other reasons veterans' housing stays with the Veterans' Administration, and promotion of home ownership through savings and loan associations stays with the independent Home Loan Bank Board.

The difficulties in deciding how to redistribute functions because of the overlap in basic goals can be illustrated in many other ways. For example, the decision was made in the reorganization planning to assign the functions of the Rural Electrification Administration to Community Development rather than to Natural Resources. In the orbit of one goal, rural electrification through cooperatives is a community-type project: in another, it could be identified with electric power policy and development of energy resources—responsibilities to be acquired by Natural Resources.

As another example, the functions of the Economic Development Administration, now in the Department of Commerce, are to be split between Community Development and Economic Affairs. The EDA's regional commissions and authority to provide grant and loan assistance for public works, and certain technical assistance and planning functions, would go to Community Development; whereas EDA's authority to provide business loans and working capital guarantees as well as to conduct research and designate areas eligible for assistance under the Public Works and Economic Development Act would go to Economic Affairs.

Whether size works for or against efficiency in administration, practical problems remain for the agencies or functions which are assimilated in larger units. In the process of subordination, independent or self-contained agencies, like the Small Business Administration and the Rural Electrification Administration, are swallowed up, so to speak, with consequent diminution of their public visibility, influence, and (hoped-for) access to the President or Congress. Other agencies, such as the Office of Economic Opportunity (in part) and the Economic Development Administration, suffer an additional handicap. They cannot retain their identity or cohesiveness, even at lower levels in departmental bureaucracies, because their functions are split up and distributed among several departments. This is not necessarily an argument against the reorganization, since other and perhaps more important benefits may be realized by redistribution of functions. It becomes a matter of trade-off in values.

ANTICIPATED BENEFITS

Reorganization of the executive branch on the scale proposed by President Nixon is justified by its advocates in terms of identified needs and anticipated benefits. These range widely across the spectrum. If the need is to restore public confidence and faith in our American institutions, then reorganization is said to be the means of achieving it. If the need is to relieve the President of administrative burdens, or to make the department heads more accountable, or to make Government more responsive, again reorganization is said to be the answer.

The promises of reorganization make up its rationale. Whether the promises are ever realized depends on the extent to which the reorganizations are effected and whether significant results can be demonstrated. Government institutions change slowly. Since reorganizations take time, are rarely executed as a whole or according to the original plan, and may have detrimental side effects, they need the perspective of years of history to get an adequate evaluation. This being the case, the promises of reorganization often stand out in bolder relief than the achievements.

In this section, the anticipated benefits of reorganization will be discussed in terms of their contributions to monetary savings and Government responsiveness through decentralization and the strengthening of departmental management.

Monetary Savings

Economy in Government—savings to the taxpayer—is one of the benefits traditionally associated with Government reorganization. Though study groups like the second Hoover Commission essayed flat savings estimates, presumably making possible a net reduction in budgetary outlays if all the proposed reorganizations were effected, claims on economy usually have been cast in terms of a fuller return on the Government dollar expended. Presidents of the past, in urging reorganization, have contended that the total costs of Government probably would not be reduced but that savings derived from reorganization could be employed on other useful public works.

None of the official Government spokesmen for President Nixon's proposed reorganizations would put a dollar estimate on expected savings. Mr. Shultz, OMB Director, testified: [83]

> When a reorganization is proposed, attention tends to be focused on the costs and savings that are expected to result, and there is an understandable desire to have firm estimates as to the expected impact on budgets and employment. In this instance, however, we are dealing with adjustments in structure, management systems, and programs that are so numerous and will take place over such a long period of time that there is no practicable way to affix a specific dollar tag to the reforms recommended by the President. There will, of course, be certain immediate economies coming out of a reduction in the number of certain headquarters positions and the consolidation of supporting services now performed for a larger number of agencies. On the other hand, there will be one-time, start-up costs involved in moving offices, changing communications, revising directives and related adjustments. These costs of activating the new departments will be relatively small in relation to the amounts being spent on the affected programs.

Of all the reorganization advocates in the administration orbit, Mr. Ash alone has hazarded an estimate of potential savings. In remarks at the National Press Club on February 10, 1971, he cited $5 billion in potential yearly savings. Queried about this figure at the subcommittee hearings, Mr. Ash acknowledged that it was a personal and subjective estimate. Considering that Federal Government outlays (exclusive of trust funds) were $50 billion a year for various types of assistance, Mr. Ash believed that 10 percent of this amount, or $5 billion, could be saved as a result of management efficiencies associated with the proposed reorganizations.[84]

No specific estimates or indications of savings through consolidations of functions and/or agencies or through reduction of overhead or administrative expenses were submitted to back up this estimate. Some reductions in personnel were anticipated by administration witnesses, but they made it clear that, as a matter of policy, such reductions would be absorbed through attrition....

---

[83] Hearings, pp. 149–150.
[84] Hearings, p. 231.

More Responsive Government

Reorganization advocates give more emphasis to effectiveness than economy in government. They see a paramount need to make government more responsive in the delivery of goods and services. The emphasis on improved delivery is relatively recent in organizational theory. As noted earlier, it signifies the greatly increased role of the Federal Government in contemporary life, including the expanded financial support of State and local activities.

In his reorganization message of March 25, 1971, President Nixon dwelt on the issue of responsiveness. Noting, for example, that community development programs of the Federal Government presently are conducted by at least eight separate authorities, including four executive departments and four independent agencies, he said: [85]

> A community that seeks development assistance thus finds that it has to search out aid from a variety of Federal agencies. Each agency has its own forms and regulations and time-tables—and its own brand of red tape. Each has its own field organizations, often with independent and overlapping boundaries for regions and districts. Sometimes a local community must consult with Federal offices in three or four different States.
>
> The result is that local leaders often find it virtually impossible to relate Federal assistance programs to their own local development strategies. The mayor of one small town has observed that by the time he finishes dealing with eight Federal planning agencies, he has little time to do anything else.

As the President's remarks imply, making Government more effective (responsive) through reorganization has dual aspects: Strengthening departmental management in Washington, and decentralizing decisions and operations to the field. Since advocates of reorganization lean more heavily on decentralization as the vehicle of responsive Government, we will consider it first. It should be pointed out here, however, that decentralization is in the nature of a derived benefit. The pattern of regional organization is not spelled out in the reorganization bills. Each Secretary would be expected to work out field arrangements best suited to the needs of his own department.

The Secretaries of existing departments have authority to form and reform existing field organizations. If decentralization as such will bring Government closer to the people, it does not necessarily have to wait upon the enactment of new reorganization measures.[86]

In associating reorganization with decentralization, the assumption is made that by increasing the size of the departments, enabling the Secretaries to have a broader command of resources, and integrating similar or competing functions and programs, the benefits will be car-

---

[85] H. Doc. No. 92–75, p. 10 (Mar. 25, 1971).

[86] By memorandum of Mar. 27, 1969, President Nixon instructed the Director of the Bureau of the Budget (later OMB) to review jointly with designated department and agency heads the existing patterns of field organizations and delegations of authority in the interest of "greater and more uniform decentralization of Federal agencies." Certain departments and agencies were instructed, at the same time, to realign their field organizations in conformity with eight (now 10) designated regional boundaries and regional office locations.

ried through to the field in a more effective way than is possible in existing departments.

DECENTRALIZATION

Although, as noted above, the manner in which departmental operations and decisions are decentralized is left wholly to the Secretary's discretion, the testimony and supporting information show that each new department would have regional directors representing the Secretary. They would provide, in President Nixon's phrase, a "Secretarial presence" in the field.[87] Presumably they would be the key agents in planning, coordination, and resolution of conflicts among field offices of component agencies in the department.

Whether in fact the regional directors would be able to mesh policy, resolve conflicts, and provide the much-touted responsiveness to claimants of Federal benefits, depends, in part, on the measure of authority they receive by delegation and the numbers and kinds of field functions within their orbit. Those that will have authority to make money grants, for example, will exert more influence and control than those who will not have such authority. Testimony and back-up information indicated variations in field authority. Thus, in the Department of Community Development, the regional directors would control the allocation and distribution of funds to sub-regional offices, whereas in the Department of Economic Affairs, with more complex field organizations, the regional directors would serve as representatives of the Secretary to help resolve conflicts and promote regional planning.[88]

The regional directors, in short, cannot automatically assume command functions in the field. The field elements ordinarily would look to the Washington heads of the operating administrations for direction and policy guidance. It is apparent that if and when the new departments are created, the vertical and horizontal lines of communication will have to be carefully sorted out.

Government could become less rather than more responsive if the problems of a Washington bureaucracy merely were shifted to the field. Considering that the new departments would encompass the field offices of numerous long-established bureaus, agencies, and administrations with operating responsibilities, viable and effective working relationships and coordinating mechanisms in the field would have to be developed anew. The more inclusive the assortment of departmental functions at the Washington level, the more complex are the ramifications in the field.

Experience suggests that there are many pitfalls in the path to effective decentralization. Without field officers who are properly selected, well trained, thoroughly conversant with departmental affairs, and prepared to assert their delegated authority in full measure, decentralization may not mean much. Department or agency heads, in turn, must have the mature understanding and will to carry out a decentralization program, to shift headquarters personnel to the field, to delegate authority in meaningful ways, and to make available the

---

[87] H. Doc. No. 92–75, p. 14 (Mar. 25, 1971).
[88] Hearings, pp. 229–30, 249, 261, 286, 293, 298, 301. Ref. Comp. pp. 59–62, 251–253.

resources for data collection, reporting, and communication essential for effective administration.[89]

Decentralization also could create additional problems in congressional oversight of departmental programs and functions and in the handling of constituents' requests or inquiries by individual Members. All Members of Congress, in principle, would favor better regional organization and making Government more responsive. In practice, Members of Congress would be greatly interested in the shift of authority, patronage, and money-disbursing privileges to regional offices for their political as well as administrative implications. For those Members who now have established points of contact and channels of communication with the various departments and agencies of the executive branch, reorganization undoubtedly would entail extended periods of readjustment.

In the context of decentralization of departmental operations, it should be noted that revenue sharing was intended to play a significant role in pulling power away from Washington. Revenue sharing was linked with reorganization in the President's state of the Union message in January 1971, and his reorganization message in March 1971. Thus he said in the latter message: [90]

> These proposals for reorganizing the Federal Government are a natural complement to my proposals for revenue sharing; there is a sense in which these two initiatives represent two sides of the same coin. Both programs can help us decentralize government, so that more decisions can be made at levels closer to the people. More than that, both programs are concerned with restoring the general capacity of government to meet its responsibilities.

Later on, as the revenue sharing proposals met a cool reception in the Congress, the administration gave less emphasis to the linkage. Though closely related, reorganization and revenue sharing can be separately considered.[91] In the event revenue sharing bills are enacted, substantial reductions in the size and number of Federal field offices and in the numbers of Federal employees could be anticipated.

STRONGER DEPARTMENTAL MANAGEMENT

It is anticipated that departmental management will be strengthened by: (1) Charging to each Secretary's direction a larger complex of functions, rationalized to the extent that they are related to a designated basic goal; and (2) allowing greater administrative discretion to the Secretary in making internal reorganization, allocating appropriated funds, and undertaking support activities. The intended results are that policy formation will be more systematic and coherent, and the department heads will be more fully accountable to the President and the Congress.

Advocates of reorganization contend that, as matters now stand, the fragmentation of policies and programs across departments and agen-

---

[89] See "Decentralizing Federal Management—Delegation with Responsiveness," reprinted from Proceedings of the Federal Management Improvement Conference, OMB, October 1971.
[90] H. Doc. No. 92–75, p. 15 (Mar. 25, 1971).
[91] For an administration statement on the relationship between departmental reorganization and revenue sharing, see hearings, pp. 772–4.

cies forces too many decisions into the President's orbit. Many of these decisions are made by "faceless" men of the President's personal or institutional staff, men who are not visible or accountable to the Congress. Also the fragmentation, it is said, contributes to the inordinate growth of interagency committees for program and policy coordination, which recently numbered about 850 in the Federal Government. President Nixon has referred to these interagency committees as "an entire new layer of bureaucracy" which has emerged because of the need for coordination and resolution of interagency disputes.[92]

It would follow, if the benefits of reorganization are achieved, that the number of interagency committees could be substantially reduced,[93] as well as the staff personnel of the White House and the Executive Office, which have expanded greatly in recent years. The hard realities of contemporary politics and administration, however, do not hold out much promise in this direction. Even while the President depicts the proposed new departments as "centers of meaningful power," he moves to assume more personal responsibility for direction or supervision of programs which draw national attention, as in those for cancer prevention and cure and drug abuse control.[94] The dynamics of policymaking, the complexities of Government, and the pressures of politics cast doubt on the supposition that Presidential involvement will be significantly altered by the proposed reorganizations.

In this context, questions were raised at the hearings about the effect of the reorganizations on the Domestic Council, created by Reorganization Plan No. 2 of 1970. The Council was established as a means for coordinating departmental policies and programs at the Presidential level. The Secretaries of the civil departments of Government sit as members of the Council, along with the Vice President and other agency heads as required, supported by a staff and an executive director (John D. Ehrlichman), who do the actual coordinating work and purportedly provide an "institutional memory" as distinguished from the President's own personal staff. Whether the Domestic Council, with attention and action centered in the work of the Council staff and its various subcommittees, does or will cause a diminution in the policy role and importance of the department heads who comprise the President's cabinet is the subject of divided opinion.

In the President's officially stated view on Reorganization Plan No. 2 of 1970, the systematizing of presidential staff work through the Domestic Council secretariat would not only serve to keep the President well informed and in a better position to make policy decisions, but it would also enable him to delegate authority to the departments and agencies with more confidence. As Mr. Nixon indicated in his message on the plan, the President will no longer need "to retain close control of operating responsibilities which he cannot and should not handle." [95] Others see the President's proposals for departmental reor-

---

[92] H. Doc. No. 92–75, p. 5 (Mar. 25, 1971).
[93] According to an OMB response to questions raised by Representative Florence P. Dwyer, consolidation of seven executive departments into four new ones "will reduce to some degree the present dependence on interagency committees as a means of effecting coordination across agency lines." It was estimated that about one-third of more than 800 presently active interagency committees would be affected by the reorganization, of which some could be eliminated outright and others reduced in size. Although the OMB did not designate a specific number of committees which might be eliminated, it anticipated that agency memberships on committees would be reduced by 600 persons. Hearings, p. 162.
[94] See hearings, p. 635.
[95] H. Doc. No. 91–275, p. 2 (Mar. 12, 1970).

ganization as running counter to the concept of Reorganization Plan No. 2 of 1970, which gives the Council secretariat a key role in policy development.[96]

Transcending Special Interests

In part, the rationale for reorganization into super departments is that the Secretaries, by commanding more resources and having broader responsibilities, will act more truly as policy makers than as advocates of particular group interests. Existing departments, such as Agriculture, Labor, and Commerce, often are described as interest-oriented—serving given clienteles or constituencies. President Nixon has referred to the "narrow missions" and "parochial interests" of existing departments, contending that departmental heads as advocates rather than adjudicators and policymakers are less useful advisers to the President.[97] Furthermore, in his view, interest groups are better served when the departmental organization is sufficiently broad to treat the problems in their complex interrelationships. As stated in his reorganizational message: [98]

> It has sometimes been argued that certain interest groups need a department to act as their special representative within the Government. In my view, such an arrangement serves the best interests of neither the special group nor the general public. Little is gained and much can be lost, for example, by treating our farmers or our workers or other groups as if they are independent participants in our economic life. Their problems cannot be adequately treated in isolation; their well-being is intimately related to the way our entire economy functions.

Unfortunately, the President undercut his own argument when he decided to retain the Department of Agriculture after opposition to its disestablishment began to develop. If Agriculture is to be retained, it can be expected that labor, transportation, and other interests will more forcefully assert opposition to breaking up departments with which they have established working relationships and economic or professional involvement. It is relevant to note that President Johnson's proposal in January 1967 to merge the Departments of Labor and Commerce in a new department more broadly concerned with economic affairs was short-lived; organized labor was credited with causing its demise.[99]

In our society, interest groups, according to their power and influence, will make their voices heard in Government. Their advice and counsel will be sought, and sometimes their active participation, as demonstrated recently in the representational roles accorded business and labor in the administrative machinery for inflation control. If the Secretaries of the new departments are to serve more in the role of

---

[96] See Mansfield cited in footnote 26, p. 492. The National Civil Service League, endorsing the President's reorganization proposals, expressed the "hope that the reorganization will help restore the Cabinet to positions of primacy in the councils of Government and arrest the trend toward excessive reliance on White House coordinating staffs evident in successive administrations since World War II." Hearings, p. 655.

[97] H. Doc. No. 92–75, p. 4 (Mar. 25, 1971).

[98] Id. at 12.

[99] The proposal was made by President Johnson in his state of the Union message, H. Doc. No. 90–1, Jan. 10, 1967. For reports on labor opposition see Congressional Quarterly, Mar. 17, 1967, p. 392, Mar. 24, 1967, p. 451; New York Times, Feb. 2, 1967; Washington Post, Feb. 20, 1967.

arbiters than advocates, presumably interest group regulation will be less publicly visible, and more of the battles among competing interests will be fought out in the lower levels of the Federal bureaucracies.

The picture that is drawn by reorganization advocates of a Secretary standing tall and strong, ruling with a firm hand, resolving conflicts and making wise policy, is overdrawn, according to some informed observers. A study, "Secretarial Leadership," by the National Academy of Public Administration, submitted to the Office of Management and Budget, suggests that the Secretary is less a commander of resources and a maker of policy than "an entrepreneur of policy" who has only a selective influence on events and must negotiate for program support with groups possessing political power. His achievements depend largely on his personal style, skill, understanding of the departmental situation, and individual strategies.[100]

As issues develop and conflicts emerge, it is likely that the Secretary will find himself an advocate willy-nilly. Major decisions are made not in a cool ivory tower but in the hot dusty arena of political contest for position, power, and influence, with interest groups arrayed for and against given policies or programs. If the Secretary does not espouse the politically popular or publicly desirable cause, he may find himself overruled by the President or challenged by key elements in the Congress.

Certain departments and agencies are established by laws explicitly intended to promote and protect designated group interests. The Small Business Act is an outstanding example.[101] The organic act which established the Department of Labor carries a mandate to advance the welfare of the American worker.[102] Similarly, the organic act for the Department of Commerce would promote business interests.[103] The bill to establish the Department of Economic Affairs, which would absorb the Small Business Administration and major functions of the Departments of Labor and Commerce, restates the congressional declaration of interest advocacy in more generalized terms and, by implication, repeals earlier and more positive declarations.

In the new legislation, it is argued, advocacy ascends from special interests to higher national purposes. The Secretary, as advocate of the higher purpose, theoretically advocates the lower one only when it is not in conflict. His role is conceived preeminently to be a balancing one. In this sense, the Secretary makes national decisions of the kind that the President would have to make if the Secretary were the mere advocate of a department with parochial interests. The Secretary becomes, in effect, an Assistant to the President or an operating Vice President for making decisions about policy formation and resource allocation. He speaks not for the interest groups but (within his area of responsibility) for the President, who speaks for all the people. This concept contrasts with the conventional one of department heads who fight hard for the interests of their departments and their constituencies, with the President or components of his office serving in an adjudicating role.

---

[100] "Secretarial Leadership," report of the National Academy of Public Administration submitted to the Bureau of the Budget, June 30, 1970.
[101] 50 U.S.C. 631.
[102] 29 U.S.C. 551.
[103] 15 U.S.C. 1512.

IMPACT ON THE CONGRESS

It must be recognized that legislative acceptance of the reorganization measures will depend in significant part on the collective judgment of the Congress that its power and influence as a separate branch of the Government are not prejudiced. The issues are subtle and complex, and judgments differ in assessing the impact of the reorganizations on Congress as they do on the Presidency. Advocates of reorganization contend that the Secretaries of the new departments, with broader and better defined responsibilities and control of the resources necessary to their missions, can be held more accountable to the Congress as well as the President. On the other hand, increased power and authority in the Secretaries must be squared with congressional prerogatives to prescribe organizational components of departments and the objectives for which expenditures may be made.

In the committee's view, the reorganizations do not pose irreconcilable issues between the legislative and executive branches of Government. The Constitution itself divides responsibility for such matters, and cooperative endeavors between the two branches are necessary to strike reasonable balances. The modern trend in Government, as noted earlier, is to emphasize executive accountability, and if department heads are to be held accountable they must have the requisite authority and responsibility.[104] At the same time, the Congress, through its legislative power and control of the purse, can do what it wills in prescribing organizational patterns and program content.

Effect on Committee Jurisdictions

The immediate question in assessing the impact of reorganizations on the Congress is not the power of Congress as a whole, which is given by the Constitution, but the bearing on committee jurisdictions and operations. None of the legislative committees, as a result of the reorganization, would lose authority over the subject matters committed to their jurisdiction. The Legislative Reorganization Act of 1946 as amended and the Rules of the House and Senate define the jurisdictional responsibilities of their respective committees and thus can be changed only by changing the Rules of the two Houses. What the reorganization would do, however, is redistribute various functions and programs among the new departments, so that the committees with jurisdiction over these functions and programs would find them in new places and at different levels in department hierarchies.

The Office of Management and Budget and the Congressional Research Service each made an analysis of the effect of the reorganization proposals on congressional committee responsibilities.[105] These studies were made on the basis of the President's initial proposals as written in the reorganization bills and do not reflect the change in plans regarding the Department of Agriculture. Furthermore, the studies were confined to the standing legislative committees of the Congress.

---

[104] See "Restoration of Effective Sovereignty to Solve Social Problems," Report of the Subcommittee on Urban Affairs of Joint Economic Committee, 92d Cong., 1st sess., joint committee print, pp. 8–9 (Dec. 6, 1971).

[105] The OMB study is printed in the hearings, p. 675 ff. The CRS study is entitled, "Some Effects of the President's Reorganization Proposals of 1971 on Congressional Committee Jurisdictions : The Legislative Committees" (July 2, 1971).

They did not deal specifically with the Appropriations Committees. Whereas the executive reorganizations would not necessarily require the legislative committees to change their internal organization, the Appropriations Committees would have to readjust their subcommittee structures to accommodate departmental reorganizations in the executive branch.

The OMB study played down the effect of the reorganization on jurisdictions of House and Senate standing committees. In some cases, it was pointed out, the committees would be dealing with a single department on program components now distributed among several departments. As an example, rural housing, now in the Department of Agriculture, would be brought together with housing programs now under the Department of Housing and Urban Development, so that the House and Senate Banking Committees could consider a more integrated program and work with one Secretary on that program. Similarly, separate disaster relief programs now managed by the Small Business Administration and the Office of Emergency Preparedness would come together in the Department of Community Development for more effective committee consideration.

In cases where programs from a single department were to be redistributed to more than one of the new departments, it was recognized that the committees would have additional Secretaries to deal with. This was said to be particularly true of those committees associated with the work of the Department of Agriculture and Commerce, and to a lesser extent, of those committees exercising overview of the Office of Economic Opportunity.

With the possible exception of the Department of Economic Affairs, the OMB study found that departmental interfaces with the standing committees, though rearranged, would be no more complex than at present. The point is made that there is no simple 1–to–1 relationship, even now, between a committee and a department. For example, eight committees of the House and six committees of the Senate were said to have a jurisdictional interest in the Department of Agriculture, and the same number of committees were involved with the Department of Commerce. The Department of Housing and Urban Development was the only Department with a 1–to–1 relationship, since one (legislative) committee in each House was said to be involved.

The CRS study, more detailed and based on somewhat different criteria of involvement, found that of the 39 congressional committees authorized to report legislation, the jurisdictions of 31 would be involved in the reorganizations (15 of the 21 standing committees in the House, 15 of the 17 standing committees in the Senate, and the Joint Committee on Atomic Energy).

Of these 31 committees, 16 (including the Joint Committee on Atomic Energy) were either extensively or significantly affected by the President's proposals, while the jurisdictions of 15 committees were only marginally affected. The jurisdictions of six House and five Senate committees and the Joint Committee on Atomic Energy would be extensively affected. These were the Committees on Agriculture, Labor, Commerce, Interior and Insular Affairs, and Public Works of both Houses, plus the House Committee on Merchant Marine and Fisheries. The House and Senate committees significantly affected are the Banking Committees, the House Committee on Ways and Means, and the Senate Committee on Finance.

According to the CRS study, under the existing structure of executive departments and committee jurisdictions, the number of committees (in both Houses) with extensive or significant program jurisdiction over a single department and its activities varies from a low of two to a high of six as follows: Agriculture (two), HUD (two), Commerce (three), Labor (four), Interior (five), HEW (six), Transportation (six). If all the original proposals were enacted, the number of committees with extensive or significant jurisdiction over each of the new departments would range from a low of seven to a high of 13 as follows: Community Development (seven), Human Resources (eight), Natural Resources (nine), Economic Affairs (13).

As specific examples, the two Agriculture Committees would have partial jurisdiction over four departments instead of a single Department of Agriculture. The two Commerce Committees would have jurisdiction over two departments with respect to activities now under the Department of Commerce, and the Joint Committee on Atomic Energy would divide its jurisdictional interest between the Atomic Energy Commission and the Department of Natural Resources. The House and Senate committees dealing with science/space matters would be affected only in minor degree.

In summary, the CRS found that for certain committees jurisdictional involvement would be substantially diversified. Instead of the single departments and independent agencies they now deal with, six committees would have to deal with two departments, three committees would have to deal with three departments, and two committees would have four departments. CRS concluded, among other things, that the reorganizations, particularly the creation of the Department of Economic Affairs, would increase jurisdictional overlaps among committees dealing with new departments, and program dispersal would make it more difficult for certain committees to oversee programs effectively.

Redirection of Responsibilities

The thrust of the OMB and CRS studies, whatever their differences in assumption and conclusion, is that jurisdictional responsibilities of some House and Senate committees would be redirected if the reorganizations were brought about. The significance of these redirections can be evaluated only in tentative fashion.

For certain committees, jurisdictional influence and control over a single department would be eliminated or reduced, but they would have jurisdictional fingers, so to speak, in more departmental pies. To the extent that they retained established working relationships with bureaucracies inside departments and interest groups outside, their effect on specific programs would not necessarily be changed. On the other hand, disestablishment of historic departments and program dispersion could affect the ability of committees to influence departmental policy and program direction and to perform oversight functions on a department-wide basis.

A similar situation would obtain in the case of committees dealing primarily with a single agency rather than a department. For example, the Small Business Committees have general jurisdiction over the Small Business Administration, and the Banking Committees have legislative jurisdiction. The Small Business Administration, in the reorganization scheme, would be transferred to the Department of Economic Affairs, where its functions would be included, along with other business loan and assistance functions, in one of the five operating administrations—the one termed "Business Development." Thereupon, the four committees involved would no longer be dealing with a single independent agency but with a subordinate unit in an operating administration of the Department of Economic Affairs.

Such developments, it should be noted, are associated with the reorganizations as originally proposed and assume that all of them would be affected. The heaviest impact on committee jurisdictions would be caused by the Department of Economic Affairs. Unlike the other proposed new departments, Economic Affairs would have no single core department upon which to build; it would draw major components from existing departments marked for oblivion. If Economic Affairs is not created, then the Departments of Labor, Commerce, and Transportation would not be disestablished, even if reduced in size by transfers of some components to other new departments. In such an event, the committees of primary jurisdiction, though affected by some of the transfers, would be dealing with the same departments as now.

The Department of Agriculture is a case in point. When the President decided, after his change in plans, to retain the Department of Agriculture comprised of agricultural functions originally earmarked for transfer to the Department of Economic Affairs, the Committees on Agriculture were assured that a departmental base for their jurisdiction would be preserved. Indeed, if the Administration's argument is accepted that the Department of Agriculture, with extraneous functions removed, would be more effective in supporting the agricultural economy, then it could be said that the committees' effectiveness is correspondingly enhanced. On the other hand, these committees might have less impact on agricultural programs transferred elsewhere, as in the rural housing and electric cooperative programs to be transferred to the Department of Community Development.

To the extent that the reorganizations cause greater diversification of committee jurisdictions, corollary problems are posed for department heads. More and more of their time would have to be spent in appearances before congressional committees. This means that they would have less time to do what the reorganizations contemplate—give strong management direction to their departments. Although the Secretary's assistants and the heads of the operating administrations within each department would do much of the work of presentation to the Congress, committees frequently insist on appearances by department heads when important (and sometimes not so important) issues are involved.

Theoretically, the problems of committee jurisdiction would be less complicated if these jurisdictions were realined to conform to the new departmental organizations. Assuming that all President Nixon's proposed reorganizations are effected, a committee realinement would involve a decrease in the number of standing committees and the loss of a few chairmanships. The prospects for such committee reorganizations are not favorable in the foreseeable future. It is well known, as the development of the Legislative Reorganization Act of 1970 attests, that changes in committee jurisdictions do not come easy. As a result of years of study and experience, existing committees have become expert in the matters under their jurisdictions. Unlike the President, who can take the initiative for the whole executive branch in proposing reorganizations, the committees of Congress, with their independent and strong-minded chairmen, do not fit into an administrative hierarchy subject to a single course of command.

ADMINISTRATIVE AND FISCAL PROVISIONS

A noteworthy feature and another anticipated benefit of the proposed departmental reorganizations is that they seek to achieve a measure of uniformity and standardization in departmental staffing and structure, based largely on the approach taken in the creation of the Department of Transportation. Thus, each department would have a small number of operating "administrations," varying from three to five, each headed by an administrator. Above the "line" or operating administrations would be the policy and management secretariat. The reorganization bills each provide for a Deputy Secretary to assist the Secretary in day-to-day operations, and two Under Secretaries: one for management and the other for policy planning (except in the Department of Human Resources where those two functions would be combined in one Under Secretary and a second would deal with field operations). A pool of Assistant Secretaries and other executive-level appointees would be available for such other assignments as the Secretary determined.

All functions of a department would be vested in the Secretary. He would be empowered to delegate, assign and reassign functions, and to reorganize his department at will, except for such statutory constraints as are imposed. For example, under the terms of the reorganizations measures, agencies transferred to a department would not necessarily retain their identity except the Coast Guard and a few others named. An agency program or function prescribed by act of Congress could not be abolished; however, the Secretary could abolish organizational entities such as the Rural Electrification Administration, the Bureau of Mines, and the Bureau of Labor Statistics, and reestablish them under other names or with a different assortment of functions. [106]

On the other hand, each department's operating administration would be established in the statutes, with the Administrator (as well as other designated top officers) appointed by the President and subject to Senate confirmation. This practice of having the first layer of program elements specified by law is found in the present Department of Transportation, which has no statutory "bureaus." The Secretary of Housing and Urban Development also is empowered to abolish or regroup the elements of his department.

Thus, the organizational restraints imposed on the Secretary of each new department would be the statutory prescription for certain officers in the secretariat and the above-mentioned operating administrations. The Secretaries would not have a clean sheet of paper, organizationally speaking, upon which to write. The top officers and the administrations, as major component organizations, would be fixed by

---

[106] For a list of statutory and nonstatutory agencies which would lapse upon enactment of the reorganization bills, see hearings, p. 744 ff. See also the discussion at p. 377 ff.

law. However, each Secretary could establish additional administrations at his discretion and assign and reassign functions within and across administrations.

REVISED APPROPRIATIONS STRUCTURE

Administration testimony and supporting documents make it clear that the departmental reorganizations are to be accompanied by a major revision of the appropriation structure of the executive branch. The administration's point is that since the regrouping of agencies, functions, personnel and facilities inevitably would "require a new appropriation structure, merging and consolidating the accounts now in use for the activities being moved to the new Department," the appropriation structure should be designed more systematically to "assist management effectiveness and provide the flexibility to respond to rapidly changing conditions." [107] In other words, changes are proposed which go beyond those necessary to accomplish the reorganizations as such.

N4

In advocating the changes, the administration asserts that "it is not the intent of the measures discussed here to freeze an appropriation pattern for all time. An appropriation structure is subject to change by Congress from year to year, and indeed should be changed as programs and organizations are modified." [108]

The administration's proposal for a revised appropriation structure involves the following elements:

1. Reduced number of appropriation accounts.—There are now about 750 appropriation accounts for the agencies and functions that would be placed in the new departments. Upon reorganization the number of accounts would be reduced to fewer than 200.[109] This does not mean a reduction in the amount of money appropriated but merely a reduction (largely through merger) of the number of accounts for which appropriations separately are made. Such a reduction, combined with a proposed practice of making one appropriation for each major grouping of agencies in a department (i.e., to each of the new administrations), could mean that the congressional statement of the purpose for which funds are appropriated would be less specific and congressional intent more difficult to ascertain.

2. Broader categories of appropriation.—Corollary to the reduction in the number of appropriation accounts, appropriations would be made in relatively broad and unrestricted terms for the groups of functions under each of the proposed operating administrations in the new departments. For example, one broadly worded appropriation for "Lands and recreation resources" under the Department of Natural Resources would cover all the functions of the Forest Service, the Bureau of Land Management, the National Park Service, the Fish and Wildlife Service, the Bureau of Outdoor Recreation, the Soil Conservation Service, and perhaps other functions, all of which now receive separate appropriations. Within this broad single appropriation, the Administrator for Lands and Recreation Resources and the Secretary of Natural Resources would be able to allocate and real-

---

[107] Ref. comp., p. 65 ; revised edition, p. 69.
[108] Id.
[109] Hearings, p. 325. The figures used are those supplied by administration witnesses before the President announced on Nov. 11, 1971, that he had decided to retain the Department of Agriculture with a large part of its existing functions.

locate the available funds as they saw fit. Of course, they would have to abide by such restrictions and guidance as the Congress may write into authorization and funding acts and accompanying reports.

3. Appropriations to the Secretaries.—All appropriations would be made to the Secretaries of the departments, and the disbursal of funds, so far as the departments are concerned, would be under their control. The Secretaries would be limited in spending the money by the broad purposes for which moneys are appropriated (except for a 5-percent transfer authority discussed in paragraph 5, below). Appropriations would not be available directly to subordinate authorities in a manner which would bypass the secretaries.

4. Preservation of statutory earmarkings.—Where a statute earmarks funds for a particular purpose (for example, the highway trust fund), the statutory requirements would be respected. However, the administration might seek changes of statutory provisions considered burdensome. It advocates, for example, combining "small earmarked funds—in one account—without in any way changing the application of funds which is contemplated by existing law." [110]

5. Transfer of funds between accounts.—Section 424 of each of the bills provides that the Secretary, when authorized in an appropriation act, may transfer funds from one appropriation to another such appropriation, provided that no appropriation shall be increased or decreased by more than 5 percent. This is largely a new provision; five of the seven departments involved in the transfer have no comparable authority at this time, while the Departments of Agriculture and Interior have very limited transfer authority. Other agencies, such as the Atomic Energy Commission and the National Aeronautics and Space Administration, have been given such authority.

The effectiveness of the 5-percent limitation on fund transfers depends on the size of the appropriations involved. For example, it would permit a billion dollar appropriation to be increased or decreased by $50 million. Further, when the transfer proposal is considered in the light of the proposed merger of 750 appropriation accounts into 200 much larger ones (item 2, above), the effect of the transfer provision is greatly increased.

The transfer authority would not be effective unless activated by a provision in an appropriation act. Of course, if Congress were to enact a transfer clause in an appropriation act, the clause would be effective whether or not language such as that contained in section 424 had been previously adopted. Apparently the justification for section 424 in the bills is the concern that a point of order would lie against a provision in an appropriation act which lacked prior authorization.[111]

6. No-year and annual appropriations.—At the same time that appropriations would be combined and reduced in number, as discussed in item 2, above, two principal appropriation accounts would be established for each major program grouping within the new departments. The first account would be established on the customary 1-year basis, subject to annual congressional review, and would finance day-to-day operating expenses and other requirements readily subject to 1-year estimates. The second proposed appropriation would be on a "no-year" basis, the funds being available until expended, and would cover "construction, land acquisition, project-oriented research and

[110] Hearings, p. 325.
[111] Hearings, p. 618.

certain types of loan and grant activity, for which there is a need for longer-term availability." [112]

Section 426 of each bill authorizes "no-year" appropriations, again for the purpose of obviating points of order in floor consideration of appropriation bills containing no-year provisions. Since section 426 could be construed as authorization generally for no-year appropriations, administration witnesses assured the committee that such a broad construction was not intended, and they agreed to delete the provision.

MISCELLANEOUS ADMINISTRATIVE PROVISIONS

Title IV of each of the four reorganization bills carries broadly stated administrative provisions relating not only to personnel and appropriations but also to internal management, contracting, and the like. They require consideration and revision to resolve possible conflicts with other existing laws, or to effect curtailment where the quest for uniformity across departments creates more authority than is demonstrably needed. Examples of possible conflicts or needed reconciliation between provisions in the reorganization bills and existing laws are as follows:

1. Concessionaires.—Section 413 of each bill authorizes the Secretary to permit concessionaires, for periods up to 30 years, to use real property and facilities, subject to regulations of the President. Existing law on the subject, as that relating to national parks, has detailed provisions regarding protection of the concessionaire's investment, reasonableness of profits, rates and charges, periodic revision of franchise fees, preference in renewal and extension of contracts, and recognition of a possessory interest in the concession property with provision for compensation if the property is taken.[113]

2. Special studies and services.—Section 416 authorizes each Secretary, either on request or on his own initiative, to make special studies on and provide services relating to matters within the jurisdiction of his department for any person, firm, or organization, public or private. They are also authorized to engage in joint projects with nonprofit organizations, research organizations, or public organizations. Charges may be made but are not required. Among existing laws which deal with this subject, section 302 of the Intergovernmental Cooperation Act of 1968 provides for special or technical services to States and political subdivisions, requires reimbursement of all identifiable direct and indirect costs, and prescribes other conditions for performing the services.[114]

3. Broad grant authority.—Section 410 of each bill (sec. 411 in the community development bill—H.R. 6962) authorizes the Secretary to make contracts and agreements, including grant agreements, to carry out his functions and further authorizes him to make payments in advance or as reimbursement. Whereas the testimony makes clear that all of the procurement laws and other general laws applicable to contracts would apply to the new departments, the unqualified authority for awarding grants suggests that procedures and restrictions applicable to Government contracts, including provision for Comptroller General access to books and records, could be avoided.

---

[112] Ref. comp., pp. 65–66 ; revised edition, pp. 69, 140.
[113] 16 U.S.C. 20.
[114] 42 U.S.C. 4222.

4. Acquisition of special service facilities.—Section 411 of each bill (section 412 of the community development bill—H.R. 6962) authorizes the Secretary to acquire, construct, improve, operate and maintain so-called special service facilities. Normally, public facilities are acquired through the General Services Administration, except for "special service facilities." As drafted, the section could be interpreted to confer new authority beyond that now given to department heads by law. After discussion with the subcommittee staff, it was agreed that the provision should be redrafted to restate "the authority of department heads to acquire special purpose facilities without in any way impinging upon the existing authority of the General Services Administration with respect to general purpose facilities or special purpose facilities." [115]

Comment on Administrative Provisions

The various sections of title IV, as well as other general provisions may be desirable but are not necessary to accomplish the regrouping of departments and agencies contemplated by the President's reorganization program. Some of the sections are novel or broader in one way or another than existing law. In several cases, Administration witnesses conceded that the sections were not well drafted or required clarification. The Office of Management and Budget has been wholly cooperative in working with the subcommittee staff to improve these provisions of the bills.

Broader authority for the department heads, as developed in the uniform pattern of fiscal and administrative provisions, reflects the larger issues of reorganization. Involved here is a conflict of values and responsibilities between the legislative and executive branches of the Government. From the executive standpoint, the departmental secretaries should have broad latitude and flexibility, not only in organizing their departments but in fund allocation and fiscal management. Lacking sufficient authority in such matters, the Secretary cannot properly manage his department nor be held fully accountable.

From the congressional standpoint, broad authority to organize the department, consolidate appropriation accounts, and transfer funds are devices working against congressional prerogatives to prescribe departmental organization and control the purse strings, which the Congress considers as among its basic constitutional responsibilities. In considering whether and to what extent the secretaries should have freedom to organize internally or to work with a revised appropriation system, the Congress will have to balance the values of greater administrative convenience and flexibility against those which enable the Congress to retain fairly precise controls over the organization of the executive branch and the appropriation and expenditure of public funds.

This committee recognizes that the modern trend in Government and executive branch administration, forcefully articulated by the first Hoover Commission and carried through in numerous reorganization plans and statutes, is to match authority and responsibility and, by broadening the Secretary's authority, make him more accountable for his stewardship. The committee believes that where executive latitude and legislative prerogatives seem in conflict, reasonable compromise arrangements can be worked out.

---

[115] Hearings, p. 860.

IMPACT ON CIVIL SERVICE

According to the Civil Service Commission testimony, some 400,000 Federal civilian employees would be involved in the departmental reorganization.[116] Since statutory programs or functions are not to be abolished by the reorganizations, transfers and consolidations of administrative support activities will result in some personnel shake-ups and displacements. Presumably these would be less pronounced in the case of the Departments of Community Development, Human Resources, and Natural Resources, which would build on existing core departments, than Economic Affairs, which would assimilate major or residual functions of Commerce, Labor, and Transportation, as well as the Small Business Administration and other agencies.

Reductions in staff would be affected through attrition. In a memorandum of March 30, 1971, to the heads of departments and agencies, President Nixon stated that "no civil servant will suffer loss of employment or reduction in compensation by virtue of the reorganization for a period of 1 year after the new departments come into existence" and, further, that any subsequent reductions in personnel resulting from reorganization would be effected through normal turnover.[117] Some of the problem areas affecting personnel are indicated below.

STATUTORY JOB PROTECTION

The four departmental reorganization bills differentiate among (a) nontemporary employees other than those holding executive level I, II, III, IV or V positions, (b) executive-level employees, and (c) personnel occupying positions expressly created by statute or reorganization plan but who are not at the executive levels. The nontemporary employees would be transferred to the new departments and protected for 1 year from separation or reduction in grade as a result of the transfer. However, this would not prevent reassignment within a new department or transfer to another locality.

The reorganization bills provide that most executive-level positions in the departments to be abolished also are abolished. Some new executive-level positions expressly are created and many others authorized. In all, the bills (as originally drawn) would abolish 140 such positions and create or authorize 177. No holder of an executive-level position is given any assurance that he would be appointed to any position at all in the new departments. However, if a person who held an executive-level position in the old organization were appointed, without a break in service, to a position in the successor department having "comparable" [118] duties, he could continue to be compensated at not less than the rate provided for his previous position, for the duration of his service in the new position.

In sum, regular civil service and nontemporary employees would be transferred with their functions and protected against separation or reduction in grade for 1 year. On the other hand, executive-level

---

[116] Hearings, p. 514. Retaining Agriculture reduces this number by 28,000.

[117] Hearings, p. 515.

[118] The Executive Director of the Civil Service Commission explained the meaning of the word "comparable" in this context as follows: "Here, the drafters of the legislation had in mind that it would be very, very similar to what the man is doing now. There might be some adjustments, but essentially the body of responsibility that the individual would have would be essentially what he has now. It was in that context and that is what is intended here." Hearings, p. 534.

employees would be neither transferred nor automatically reappointed, but if they did receive immediate new appointments to positions with comparable duties, their pay levels would be protected for the duration of their service in the new positions.

Employees serving in positions expressly created by statute or reorganization plan, but who are not at the executive level, would not receive any statutory protection. This, however, is a very small category, since almost all positions expressly created by statute or reorganization plan have been placed in the executive levels.

According to the testimony, veterans' preference would not be affected by the reorganizations.[119]

Transfers to the Field

Since decentralization is so strongly emphasized, enactment of the reorganization bills undoubtedly would result in additional functions, activities, offices, and employees being decentralized to field offices. Positions in Washington would be reduced, those in the field increased. In some departments, particularly Economic Affairs, consolidation of field offices could lead to substantial displacement of support personnel.

Though the four bills specifically provide that nontemporary employees (other than executive-level officials) are to be protected for 1 year from separation or reduction in grade or pay as a result of being transferred to a new department, this protection would not prevent the new departments from transferring employees from one position, one office, or one location, to another. On this point, the Executive Director of the Civil Service Commission stated:[120]

> The authority of the Department to transfer people geographically is in no way intended to be affected by this guarantee. * * * In other words, the guarantee has to do entirely with the matter of separation or reduction in grade or compensation only.

Union-Management Relations

In his March 30, 1971, memorandum, the President stated:[121]

> It is also my intent that the Secretaries of the new departments work closely with the representatives of those employees covered by existing collective-bargaining agreements established under Executive Order 11491 to minimize any possible impact on the constructive relationships that have developed.

The Executive Director of the Civil Service Commission stated at the subcommittee hearings that union-management relationships in Government had been extensively studied in the development of the reorganization measures; also that union officials were informed of developments and invited to express their views at a White House meeting called for this purpose. He anticipated that in cases where agencies or components were transferred intact to a new department,

---

[119] Hearings, p. 527.
[120] Hearings, p. 536.
[121] Hearings, p. 515.

without being divided up or added to, employees' union bargaining units would remain basically unchanged. In other cases, where agencies or offices were broken up or recombined, new bargaining units would have to be formed and new agreements reached.[122] The governing document for procedures and decisions in such matters is Executive Order 11491.

A statement submitted by the American Federation of Government Employees, making preliminary comments on the reorganization proposals, expressed concern about the abolition of the Office of the Secretary of Labor and of the Assistant Secretary of Labor for Labor-Management Relations. Foreseen was the possibility of additional delays in resolving labor-management impasses in Government. Although transitional problems were to be expected, it was noted in the Civil Service Commission testimony that upon the creation of the new departments, an appropriate official would succeed to the duties of the Assistant Secretary for Labor-Management Relations.[123]

AUTHORITY TO USE MILITARY PERSONNEL

Each of the bills contains a provision (sec. 408) authorizing the Secretary of the new department to appoint or use military personnel, Coast Guard personnel, and commissioned officers of the National Oceanic and Atmospheric Administration and of the Public Health Service in the civilian positions in each of the four new departments.

Administrative witnesses justified this broad grant of authority to fill civilian positions with military personnel as being similar to authority given to the Secretary of Transportation when the department was created.[124] It should be noted that when the Department of Transportation was created, authority to use military personnel was given to it "because of the special relationships between the Coast Guard and the Federal Aviation Agency and the Department of Defense." [125] No such specific or unusual need to extend this authority to other departments has been shown.

The grant of authority to use military personnel to fill civilian governmental positions poses obvious political and other considerations which have not been developed in the administrations rationale for reorganization. The committee recognizes that a restraining effect on the use of military personnel would be the need to get agreement from the Secretary of Defense and funds from the Congress. Agencies such as FAA, AEC, and NASA make sparing but effective use of military personnel.

COMMENT ON PERSONNEL PROVISIONS

Reorganizations of the magnitude contemplated in the President's proposals have positive and negative aspects, so far as the welfare

---

[122] Hearings, p. 517. According to the Civil Service Commission testimony, in the seven departments that would be merged into four under the proposed reorganizations, as of November 1970, there are 868 bargaining units with 111,735 employees. Because of the mergers, "the odds would be heavy against 868 units coming over in toto." Hearings, p. 528.

[123] Hearings, pp. 657–658.

[124] Hearings, p. 521.

[125] "Creating a Department of Transportation (Pt. 2)," hearings before a subcommittee of the Committee on Government Operations. House of Representatives, 89th Cong., 2d sess., May 2, 3, 17, 18, 19, 24, and June 21, 1966, p. 856.

and career opportunities of Federal employees are concerned. The Administration stresses the primary purpose of the reorganizations to improve Government service rather than to reduce the number of employees and points to the protective features in the legislation. Also, it stresses the potential broadening of the range of opportunities for promotion and career development.

There are those who believe that reorganizations have beneficial effects in shaking up the status quo and stirring personnel to greater achievement. Routines are broken, and all but the hopeless and the time-servers are energized to do more productive work.

At the same time, it must be recognized that numerous transfers of functions and personnel create turbulence and uncertainties for extended periods, which could result in lower morale and reduced productivity of Federal employees. Not all the reorganizations can be effected simultaneously. Assuming the new departments are created, it will take years before the process is completed. For those employees who are left in truncated departments or dangling agencies while the reorganization process moves along, the hazards to morale N6 and career advancement are apparent.

The negative features of reorganizations, though exacting money and psychic costs of unknown magnitudes, are rarely considered by advocates of reorganization, who understandably are preoccupied with the anticipated benefits.

EDITORS' EPILOGUE

The House Government Operations Committee report on the Nixon reorganization plan concluded its summary with the following prospect: ". . . there are factors working against early enactment. This is the year of a national election, the President's party does not hold a majority in the Congress, and there is considerable skepticism about wholesale reform packages." The authors of the Committee report were concerned with technical legislative problems and the difficulty of sorting out shifting political prerogatives between units of government. Subsequent events served to reinforce their conclusion.

By the time the report was released in March 1972, the "Ellsberg papers" (Pentagon Papers), detailing the decision-making processes on U.S. involvement in Vietnam, had also been released. The White House had already supervised plans to burglarize the office of Daniel Ellsberg's psychiatrist; and in June the Watergate breakin occurred. In November, Richard Nixon won reelection to the Presidency by a landslide—97 percent of the electoral vote. Ordinarily, that would have been sufficient mandate to push through any reasonable reorganization proposal. But the times were different.

The Executive branch's almost unilateral prosecution of the war in Vietnam had led many members of Congress to be wary of concentrated Executive power. Committees in both the House and Senate moved slowly, even after the election. By the time the 1949 Reorganization Act was due to expire, the Watergate investigation had begun, and the reorganization authority was not renewed by Congress. In due course, through investigations of the media and Congress, it became clear that the president of the United States and his closest aides had manipulated the structure and processes of government in pursuit of illegal ends. The work of the Ash Council, Office of Management and Budget experts, and congressional committees was dropped and lost in the backwash of Watergate. Nevertheless, their research represents a useful contribution and a base on which future approaches to reorganization can be built.

NOTES AND REFERENCES

1. The "Green Book" was issued by the Office of Management and Budget in February 1972. It reflects the revision of Nixon's reorganization proposal to retain the Department of Agriculture. Portions of the "Green Book" ([3]) outlining the creation of four new departments are reprinted in Chapter 2.

2. Of all the proposals for Executive branch consolidation addressed in the 1971 Ash Council report, those affecting the agencies responsible for energy matters are the most obsolete. The possibility of an energy crisis had certainly been perceived by many at that time, but it was the 1973 Arab oil embargo which prompted an urgent reexamination of administrative authority over energy policy, as well as a restructuring of energy agencies to focus more attention on energy alternatives (i.e., coal, nuclear, and solar energy). For a more recent approach to the energy situation, see [71], a portion of which appears in the appendix section of this volume.

3. The 1971 Ash Council report on regulatory agencies is partially reprinted in Chapter 3.

4. Since the report of the House Government Operations Committee was prepared in March 1972, legislation was passed to create a congressional budget review process and oversight body. This legislation created the Congressional Budget Office in 1974. The CBO mandate is described in the appendix section of this volume.

5. The Civil Service Commission was created by Congress on January 16, 1883; it is the personnel agency of the Executive branch of the U.S. government. The Commission's responsibilities include recruiting, examining, training, and promoting, as well as providing personnel services to federal employees.

6. What is not included in this comment is the significant fact that an administration can use structural reorganization to create new positions and move career people out of existing ones. "Box shuffling," as it is sometimes called, allows a president and his staff to penetrate the ranks of bureaucracy with those who may be more politically attuned to the administration.

Chapter 2
Departments Proposed in the 1971 Reorganization

This chapter provides descriptions of four new departments of the Executive branch to have been created under the 1971 Nixon reorganization proposal: Community Development, Natural Resources, Human Resources, and Economic Affairs. As stated in Chapter 1, a large portion of President Nixon's plan was derived from the recommendations of the Ash Council, headed by Litton Industries' President and subsequent OMB Director, Roy Ash. The text here was drawn from the "Green Book," officially titled, "Papers Relating to the President's Departmental Reorganization Program: A Reference Compilation." The "Green Book," a revision of the March 1971 "Gray Book" (with the same official title), was issued in February 1972 and is a compilation of reference materials prepared by the President's Office of Management and Budget for use in the study and analysis of the administration's proposal.

By the time the "Green Book" was prepared, the idea of eliminating the Agriculture Department had been withdrawn by the administration—perhaps in response to alert parochial interests who foresaw diminution of their power in the reorganization scheme. The proposal to allocate some of the Agriculture Department functions to new bodies, however, was retained and is addressed in this material. The departments of State, Treasury, Justice, and Defense were to keep their functional jurisdictions and were not effected by the reorganization plan; for that reason, they are not described here.

Congressional hearings were held by both the House and Senate on the overall proposal ([25], [70]), while the legislation creating the Departments of Community Development and Natural Resources underwent more intensive hearings ([21], [26], [68], and [94]). The material included in this chapter is somewhat dated, particularly regarding energy related agencies. However, the principles of public administration set forth are still current and the proposals remain the only detailed approach to Executive branch consolidation available for consideration.

DEPARTMENT OF COMMUNITY DEVELOPMENT ([37], pp. 46–74)

One of the central missions of government which should provide a focus for the departmental organization of the executive branch is community development.

Community development is the process by which we seek to create and preserve a wholesome living environment for all citizens. Such an environment should provide not only an adequate supply of decent housing accessible to all, balanced community transportation systems, and reliable public facilities and services, but also effective and responsive institutions of government and opportunities for the participation of private individuals and voluntary organizations in government decisions affecting the community. The goal of the community development process should be the establishment of vital communities—in metropolitan and nonmetropolitan areas, in cities, suburbs, and rural towns and villages—and the stimulation of a pattern of balanced growth which links together opportunities for housing, jobs, education, recreation, culture, and basic social services for every American, no matter where he lives.

Many factors have combined to place heavy strains on the ability of existing public and private institutions to assure safe and wholesome living environments for all Americans.

Population growth, rapid urbanization, the stagnation of many rural areas, lack of coordination among local and State jurisdictions, deterioration and social isolation in central cities, and accelerating social, technological, and economic change have had a major impact on the pace and quality of community development in recent years.

There is an urgent need and a clear national interest in enhancing the capacity of State and local governments to improve the quality of the physical facilities and services for our communities in cooperation with private institutions and local citizens. As the responsibilities of State and local governments and the demands upon them grow, their authorities must be enhanced, their resources expanded, and their capacity to deliver services improved.

The creation of a new Department of Community Development is not dependent upon the enactment of the President's revenue sharing proposals, but it reinforces their objectives in that it also stresses the importance of general purpose units of government. In the same manner that revenue sharing will provide flexible resources for States and localities to address their unique problems, a broad-based department will permit the Federal Government to respond to communities on the basis of locally determined needs, priorities, and plans for community improvement and will help strengthen State and local government capabilities to carry out their increased responsibilities effectively.

The present Federal structure is not adequate to meet community development requirements. The delivery of community development assistance by the Federal Government to the States, areawide agencies, and localities must be improved and a more effective tool must be made available for meeting Federal responsibilities in this area.

BACKGROUND OF THE PROPOSAL

The need for improved executive branch management has been a major concern of every President since the Second World War. In reviewing previous studies of this problem, the evolution of the community development concept is readily apparent. In 1953, the President's Advisory Committee on Government Reorganization, under Nelson Rockefeller, urged the consolidation of housing programs and the creation of a stronger secretarial role in the planning and management of a comprehensive and balanced housing program. In 1964, the President's Task Force on Government Reorganization, chaired by Don K. Price, took a broader view of community development and proposed that urban highways, waste treatment facilities, and community water supply systems be placed under the purview of a proposed Department of Housing and Community Development. More recent studies have stressed social needs as well as housing and community facilities programs and underscored the need for decentralization of program operations and decisionmaking to a strong field organization. The Ash Council Report of 1970 thus reflects a consistent theme that the Federal Government should become more responsive to the needs of today's communities.

PROBLEMS WITH EXISTING ORGANIZATION

Current Federal responsibilities for community development are severely fragmented—scattered in four Departments and four independent agencies. There is no single organization with the responsibility—and authority—to coordinate and direct Federal assistance for community development. For example, both the Department of Housing and Urban Development and the Department of Agriculture provide assistance for the construction of physical facilities critical to the community development process—housing, water and sewer lines, and recreational areas. The Department of Commerce has responsibility for regional economic development, but does not administer the functional programs related to that broader objective. The Department of Transportation provides assistance for community transportation systems which frequently determine the overall pattern of development, but is not responsible for the general development of localities.

The Ash Council has pointed out, "The present organizational structure encourages fragmentation when comprehensive responses to social and economic problems are needed. Problems are defined to fit within the limits of organizational authority, resulting in piecemeal approaches to their solutions by separate departments and agencies."

Most seriously, the fragmentation in the Federal response has undermined the capacity of State and local general purpose governments to coordinate and integrate developmental activities, programs, and projects at the community level.

A Council of Governments director from Tulsa stated:

The examples of fragmentation on the local level are almost too numerous to list. There are parts of four OEO Community Action Agencies in this planning region. HUD recognizes and funds one county as a planning organization and refuses to even recognize the plans made by the other counties. There are parts of three HEW health facilities planning areas in this region. For the most part, these boundaries subdividing the Federal agency regions were drawn before the concept of uniform substate planning regions was adopted, but the fragmentation process continues yet.

In another case, Monroe, Ohio, requested assistance in submitting an application to the Federal Government for sewers in a portion of newly annexed territory. A State field adviser discovered that the community was eligible for grants from the following Federal agencies: the Economic Development Administration, the Farmers Home Administration, and the Department of Housing and Urban Development. At that time the field offices of these agencies were widely scattered, placing a heavy burden on the community seeking aid.

The same official also pointed out: "Each agency, of course, has specific criteria for funding applications—the size, population, location (whether in or out of a standard metropolitan statistical area), and the severity of the problem is taken into consideration. The dilemma of the communities such as this is to determine which agency to contact and which agency would have jurisdiction to fund such a project."

The reorganization proposals for the Department of Community Development adhere closely to the recommendations of the Ash Council report. Most of the present programs of Federal aid for community development will now be consolidated in a single department.

In addition, key components of the Department of Transportation which are fundamental to achieving balanced growth within and between communities would be included in the new Department. They include all highway construction programs as well as urban mass transportation. Thus, the new Department will encompass a broad range of programs involving key elements of community development—housing, transportation, and community facilities—under unified Federal leadership as called for by the Ash Council.

Organization and Program Substance

The proposal for a Department of Community Development deals, as does all of the President's Departmental Reorganization Program, only with organizational and administrative matters. *It does not affect program substance.* While the statutory purposes and functions of each program are unaffected, these organizational proposals deal with the question of how programs can be made more effective by improving the structure and mechanisms by which they are carried out.

Objectives and Functions

GENERAL OBJECTIVES

The Department of Community Development will strengthen the capacity of State and local general purpose government and areawide and regional agencies to undertake programs of balanced growth and development in a manner responsive to citizen needs. The establishment of this Department recognizes the interrelationships among rural, suburban, and urban problems and the need to strengthen the essential social and economic partnership between the towns and villages of rural America and our great metropolitan areas. This Department must assist rural America to share in the Nation's affluence and growth, as well as coordinate programs for a livable urban America.

Similar and interdependent programs assisting community development should be located in a single department. This facilitates the delivery of assistance to States and localities by permitting the formulation of consistent program policies, procedures, and requirements. It also gives the Federal Government a clearer perception of national community development needs. This, in turn, should lead to more responsive Federal laws, policies, and priorities in meeting these needs. At present, assessment of national needs in this broad area depends on the perceptions of dispersed program managers in a number of departments and agencies, none of which are clearly focused on the total problem of community development.

MAJOR FUNCTIONS

The Department of Community Development will be concerned with the total problem of planning and developing the best communities possible. The specific functions of the Department are as follows:

1. To strengthen public and private community institutions through the provision of financial and technical assistance to States, areawide agencies, and localities in order to enhance their capacity to coordinate and manage public services, and to plan for growth and development. This function recognizes the need for responsible institutions through which local communities will be able to make decisions, expand the levels of economic activity, allocate resources, and establish goals and priorities.

The focus of such assistance will be on State and local general purpose government—particularly, the office of the chief executive. Recognizing that balanced growth and development depend upon expanded regional and areawide cooperation and program coordination, the Department of Community Development will also seek to strengthen interlocal government institutions such as councils of government on which such comprehensive development depends.

2. To encourage and assist citizens, private groups, voluntary organizations, and private economic entities to contribute ideas, skills, and resources to solving community problems and meeting community needs.

3. To provide financial and technical assistance to public and private institutions for the planning, financing, construction, and maintenance of certain basic community facilities such as water and waste disposal facilities, as well as libraries, parks, and open space; for the revitaliza-

tion of deteriorating neighborhoods and for meeting the special developmental needs of rural areas. This function includes the provision of electric power and telephone services in rural areas and the coordination of rural development with the development of related urban growth centers.

4. To provide assistance for the development of balanced and integrated transportation systems for communities. This function includes highway construction grants for communities and interstate highway networks linking communities, safety improvements, urban mass transportation assistance, and support for overall State and local transportation planning.

5. To support a broad range of activities for the planning, financing, construction, rehabilitation, maintenance, and management of housing, pursuant to the national goal of providing decent housing for every American.

This function includes departmental leadership in formulating national policies that will encourage private construction of decent housing at prices citizens can afford, assuring the availability of housing credit in rural areas, and operating programs of housing subsidies for urban and rural families with incomes too low to afford decent, safe, and sanitary housing.

6. To implement certain community disaster assistance and relief programs on behalf of the Federal Government.

7. To design and conduct basic and applied research on community development and related matters.

In carrying out all of the above functions, the Department of Community Development will undertake programs of research, demonstration, and training. It will give particular attention to the impact of community development on the national economy and markets for private capital, and will assist States, localities, and public and private sponsors of housing and community facilities in meeting demands for private investment. The Department will also assist in the planning, financing, and development of new communities.

ADVANTAGES OF CREATING A NEW DEPARTMENT

The creation of a new Department of Community Development will provide an effective framework for resolving the current problems of fragmentation and duplication. Through this Department, a coordinated Federal response to the problems of community growth and development will be possible. In addition, the proposed departmental structure will make it possible to determine accountability for performance and to overcome obstacles to leadership and initiative which presently exist in the community development area.

Beyond these general considerations, the creation of a new Department of Community Development promises various specific advantages, such as:

- Providing a central point in the federal system for formulating policy, advising the President on community development, transportation, and housing problems and needs, assigning accountability for Federal performance, and reducing jurisdictional disputes and the need for interagency coordination.

An example cited by an official from Little Rock, Ark., illustrates the clear need for a central point of responsibility. The community's plans called for Federal assistance requests in economic development and transportation. The first application went to the Economic Development Administration regional offices but was returned to Little Rock for a review by the local HUD office on its urban renewal impact. The second request was sent to the Department of Transportation in Washington and later was returned to the same local HUD office for review and concurrence. Placing these programs in a single agency will reduce the burdensome and time-consuming job of securing clearances from an outside agency for community programs that are not that agency's primary responsibility.

- Establishing a better balance between rural and urban areas in terms of Federal concern and resource allocation.

There is no neat dividing line between "urban" and "rural." Small towns and rural communities have many of the same problems as large cities. Moreover, with the passage of time, many smaller communities become urban in character. The decline of rural communities and the overcrowding of urban areas are parts of the same problem. Thus, there is no rationale for splitting the Federal response to the needs of communities based on size alone. Solutions must be tailored to the specific needs of each community which relate to factors other than size. Concentrating programs to assist rural communities in a single department, however, will help to accelerate development of rural communities.

- Assuring that development of physical aspects of an area are planned within the context of total community needs.

The new Department, by offering a broad range of programs—transportation, housing, and community facilities and services—aimed at total community development needs, will move away from the narrow functional orientation which currently exists. In many communities, the pattern of development is determined by the arterial transportation system. In others, the key factor may be sewer lines or housing developments. A single department will be capable of working with State and local governments from overall planning through execution of community development activities.

PROGRAMS OF THE NEW DEPARTMENT

Within the new Department, there are logical groupings of programs. For example, urban and rural development programs include two broad areas. One would be assistance to State and local governments and private institutions. This would include programs of grants for planning and management, designed to build the capacity of State and local government to develop and carry out their policies and programs. It would also include programs to encourage and assist citizen involvement in community development efforts and to direct attention to the needs of poor and minority groups in community decisionmaking. Model Cities, community action and special impact programs, and disaster assistance are included in this category.

A second grouping would cover assistance for development of the physical community. This would include such programs as urban renewal, water and waste disposal, open space, regional economic development programs, and rural electric and telephone facilities. Assistance for electric and telephone facilities are included with the others in this group because they are basic to viable communities in rural areas.

The community transportation programs include two closely linked programs: highway development and urban mass transportation. The major elements of intercity and interstate highway systems are in place so that the major thrust of the highway program is now more local in nature, being more focused on providing balanced community and areawide ground transportation. The linkage with mass transportation is vital inasmuch as, in all except major metropolitan areas where rail systems are feasible, mass transportation systems are highway based.

In housing, again, there are two distinct but compatible groupings. In one would be the activities related to production of housing (including loans, grants, mortgage insurance, and subsidy contracting). The other set of activities relates to Federal responsibility for assisted housing once it is completed. This would include payment of subsidies and the management and disposition of acquired housing.

The following transfers are planned from existing agencies to the broad functional areas of the new department:

Urban and Rural Development

HUD:

Urban Renewal
Model Cities
Water and Sewer Facilities
Open Space
Neighborhood Facilities
New Community Programs
Planning Assistance
Relocation

Commerce:

Public Works and Related Community Development Programs
Regional Commission Oversight

USDA:

Water and Waste Disposal Programs
Rural Electric and Telephone Systems
Rural Community Research and Planning
Rural Telephone Bank

HEW:

Library Construction Grants

OEO:

Community Action Program
Special Impact Program

SBA:

Residential Disaster Loans

Community Transportation

DOT:

Federal Highway Programs (excluding motor carrier safety)
Urban Mass Transportation Programs

Housing

HUD:

Mortgage Insurance
Government National Mortgage Association Programs
Housing Subsidies
Housing Management
Property Disposition

USDA:

Rural Housing

Federal Insurance

HUD:

Flood Insurance
Riot Reinsurance
Crime Insurance

The initial organization of the Department of Community Development will reflect its mission while taking into account the integrity of existing agencies and organizations which are transferred into the new Department. Realignments will be made only when such changes will substantially contribute to the effectiveness of the new Department. For example, the functions of the Farmers Home Administration transferred to the Department cover two basically distinct objectives. The largest is assistance for rural housing. To minimize problems of coordination with the housing programs transferred from HUD, these programs will be placed under a single housing administration. In creating this broad-based unit, measures will be taken to assure continued recognition of the special problems of housing in rural areas.

For example, the system of county offices established under the Farmers Home Administration is being retained in order to serve the needs of rural residents most effectively.

The second broad category of present Farmers Home Administration assistance is for community water and waste disposal facilities. This activity will be placed with similar programs from other agencies under the Urban and Rural Development Administration, where a major emphasis will be placed on the development of rural communities. These programs will also continue to be administered out of the county offices now in the Farmers Home Administration.

Management and Organization

BASIC MANAGEMENT STRUCTURE

The organization of the Department contemplates—(1) strong national level leadership and coordination through line program administrators who head groupings of related functions and the Under and Assistant Secretaries; and (2) strong local level program leadership and coordination through the decentralization of operations to regional directors and the subregional organization. Program authority will flow from the Secretary to the program Administrators to the regional directors. An overall organization chart appears on page 52.

The overall management team of the Department of Community Development will be headed by the Secretary and Deputy Secretary and includes the three major program Administrators, two Under Secretaries, four Assistant Secretaries, and the General Counsel.

a. The Secretary.—The position of the Secretary of Community Development is to be created with full power and authority over the organization and management of the Department and with full power of delegation. He will thus be in a position to organize the Department in the way best suited to accomplishing its purposes. The Secretary will have the authority (subject, of course, to the limitations of authorization and appropriations acts) to allocate the funds, personnel, and other department resources to implement Federal programs. The authority and flexibility of this position would permit the Secretary to mold and adapt the Department so that it will be responsive to national interests, and changing needs and conditions. He will be empowered to assign responsibilities and delegate authority so that his departmental subordinates can effectively administer the programs of the Department. Lines of control and points of accountability will thus be clearly established by the Secretary, pursuant to his wishes and needs.

b. The Deputy Secretary.—Because a substantial part of the Secretary's time and attention must be devoted to relationships external to departmental management, a strong role is visualized for the Deputy Secretary as the second ranking official in the Department and the Secretary's "alter ego" on all matters affecting the Department. The exact duties and functions of the Deputy Secretary will, of course, depend on the wishes of the Secretary.

The Deputy Secretary is expected to be closely involved in matters of internal management, but his responsibilities will not be limited to day-to-day operating decisions. Rather, it is contemplated that he will be responsible to the Secretary for insuring that policy decisions are translated into action. The key role played by the Deputy Secretary in the management of the Department can be underscored by indicating some of the responsibilities which could be discharged by the Deputy Secretary on behalf of the Secretary:

- Developing the overall operational guidelines of the Department; deciding what resources are needed to carry out the Department's programs; how those resources can be obtained, and how they can be deployed most effectively.
- Assuring that the Department's management structure—its organization, management systems, financial controls, and operating guidelines—effectively relates to and supports the policy objectives of the Department.
- Integrating and coordinating the efforts of the line and staff elements of the Department, maintaing effective channels of communication among these officials and between them and the Secretary.

c. The Under Secretaries.—Two Under Secretaries are proposed so that the Department will have strong, crosscutting managerial capability independent of the more narrowly defined interests of the four program administrators:

Under Secretary for Planning and Policy Analysis.—A major responsibility of the Secretary will be the planning, development, and evaluation of policy and programs. Accordingly, it is important that the Secretary be served by a single official of appropriate rank, who can provide continuous staff leadership in formulating the Department's overall strategy. The Under Secretary for Planning and Policy Analysis would be responsible for assisting the Secretary in the early recognition of national needs and priorities, in assuring consistency of policies within the Department and with other departments, and in coordinating the Department's planning and program evaluation processes.

In the shaping of departmental policies and plans, the Under Secretary will assist the Secretary in carrying out his principal responsibilities—providing advice to the President, furnishing testimony before the Congress and establishing priorities for the Department's substantive programs to meet national needs.

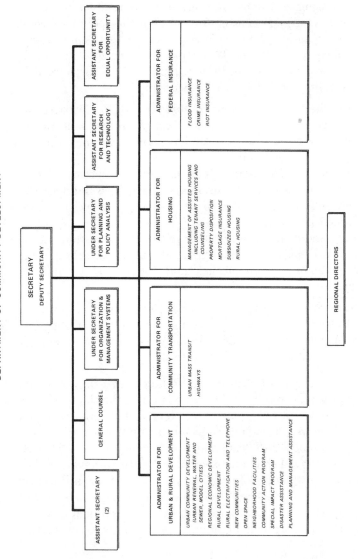

PROPOSED
DEPARTMENT OF **COMMUNITY DEVELOPMENT**

SECRETARY
DEPUTY SECRETARY

ASSISTANT SECRETARY (2)

GENERAL COUNSEL

UNDER SECRETARY FOR ORGANIZATION & MANAGEMENT SYSTEMS

UNDER SECRETARY FOR PLANNING AND POLICY ANALYSIS

ASSISTANT SECRETARY FOR RESEARCH AND TECHNOLOGY

ASSISTANT SECRETARY FOR EQUAL OPPORTUNITY

ADMINISTRATOR FOR URBAN & RURAL DEVELOPMENT

URBAN COMMUNITY DEVELOPMENT
(URBAN RENEWAL, WATER AND
SEWER, MODEL CITIES)
REGIONAL ECONOMIC DEVELOPMENT
RURAL DEVELOPMENT
RURAL ELECTRIFICATION AND TELEPHONE
NEW COMMUNITIES
OPEN SPACE
NEIGHBORHOOD FACILITIES
COMMUNITY ACTION PROGRAM
SPECIAL IMPACT PROGRAM
DISASTER ASSISTANCE
PLANNING AND MANAGEMENT ASSISTANCE

ADMINISTRATOR FOR COMMUNITY TRANSPORTATION

URBAN MASS TRANSIT
HIGHWAYS

ADMINISTRATOR FOR HOUSING

MANAGEMENT OF ASSISTED HOUSING
INCLUDING TENANT SERVICES AND
COUNSELING
PROPERTY DISPOSITION
MORTGAGE INSURANCE
SUBSIDIZED HOUSING
RURAL HOUSING

ADMINISTRATOR FOR FEDERAL INSURANCE

FLOOD INSURANCE
CRIME INSURANCE
RIOT INSURANCE

REGIONAL DIRECTORS

FEBRUARY, 1972

Under Secretary for Organization and Management Systems.—This would be the leading official on whom the Secretary can rely for strong management of the Department's resources—men, money, material, and information. He would provide department-wide leadership in the development and installation on a timely basis of improvements in management systems and administrative arrangements, thereby increasing the responsiveness of the Department to policy and programmatic changes. He is concerned with and involved in the substantive programs of the Department, but with a perspective which aims at augmenting the Secretary's capacity to manage those programs without sacrificing the advantages of a decentralized operation. Accordingly, the Secretary will look to him as a force for balancing and integrating judgments on the organization and management of departmental activities. His specific responsibilities would include the following:

- Assuring an effective plan of organizational and functional responsibilities for all elements of the Department so as to assure orderly program implementation and the proper flow of management information.
- Development of an effective personnel system supporting a single career service in which employees may aspire to advancement in any component of the Department and through which can be developed a cadre of senior staff people capable of bringing departmentwide perspectives to their work.
- Development of budget, costing, ADP, and other systems which serve the entire Department and which will permit data, wherever originated, to be used for departmental purposes with assurance as to their meaning and reliability.
- Improvement of program implementation, including adequate administrative support, and the development of techniques to utilize fully resources available in the Department.
- Design of an effective communication system to support the flow of timely and pertinent information between headquarters and the field in both directions.
- Assuring the necessary integration of the budgeting, financial management, auditing, and inspection functions under his jurisdiction with the policy functions of the Under Secretary for Planning and Policy Analysis, so that performance data may be used for reassessing departmental policies and plans.

Under this concept the Under Secretaries would be principal staff officers rather than links in the chain of command. Accordingly, their broad functional assignment would be to assist the Secretary in matters of departmentwide scope, but they would not exercise line control over the Administrators for operating programs. The Under Secretaries would, therefore, rely greatly on initiating coordinated action and the direct participation of the program administrators in the formulation of departmental resource requirements, systems, and controls.

d. Assistant Secretaries.—The Secretary and Deputy Secretary will also be served by several assistant secretaries, with department-wide functions in specific areas of activity. The functions for which the assistant secretaries are responsible, while less comprehensive and broad ranging than those of an Under Secretary, are crosscutting and related to all program groups. Included at this level are the General Counsel, the Assistant Secretary for Equal Opportunity, the Assistant Secretary for Research and Technology, and the Assistant Secretary for Financial Policy.

It is also contemplated that two assistant secretary positions would be used to give special attention to the audit and inspection functions and to the area of financial policy and programs. The latter area involves responsibility for advising the Secretary on the impact of the Department's policies and programs on the national economy, for management of the Government National Mortgage Association and various other loan fund operations for which the Department is responsible, and for assistance to States, localities, and other public bodies in raising capital.

e. Program Administrators.—Programs are to be grouped into three major organizational elements, each under the direction of an Administrator. These are Urban and Rural Development Administration, Community Transportation Administration, and Housing Administration. In addition, there will be a Federal Insurance Administration which will be substantially smaller than the others and more specialized in nature.

In general, the three major program Administrators would, along with the Secretary, Deputy Secretary, Under Secretaries, and the Assistant Secretaries comprise the top management team of the Department. The Administrators report directly to the Secretary and are each responsible for a broad, major purpose-oriented organizational grouping, which includes all of the activities and programs of the Department which serve that purpose. An Administrator is a line official responsible for carrying out a major national objective(s), including the planning and organization of his programs, the establishment of goals, priorities, and schedules, and the monitoring and evaluation of performance and implementation. Program authority and direction will flow from the Secretary to the Administrators.

It is expected that the Secretary will delegate to the maximum reasonable extent to his Administrators the authorities and resources necessary to carry out the program goals of the Department.

Normally, program implementation is the responsibility of the field structure, with the respective roles of the Administrator and field official defined by the Secretary. Each Administrator will, however, have under him a broad range of subordinate activities which can be organized in different ways. Within his delegation from the Secretary, the Administrator would set up both line and staff groups under him to which he may redelegate authority. He would generally delegate substantial authority to regional directors for effective implementation of programs. In the case of the Federal Insurance Administration, however, there will be an exception to this rule, because of the centralized nature of the Federal role.

Urban and Rural Development Administration.—The Urban and Rural Development Administrator will be responsible for all programs of the Department which are designed to assist the basic physical facilities and institutional development of communities. This official will be responsible for three broad groups of activities.

The first would be public planning and management in which the primary objectives are: (*a*) Assisting State, area, and community planning activities; and (*b*) improving the capabilities of governments. These include planning assistance programs, administration of planning requirements, intergovernmental relations, and technical assistance to States and communities.

The second area is development assistance, including programs providing financial assistance for physical development, excluding transportation and housing. This includes both loans and grants to urban and rural areas. It includes both the proposed urban and rural community special revenue sharing programs, plus other categorical grant and loan programs such as the water and waste disposal programs of the Farmers Home Administration, the programs of the Rural Electrification Administration, Rural Telephone Bank, library grants, urban renewal, open space land grants, neighborhood facilities grants, and the group of programs encompassed in the new communities development program. Not only are these programs similar in substance and intent, so that similar skills are required in their administration, but in many instances they will operate together to help carry out a community's overall plan.

The third grouping under the Administrator for Urban and Rural Development covers the "social development" activities and the development of private organizational capabilities. These include the community action program, the special impact program of OEO, Model Cities demonstration program, disaster assistance activities (which are both social and physical), and relocation policies and procedures for all Department programs.

The Deputy Administrator will have special responsibility for rural development and will be in charge of an Office of Rural Development that will carry out planning, evaluation, and research directed at the special development needs of rural communities.

Community Transportation Administration.—The Community Transportation Administrator will be responsible for the large transportation component of community development. This will include programs transferred from the present Federal Highway Administration (excluding motor carrier safety) and the Urban Mass Transportation Administration. These activities have a direct and major impact on community development, since the local and regional transportation system is a key element in a viable community. It is, in fact, a fundamental shaper of the community. It can serve to create or define communities, neighborhoods, and service districts—or can destroy them. Over the years, efforts to coordinate highway and transportation planning with community development planning have been frustrated by organizational fragmentation at the Federal level. This has prevented the melding of transportation and community development policy which is necessary to realize the beneficial potential of highways and mass transportation for community development. The Department of Community Development can provide this unified policy control.

At the same time, however, unlike water and sewer grants, for example, transportation programs have an impact beyond the community and must be integrated with statewide and national systems. Thus, transportation activities will be maintained as a single grouping and assigned to a single Administrator. This official will be responsible not only for the transportation programs themselves, but for facilitating the integration of transportation systems into State and local development objectives. This will include coordination with national transportation systems in order to assure, for instance, that airport location and access facilities are integrated with local and areawide plans.

Housing Administration.—The Housing Administrator will be responsible for two functions:

Housing production covers the direction of all housing programs through the completion of construction. These would include the mortgage insurance programs, the housing subsidy programs for low- and moderate-income housing, the rural housing programs of Farmers Home Administration, and the low-rent public housing program.

Housing management covers all matters relating to Department-assisted housing after completion of construction. This would include loans and mortgage servicing, housing management, and improvement of public housing, operation and disposition of Government-held housing, and tenant assistance services and counseling.

Federal Insurance Administration.—The Federal Insurance Administrator will be responsible for three programs involving Federal insurance or reinsurance. These are flood insurance, riot reinsurance, and crime insurance. In contrast with the other program Administrations, the Federal role in these activities is highly centralized. There is little or no involvement by Federal employees in the field, since the programs operate through private insurance companies. The

Administrator will be responsible for establishing and maintaining contact with these firms, assuring that their operations are responsive to the national interest in the area of specialized insurance.

FIELD ORGANIZATION

a. Regional Organization.—The departmental regions will conform to the 10 Standard Federal Regions established by the President by Executive order on March 19, 1969. The field organization, in general, and the regional director, in particular, have unique importance for the Department of Community Development. To a much greater extent than most all other Federal departments, activities of the Department of Community Development bear on local governmental functions. The particular mission of this Department relates to strengthening local government's capacity for formulating and carrying out strategies of development in a manner responsive to local institutional and citizen needs. Thus, in implementing its program responsibilities, the Department of Community Development has a peculiar need to "decentralize." Programs must be coordinated at the State and local levels—and the coordination and implementation of programs must be suited to the particular needs, problems, and opportunities of each community. Communities must be encouraged to create areawide comprehensive development strategies and to fit categorical program assistance for planning, management, development, community services, housing, and transportation into these strategies.

The organization contemplates a departmental field structure headed by strong regional directors. This is in keeping with the general objectives of the broad departmental reorganization—to strengthen responsible management and to base the internal organization of each department on major purposes. A chart illustrating this organization appears on page 58.

While the Department's leadership makes and interprets policy, establishes priorities, promulgates standards, criteria, and procedures for all levels of field operation, and provides for overall program administration, the regional director will be responsible for coordinating and integrating all programs and activities of the Department in his assigned geographic jurisdiction. Most significantly, the regional director will control the allocation and distribution of funds to subregional offices in his jurisdiction.

All other departmental staff in the region are subordinate to the regional director, and the regional office will provide technical assistance and staff support to the subregional offices and to States and communities in each region. As indicated, the regional director does not establish program policy but is responsible for coordinated and effective implementation. Therefore, he will have authority, under

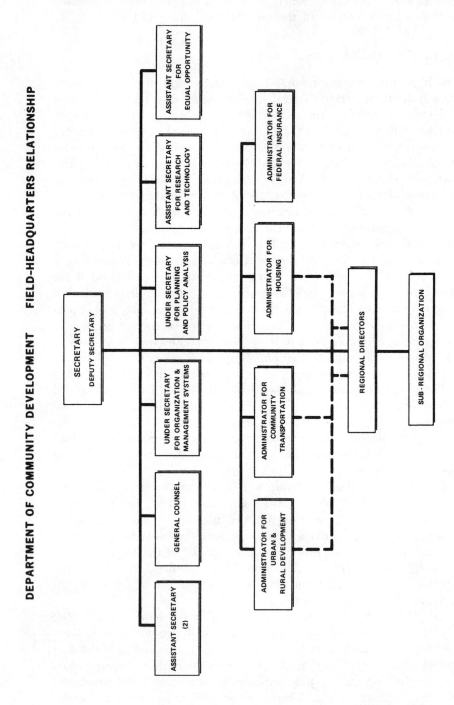

DEPARTMENT OF COMMUNITY DEVELOPMENT   FIELD-HEADQUARTERS RELATIONSHIP

SECRETARY
DEPUTY SECRETARY

ASSISTANT SECRETARY
(2)

GENERAL COUNSEL

UNDER SECRETARY
FOR ORGANIZATION &
MANAGEMENT SYSTEMS

UNDER SECRETARY
FOR PLANNING
AND POLICY ANALYSIS

ASSISTANT SECRETARY
FOR RESEARCH
AND TECHNOLOGY

ASSISTANT SECRETARY
FOR
EQUAL OPPORTUNITY

ADMINISTRATOR FOR
URBAN &
RURAL DEVELOPMENT

ADMINISTRATOR FOR
COMMUNITY
TRANSPORTATION

ADMINISTRATOR FOR
HOUSING

ADMINISTRATOR FOR
FEDERAL INSURANCE

REGIONAL DIRECTORS

SUB - REGIONAL ORGANIZATION

delegation from the Secretary, to make changes in organization, staffing patterns, and other related administrative matters within the limitations of resource availability and of priorities and plans established by headquarters.

The regional directors represent the Secretary in the regions to Governors and local officials and with other Federal agencies, especially as members of the Federal Regional Councils. They are line officials, responsible to the Secretary for the execution of all the Department's activities in the region. Basic policy direction and resources flow to the regional directors from the Secretary and Deputy Secretary. At the same time, while they are line officials, accountable to the Secretary, the regional directors receive specific program authority and direction from the Secretary through the appropriate program Administrators at the national level. The authority to administer programs runs from the regional directors to the subregional organization.

b. Subregional Organization.—Effective operation of the Department of Community Development along these lines necessarily depends on the capacity of the Department's subregional offices and staff to work with individual communities. Genuine decentralization of Federal authority is perhaps more important for this process and these programs than any others. Such program administration will be the primary focus of the Department's subregional offices. The regional director and his supporting staff at the regional level thus have special responsibilities for this Department—to allocate program funds to subregional offices and to individual States or cities on the basis of fund availability in each separate categorical (national) program *and* on the basis of the community development strategies for each of the States and localities in the region. They also provide support and technical assistance to both the recipients and the Department's subregional staff.

The Department's field organization, under the regional director, is the operating arm of the Department. The Department's day-to-day program decisions and operations are made and carried out at the subregional level, subject to the direction, guidance, assistance, and evaluation of the regional office. Subregional offices are responsible for operating and decisionmaking functions in the field and are the Department's principal points of contact with program participants and sponsors. The directors of the subregional offices are responsible to the regional director for the supervision and direction of their offices. They are responsible for the management and execution of the programs and functions assigned them in accordance with law and regulation, and the policies, procedures, and criteria established by the appropriate program Administrators.

Subregional organization would follow two main lines and, generally, would be established on a State-by-State basis. There would be a State office responsible for all nonhighway departmental programs and one responsible for highway programs. Because of the very effective relationships established over the years, the State offices of the highway program division engineers will be maintained as distinct entities, although the main subregional departmental offices and the division engineers' offices would be co-located wherever practicable. The two offices would be closely coordinated.

The Director of a departmental subregional office would have full authority over all Department personnel and activities in his jurisdiction. He would reflect a generalist approach to community development needs and problems. Under this concept, the subregional offices would deal with the problems of specific communities as a whole, using the range of Department programs to provide a package of assistance suited to the needs of the community.

Directors of the subregional offices would have full authority to operate the programs of the Department which are decentralized to the field, including the authority to approve specific projects and to authorize financial and other assistance without referral to a higher level. He would operate under the direction of the regional director, and in accordance with the procedures, policies, and guidelines established by the appropriate program Administrators.

Below the subregional offices would be local Federal Housing Administration insuring offices and the local offices established under the Farmers Home Administration. The latter offices would continue to administer the rural housing and community facilities programs transferred from the Department of Agriculture; in addition they would continue to administer the FHA farm loan programs as an agent of the Department of Agriculture for as long as the arrangement proves effective. In addition, it is expected that, in general, the county office would provide the primary contact in rural areas and communities for the other housing and community facilities programs of the Department of Community Development.

c. Advantages of the Proposed Field Organization.—Briefly, the advantages of this field organization are as follows:

- Emphasis is placed on the role of States, areas, and localities;
- A unified approach to local and community problems is encouraged;
- Regional headquarters is freed from detailed day-to-day program operations and can emphasize coordination with other Federal agencies, the development of State and local program strategy, and the evaluation of subregional performance;
- Significant field input into the headquarters budget, policy, and resource allocation systems is realized;
- The concept is flexible—new activities can be added, present ones changed or eliminated, relatively easily;
- Management, coordination, and evaluation activities are emphasized;

- The number of field officials reporting to the Secretary is limited;
- Field activities are focused under one individual, who is given the necessary authority and resources, and can be held accountable for his performance;
- A focal point for strong liaison with States and other Federal agencies in the field is provided; and
- Clear and direct channels of authority in the field are established.

SELECTED MANAGEMENT CONCEPTS

To give added substance to the general organizational structure, it is useful to describe in broad outline a few specific concepts to illustrate how the Department's management system should function. The central theme of each of these concepts is highlighted below:

- *Manpower and Personnel.*—Manpower will be the most important resource of the Department. The development, deployment, and utilization of manpower will be major responsibilities of the Secretary and Deputy Secretary, relying heavily on the advice and assistance of the Under Secretary for Organization and Management Systems. A key element will be the development of a comprehensive plan for keeping employees informed of changes and events which will affect them. This is vital in the long run, as well as during the transition to a new Department. Equally important will be the establishment of a departmentwide manpower system, permitting employees to develop their full potential by working in various programs or crosscutting functions. Employees will have greater opportunity to move from, for example, housing to the broader development fields (or vice versa) as their special abilities match the changing needs of the Department.
- *Planning and Evaluation.*—At a different level, planning and evaluation will be established as primary responsibilities of the top management of the Department, including the Secretary, Deputy Secretary, Under Secretary for Planning and Policy Analysis, program administrators, and regional directors. Staff elements will be given an advisory and supportive role. The integration of long- and short-term planning is essential. Both are dynamic processes keyed to results of current evaluations to assure their validity, relevancy, and realism. Both planning and evaluation are oriented toward concern with resources, objectives, goals, organization, and the other factors having a bearing on program success or failure. The planning process provides boundaries within which managers can operate, such as specifying the housing that should be produced and the resources available for the objective. The evaluation system focuses on the quality of performance and the identification of preventive action, such as examining the probable cost per unit of housing under alternative

methods of production. The overall approach establishes an attitude and conceptual framework for the construction of approaches, tailored to the special needs of the Department, that will reinforce decentralization and encourage creativity.

The creation of the Department itself will encourage an evaluation process that permits broader and more comprehensive assessments of the impact of Federal programs to be undertaken within a single department. The resulting evaluation system will be responsive to the needs of the Congress as well as the executive branch.

- *Budget Preparation.*—Within the context of the planning system described above, budget preparation is an integral part of the planning process, determining, for example, the resources in men and money which will be needed to achieve housing production (or any other) objectives in a specified period. It is a major element in the development of the short-term plan, but may involve such supplemental data and reviews as are dictated by need. This assures that the annual budgets are consistent with current and longer range plans.
- *Audit, Inspections, Investigations.*—These functions are concerned with determining what actually happened as contrasted with the effort to look ahead that is the focus of the planning and evaluation process. These activities take on a new importance in a highly decentralized organization. Particular attention will be given to the opportunity for simplification and reduction of requirements with the enactment of revenue sharing. Throughout, increased reliance will be placed on local efforts with Federal audit and inspections taking on the role of assuring that adequate financial and program controls are maintained.
- *Grants Management.*—Even with the enactment of the President's revenue sharing proposals, the problem of rationalizing the balance of the grants system must be addressed. Within existing authorities there are a number of changes which could be made that would serve to simplify the present maze of rules and requirements with the result that the effectiveness of existing grants would be significantly improved. For example, the creation of the Department itself will substantially reduce the need for coordination and multiple-agency review of applications. Other steps can be taken to reduce or eliminate detailed project reviews which no longer serve a useful purpose.
- *Co-location and Common Service.*—In order to promote more effective coordination and to make better use of manpower and other resources, the Department will, to the extent possible, co-locate functions in each region and in subregional offices. By bringing all its resources together in each area the Department will be better able to assure the systematic analysis of all the common services at each location and the determination, based

on the best interests of the Government, whether or not a multi-user single service such as supply, graphics, ADP, etc., is to be prescribed.

- *Information Systems.*—This is generally thought of as the means by which data on program activity flow from the field structure to the headquarters and up to the Secretary, assuring that program managers and policy officials at each level have access to the information which they need for responsible decisionmaking. Equally important, however, is the fact that information must flow down as well as up throughout the organization. Policy guidance and directives must flow efficiently from the Secretary to the line Administrators and to the field structure with effective feedback from field to headquarters.

The highly decentralized operations of the new Department will necessitate sensitive and effective information systems. This will be a major responsibility of the Under Secretary for Organization and Management Systems. During the transition phase he will have particular responsibility for avoiding conflict and eliminating duplication, while at the same time assuring continuity of information flows. In the longer run he must develop systems that are adaptable to the changing needs of the Department.

APPROPRIATION STRUCTURE

The new Department of Community Development will require a new appropriations structure, merging and consolidating the accounts now in use for the activities being moved to the new Department. The revised appropriations structure should assist management effectiveness and provide the flexibility to respond to rapidly changing conditions.

To facilitate effective management, the appropriations structure should correspond to the organization of the new Department. Further, it is proposed that appropriations be made to the Secretary, with some appropriation items identified to the level of the first major program grouping of the Department. With the concurrence of the Congress, this would result in a simplification of the appropriations structure and would facilitate legislative review of the President's budget requests.

The existence of many relatively small "pockets" of appropriations, transferred from the existing departments and agencies, could be a handicap to the new Department in integrating its operations, as well as a handicap to the Congress and the public in understanding the Federal budget. It is not the intent of the measures discussed here to freeze an appropriation pattern for all time. An appropriations structure is subject to change by Congress from year to year, and indeed should be changed as programs and organizations are modified.

One means of achieving this objective would be to provide two principal appropriation accounts for each major program grouping of the Department. The first includes financing for day-to-day operating expenses and the other would cover funds for construction, land acquisition, project-oriented research, and certain types of loan and grant activity.

In addition, the financial accounts of the Department will continue to provide separately for the highway trust fund and for the various public enterprise funds transferred to the Department. A working capital fund at the departmental level to finance departmentwide administrative services is also desirable. Service funds could also be established where necessary, to merge accounts which provide for services performed for others at a charge approximating cost, or which continue earmarking now required by law in connection with programs of the Department.

COORDINATION WITH OTHER DEPARTMENTS

The programs of the proposed Department of Community Development will emphasize physical development and institution building. However, it will be necessary to establish appropriate coordination with Federal departments and agencies concerned with social, environmental, and economic programs.

The shift of community-based transportation programs will substantially reduce the coordination now required between DOT and HUD by recognizing that these transportation programs have a major impact on the development of communities. The need to integrate these programs with other community development efforts is, indeed, a strong reason for the new organization. At the same time, however, an element of coordination will be necessary between the Department of Community Development and the Department of Economic Affairs. Local and regional transportation systems must continue to serve national needs as well, and must constitute part of integrated national systems.

At the community level, location and accessibility of airports, railroad stations and facilities, and port facilities are extremely important. All of these elements of national transportation systems must be so planned that they are not disruptive of the community and are melded with the local and areawide highway and mass transportation systems so that transfers of people and goods from national to local transportations systems can be easily and effectively accomplished. Provision is made for such coordination in the departmental legislation.

The growth and economy of rural towns and villages is often dependent on the argicultural economy, and farm areas are dependent on the quality of local community services. This interdependency will require close collaboration between the Department of Community Development and the Department of Agriculture at key points. Collaboration at the grassroots level will be facilitated by the county offices of the Department of Community Development which, in addition to providing community facilities and housing assistance, will continue to make and service the farm loans for the Department of Agriculture.

It will also be necessary to assure coordination with the Department of Human Resources. For example, while grants for construction of schools and hospitals are primarily related to Federal purposes in the human resources area, the programs do have an impact on the development of communities. It will be important to assure that this impact is recognized and considered. Similarly, certain community development programs (such as Model Cities and Community Action) will have an impact on human resource objectives. Thus, while the creation of the Department will reduce substantially the need for interagency review and coordination, a certain amount of communication and coordination will continue to be necessary.

IMPACT OF REVENUE SHARING

Enactment of the revenue sharing proposals would have a major impact—at all levels—on the operations of the proposed Department of Community Development, although not on housing assistance programs.

Revenue sharing will provide States and localities with the resources and the flexibility to undertake programs of community development suited to their particular needs. Along with the proposed community planning-management grant program, it will also act to improve the capacity of State and local governments to exercise their responsibilities and to enhance their authority to govern. The restructuring of the Federal executive branch, including the creation of a Department of Community Development, parallels this effort to build up States and localities. The reorganization will allow Federal Departments, structured around broad purposes and with decentralized authority, to deal more effectively with the other levels of the Federal system and to implement a more productive and responsive process of community growth and development.

With the enactment of the special revenue sharing proposals, the Department of Community Development (particularly the Urban and Rural Development and the Community Transportation Administrations) would be able to give greater priority to broad policy development and implementation, research, evaluation, and technical assistance and to reduce attention to daily program administration in the form of individual project approvals.

It should be emphasized that while the establishment of a Department of Community Development is an independent initiative, it would complement revenue sharing in this program area. With this new departmental structure, States and localities would be able to obtain assistance for broad and comprehensive strategies of growth, physical development, and institutional improvement from a single department. Moreover, the decentralized authority of this Department will make such Federal community development assistance more accessible to States, areawide agencies, localities, the private economic sector, voluntary organizations, and individual citizens. Thus, the establishment of a Department of Community Development, along the lines suggested in this report, would combine with the special revenue sharing proposals to improve greatly the delivery of Federal community development assistance.

Budget and Manpower

The new Department will consist of four program administrations, plus general departmental management and support offices. The following table provides a breakdown of estimated manpower and budget resources based on data in the President's fiscal year 1973 budget.

N1

	Fiscal year 1972	
Major components:	Program outlays (in millions)[1]	Employment
Urban and Rural Development	$3,546	11,360
Community Transportation	5,115	4,769
Housing	[2]1,558	11,058
Federal Insurance	2	50
General Departmental Management	60	2,973
Total	$10,281	30,210

[1] Net of receipts and collections which are offset against outlays.
[2] Reflects impact of sale of assets.

Safeguards for Civil Service Personnel

The new Department of Community Development will directly involve four of the present Cabinet departments and several independent agencies. Their programs will become a part of the new department.

These changes, while primarily affecting programs, also will affect many Federal employees who will participate fully in accomplishing the reorganization. To that end, current plans include sound provisions to insure that disruption to employees will be kept to an absolute minimum; that cutbacks in staffs, where necessary, will be accomplished by normal turnover; and that actions which could adversely affect employees will be avoided.

No employee will be separated because of the reorganization.—In addition, the reorganization bills include a provision that no employee will be reduced in classification or compensation as a result of the plan for a period of 1 year after the reorganization becomes effective. All movements of functions and jobs will be governed by current law and Civil Service Commission regulations with full employee protections and appeal rights. From another standpoint, the reorganiza-

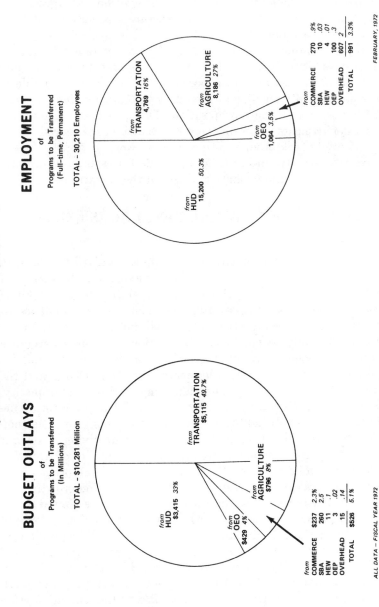

The Proposed
Department of Community Development

BUDGET OUTLAYS
of
Programs to be Transferred
(In Millions)

TOTAL - $10,281 Million

from
TRANSPORTATION
$5,115 49.7%

from
AGRICULTURE
$796 8%

from
HUD
$3,415 33%

from
OEO
$429 4%

from		
COMMERCE	$237	2.3%
SBA	260	2.5
HEW	11	.1
OEP	3	.02
OVERHEAD	15	.14
TOTAL	$526	5.1%

ALL DATA – FISCAL YEAR 1972

EMPLOYMENT
of
Programs to be Transferred
(Full-time, Permanent)

TOTAL - 30,210 Employees

from
TRANSPORTATION
4,769 16%

from
AGRICULTURE
8,186 27%

from
OEO
1,064 3.5%

from
HUD
15,200 50.3%

from		
COMMERCE	270	.9%
SBA	10	.03
HEW	4	.01
OEP	100	.3
OVERHEAD	607	.2
TOTAL	991	3.3%

FEBRUARY, 1972

tion can be viewed as improving the range of opportunities for promotion and career development, as more broadly conceived program management and staff positions evolve in the new departments.

Full consideration is also given to avoiding any adverse impact of reorganization on the existence of union recognition and agreements as a result of possible changes in unit structure that may result from transfers and realignments.

The reorganization bill will provide for salary retention for an executive level officer (Levels I to V) who is transferred to a new department and is assigned to a position with duties comparable to those he performed immediately preceding the transfer, for the duration of his service in the new position. This provision permits the proposed departments to retain the services of its experienced executives, who might seek other positions if they were to suffer a loss in executive level or pay, and thus help provide for essential continuity of operations during the formative phases of the Department.

DEPARTMENT OF NATURAL RESOURCES ([3], pp. 112–143)

The people of this Nation enjoy the highest standard of living in the world, in large part as the result of having an abundance of natural resources and the technological capability to develop and operate a sophisticated, industrialized economy. This abundance of natural resources has served the Nation well, but the needs of future generations can only be met if effective action is taken to recognize not only the demands of a growing population, but the effects of increased per capita consumption, higher standards of living, and the need for restoring, protecting, and enhancing environmental quality.

Population growth is a major factor that will determine future demands for resources. In addition, the impact of this growth is compounded by rapid improvement in standards of living, economic growth, and a general public desire for improved quality of life. As a result of the combination of these factors, the consumption of resources will increase at a rate far greater than population growth. Currently, with only 6 percent of the world population, the United States consumes 30 percent of the total world mineral production. If present trends continue, the U.S. demand for primary minerals could increase by more than 400 percent by the year 2000, energy requirements could more than triple, and water withdrawals could be over four-fifths of the entire national streamflow. We will have to construct as many additional houses and other structures as now exist. In the remaining years of this century, the United States will use more energy and other key resources than it has consumed since its beginning.

In addition to satisfying future demands for water, timber, minerals, and energy, our people also will need and demand the preservation of forests, lakes, wilderness, beaches, and the general environment for increased recreational use, and to maintain the quality of life for the Nation.

The world is an ecological system—the sum of all of the living and nonliving components that support the chain of life. As some natural resources are being depleted, as foreign sources of supply become less plentiful and less secure, and as environmental problems become more evident, the Nation suddenly has become aware of the full importance and significance of the need for the conservation and management of natural resources and the protection and preservation of the environment, not only to sustain and provide for continued social and economic growth but for man's well-being and survival.

The Nation needs a better understanding of the total environment—the oceans, the atmosphere, and lands and their interaction—to enable us to monitor more effectively and predict environmental actions, and to exercise some degree of control over the environment for the better protection of life and property from natural or manmade hazards. There is also need for exploration and development leading to more intelligent use of our resources, wherever they are found, with full consideration of the environment.

In summary, the natural resource and related environmental challenges facing the Nation are:

- To provide sufficient supplies of water, minerals, fuel, and timber to support our energy and other needs for future economic development.
- To maintain and enhance our forests, unique natural areas, historic properties, lands, waters, fish and wildlife, beaches, and estuaries in a manner which meets the aesthetic, cultural, and recreational needs of the people.
- To understand our physical environment and the natural and manmade changes that are taking place so that modifications can be made when advantageous and possible and, when modifications are not possible, to provide advance hazard warnings.
- To manage our resources in ways which will assure ecological balance and thus sustain the basis on which public needs can continue to be fulfilled.

If this Nation's future resource requirements are to be met through the wisest conservation and management of natural resources, there is urgent need to provide that governmental organization and managerial capability which can most effectively develop and implement comprehensive natural resource policies and programs. Both operational programs and scientific investigations for the land, oceans, and atmosphere need to be integrated as elements of a total system rather than as separate entities under diverse administration. Since natural resources policies and programs involve more than the conservation and management of federally owned resources, there needs to be consistency of treatment by the Federal Government in its policies and programs affecting natural resources owned or administered by State and local governments, Indian tribes, private organizations, and individuals.

The distribution and mixed ownership of natural resources is a major consideration which requires a more effective and efficient Federal organization to assure that these resources most effectively meet future needs. This Nation's resources are distributed over some 3.6 million square miles of onshore lands and 527,000 square miles of the Continental Shelf. Ownership and management responsibilities are divided among Federal, State, local governments, Indian tribal governments, and the private sector.

Responsibility for management of the Federal lands which comprise one-third of the Nation's onshore lands is divided among a number of organizations:

	Millions of acres
Bureau of Land Management	475
Forest Service	187
National Park Service	30
Bureau of Sport Fisheries and Wildlife	30
Bureau of Reclamation	9
Defense and other	35
Total	766

Future planning and management must adequately recognize and provide for the most effective use and productivity of all resources, both publicly and privately owned. For example, only about 30 percent of rainfall can be intercepted and managed as it flows toward the sea through surface and subsurface systems involving lands of all ownerships and uses. Water resource management therefore must recognize and provide for all lands and uses if the regions of the Nation are to be assured that their water needs will be met. Other examples of closely related public-private resource ownership relationships which affect future availability of resources are:

	Percent	
	Federal land	Non-Federal land
Outdoor recreation visits	14	86
Petroleum reserves (including Outer Continental Shelf)	52	48
Natural gas reserves (including Outer Continental Shelf)	52	48
Coal	39	61
Shale oil potential	75	25
Uranium	40	60
Geothermal steam	60	40
Saw timber inventory	48	52
Commercial forest land area	22	78
State and county		(6)
Industry		(13)
Farm and miscellaneous private		(59)

The close relationships among resource uses also must be recognized. Forestry practices directly affect water supplies, fish and wildlife, and outdoor recreation. Flood control or water supply projects likewise have similar impacts on other resource values. Mineral development and utilization can, if carelessly done, destroy other resource values and result in serious water and air pollution. The need for environmental protection is linked directly to every form of natural resource use.

To better meet these challenges, the Department of Natural Resources will bring together into one agency most of the numerous natural resources and physical environmental programs which currently are scattered throughout several Federal organizations. It will provide the essential governmental capabilities required to plan, establish priorities, weigh alternatives and priorities, and operate programs so that this Nation's natural resources will make their optimal contribution to national objectives.

The availability of adequate water, energy, timber, forage, outdoor recreation, and other resources contributes to individual well-being, community development, and economic growth and productivity. For example, sufficient energy is essential for general economic development, for the growth of communities, and for the public well-being. The same is true for water and for recreation resources.

Thus, the purposes of the Department of Natural Resources are interrelated with the purposes of the other three proposed departments. However, since natural resources involve a coherent system of relationships among resources and with the environment, they need to be managed within a single organizational framework. The management of natural resources also requires conservation to meet future, as well as current, needs. Immediate pressures for short-term development and utilization must be evaluated in the light of requirements of future generations.

Accordingly, the proposed Department will be so structured and organized as to integrate resource utilization and environmental values. Through its policy formulation and program operation functions the Department will be able to respond more vigorously and coherently to the needs for economic and community development, for environmental protection and enhancement, for the conservation and wise use of resources, and for other national goals than can present agencies.

PRIOR REORGANIZATION STUDIES AND RECOMMENDATIONS

Over the past 50 years, a number of studies have focused on the management problems posed by the fragmentation and proliferation of natural resource functions among departments. For example, after laboring for several years, the Congress' Joint Commission on Reorganization of Government Departments rendered its report to President Harding who, in turn, transmitted it to the Congress with his recommendation for adoption. The report recommended transfer of the nonmilitary engineering activities of the War Department to the Department of the Interior and the transfer of the functions of the

Federal Power Commission to Interior. There were joint House and Senate hearings on those recommendations but no further action.

Late in 1932, President Hoover submitted a plan to Congress that, among other things, would have transferred the Corps of Engineers' civil functions to Interior and the General Land Office from Interior to Agriculture. All of President Hoover's reorganization recommendations, including those affecting natural resources, were disapproved by a House resolution of January 19, 1933.

The President's Committee on Administrative Management in 1937 recommended creation of a National Resources Planning Board which was established in 1939. It functioned largely in the natural resources field and helped coordinate agency activities and Federal-State relationships until its abolition in 1943. The President's Committee also recommended a basic structure of 12 departments, one to be the Department of the Interior retitled the Department of Conservation.

N2　　In 1949, a majority of the Hoover Commission overrode the recommendation of its Task Force and its Committee on Natural Resources which would have consolidated water resources and public land management functions in a Department of Natural Resources. Instead, the Commission recommended that public land management be consolidated by transferring the Bureau of Land Management to the Department of Agriculture and that civil functions of the Corps of Engineers be transferred to Interior.

The second Hoover Commission, reporting in 1955, recommended creation of a Water Resources Board and that the Corps of Engineers assume the Soil Conservation Service function of constructing headwater dams for flood control. The proposal to establish a Board was similar to one going back to the Inland Waterways Commission established by Theodore Roosevelt. The present Water Resources Council represents to some degree the kinds of coordinating mechanism advocated by the two Commissions.

President Eisenhower, in his final budget message of 1961, recommended consolidating the water resources functions of the Corps of Engineers, the Department of the Interior, and the river basin survey work of the Federal Power Commission.

The June 1970 report to the President by the Public Land Law Review Commission, entitled "One Third of the Nation's Land", recommended the establishment of a Department of Natural Resources which would bring together the major public land agencies.

PROBLEMS WITH EXISTING ORGANIZATIONS

Federal natural resources programs have developed historically on a piecemeal basis in response to problems, specific needs, various pressures and urgencies over a long period. This has resulted in programs scattered among agencies, with attendant overlaps, duplications, inefficiencies, and also voids. For instance:

- Major water resource development programs are located in three departments: Agriculture, Interior, and Army. A separate agency, the Water Resources Council, was established for the purpose of providing a mechanism to coordinate the several agencies' planning efforts and water resources policy. The Council has had limited effectiveness since it is basically an interagency committee. While some improvements have been made, interagency rivalry, duplicative planning, and conflicting policies still persist.
- Nonmilitary Federal lands are administered by five agencies in two departments. Agriculture's national forest lands and Interior's public domain lands generally involve the same types of resources and uses. These lands often are adjacent to each other and sometimes intermingled. Even though these lands are managed to meet similar objectives and frequently are used by the same clientele, management policies and procedures have been dissimilar or not uniformly applied. Their separate administration results in unnecessary problems for forest and range users, overlapping efforts, and less effective land use planning for public uses.
- Federal recreation areas are administered by six different agencies in three departments and by one independent agency. Each agency tends to plan its own recreation development without appropriate recognition of the regional public need or the interaction among Federal and non-Federal public and private facilities and programs to meet total needs.
- A variety of marine resources and environmental programs were located in several agencies of the Government, inhibiting the development of a cohesive national effort. Many of these were transferred to the National Oceanic and Atmospheric Administration by Reorganization Plan No. 4 of July 9, 1970. However, this still left the related offshore oil, gas, mineral resource, and earth sciences programs separately managed by Interior.
- Energy programs consist of separate activities concentrating on particular sources of energy. They are scattered among several agencies with no single agency charged with formulating and implementing a unified policy and approach to assure effective energy resources utilization and conservation and, at the same time, to meet future energy requirements and the achievement of environmental objectives.

The present government organizational structure is not conducive to effective natural resource management because there is no mechanism for the effective coordination of policies, authorities, programs, activities, and services, as discussed above. Specific results have been:

- In the Southeastern States, stream channel straightening and deepening (Agriculture) has been protested vigorously by the

Department of the Interior, supported by certain conservation interests.

The process of balancing fish and wildlife and scenic values against economic development needs is unnecessarily frustrated by fragmented planning and evaluation responsibilities within the Federal Government.

- A Corps of Engineers project for flood control and agricultural water supply had serious impacts on the Everglades National Park and on fish and wildlife values in south Florida as a result of incomplete planning and coordination. Settlement of the conflict would have been expedited had one department been responsible for consideration of all facets of the problem.

- Frequently the management objectives for coterminous lands administered by two or more agencies are significantly different. For example, in California there are three national parks—Lassen Volcanic, Yosemite, and Sequoia-Kings Canyon—that are almost completely surrounded by contiguous national forest lands of the Department of Agriculture. Forest infestation by the mountain pine beetle in epidemic proportions is a recurrent problem. Multiple-use forest management objectives usually call for rapid suppression of such outbreaks while national park management objectives call for letting ecological forces take their course in reaching a natural balance. Another example is the proposed recreational development of the Mineral King Valley in California which has resulted in significant interdepartmental disagreements between Interior's National Park Service and Agriculture's Forest Service. Thus, there are apparent conflicts of management principles between two agencies now in separate departments that could be more readily resolved within a new Department of Natural Resources.

- A proposed Corps of Engineers' water supply and flood control project on the Rappahannock River has direct impact on river recreational and scenic values, estuary areas, and sports fish and wildlife resources which are the responsibility of the Department of the Interior. There also are possible impacts on oyster beds used for commercial purposes which fall within the program area responsibilities of the National Oceanic and Atmospheric Administration, currently in the Department of Commerce.

- In California and in Oregon, the Corps of Engineers and the Bureau of Reclamation each contended it should build certain projects. These jurisdictional problems, which the Executive Office of the President has had to handle, often inadequately, need not arise if there were one water resource agency.

- The Bureau of Land Management typically manages lands of lower elevation while the Forest Service manages the higher areas.

Quite often, a rancher desires to graze his livestock in the lower areas in the spring and the higher areas during the summer. Dual management of these lands is an undue hardship to the rancher who must obtain permits from the two agencies.

The grouping together of natural resources programs with broad common purposes and the establishment of a coordinated natural resources management policy through the Department of Natural Resources will eliminate many of these problems, or enable the resolution of them within one department.

POLICY OF MINIMUM CHANGE CONSISTENT WITH DEPARTMENTAL GOALS

In planning the new department, consideration has been given to how to preserve necessary program continuity and effectiveness in meeting current needs. Upon enactment of the proposed legislation, existing organizational units transferred to the Department of Natural Resources will lapse. The Secretary will administratively reestablish these units so that they will remain relatively intact to avoid serious disruption of essential functions or services. However, he may be expected progressively to reorganize his department so that various programs and activities will come to be grouped around common purposes and functions to achieve the maximum potential benefits associated with the new departmental concepts. Making such transitions on a well-planned schedule will afford sufficient time to consider all factors and to assure the most orderly achievement of departmental objectives with a minimum of adverse impacts.

Objectives and Benefits

OBJECTIVES OF THE PROPOSED DEPARTMENT

To achieve national objectives the Department of Natural Resources must incorporate the necessary planning, policy formulation, program management, research, and other activities required for it to provide effective Federal leadership. However, Federal responsibilities will vary, depending on a number of factors such as ownership of resources and the responsibilities of the private sector and of the States and local governments. Recognition of these responsibilities is germane to the development and operation of the various functions of this Department.

It will be the function of the Department of Natural Resources— by providing national leadership and establishing effective working relationships with private organizations and individuals, State and local governments, and other Federal agencies, to:

- Foster the conservation, management, and utilization of natural resources, based upon studies and analyses of supply and demand and alternative measures for meeting such demand.
- Plan and undertake programs for the conservation, management, and utilization of land, water, forest, range, mineral, fish and wildlife resources.
- Help assure maintenance of the ecological balance necessary to sustain human and vital plant and animal life systems.
- Explore and survey the earth, the atmosphere, and the oceans and to assess their physical characteristics.
- Conduct scientific research and to encourage development of technology to conserve and effectively utilize natural resources with minimum impact on the environment.
- Undertake programs for the optimal development of various energy sources, including research on nuclear power and management of uranium raw materials and uranium enrichment.
- Provide physical and economic data, maps, charts, and hazard warnings, and other information regarding the earth, its atmosphere, and its oceans.
- Provide and enhance opportunities for outdoor recreation.
- Manage Federal public lands and other resources, including national parks, forests, wildlife refuges, and fish hatcheries.
- Preserve irreplaceable and unique park, wilderness, scientific, historic, fish and wildlife, and other biotic resources.
- Facilitate the development and protection of commercial fisheries.
- Foster the health and safety of miners.
- Assist in achieving oil and gas pipeline safety.
- Assist Indians, Alaskan Natives, and territorial peoples to achieve their cultural, social, and economic objectives.

EXPECTED BENEFITS AND IMPROVEMENTS

The general welfare of the Nation requires that its limited natural resources, including energy sources, be conserved, managed, and utilized so as to help achieve the highest practicable environmental quality; harmony between man and nature; social, economic, and community development; individual fulfillment; and the security of the American people of this and future generations. The establishment of the Department of Natural Resources will provide the necessary organizational capability for best achieving natural resources objectives, improving government operations, and assuring the coordinated and effective administration of programs. It will bring together and provide leadership and direction for all of those Federal activities which most directly relate to the discovery, assessment, preservation, development, utilization, future adequacy and enjoyment of natural resources, including energy sources, and achieving a sound balance between preservation and development. By grouping together all natural resources programs with broad common purposes in the Department of Natural Resources, it will be possible to:

(*a*) Establish a center of responsibility for developing essential, broad, unified natural resources policies, such as energy policy and water policy, for consideration by the President, the Congress, and the people.

(*b*) Provide for necessary accountability to the public through discrete assignments of responsibilities on such matters as public land management.

(*c*) Simplify relationships of States, local governments, and the private sector with the Federal Government in natural resources matters.

(*d*) Allow the President to look to a single key official, the Secretary of Natural Resources, to carry out his administration's natural resources policies and programs.

(*e*) Provide greater effectiveness in the development of policies, plans, and evaluation of performance than is now possible with responsibilities and programs scattered among several agencies and with the small staff available to the President.

(*f*) Provide broader organizations to permit more adequate consideration of possible tradeoffs among competing programs.

(*g*) Rationalize balance among conflicting demands, for example, preservation versus development, in planning and managing resources.

(*h*) Encourage the resolution of most disagreements on resource problems at a departmental level rather than a higher level, or by having to resort to often inconclusive interagency coordinating mechanisms.

The proposed Department of Natural Resources will bring together in one agency most of the primary responsibilities and functions required to assure the most effective achievement of natural resources and related environmental objectives. The Secretary of the Department will have the necessary overall perspective and responsibility so that alternatives can receive proper consideration and conflicts can be resolved in the public interest. Federal policies and programs can be more responsive and coherent with appropriate emphasis and vigor as required to meet current and future social, cultural, and economic needs. Priorities can be better weighed in the development and implementation of national policies and programs. A wider range of alternative actions can be taken without jeopardy of administrative conflict. A clearly defined center of responsibility will mean that a continuous effort can be sustained to match national requirements for resources with action programs geared to meet them.

In addition to the substantive improvements for more effective planning, policy formulation, and programs set forth in the previous sections, there will be opportunity for administrative efficiencies and savings over the long run. The simple act of consolidating the related programs of existing agencies will permit some consolidation of common services and reduction in overhead staffing. Specific examples can be mentioned which will result in considerable improvement in operating efficiency, such as the combined use of data processing systems, ships, aircraft, and laboratories, which now separately exist in NOAA and USGS. Elimination of much of the need for coordination among agencies will reduce workload in such areas as remote sensing, coastal zone and Outer Continental Shelf mapping, and water supply forecasting. Other economies should result from the unified administration and management of Federal lands and the simplification of the present checkerboard pattern of administrative jurisdictions.

Organizational Structure

There is much interdependence among natural resources programs. For example, the various sources of energy often are substitutable and competitive. How minerals are mined has an impact on other land and resource management activities, water quality, and on scenic value. Recreation depends on scenic value and on a number of resources such as land and water.

By not recognizing the interdependence, the present structure encourages fragmentation. Thus, a comprehensive response to natural resource problems is most difficult to make. By bringing together related programs and organizations with similar missions, the Secretary will have in one organization the necessary capabilities to make a comprehensive response to such problems.

Considerable thought and planning has been directed to this structure which will bring together under common direction, at the Administrator level, formerly competitive organizations and activities such as the Forest Service and the Bureau of Land Management; the Bureau of Reclamation, the Corps of Engineers' civil functions, and the Soil Conservation Service; and the conventional sources of energy (coal, gas, and oil) and nuclear energy. At the same time, the organization structure will be made more comprehensive and more manageable.

Natural resources programs are conducive to being grouped into a small number of major components on the basis of common purposes. The reorganization will, therefore, bring together related resource functions in the following administrations: Land and Recreation Resources; Water Resources; Energy and Mineral Resources; Oceanic, Atmospheric, and Earth Sciences; and Indian and Territorial Affairs.

a. Land and Recreation Resources Administration.—This Administration will have two principal resource management objectives: land and recreation.

Land resources deal with both publicly and privately owned lands.

Federal land management and development programs cover all non-military Federal lands—some 760 million acres, of which 90 percent are in the West. Sixty percent of the Nation's softwood saw timber grows on federally owned lands, and the value of the Federal timber inventory is estimated at $30 billion. Some 19 million livestock in 31 States graze at least part of the year on these lands. A third of the Nation's big game and 10 percent of all other game is taken from them. Recreational use is heavy—some 500 million visits annually—and growing.

Consolidation of management responsibility for public lands will provide more effective management of resources and provide the maximum benefits to the public from this rich national asset. Resource conservation and development must effectively incorporate and use the principle of multiple-use management. Management also must recognize the commonality of functions shared by the Federal land management agencies in such things as fire protection, recreation facility development, forestry, grazing, wildlife management, and visitor services. Resource conservation and development can be met most effectively by a single department responsible for managing interrelated Federal activities in the public interest. This component of DNR will effectively group together the land management and recreation resource agencies and their functions.

The emphasis on outdoor recreation opportunities also requires a focal point within the Government for the formulation and implementation of national policies. There is great national concern for the preservation and enhancement of the environment so it may be enjoyed. Part of this concern centers on having access to adequate parks, open spaces, fish and wildlife, and other outdoor recreation resources and facilities. Recreation demand is increasing rapidly and varies widely depending on the desires of people and the nature of lands and facilities available. The provision of outdoor recreation opportunities depends on the private sector, local governments, States, and the Federal Government. The DNR will provide a center for coordinated relationships with the States and communities on outdoor recreation matters. The DNR will also provide the focus that considers all relevant factors so that Federal land and water recreation programs can be planned and evaluated, have priorities established, and be administered effectively.

Planning for the most effective development and utilization by the public of Federal recreation areas will be better coordinated with other land use, resource, and environmental factors. Water-based recreation is one of the most desired forms of outdoor recreation. Bureau of Reclamation and Corps of Engineers water projects provide significant recreation opportunities as part of national multiple-purpose water resources development. National forests and public domain lands pro-

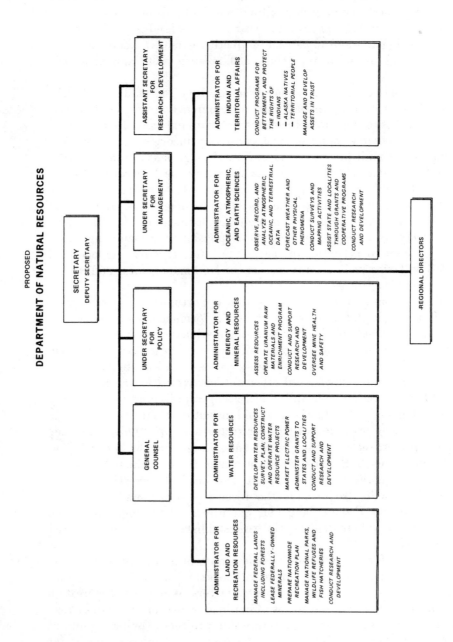

PROPOSED
DEPARTMENT OF NATURAL RESOURCES

vide outdoor recreation opportunities as part of multiple-use management of lands. The Forest Service and the Bureau of Land Management also administer wilderness and primitive areas, wild and scenic rivers, fish and wildlife, historical and other sites of cultural and recreation value. National parks and wildlife refuges have the primary mission of preservation and availability of unique natural, historic, or scientific areas, and fish and wildlife species for public enjoyment.

The functions of the land and recreation component are:

Formulation and implementation of national recreation policy;

Nationwide recreation planning;

Technical and financial assistance to States (including grants) for planning, land acquisition, facility development, fish and wildlife, historic sites preservation;

Formulation and implementation of national timber policy based on supply and demand projections;

Technical and financial assistance to States (including grants) for fire protection, forest management, tree planting, insect and disease control;

Research and information services;

Management of federally owned lands:

Timber resource management;

Range resource management;

Provision of outdoor recreation resources and facilities;

Fish and wildlife management and preservation;

Preservation of unique natural resources and historic sites;

Mineral resource management;

Natural resource preservation;

Soil and moisture conservation;

Resource protection; and

Related environmental considerations.

The organizational entities that would be transferred to this component are:

From Agriculture: Forest Service.

From Interior:

Bureau of Outdoor Recreation;

Bureau of Land Management;

National Park Service; and

Bureau of Sport Fisheries and Wildlife.

The Forest Service is a land management agency devoted to the same basic purposes as most of the other land management agencies of the Federal Government. Over 85 percent of its funds are spent on managing 187 million acres of public forest and range lands, a function similar in purpose and scope to that of the Bureau of Land Management. The importance of the national forests as a recreation resource is attested to by 190 million annual visits. The Forest Service not only shares activities with common purposes with the Bureau of Land Management, but also fish and wildlife management with the Bureau of

Sport Fisheries and Wildlife, and recreation with the Bureau of Outdoor Recreation and the National Park Service. It also has the Federal Government's principal forest resources research capabilities, which play an essential role in improving the management of all of the Nation's forest resources—Federal, State, and private.

But it is not only the commonality of purposes which justifies placing the Forest Service with other Interior bureaus in the DNR. Common management would enable better planning of timber harvests, better location of facilities to meet recreational demands, and other improvements for more efficient and consistent management of the now separate tracts which make up the aggregate of Federal lands.

The rapidly increasing use of forest lands for timber and forage, recreational areas, management of wildlife, preservation of scenic beauty, and protection of downstream lands from floods and erosion dictates their placement in the DNR, where all competing claims may be balanced. This should result in more effective land management and a greater overall contribution to the public good.

b. Water Resources Administration.—Planning, development, and management of the Nation's water resources are the responsibility of many Federal, State, and local agencies, as well as private interests. There is little dispute that the Federal Government should encourage comprehensive river basin planning in which all interested parties participate to meet immediate and long-range water-related needs. Construction of projects by Federal agencies should be integrally incorporated to fit these plans in proper sequence and timing.

With this objective in mind, the Congress established the Water Resources Council to take the lead in water resources planning, guide the activities of the several Federal agencies, and bring order to water resources policy. While the Council has made progress, it has had limited effectiveness in policy development and guidance of Federal water resources programs due, in part, to its interagency character.

Critical to the realization of an integrated national policy for water resources management and use are the water planning and project evaluation functions. The responsibility for the determination of national water resource policy and the preparation of water resource plans needs to be transferred from the Corps of Engineers (Army), the Soil Conservation Service (Agriculture), and the Bureau of Reclamation (Interior) to the Department of Natural Resources. That Department would then have clear responsibility for evaluating water resources projects for their compliance with national policy and plans and for making decisions as to which projects should be recommended for implementation.

The functions of the Water Resources Administration of DNR are:

Formulation and implementation of national water resources policy;

Assistance (grants) to States;

Water resources planning, development, and management;

Provision of certain outdoor recreation facilities;

Fish and wildlife management;

Flood control and hurricane protection;

Improvement of navigation;

Provision of irrigation and municipal and industrial water supply;

Conservation of soil;

Marketing of electric power from Federal water projects;

Research and informational services; and

Related environmental activities.

The organizational entities and programs that would be transferred to this component are:

From Interior:

Bureau of Reclamation;

Office of Saline Water;

Office of Water Resources Research; and

Power marketing agencies.

From Army: Corps of Engineers—civil functions (policy, planning, and funding).

From Agriculture:

Soil Conservation Service (including watershed loans and resource conservation and development loans made by the Farmers Home Administration);

Economic Research Service—natural resource economics research; and

Agricultural Research Service—soil and water conservation research.

From Water Resources Council: all functions (planning, policy, and grants).

The construction capabilities of the Soil Conservation Service and the Bureau of Reclamation would be more closely integrated and coordinated to accomplish detailed project cost estimating, engineering, and construction.

The planning, project evaluation, and policy formulation functions of the Corps of Engineers would be transferred to DNR. This will allow a single Federal agency, the DNR, to consider all facets of water problems and programs, and their interrelationships with land use and other resource programs and to assess priorities. The Corps civil works program would be funded through the DNR. Regional planning offices of DNR would provide comprehensive river basin planning and overall direction and monitoring of the Corps project planning. The Corps would continue to carry out the design, construction, and operation of projects. This arrangement will retain the opportunity for training military officers and the quick-response construction capability of the Corps to meet mobilization requirements and to provide assistance in times of natural disasters and other emergencies.

The Office of Saline Water and the Office of Water Resources Research would also be included in the Water Resources component of the DNR.

The Secretary of the Department of Natural Resources would receive the statutory powers of the Water Resources Council, including policy formulation, comprehensive river basin planning, and the administration of planning grants to the States.

One of the most significant changes from present organizational and program arrangements will be the centralized development of water resource policy, comprehensive planning, and project evaluation within the DNR. The DNR planning offices, cooperating with State and local interests, would do the multiobjective comprehensive planning and advise as to which potential projects fit properly into regional and national plans. Use will be made of uniform principles, standards, procedures and processes for planning, and evaluation of water and related land resource development projects.

With these consolidations, all of the significant policy formulation, planning, and project evaluation activities associated with water resources projects will be placed in the hands of a single Cabinet officer. This will make it possible for him to shape water resources programs to meet effectively the needs of our Nation in the decades ahead.

c. Energy and Mineral Resources Administration.—Energy is a vital ingredient in our national life. Without it, nearly everything stops—as we discovered in the Northeast blackout several years ago. Energy consumption is growing five times as fast as population, and countless industrial processes depend on increasing amounts of fuels and electric power. Our affluent society has come to depend upon conveniences using energy to a degree unknown a few decades ago.

Insuring an adequate energy supply to meet these future needs, while preserving the quality of our environment, is a fundamental priority for our Nation. The Federal interest in the energy field is all the more sharpened by the fact that more than half of our oil and gas resources, and over one-third of our coal and uranium, are on N3 Federal lands.

The function of the Energy and Mineral Resources Administration are:

  Formulation and implementation of national energy resources policy;

  Development of energy production technology;

  Development of resource development and utilization technology;

  Management of uranium stockpile;

  Production of enriched uranium;

  Ore body and resource delineation and information;

  Resource conservation;

  Supply, demand, and other economic information;

Mining, recovery, processing, and utilization studies;

Waste disposal, reuse, recycling, and substitute studies;

Protection and restoration of mined areas;

Research and information services;

Fostering mining health and safety;

Fostering oil and gas pipeline safety; and

Related environmental considerations.

The organizational entities and programs that would be transferred to this component are:

From Interior:

Bureau of Mines;

Office of Coal Research;

Office of Oil and Gas;

Defense Electric Power Administration; and

Underground power transmission research.

From Atomic Energy Commission:

Raw materials management;

Uranium enrichment;

Civilian nuclear power and nonnuclear energy programs (policy, planning, and funding); and

Natural resource activities of Peaceful Nuclear Explosives (Plowshare) program (policy, planning, funding, and industry relations).

From Transportation: Office of Pipeline Safety.

Some Federal energy programs are administered by separate agencies which promote particular forms of energy, such as the Bureau of Mines, the Office of Coal Research, or the Atomic Energy Commission. These programs were initiated to meet a specific problem. No responsibility was assumed for considering the impact of one program on the other. It is now time to take steps to assure the adequacy of government organization for formulating a cohesive energy policy to meet future needs.

Since a change in policy regarding one form of energy may profoundly affect competitive forms, energy programs should be organized as a unit. Only in this way can competing interests be adequately evaluated. In the future, certain energy materials may need to be conserved for other purposes, such as the production of plastics. One agency which includes all the energy programs, and is charged with optimizing the use of natural resources, can make the necessary tradeoffs.

International negotiations, such as those with Canada and Mexico to develop a North American energy policy, would be simplified with the establishment of a single energy agency.

Federal energy policy could be better integrated since it would be formulated with all energy activities in mind. Broader scope and greater balance would be given to nationally supported research and development work in the energy field. Finally, an energy organization would help assure more economic and effective use of our total energy resources.

Nonfuel mineral activities of the consolidated agencies would continue to be located with their energy-mineral counterparts, as separation would offer no significant benefits and would unnecessarily disrupt existing organizations. The Bureau of Mines' health and safety activities would be transferred to DNR along with the other programs of that Bureau because of the close interrelationship of health and safety activities to research on mining technology.

Many of the constituent agencies of the "Energy and Mineral Resources" component are presently located in the Interior Department—the major shift involves transfer of the civilian power programs from the AEC.

The Atomic Energy Commission was created in 1946 to handle all aspects of atomic energy. It has been successful in its various missions, including advancing technology to the point where nuclear power is becoming a realistic alternative to other forms of energy. With this fact in mind, certain of the AEC's energy activities should be consolidated with other energy activities in an agency charged with the mission of insuring that the total energy resources of the Nation are effectively used.

The benefits to be obtained from a balanced and integrated power program are the overriding consideration. The time has come when the need to nurture a new energy technology, which was part of the justification for the separate organization of the AEC in 1946, should give way to an organization formed around the purpose to which that technology was directed.

The uranium raw materials and enrichment programs are proposed for transfer to DNR. The DNR would fund and establish policy and priorities for the natural resources related aspects of Plowshare, nonnuclear energy programs, and the development of civilian nuclear power reactors, based upon overall energy needs and competitive resources. However, the AEC will continue to conduct the research, development, and demonstration (including safety) in the latter three programs because of its expertise and facilities, and the close interrelationship with other nuclear programs conducted by AEC. Section 201(a) of Public Law 92–84, August 11, 1971, amended the Atomic Energy Act of 1954, extending AEC's research authority to include nonnuclear energy research. Transfer of this authority is also necessary to assure DNR's leadership role in Federal energy matters. The AEC will continue its program of controlled thermonuclear research until such time as the scientific feasibility has been demonstrated.

d. Oceanic, Atmospheric, and Earth Sciences Administration.— Federal efforts to increase knowledge of the physical environment and to improve our ability to predict and modify geophysical phenomena, would be brought together into one component. So organized, these programs can better serve to help us understand the earth, its waters and atmosphere, and the physical processes that govern our planet. There is now a realization of the interactions of the oceans, the atmosphere, and lands in predicting weather and understanding the causes of natural disasters.

The functions of the Oceanic, Atmospheric, and Earth Sciences Administration are:

National weather services;

Resource and environmental remote sensing studies;

Operation of environmental satellites;

Geologic and soil investigations and surveys;

Water data collection and investigations;

Environmental data services;

Earth hazard programs (earthquake, volcano, landslides, etc.);

Predictions of natural hazards and warnings for public health and safety;

Topographic and other mapping and charting services;

Ocean and lake surveys, investigations, and research;

Fishery resources management, research, and assistance to industry;

Research and information services; and

Technical and financial assistance to States.

The organizational entities that would be transferred to this component are:

From Interior: Geological Survey.

From Commerce: National Oceanic and Atmospheric Administration.

Both the Geological Survey and NOAA combine scientific skills with data gathering and dissemination services required by many different users. Much of the activity of both agencies is carried out for other Federal agencies. In some earthquake, hydrology, and mapping activities, they conduct similar and sometimes overlapping operations. These duplications should be eliminated by bringing the two organizations together. For example, there is no comprehensive system in a single organization for the forecasting of extreme water supply conditions (floods and droughts). The USGS keeps data on ground water levels, reservoir storage, river flow, river stage, and snow cover. At the same time, NOAA gathers similar data to provide forecasts of river flow, precipitation, and warnings of flood and low water.

There are also major opportunities for consolidating and improving related surveying, mapping, and charting programs that now exist within these organizations.

Because the services of NOAA are widely used, no compelling logic dictates its location in any specific department. However, when NOAA is combined with the Geological Survey and related science service activities, the resulting entity has closer ties to the proposed DNR than to any other department. For example, the marine resource programs of NOAA are related to DNR responsibilities regarding the development and use of offshore oil, gas, and other mineral resources. For that reason, an "Oceanic, Atmospheric, and Earth Sciences" component of the DNR is proposed to emphasize that this agency serves all components of the new Department, as well as other government agencies and private users.

e. Indian and Territorial Affairs Administration.—The social, cultural, and economic needs of Indians, Alaskan Natives, and territorial peoples are acute and require special handling. The President has enunciated his policy of providing Indians with greater self-determination over the management of their affairs. The challenge is to focus the resources of the Federal Government to meet the unique needs of different cultures in ways that allow the recipients to determine their own priorities.

The functions of Indian and Territorial Affairs Administration are:
    Education;
    Natural resource and economic development;
    Public safety;
    Job training and placement; and
    Community services and facilities.

The organizational entities that would be transferred to this component are: From Interior—Office of Territories; Bureau of Indian Affairs.

The Indian and territorial programs are included in the Department of Natural Resources at this time because of their historical association with the natural resource functions of the Department of the Interior. Most Indians in the past have rejected proposals for transfer of the Indian programs to other departments. Any transfer proposal will have the full involvement and participation of the Indian and territorial peoples. These programs therefore are proposed for inclusion in the Department of Natural Resources, subject to further study.

BUDGET AND MANPOWER SUMMARY

Total fiscal year 1972 outlays for the proposed Department of Natural Resources, based on the President's 1973 budget, would be approximately $6 billion. Permanent employment would total approximately 106,500. Distribution by major program components would be approximately:

	1972 outlays (dollars in millions)	Permanent employment
Land and recreation resources	$1, 535	35, 697
Water resources	2, 536	28, 286
Energy and minerals resources	782	6, 089
Oceanic, atmospheric, and earth sciences	427	20, 454
Indian and territorial affairs	657	14, 272
Other	28	1, 677
Total	$5, 965	106, 475

FIELD ORGANIZATION

Over 3,000 field offices from the various components proposed for inclusion in DNR will comprise the Department's field organization. The offices include research laboratories, weather stations, national forests and parks, wildlife refuges, public domain lands, water development projects, and fish hatcheries. The heads of these various field stations and offices will be responsible for the management and execution of the functions assigned them in accordance with policies and criteria established by the Secretary and his program administrators. Their field counterparts are the regional director and the regional administrator.

The field organization has key importance for the Department of Natural Resources. It is at the field office that the public has its principal point of contact with the Department. Of equal importance, the Department of Natural Resources deals to a great extent with problems of a regional nature. The particular mission of this Department relates to land, sea, and air values which frequently have an initial effect on the adjacent geography, before any national effect is felt. Thus, in implementing its program responsibilities, the Department of Natural Resources has a particular need to "decentralize." Many natural resource programs must be coordinated and implemented at the State and local levels according to the particular needs, problems, and opportunities of each region. State and local governments must be encouraged to participate in the overall resource planning and to mesh their assistance, management, and development into the national strategies.

a. Regional Directors.—The Department's Washington leadership makes and interprets policy, establishes national priorities, promulgates standards, criteria, and procedures for all levels of field operation, and provides for overall program administration. Most natural resources program execution takes place in the field and requires direction by key regional officials.

The Proposed
Department of Natural Resources

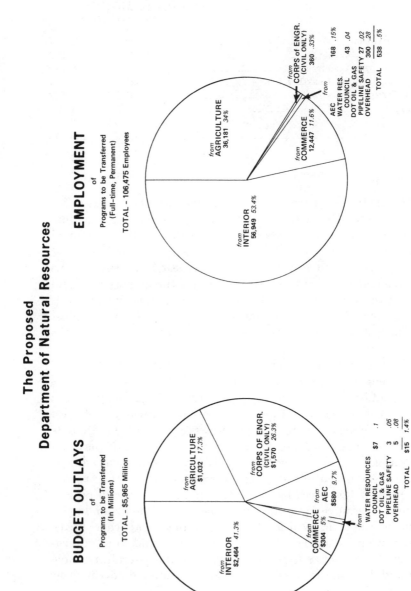

BUDGET OUTLAYS
of
Programs to be Transferred
(In Millions)

TOTAL - $5,965 Million

from INTERIOR $2,464 41.3%

from AGRICULTURE $1,032 17.3%

from CORPS OF ENGR. (CIVIL ONLY) $1,570 26.3%

from COMMERCE $304 5%

from AEC $580 9.7%

from WATER RESOURCES COUNCIL $7   .1
DOT OIL & GAS 3   .05
PIPELINE SAFETY 5   .08
OVERHEAD

TOTAL $15   1.4%

EMPLOYMENT
of
Programs to be Transferred
(Full-time, Permanent)

TOTAL - 106,475 Employees

from INTERIOR 56,949 53.4%

from AGRICULTURE 36,181 .34%

from COMMERCE 12,447 11.6%

from CORPS of ENGR. (CIVIL ONLY) 360 .33%

from
AEC 168 .15%
WATER RES. COUNCIL 43 .04
DOT OIL & GAS
PIPELINE SAFETY 27 .02
OVERHEAD 300 .28

TOTAL 538 .5%

ALL DATA — FISCAL YEAR 1972

FEBRUARY, 1972

The regional director will be appointed by the Secretary and will be delegated selective authority to perform regional planning which cuts across program lines, to coordinate operations, and to resolve conflicts between programs. The regional director is responsible for facilitating the coordinated implementation of DNR's programs within his region. Therefore, he will recommend or implement changes in organization, staffing patterns, and other related administrative matters, within the limitations of available resources and of priorities and plans established by the Secretary and his central program administrators. As the Secretary's field representative, he will also be the chief administrative official in the region with authority over personnel, space, budget, housekeeping services, data systems, and evaluation of regional services.

The regional director will serve as the Department's representative in relationships with Governors, other State and local officials, and public interest and clientele groups. He will represent his Department on the Federal Regional Council and other regional coordinating groups.

b. Regional Administrators.—Line authority over programs representing the five broad program areas (with the likely exception of the Indian and Territorial Affairs Administration) will be exercised by the regional administrators. They will report directly to their counterparts in Washington. Regional administrators will generally be responsible for the regional operations within their respective program areas. They will be held accountable for the day-to-day program decisions and operations. The magnitude of a regional administrator's responsibility will vary significantly from one administration to another, depending upon the nature of the regional programs involved.

c. Regional Boundaries.—The oversight of the Department's extensive field organization requires, to the extent practicable, regional boundaries coterminous with those of other departments and agencies administering related activities. Under the Federal assistance review (FAR) plan, 10 common regional boundaries have been established for most Federal domestic departments and agencies, including the Department of the Interior. The Secretary of the Interior has directed that his Department conform with the common regional boundaries by July 1, 1972, with the possible exception of the Bureau of Indian Affairs which is receiving special consideration.

While all programs and functions of the DNR may not require a regional structure, such an organizational level is necessary to carry out effectively most of the missions of the Department. The proposed units of the Department of Natural Resources have developed over the years their respective regional organizations so as best to accommodate their individual administrative needs. In the past, no overall departmental standard or guidance dictated common regional organizations or boundaries; hence, no two of the existing regional boundary patterns are alike. The current national emphasis on problems of the environment, management of natural resources, and the quality of life has increased the need for a coordinated and integrated approach to insure that natural resources planning, acquisition, development, and use are consistent with environmental considerations and other national goals.

The basic field structure of DNR generally will conform to the 10 common regional boundaries with appropriate modification to allow for special natural resource considerations. An exception might be the combining of contiguous regions, such as Regions II and III in the Northeast, where insufficient program activities so dictate. The regional headquarters for the DNR will be the same as for other departments and agencies conforming with the 10 standard regions, except in those instances where natural resource management needs can be more effectively met by use of a different headquarters location within the region.

Management

The management of the Department of Natural Resources will be achieved through effective management techniques and methods. In addition, the proposed reorganization, by establishing a clear purpose for the Department and by bringing together programs of similar purpose, will further enhance manageability.

PERSPECTIVE

The management concept for the four new Departments is based upon three key principles derived from the recommendations of the President's Advisory Council on Executive Organization. These are:

(a) That each Department should represent a broad purpose and have sufficient breadth to accomplish its mission.

(b) That the Secretary should be the sole repository and source of all authority within his Department.

(c) That, to the maximum extent practicable, authority and responsibility for the operation of each Department's programs should be decentralized to the field.

The implementation of these principles will produce an organization fully responsive to the needs of the people. The proposed legislation for the establishment of the new Departments is based on these principles.

CLARITY OF PURPOSE

By creating a Department of Natural Resources, the objective of conserving and managing the Nation's natural resources becomes clearly the purpose of a single department of government for the first time. Until now, this important purpose was shared by several major departments, so that the President was the only person who had full responsibility, and he had to be concerned with coordinating the various programs. Now, the major responsibility for natural resources functions of the Federal Government will be vested in the Secretary of the Department of Natural Resources and he can be held accountable for results.

KEY OFFICIALS

The key officials of the Department are as follows:

(a) The Secretary who, once he has selected his key officials, will concern himself primarily with the strategy for his Department, its goals and priorities, and its overall performance, and will be its spokesman to the President, the Congress, and the public.

(b) The Deputy Secretary who, as the "alter ego" of the Secretary, serves as the general manager for the Department with responsibility for allocating resources, assessing the quality of program performance, and harmonizing the efforts of the line and staff elements.

(c) Two Under Secretaries to serve as staff arms of the departmental leadership in such areas as the development of overall policy, strategy, and plans for implementation, and to be responsible for organization, business management, information systems, resources deployment, and the efficiency and effectiveness of the Department.

(d) An Assistant Secretary for Research and Development who, in direct support of the departmental leadership, guides, promotes, evaluates, and coordinates the research, technology, and technology transfer activities of the Department.

(e) Administrators with line authority over programs representing broad subdivisions of the Department. There would be an administrator for each of the first tier organizations; for example, Land and Recreation Resources Administration, and Energy and Mineral Resources Administration. These key officials appointed by the President and confirmed by the Senate will be accountable for the success or failure of those programs under their purview. They will be the managers and implementors of the Department's programs.

ADEQUATE AUTHORITY

The Secretary must have wide flexibility to manage his Department effectively. This depends on the Secretary having:

- Statutory authority rather than his subordinates;
- Authority to organize his Department;
- Authority to appoint his subordinates; and
- An appropriate appropriation structure.

Statutory Authority.—The Secretary is responsible for his Department and he is held accountable. Thus, statutory authority regarding his Department must reside with him rather than his subordinates. He can then delegate authority to them with commensurate accountability for results. The proposed reorganization legislation will place all statutory authority in the Secretary.

Authority To Organize.—The Secretary must be able to organize his Department in a manner that will group interdependent programs with similar missions so that the Department's objectives can be effectively and efficiently achieved. He must be able to centralize policy formulation and decentralize operations so that program outputs may be delivered on a timely basis for the benefit of the people. The proposed reorganization legislation will give the Secretary power to organize his Department.

Authority To Appoint.—The Secretary must be able to select subordinates. The Secretary is held accountable for his Department and he should have the authority to run it. The proposed reorganization legislation will give him this capability.

Appropriation Structure.—The existing multitude of appropriations to the various constituent units of a department forms an obstacle to effective management. It causes compartmentalization and rigidity—making it difficult to cope with changing conditions and shifting priorities. An appropriation structure for the new Department will be proposed to help correct this situation.

ADEQUATE STAFF

The Secretary must have adequate staff to effectively manage his Department. The Secretary especially needs staff for:

- Planning, policy formulation, program evaluation; and
- Establishment and operation of management systems.

Planning, Policy Formulation, and Program Evaluation.—Attainment of departmental goals will be enhanced by a plan of operation which sets concrete objectives for each element of the organization; milestones of progress; clear and specific assignments of responsibility; and a reporting system for regularly monitoring progress. As part of this anticipatory planning process, programs and policies can be formulated and evaluated and recommendations made to the Secretary. This will decrease the need to adopt ad hoc policies in response to crises and assist the Secretary in keeping on top of his Department.

The Secretary needs staff that is concerned with the entire Department so that policies are consistent and tradeoffs among programs can be considered. He needs staff who can assist and work with the program administrators to solve a host of problems so that only the larger problems need the attention of the Secretary.

While the proposed reorganization is not necessary for planning, policy formulation, and program evaluation, the reorganization will bring together related programs with similar objectives so that a more effective job can be done.

Management Systems.—Effective management systems for the control and improvement of departmental operations will enable the Secretary and other top managers to make the best use of manpower, funds, and facilities. Such systems will also facilitate corrective actions where program execution needs improvement.

APPROPRIATION STRUCTURE

The new Department of Natural Resources will require a new appropriation structure, merging and consolidating the accounts now in use for the activities being moved to the new Department. The revised appropriation structure should assist management effectiveness and provide the flexibility to respond to rapidly changing conditions.

To facilitate effective management, the structure must correspond to the organization of the new Department. Further, appropriations should be made to the Secretary, with some appropriation items identified to the level of the first major program grouping of the Department. With the concurrence of the Congress, this should result in a simplification of the appropriation structure and facilitate legislative review of the President's budget requests.

The existence of many relatively small "pockets" of appropriations, transferred from the existing departments and agencies, could be a handicap to the new Department in integrating its operations as well as a handicap to the Congress and the public in understanding the Federal budget. It is not the intent of the measures discussed here to freeze an appropriation pattern for all time. An appropriation structure is subject to change by Congress from year to year, and indeed should be changed as programs and organizations are modified.

It is contemplated that two principal appropriation accounts will be proposed for each major program grouping of the Department. The first includes financing for day-to-day operating expenses and other activities for which the requirements for a specific year can be readily estimated. This 1-year appropriation would facilitate annual congressional review.

The second proposed appropriation would cover funds for construction, land acquisition, project-oriented research, and certain types of loan and grant activities for which there is a need for longer term availability. In these cases, "no year" appropriations would be proposed; that is, such amounts would be available until expended.

In addition, the financial accounts of the Department will continue to provide separately for the major trust funds and for the various public enterprise funds transferred to the Department. To the extent that the Department receives and administers "earmarked" funds which have been created by statute, the statutory provisions would be observed; e.g., the Land and Water Conservation Fund and the Migratory Bird Conservation Fund. A working capital fund at the departmental level to finance departmentwide administrative services is also desirable. Service funds could also be established where necessary to merge accounts which provide for services performed for others at a charge approximating cost, or which continue earmarking now required by law in connection with programs of the Department.

Consolidation and Coordination of Natural Resources and Related Programs

RELATIONSHIP TO STATE AND LOCAL GOVERNMENTS, THE PUBLIC, AND OTHER FEDERAL AGENCIES

The basic concept of the President's reorganization plan is to enable the Government to do a better job in meeting the needs of the people. This is the primary reason for organizing the four new Departments around the major purposes of Government. The responsibility for solving problems related to the conservation, development, and utilization of natural and energy resources will be focused and concentrated in the Department of Natural Resources. Most of the major natural resources and related environmental programs will be brought together in one governmental organization, and the Secretary will be held accountable.

State and local governments and the public will be able to do business relating to natural resources with one department rather than several agencies. Thus, the reorganization will simplify their relationship to the Government. Furthermore, it will be possible to assist them more efficiently and effectively.

Federal interagency coordination and relationships also should be significantly improved. Questions regarding such matters as energy and water resources policies and programs can be resolved within one responsible and accountable department.

However, because of the interrelatedness of the various sectors of modern society and some commonality of purpose between the Department of Natural Resources and other Federal agencies, coordination will continue to be required. For example, the responsibilities of the Environmental Protection Agency relating to air and water pollution, pesticides, and disposal of solid wastes have an impact on the development and utilization of natural resources. The weapons development program and technical expertise of the Atomic Energy Commission bear some relationship to the civilian nuclear power programs proposed for transfer to DNR. Forest, water, and energy resources contribute to economic and community development.

All factors considered, external relationships should be improved greatly with a corresponding improvement in the effectiveness of the total Federal-State-local government-private sector effort for achievement of overall national goals.

RELATIONSHIP TO REVENUE SHARING PROPOSALS

The revenue sharing plan proposed by the President will provide funds for State and local governments in a way that will:

- Assign both revenues and management discretion to those levels of government closest to the problem;
- Alleviate the fiscal problems of State and local governments by providing additional unrestricted revenues through general revenue sharing and by eliminating the present matching requirements of the categorical grants being absorbed into special revenue sharing; and
- Make State and local elected officials responsible for capably dealing with their problems.

Under the President's proposal, only those existing grant programs for which there is a clear, continuing national requirement will be maintained; for example, the Land and Water Conservation Fund which provides grants for planning, land acquisition, and development of land, water areas, and facilities needed to provide people with recreation opportunities.

Characteristically, the programs recommended for conversion to special revenue sharing programs deal with top priority national problems which have State and local solutions and benefits. These are in six broad functional areas: transportation, education, urban and rural community development, manpower training, and law enforcement. Of the programs to be transferred to the Department of Natural Resources, four categorical grant programs are proposed for conversion to the special revenue sharing program. These are the Forest Service's grants for forestry assistance ($25 million) and tree planting assistance ($1 million) and the Soil Conservation Service's grants for Resources Conservation and Development ($4 million) and the Great Plains Conservation program ($11 million). These are planned for conversion to special revenue sharing for rural community development.

These four grant programs will continue in the Department of Natural Resources until the special revenue sharing legislation is enacted. However, if the revenue sharing legislation is enacted prior to the establishment of the Department of Natural Resources, the four grant programs would not transfer to the new Department. The revenue sharing program for rural community development will be administered by one of the existing departments or the new Department of Community Development, depending on which is in existence at the time. In any event, appropriate arrangements would be made to serve existing Federal commitments.

No changes are contemplated in the revenue sharing associated with receipts from the sale or lease of federally owned resources such as land, timber, forage, and minerals, or from excise taxes on hunting and fishing equipment.

SAFEGUARDS FOR FEDERAL PERSONNEL

The proposed governmental reorganization will directly involve seven of the present Cabinet Departments and several independent agencies. Programs and services will be grouped according to similarity of purpose. The changes proposed are not in what the Government does, but, rather, in the manner in which the Government's business is conducted. These changes, while primarily affecting programs, also will affect each Federal employee and it is expected that they will participate fully in accomplishing the reorganization. To that end, current plans include sound provisions to insure that disruption to employees will be kept to an absolute minimum, that cutbacks in staffs, where necessary, will be taken care of by attrition, and that actions which could adversely affect employees are to be avoided.

More specifically, it can be stated that no employee will be separated because of the reorganization. In addition, the reorganization bills include a provision that no employee will be reduced in classification or compensation as a result of the plan for 1 year after the reorganization becomes effective. All movements of functions and jobs will be governed by current law and Civil Service Commission regulations, with full employee protection and appeal rights. From another standpoint, the reorganization can be viewed as improving the range of opportunities for promotion and career development, as more broadly conceived program management and staff positions evolve in the new departments. Full consideration is being given to the impact of reorganization on the existence of union recognition and agreements, in light of possible changes in unit structure that may result from transfers, realinements, and combinations.

The reorganization bills provide salary retention for an Executive Level Officer (Levels I to V) who is transferred to a new department and is assigned to a position with duties comparable to those he performed immediately preceding the transfer, for the duration of his service in the new position. This provision permits the proposed departments to retain the services of its experienced executives, who might seek other positions if they were to suffer a loss in pay, and thus provides for essential continuity of operations during the formative phases of the Department....

DEPARTMENT OF HUMAN RESOURCES ([3], pp. 190–210)

In the human resources area, the Government has failed to take into account the close interrelationships among the needs of individuals and families. The need for minimum income, education, training, social and health services cannot be met effectively by a piecemeal approach. It does little good, for example, to provide additional instruction to a poor child if he is so hungry or in such poor health that he cannot benefit from his expanded educational opportunities. The child's problems must be addressed on a comprehensive basis if he is to overcome his learning difficulties.

The proposed organizational structure would bring together in a single new Department of Human Resources all programs directed at the development and well-being of individuals and families. These would include virtually all of the present Department of Health, Education, and Welfare (HEW), as well as major existing programs from the Departments of Labor and Agriculture, and the Office of Economic Opportunity (OEO). In fiscal year 1972, the proposed new Department of Human Resources would employ approximately 120,000 full-time personnel. Total Federal outlays in 1972 for programs administered by the Department would approximate $30 billion in Federal funds and $57 billion in trust funds.

MISSION OF THE NEW DEPARTMENT

The new Department would have the overall mission of promoting the development and well-being of individuals and families in partnership with State and local governments, public and private institutions, and individual citizens. Its activities would fall into three general areas: Income security, health, and human development.

The Department's functions will be:
- Assisting in the enhancement of intellectual growth and development;
- Maintaining and improving the skills of individuals through training;
- Maintaining and improving physical and mental health;
- Extending opportunities for participation in the Nation's labor force to all individuals;
- Protecting the quality, purity, and safety of foods, medicines, and other consumer products;
- Assuring basic income security for those temporarily unemployed and those withdrawn from the work force, their survivors and dependents, and for those who cannot provide for themselves; and
- Providing basic social services to individuals and families unable to meet basic needs for themselves, and providing for those who have not been able to compete in and participate fully as citizens in a free society.

To accomplish these functions, the Department will make grants, conduct and support research and studies, provide technical assistance, and administer direct Federal services.

Rationale for the New Department

PROBLEMS WITH PRESENT ORGANIZATION

Under the present structure of the Federal Government, human resource program responsibilities are shared by the Department of Health, Education, and Welfare, the Office of Economic Opportunity, the Department of Agriculture, and the Department of Labor. The formation of a new Department of Human Resources will create a

N4

unified system of programs designed to overcome the serious problems resulting from this dispersal of Federal programs. Chief among these problems are:

Poorly coordinated, fragmented, and overlapping Federal programs.—The effectiveness of present programs and efforts to assist the individual is seriously impeded by ambiguity in the definition of Federal organizational missions, lack of coordination or outright duplication among programs, and jurisdictional rivalry among agencies. This has frequently led to confusion and frustration on the part of both recipients and State and local officials who deal with these programs. For example:

- In a Southwestern city, a large and modern skills training center for vocational education was constructed using funds supplied by the Department of Health, Education, and Welfare. At about the same time, a private corporation, operating under a contract from the Department of Labor to train workers, constructed a similar skills training center three blocks away. This is an extreme example of the problems resulting from divided authority for programs having similar purposes.
- The Food and Drug Administration of HEW has the responsibility for inspecting eggs, meat, and milk products for salmonella and other unhealthful conditions. To do this they make regular inspection visits to meat and egg plants. The Department of Agriculture also has a food inspection program which maintains government employees in these *same* plants on a full-time basis. Were it not for legislative requirements and jurisdictional disputes, the functions could easily be combined.
- Recognizing the conditions migrant workers and their families are forced to endure, a community mobilizes to assist the migrant in overcoming serious health, nutritional, educational, and social problems. In addition to local and State resources, Federal assistance is sought. The community finds the Federal organizational structure a frustrating obstacle to developing a coordinated attack on the problems of the migrant. They find HEW supports health and education programs; that OEO operates a broad migrant service program while financing a migrant Head Start program whose operation has been delegated to HEW; the Department of Labor registers migrant crew leaders, provides for guarantees of safety and insurance coverage, and arranges an annual sequence of work opportunities. The loser is the migrant and his family who fail to receive the assistance that might have been available to them.

Programs organized along narrow functional lines.—Most operating agencies in existing departments responsible for human resources activities oversee relatively limited programmatic groupings of narrow functional programs. These agencies and their administrators are, by nature of this narrow focus, often closely alined with clientele and professional groups; they often do not see the well-being of individual citizens as their primary responsibility. Past efforts to decentralize program responsibility to the field in order to increase responsiveness to local needs have, in some agencies, been seriously impeded, or even halted by pressures brought to bear by groups focused on narrow program interests. For example, in 1967, a government agency undertook a large decentralization drive. Positions were transferred to the regional offices and people hired to fill them. However, an organization comprised of influential interest groups quickly mobilized their forces and brought about a hasty agency retreat.

Decisionmaking authority unresponsive to local and regional needs.—The Federal Government must focus its efforts on aiding State and local governments and responding to community problems and needs if an effective attack on problems affecting the individual and family is to be carried out. The current Federal organization for the management of human resources programs is seriously deficient in this respect.

Many programs support narrow program categories on a project-by-project basis, with decisions made centrally. The system of reviewing applications for these grants often involves as many as seven or eight different reviews—by State agencies, regional offices, headquarters staff, and advisory committees. In many instances, these additional levels of review make minimal contributions or have negligible effect on the outcome. In one program, of 657 grants reviewed, the advisory committee differed with the headquarters recommendation in only two instances. Not only did this review process add 2 months to the approval time and several thousand dollars to the cost, but it diluted the influence of community concerns and needs in the decision process.

Lack of accountability.—A serious impediment to effective management of human resources programs posed by the current organizational structure is the difficulty of establishing accountability. The public holds the President accountable for effective operation of the Government. But without relatively clear assignment of responsibility, it is difficult for the President to hold operating officials accountable. Accountability for broad objectives is often so diffusely spread among departments and agencies in the field of human resources that attempts to establish measures of success or failure, or to take effective corrective action when problems arise, are frustrated. For example:

- The work incentive program (WIN) is intended to provide public assistance recipients with the training and work experience needed to enable them to obtain and maintain employment. A key element in the program is the provision of child care for children of WIN enrollees. The program, to operate effectively, requires an integrated effort involving the public assistance system, manpower training offices, and child care activities. Child care and public assistance services are administered by HEW; manpower training functions are delegated to the Department of Labor. No administrator has clear responsibility for success or failure in the overall program, and each can attribute difficulties to shortcomings in someone else's portion of the program. In this situation, corrective action tends to be fragmented and ineffective.

- The concentrated employment program (CEP)—through which the Federal Government has committed nearly $600 million since 1967—is another example where problems of accountability and coordination exist. The Department of Labor enters into "prime" contracts with local governments and community action agencies to provide a comprehensive program of manpower services in ghetto areas. These services include institutional training components which are approved and funded through a channel completely independent of the prime contractor. The Office of Education in HEW approves and funds these projects through the State vocational agencies, using Manpower Development and Training Act funds which have been appropriated to the Department of Labor and transferred to HEW. If the State vocational agency is unwilling to approve the necessary institutional training, the CEP program is left with no capacity to provide the manpower training which is essential to success of the comprehensive program.

RECENT REORGANIZATION STUDIES OF HUMAN RESOURCES PROGRAM

A number of reorganization studies in the postwar period have proposed changes in executive departments dealing with human resource programs. In 1949, the Hoover Commission recommended a consolidation of labor functions into the Department of Labor and a grouping of activities according to major purpose in a new agency for Social Security, Education, and Indian Affairs. The report highlighted the fluid nature of Federal responsibility for human resource programs as follows:

American concern over the problems of education, health, relief of the needy, aid to the handicapped, and old age is as old as the Republic. Responsibilities in these fields were originally considered to be those of State and local governments. With the growth of the Nation, these problems have become wider than local and State boundaries. There is a common interest in the advancement of science and in the common dangers from disease * * *. The problems of unemployment extend beyond State borders. There is generally a recognition of the practical problems which lie in our obligation as "our brothers' keeper."

* * * In dealing with these matters, the Federal Government has usually sought to preserve the responsibilities of local government and their agencies of administration in effecting the national purpose.

In 1953, the President's Advisory Committee on Government Organization recognized the "astonishing variety of responsibilities, which collectively touch virtually every citizen, but in numerous scattered ways." In recommending the initiation of HEW as successor to the Federal Security Agency, the report said:

> The one common thread that weaves through these varied activities is that all are concerned with what might be called the human side of the Nation's problems. In this complex, rapidly changing world it is vital that human problems should be given the fullest consideration at the highest level of government.

More recently, the 1965 report of the Task Force on Intergovernmental Program Coordination, chaired by Stephen K. Bailey—then the distinguished Professor of the Public Administration at Syracuse University—clearly pointed out the difficulties of delivering the services of the varied human resource programs to their intended beneficiaries. The Ash Council recognized these difficulties, making these statements:

> Assisting the development and well-being of its citizens is an essential purpose of Government. * * * The creation of * * * a Department (organized around this purpose) would provide, for the first time, a single Federal focus by bringing together the now fragmented array of programs and services dealing with the problems in this area.
>
> This single focus is critical for two reasons. First, assisting the development and well-being of individuals often requires the application of several programs and services. The needs are interrelated but the existing organization of Federal assistance prevents an effective, integrated response. Second, due to the expanding demands and the limited resources available, we must have the capability to set priorities and make the required tradeoffs in this area.

SCOPE AND BENEFITS OF THE REORGANIZATION

The President's proposal for a Department of Human Resources makes three major changes in the administration of human resources programs at the Federal level. It will:

- Provide a single, integrated focus to meet the Federal responsibility for individuals by bringing human resources programs together within a single organizational entity.
- Assure a strong management team to assist the Secretary in his responsibilities for all operations of the Department, to develop policy embracing all human resources functions, and to plan and implement a balanced program of Federal activities affecting individuals and families.
- Create three administrative units oriented to the broad human resource purposes of income security, health, and human development.

The Department will have a Secretary and a Deputy Secretary directly under him who will concentrate on internal management. It will also have two Under Secretaries to assist the Secretary in matters relating to the performance of planning, policy, and management functions and in the direction and coordination of field operations.

Regional directors of the Department will be given full authority for all service programs involving payments to State, local, and private institutions with the exception of experimental and R. & D. activities.

Operating programs would be grouped under three "administrators" with wide authority for administration of programs and development of policy in income security programs, health, and human development.

The income security functions of the Department will encompass:

• Administration of contributory social insurance systems currently authorized under the Social Security Act—retirement and survivors' insurance, disability insurance, and Medicare.

• Administration of other social insurance programs of the Federal Government—railroad retirement and unemployment insurance.

• Provision of assistance benefits for the poor and near-poor through public assistance, food stamp, commodity distribution, supplemental food, and Medicaid programs, and upon enactment, the family assistance plan, and the family health insurance plan.

The functions of the Department related to the health of individuals and families will include:

• Development of improvements in the health care delivery system to make it more effective and accessible.

• Conduct of research to develop new and improved means of preventing and curing illness.

• Assurance that the individual is protected from possible health hazards.

• Assurance that personnel needed to perform health functions throughout the Nation are trained and available.

In the third major area, human development, the Department's functions will include:

• Assurance that a quality basic education is available to all.

• Aid for school systems in achieving desegregation and preventing racial isolation.

• Assistance and encouragement in improvement of the Nation's system of higher education and increasing its accessibility to all qualified individuals.

• Support of occupational training, apprenticeship, work experience, and employment for those individuals in the labor force whose skills and/or work experience are insufficient to qualify them for available jobs.

• Provision of services to individuals and employers designed to place workers in appropriate occupations and facilitate more efficient distribution and use of our manpower resources.

- Assistance for State and local organizations to provide and improve services that help individuals and families overcome problems which prevent or hinder them from functioning normally in our society.

The integrative, structural, and management features described in the foregoing paragraphs will result in major advantages as described below:

Creation of a coordinated Federal response to human resources problems.—Administration by a single Department of functions which affect individuals and families will permit a linking of manpower training and welfare, of education and health, which will view the individual as an entity and stress the interrelatedness of program areas as they affect individuals. It will facilitate development of a comprehensive income strategy. The management team will play a strong role in insuring overall program and policy coordination and a strong regional structure will insure coordination of programs of State and local assistance.

Development of a structure to organize programs around comprehensive and interrelated objectives.—Grouping of several existing operating agencies into three purpose-oriented administrative units will facilitate a comprehensive view of the national purpose. Groups having particular interest in education, or manpower, or social service programs, for example, will continue to receive a sympathetic hearing within the new Department. Combining these program areas under a single administrative official for Human Development will permit a focus on the interrelationship between these programs in a way that was not previously possible, and will provide increased responsiveness to special concerns in each area. For example, the objective of both the vocational education and the manpower training program is to provide individuals with essential job skills. Having both programs under one administration will make it possible to assign the most appropriate role to each in accomplishing the overall mission. This should increase the effectiveness of the overall human development effort in accomplishing its primary purpose of aiding people to achieve their full potential.

More effective response to State and local needs and priorities.— The new Department will provide that decisions affecting programs for States and communities will be made in the field rather than in Washington. Regional directors, appointed by the Secretary, will have complete decisionmaking authority over Federal grants-in-aid to State and local governments, and will exercise coordinating responsibility in their regions for all programs administered by the Department. This will enable the Federal Government to be responsive to State and local needs, and will assist in development of an effective partnership between governments at all levels.

Establishment of clear accountability and responsibility for Federal programs aiding individuals and families.—One Department will have responsibility for the whole spectrum of Federal activities affecting individuals and families. Decisions involving the most effective allocation of resources among these activities will be made at the departmental level, in contrast to the present system which frequently requires the President and his staff to consider issues that should have been resolved at lower levels.

Organization and Management

OVERVIEW

The management system of the Department of Human Resources has been designed around three key principles:

- The Department should represent broad purposes. Similar and interdependent programs should be grouped together and lines of authority clarified to provide a single organizational location for each given purpose.
- The Secretary should be the sole repository and source of authority within the Department. He should be free to delegate this authority as he deems appropriate.
- To the maximum extent practicable, authority and responsibility for the operation of the programs of the Department should be decentralized.

The organization of the Department has the following principal features:

- The Secretary will provide overall executive direction, concentrating his attention on new policy initiatives, assessment of the Department's performance, working with the President and other Cabinet executives, and relations with the Congress and the public.
- A Deputy Secretary will be the alter ego to the Secretary; he will carry a portion of the burden in policy, communications, and external relations, but will concentrate primary attention on overseeing the internal operations of the Department.
- Two Under Secretaries will coordinate Department-wide policy development and management improvement, arrange for the provision of essential managerial services, and help oversee the regional activities of the Department. Full authority for State and local assistance programs supporting the provision of services will be decentralized to the regional directors.
- Assistant Secretaries will be assigned human rights and various other Department-wide responsibilities to aid in overall management.
- All operating programs will be grouped under three "Administrators," appointed by the President with Senate confirmation, each with considerable authority delegated from the Secretary for both operating and policy decisions.

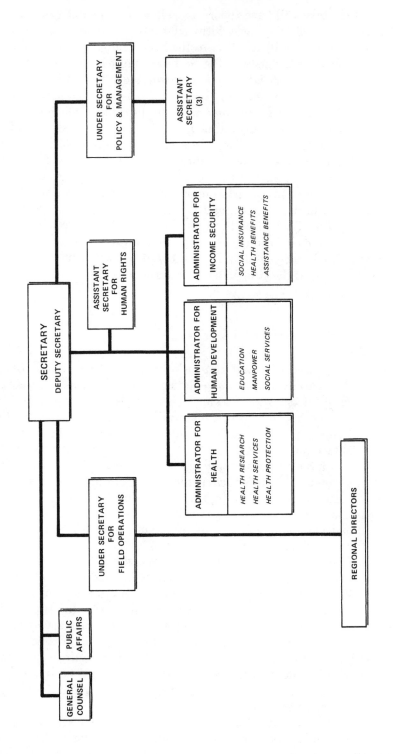

PROPOSED

DEPARTMENT OF HUMAN RESOURCES

The Secretary will have reporting to him on a regular basis six key departmental officials, each with substantial authority and clearly delineated responsibilities. Due to the broad range of programs and major external relationships, the Secretary must have the support of this top "team" of officials who are empowered to act on his behalf in specific assigned spheres. This team of top policy and management officials constitutes a forum and management council which can assist the Secretary by providing an integrated and coordinated view of the Department's mission. The members of this group of officials, as discussed below, have two major types of responsibilities:

- Delegated responsibilities for major operating programs. These will be lodged in the Administrator for Income Security, the Administrator for Health, and the Administrator for Human Development. Each official has responsibility for program execution and for policy formulation within his respective sphere.
- Delegated responsibility for the broad management functions as in the case of the two Under Secretaries and the various Assistant Secretaries.

OFFICE OF THE SECRETARY

All basic authorities and responsibilities for the activities of the proposed Department of Human Resources will be vested in the Secretary. He will delegate substantial authorities and responsibilities to other executives, and spend a substantial portion of his time dealing with persons outside the Department—the President, the Congress, other Cabinet officers, State and local government officials, and representatives of the various major groups. His personal attention will also be devoted to matters such as the determination of priorities and the allocation of resources, approval of basic plans and policies, resolving major conflicts among operating or staff units, and assuring on a broad basis that effective direction and control are maintained over all parts of the Department.

The Deputy Secretary will aid the Secretary in performing his duties. The Deputy will act in the Secretary's absence and will be delegated various policy responsibilities as the Secretary deems appropriate, including responsibilities for general, day-to-day supervision of the operating agencies. He will concentrate his primary attention on overseeing the operations and management of the Department.

The Under Secretaries will be assigned responsibilities in such a way as the Secretary believes can best assist him. The paragraphs below describe one way in which they might be utilized in the Department of Human Resources.

An Under Secretary for Policy and Management will create an integrating force, responsive to the Secretary, to balance the various major programs and interests of the component agencies of the new

Department. The Under Secretary for Policy and Management will be responsible for crosscutting departmental staff functions relating to: (1) Policy development, (2) liaison with the Congress, and (3) departmental management. These activities, for example, would be grouped under several officials at the Assistant Secretary level, with the following types of responsibilities:

- *Planning and Analysis.*—Responsible for basic policy and program planning, program development, evaluation, and analysis.
- *Research.*—Responsible for developing and implementing an overall research and development strategy for the Department.
- *Congressional Relations.*—Responsible for facilitating communications between Members of Congress and the Department and contributing to development of legislation before it is sent to Congress.
- *Comptroller.*—Responsible for preparation of the budget and for management of the Department's financial affairs. In addition, he will promote uniform grant administration practices and policies and oversee audit activities within the proposed Department.
- *Administration and Management.*—Responsible for management support to the Secretary and Deputy Secretary in areas such as organizational planning, the development and maintenance of management information systems, and the evaluation of overall performance of the Department. He will be responsible for personnel matters and administrative services.

An Under Secretary for Field Operations will oversee the regional activities of the proposed Department. He will have responsibility for operation of the regionalized grant-in-aid programs of the new Department and coordinating responsibilities for "national" programs. As such, he will be a key official in carrying out the purposes of the Department through programs closely in touch with and responsive to the needs of local citizens. To give a strong emphasis to decentralization and to support the role of the regional director, an Under Secretary for Field Operations will:

- Be responsible for developing ways to strengthen relationships with general purpose governments at the State and local level and to promote the integration of services.
- Provide an important, visible, high-level contact for Governors, mayors, other officials, and the public on their concerns, over the entire range of decentralized departmental operations.
- Provide authority, short of the Secretary, to make decisions on important operational problems in the field.
- Assure a hearing of regional views at the highest levels in the Department.
- Provide a channel to inform regional directors of policy decisions by the Secretary.
- Provide for supervision of regional operations to assure a common approach to basic departmental problems.

Other positions could be established at the Secretary's level for Public Affairs and General Counsel. Because of the nature of their responsibilities, such officials would most likely deal directly with the Secretary and Deputy Secretary on a more frequent basis than the staff Assistant Secretaries.

It will also be appropriate to establish an Assistant Secretary for Human Rights. An Office of Human Rights will be responsible for assuring that beneficiaries of Federal programs receive services on a nondiscriminatory basis. The Office will also act as point of contact and spokesman for groups of special Federal concern.

REGIONAL OFFICES

The departmental regions will conform to the 10 Standard Federal Regions established by the President by Executive order on March 19, 1969. Each of the 10 offices will be headed by a regional director reporting to the Under Secretary for Field Operations. The regional director will carry these responsibilities and have these attributes:

- Highest ranking departmental official in the field and the Secretary's representative.
- Point of contact with Governors, mayors, other officials, institutions, and members of the public and interest groups on matters of departmental policy.
- Chief administrative official in the region with authority over personnel, space, budget, housekeeping services, data systems, and evaluation of regionalized activities.
- Final point of decision for assignment of Federal personnel to provide assistance requested by States and localities or other institutions.
- Communicate and interpret policy from the President and the Secretary to all DHR units in the region.
- Participate in regional planning and act as a member of the regional council of Federal regional agency representatives.

The regional director will have line authority over programs whose primary purpose is the support of services provided by State and local governments or by institutions. He will not have line authority over national, direct service programs such as social security or health research. But he will, however, work with officials stationed in the field for administration of these programs for the purpose of transmission of Presidential and departmental policy; when there is contact with elected officials; when issues arise with general purpose governments; when there is an impact of any national program on other regionalized functions; and when other Federal agencies are involved.

Under the administration's proposals for revenue sharing, a new approach to domestic policy, the role of the Department of Human Resources regional offices will be critical. The revenue sharing funds will be granted to States without restriction under general revenue sharing, and in addition, DHR will administer "special" revenue sharing grants in education and manpower training. Under these measures, States and localities would determine how best to achieve the broad purposes for which the funds are made available. The role of the Department of Human Resources will increase as a source of support for developing new techniques in solving social problems. Its role will increase, also, in transmitting the results of research and experimental projects and other new information and expertise back to the States and localities. The regional offices will bear primary responsibility for this dissemination process. The critical importance of this role is demonstrated by the fact that approximately 50 percent of all State and local spending is for human resources programs.

ADMINISTRATIONS

Under the proposed legislation for the new Department of Human Resources, principal operational arms, called "administrations," will be established to oversee broad program areas. The heads of these units, to be known as "administrators," will have significant responsibilities and authorities delegated to them from the Secretary and Deputy Secretary.

The staffs of each of the administrators will be sufficient to perform such functions as policy planning, program evaluation, operational planning and control, budget preparation, financial management, and administration and management.

The programs and activities that would be transferred to the Department of Human Resources would be grouped as follows:

Income Security Administration.—A number of programs within the proposed Department of Human Resources have the goal of providing basic resource support to eligible individuals and families. This eligibility is the result of either a personal economic contribution to the system ("social insurance") or of a disadvantage. Such programs would be grouped together under the Administration for Income Security. The purposes and functions performed by this organization are related and the target groups are similar. For example, all the programs include an eligibility determination requirement. They are also all involved in checkwriting, extensive data processing, and sophisticated recordkeeping activities. The proposed grouping provides the opportunity for significant operating efficiencies.

Many of the programs under the Income Security Administration have similar target groups. The blind, aged, and permanently disabled receiving aid under the adult categories assistance payments programs are also people who receive social security benefits. The collocation of these programs will provide the framework for efficiently reaching similar target groups. It will lead to development of an optimum field structure for fulfilling the missions of the various income security programs.

Perhaps most importantly, the Income Security Administration will provide an explicit organizational focus for the emerging income strategy of the Federal Government. The agency would be charged with identifying inconsistencies, overlaps, and deficiencies in income security programs that have evolved over decades of unconscious development. It will also be responsible for rationalizing its programs more closely with in-kind benefits.

The distribution of functions under the Income Security Administration will be as follows:

- Social insurance includes the functions of the Social Security Administration of HEW; the Railroad Retirement Board; and unemployment insurance from Labor.
- Assistance benefits includes the functions of AFDC of HEW and family assistance when passed; the family food programs of Agriculture, including food stamps and commodity distribution.
- Health benefits includes the functions of Medicaid, and family health insurance when passed.

Health Administration.—Health activities including research, manpower, protection, and services will be consolidated under the Administrator for Health. He will have the principal responsibility for articulating national health goals and implementing a national health strategy.

The Administrator will be in a position to make policy and priority setting decisions. For example: How should resources be split between health research and health services delivery? How can we develop a system which focuses on preventive as well as curative medicine? Do we need more physicians, or a more efficient use of the doctors we now have, through increased use of paraprofessionals and sophisticated technology? The Administrator will insure that the delivery of educational and social services is linked with the delivery of medical services so that the problems of individuals are approached as an integrated whole, and not in piecemeal fashion.

The distribution of functions under the Health Administration will be as follows:

- Health research includes the functions of the National Institutes of Health of HEW.
- Health services includes the functions of the Health Services and Mental Health Administration of HEW and the health programs of OEO.
- Health protection includes the functions of the Food and Drug Administration of HEW; the meat, poultry, egg and egg product inspection services of Agriculture; human nutrition and home eco-

nomics research of Agriculture; and the fabrics and related consumer protection services of Commerce.

Human Development Administration.—Human development programs are those affecting education, social services, and manpower training. As Federal concerns in education have expanded beyond education "in school," and as social services are separated from welfare payments, the concept of human development takes on new meaning.

An example of the tie between these two areas lies in the community school concept. It is increasingly being recognized that education can be broadened to involve the entire community in developmental activities centered around the school. This could include programs for the aged, youth, and day care for both school-age and preschool children.

A second example of the interrelationships among human development programs is Head Start, a federally supported, preschool program enrolling 263,000 3-, 4-, and 5-year-olds. This program is closely linked with both education and social services. Many Head Start projects are located in schools. The program will be administered at the national level as part of the Social Services unit in the Human Development Administration. Having the same Administrator for both education and social services will encourage development of integrated and coordinated systems for dealing with similar target groups.

A third illustration is the strong tie which must exist between the counseling and placement services of manpower programs and both education and social services. In one sense manpower deals with the failures of the educational system. Manpower contracts with local agencies for some of its training programs. Having the two reporting to the same Administrator will encourage a realistic educational focus on the job-oriented training needs of the country, as well as strengthen the training elements of manpower programs.

The distribution of functions under the Human Development Administration will be as follows:

- Education would include the functions of the Office of Education (less community library construction) of HEW; the school lunch, school breakfast, and other child food assistance programs of Agriculture; the college housing program of HUD; the National Institute of Education (legislation pending); the National Foundation of Higher Education (legislation pending); and the Follow Through program of OEO, administered by HEW.
- Manpower would include the functions of the Manpower Administration of Labor (less unemployment insurance) and the Women's Bureau of Labor.
- Social services would include the functions of the Social and Rehabilitation Service (less the Medical Services Administration and the Assistance Payments Administration) of HEW, the Office of Child Development of HEW, and the President's Committee on Employment of the Handicapped.

Budget, Administrative, and Technical Provisions

BUDGET AND MANPOWER

The programs to be included in the Department of Human Resources total $87.7 billion in outlays for fiscal year 1972 and employ more than 119,000 permanent employees. Included in the spending total is $57.3 billion in outlays for social security, railroad retirement, and unemployment insurance trust funds.

As contained in the President's 1973 budget the fiscal year 1972 budget outlays and employment would be distributed as follows:

	Full-time permanent employment	Outlays (millions)
Income Security	55, 278	$73, 707
Health	48, 474	3, 945
Human Development	10, 230	9, 948
Departmental Management	5, 598	76
Total, DHR	119, 580	$87, 676

APPROPRIATION STRUCTURE

The new Department of Human Resources will require a new appropriation structure, merging and consolidating the accounts now in use for the activities being moved to the new Department. The revised appropriation structure should assist management effectiveness and provide the flexibility to respond to rapidly changing conditions.

To facilitate effective management, the appropriation structure must correspond to the organization of the new Department. Appropriations will generally be made to the Secretary, with some appropriation items identified to the level of the first major program grouping of the Department. With the concurrence of the Congress, this should result in a simplification of the appropriation structure and facilitate budget review of the President's budget requests. The existence of many small "pockets" of appropriations transferred from the existing departments and agencies, if not consolidated, could be a handicap to the new Department in integrating its operations, as well as a handicap to the Congress and the public in understanding the Federal budget. It is not the intent of the measures discussed here to freeze an appropriation pattern for all time. An appropriation structure is subject to change by Congress from year to year, and indeed should be changed as programs and organizations are modified.

A highly desirable approach would be to establish two principal appropriation accounts for each major program grouping of the Department. The first would provide for financing day-to-day operating expenses and other activities in which the requirements for a specific year can be readily estimated. This 1-year appropriation would facilitate annual congressional review.

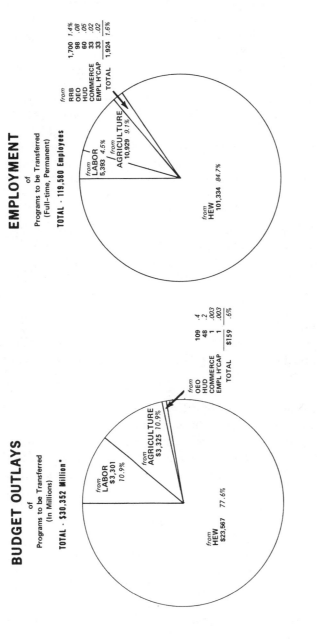

The Proposed
Department of Human Resources

BUDGET OUTLAYS
of
Programs to be Transferred
(In Millions)

TOTAL - $30,352 Million*

from
LABOR
$3,301
10.9%

from
AGRICULTURE
$3,325 10.9%

from
HEW
$23,567 77.6%

from		
OEO	109	.4
HUD	48	.2
COMMERCE	1	.003
EMPL H'CAP	1	.003
TOTAL	$159	.6%

EMPLOYMENT
of
Programs to be Transferred
(Full-time, Permanent)

TOTAL - 119,580 Employees

from
LABOR
5,393 4.5%

from
AGRICULTURE
10,929 9.1%

from
HEW
101,334 84.7%

from		
RRB	1,700	1.4%
OEO	98	.08
HUD	60	.05
COMMERCE	33	.02
EMPL H'CAP	33	.02
TOTAL	1,924	1.6%

FEBRUARY, 1972

* Total excludes $57.3 billion in Social Security, RRB, and Unemployment Benefits Trust Funds

ALL DATA — FISCAL YEAR 1972

The second proposed appropriation would cover funds for construction, land acquisition, project-oriented research, and certain types of loan and grant activity, for which there is a need for longer term availability. In these cases, "no year" appropriations would be proposed; that is, such amounts, upon the concurrence of the Congress, would be available until expended.

In addition, the financial accounts of the Department will continue to provide separately for the major trust funds and for the various public enterprise funds transferred to the Department. A working capital fund at the departmental level to finance departmentwide administrative services is also desirable. Service funds could be established to merge accounts which provide for services performed for others at a charge approximating cost, or which continue earmarking now required by law in connection with programs of the Department.

SAFEGUARDS FOR FEDERAL PERSONNEL

The proposed governmental reorganization will directly involve seven of the present Cabinet Departments and several independent agencies. Programs and services will be grouped according to similarity of purpose. The changes proposed are not in what the Government does, but, rather, in the manner in which the Government's business is conducted.

These changes, while primarily affecting programs, also will affect each Federal employee and it is expected that they will participate fully in accomplishing the reorganization. To that end, current plans include provisions to insure that disruption to employees will be kept to an absolute minimum, that cutbacks in staffs, where necessary, will be taken care of by attrition, and that actions which could adversely affect employees will be avoided.

More specifically, it can be stated that no employee will be separated because of the reorganization. In addition, the reorganization bills include a provision that no employee will be reduced in classification or compensation as a result of the plan for 1 year after the reorganization becomes effective. All movements of functions and jobs will be governed by current law and Civil Service Commission regulations, with full employee protection and appeal rights. From another standpoint, the reorganization can be viewed as improving the range of opportunities for promotion and career development, as more broadly conceived program management and staff positions evolve in the new Departments.

Full consideration is being given to the impact of reorganization on union recognition and agreements, in light of the possible changes in unit structure that may result from transfers, realinements, and combinations.

The reorganization bills provide salary retention for an Executive Level Officer (levels I to V) who is transferred to a new department and is assigned to a position with duties comparable to those he performed immediately preceding the transfer, for the duration of his service in the new position. This provision permits the proposed departments to retain the services of its experienced executives, who might seek other positions if they were to suffer a loss in pay, and thus provides for essential continuity of operations during the formative phases of the Department.

PROGRAM CONTINUITY

In forming the new Department, consideration has been given to existing organizational units and to individuals presently employed in those units. As the new Department takes form, care will be taken to preserve program continuity and to assure effectiveness in meeting current needs. Savings clauses and hiring policies based on attrition will preserve the rights of those presently employed.

Initially most of the existing program units will remain intact, although they will be administered differently. Manpower programs will be linked with education and social service programs under a single Administrator; however, social service programs may be grouped differently from current groupings in the Department of Health, Education, and Welfare. Additional changes will be made as benefits of the new organization become apparent. New policy and planning machinery will permit an orderly transition to the new departmental missions, and will insure minimum disruption of departmental programs....

DEPARTMENT OF ECONOMIC AFFAIRS ([3], pp. 246–278)

Assuring our economy's continued growth and proper functioning is one of the great purposes around which national government should be organized. Vigorous economic growth provides tangible benefits to increasing numbers of individual and organizational participants. Sustained high economic performance is essential to the success of basic social and economic programs. And finally, the way in which our complex and abundant economy operates—including work conditions and opportunities, business efficiency and productivity, transportation services and safety, market information and international trade flows—profoundly affects our individual, corporate, and national well-being. We have a common interest in the sustained growth and smooth operation of our economy which transcends individual, business sector, and agency program perspectives, and the Federal Government must effectively respond to this pervasive national concern.

Our system places basic reliance on individual initiative and private enterprise to develop and direct the Nation's economy. The Federal

Government has special supporting responsibilities with regard to interstate and foreign commerce, and promotion of the useful arts and sciences. Current Federal Government program activities which guide and service the Nation's economy include:

- Compiling and disseminating basic economic data and analyses.
- Establishing and enforcing selected policies and standards.
- Conducting diverse operations having direct and indirect economic impact.

These activities are reflected in programs scattered throughout the Federal establishment, including several cabinet departments, and numerous executive and independent agencies. While these widespread organizational and program responsibilities span much of our economy, the focus of each effort is much narrower and overall economic performance accountability is undermined.

The Department of Economic Affairs will provide a cabinet-level Federal organization whose perspective is the overall operation of our economy, whose objective is fostering optimum economic growth and performance, and whose responsibility is the practical assistance and assessment of national economic activities and initiatives. The new Department will consolidate existing programs from four cabinet departments, and four executive and independent agencies. It will have initial responsibility for Federal programs which affect labor standards and relations; small, minority, and domestic business development; mediation and conciliation services; transportation safety and service; social, economic and technical information; and international labor and commercial activities. The new Department will be in a position to administer more effectively the consolidated Federal economic programs, provide more balanced economic data and analysis, render improved services to the public and private sectors, present more comprehensive and practical perspectives in developing economic policy, and to assure more integrated implementation and evaluation of Federal economic program initiatives.

PRIOR REORGANIZATION STUDIES

The need for major reorganization of the executive branch is well documented. Previous reorganization studies have proposed the consolidation of programs concerned primarily with economic affairs.

For example, the President's Task Force on Government Reorganization, chaired by Don K. Price, a leading authority in governmental administration, suggested to President Johnson in 1964 the creation of a "Department of Economic Development." A key point made by the Price task force was that "reorganization is needed from time to time as the pace of economic, social, and technological progress leads to the adoption of new action programs for which the old structure is poorly suited." With reference to the present separation of

Commerce and Labor, the task force found that "the separation of the Commerce and Labor Departments, originally established as one, has been justified by the conflict between management and labor, and the need to give each a department to represent it. That concept is obsolete in theory, and has been growing more obsolete in practice."

WEAKNESSES IN EXISTING ORGANIZATIONAL ARRANGEMENTS

During the past two decades, executive departments have grown in size and complexity with the addition of many new programs enacted in response to an array of specific needs. While most of these programs have sound objectives, very little consideration has been given to where responsibility for program operations should be placed to insure maximum overall effectiveness. It is not surprising, then, that many people believe that the Federal Government has not met its obligation to deliver required services and assistance where needed on a timely basis. A number of weaknesses are inherent in the government's existing organization structure. To illustrate, the current structure inhibits:

- Formulation and execution of integrated economic policies and programs.
- Realistic program evaluation and accountability.
- The orderly resolution of differences in interests among economic sectors and their representatives in government.
- Effective coordination and client communication of related program initiatives.

1. *The dispersal of related responsibilities inhibits the formulation of integrated economic policies and the coordinated execution of comprehensive programs.*—The current structure not only encourages but forces agencies concerned with economic policy planning and the operation of economic programs to take narrow, parochial views of the economy. As a consequence, wide-ranging economic problems which should receive unified analysis and treatment are dealt with in more narrowly defined contexts. Too often this piecemeal response is poorly coordinated and, on occasion, even counterproductive. As the Ash Council pointed out, "The present organizational structure encouraged fragmentation when comprehensive responses to social and economic problems are needed. Problems are defined to fit within the limits of organizational authority, resulting in piecemeal approaches to their solutions by separate departments and agencies."

For example, the complex practices and documentation involved in the transshipment of cargo in international trade have long been recognized as inhibiting the free and rapid movement of goods, and contributing to unnecessary shipping costs. Failure to expand the intermodal use of shipping containers similarly and adversely affects domestic and international commerce. The United States is mounting an important effort to simplify such transshipment practices and documentation, yet a number of separate departments and agencies are vitally interested in the nature and extent of any changes made to facilitate domestic and international commerce. The agencies involved in the present simplification efforts would include:

Department of Transportation—
   Federal Aviation Administration
   Federal Railroad Administration
   Saint Lawrence Seaway Development Corporation
   U.S. Coast Guard
   Bureau of Motor Carrier Safety
Department of Labor—
   Bureau of International Affairs
   Labor-Management Services Administration
   Bureau of Labor Statistics
Department of Commerce—
   Social and Economic Statistics Administration
   Bureau of International Commerce
   Maritime Administration

Small Business Administration

Under the proposed Department of Economic Affairs, these program activities would be brought together in a single cabinet department. The number of separate agency concurrences now required to establish a U.S. position, and the coordination required to implement resulting programs, would both be substantially reduced.

2. *The current organization structure inhibits realistic program evaluation and accountability.*—Recent Presidents have found it difficult to hold any single agency accountable for the accomplishment of their stated policy objectives. The organizational fragmentation of economic programs among departments and agencies, primarily on the basis of special interest groups or functional areas, results in a splitting of common activities and national concerns with little attention to the interrelatedness of the country's overall economic needs. The President's broad economic policies and programs are thus implemented only in those areas directly related to an agency's mission. Problems which transcend the boundaries of an agency's mission often receive partial treatment, because the programs are designed to deal with those aspects of the problem which fall within agency boundaries.

The diffusion of responsibilities for closely related areas is illustrated by the split of programs relating to the dissemination of technical information between Commerce and the National Aeronautics and Space Administration. At present, businessmen seeking information about federally developed manufacturing technology or new products technology are uncertain about which agency to contact for the desired information. Commerce's National Technical Information Service will sell already published Government technical reports, but will not provide the more sophisticated technology utilization services that NASA's Technology Utilization Office provides for NASA-generated technology. Thus, gaining access to federally generated technology, whose sources are spread throughout Federal agencies, is both time consuming and expensive. The Commerce and NASA information activities will be centralized in the Department of Economic Affairs, and the President, the Congress, and the public will have a single agency to hold accountable for the availability of this information.

3. *The current organization structure provides no mechanism for the orderly resolution of differences between economic sectors and their representatives in Government.*—The organization of the departments and agencies concerned with economic affairs along functional lines inhibits consideration and resolution of relative policy and program priorities within the executive branch. Decisionmaking responsibility is often shifted to the Executive Office of the President because no official at the departmental level has the authority to decide the issues presented. This forced centralization of conflict settlement on issues related to economic programs raises to the presidential level questions which would not otherwise require a high policy-level decision. The escalation of the level of conflict resolution adds seriously to the timelag between initial issue identification and its final resolution. In an era in which the pace of change is accelerating, such unnecessary delay in decisionmaking is unacceptable.

The existing structure's weakness in this area is illustrated by two cases. The first has resulted from the existence of several statistical agencies which collect, analyze, and publish a wide array of social and economic statistical reports and research studies. These agencies often secure their basic data from the same sources, causing inconvenience for the respondents, creating doubts as to data comparability, and increasing overall data collection costs. The differences in each agency's terminology, definitions, and statistical techniques produce results which conflict or contradict each other, at worst, and which at best are often noncomparable.

The second illustration involves crew sizes for merchant marine vessels. The Maritime Administration, Department of Commerce, provides subsidies for the construction and operation of U.S. cargo ships, and is therefore interested along with the operators in the most economical operation of the ships. Crew size is an important factor in operating costs, and from that standpoint small crews are also desirable. However, the Coast Guard, Department of Transportation, is responsible for safety measures on the high seas, and for this reason is authorized to set qualifications and manning levels for crews of vessels of U.S. registry. This example illustrates how safety and economy of marine operation can be in opposition. A third factor is the Department of Labor's role as the Federal agency responsible for the conditions of employment of merchant mariners and for the maritime unions. These conflicting interests are a frequent source of friction and strife among the various elements of the maritime shipping business.

Bringing the affected agencies together in the Department of Economic Affairs 'will permit resolution of the differences outlined above at a level below the Executive Office of the President.

4. *Currently divided and sometimes overlapping responsibilities inhibit effective coordination and client communication of related Federal program initiatives.*—A prime illustration of this kind of weakness results from the lack of clear demarcation between the role of the Office of Minority Business Enterprise (OMBE), in the Commerce Department, and the Small Business Administration. For example, OMBE-funded organizations furnish information and preliminary counseling to prospective entrepreneurs; help businessmen to prepare business plans and loan applications and obtain funds from financial institutions; and provide management services and technical assistance to businessmen. SBA also offers these services to minority businessmen. Conversely, the SBA licenses, regulates, and partially finances special corporations designed to invest particularly in minority enterprises (MESBIC's); and administers a minority-oriented procurement program under section 8(a) of the Small Business Act. The OMBE has undertaken a major effort to stimulate minority interest in and use of the MESBIC and section 8(a) procurement programs. Both the OMBE and the SBA have become popularly associated with these programs, and have maintained considerable contact with minority firms and other affected Government agencies. Both OMBE and SBA are staffed with field representatives primarily charged with the responsibility for assisting minority applicants seeking Government assistance. The new Department of Economic Affairs will incorporate the minority business programs of both OMBE and SBA, with a commensurate increase in program coordination and decrease in confusion by minority businessmen seeking program assistance and information.

Rationale for the New Department

HISTORICAL PERSPECTIVE

American economic abundance is unsurpassed in the world community. Our free enterprise system, energetic and resourceful working force, and abundance of natural resources have combined to enable the United States to develop unprecedented levels and means of production.

The U.S. economy provides the basis for a relatively high standard of living, for the development of human and natural resources, for meeting national security needs, for an increasingly viable and healthful environment, and for continuous improvement in health, education, and recreation capabilities. In a relatively short span of history, we have moved from an agrarian to an industrial society that has penetrated the boundaries of space. Concrete evidence of our economic and technological advance is provided by the annual production of over a trillion dollars worth of goods and services.

The process of changing to a more specialized, interdependent economy began during the early 19th century, but the pace has greatly accelerated in recent decades. Productivity gains have come rapidly, permitting a large part of our manpower to shift from manufacturing and construction activities to providing the services which are popularly demanded in this age of consumer affluence and conveniences.

Also in recent years, the growing force of white collar workers has outstripped the number of production workers, and the number of Americans who gain their livelihood as craftsmen or farmers has dwindled. The work force is employed largely in offices or factories where the production processes are increasingly automated. Long ago the 40-hour week became a national standard, and is now being challenged as an inhibiter of a fuller life and higher employment. Our success in producing goods and services has created new problems, and exacerbated some of those of longer standing. Against this background of continuing change the Federal Government has provided assistance in:

- Devising ways to utilize fully America's manpower and other resources.
- Maintaining reasonable price stability so as to permit continued growth in living standards, to prevent breakdowns in our financial and business machinery, and to avoid gross inequities to retired persons and others dependent on fixed incomes.
- Keeping the United States competitive in world markets in the face of increased foreign competition.
- Promoting economic growth while maintaining a healthful environment.
- Bringing more poverty-stricken and low-income people into full participation in our economy.
- Opening avenues for greater participation by minorities and others disadvantaged as business owners and managers.
- Preventing the development of conditions which would cause severe adverse economic impact on any segment of society.
- Seeking means of effectively protecting consumers against substandard goods and practices where market forces provide inadequate protection.

INTEGRATED APPROACH TO ECONOMIC GROWTH

In the real world the major elements of our private enterprise economy are highly interdependent. Labor and management may still negotiate respective shares of specific economic gains, but both now recognize a more overriding stake in increasing the total productivity and profitability of our economic system. The national transportation system is a major economic sector in itself, but it is also the vital service linkage which moves raw materials to processing plants, finished products to wholesalers, retailers, consumers, and the traveling public from place to place. The increasing movement of goods in world markets has made the competitive posture of American goods in international trade a matter of basic concern to worker, manufacturer, transporter, and purchaser alike. Even the impact of highly specialized economic actions, such as financial or agricultural matters, eventually have a real effect on more generalized economic pursuits.

In this real world of interdependence, it is increasingly unrealistic for those agencies of the Federal Government which deal directly with various elements of the economy to remain organizationally separate and programmatically fragmented. The President and the Congress can no longer afford to view the elements of the economic system as separate and independent entities. The forces which draw these elements together, and demand an integrated Federal economic approach, are now far greater than the forces which have previously caused them to be treated separately. Separate Federal organizations increasingly represent an artificial and unwarranted barrier to unified Federal policy and programs which are responsive to the operating needs of our free enterprise system.

The Department of Economic Affairs will recognize contemporary economic reality and, for the first time, bring together in one agency the principal elements, exclusive of Agriculture and specialized financial agencies, by which the Federal Government helps the economy function most effectively. The special province of the Department of Economic Affairs will not be general fiscal policy, but rather a service and assistance role of a real, comprehensive and practical nature, which directly aids the work force, the manufacturer, the merchant, and the transportation system. However, as a result of these direct program activities, the DEA will also bring new and broader practical perspectives to bear in the establishment of general economic policies.

DEA will create the capability to develop, under a single cabinet Secretary, an integrated approach to orderly economic growth and increasing productivity. Those economic development and assistance programs can be selected which benefit all and are mutually reinforcing. Program initiatives can be better orchestrated, both internally and with more general economic policies. The concerns of each clientele group can be reflected directly to the Secretary and can be factored into all of the policies and actions of the Department. All of the technical assistance resources of the Department such as international development, science and technology capability, statistics and information services, and economic planning will be available to all the groups in the economy which the Department will serve.

BASIC PROGRAM OBJECTIVES

The objectives of the Department of Economic Affairs will be to provide Federal leadership and conduct programs for assuring:
- Full employment with reasonable price stability.
- Effective participation in the world economy.
- Profitable and productive use of economic resources.
- Continuous improvement in America's standard of living.
- A fair distribution of the benefits of economic growth.
- The efficient, safe, economical, and convenient movement of people and economic goods.
- A stable economic base to meet national security needs.
- Effective standards for worker protection.
- A safe and healthful work environment.
- Increased participation of disadvantaged and small business enterprises in the economic mainstream.
- Prompt economic relief to areas or elements of the economy affected by disasters.
- Increased harmony between management and labor.
- The availability of meaningful and current economic data and analyses.

In pursuing these objectives the Department of Economic Affairs will provide four essential types of Federal services:
- Technical and financial assistance to individual enterprises.
- Social, economic, and technical information and analysis to all users.
- Standards for businesses, workers and labor unions.
- Transportation and other public services which are not, and often cannot be, provided by the private enterprise system.

MAJOR DEPARTMENT FUNCTIONS

The Department of Economic Affairs brings together Federal programs which facilitate the growth and functioning of the U.S. economy and its relationship to the world economy. To achieve its objectives, the Department of Economic Affairs must incorporate the necessary policy formulation, planning, program management, standard setting, research, and other activities required to provide adequate Federal leadership. In carrying out these activities, the Department will perform the following functions:

1. Provide advice to the President and Congress, in concert with other economic advisors, as to policies affecting the development and functioning of the economy and U.S. participation in the world economy.

2. Assist in the creation and expansion of domestic and foreign markets for American products and services.

3. Enhance the productivity and profitability of our factories and other workplaces by promoting and facilitating the development, dissemination, and application of American science and technology.

4. Provide and promote the use of mediation, conciliation, and arbitration services to increase industrial harmony.

5. Promote and stimulate programs of worker protection in all areas pertaining to employment and well-being on the job, and insure a safe and healthful work environment.

6. Assist the President, Congress, Government agencies, and members of the private economy in analyzing and interpreting economic events and in formulating economic policy by providing basic economic, demographic and social data, and other information.

7. Assure workers, investors, employers, and consumers a full opportunity to share and participate in the benefits of national economic development by promoting balanced growth of all sectors.

8. Promote and facilitate the efficient, safe, reliable, and convenient movement of goods and people by fostering the development of balanced national systems of air, ground, and water transportation.

9. Facilitate the establishment and growth of small and other businesses by assuring adequate sources of capital and furnishing management and technical assistance.

10. Assist minority and disadvantaged persons to participate effectively in the Nation's economy and share fully in its benefits as workers, employers, and investors.

11. Promote fair competition within a free enterprise system and facilitate the orderly and uninterrupted flow of goods and services.

PROGRAMS OF THE NEW DEPARTMENT

To carry out these functional responsibilities, existing Federal programs will be transferred from their present departments and agencies, and consolidated in the department. Programs to be transferred are summarized below:

From Commerce:

Programs which furnish economic, social and technical information, support the development and application of technology, assist minority and other disadvantaged firms, and facilitate domestic and foreign marketing of U.S. goods.

From Labor:

Programs which promote industrial harmony between labor unions and employers, assure the well-being of workers, including a safe and healthful work environment, provide labor statistics and analyses, and represent the Government in international labor matters.

From Transportation:

Programs which promote and facilitate balanced, safe, reliable and efficient national systems for the movement of goods and people.

From Small Business Administration:

Programs to strengthen small business participation in the economy and to assist minority and other disadvantaged persons to participate as owners and managers of businesses.

From other agencies:

- Federal Mediation and Conciliation Service.
- Nonadjudicative functions of the National Mediation Board.
- Technology dissemination functions from the Technology Utilization Office of the National Aeronautics and Space Administration.

EXPECTED BENEFITS AND IMPROVEMENTS

The establishment of the Department of Economic Affairs as an executive department consolidating key Government programs dealing with the national economy will produce significant benefits for the American people. Among these are the following:

N5

1. *The experience and voice of business and labor will be more effectively brought to bear in formulating national economic policies.*—The Departments of Labor, Commerce, and Transportation have a close and continuing relationship with their respective clientele groups, and are sensitive to their points of view on economic issues. However, their existence as separate departments, each with its own distinct clientele has reduced their effectiveness in formulating advice on national economic policy for the President.

The Secretary of Economic Affairs will be well equipped to participate effectively in economic policy formulation since he will have a close relationship with most sectors of the economy. For example, in discussions of price stability he would have direct inputs on labor's sensitivity to employment levels and business' views on price levels and profitability.

2. *A single source of social and economic data will produce more comprehensive and consistent intelligence to guide economic decisions.*—Bringing together all the major statistical and economic analysis programs under common direction will resolve inconsistencies, gaps, and overlaps in the information now provided. The users of these data—including business firms, labor unions, common carriers, and governmental agencies at all levels—will have the convenience of a single source of data as well as more comprehensive analysis. This, in turn, will assist in better informed economic decisionmaking throughout the private and public sectors.

3. *American business will receive more effective assistance in reaching world markets.*—The promotion of exports is an objective of common interest to most areas of economic endeavor. It also stabilizes and expands employment opportunities for American labor. Consolidation of Commerce and Labor programs which promote and assist exporters in a Department broadly concerned with the economy will increase

their impact, and provide a single cabinet official to whom those interested in export policies and activities can appeal for assistance.

4. *Transportation policies can be more effectively related to total national economic policies.*—The efficient and economical movement of materials and finished goods is vital to the functioning of the entire economy. Transportation systems must be balanced internally as to alternative modes, and externally with other factors affecting the entire economy. This external balance will be achieved by the incorporation of national transportation programs and policy in the Department's National Transportation Administration.

5. *The progressively greater decentralization of economic program management to regions which utilize standard Federal boundaries will promote meaningful contact between interested citizens and the programs which affect their interests.*—Related programs, which are now scattered among several Departments and agencies, will be consolidated into administrations of the Department. This will facilitate consistency and a maximum degree of decentralization of decision-making authority to the regional officials. As a result, regional officials of the various administrations of the Department will be able to relate more meaningfully to State, local, and private officials in their regions.

6. *The new Department of Economic Affairs will provide many points for access by interested citizens.*—The existence of a Secretary who is responsible and accountable for Federal programs relating to most major economic sectors will improve communications between the public and the Government. He and the heads of the components of the Department will have many access channels for interested citizens. Under the existing structure most queries and appeals from the public must go to higher levels, where generally resources are insufficient to analyze the situation and develop responsive reaction. The Department will have these resources, and the ability of Government to respond to the needs of its citizens will be improved.

Organization and Management

MANAGERIAL SCOPE AND REQUIREMENTS

The President's proposal for a sweeping reorganization of the executive branch brings together in each of the four new departments many varied and complex programs. Some of the new departments will be quite large. The Department of Economic Affairs will be the largest of the new departments in terms of Federal manpower with approximately 126,000 full-time employees, and will have an annual budget of approximately $5 billion. Its range of programs will be wide and varied. These factors of variety, complexity, and magnitude require very careful consideration to insure the manageability of such a large enterprise.

The Department of Economic Affairs must have a carefully designed internal organization if the Department is to perform its assigned mission effectively. At a minimum, such an internal organization must have three broad features:

- The Secretary must have adequate authority and supporting staff resources to enable him to carry out his responsibility for controlling policy development and program execution at all levels.
- Substantive programs must be coherently grouped into major manageable units at the first-tier organizational level.
- The field structure and management system must lend itself to extensive decentralization of program execution, including the capacity to tailor Federal services delivery to local conditions.

THE DEPARTMENTAL MANAGEMENT SYSTEM

The manageability of a large organization in great part depends upon the clear delineation of the functions the Secretary and his top management team are expected to perform. However, the functions should, and will often have to, be carried out by these officials in a way which allows maximum flexibility of roles and a minimum of rigidly conceived specialization.

a. The Secretary.—The Secretary will be responsible for the management and direction of his Department. This is underscored by the fact that all statutory authorities and Presidential authorities vested in the Department will be assigned to the Secretary, including matters of program substance and of management. Thus, the Secretary has ultimate managerial responsibility to the President and the Congress. The Secretary will thus be in a position to:

- Assign or reassign responsibilities and authorities within the Department and place any necessary limitations on the exercise of authority.
- Select policy-level officials, except a small number to be named by the President with Senate confirmation.
- Set the goals and objectives of the Department.
- Organize the Department in the way best suited to carry out its assigned purposes and give effect to the principle of decentralization.
- Allocate the funds, manpower, and other resources of the Department in the manner best calculated to assure the accomplishment of the President's programs and the enactments of the Congress.

b. The Deputy Secretary.—The Secretary of this Department will require the support and services of a strong deputy with whom to share the management of the Department.

The role of the Deputy Secretary will be that of the Secretary's alter ego in all matters affecting the Department with particular reference to internal management. His role can be characterized as assisting the Secretary to:

- Determine the program activities and operational guidelines of the Department's operations, including determination of requirements and deployment of resources among the programs.
- Evaluate the performance of all elements of the Department in meeting these objectives.
- Determine how well the Department's management structure and systems are functioning and effect necessary changes.
- Integrate and coordinate the efforts of the line and staff elements of the Department and resolve conflicts as necessary.

c. Top management team.—Due to the broad range of programs and major external relationships, the Secretary and Deputy Secretary clearly must have the support of a top team of officials empowered to act on their behalf in assigned spheres. This team will constitute a management council to assist the Secretary by providing an integrated and coordinated view of the Department's functioning. The members of this group, as discussed below, will have responsibilities which may be described as either of two types:

(*a*) Delegated responsibility for a major operating program segment. In the Department of Economic Affairs these segments will be administrations with an administrator at the head of each. They will be:

- Administrator for Business Development;
- Administrator for Labor Relations and Standards;
- Administrator for National Transportation;
- Administrator for International Economics;
- Administrator for Social, Economic, and Technical Information.

Each administrator will have responsibility for program execution and policy formulation within his assigned sphere.

(*b*) Delegated responsibility for the broad management of key functions critical to the central direction of the entire Department. These functions will be directed by:

- Two Under Secretaries;
- General Counsel;
- Assistant Secretary for Science and Technology;
- Other Assistant Secretaries.

The roles and relationships of these officials are described as follows:

The Two Under Secretaries.—The Secretary and Deputy Secretary will require the support of two top level officials to provide a departmentwide perspective on such matters as policy formulation, planning and budgeting, resource utilization, management structure and controls, information systems, program audits and field operations. Thus, the Secretary will have a strong, cross-cutting managerial capability independent of the more narrowly defined interests of each program administration.

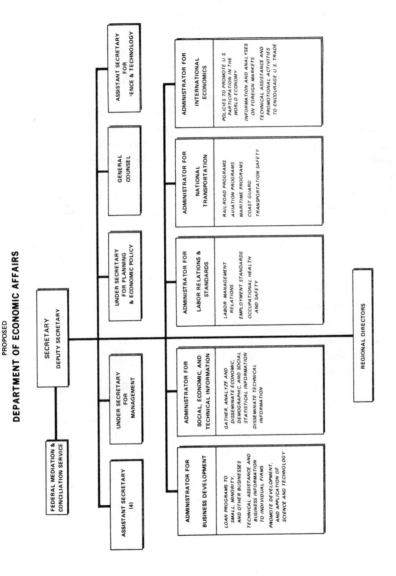

PROPOSED
DEPARTMENT OF ECONOMIC AFFAIRS

FEDERAL MEDIATION &
CONCILIATION SERVICE

SECRETARY
DEPUTY SECRETARY

ASSISTANT SECRETARY
(4)

UNDER SECRETARY
FOR
MANAGEMENT

UNDER SECRETARY
FOR PLANNING
& ECONOMIC POLICY

GENERAL
COUNSEL

ASSISTANT SECRETARY
'ENCE & TECHNOLOGY

ADMINISTRATOR FOR
BUSINESS DEVELOPMENT

LOAN PROGRAMS TO
SMALL, MINORITY,
AND OTHER BUSINESSES

TECHNICAL ASSISTANCE AND
BUSINESS INFORMATION
TO INDIVIDUAL FIRMS

PROMOTE DEVELOPMENT,
AND APPLICATION OF
SCIENCE AND TECHNOLOGY

ADMINISTRATOR FOR
SOCIAL, ECONOMIC, AND
TECHNICAL INFORMATION

GATHER, ANALYZE AND
DISSEMINATE ECONOMIC,
DEMOGRAPHIC, AND SOCIAL
STATISTICAL INFORMATION

DISSEMINATE TECHNICAL
INFORMATION

ADMINISTRATOR FOR
LABOR RELATIONS &
STANDARDS

LABOR MANAGEMENT
RELATIONS

EMPLOYMENT STANDARDS

OCCUPATIONAL HEALTH
AND SAFETY

ADMINISTRATOR FOR
NATIONAL
TRANSPORTATION

RAILROAD PROGRAMS
AVIATION PROGRAMS
MARITIME PROGRAMS
COAST GUARD
TRANSPORTATION SAFETY

ADMINISTRATOR FOR
INTERNATIONAL
ECONOMICS

POLICIES TO PROMOTE U.S
PARTICIPATION IN THE
WORLD ECONOMY

INFORMATION AND ANALYSES
ON FOREIGN MARKETS

TECHNICAL ASSISTANCE AND
PROMOTIONAL ACTIVITIES
TO ENCOURAGE U.S. TRADE

REGIONAL DIRECTORS

FEBRUARY, 1972

The Under Secretaries will be equivalent in rank and stature to the program Administrators, and thereby able to participate to the fullest possible degree as members of the top management team.

Some of the major functions which will be assigned to the Under Secretaries are:

- Assist in formulating the overall policy of the Department and in carrying out the presidential and congressional intentions.
- Oversee and coordinate the preparation of legislative proposals needed to strengthen national or Departmental policy and programs.
- Serve as effective witnesses before Congress on the policies, plans, requirements, and operations of the Department.
- Provide a source of innovation and evaluation in the systems for managing and administering the programs of the Department.
- Assure an effective plan for organizational relationships and responsibilities necessary for orderly and efficient management.
- Provide an independent evaluation of the accomplishment of program objectives and conformance with established policy.
- Develop a field/headquarters balance in which program decisions are made and executed at field levels to the fullest possible extent.
- Assure the compatibility of field locations and boundaries internally and with other agencies, in order to provide necessary services to the public in an effective and convenient manner.
- Provide policies, programs, and controls to assure that manpower and financial resources are utilized fully and effectively in the accomplishment of program objectives.
- Design and operate an effective flow of timely and pertinent management information between the Secretary and the several levels of management.

The General Counsel.—The General Counsel will occupy the top legal position in the Department and will be charged with furnishing legal advice and support to the Secretary and Deputy Secretary. In addition, the General Counsel will be responsible for furnishing legal assistance to officials throughout the Department and for assuring consistency and high professional competence in legal services at all levels. Finally, the General Counsel will also assist in the drafting of proposed legislation of interest to the Department.

Assistant Secretary for Science and Technology.—Many of the policy and operational issues which will confront the Department of Economic Affairs at the Secretarial level involve sophisticated matters of science and technology. In view of these considerations and in order to provide expert leadership and strong support to the Secretary and Deputy Secretary in matters of research and technical development, an Assistant Secretary for Science and Technology will be appointed. The Assistant Secretary will develop and recommend plans, policies, resource allocations, and other activities to make the best use of research and technology in meeting the goals and objectives of the Department. He will also serve as principal adviser to the Secretary on science and technology matters and assist the Secretary in relationships with the White House and Congress on scientific matters.

Other Assistant Secretaries.—In addition to the two Under Secretaries, the General Counsel and the Assistant Secretary for Science and Technology, there will be a need for several other Assistant Secretaries to concentrate departmentwide managerial attention on matters of key secretarial interest. The most effective utilization of these positions should be left for final determination by the Secretary on the basis of his assessment of priorities. Areas which may merit the attention of an Assistant Secretary separate from the officials cited above are such things as:

- Civil rights and equal opportunity;
- Environmental and consumer affairs;
- Minority business enterprise;
- National economic policy; and
- Audit and inspection

Those areas which are not given separate status under an Assistant Secretary can be subsumed as a responsibility of one of the Under Secretaries.

d. Field/Headquarters Relationships.—The field/headquarters relationship is a vital and integral part of the overall management system of the Department of Economic Affairs. This is particularly true in the light of the President's objective of decentralizing operations and decisionmaking to the regions and field offices to the greatest possible extent. The importance of field operations to overall departmental management is discussed later in this report.

PRIMARY GROUPINGS OF PROGRAMS

The grouping of programs into Administrations has been developed to minimize the need for continuous and close coordination across Administration lines, thus eliminating to the greatest possible degree the amount of overlap and duplication of functions and skills among the Administrations. Above all, this grouping of programs will facilitate the access of citizens to Government programs which affect their vital interests. This grouping is conducive to the development of a unified field system which allows maximum decentralization of decisionmaking authority. The grouping of programs into Administrations also reflects the President's policy that uninterrupted provision of vital Government services must be assured by avoiding unnecessary disruption of established organizational structures and relationships.

1. *Proposed Administrations.*—The Department will be organized into five Administrations:

- Business Development;
- Labor Relations and Standards;
- National Transportation;
- International Economics; and
- Social, Economic, and Technical Information.

2. *Description of Each Administration.*—In the following pages each of the five proposed Administrations is described as to its general concept or mission, its principal functions, and the existing Federal programs which it will manage.

Business Development Administration.—American business enterprises provide the effective combination of capital, management, labor, and technology to expand and adjust the Nation's economy. The Federal Government assists business by providing standards and services which promote the growth of private enterprise and provide a structure of opportunity and fair competition. The Nation has recognized the importance of fostering small business. Many small enterprises provide an environment which encourages constructive innovation and an opportunity for individuals to participate more fully in the Nation's prosperity. This Administration will have the broad purpose of assisting all businesses to prosper and to adjust to the changing economic environment. Consolidation of these business assistance services will promote uniform policies and facilitate access by interested members of the public. The functions of this Administration include:

- Development of policy to assist in the growth and development of private business enterprise.
- Provision of capital, managerial, and technical assistance to small and other businesses.
- Assistance to minority and other disadvantaged businesses through the provision of capital and technical services.
- Basic and applied research and technical services to strengthen and advance the Nation's science and technology and facilitate their effective application to increases in productivity and other uses for the benefit of the general public.
- Dissemination of useful business information to enhance marketing and management.

The Administration will encompass the functions of the following units.

From the Department of Commerce:

- Bureau of Domestic Commerce;
- Office of Minority Business Enterprise;
- National Bureau of Standards;
- Patent Office;
- Office of Telecommunication; and
- Business loans, technical assistance, and economic research functions of the Economic Development Administration.

From the Small Business Administration:

- Entire Administration except residential disaster loans.

From the National Aeronautics and Space Administration:

- Dissemination functions of the Technology Utilization Office.

Labor Relations and Standards Administration.—Since 1913, when the Department of Commerce and Labor was divided into two Departments, the rights of working men and women to decent wages, working conditions, and employment opportunities, have been substantially recognized and facilitated by new legislation, court decisions, and widespread union participation in collective bargaining with employers. Placing the Government's labor relations and standards programs and services in a Department charged with a broad economic mission will enhance the position of labor and is consistent with its economic objectives. The Administrator responsible for this component will be the spokesman for the labor force in the consultations of the Secretary and his advisers on economic policy matters. His participation in these deliberations will provide for the full and equitable consideration and integration of the workingman's concerns in all departmental programs. As a result, insuring the American worker's share in the benefits of increases in economic growth and productivity will be identified as a major purpose of all economic policies and programs. Functions of this Administration will include:

- Development of national labor policy.
- Provision of services to labor and management to promote industrial harmony.
- Development and enforcement of standards to protect workers.
- Improvement of occupational safety and health.
- Labor standards research, information, and implementation.

The Administration will be responsible for the functions performed by the following units.

From the Department of Labor:

- Labor-Management Services Administration.
- Employment Standards Administration (exclusive of the Womens Bureau and the Bureau of Employee Compensation).
- Occupational Safety and Health Administration.

From the Department of Health, Education, and Welfare:

- National Institute for Occupational Health and Safety.

National Transportation Administration.—The National Transportation Administration will be responsible for promoting and assuring the safe, convenient, economical, and efficient transportation of goods and people. The Administration will facilitate, establish standards, inspect, regulate, but generally will not operate total transportation systems. The National Transportation Administration will have responsibility for those major Federal transportation programs which must be planned and conducted on a national basis, to assure satisfactory performance and integration with other elements of the economy. Although all transportation programs contribute to economic growth and development, certain transportation programs have a predominant influence on land use, and the development, growth and, in sum, on the character of our communities. Such programs will be transferred to the Department of Community Development. However, the National Transportation Administration will closely coordinate the development of these community-oriented transportation programs with national transportation investment policies, thus achieving a balance among Federal programs designed to assure that the economy will be supported by an efficient and effective national transportation system.

This transfer of transportation functions according to overall purpose dictates a transfer of the community-oriented highway programs to the Department of Community Development. The Interstate Highway program is deeply involved in both urban and rural community planning and development, and is also being transferred to avoid the creation of two Federal highway agencies. While the importance of the Interstate System to the American economy is fully recognized, the system is basically in place and the remaining segments will have their greatest impact on communities.

The maintenance of high level attention to all aspects of transportation safety will be assured by continuing the independence of the National Transportation Safety Board within the new Administration. The Board Chairman will report directly to the National Transportation Administrator. The functions to be performed by the National Transportation Administration are:

- Development of national transportation policy.
- Promotion of transportation safety.
- Management of the National Airways System.
- Federal aid to airport construction.
- Provision for law enforcement, navigation aids, and the overall safety of life and property at sea and in the navigable waters of the United States.
- Improvement of motor carrier, automotive, and highway traffic safety.
- Maintenance of the merchant marine.
- Assistance to the rail transportation system.
- Operation of the U.S. portion of the Saint Lawrence Seaway.
- Transportation research and information service.

The National Transportation Administration will be responsible for functions of the following units.

From the Department of Transportation:
- National Transportation Safety Board.
- U.S. Coast Guard.
- Federal Aviation Administration.

- Bureau of Motor Carrier Safety.
- National Highway Traffic Safety Administration.
- Federal Railroad Administration.
- Saint Lawrence Seaway Development Corporation.
- Transportation Systems Center.

From the Department of Commerce:

- Maritime Administration.

International Economics Administration.—This Administration will consolidate and give unified policy and program attention to Federal programs which foster and assist effective U.S. participation in world markets. The span of programs thus consolidated will include those related to commercial and labor interests. The Administration also will promote participation of U.S. private capital and expertise in the total international economic development effort.

Maintenance of our competitive position in the world economy involves activities beyond those proposed for this Department, and close coordination with the Council on International Economic Policy and other affected agencies will be necessary.

The International Economics Administration will perform the following functions:

- Formulation of international economic policy advice.
- Collection, analysis, and dissemination of information on international trade and investment.
- Promotion of foreign travel to the United States.
- Regulation of U.S. foreign investment and exports.
- Promotion of U.S. exports and other activities to strengthen U.S. participation in the international economy.

The functions assigned to the following units will be performed by this Administration.

From the Department of Commerce:

- Bureau of International Commerce.
- U.S. Travel Service.
- Office of Foreign Direct Investment.

From the Department of Labor:

- Bureau of International Labor Affairs.

Social, Economic, and Technical Information Administration.— This Administration will serve as a focal point for the collection, compilation, analysis, and publication of a wide range of economic, social, demographic, and technical data. This information is essential for effective planning and sound decisionmaking by the Federal Government, State and local governments, business and agriculture interests, labor unions, and the public at large. The functions of the Administration will be:

- Provision of basic statistics and research findings about population characteristics and the economy including the Nation's economic accounts.

- Conduct of special economic analyses in the fields of industry, labor, and transportation.
- Dissemination of technical, statistical, and economic information.

This Administration will be responsible for the functions of the following units.

From the Department of Labor:

- Bureau of Labor Statistics.

From the Department of Commerce:

- Social and Economic Statistics Administration.
- National Technical Information Service.

Federal Mediation and Conciliation Service.—The Federal Mediation and Conciliation Service will report directly to the Secretary and Deputy Secretary. The mediation and conciliation services are made available impartially to all sectors of the economy; freedom from dominance by the interests of any one sector will be achieved by assigning this service independent of any one administration. Functions performed will be:

- Dispute mediation by rendering assistance to the parties, when needed, in connection with the negotiation or renegotiation of a collective bargaining agreement.
- Preventive mediation through the long-term improvement of the labor-management relationship by encouraging the parties to discuss their problems apart from the tensions of imminent contract expiration or strike deadlines.
- Public information and educational activities in support of the total mediation effort.
- Arbitration activity through maintenance of a select roster of well-qualified persons from which the involved parties can select an arbitrator to hear and decide disputed issues.

The Federal Mediation and Conciliation Service of the Department of Economic Affairs will include the mediation functions of the National Mediation Board. The NMB provides services for two industries—railways and airlines. The consolidation of these functions with similar services to other industries will provide more effective and uniform mediation services to all segments of American labor and business.

REGIONAL STRUCTURE AND SYSTEM

1. *Existing Systems.*—The Department of Economic Affairs will initially inherit from its component programs a complex set of field or regional systems with the following general characteristics:

- Approximately 20 regional or subregional field systems exist.
- A number of specialized office units exist which are physically removed from Washington, but which do not function in relation to the programs of a given territory.

- Partial observance of the President's standard regional boundaries and regional headquarters location exists (SBA, Labor Department, and many Transportation Department field systems are so alined and located, but field systems to be transferred from Commerce do not fully conform to the standard Federal regions).
- Many field systems transferring to the Department have a considerable range in the degree of authority delegated to the field for program actions and management.
- There is no Department or agencywide regional official with direct authority over field units except for the Small Business Administration regional directors (Transportation and Labor have Secretarial representatives in a coordinative capacity, and Commerce has no Secretarial counterpart in the field).
- Overseas field offices are maintained by three component organizations.

2. *General Plan.*—The basic field plan for the Department will have characteristics summarized as follows:

- The Secretary's policy and managerial influence will be extended to the field level to the greatest feasible degree by establishing a secretarial representative in each of the 10 standard regions to work with related interest groups.
- Continuity of current operations will be assured by utilizing existing headquarters/field relationships for line direction to the maximum feasible extent with broad delegations of authority to the field.
- Existing boundaries and regional office locations will be utilized initially. Where these deviate from the Federal standard regions, efforts will be made to aline them over a period of years. This will give the public greater convenience in contacting Department of Economic Affairs program officials.
- As the Department evolves, the Secretary's management authority will be utilized to move in a deliberate and planned way toward a progressively more unified field management system. That is, where possible, the several field systems within each Administration will be merged under a common regional Administrator.
- Field installations which are dispersed headquarters operations will remain separate from any regional management system and will be administered directly as part of their parent organization.

3. *Description of Initial Field System.*—(*a*) *Secretarial Representation.*—The Secretary will exercise a direct influence and obtain departmental representation in the field operations by placing a secretarial representative or regional director in each of the 10 Federal regions. These officials will be appointed by the Secretary and will serve at his pleasure. They will report to the Secretary/Deputy Secretary. These appointees will not initially be line supervisors of Department field operations, but will fill the following role:

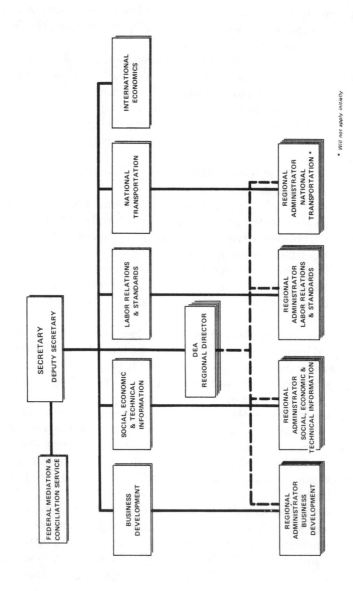

DEPARTMENT OF ECONOMIC AFFAIRS

FIELD-HEADQUARTERS RELATIONSHIP

FEBRUARY, 1972

* Will not apply initially

- They will be delegated authority by the Secretary to help resolve conflicts in their regions among program elements or program and support elements.
- They will represent the Secretary in their regions dealing with senior State and local officials and, in particular, with the elected heads of State and local governments.
- They will communicate and interpret policy from the President and the Secretary to all departmental units in their regions with particular reference to policy on matters which affect relationships between programs.
- They will evaluate the performance of Department programs in the region, deal with criticisms and complaints from groups including labor, business, and public officials, and provide a separate and independent communication channel to the Secretary.
- They will further exercise departmental influence in the regions by assuring consistency in regional planning, by helping to achieve program integration and coordination, and by management of common services.
- They will be members of the regional councils and encourage interdepartmental cooperation through the councils and in other ways.

(*b*) *Direction to Field.*—Paralleling the above system of secretarial representation and influence, the Department will move toward a headquarters/field system of line direction which will link the Administrator of each component with his counterparts in the field (see chart). To illustrate, the Administrator for Labor Relations and Standards could delegate program and management authorities to 10 regional Administrators of Labor Relations and Standards, and they would be accountable to him for performance. The 10 regional Administrators, in turn, would redelegate appropriate authority to field operating components within their region.

The Labor Relations and Standards Administration can move directly to this type of regional management system when the Department of Economic Affairs comes into existence. The Business Development Administration and the Social, Economic and Technical Information Administration will be organized with counterpart regional Administrators as soon as feasible after the Department is created. The desirability and practicality of this regional management system for the National Transportation Administration has not been established. The programs of these component Administrations will be reviewed to determine how they can best achieve the objectives of effective decentralization and responsive administration.

4. *Special Field Arrangements.*—In a few cases field units will have special relationships:

- *Federal Mediation and Conciliation Service.*—The FMCS at headquarters level will be organizationally separate from all of the Department's Administrations. Its field officials similarly will be independent of the other regional Administrators. However, FMCS field offices could receive administrative support from the Secretary's regional director.

- *National Transportation Safety Board.*—Within the National Transportation Administration, the field officials will report directly to the NTSB headquarters. However, the NTSB field offices could receive administrative support from the Secretary's Regional Director or other National Transportation Administration field office.
- *National installations in the field.*—In the Department, there are installations located outside of Washington which have only incidental relationship to the area in which they are located. They are not part of a regional scheme and, in fact, are considered to be decentralized national offices. These field installations will report directly to the Washington offices for which they operate. The National Bureau of Standards complex at Boulder, Colo., is an example of this type of field/headquarters relationship.

ORGANIZATION/APPROPRIATION STRUCTURE RELATIONSHIPS

The new Department of Economic Affairs will require a new appropriation structure, merging and consolidating the accounts now in use for the activities being moved to the new Department. The revised appropriation should enhance management effectiveness and provide flexibility to respond to rapidly changing conditions. To facilitate effective management, the appropriation structure must correspond to the organization of the new Department. Further, appropriations will be proposed to be made to the Secretary, with some appropriation items identified to the level of the first major program grouping of the Department. With the concurrence of the Congress, this should result in a simplification of the appropriation structure, and facilitate legislative review of the President's budget requests. The existence of many relatively small appropriations, transferred from the existing departments and agencies, could be a handicap to the new Department in integrating its operations, as well as a handicap to the Congress and the public in understanding the Federal budget. It is not the intent of the proposals discussed here to fix an appropriation pattern for all time. Appropriation structures are subject to change by the Congress from year to year, and indeed should be changed as programs and organizations are modified.

A highly desirable approach would be to establish two principal appropriation accounts for each major grouping of the Department. The first includes financing for day-to-day operating expenses and other activities for which the requirements for a specific year could be readily established. This annual appropriation would facilitate continuing congressional review.

The second appropriation would cover funds for construction, land acquisition, project-oriented research, and certain types of loan and grant activity, for which there is a need for longer term availability of appropriated funds. In these cases, "no year" appropriations would be proposed; e.g., such amounts as, upon the concurrence of Congress, would be available until expended.

In addition, the financial accounts of the Department would continue to provide separately for the major trust funds and the various public enterprise funds transferred to the Department. A working capital fund at the departmental level to finance departmentwide administrative services would also be desirable. Service funds could be established where necessary, to merge accounts which provide for services performed for others at a charge approximating cost, or which continue earmarking now required by law in connection with programs of the Department.

PRINCIPAL ADMINISTRATIVE IMPROVEMENTS

The President's Departmental Reorganization Plan affords the executive branch an opportunity to make significant improvements in management practices and procedures. The primary thrust of these improvements will be to create an environment where innovation can flourish, and management can readily adapt to future needs. The theme of adaptability and flexibility is built into the structure of each department. This has been achieved by:

1. Providing the capability to react swiftly to changes in emphasis and established priority by authorizing the Secretary to organize and manage the Department internally.

2. Emphasizing maximum decentralization of authority and responsibility so as to place the power of decision where the problem is best solved in the interest of the public.

3. Providing the authority to draw upon the whole range of national capability in carrying out the missions of the Department.

4. Providing greater discretion in the management of financial resources.

These administrative improvements will not only make possible but necessitate new and improved ways of doing business. Some of the significant opportunities are:

(1) The simplification and reorientation of information systems to furnish current program status and for such common purposes as payroll, supply control, and accounting.

(2) The introduction of a comprehensive planning process to enable the integration of long- and short-range planning. It will also serve as a basis for management evaluation.

(3) The upgrading of the contracting process to allow the best practices to be adopted for general use. Improved selection processes,

requirements definition, and administrative procedures can be employed, and procurement leadtime can be reduced.

(4) The unification of research and development to permit technology assessment and goal selection to be conducted in terms of departmental objectives, thus producing a balanced, cohesive, and responsive research and development effort.

Budget and Manpower

The approximate size of each of the major administrations of the Department of Economic Affairs is displayed in the following table. Outlays are generally used as the measure of program level except in the case of some programs where obligations or loan level is a more accurate indicator of the dimension of the program. Manpower estimates are end of year employment. All data are for fiscal year 1972, based on the President's 1973 budget.

	Fiscal year 1972	
	Employment	Budget outlays [1] (in millions)
Business Development Administration	12, 606	$1, 720
Labor Relations and Standards Administration	5, 079	139
National Transportation Administration	[2] 63, 072	3, 217
International Economics Administration	1, 375	42
Social, Economic, and Technical Information Administration	5, 302	100
Federal Mediation and Conciliation Service	473	11
Total	[2] 87, 907	5, 229

[1] Adjusted to reflect program levels in some cases.
[2] Exclusive of 38,128 military personnel.

Transition to New Department: Structural Continuity

POLICY OF MINIMUM TRANSITION CHANGE

In establishing the new Department, it is planned that initially most of the existing organizational units and programs transferred to the Department of Economic Affairs will remain intact. This will avoid serious disruption of essental functions or services, and avoid uncertainty on the part of the public and other Federal agencies in making contact with units serving their needs. Changes will be made over time to achieve the maximum benefits the new departmental concept offers. This will afford sufficient time to consider all factors so as to assure the most orderly achievement of departmental objectives with a minimum of disruption and confusion to the public and to employees.

CONTINUITY OF STRUCTURE

The bill to establish this Department provides that whenever all of the functions of a department, agency, or other component are transferred to the Secretary of the new Department, the old Depart-

The Proposed
Department of Economic Affairs

BUDGET OUTLAYS
of
Programs to be Transferred
(In Millions)

TOTAL - $5,229 Million

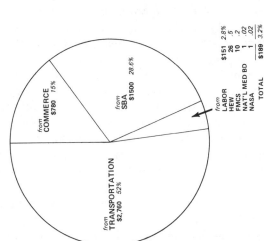

from
TRANSPORTATION
$2,760 52%

from
COMMERCE
$780 15%

from
SBA
$1500 28.6%

from
LABOR $151 2.8%
HEW 26 .5
FMCS 10 .2
NAT'L MED BD 1 .02
NASA 1 .02
TOTAL $189 3.2%

ALL DATA — FISCAL YEAR 1972

EMPLOYMENT
of
Programs to be Transferred
(Full-time, Permanent)

TOTAL - 126,035 Employees*

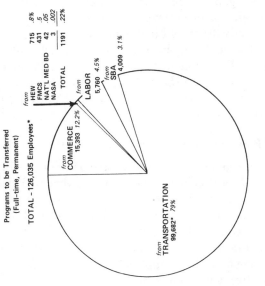

from
HEW 715 .8%
FMCS 431 .5
NAT'L MED BD 42 .05
NASA 3 .002
TOTAL 1191 .22%

from
LABOR
5,760 4.5%

from
SBA
4,009 3.1%

from
COMMERCE
15,393 12.2%

from
TRANSPORTATION
99,682* 79%

*INCLUDES 38,128 COAST GUARD MILITARY PERSONNEL

FEBRUARY, 1972

ment, agency, or other component shall lapse. The purpose of this provision is to clarify the authority of the Secretary of the new Department to consolidate or reorganize the existing bureaus or agencies in order to better achieve the expected benefits and improvements afforded by the reorganization. This does not necessarily mean that any particular bureau or agency will be discontinued. Where the existing agency is already organized in the most efficient manner to carry out its mission and serve the public, it can be continued in effect by the Secretary of the new Department. Upon activation of the new Department, the Secretary will have the authority administratively to issue an order continuing all existing agencies in effect until such time as he makes other provisions for them.

RELATIONSHIP TO REVENUE SHARING PROPOSALS

The revenue sharing plan proposed by the President will provide funds for State and local governments in a way that will assign both revenues and management discretion to those levels of government closest to the problem. Revenue sharing will ease the fiscal problems of State and local governments by providing additional unrestricted revenues through general revenue sharing and, by eliminating the present matching requirements of the categorical grants, through special revenue sharing. Finally, it will make State and local elected officials responsible to the electorate for capably dealing with their problems.

Characteristically, the programs recommended for conversion to special revenue sharing deal with those top priority national problems which can benefit from State and local analysis and decisionmaking. Six broad functional areas are included: Transportation, education, urban community development, rural community development, manpower training, and law enforcement. Several of the programs transferred to the Department of Economic Affairs will be affected by special revenue sharing. These are: (1) The business loans and technical assistance programs of the Economic Development Administration, Department of Commerce, and (2) the airport grant and highway traffic safety programs of the Department of Transportation. These programs will go into the rural community development and transportation portions of special revenue sharing, respectively. They will continue in the Department of Economic Affairs, however, until these portions of the special revenue sharing programs are enacted. Then they will be administered by the Department of Community Development.

If the revenue sharing legislation is enacted prior to the establishment of the Department of Economic Affairs, these programs will not transfer to the new Department. The revenue sharing programs for rural community development and transportation will be administered by one of the existing Departments or the new Department of Community Development.

No other changes in the Department of Economic Affairs are contemplated as a result of the enactment of general or special revenue sharing.

EMPLOYEE SAFEGUARDS

The bill contains savings clauses which are designed to protect the interests of present officers and employees. The bill provides that no executive pay level official whose position is abolished by the act will be compensated at less than his present executive pay level as long as he serves in a position in the new Department with comparable duties. This will enable the new Department to retain the services of experienced executives, who might seek other positions if they were to suffer a loss in pay or status. The bill also provides that other employees' grades and compensation will not be adversely affected by the reorganization for a period of at least 1 year after transfer.

These organizational changes, while primarily affecting programs, also will affect each Federal employee and it is anticipated that they will participate fully in accomplishing the reorganization. To that end, current plans include sound provisions to insure that disruption to employees will be kept to an absolute minimum, that cut-backs in staffs, where necessary, will be accomplished through attrition, and that actions which could adversely affect employees will be avoided.

More specifically, it can be stated that no employee will be separated because of the reorganization. In addition, the reorganization bills include a provision that no employee will be reduced in classification or compensation as a result of the plan for 1 year after the reorganization becomes effective. All movements of functions and jobs will be governed by current law and Civil Service Commission regulations, with full employee protection and appeal rights. From another standpoint, the reorganization can be viewed as improving the range of opportunities for promotion and career development, as more broadly conceived program management and staff positions evolve in the new Department.

Full consideration is being given to the impact of reorganization on the existence of union recognition and agreements, in light of the possible changes in unit structure that may result from transfers, realinements, and combinations.

In these ways the bill provides for essential continuity of operations during the formative phases of the Department.

NOTES AND REFERENCES

1. "Manpower," as used here and subsequently in this chapter, refers to the number of full-time federal employees of the proposed Department of Community Development. This should not be confused with HEW's Office of Manpower, which coordinates programs to improve the employment opportunities of all Americans who are unemployed, underemployed, or in need of training.

2. Hoover Commission I (1947–1949) and Hoover Commission II (1953–1955), both officially named the Commission on Organization of the Executive Branch of the Government, were established by Congress. The reports of the earlier commission stressed the need for centralization of policymaking responsibility and improved presidential control over management of the government. Hoover Commission II was less concerned with the organization and management of the government than Hoover Commission I. It focused on the functions of the federal government, recommending a reduction in federal government functions and less competition with private enterprise.

3. It is interesting to note the White House/OMB perception of the nation's energy situation in 1972. Subsequent realization of an emerging energy crisis has overtaken this assessment, leaving the plans it justified a curious anachronism. More recent thinking on how the energy agencies should be organized is found in [22] and [71], a portion of which is reprinted in the appendix section of this volume.

4. On August 4, 1964, the Johnson administration established the Office of Economic Opportunity within the Executive Office of the president. On July 6, 1973, all OEO programs except three were transferred, by administrative action under President Nixon, to the departments of Health, Education, and Welfare; Labor; and Housing and Urban Development. The three programs which were not transferred were Community Action, Economic Development, and Legal Services; however, they were transferred to the Community Services Administration in HEW on January 4, 1975.

5. The consolidation of broad policy programs and functions under one department that might provide an additional benefit is not included in this reprinted document. That benefit would be to lessen the domination of more narrowly defined departments by the constituencies they serve, both business and labor. Such special interest constituencies, or parochial interests, are discussed in the reports to President Johnson of the 1964 and 1966 Task Forces on Government Organization, chaired by Don Price and Ben Heineman respectively. See [11] and [12].

6. An unstated, political dimension is at play in the attempt to insulate the department secretary from the administrative levels. Throughout government, the constituencies, some of which are large and politically powerful, exert strong influence on administrators. This extends to cabinet levels in Agriculture, Labor, and Transportation. Cabinet members often become advocates for the "narrowly defined interests" of the constituency and relay such interests to the president, if they have access to him for decisions. This puts the president very close to the wellspring of political influence. Ash, as well as Price and Heineman before him, wanted to interpose a "super secretary" between the president and the administrators. Price and Heineman referred to this as protecting the president from parochial interests and getting the "president's own man" into the decision-making process.

PART II

REGULATORY REFORM

Introduction

The Constitution grants regulation of commerce to Congress, but federal regulatory bodies are so intertwined with the Executive branch that they fall within the scope of reorganization of Executive departments and agencies. The commissions and boards commonly referred to as "independent regulatory bodies" were created by Congress, with delegated congressional authority to regulate commerce. Historically, they have had a special relationship with Congress, but that relationship has changed. Today the place of regulatory bodies within the structure of government is ambiguous. The Executive branch asserts de facto control over many aspects of their work, and some strictly Executive agencies effectively engage in regulation of commerce. The ambiguity over the jurisdiction of regulatory bodies has, of course, had an effect on efforts to administer, oversee, and reform them.

The influence of these bodies on the American economy is profound and affects virtually every citizen every day because of their impact on such diverse matters as purity of food and drugs, freight rates, television programming, and auto emissions. Their performance has been subjected to critical scrutiny, particularly in the last five years. The reason for this scrutiny is due partly to the failures of regulatory agencies, and partly to growing congressional concern over which branch of the government is to oversee and control their operations.

The documents in Part II pertain to reform of the regulatory process and to a restructuring of the agencies responsible for regulation. Chapter 3 includes an exposition of the issues of regulatory reform, a chronological summary of recent proposals, and portions of the Ash Council proposal. This proposal would further entrench Executive branch control over the regulatory bodies. Chapter 4 deals with selected issues concerning the effectiveness of the regulatory agencies and the views of past regulators, as presented in testimony before congressional committees. Finally, Chapter 5 discusses congressional initiative to reassert its authority over the regulatory process through improved oversight and the utilization of so-called sunset procedures for periodic review of programs.

The Senate Committee on Government Operations' study on federal regulation defines a regulatory agency or office as one which (1) has decision-making authority; (2) establishes standards or guidelines conferring benefits and imposing restrictions on business conduct; (3) operates principally in the sphere of domestic business activity; (4) has its head or members appointed by the president, and, in all but one instance (the Food and Drug Administration), is subject to Senate confirmation; and (5) has its legal procedures generally governed by the Administrative Procedure Act.[1] The committee's definition encompasses such matters as regulation of market entry and exit, regulation of rate, price, and profit structures, preservation of competitive environments (systems), protection of consumer health and safety, environmental protection, and protection from deceptive and misleading trade or marketing practices.

Under its working definition, the committee's attention is directed to the following regulatory bodies: Civil Aeronautics Board, Consumer Product Safety Commission, Environmental Protection Agency, Federal Communications Commission, Federal Energy Administration, Federal Maritime Commission, Federal Power Commission, Federal Reserve Board, Federal Trade

Commission, Interstate Commerce Commission, Nuclear Regulatory Commission, Securities and Exchange Commission. Consumer and Marketing Services (Department of Agriculture), Food and Drug Administration (Department of Health, Education, and Welfare), Federal Aviation Administration, National Highway Traffic Safety Administration (both of the Department of Transportation), and the Occupational Safety and Health Administration (Department of Labor). It is evident from this list that the work of these agencies is mutually related to that of the Executive branch departments. While others might work with a slightly different list, the issues faced in examining their future course would not change significantly.

Two broad issues underlie regulatory reform: one concerns the place of regulatory structures within or between the Executive and Legislative branches of government; the other concerns the effectiveness and fairness provided by present regulatory structures. The status of regulatory functions within the federal establishment was less ambiguous in earlier times. For approximately the first century of U.S. government operations, Congress exercised direct control over many functions of government departments, including the Treasury and the Post Office. Towards the end of the nineteenth century, the concentration of economic power in the railroads led to the creation of the first "independent" regulatory body, the Interstate Commerce Commission. It was delegated certain responsibilities by Congress, which had neither the time nor the staff to keep check on the increasingly powerful transportation industry.[2] As the American industrial economy grew stronger and more complex, the abuse of concentrated power became more widespread. Congress decided to designate other regulatory functions to new commissions and boards or to Executive departments with either tacit or statutory approval. Today there are more than 65 units of the federal government directly involved in some form of economic regulation. They employ over 100,000 people and have direct budget outlays in excess of $3 billion. The dollar impact of their activities is, of course, many times greater.[3]

Determining the place of the regulatory bodies within the federal structure is an issue of profound implications as to the balance between the Executive and Legislative branches. Proposals to alter the authority asserted by either branch have generated much public discussion of the issues, but this discussion has been obscured by revelations of wrongdoing and inefficiency within the regulatory agencies. The Ash Council proposals on regulatory bodies, which appear in Chapter 3, implied recognition of their de facto place within the Executive branch and contained recommendations on the appointment of regulators that would place effective political control in the White House. These Ash proposals got nowhere, partly because of the collapse of the Nixon administration, but they did serve to renew Congress' attention to its regulatory responsibilities.

Congressional hearings were held in 1974 and 1975 by the Senate Committee on Government Operations under the general heading of "Regulatory Reform." Those inquiries, uncovering stories of waste, inefficiency, and abuse, not only made headlines but aroused fear that the "antiregulation" mood created by them would lead to the repeal of basic measures vital to the protection of public health and safety. Portions of these hearings, including both exposés of failures and defense of continued regulation, are presented in Chapter 4. Much of the material from the Regulatory Reform hearings has no bearing on where regulatory bodies fall between the Executive and Legislative branches; rather, it concentrates more on the manner in which regulation is to be implemented. During the year 1977, the Senate Government Operations Committee will release its complete six-volume report regarding federal regulation. It will address the question of how Congress might reassert its constitutional prerogative and develop mechanisms for effective oversight and control of the regulatory process.[4]

Even before the Government Operations Committee studies were completed, legislative initiative had begun. Senators Robert Byrd and Charles Percy introduced the Regulatory Reform Act of 1976 in the 94th Congress as S. 2812. The bill provided that the president must submit to Congress, over a five-year period, annual plans to eliminate unnecessary or harmful regulation. Each plan would address a different area of government regulation. If the Congress did not enact a reform by a given date, the president's plan would become law, unless disapproved by the House or Senate. If there were disapproval, Congress would have six months to enact reforms, or the rules of the affected agencies would expire. This act represents a sunset type proposal, applied solely to regulatory agencies. (A discussion of the sunset concept follows in Chapter 6, with considerable attention given to the legislative veto arrangement.) This and similar measures hardly reclaim regulatory functions as the exclusive domain of Congress.[5] They do, however, assert congressional interest, and seek also to recognize the legitimate role of the Executive branch in regulatory processes.

The revelations of abuse associated with the Nixon administration and the Watergate affair have made both Congress and the public more aware of and cautious about unchecked Executive power. Therefore, it seems unlikely that Executive branch control over regulatory agencies will be allowed to reach the degree proposed by the Ash Council. Congress is intent on reaffirming its role and on clarifying the manner in which it shares regulatory oversight power with the Executive. As debate and deliberation progress, the issues set forth here and in the documents that follow will be significant. The impetus for regulatory reform exists and the outcome may be a milestone in the history of federal reorganization.

1. U.S. Congress. Senate Committee on Government Operations. *Study on Federal Regulation.* Vol. II: *Congressional Oversight of Regulatory Agencies.* Chapter 1. To be issued in 1977. [The official name of the Senate Committee on Government Operations was changed to the Committee on Governmental Affairs in February 1977.]

2. Ibid.

3. Ibid.

4. Volume II of the Government Operations Committee report is entitled *Congressional Oversight of Regulatory Agencies.* It examines the relationship of Congress to the regulatory agencies and contains historical, as well as legal, analysis.

5. Another major bill with sunset components, applicable to the regulatory agencies, is the Government Economy and Spending Reform Act (S. 2925 in the 94th Congress and S. 2 in the 95th). That measure addresses all government programs and contains zero-base budgeting provisions. It is the subject of Chapter 8.

Chapter 3
Regulation within the Federal Structure: Issues and Initiatives

ISSUES IN FEDERAL REGULATORY ACTIVITIES ([46], pp. 1–6)

The following reprint is a Congressional Research Service Issue Brief (of the Library of Congress). It provides a useful overview on the development and status of regulatory reform from a legislative perspective. Some liberty has been taken with the author's very orderly exposition by inserting portions of the Ash Council report on regulatory bodies ([104], pp. 3–7, 13–26) into the section following the issue brief's summary of the Ash Council report.

The economic regulation of private and public activities by the Government has been the subject of much controversy and of numerous congressional and independent studies. Today there is no single accepted definition of what constitutes regulation or a list of "regulatory agencies." Although many Federal agencies perform regulatory functions as a subsidiary responsibility, some "independent regulatory commissions" operate primarily (if not solely) for that purpose. Indeed, no small part of the contemporary "regulatory problem" appears to be conceptual in nature. Difficulty is experienced in defining objectives sought in regulating the economy and in describing who is responsible to whom, and for what. Various institutions are presently involved in reassessing the nature and objectives of regulation, its impact, and the organization required to best achieve these objectives.

Congress has long pursued two principal economic objectives: to encourage competition within industries and to protect the public from unfair and unsafe business practices. For the most part, these goals are complementary. However, there are instances (now more frequently than in the past) when these goals appear to conflict. As a consequence, the following issues have arisen, and have continued to resist resolution:

(1) Does economic regulation, beyond ensuring minimum safety provisions and honest transactions, tend to encourage or inhibit competition within an industry?

(2) Should the agency responsible for administering economic regulations be located within a department of the executive branch, be an independent executive agency, or be an independent regulatory commission?

(3) Regardless of the location of the agency within the government, should the leadership of a regulatory agency be furnished by a single administrator or by a plural-member board?

(4) If the agency is an independent regulatory commission, what type of relationship should it have with the President, the Congress, and the Courts?

(5) With regard to the relationship of independent regulatory commissions and the President, what whould be the method of appointment for members of the commissions? What procedures and limitations should be imposed with regard to removal of commission members? Should the Office of Management and Budget review the commission's budget request? Should the Department of Justice be involved in decisions regarding commission litigation? Should the commission be required to submit legislative requests through the Office of Management and Budget?

(6) Should an agency regulate an industry or a field and at the same time confer benefits (subsidies, routes, licenses, etc.) on those it regulates?

(7) What relationship should exist between the regulator and the regulated? How can a regulator resist becoming identified with the interests it is charged with regulating?

(8) How can a regulatory agency resist the tendency toward over-judicialization of its rulemaking and procedures?

(9) How can the regulatory agency, whatever its organization and function, be made more accountable to the public? And is it possible to achieve accountability to the public outside of the representative political process?

The first independent regulatory commission, the Interstate Commerce Commission, was established in 1887 by the Congress in response to what were considered to be economic abuses practiced by the railroad industry. It marked a significant departure from earlier administrative doctrine in that it provided for a regulatory commission outside the framework of the executive branch, deliberately designed to operate with a substantial degree of autonomy.

Since the establishment of the Interstate Commerce Commission, there has been a degree of constitutional ambiguity regarding the status of the commissions. Article I of the Constitution entrusts to the Congress the regulation of commerce. Under this power, the Congress justified its decision to establish a commission largely independent of the executive branch, to which was delegated a limited amount of legislative and judicial authority. Article II, on the other hand, grants to the President the executive power of the government, e.g., the general administrative control of those executing the laws. He is held responsible for the actions of the Federal Government, yet in substantial fields of public policy he has purposefully been denied authority to insure that the administration of laws, according to his interpretation, does occur.

While these commissions possess numerous characteristics of organizational independence, it is important to recognize also that their independence is tempered by relationships to the three branches of government.

The independent regulatory commissions are not totally independent of the Congress, for it is the Congress which created them, vested them with authority, and supplies them with funds. Congress may terminate them, modify their powers and jurisdictions, and expand or diminish their financial resources. The commissions are not independent of the courts either, for upon petition of the parties involved the courts may review commission decisions and conform, modify, or nullify them. Finally, the commissions are not wholly independent of the President, for it is he who nominates, and renominates, members to be later confirmed by the Senate, and appoints the chairmen of the commissions. The Office of Management and Budget, on behalf of the President, approves their budgets (with one exception) before they are submitted to Congress. The Department of Justice, with certain exceptions, determines what litigation will be pursued.

Today, while there is no universally agreed-upon list of independent regulatory commissions, there are ten commissions that appear on all lists and share several common characteristics.

Regulatory Agency	Year Estab.	Regulatory Areas
Interstate Commerce Commission	1887	Railroads, motor carriers, domestic water carriers, oil pipe lines
Federal Trade Commission	1914	Antitrust, trade practices
Federal Power Commission	1920	Hydroelectric power, electric energy, natural gas
Federal Communications Commission	1934	Broadcasting, licenses, domestic and international communications carriers
Securities and Exchange Commission	1934	Security issues, security exchanges, companies controlling electric or gas utilities
Civil Aeronautics Board	1938	Civil air transport industry
Federal Maritime Commission	1961	Oceanic transportation
Consumer Product Safety Commission	1972	Consumer product safety
Nuclear Regulatory Commission (formerly AEC)	1974	Nuclear energy licensing
Commodity Futures Trading Commission	1974	Commodity exchanges and futures trading

In addition to these commissions, a number of plural-member commissions, such as the Federal Reserve Board, the National Labor Relations Board, and the recently established Federal Elections Commission, are considered by some to be independent regulatory commissions.

The independent commission is not the only form of agency involved in regulation. There are a number of single-administrator executive agencies which perform regulatory functions, such as the Food and Drug Administration in the Department of Health, Education, and Welfare and the independent Environmental Protection Agency (EPA). Such single-administrator executive agencies may be located either within an executive department (as in FDA) or exist as an independent executive agency (as in EPA).

Although regulatory agencies are usually classified by organizational structure, they can also be considered in terms of functions. Some agencies are principally concerned with regulating one industry, and hence are frequently considered to have a vertical perspective, while other agencies are concerned with making and enforcing rules and standards across the economy, and hence tend to have a horizontal perspective. To cite examples, it appears that eight of the ten independent regulatory commissions listed above are vertical in function (regulate one industry), while two commissions, the Consumer Products Safety Commission and the Federal Trade Commission, are horizontal in perspective (regulate a number of industries). Among executive branch regulatory agencies, a similar distinction may be made. For example, the Food and Drug Administration would be "vertical" while the Environmental Protection Agency would be "horizontal."

EARLY STUDIES

The subject of reorganizing the independent regulatory commissions has arisen in every modern Administration. A pattern has been established: a major study is undertaken, a report is published, and "reform" proposals are offered. The first report was issued in 1937 by President Roosevelt's Committee on Administrative Management (Brownlow Committee). The Brownlow report is properly viewed as a tool in Mr. Roosevelt's strategy to gain greater Presidential control over the policies and operations of administrative agencies. The report charged that the independent regulatory commissions were a "headless fourth branch" of government.

> "The independent commissions present a serious immediate problem. No administrative reorganization worthy of the name can leave hanging in the air more than a dozen powerful, irresponsible agencies free to determine policy and administer law. Any problem to restore our constitutional ideal of a fully coordinated Executive Branch responsible to the President must bring within the reach of that responsible control all work done by these independent commissions which is not judicial in nature. That challenge cannot be ignored."
> ([7], p. 7)

The Committee recommended that the commissions be abolished and their functions be distributed among the departments. Once relocated, the functions would be divided between an administrative section directed by a single administrator and a judicial section that would remain independent in the making of regulatory decisions. While few results can be traced to the recommendations emanating from the Brownlow report, the report did inaugurate what has come to be a rather substantial body of government reports and academic literature critical of the theory, organization, and operations of the independent regulatory commissions.

The first Hoover Commission (1947-1949) conceded that the regulatory commissions had a rightful place in the political system but had generally failed to live up to original expectations. The recommendations tended to be concerned with structure rather than substance and were modest in scope.

The Commission argued that the commissions would be more effective and efficient if the administrative responsibilities were vested in the chairmen. The Commission also noted with concern that there was little coordination between the commissions and the agencies in the executive branch with similar regulatory responsibilities. The Commission therefore recommended that there be established an Administrative Management Director in the Bureau of the Budget to "suggest ways and means to improve and thereby reduce the cost of disposing of business before administrative agencies."

The report of the second Hoover Commission (1953-1955) supported the concept of an integrated legal staff within agencies under a General Counsel, improving internal procedures and separating--where possible-- the judicial and executive functions of administrative agencies and increasing the independence of hearing examiners. Critics argued that the second Hoover Commission was promoting the concept of judicialization of policymaking. The Commission also recommended the establishment of an administrative court at trial level to handle cases then handled by administrative agencies, and not a specialized court to review actions of administrative agencies. No significant changes in the organization and functions of independent regulatory commissions resulted from this Commission and its report.

During the Kennedy and Johnson Administrations, there were no large public studies of governmental organization comparable to the earlier Hoover Commissions. In 1960, President-elect John Kennedy requested James M. Landis to write a report on regulatory commissions and to suggest methods to improve the operations of these agencies. Landis proposed that the administrative powers of the chairman of the respective commissions be enhanced and that staff positions be made more attractive by delegating some authority. He further suggested that regulatory policy formulation come under Presidential guidance to insure uniformity, such guidance to be provided by the establishment of several offices in the Executive Office of the President. During the Johnson Administration there were three "unpublished" reports which dealt in part with the regulatory commissions.

N1

ASH COUNCIL REPORT OF 1971

The tradition of major published reports on governmental organization was resumed during the Nixon Administration. In 1971, three reports were issued by the President's Advisory Council on Executive Organiza-

tion (Ash Council), two concerning executive departments and one dealing
N2   exclusively with independent regulatory commissions.

The Ash Council report on independent regulatory commissions, like
the earlier Brownlow report, was highly critical of the regulatory commissions. The underlying theme of the report was that the commissions
were not sufficiently accountable to either the President or the Congress. Insofar as these commissions could be brought under Presidential
guidance for purposes of policymaking, the Council argued, Congress
would also be a beneficiary since such an arrangement would enhance congressional ability to oversee.

The regulatory commissions were viewed by the Ash Council as being
essentially ineffective and unable to respond adequately and in a timely
fashion to economic, technological, and social changes. This apparent
inability to adapt to changing conditions was attributed by the Council
to three factors: "collegial organization, the judicial cast of agency
activities, and the misalignment of certain function responsibilities."

The Council recommended a major restructuring of the independent
regulatory commission system.

> "To assure coordination of regulatory matters with national
> policy goals, to improve the management efficiency of regula-
> tory functions, to improve accountability to the Congress and
> the executive branch, and to increase the probability of
> superior leadership for regulatory activities, the trans-
> portation, power, securities, and consumer protection regula-
> tory functions should be administered by a single adminis-
> trator, appointed by the President. These functions should be
> performed by agencies respectively designated: Transportation
> Regulatory Agency, Federal Power Agency, Securities and Ex-
> change Agency, and Trade Practices Agency."

In short, the Interstate Commerce Commission, Civil Aeronautics
Board, and the Federal Maritime Commission would be combined within a
new Transportation Regulatory Agency. The promotional subsidy-granting
activities of the Civil Aeronautics Board would be transferred to the
Department of Transportation. The Federal Trade Commission's consumer
protection responsibilities would be vested in the Federal Trade Practices Agency while its antitrust enforcement responsibilities would
be vested in a new Federal Antitrust Board, the latter to consist of
a chairman and two economist members each appointed by the President
with the consent of the Senate. Finally, the responsibilities of the
Securities and Exchange Commission under the Public Utilities Holding
Company Act would be transferred to the Federal Power Agency.

The Federal Communications Commission was specifically omitted from
this list of plural-member commissions which were slated to become
single administrator executive agencies. The official reason given
for this omission was "the uniqueness of Federal Communication Commission regulation over broadcast content which requires continuation of
the collegial form." Critics of the report speculated that the retention of the Federal Communications Commission independence was in the
nature of a politically prudent move to ease the likelihood of charges
that the Administration was attempting to harass the broadcasting industry. Like the majority of previous reports with recommendations,
the results directly attributable to the Ash Council were marginal....

Findings and Recommendations ([104], pp. 3–7, 13–26)

Major and fundamental change pervades each of the areas of economic enterprise under regulation by the independent regulatory commissions.

- In transportation, increasing interaction between the various modes reflects a persistent striving for greater efficiency in the movement of goods and people;
- In trade, new and probably enduring levels of public and producer attention are being given to the quality of goods and services, and to the operation of the marketplace;
- In securities, even as the structure of the industry itself and the relationship between Government and industry are experiencing major changes, a well-established trend toward institutional investment and new methods of financing are significantly altering the characteristics of securities trading;
- In power, where industry structure is also undergoing change, supplies of electrical energy and natural gas have not consistently kept pace with increasing demands in certain areas, and new technologies have yet to take up the slack;
- In communications, burgeoning technology has created new avenues for service and new products which together complicate the task of regulation and blur distinctions between the various forms of communications.

The independent regulatory commissions play a critical role in balancing the changing demands of the Nation for the goods and services of regulated industries and the related need for financially sound and effectively managed industries in the regulated sectors of our economy. Unfortunately, obsolete organizational forms limit the effectiveness of these commissions in responding to economic, technological, structural, and social change. Inappropriate regulatory structures and cumbersome procedures impose burdens that impede good public service, sound financial and operational planning, and adjustment to changes in growing industries—contrary to the purposes of regulation.

Our proposals for change in the organizational forms of several independent regulatory commissions are directed at improving agency effectiveness, while assuring fairness to those involved in or affected by the regulatory process.

The regulatory commissions are not sufficiently accountable for their actions to either the Congress or the President because of the degree of their independence and remoteness in practice from those constitutional branches of government. Regulatory activities, therefore, are not adequately supported and are not effectively coordinated with national policy goals.

Inherent deficiencies in the commission form of organization prevent the commissions from responding effectively to changes in industry structure, technology, economic trends, and public needs.

Deficiencies in the performance of the regulatory commissions are partly due to the difficulty of attracting highly qualified commissioners and retaining executive staff. Even able administrators have difficulty in serving as coequals on collegial commissions.

- While there are notable exceptions, it is difficult to attract to regulatory positions men of skill in administration and breadth of perspective largely because of the procedures and traditions associated with appointment to the regulatory commissions.

- Given these traditions and the shared responsibility of the collegial form, it is not likely that commission positions will generate greater interest in the future.

Certain judicial activities of the commissions conflict with their policymaking responsibilities and generate an organizational environment inimical to regulatory efficiency and constructive response to industry and the public.

- Many commissions engage excessively in case-by-case adjudication as a basis for policy formulation rather than using less formal procedures such as exchanges of written or oral information, informal regulatory guidance, or rulemaking.
- The judicial cast of agency review proceedings place too great an emphasis on legal perspectives to the detriment of economic, financial, technical, and social perspectives. One result is a high level of legal skill among agency professionals and commissioners, but generally insufficient capability in other disciplines.
- The judicial cast of agency review proceedings delays final administrative determinations and invites dilatory appeals.
- Overjudicialization encumbers the time and energies of commissioners and staff, causes undue case backlogs, imposes high costs upon litigants, prevents anticipatory action through rulemaking, deters informal settlements, and precludes coordination of agency policy and priorities with those of the executive branch.

Certain functional responsibilities are inappropriately distributed among the various commissions.

N3
- Responsibility for regulation of transportation is distributed among the ICC, CAB, and FMC, impeding formulation of broader regulatory policy covering the several transportation modes and coordination with the Department of Transportation, and thus forestalling consistency in national transportation policy.
- Responsibility for promotion of transportation, vested in some regulatory commissions, conflicts with the regulatory activity of those agencies.
- Combination of antitrust enforcement and consumer protection in the FTC deprives that agency of a central purpose, fostering an uncertainty of emphasis as between its functions, inordinate delay, and preoccupation with routine matters.
- Regulation of public utility holding companies by the SEC is no longer best performed by that agency. Regulatory expertise regarding public utility holding companies rests with the FPC.

To assure coordination of regulatory matters with national policy goals, to improve the management efficiency of regulatory functions, to improve accountability to the Congress and the executive branch, and to increase the probability of superior leadership for regulatory activities, the transportation, power, securities, and consumer protection regulatory functions should be administered by single administrators, appointed by the President. These functions should be performed by agencies respectively designated: Transportation Regulatory Agency, Federal Power Agency, Securities and Exchange Agency, and Federal Trade Practices Agency.

- The authority and responsibility attending the single administrator form should enable the agencies to attract and retain the most highly qualified administrators and executive staffs.
- Unambiguous placement of authority for agency policy and operations in a single administrator should increase accountability to both the Congress and the President.
- Agency work should be expedited by utilizing more effective administrative techniques made possible by one-man management of agency activities.

The communications regulatory function and the antitrust enforcement function should, as now, be carried out by multimember bodies for reasons supervening the advantages of a single administrator. The FCC should be reduced in size from seven to five members, to serve 5-year terms.

To prevent the overjudicialization of agency procedures and attitudes and to assure comprehensive and anticipatory policymaking, internal agency review of proceedings should be limited in time and focused primarily on the consistency of the decision with agency policy. Appeals from final agency decisions should be heard by an Administrative Court of the United States.

- A 30-day period should be allowed after a hearing examiner's decision for review by the single administrator. The administrator should have the power to modify or remand an examiner's decisions. The limited time and scope of policy review by agency administrators should help make initial decisions of agency examiners, in many cases, final determinations of the agency.
- The Administrative Court should review appeals by an aggrieved party from final agency determinations of the transportation, securities and power agencies. Decisions of the antitrust, trade practices, and communications agencies would be reviewed in the Federal courts as they are today.
- The court should consist of as many as 15 judges, appointed by the President and confirmed by the Senate for terms sufficiently long as to attract men of quality. We suggest 15-year staggered terms, with judges sitting in three-man panels for each case reviewed by the court.

Certain functional responsibilities of the agencies should be realigned.

- To reflect the increasing interdependence of the structure, economics, and technology of the transportation modes, regulatory responsibilities of the ICC, CAB, and the FMC should be combined within a new Transportation Regulatory Agency.
- To correct the conflict inherent in performing regulatory and promotional functions in the same agency, the promotional subsidy-granting activities of the CAB should be transferred to the Department of Transportation.
- To assure that each of its missions is more effectively performed, the FTC's consumer protection responsibilities should be vested in a new Federal Trade Practices Agency and its antitrust enforcement responsibilities should be vested in a new Federal Antitrust Board. The Board should consist of a chairman and two economist members, each appointed by the President with the consent of the Senate.
- To provide an organizational placement which better reflects current realities, the regulatory responsibilities of the SEC under the Public Utility

Holding Company Act should be transferred to the Federal Power Agency.

Analysis of Structure and Relationships of Regulatory Bodies

The independent regulatory commissions, now mature institutions of the Federal Government, are characterized by rigidity in their process and in their patterns of relationship with Congress and the executive branch, the regulated industries, and the public. They lack the adaptive force which might regenerate or redefine their roles in helping shape the American economy. Both rigidity and lack of adaptability impede regulatory effectiveness at the very time when persistent trends and new directions in the economy demand flexibility and imagination to carry out regulatory objectives and to formulate action in the interest of the public, including the regulated segments of the private sector.

REGULATION AND GOVERNMENT STRUCTURE

The ICC, CAB, FMC, FTC, SEC, FPC, and FCC, established by Congress in the years since 1887, have long been considered an anomaly in government structure.[1] They are institutions housed in the executive branch, carrying out legislative functions, and behaving like courts. In the past quarter century, the growth of the regulated industries and the pace of the national economy have largely outdistanced the ability of the commissions to cope constructively with regulatory problems.

To have practical meaning, the commissions' charge to regulate in the interest of the public must include regard for economic, technological, and social developments, as well as the capability of the regulated industries to provide good public service.

Inadequacies in regulatory structure have adversely affected the implementation of Congressional mandates, the management of executive branch functions, the interests of the public generally, and the ability of the regulated industries to operate their businesses profitably or to plan future actions with reasonable assurance of what regulatory policy will be.

The history of the regulatory commissions reflects an attempt to respond practically to national needs with institutions outside the three constitutional branches of government. Congress initially undertook to perform some regulatory responsibilities, but later conferred these responsibilities on independent commissions, a form that it believed would provide fairness and expertise, without delay or partisan influence. The commissions, however, soon became part of a highly specialized, independent "fourth branch" of the Federal Government. Today, they are not sufficiently accountable to either Congress or the executive branch. Perhaps because of this, they have become less

---

1. "It [the committee] is not persuaded of the soundness of the view sometimes asserted that, to the traditional threefold classification, there must be added a fourth power, conveniently called 'administrative,' which somehow involves the exercise of functions which are neither executive, legislative, nor judicial and thus escapes the necessity for safeguards which centuries of experience have built around the exercise of such functions." Report of the Special Committee on Administrative Law, before the 57th Annual Meeting of the American Bar Association, Milwaukee, Aug. 28-31, 1934, in "Separation of Powers and the Independent Agencies: Cases and Selected Readings," Committee on the Judiciary, S. Doc. No. 91-49, at 216 (1970).

effective in balancing the needs of the public with those of the industries they regulate consistent with Congressional intent and executive policy.

ACCOUNTABILITY

More than 30 years ago, the President's Committee on Administrative Management highlighted the lack of accountability of independent regulatory commissions:

> They constitute a headless "fourth branch" of the Government, a haphazard deposit of irresponsible agencies and uncoordinated powers * * * . The Congress has found no effective way of supervising them, they cannot be controlled by the President, and they are answerable to the courts only in respect to the legality of their activities.[2]

The point has been made many times since, but the scope of the problem has changed little, if at all, over the years. The independent commissions persist more from inertia than from an analysis of how regulatory bodies should properly function within the context of a comprehensive political and economic system.

Congress has conceived of these commissions as independent of executive branch control, but in fact the commissions are almost as independent of Congress itself. Apart from inappropriations approval, periodic program review, and the intermittent interest of one or several of its members, Congress does not exercise the degree of oversight with respect to regulatory commissions that it does for executive departments and other agencies of the executive branch. Congress has sought to preserve the independence of the regulatory commissions, even as their activities increasingly affect the implementation of national policy. The executive branch, responsible for carrying out national policy, has been reluctant to support reforms needed to integrate regulatory activities with executive programs because the President does not have sufficient responsibility for commission direction.

Yet congressional and executive attention to regulatory needs is required more today than ever in the past because of the increasing interdependence of national economic policies which emerge from budget and fiscal action, economic regulation, and industry promotion by government. Proponents of the commission form tend to ignore that interdependence.[3] In doing so they perpetuate processes and relationships which may frustrate national policy and sound economic growth.

Independence, and the resulting absence of regulatory accountability, has transferred to a generally shielded arena those questions which should be settled in a more open forum. The public—the intended beneficiary of regulation—has found it difficult to understand the issues and lacks a practical mechanism through which to communicate its views.

All this, together with significant impediments to regulatory performance inherent in the commission form itself, has led the commissions to become less responsive to economic and social trends and changes in industry structure.

---

2. The President's Committee on Administrative Management, "Report of the Committee With Studies of Administrative Management in the Federal Government," pt. I, at 40 (1937) (hereinafter referred to as Brownlow report).

3. See M. Bernstein, "Regulating Business by Independent Commission" 283 (Princeton University Press, Princeton, 1955) (hereinafter referred to as Bernstein).

Most studies and commentary relating to reform of the regulatory commissions over the years emphasize their separateness from an integrated governmental structure.[4] These studies, and subsequent attempts to implement proposals stemming from them, have concentrated on reordering personnel, procedures, or functions to improve commission performance. Such efforts are commendable, but internal revision and redefinition are not enough. The regulatory apparatus requires a fundamental restructuring to enhance overall effectiveness and responsibility.

TO CONGRESS

Congress' powers under article II of the Constitution to regulate interstate and foreign commerce is the primary basis for regulatory controls. Through legislation, Congress has vested in regulatory commissions the powers necessary to carry out broad statutory mandates. But congressional statements of policy are understandably general, leaving to the commissions the task of making specific policy to implement those objectives. One result is that the commissions, in the course of time, have developed policies affecting the economy without sufficient guidance or check by Congress.[5] This condition is aggravated in the view of some commentators by the commission form of organization which makes it hard to pinpoint those within the regulatory agencies responsible for setting policy.[6]

With greater coordination between the agencies and the executive branch and an organization structured to focus responsibility, Congress would be better able to oversee agency policy and, in concert with the President, improve regulation.

TO EXECUTIVE BRANCH

The President is responsible under article I of the Constitution to "take care that the laws be faithfully executed." That duty extends to the activities of the

4. See generally "Report of the Special Committee on Administrative Law" before the 57th Annual Meeting of the American Bar Association supra note 1; Brownlow report, supra note 2; "The U.S. Commission on Organization of the Executive Branch of the Government, the Independent Regulatory Commissions," Rept. No. 12, March 1949 (U.S. Government Printing Office, Washington, D.C., 1949) (hereinafter referred to as First Hoover Commission Report); Bernstein, supra note 3; J. Landis, "Report on Regulatory Agencies to the President-Elect," printed for use of the Senate Committee on the Judiciary, 86th Cong., Second sess. (1960) (hereinafter referred to as Landis report).

5. "Usually these investigations or hearings are sporadic in nature having been sparked by some incident that has caught the attention of the press. Regular surveys of their activities would be far more valuable." Landis report, supra note 4, at 34-35; "Congress has found no effective way of supervising them, they cannot be controlled by the President, and they are answerable to the courts only in the respect to the legality of their activities." Brownlow report, supra note 2, at 40.

6. "This arrangement [a chairman designated by the President and responsible for administration and staff] has advantages for the Commission as well. Over the long pull, it must function as a part of the Government as a whole. For one thing, it can accomplish its duties only with proper appropriations and that may require sympathetic help from the Chief Executive with respect to its budget." The U.S. Commission on Organization of the Executive Branch of the Government, Committee on Independent Regulatory Commissions: A Report with Recommendations, Jan. 13, 1949 (U.S. Government Printing Office, Washington, D.C., 1949) (hereinafter referred to as "First Hoover Commission Task Force Report"); "So far an administration carried on by a group is concerned, there there is little to commend it. It is on the purely administrative side that the independent commissions are weakest, and gain rather than loss would result from centralizing control and responsibility. * * * For purposes of management, boards and commissions have turned out to be failures." Brownlow report, supra note 2, at 21; "Administration by a plural executive is universally regarded as inefficient." "First Hoover Commission Report," supra note 4, at 5.

regulatory agencies to assure that the laws enacted by Congress are carried out effectively and fairly. The American public—to whom the President is directly answerable—looks to the President for leadership in pursuing national policy goals, including those affected by the regulatory process. The success of many Congressional and executive programs ultimately depends on a coordinated regulatory response.

Several recent Presidents have recommended changes in the regulatory process.[7] Although many proposed reforms have fallen short of enactment, these Presidents presumably felt that such recommendations were part of their responsibility to oversee faithful execution of the laws. Congress has repeatedly recognized the President's role in the regulatory scheme by authorizing him to make organizational changes in all agencies of the executive branch without distinction between executive agencies within the Departments and independent regulatory commissions.[8]

If regulation is to be more responsive to the public interest and coordinated with national programs, it must first be brought within the ambit of elective government, with accountability to those officials to whom the public and the regulated industries alike look for fair and constructive application of national policy.

CONCEPT OF INDEPENDENT COMMISSIONS

Historically, at least four premises have been offered to support regulation by independent commission.

The first is that Congress delegated unique legislative authority to carry out certain critical regulatory functions and created a unique form of organization, the independent commission, for that purpose. Yet, most executive departments also possess delegated regulatory powers. For both, Congress enacts skeletal legislation setting forth principles, mandates, and limitations within which the traditional executive departments and agencies develop rules, standards, and regulations to give substance to a legislative program.[9] It is difficult today to discern the distinction which justifies wide differences in the structure and processes of the Federal Trade Commission on the one hand and the Food and Drug Administration or Federal Aviation Administration (both headed by single administrators) on the other. The most recent agency to be vested with regulatory functions, the Environmental Protection Agency,[10] incorporates the concept of unitary leadership in place of the commission form.

7. Eisenhower administration: "U.S. Commission on Organization of the Executive Branch of the Government, Legal Services and Procedure" (U.S. Government Printing Office, Washington, D.C., 1955) (hereinafter referred to as "Second Hoover Commission Report").

Kennedy administration: Landis report, supra note 4.

Johnson administration: "President's Task Force Report on Government Organization"; "Price Task Force 1964"; "Heineman Task Force Report 1967" (unpublished).

8. See, e.g., 5 U.S.C. 901 (a), 902 (1) (a) (supp. IV, 1965–68); see also 5 U.S.C. 105 (supp. IV, 1965–68); 31 U.S.C. 2, 18(a) (b) (1964).

9. See, e.g., Packers and Stockyards Act, 7 U.S.C. 181–231 (1964) as amended (supp. IV, 1965–68), administered by the Department of Agriculture; Federal Food, Drug, and Cosmetic Act, 21 U.S.C. 301–392 (1964), as amended (supp. IV, 1965–68), administered by the Food and Drug Administration; and the Commodity Exchange Act, 7 U.S.C. 1–17(a) (1964), administered by the Commodity Exchange Commission under the executive branch.

10. Reorganization Plan No. 3 of 1970, prepared by the President and transmitted to the Senate and the House of Representatives, July 9, 1970, pursuant to the provisions of 5 U.S.C. ch. 9.

Second, it is argued that to deal with complex and technical regulatory problems, special expertise is required of decisionmakers and that the commission form alone best develops that expertise. The commissions have not, however, demonstrated consistent mastery of the subjects within their jurisdictions.[11] Nor does their technical capability visibly surpass that of regulatory counterparts within executive departments.

Third, it is urged that the application of regulatory statutes, rules, and regulations requires a bipartisan, multimember body that can act without regard to the partisan considerations which affect Congress or the executive branch. Political pressure coming from Congress or the executive branch unquestionably impinges on the impartiality of commission proceedings. But the procedural requirements of adequate notice and fair hearing, as well as the availability of judicial review, help to assure, as much as anything, a just result in particular proceedings. In the opinion of several observers of the regulatory process, the fairness of regulatory decisions results more from the mechanics of internal decisionmaking and breadth of perspective of the regulators than from the fact of bipartisan representation on the commissions.[12]

A fourth premise often asserted in support of the commission form is that commissions can better serve the public interest in regulatory matters because their independence makes them immune from control by the industries they regulate. The assumption which lies behind these assertions is that the interest of the industries and of the public are in fundamental conflict. But today, those interests are closely related, for the success of an industry will have a marked impact on the extent, quality, and price of available goods and services. Nevertheless, undue or unbalanced influence upon the commissions by the industries regulated is undesirable. While the adversary nature of commission proceedings decreases the likelihood of such influence, when it occurs, it is an outgrowth of the dependence of the regulator on the regulated—a relationship which may occur regardless of form.[13] To the extent the form of organization is responsible at all, the very anonymity of the commission structure which heightens unaccountability tends to prevent public exposure of relationships which may be improper.

The foregoing does not set forth all the premises underlying the commission form for use in economic regulation.[14] Other arguments for the establishment of the commissions range from the discomfort of many courts with complex economic and technological problems to the need for expeditious procedures in regulating commerce.

At the very least, these reasons for regulation by independent commission, if ever valid, are today of questionable validity. In practice, the commission form has proven most of them to be invalid.

---

11. "In both the ICC and the FTC, long tenures and the tradition of reappointment have tended to make incumbent commissioners relatively insensitive to new industrial developments and rather hostile to new ideas about regulatory policy and administrative practice." Bernstein, supra note 3, at 108.

12. "There is a little evidence that commissioners divide on major policy issues according to their party affiliations." Bernstein, supra note 3, at 104. See generally E. Herring, "Federal Commissioners—A Study of Their Careers and Qualifications" (Harvard University Press, Cambridge, 1936).

13. See E. Redford, "American Government and the Economy" 587–590 (Macmillan, New York City, 1965).

14. For an indepth historical analysis see "Final Report of the Attorney General's Committee on Administrative Procedure," ch. 1 (U.S. Government Printing Office, Washington, D.C., 1941); J. Anderson, "The Emergence of the Modern Regulatory State" (Public Affairs Press, Washington, D.C., 1962) (hereinafter referred to as Anderson).

REGULATION WITHIN THE INDUSTRIAL ECONOMY

The form of the regulatory commissions, compatible with another era prevents them from responding effectively to economic trends and changes in technology, industry structure, and public needs

The Interstate Commerce Commission, first among the Federal regulatory commissions, was established in 1887 to achieve rate stability, prevent discrimination in favor of large shippers and certain geographical areas, and protect farmers from undue charges by railroads. Today some of the surface transportation industries suffer major economic hardship partly caused by the regulatory processes themselves.

Given the likely impact of such developments as containerization, jet freight carriage, and the interstate highway system, as well as the needs of a growing and concentrated population, modes of transportation within ICC jurisdiction must be viewed together with other modes as an integral part of a unified transportation network. Other carriers not regulated by the ICC affect and are affected by ICC decisions. Urban mass transit is a concern of the ICC, CAB, and the Department of Transportation. The ICC and the CAB exercise jurisdiction over inland segments of overseas shipments while the FMC and CAB exercise jurisdiction over the ocean segment of such shipments, even though containerization has made possible a continuous flow of commerce from the interior of the United States to the interior of other continents. Fragmented regulation of the transportation industry is inconsistent with efforts to develop a coordinated transportation system. It frustrates the development of management and financial capability in the industries involved, and impedes the rate at which new technology can be utilized.

The Federal Trade Commission was created in 1914 to prevent unfair methods of competition by businesses in interstate commerce. Originally intended to augment antitrust enforcement, the FTC has become a repository for many bits and pieces of legislation that did not seem to fit neatly into any other agency of government. Consequently, FTC jurisdiction now ranges from the complexities of large corporate mergers to the comparatively simple task of accurate labeling of fabrics and furs.

The Federal Power Commission originated in 1920 with the relatively tidy mandate of licensing construction and operation of hydroelectric power plants on bodies of water within the jurisdiction of the Federal Government. It now also regulates transmission and wholesale marketing of electric energy in interstate commerce, including rates, accounting procedures, mergers, consolidations, interconnections, and coordination of interstate electric energy systems. The FPC similarly regulates transmission and wholesale marketing of natural gas in interstate commerce. An increasingly complex interstate energy system affecting the well-being of every citizen makes these regulatory tasks monumental.

The Federal Communications Commission was set up in 1934 to bring order to radio spectrum allocation and to regulate the existing telephone systems as a monopoly service under legislation that authorized exclusive operation in the public interest. To these has been added regulatory responsibility for standard television broadcasting, cable and subscription television, satellite communications, and computer utilities.

The Securities and Exchange Commission, also a product of regulatory legislation in the 1930's, was established to promote public confidence, through government oversight, in the issuance and trading of securities. But today, the SEC must deal with related problems of public ownership of brokerage firms, the operations of securities exchanges, the effects of computerization and new financing techniques, and the advent of major institutional investors.

The Civil Aeronautics Board, created in 1938, dramatically illustrates the way in which technology has challenged the ability of regulatory commissions to respond to change. The CAB initially concentrated on safety regulations and awards of mail routes. Today, the Board oversees an industry experiencing recurring economic problems and faced with crowded airways, jumbo jets, inadequate terminal facilities, and problems yet to be generated by the SST. These factors materially affect the ability of the industry to provide good service and at the same time impinge on the economy, our physical environment, and transportation modes not regulated by the CAB.

The Federal Maritime Commission, which in 1961 replaced the Federal Maritime Board established under the Shipping Act of 1916, today is involved in tasks of international importance. The FMC must deal with the effects of containerization and other technological innovations in ocean shipping. The Commission must also resolve problems relating to joint through rates and single bills of lading, its impact on modes (including foreign carriers) it does not regulate, and pricing through international shipping conferences.

The end result of this period of unparalleled technological change, industry expansion, economic growth, and environmental and social concern is that new responsibilities and workloads generated by routine matters have outdistanced the commissions' ability to respond. As the volume of proceedings has increased with each new responsibility, internal commission structure and process has become more complex. While some attempts have been made to remedy these problems through internal reforms, little thought has been given to restructuring the entire regulatory apparatus.

But it is not the mounting ineffectiveness of the regulatory framework alone which compels change. The world is in an era of transition that challenges government and private sectors alike to deal constructively and cooperatively with the economic issues, current, prospective, and unforeseen. The independent regulatory commission's inflexible institutions attuned to a simpler day, cannot be expected to deal constructively with economic issues yet to be generated if they are unable to deal with current ones. More than ever, a new framework is needed for improved regulation and as a necessary first step to reconsidering the statutes which authorize economic regulation.

An Alternative Conceptual Framework

The failure of regulatory commissions to respond to current demands and the unlikelihood of their responding to new ones is principally attributable to collegial organization, the judicial cast of agency activities, and the misalignment of certain functional responsibilities.

The collegial form is today inappropriate for regulating highly complex, everchanging areas of the economy. What is needed is a regulatory structure which is more adaptable to changing conditions and better able than a collegial body to articulate policy. Plural-headed administration is usually characterized by shared powers, shared responsibility, and, for that reason, shared indecision and unaccountability.

In addition, overjudicialization, resulting from full commission review of initial agency decisions as a matter of course, has upset commission priorities and obscured the formulation of comprehensive, timely, and anticipatory agency policy. Moreover, the admixture of certain judicial functions with policymaking and prosecutory responsibilities has created a condition of apparent bias in certain proceedings, subjecting agency determinations to criticism on that ground and generally undermining confidence in the regulatory process.

Finally, certain regulatory activities are improperly divided among, or unwisely combined in existing commissions.

AGENCY ADMINISTRATION

We have considered several alternatives and have concluded that the best approach to solving the problems created by the commission form is to replace commissions—for transportation, power, securities, and trade practices regulation—with single administrators. These officials should be appointed by the President, upon the advice and consent of the Senate, to serve at the pleasure of the President.

We believe single administrators will enhance leadership, improve the management of operations, and insure accountability in the regulatory agencies, where these vital requirements for program effectiveness are now often weak. This form of organization would also strengthen program coordination where two or more agencies need to work together to achieve a common goal.

Specifically . . . the single administrator would:

- Enable an agency to attract and retain highly qualified executives and staff because of better-defined, singular authority and responsibility;
- Encourage formulation of policy through informal procedures and rule-making rather than case-by-case adjudication;
- Foster improved policy coordination among the agencies and with executive departments;
- Facilitate more immediate response to the needs of the public and to structural, economic, and technological changes in the regulated industries; and
- Promote more efficient allocations of agency resources by encouraging the use of modern management methods, including greater delegation of authority and more direct staff accountability.

Unitary leadership will not solve all regulatory problems. An agency so led may flounder for lack of the right kind of leadership or suffer from misguided efforts. But fault for that lies in the quality of the appointment not the form of organization. In such a case, responsibility lies with the President who has power to make the necessary change.

We suggest retention of plural leadership in the communications and antitrust areas because of overriding considerations which in our view supervene the benefits of the single administrator form. . . .

REVIEW OF AGENCY DECISIONS

The regulatory commissions have tended over the years to overjudicialize agency process by adopting a case-by-case approach. Excessive judicialization has fostered the development of ad hoc policies often limited to the particular fact situation at hand and therefore without general applicability or future effect.

Such judicial preoccupation, seen most readily in the course of systematic full commission review of decisions by agency hearing examiners, generally has precluded early, comprehensive statements of policy through rulemaking proceedings and other informal policymaking procedures. It has prevented the application of current agency policy by examiners while implicitly encouraging appeals to the full commission for a de novo review of findings and legal issues raised in hearings. It has spawned an overly legalistic attitude which permeates all agencies and narrows the perspectives of staff and commissioners. The judicial attitudes and procedures of the commission have unduly prolonged proceedings and nurtured high case backlogs leading to ineffective uses of agency resources.

To rectify this situation, we propose that, instead of reviewing each initial decision as a matter of course, the single administrator of the restructured transportation, securities, and power regulatory agencies, and the new trade practices agency, review selected cases primarily for consistency with agency policy. Action by the administrator to overturn, modify, or remand an examiner's decision should be taken within 30 days and should set forth the reasons underlying such action.

Final agency action would be subject to review in the Federal courts. Whereas judicial review is presently exercised by the U.S. Courts of Appeals, we propose that, except for trade practice proceedings, review be transferred to a new Administrative Court of the United States. That court would be expert as to both the substantive issues involved in transportation, securities, and power legislation and the procedural intricacies of the Administrative Procedure Act which governs agency and review process. Moreover, the court's familiarity with problems of regulatory administration and the need for expedited procedures can be expected to aid in displacing the court-like posture of the agencies while maintaining regulatory fairness. We anticipate that removing judicial review of agency process from the Courts of Appeals will reduce somewhat the load on those courts and eliminate much of the agency preoccupation with judicial procedures which derives from review by common law courts.

The Administrative Court should consist of as many as 15 judges, appointed by the President, upon the advice and consent of the Senate, to serve staggered terms. We suggest terms up to 15 years. Appointments should be made initially on a bipartisan basis, with no more than a bare majority from one political party. Subsequent appointments or reappointments, just as those to other Federal courts, should be made without regard to political affiliation. The length of judicial terms should be long enough to insure continuity of expertise and at the same time short enough to permit revitalization of the judicial process compatible with an expanding economy, new technology, and changes in industry structure. A Chief Judge designated by the President should assign judges to cases on a rotating basis rather than to specialized panels. This would allow judges to maintain an open perspective and avoid identification of particular judges with specific types of proceedings.

RESTRUCTURING REGULATORY AGENCIES BY SECTOR

The single administrator form, limited internal review, and the Administrative Court create a structure within which several regulatory functions can be realigned to reflect a more rational and potentially more effective placement of responsibilities.

TRANSPORTATION

Three agencies presently regulate transportation: the ICC (railroads, trucks, buses, freight forwarders, barge lines, and pipelines), the CAB (air carriers), and the FMC (maritime shipping). While the reasons for dividing responsibility among three agencies may have been compelling as transportation regulation evolved, we found no persuasive reasons to justify the continuation of these divisions. To the contrary, grouping these responsibilities within a single Transportation Regulatory Agency has many advantages. These are set forth at length in chapter 3.

Today, there is a singularly vital need for a regulatory facility which is consonant with the increasing interdependence of transportation modes, competition among the modes, and integration of transportation into effective networks. The proposed Transportation Regulatory Agency would be charged with weighing the interests of each transportation mode in terms of the public interest. Rules and procedures for uniform classifications and for coordinated rates, routes, and industry practices would be possible when now such action is virtually impossible.

Promotional as distinct from regulatory functions of the existing transportation agencies—such as the subsidy-granting activity of the CAB—should be consolidated in the Department of Transportation which has primary concern for industry promotion. This would eliminate conflicting responsibilities for promotion and regulation within a single agency.

TRADE

While transportation regulation is in our view better administered by one agency, regulation of antitrust enforcement and consumer protection is ill-combined in the FTC.

Although both activities aim at assuring fair business practices and preserving competition in American industry, methods of investigation, negotiation, and enforcement of their respective statutory mandates differ widely. Each requires different expertise and procedures. Consumer protection relies primarily on the promulgation of rules and regulations together with field investigations. Antitrust enforcement entails intensive study of the industry and of the economic impact of industry practices.

. . . To fulfill these separable responsibilities the FTC should be abolished and in its place created a new Federal Trade Practices Agency for protecting consumers and a new Federal Antitrust Board for antitrust enforcement.

The Federal Trade Practices Agency would establish trade practice policies, both on its own initiative and in response to public initiatives. It would also investigate actual instances of alleged violations of fair trade practices. Since many such complaints are of limited financial consequence and are amenable to prompt resolution, hearing examiners situated in regional offices of the agency could most expeditiously deal with them. In fact, today many such situations are resolved quickly through the most informal discussion between the FTC and alleged offenders. In those cases where substantial issues are involved, examiners' decisions should be subject to appeal in appropriate Courts of Appeals after opportunity for policy review by the agency administrator.

The Federal Antitrust Board, consisting of a chairman and two economist administrators, would continue dual antitrust enforcement with the Department of Justice. The chairman would be responsible for all executive and administrative duties, and would articulate agency policy. The multimember Board would permit comprehensive micro- and macro-economic analysis by drawing upon the special expertise and perspectives of its members. Actions brought by the Board should be heard in the Federal district courts.

SECURITIES

A new Securities and Exchange Agency should supplant the SEC. Internal review of certain judicial proceedings presently commenced before hearing examiners should be limited to 30 days and directed principally to assuring that decisions correctly reflect agency policy. Appeals from agency decisions should be to the Administrative Court. Original actions taken by the SEC in the Federal district courts should continue as they do today. . . . Application of these structural changes would enable the agency to adapt readily to present and future needs of the securities industry and the investing public.

Regulatory responsibilities of the SEC under the Public Utility Holding Company Act of 1935 should be vested in the proposed power regulatory agency, since problems relating to the structure of public utility holding companies are properly within the competence of that agency. For many years, in fact, the SEC has drawn upon FPC expertise in administering the act. This proposal has long had substantial support from both the SEC and FPC.

N4

POWER

A new Federal Power Agency should replace the FPC. As with the proposed transportation and securities agencies . . . the power administrator would be able to respond more effectively than a multimember commission to the needs of the electric power and natural gas industries, their customers, and the public generally. Appeals from final agency decisions would be to the Administrative Court. As noted, the power agency should assume regulatory responsibilities under the Public Utility Holding Company Act.

COMMUNICATIONS

The FCC regulates, among other things, radio and television broadcasting, both important sources of public information. To an extent not present in other agencies, regulation in this area involves personal value judgments as to the type, quality, and substance of programming—the product of the industry which the FCC oversees. Clearly, the public has come to rely on the broadcast media for much of its information. The mere appearance of possible undue influence over program content might undermine public confidence in the sources of its information. Thus, we believe it would be inadvisable to place in the hands of a single administrator the power to exercise control over industry members through licensing and programming decisions.

Moreover, because broadcast regulation is uniquely subjective in character, we believe that decisions in this area should reflect the personal values of more than a single individual. This is especially important in view of the fact that even though the damage to society from control of information sources may be substantial, there is no satisfactory remedy for undoing the harm. Accordingly, it is imperative, in the first instance, to build in added safeguards for assuring an uncontrolled flow of ideas and information.

For these reasons . . . the FCC should be retained as a multimember commission. To offset some of the disadvantages of plural administration, the number of FCC commissioners should be reduced from seven to five, to serve 5-year terms.

CONCLUSION

Most deficiencies and problems of the regulatory agencies stem from an inapposite wedding of form and function. The present commissions combine the passive, judicial characteristics of a court with the active policymaking responsibilities of an administrator, to the detriment of both.

Substantial changes are advisable in the present structure of regulation by collegial bodies. The transportation, power, securities, and trade practices agencies are in need of the vigorous reform which a single administrator is most likely to bring about.

We have not recommended single administrators for all the regulatory agencies because organizational theory should give way when other factors bear greater weight. Although we emphasize organizational principles, we think exceptions should be made where, on balance, supervening considerations apply or greater effectiveness is likely by retaining collegial bodies. Hence, we believe that the overriding needs for a mixture of views in the communications area and for extensive economic judgment at the point of decision in the antitrust field justify plural-headed organizations in these areas.

There has been no attempt to catalog all the flaws of the regulatory structure nor to set forth solutions to all problems. But we have identified the major problems; and we have suggested a constructive plan for refashioning the regulatory structure so that the agencies can perform more effectively and at the same time more fairly.

We do see, moreover, that in our complex and growing society economic regulation must be consistent in its purpose, constructive in its policies, and objective in its decisions. Regulators have the difficult task of balancing the interests of industries and of the public to insure that the latter is well served and that the former remain vigorously able to provide that service. Such is the goal of the proposals we have made.

RECENT INITIATIVES ([46], pp. 6–16, 19–20)

The Ash Council recommendations of 1971 were presented just prior to the collapse of the Nixon administration and were obscured by the turmoil of Watergate. For all practical purposes, they were not subjected to any significant degree of public debate or examination. It is not because of its association with Nixon that the Ash Council proposal would have faced serious resistance from Congress. In stark political terms, the Ash Council proposed an Executive branch takeover of the regulatory agencies through control of the appointment process. What Ash proposed was the appointment of a single administrator to replace the collegial structure of most of the existing regulatory boards and commissions, which was marked by a more equalized sharing of responsibility. Ash recommended that a single administrator serving at the pleasure of the president head the regulatory body, as opposed to the administrative functions being shared by various commissioners. This would, in effect, weaken the semi-independent structure of regulatory body administration which the Congress has established over the years.

Currently, the regulatory bodies are headed by bipartisan commissioners, who serve staggered terms and are removable from office by the president only if there is cause. This structure insulates the regulatory agencies from precipitous action by the Executive branch. To undo that structure and tilt its control toward the Executive branch would be a profound change in the balance and exercise of power within the federal government. Such a shift would have been politically difficult even before Watergate and was out of the question once Congress began examining articles of impeachment. Included in those articles of impeachment was the charge against President Nixon of the abuse of Executive power. In the 93rd and 94th Congresses, attention was turned to a more traditional involvement in oversight and control of the regulatory bodies, and some progress was made in defining a continuing approach to regulating the regulators.

CONGRESS

...Interest in regulatory agencies, particularly the independent regulatory commissions, resurfaced during the 93rd Congress in both the executive and legislative branches. While those interested in regulatory policy espoused the cause of "reform," their definitions of reform and the motivations underlying their interest varied greatly. Viewed on a spectrum, at one end were those who believed that reform would follow only if the path of less regulation were followed. Economic "deregulation" became a major theme for a large number of economists. At the other end of the spectrum were those who believed that economic regulation by government is not only desirable, but should be intensified in certain fields to protect the consumer. The latter group generally seeks to make the independent regulatory commissions even more "independent" of the executive branch. The bulk of opinion, as might be expected, fell somewhere between these two extremes.

A number of bills proposing the establishment of a commission to study the role and operations of independent regulatory commissions were introduced in the House and Senate during the 93rd Congress. In addition, the President urged Congress on Oct. 8, 1974, to establish a national commission to examine Federal regulatory practices and their economic impact. With the impetus provided from the members themselves, certain interest groups, and the President, two Senate committees held hearings on the several bills after the 1974 congressional elections. The Government Operations Committee held hearings on S. 4145, S. 3604, S. 770, and S. 740 on Nov. 21, 22, 25, and 26, 1974. The Commerce Committee held hearings on S.J.Res. 253 on Nov. 12-21, 1974.

N5

The two principal bills were S. 4167, introduced by Senator Percy, and S. 4145, introduced by Senator Metcalf on behalf of the Administration. The distinctive characteristic of these bills was that both proposed the establishment of a commission composed of representatives from the executive and legislative branches, as well as the public, to study all aspects of the roles played by regulatory commissions. No action was forthcoming before the close of the 93rd Congress.

As the 94th Congress opened, it was apparent that the prevailing sentiment in both chambers was against attempting to establish a separate "Hoover-type" commission to study the regulatory agencies. Rather, the congressional and committee leaderships opted for hearings and studies conducted under congressional committee supervision with emphasis on proposing legislation as soon as possible.

The evaluation of Federal regulatory policies and the institutions responsible for implementing these policies has been the focus of a series of hearings and symposiums held by the Senate Committees on Commerce and Government Operations, and the House Oversight and Investigations Subcommittee. The committees have been authorized by their respective bodies under S.Res. 71 and House Rule 10 to undertake a thorough investigation of the basic structure, procedures, organization, and substance of Federal regulatory activities.

In May 1976 the Government Operations Committee held hearings on several related bills, notably S. 2812 and S. 3428, designed to provide regular review of all regulations in specified areas of the economy with an eye toward eliminating those regulations, programs, or agencies that are shown to be counter-productive. The two principal bills provide that the President must make recommendations on a scheduled

basis as to whether certain programs and the related agencies should be
continued or modified. These recommendations must be acted upon, either
affirmatively or negatively, by Congress. In a related action, the
Senate on May 19, 1976, passed a bill (S. 3308) that would require independent regulatory commissions involved in transportation to regularly submit to Congress proposals to revise and modify the laws and
regulations administered by that agency.

A number of bills passed or under consideration by Congress have an
impact on regulatory agencies even though they may not be specifically
considered as regulatory legislation. In this category is H.R. 11656,
"Government in the Sunshine Act." The House passed this bill on July
28, 1976, while the Senate had passed a similar bill (S. 5) in late
1975. This bill amends the Administrative Procedures Act (5 U.S.C.
552(b)) to require approximately 50 Federal agencies--almost all but
those located in Cabinet departments--to open their meetings to the
public. Exceptions to this rule were limited to ten specific matters.
The House bill also barred ex parte contacts between agency officials
and interested outsiders to discuss pending agency business.

The Oversight and Investigations Subcommittee of the House Interstate and Foreign Commerce Committee has been involved on a continuing
basis with regulatory issues. It has held hearings in late 1975 and
1976 on a variety of questions, e.g., "quality of regulators," with a
view towards making regulatory agencies more "independent" of Presidential direction.

Numerous committees and subcommittees have been interested in
particular aspects of economic regulatory policy. Especially active
in the regulatory area has been the Senate Judiciary Committee. The
Subcommittee on Administrative Practice and Procedure has reviewed
critically the policies and operations of the Civil Aeronautics Board,
Federal Energy Administration, and the Food and Drug Administration.
The Subcommittee, while not having jurisdiction over the substantive
fields, has circulated its studies and recommendations. A second subcommittee, Antitrust and Monopoly, held hearings on S. 2028, Competitive
Improvements Act, in late 1975. This bill would require regulatory
agencies to weigh the effect of their rules and orders on competition
and to issue "pro-competitive" rulings unless they would have an adverse
impact on the general public. After approval by the Judiciary Committee, the bill was referred to the Commerce Committee.

PRESIDENTIAL AND DEPARTMENTAL INITIATIVES

The President, perceiving the prospect that Congress would not establish a national commission to study regulatory agencies, announced on
Apr. 8, 1975, his intention to summon all commissioners of the major
regulatory commissions, plus selected key executive officials, to a
White House "summit meeting," The President met on June 25, 1975, with
24 members of Congress with major oversight responsibilities for regulatory agencies to discuss problems relating to economic regulation.
According to press reports, there was significant agreement between executive and legislative branch participants on the need for "reform,"
although there was little discussion of specific proposals.

The meeting of commissioners of 10 major independent regulatory
commissions took place in the White House on July 10, 1975. At this
2-hour meeting, the President called upon the commissioners to explore
ways and means to simplify the regulations they enforce as a step
towards increasing competition within and between industries.

N6

To assist the President in developing a strategy and set of programs to increase competition through less regulation, the President
announced on June 17, 1975, the establishment of a Domestic Council
Review Group for Regulatory Reform (DCRG). This group consists of approximately twelve key economists, lawyers, and legislative tacticians
from various Executive Office units and several departments. The number of participants varies depending on the issue under consideration.
The two co-chairmen are Edward Schmults, Deputy Counsel to the President, and Paul W. MacAvoy, member of the Council of Economic Advisors.

The DCRG has not followed a consistent pattern in developing the
various parts of what has been referred to as the "President's regulatory package." On some issues, agencies may take the lead while in
other areas a unit within the Executive Office, such as the Council on
Wage and Price Stability, will be the lead unit. The purposes of the
DCRG, broadly speaking, are to be a catalyst, coordinator, and monitor
of the various aspects of the executive branch's efforts to review all
N7   regulatory policies.

While the DCRG is not an agency of government and is somewhat amor-
phous as to membership, it does possess certain institutional characteristics. For example, the DCRG held public hearings, its first such
venture, on the Robinson-Patman Act in December 1975. The Antitrust
Division of the Department of Justice took the lead role in this exercise. Among the fields currently receiving the attention of the DCRG
are agriculture, insurance, and communications.

Thus far in the 94th Congress, the President has proposed changes in
regulatory statutes in five fields: railroads (enacted as P.L. 94-210),
repeal of fair trade enabling laws (enacted as P.L. 94-145), elimination
of fixed brokerage commissions (enacted as P.L. 94-29), entry and fare
structures of domestic airlines, and reorganization of motor carrier
rules and regulations. In each instance, enacted legislation has reflected major Congressional input.

The DCRG was the principal agent in developing a major bill (S. 3428)
submitted by the President to Congress on May 13, 1976. This bill,
titled "Agenda for Government Reform," would require the President to
develop legislative and administrative proposals over a 4-year period.
The regulatory agencies to be covered fall into four major sectors of
the economy with one sector, e.g., transportation and agriculture, being
reviewed each year. The President will submit recommendations to Congress, which in turn is required to act upon these proposals. The objective of these proposals will be to insure that programs and regulations are evaluated in a systemmatic manner. One important element of
this evaluation will be the publication of analyses as to the costs and
benefits accruing from various regulatory programs. The Senate Government Operations Committee held hearings on this bill and others in May
1976.

Departments and agencies within the executive branch having regulatory responsibilities are reviewing economic and social regulations not
only in terms of objectives, utility, need, and cost, but in terms of
the procedures for making regulations and amending the regulations once
in force.

As noted previously, the majority of agencies are regulative in
the broad sense of the term and most regulations have an economic
impact, however indirect. One of the most comprehensive changes in the
procedures for making regulations has occurred in the Department of

Health, Education and Welfare (DHEW). On July 25, 1976, Secretary
Mathews announced that henceforth any proposed regulation of "major
program significance" will be first brought to the public's attention
in the form of a Notice of Intention stating the problem and possible
options available. After comments are received, a draft regulation will
be published and public hearings held. Only after the inputs received
from the public are considered will a regulation be promulgated by the
Department....

REGULATORY COMMISSION INITIATIVES

   Partially in response to Congressional and Presidential pressures,
the independent regulatory commissions have studied their own policies
and procedures with the objective of increasing competition within their
industries and decreasing the complexities of their reporting and adjudicating procedures.

   The Federal Communications Commission, for example, submitted to
President Ford, on Jan. 15, 1976, an internal Task Force Report on
procedures utilized by the Commission in handling its case workload.
The Report contends that the FCC "has no real control over its workload," and that "delay is endemic to such a situation and procedural
changes are unlikely to have a palliative effect." The Report further
concluded that previous attempts by Congress to place time limits on
proceedings as a countermeasure to delay have mostly failed. Notwithstanding the relatively pessimistic tone of the Report, the Task Force
did make 10 recommendations as to ways to reduce the time necessary to
resolve cases. For instance, the Task Force recommended that the Commission allow the option of using written testimony in all cases in
substitution for oral testimony.

   In their April 1976 meeting with the President, the chairmen of the
commissions outlined their current efforts to improve the efficacy of
the regulatory process. Each commission has undergone some degree of
self-evaluation and in most instances policy and procedural changes have
resulted which were reported to the President. One agency, the Consumer
Products Safety Commission, even recommended its own abolition within 6
years. Speaking to the President, the then chairman, Richard Simpson,
stated: "We have put together a plan, a 6-year plan, and we have submitted it last September to OMB and the Congress and that plan predicts
the ability to abolish this agency, an agency only 3 years old, in 6
more years. It would abolish it because we believe our task is a finite
task, and we believe rational people would come to the conclusion consumer products no longer present a grave risk."

   The commissions have not been reticent to forward legislation on
their own to Congress. The Interstate Commerce Commission sent to
Congress on Aug. 20, 1975, a legislative proposal that would permit
the commission to experiment with regulatory changes. The commission
further requested authority to control the growth of conglomerate holding companies owning major segments of the surface transportation industry.

   For the most part, the trade associations of the industries currently functioning under regulations being reviewed have taken a non-
committal, if not negative, view towards Congressional, Administration,

and regulatory commission proposals. The principal argument offered by the associations is that proposed changes will "disrupt the essential stability" of the industry leading to unanticipated and deleterious consequences for the economy as a whole.

LEGISLATION INTRODUCED IN THE 94TH CONGRESS

H.R. 1951 (Moss)

Regulatory Commissions Independence Act. Proposes amendments to existing statutes which would (1) provide for concurrent submission of budget estimates by the independent regulatory commissions to the Congress and the President; (2) provide that whenever an independent regulatory commission submits any legislative recommendations, testimony, or comments on legislation to the President or the Office of Management and Budget, it shall concurrently transmit a copy to the Congress; and (3) provide that commissions shall have control over litigation independent of the Department of Justice. The bill was introduced in the House on Jan. 23, 1975, and was referred to the Committee on Government Operations.

H.R. 2277 (Heinz)

National Commission on Regulatory Reform Act of 1975. Provides for the establishment of a National Commission on Regulatory Reform to conduct a study of such regulatory activities of the independent regulatory agencies of the Federal Government as determined by the Commission to be primarily economic in nature and to have a significant effect on the segments of the economy involving transportation, communications, the development and distribution of energy resources, or financial institutions. The Commission would be composed of 14 members; six appointed by the President from the public, four appointed by the President from among the senior officers of the executive branch, two appointed by the President pro tempore of the Senate from among its Members, and two appointed by the Speaker of the House from among its Members. The Commission would have a professional staff. The Commission would submit its report with recommendations to the President and the Congress one year after its appointment. The bill was introduced in the House on Jan. 28, 1975, and was referred to the Committee on Interstate and Foreign Commerce.

H.R. 3468 (Moss)

Independent Regulatory Agencies Reform Act. Seeks at once to increase the independence of the agencies while increasing their accountability to Congress. Included in the changes proposed for the commissions are that Presidential appointments for chairmen would be made subject to the advice and consent of the Senate, that the right of the President to remove members would be limited to "neglect of duty," that civil actions could be brought by the commissions themselves and not require that the Justice Department represent the commissions, that appropriations requests be submitted simultaneously to the OMB and Congress, that information be made readily available to congressional committees, and that political clearance be prohibited in the regulatory agencies. The bill was introduced in the House on Feb. 20, 1975, and was referred to the Committee on Interstate and Foreign Commerce.

H.R. 3658 (Levitas)

Administrative Rulemaking Control Act. Establishes a procedure
whereby Congress may review certain rulemaking activities of executive
agencies, thereby exercising greater control and oversight of the operations of such agencies. Section 553 of title 5, U.S. Code, is amended
to provide procedures for interested parties to submit data, views, and
arguments on proposed rule changes. Such rule changes may take effect
only if published in the Federal Register and if, after a period of 30
calendar days of continuous session of Congress following the publishing date, neither House passes a resolution stating in substance that
the House does not favor the rule change. The bill was introduced in
the House on Feb. 25, 1975, and was referred to the Committees on the
Judiciary and Rules.

H.R. 9125 (Mikva)

Regulatory Agency Self-Destruct Act. To abolish as of July 4, 1976,
certain Federal regulatory agencies (most notably the "independent regulatory commissions") which "the President and the Congress determine
have inadequately promoted the public welfare, unnecessarily fostered
unwieldy and costly bureaucracies, unsuccessfully carried out the purposes for which they were established, and otherwise outlived their
usefulness"; and "to cause the self-destruct of those remaining agencies, their successors, or new regulatory agencies established after the
date of enactment of this Act, which are determined to have failed to
accomplish such purposes seven or fifteen years after July 4, 1976, depending on how long such agencies have been in existence." The President is empowered to submit a plan to Congress to provide successor
agencies for those scheduled to "self-destruct," which either chamber
may reject by passing a resolution of disapproval within thirty calendar days of continuous session of Congress. The bill was introduced in
the House on July 31, 1975, and was referred to the Committees on Government Operations and Rules.

H.R. 10507 (Howe)

Federal Regulatory Agency Review Act of 1975. Proposes to establish a Federal Regulatory Agency Review Commission to study the structures, policies, practices, regulations, and controlling statutes of
the regulatory agencies and make recommendations to the Congress. This
Commission would study all agencies that exercise regulatory functions
as one of their principal activities. Its objective will be to determine those areas which are overregulated or underregulated, overlapping
jurisdictions, conflicting statutory mandates, and the costs and benefits of regulation. The Commission shall be composed of six members:
two appointed by the President, two by the President pro tempore of the
Senate, and two by the Speaker of the House. A final report shall be
transmitted to each House not later than one year after the first meeting of the Commission. The bill was introduced on Oct. 31, 1975, and
was referred to the Committee on Interstate and Foreign Commerce.

H.R. 10836 (Mikva)

Regulatory Agency Appointment Reform Act. Alters the appointment
process by which commissioners of Federal regulatory agencies are selected. Would establish a bipartisan Federal Regulatory Agency Nominating

Board of 12 members which would recommend three names to the President to fill any vacancy. The President must select one of the three individuals recommended. There would be a prohibition against reappointments. The bill was introduced in the House on Nov. 19, 1975, and was referred jointly to the Committee on Interstate and Foreign Commerce, Public Works and Transportation, Agriculture, Banking, Currency and Housing, and Merchant Marine and Fisheries, and the Joint Committee on Atomic Energy.

H.R. 11094 (Archer)

Occupational Safety and Health Reform Act of 1975. This legislation recommends 21 specific changes to the Occupational Safety and Health Act of 1970 to correct deficiencies. Those aspects of the 1970 law that have an adverse economic impact because they force companies out of business or to cut back on employment are either amended or deleted. This legislation, in the view of the sponsors, represents a congressional reassertion over a field which through poor legislative drafting left an executive agency with a vague mandate and excessive discretion. The bill was introduced on Dec. 10, 1975, and was referred to the Committee on Education and Labor.

H.R. 11450 (Anderson and Jordan)

Regulatory Reform Act of 1976. Identical to S. 2812. This bill was introduced on Jan. 22, 1976, and referred to the House Committee on Government Operations and Committee on Rules.

S. 5 (Childs)

Government in the Sunshine Act. This bill would amend the Administrative Procedures Act (5 U.S.C. 500-559) by requiring that meetings of listed multi-member Federal boards and agencies be open to the public subject to exceptions similar to that found in the Freedom of Information Act (5 U.S.C. 552(b)). The bill passed the Senate on Nov. 6, 1975. H.R. 5075 (Fascall) was introduced in the House on Mar. 18, 1975, with provisions regarding open executive branch meetings and regulation of ex parte communications virtually identical to S. 5. Hearings were held before the Government Information and Individual Rights Subcommittee of the House Committee on Government Operations on Nov. 6 and 12, 1975, on this and companion bills (H.R. 9868 and H.R. 10315). On Mar. 2, 1976, the House Committee on Government Operations agreed, 32 to 7, to report (H.Rept. 94-880, Part I) a companion bill (H.R. 11656). At the direction of the Speaker, the measure was then referred to the Committee on the Judiciary which, by a voice vote, reported the bill with amendments on Apr. 6, 1976 (H.Rept. 94-880, Part II). The measure was given a ruling (H.Res. 1207; H.Rept. 94-1180) on May 19 and placed on the House Calendar. By a vote of 390 to 5, the House adopted H.R. 11656 on July 28 after agreeing to an amendment in the nature of a substitute incorporating all amendments recommended by the Committee on Government Operations and the Committee on the Judiciary. (For further information on this bill, see Issue Brief 74103, "Secrecy in Government.")

S. 363 (Metcalf, Percy)

Regulatory Commissions' Independence Act. Provides that seven designated independent regulatory commissions submit budget estimates and requests to the Congress and to the President or the Office of Management and Budget concurrently. Legislative recommendations, testimony or comments on legislation would be concurrently transmitted. Also places litigation under the authority of the commissions rather than the Justice Department. The bill was introduced in the Senate on Jan. 23, 1975, and was referred to the Committee on Government Operations.

S.Res. 71 (Glenn)

Authorizes expenditures of $750,000 for an 18-month joint study of Federal Government regulation by the Senate Committees on Commerce and Government Operations. The Commerce Committee would concentrate its resources on a comprehensive evaluation of transportation regulation. The Government Operations Committee would take a two-fold approach: a study of certain common organizational or management problems which are hindering the effectiveness of almost all regulatory agencies, and a study of the efficiency and economy of several different agencies and departments under the jurisdiction of various congressional committees that regulate a single area of the economy. Legislative proposals are expected to result from these studies. Where such proposals are not within the jurisdiction of the Committees conducting the study, they will be forwarded to the appropriate committees. The resolution was introduced in the Senate on Feb. 7, 1975, and was referred to the Committee on Rules and Administration. The Committee recommended that the expenses of the Committee on Government Operations not exceed $250,000, of which not over $166,700 may be expended for the procurement of the services of individual consultants or organizations thereof. The expenses of the Committee on Commerce under the amended resolution were not to exceed $216,700, of which amount not over $208,000 may be expended for the procurement of the services of individual consultants or organizations thereof. The joint report of these two committees is to be submitted not later than July 1, 1976. The resolution, as amended, passed the Senate on July 26, 1975.

S. 857 (Hart of Mich.)

Provides for increased independence of the independent regulatory commissions from executive branch influence. The bill also seeks to increase the accountability to the public of such commissions. The commissions would be required to submit budget estimates and legislative recommendations directly to Congress without clearance by the OMB. Each commission would be given authority to decide whether its own lawyers or the Department of Justice would represent the commission in civil litigation. The President's power to remove commissioners would be restricted to a finding of neglect of duty and malfeasance in office, and the Presidential appointments to chairmanships would be made subject to the advice and consent of the Senate. The bill was introduced in the Senate on Feb. 26, 1975, and was referred to the Committee on Government Operations.

S. 2290 (Taft)

Regulatory Agency Revision Act of 1975. To establish a Consumer Protection Study Commission for the sole purpose of making revised and updated recommendations relative to the desirability and feasibility of transferring the adjudicatory, licensing, and rulemaking functions of the regulatory agencies of newly created administrative law courts.

This study commission would be charged with restudying recommendations of the second Hoover Commission (1955) that adjudicatory functions of regulatory agencies be transferred to administrative courts. Further, this Commission would make recommendations with respect to maintaining within the agencies studied a prime responsibility for protecting the interests of consumers as they relate to the functions performed by such agencies and administrative courts. The Commission would submit its findings and recommendations to the President and the Congress not later than 6 months after the appointment and confirmation of all members of the Commission. The bill was introduced in the Senate on Sept. 4, 1975, and was referred to the Committee on Government Operations.

S. 2551 (Magnuson and Pearson)

Aviation Act of 1975. This bill, introduced on behalf of the Administration, provides for altering the regulations that determine the entry rights of airlines into new or additional routes. It further requires that the Civil Aeronautics Board (CAB) act within 180 days or any airline proposal with regard to rates goes into effect and cannot be challenged. Supplemental or charter air operations are encouraged in this legislation. The bill was introduced in the Senate on Oct. 22, 1975, and was referred to the Committee on Commerce. An identical bill, H.R. 10261, was introduced in the House by Representatives Jones, Harsha, and Anderson on Oct. 21, 1975, and was referred to the Committee on Public Works and Transportation.

S. 2677 (Biden)

Regulatory Agency Responsibility Act. The purpose of this bill is to abolish not later than Oct. 1, 1976, certain Federal regulatory agencies determined by the President and the Congress to have inadequately promoted the public welfare, unnecessarily fostered unwieldy and costly bureaucracies, unsuccessfully carried out the purpose for which they were established, and otherwise outlived their usefulness. The remaining agencies, their successors, or new regulatory agencies established after the date of enactment of this legislation, which are determined to have failed to accomplish such purposes, shall be terminated 7 or 15 years after Oct. 1, 1976. The bill was introduced on Nov. 11, 1975, and was referred to the Senate Committee on Government Operations.

P.L. 94-210 (S. 2718)

Railroad Revitalization and Regulatory Reform Act of 1976. The purpose of this legislation was to provide means to rehabilitate and maintain the physical facilities, improve the operations and structure, and restore the financial stability of the railway system of the United States. Included among the numerous provisions of the bill were structural and procedural changes for the Interstate Commerce Commission (ICC), increased responsibilities for the Secretary of Transportation over rail planning, reorganizations, mergers, and consolidations, the establishment of the Railroad Rehabilitation and Improvement Fund to finance loans to railroads, the establishment of the United States Railway Association (USRA), and implementation of the Northeast Corridor Project. The bill, as amended, passed the Senate Dec. 4, 1975, and the House, in lieu of H.R. 10979, on Dec. 17, 1975. The House and Senate agreed to a conference report on Jan. 28, 1976, and the President signed the bill Feb. 5, 1976.

S. 2792 (Fannin)

Regulatory Reform Act. This legislation requires that the House and
Senate approve every major regulation proposed by any agency. Such approval would require that the agency demonstrate that the economic benefits of a proposed rule exceed its anticipated costs to the public.
The bill would make employers and employees jointly responsible for
compliance to regulations. It would decrease paperwork, report-filing,
and record-keeping requirements, and penalize agencies for not taking
action in a timely manner. The bill was introduced on Dec. 16, 1975,
and was referred to the Senate Committee on the Judiciary.

S. 2812 (Percy and Byrd of W. Va.)

Regulatory Reform Act of 1976. The bill provides that over a period
of 5 years, from 1977 through 1981, the President would submit to the
Congress by March 30 of each year comprehensive plans for reforming
regulation in five specific areas of the economy: banking and finance;
energy and environmental matters; commerce, transportation and communications; food, health, and safety, and unfair and deceptive trade
practices; housing, labor-management relations, equal employment opportunity, Government procurement and small business. Each plan would
include recommendations for increasing competition, and for procedural,
organizational, and structural reforms--including the merger, modification, establishment or abolition of Federal regulations, functions and
agencies. The plans are referred to the respective congressional committees. An "action-forcing mechanism" is proposed whereby the abolition of agencies and regulations would occur unless a comprehensive
statute is enacted by a certain date. The bill was introduced on Dec.
18, 1975, and was referred to the Committee on Government Operations
and the Committee on Rules and Administration.

S. 2878 (Javits)

Congressional Office of Regulatory Policy Oversight Act of 1975. The
legislation has two titles: Title I would create an Office of Regulatory
Policy Oversight within the legislative branch somewhat analogous to the
Congressional Budget Office and the Office of Technology Assessment. It
would be run by a board of Congressmen and Senators with executive authority vested in a Director appointed by joint Congressional leadership. The Office would be responsive to all oversight committees. At
request of the appropriate Senate committee, the Office shall conduct
an independent investigation of any regulatory commission nominee.
Title II sets forth a procedure whereby every regulatory agency of the
government, when it proposes to promulgate a rule of general applicability pursuant to statutory authority that deals with economic regulation or licensing matters, would have such rule subjected to review,
and potential veto, by the Congress. The bill was introduced on Jan.
27, 1976, and was referred to the Senate Committee on Government
Operations.

S. 3308 (Pearson)

Interim Regulatory Reform Act of 1976. Requires certain Federal
regulatory agencies that have jurisdiction over transportation regulations to review their administrative authorities. The bill directs
each such agency to submit to Congress a proposed modernization, revision, and codification of the laws and other authorities administered

by it.   The Administrative Conference of the United States shall submit to Congress its comments on each proposal forwarded by the agencies.   Each agency shall have a law revision staff assisted by an
Advisory Committee on Law Revision.   The bill provides procedures
designed to make for more timely consideration of petitions.   The bill
further provides for amendments in each of the enabling acts for the
listed agencies intended to insure the members against conflict of
interests.   The bill was introduced on Apr. 13, 1976, and referred to
the Committee on Commerce.   The bill, as amended, passed the Senate on
May 19, 1976.

S. 3428 (Scott of Pa.)

Agenda for Government Reform.   Administration sponsored legislation
that would require the President to develop legislative and administrative proposals over a 4-year period.   The regulatory agencies to be
covered fall into four major sectors of the economy with one sector,
e.g., transportation and agriculture, being reviewed each year.   The
President will submit recommendations to Congress, which in turn is
required to act upon these proposals.   The objective of these proposals
will be to insure that programs and regulations are evaluated in a
systemmatic manner.   One important element of this evaluation will be
the publication of analyses as to the costs and benefits accruing from
various regulatory programs.   The bill was introduced on May 13, 1976,
and referred to the Committee on Government Operations.   Hearings were
held on May 19, 1976.

CHRONOLOGY OF EVENTS

This Congressional Research Service chronology was published in August 1976. In updating
the chronology, the following items should be noted.

1/20/77   Jimmy Carter inaugurated as 39th president of the United States and pledges to undertake a major reorganization of the Executive branch.

10/1/76   94th Congress adjourns without taking action on any of the several reorganization
proposals or without extending the president's authority to submit reorganization plans.

05/13/76 -- President forwarded to Congress a bill (S. 3428) to require
review of all economic regulatory agencies and programs
within 4-year period.

04/08/76 -- Second White House "summit meeting" of commissioners of 10
independent regulatory commissions and other key executive
officials to hear the chairmen of the commissions report to
the President on progress being made to improve efficacy of
regulatory process.

12/08/75 -- Domestic Council Review Group held 3 days of public hearings
on the Robinson-Patman Act (15 U.S.C. 13).

11/13/75 -- The President submitted to the Congress legislation to alter
the regulations governing the motor carrier industry.

11/06/75 -- The Subcommittee on Oversight and Investigations of the
House Committee on Interstate and Foreign Commerce held
hearings on problems of Federal regulation, concentrating
on the process of selection of regulators and confirmation
under recent Administrations.

10/29/75 -- The Senate Committee on Government Operations held hearings
on the problems of Federal regulation of the economy.

10/08/75 -- The President submitted to Congress legislation to alter the
organization and fare structures for domestic airlines.

10/01/75 -- Chairman Ribicoff of the Senate Committee on Government
Operations announced the appointment of an Advisory Panel
of authorities on regulatory problems and practices to
assist the Committee on Government Operations and Commerce
in their joint study.

09/20/75 -- The Interstate Commerce Commission forwarded to Congress
legislation that would permit the Commission to experiment
with regulatory changes. The Commission further requested
authority to control the growth of conglomerate holding
companies among major segments of the surface transportation
industry.

07/26/75 -- The Senate passed S.Res. 71, as amended, providing funds
for joint study of Federal regulatory agencies by the
Senate Committees on Commerce and Government Operations.

07/10/75 -- A White House "summit meeting" of commissioners of 10
independent regulatory commissions and other key executive
officials was held to discuss problems related to the impact on the economy of regulatory policies and practices.

06/25/75 -- The President met with 24 Members of Congress with oversight responsibilities to discuss problems relating to
economic regulation.

02/20/75 -- Rep. Moss introduced H.R. 3468, to further ensure the in-
dependence of the Federal Communications Commission, the
Federal Power Commission, the Federal Trade Commission, the
Interstate Commerce Commission, the Securities and Exchange
Commission, the Consumer Products Safety Commission, and
the Civil Aeronautics Board.

02/07/75 -- Sen. Glenn introduced S.Res. 71, requesting that $750,000
be authorized for an 18-month joint study of Federal Government regulation by the Senate's Committees on Commerce
and on Government Operations.

11/21/74 -- Hearings were commenced by the Senate Government Operations
Committee on the question of whether it is desirable to
establish a commission to study the independent regulatory
commissions.

01/30/71 -- The President's Advisory Council on Executive Organization
(Ash Council) submitted its report on independent regulatory
agencies to President Nixon.

12/21/60 -- James M. Landis submitted his Report on Regulatory Agencies
to President-Elect Kennedy.

02/05/49 -- The Commission on Organization of the Executive Branch of
the Government (First Hoover Commission) submitted its
report to President Truman.

01/00/37 -- The President's Committee on Administrative Management
            (Brownlow Committee) submitted its report to President
            Roosevelt.

NOTES AND REFERENCES

1. Two of the unpublished reports cited in this portion of the text were prepared by the 1964 and 1966 Task Forces on Government Organization ([11] and [12]). These task forces of the Kennedy and Johnson administrations were chaired by Don Price and Ben Heineman, respectively. They are included in the Lyndon B. Johnson presidential papers at the Lyndon B. Johnson Library in Austin, Texas.

2. The findings and recommendations of the Ash Council report on regulatory agencies are reprinted in this chapter. Another report, "The Powers and Responsibilities of the President," was prepared for the Ash Council and detailed the legislated powers of the president. It was published in 1970 by the Aspen Systems Corporation in Pittsburgh, Pennsylvania.

3. A listing of commonly used acronyms for government agencies appears in the appendix section of this volume.

4. The Public Utility Holding Act, passed in 1935, provides for regulation by the Securities and Exchange Commission of the purchase and sale of securities and assets by companies in electric and gas utility holding company systems. Proposals for reorganization, merger, or consolidation of such holding companies must meet the satisfaction of the SEC so that the objectives of the 1935 act are met.

5. These and other references to hearings are cited in the bibliography of public documents under the specific names of the congressional committees.

6. Reference is made in this document to the "president," who is President Ford.

7. No documents were released by the Domestic Council Review Group for Regulatory Reform (DCRG). However, several internal memoranda are available for copying under Freedom of Information Act procedures at the DCRG office, Executive Office Building, Washington, D.C.

Chapter 4
Performance of Regulatory Bodies: Problems and Perspectives

JOINT STUDY BY SENATE COMMERCE AND GOVERNMENT OPERATIONS COMMITTEES PURSUANT TO SENATE RESOLUTION 71 ([76], pp. 9–16)

Congressional hearings on regulatory reform have generated a substantial body of opinion on how and where reform should take place within the regulatory bodies. A Senate study of the subject to be made jointly by the Senate Commerce and Government Operations Committees was authorized in July 1975 by passage of Senate Resolution 71. (The official name of the Government Operations Committee was changed to the Governmental Affairs Committee in February 1977.) The study is described here by Richard Wegman, chief counsel and staff director of the Senate Committee on Government Operations. This joint study had not yet been published when the 94th Congress adjourned.

Transcripts of the Senate hearings held between November 1974 and May 1976 are found in documents [73], [75], [76], and [77]. House hearings on regulatory agencies, held between November 1975 and April 1976, are found in documents [36], [37], and [38], and the joint Senate-House hearings of November 1975 on regulatory reform are available in document [35]. While the Senate study was a joint effort of the Commerce and Government Operations Committees, the committee issuing the report is the Senate Government Operations Committee. The entire report of this study on federal regulation will be issued in 1977, in six parts under the following headings: The Regulatory Appointments Process; Congressional Oversight of Regulatory Agencies; Public Participation in the Regulatory Process; Undue Delay in Regulatory Administration; Regulatory Organization and Coordination; Framework for Regulation, and Case Studies in Federal Regulation. Such studies are generally available, for a time, through the Government Printing Office for $3 to $6 per volume. They contain summary material from the hearings, staff analyses, appended exhibits, and, at times, dissenting views of committee members.

The joint study on regulatory reform is authorized by Senate Resolution 71, which the Senate passed on July 26, 1975. The two committees have been allocated just under $500,000 for purposes of the study.

To our knowledge, this is the first time a comprehensive study of the Federal regulatory agencies has ever been undertaken by the Congress. Although there have been a number of studies of Government organizations and Federal regulations in the past, this study by two congressional committees is unique in that they will have the ability to convert study recommendation into legislative action where they decide it is appropriate and needed.

The mandate of Senate Resolution 71 is rather broad. Among other things, the resolution directs the two committees to make findings and recommendations with respect to:

The most serious deficiencies within the regulatory process which tend to contribute to inflation, lessen competition, or which adversely affect the public and regulated companies.

The extent to which certain areas of the national economy are over-regulated or under-regulated.

The economic costs and benefits of regulation.

The anticompetitive effects of regulation, and the degree of market concentration in regulated industries.

An evaluation of the purposes and objectives which regulation should now serve.

The consequences to the Nation of selective deregulation in specified areas.

Elimination, transfer, or separation out of the subsidy-granting or other forms of promotional activity performed by regulatory agencies.

Revising procedures for selecting commissioners and reviewing their qualifications.

Modifying agency rules to expedite regulatory agency proceedings as a means of facilitating more timely decisionmaking.

As one can see from this partial list, this study is neither proregulation nor antiregulation, neither probusiness nor antibusiness. Individuals and institutions representing all segments of the economy, and all elements of the political spectrum, have raised concerns about the present state of Federal regulation. The witnesses at this morning's hearing, who will speak of the difficulties they have encountered with the Federal regulatory agencies, range from consumer advocate Ralph Nader to the chairman of the board of one of the Nation's leading railroads.

Of course, different groups are concerned with different aspects of regulation. Consumers may be concerned with the imbalance of public interest advocacy, and with the close ties between the regulatory agency and the industry it regulates. Small businesses may be concerned with the inordinate paperwork burden, and with the variety of regulations which affect them. Independent businesses may be concerned with barriers to entry created by a regulatory agency, and with the negative attitude toward technological innovation. Large, regulated corporations and utilities may chafe at the regulatory lag in approving rate-increase requests, and at regulatory indecision in general. The joint study will examine these concerns and many others, and will seek ways to make the regulatory process more responsive, more decisive, more accessible, and swifter.

At the outset, the Senate Resolution 71 study has been tentatively divided into seven working segments. They are:

(1) Eliminating undue delay in the regulatory process.

(2) Eliminating or modifying inconsistent or overlapping regulatory functions.

(3) Increasing public participation in the regulatory process.

(4) Insuring agency independence from (a) undue political pressures and (b) influence by the regulated industry.

(5) Upgrading the quality of regulators.

(6) Improving and increasing congressional oversight.

(7) Determining the extent to which regulation is appropriate or necessary.

ADMINISTRATIVE DELAY

Examples of enormous delay in the regulatory process are legion. Delay has probably been talked about and written about more than just about any other problem in the regulatory field. It is not at all difficult to find cases when the administrative process has dragged on for years and years, exhausting both the funds and the patience of all parties concerned, and in the end yielding a result that is satisfying to no one.

For example: For over 34 years, the Federal Communications Commission has been unable to resolve a dispute between radio stations KOB in Albuquerque and WABC in New York, which arose because the agency placed the two stations on the same frequency. Since 1941 when an international agreement required the FCC to assign a new frequency to KOB the FCC has been unable to figure out how to restrict the broadcast frequency of one of the stations to eliminate interference. Since 1969 the FCC has had a proposed rulemaking pending on this issue. Meanwhile, the delay has caused a paperwork nightmare at the FCC, cost the respective companies a fortune in legal fees, and left listeners of either station with interference from the other.

On July 2, 1959, the Food and Drug Administration proposed new rules setting the percentage of peanuts that should go into peanut butter. After originally proposing a higher figure, the FDA said it should be 90 percent; the Peanut Butter Maufacturer's Association thought it should be only 87 percent. On the opening day of the hearing before the FDA, the first Government witness presented a survey of cookbooks, patent applications, and general testimony concerning the historical composition of peanut butter. On cross-examination, the witness was questioned about his personal tastes in peanut butter, omissions in his list of patent applications, and about a number of cookbook formulations of peanut butter that he had failed to refer to in his direct testimony.

This kind of attention to unimportant detail set the pattern for the FDA's hearings: 6½ years and 7,736 pages of testimony later, the lawyers finally rested their case. Still, it took the FDA another 2 years and 3 months—until July 24, 1968—to issue its final order in the case. Then the case was appealed to the Third Circuit Court of Appeals. On May 14, 1970, the third circuit finally disposed of the case by affirming the FDA's regulation. Thus, it took nearly 11 years, and millions of dollars in staff time and legal fees, to decide by what amount peanut butter manufacturers should be required to increase the composition of peanuts in peanut butter. The answer was: 3 percent.

Several of the witnesses at this morning's hearings will describe in detail their experiences before Federal regulatory agencies, and the enormous wastes of time and money that were incurred as a result of administrative delay.

What causes administrative delay of this magnitude, what costs does it impose, and what can be done to prevent it? It has been suggested that regulatory agencies have become over-judicialized, that they tend to act on a case-by-case basis rather than utilizing generic rulemaking. It is also suggested that the fear of judicial review and reversal is so pervasive that agencies tend to amass mammoth records and to dot every "i" and cross every "t" in an effort to insure that the agency action will not be reversed.

Many suggestions have been offered for dealing with the problem of undue delay—ranging from the Ash Council's proposal that a new administrative court of appeals be established and that review at the Commission level be sharply curtailed, through procedural reforms which would require written instead of oral testimony, limit the time or the scope of discovery, limit the number or types of intervenors, and increase the discretionary powers of administrative law judges to broader reforms which would impose far greater rulemaking responsibilities on the agencies and discourage the use of case-by-case adjudication as a policymaking tool. The joint study will explore these proposals, and seek to find ways to speed up the process without depriving interested parties of an opportunity to be heard and to participate fully in the process.

OVERLAP

As the Federal regulatory scheme has developed since the establishment of the Interstate Commerce Commission in 1887, numerous instances of overlap, duplication, or inconsistent regulation have come to exist. The transportation regulatory agencies are a case in point, as the Ash Council noted. For example, if a manufacturer of television tubes in Chicago wants to send his wares to Zurich, Switzerland, he has to be concerned with a regulatory patchwork covering three different modes: The first part of the trip by truck is regulated by the ICC under the Motor Carrier Act of 1935; the second portion of the trip, by rail, is also regulated by the ICC, under the Interstate Commerce Act of 1887; and the final leg—before reaching Europe—of the journey is on an oceangoing vessel, regulated by the FMC under the Shipping Act of 1916.

The problem is not limited to transportation. Consider, for example, the maker of a pesticide. Before he can sell it, it must be registered with the Environmental Protection Agency (EPA). If it is bought by a homeowner, it has to conform to the requirements of the Consumer Product Safety Commission (CPSC). And, if the maid in the home uses it, it has to satisfy the requirements of the Occupational Safety and Health Administration (OSHA).

Nor are these problems limited to the Federal level. In many instances, Federal regulations overlap or are inconsistent with regulations imposed by State regulatory agencies, and a business attempting to comply with both may be caught in the middle. At a minimum, better coordination between Federal and State regulatory agencies seems desirable. Possibly, the joint study may develop an organizational mechanism to avert problems of this nature before they occur.

PUBLIC PARTICIPATION

Testimony before both Houses of Congress over the past several years have attested to the imbalance of the advocacy before the Federal regulatory agencies—testimony by Robert Pitofsky estimating that business advocacy outweighs consumer advocacy by a ratio of 100 to 1—before the House Government Operations Committee, March 1973; testimony by Anthony Roisman that public utilities budget 5 to 10 times as much as consumers in presenting their case for a Federal license—before the Senate Government Operations Committee, March 1974; statement by Carol Foreman of the Consumer Federation of America that consumer groups are outspent 50 to 1 by trade association organizations.

One response by these two committees and by the full Senate this year has been legislation to create an Agency for Consumer Advocacy, which would be empowered to represent the consumer's interests, with full party rights where appropriate, before the Federal regulatory agencies and other Federal decisionmakers. That legislation is now pending before the House, and action is expected shortly.

But the ACA addresses only part of the problem. Roisman's testimony, for example, suggests that there may be a case for providing direct public assistance to public interest intervenors—possibly in the form of assisting with research, providing reports on request, or even reimbursement for witness costs and attorneys fees. Congress is already beginning to respond to this need. The Magnuson-Moss Act passed by Congress last year, provides up to $500,000 per year for funding public interest advocates in FTC rulemaking proceedings. A similar provision was adopted by the Senate last year as part of the Energy Reorganization Act of 1974—the legislation that abolished the Atomic Energy Commission and established the Energy Research and Development Administration (ERDA) and the Nuclear Regulatory Commission (NRC). However, the provision was dropped in conference, in favor of conference report language urging the NRC to decide this question for itself at the administrative level. We understand that Senator Kennedy is now working on a comprehensive bill which would provide reimbursement, under certain conditions, for costs of public participation before any Federal regulatory agency.

The addition, the Senate Resolution 71 study will review questions of standing and access to determine whether agency procedures permit the fullest possible public participation.

AGENCY INDEPENDENCE

Questions under this segment of the study fall into two categories: How can the regulatory agency be better insulated from the industry it is charged with regulating? And to what extent should the agency be insulated from political pressures?

The need to better insulate the agency from close ties with the regulated industry is illustrated by the case of the DC–10—a case which Senator Cannon's Aviation Subcommittee has thoroughly investigated. In June 1972 an American Airlines DC–10 flying from Detroit to Buffalo, suddenly went out of control. The rear cargo door had blown off the plane in midflight, which caused the plane to depressurize, which caused the rear floor to buckle, and which in turn caused the pilot to lose control of the aircraft. Fortunately, the pilot succeeded in guiding the plane down safely and the 67 people on board survived.

An investigation immediately thereafter by the Federal Aviation Administration determined that a locking mechanism on the rear cargo door was at fault. Thereupon, the Western Regional Office of the FAA prepared an airworthiness directive (AD) requiring that the plane be repaired. An AD carries the force of law, and requires that the modification be made by a set date.

However, before the AD went out, the president of McDonnell Douglas, the plane's manufacturer, talked with John Shaffer, then head of the FAA. He persuaded Shaffer that an AD—which is considered a black mark against the plane—should not go out. He asked that a simple service bulletin be issued. Service bulletins do not require that the modification be made; they simply alert the aircraft manufacturer and the airlines that the problem exists, and it sets no time limit for the modification to be carried out.

As of March 1974, the modification of the DC–10's cargo door had been made on almost all of the DC–10's then in service—but, unfortunately, not all of them. Two of the planes had not been modified. One was owned by Laker Airways of Britain, the other by Turkish Airlines. On March 3, 1974, the Turkish Airlines DC–10 took off from

Paris heading to London. Nine minutes after takeoff the rear cargo door of the DC–10 blew off the plane. Again the plane depressurized, again the rear floor buckled, and this time the control cables were severed completely. The pilot was helpless, the plane went completely out of control, and crashed in a field outside of Paris. There were 346 people on board. No one survived the crash.

This case is perhaps an extreme example, but it suggests the types of problems that may arise when a too-close relationship exists between top regulatory officials and the industry under its jurisdiction.

Another example, in a lighter vein, is the yak fat case at the Interstate Commerce Commission. In March 1965, a trucker named Leroy Hilt, who owns Hilt Trucking, Inc., was upset by what he viewed as the ICC's favoritism toward the railroads. On a number of occasions, he had his own tariffs rejected by the ICC because his rates were too low, and would take business away from the railroads. To see how far the ICC would go in protecting the railroads, Hilt concocted a phony tariff—a tariff for a nonexistent commodity—yak fat. Hilt had once seen a yak at the local zoo. The tariff he prepared read as follows:

Yak Fat, Omaha to Chicago—45 cents per 100 pounds—Effective April 11, 1965.

The tariff went on to specify that the yak fat was to be shipped in minimum quantities of 80,000 pounds per shipment. The trucker indicated that he would accept shipments in glass or metal containers, boxes, barrels, pails, or tubs.

Hilt then sent his seven-page tariff off to Washington, D.C., and waited to see what would happen. And the predictable happened. A group of the Nation's leading railroads, upset by the noncompensatory rate, immediately formed a yak fat arguing committee. The railroads pointed out to the ICC that the minimum it should cost to ship yak fat from Omaha to Chicago was 63 cents, and that the tariff was, therefore, 18 cents below cost. The ICC agreed, and on April 7, 1965, it suspended Hilt's rate. It offered Hilt 30 days to come in and argue on behalf of the rate, and when Hilt declined the offer, the ICC ruled that Hilt had failed to sustain his rate, and it was, therefore, rejected.

These cases also argue forcefully for the establishment of an Agency for Consumer Advocacy. Beyond this, other suggestions for dealing with the problem range from Senator Hart's S. 857 now pending before this committee, which proposes that a majority of commissioners shall not have been employed by the industry regulated by the Commission prior to their appointment, to Senator Proxmire's proposal which would sharply limit the ability of Commissioner and staff to go to work for the regulated industry upon leaving the regulatory agency. At a minimum, there is certainly a need to look at existing conflict-of-interest statutes, and at provisions which govern ex parte contacts with members of an agency.

On the question of agency independence from the executive branch, there is some difference of opinion. Senator Metcalf's bill before this committee, S. 363, proposes that agency budgets and legislative recommendations be submitted directly to Congress at the same time they are submitted to the Office of Management and Budget, as a means for securing greater independence from the executive branch. It would also empower agencies to conduct their own litigation. On the other hand, the Ash Council recommended that agencies be headed by single administrators, serving at the pleasure of the President, in order to make them more accountable to the executive branch.

There seems to be a general agreement, however, that regulation of an industry should not be handled by the same individuals who are responsible for promotion of the industry. Last year Congress enacted the Energy Reorganization Act, which split the promotional responsibilities of the old Atomic Energy Commission off from its regulatory responsibilities, and vested them in entirely separate bodies. This approach may be worth considering elsewhere.

QUALITY OF REGULATORS

A team of researchers at the Georgetown University Law Center has been studying the quality of regulatory appointments to the FTC and FCC since World War II. The study analyzed regulatory appointments and we understand they came up with some striking conclusions:

The current appointment process has consistently failed to provide the commissions with able, energetic, and forceful leadership.

Except for minimal statutory requirements, the appointment process operates without any announced standards or qualifications for appointments.

The appointment process operates without consistency. For example, FBI checks on prospective appointees sometimes have been delayed until after the nominee has been announced to the public.

The public is never informed who is under consideration for an appointment before it is made, or what criteria governed a particular nomination. However, the regulated industry is actively consulted by the White House before a nomination is announced.

Most regulators are not picked as a result of a systematic search for talent, nor are they appointed on the basis of special qualifications or ability.

Partisan consideration dominates the selection of regulators to an alarming extent, even on occasions where the law requires a partisan balance.

The Ash Council, in recommending that administrators replace collegial bodies at the heads of regulatory agencies, cited the need to upgrade the quality of regulatory appointments. The council believed that a President would find it easier to attract first-rate people if the job was that of a single administrator rather than as a commissioner on a multimember commission. Senate Resolution 71 will certainly explore this issue.

CONGRESSIONAL OVERSIGHT

Almost everyone agrees on the need to improve the quality and extent of congressional oversight. Much of this lies in the hands of the committees themselves, and no legislation is necessary. Several proposals, however, have been offered to make the process easier. Senator Metcalf's S. 363, which is mentioned earlier, would give Congress easier access to agency budgets and legislative recommendation, and might make it easier to go to bat for increased agency funding. Senator Hart's S. 857 would require regulatory agencies to submit annual regulatory activity reports to Congress, and planning reports every fourth fiscal year. Senator Brock has introduced a bill, S. 2258, which would require that each regulation promulgated by a regulatory agency lay over for 60 days during which period Congress would have an opportunity to consider and reject such regulation. Only after the expiration of such a period would the regulation take effect. Senate Resolution 71 will consider these and other means of insuring better congressional oversight.

As part of this segment of the study, the question should be asked: Do agencies have their priorities straight? Problems of excessive agency attention to trivial details, imposition of enormous paperwork burdens, a tendency to focus on violations by small businesses and to ignore transgressions by the corporate giants—all of these bear looking into. The yak fat and peanut butter cases mentioned earlier suggest that in those cases at least, agency priorities could use reordering.

On a broader basis, Senator Brock has proposed a cost and benefit assessment as a means of keeping agency priorities in order. A requirements that each regulatory agency undertake such an assessment whenever regulations are issued has been made a part of S. 200, which passed the Senate earlier this year.

REGULATION VERSUS DEREGULATION

This aspect of the Senate Resolution 71 study may be the most significant of all, since it raises questions relating to the basis of regulation in the first place.

The joint study will make an effort to identify fundamental criteria for justifying regulation. Does a natural monopoly exist? Is the existing regulatory scheme required in order to assure service to small communities? If Congress decides to deregulate, what would replace regulation? Increased antitrust enforcement? State regulation? Subsidies? Nothing? Does regulation of one particular mode—for example, railroads—justify regulation of a competing mode—for example, motor carriers?

This segment of the Senate Resolution 71 joint study will attempt to answer some of these questions, and perhaps suggest alternatives. It may be useful to focus on three or four case studies, and assess competing industries.

Finally, in considering these questions, it is essential to distinguish between economic regulation and health and safety regulation. This is a distinction which has been blurred somewhat in a number of the recent calls for regulatory reform, and very different considertions often apply. The answer may well be deregulation when one considers the effect of ICC rules which require interstate motor carriers to travel empty on return trips. But few would suggest that the Government should have nothing to say about whether a nuclear reactor is safe before it issues a license for construction, or that the Food and Drug Administration should not have the authority to seize cans of soup suspected of containing botulism.

We have tried to indicate by examples the scope of the problems which the committee has decided to study. Obviously for each illustration there are 100 others. These serious concerns about the Federal regulatory process, as expressed by so many Members of the Senate, are what this study will seek to address.

OVERREGULATION AND DELAY: TWO CASE STUDIES ([76], pp. 38–49)

Laker Airways

The Senate Government Operations Committee held hearings on regulatory reform from 1974 to 1976. In the course of those hearings, the committee heard many complaints as to the inadequacies of regulatory agencies. Small businesses objected to the paperwork burdens, the number of offices with which they had to deal, and the variety of regulations to which they had to adhere. Larger enterprises complained the most about delays in getting licenses or permissions, especially those industries subject to explicit regulation, or the so-called regulated industries, such as broadcasting and transportation. Representatives from businesses, both large and small, joined with consumer advocates in agreeing that indecision and delay were costly to all concerned.

The Laker Airways and Rock Island Railroad "horror stories," reprinted here, are often cited as examples by advocates of reform. These two case studies illustrate the failures of regulatory agencies: failure as to delay and failure to protect the public interest. Some regulatory agency officials may view them as extreme cases and unrepresentative. Their inclusion here is not intended to suggest that this is how the agencies normally operate, but rather to provide examples of their deficiencies. The subject of the first case study is Laker Airways. Robert Beckman, an attorney, testified before the Senate Committee in late 1975. He represented Laker Airways, a British aviation firm seeking approval from the Civil Aeronautics Board for the operation of a transatlantic shuttle or air bus. What Laker proposed was to offer substantially reduced fares to passengers, who presented themselves on a first-come, first-served basis, for a "no frills" flight to London. Laker claimed it could offer fares as low as $135 on that basis; this amount was less than half that charged by most other carriers.

...Mr. BECKMAN. Mr. Chairman, it is an honor to appear before this respected committee, now in its second half-century of distinguished service to the Nation. The task the committee has undertaken is formidable: an examination in depth of the functioning of the Federal regulatory agencies to determine if they are carrying out the purposes set for them by Congress and, even more formidable, to devise corrective action where appropriate.

My point of view is the aviation industry and the regulation of air transportation by the Civil Aeronautics Board. I am a practitioner representing airlines and also communities throughout the country who seek better air transportation service of persons, cargo, and mail.

I can say, without overtsatement, that we are in bad shape. I do not mean we have a bad air transportation system. We have a very good one. Our domestic air transportation system is the best air transportation system to be found on any continent in the world. Our international air transportation system offers a variety of convenient air services. We have every reason to be proud; but not to be satisfied.

There are many disquieted observers of the Civil Aeronautics Board:

Congress set forth in the Federal Aviation Act that people and goods were to fly at the lowest possible rates—fares have escalated, there is a hostility toward innovative low-fare proposals.

Congress set forth in the Federal Aviation Act that there should be competition in the air transport industry.

The Civil Aeronautics Board has a negative attitude toward new entrants. Worse, the Board has actively encouraged and approved agreements between existing carriers limiting and allocating market shares between them.

The CAB just approved another capacity limitation agreement for New York-London services this winter. You can rest assured, Mr. Chairman, that Pan American, TWA, and British Airways will continue to serve you when it suits their convenience and at the highest possible prices.

Congress set forth in the Federal Aviation Act that five Board members, appointed by the President and confirmed by the Senate, should decide all significant matters and hold evidentiary hearings in licensing and fare cases.

The Board's staff makes most decisions and holds the hearing process hostage through its control of what matters will be set for hearing.

Most important of all, the Congress sets forth in the Federal Aviation Act that the interest of the public and the convenience and needs of the public were to be the sole criterion, the sole objective, indeed the only reason for the regulatory activities of the Civil Aeronautics Board.

The Board has devoted itself to the interests of the air carriers. Assuring a rate of return on investment of 12-percent to 16-percent a year has become the CAB's overriding concern and guide. Let me illustrate what I mean.

If a carrier wants to provide a new service, or a community wants better service, an application is filed with the Board.

The law says that the application shall be set for public hearing and promptly decided. If it worked that way, there would be public accountability and decisions would have to be rationally explained in terms of the public interest.

But it doesn't work that way.

The staff of the CAB, the institutional staff, decides whether the application should be set for hearing or not.

The euphemism for denying an application is determining priority of hearing. It is never heard at all.

What criteria, what standards does the staff use in determining what ideas should see the light of the hearing room?

Nobody knows. Who actually decides? Nobody knows. There is no public accountability. How many applications are heard? Very, very few.

It has even happened, Mr. Chairman, that the staff of the CAB has refused to set an application for hearing because they thought, wrongly, that one of their clients, an established airline, might not like it.

I represent Tampa, Fla. A new carrier wanted to provide a badly needed cargo service between Tampa and Honduras to serve the tobacco and fresh fish industries. There is no direct air service at all between Tampa and Honduras.

We could not get a hearing. I went to the CAB staff official who was sitting on the application and asked him, why? He told me that this service was contrary to Pan American's interest.

Now, Pan American does not serve between Tampa and Honduras and has no interest in this route whatsoever. I had to call Pan American and have them tell the CAB staff official that Pan American didn't care. After I did that, we got our hearing and our service.

Let me tell you about an innovative new fare proposal for New York-London service. A British independent carrier, named Laker Airways, in 1971 came up with the idea which had never been tried in international aviation: a scheduled jet no-reservation service between New York and London for a fare of $135 each way. This is not a no-reservation service like the Eastern shuttle which guarantees you a seat. This was an entirely new idea of selling tickets only at the airport for one flight a day. You had to get in line and buy a ticket on the day of the flight, like you do to get on a train. When the flight is sold out, you have to line up again the next day. There are no reservations.

The service was called skytrain and it had other innovative features. Freddie Laker, the owner of Laker Airways, thought there was a market for just air transportation with none of the frills you get included in your high-priced ticket on Pan American, TWA and the other IATA airlines. For $135 you get just air transportation on Laker's skytrain. You get your seat on a modern McDonnell-Douglas DC–10 jet, but nothing more unless you want it.

If you want to bring your own food in a brown paper bag, you could. If you want to buy a meal on the plane, he would sell it to you, just like on a train. If you want to see a movie, you pay for it; if you want a cocktail, you pay for it; if you want stereo, you pay for it.

Unlike Pan American and TWA, with language lessons, hotel reservations, rental car reservations, and on and on, which you pay for in the price of your ticket whether you want them or not, Laker offered good, reliable, comfortable air transportation at a low price because he is an efficient operator and had none of the costs of a reservation system and the other frills.

What happened? As a British carrier, he was designated by the United Kingdom under the International Air Service Agreement between the United States and the United Kingdom. By virtue of this agreement, the United States was bound to issue Laker authority to operate the service without undue delay. He already had authority from the British.

The frustration of Laker's authorization by staff officials of the State Department and the Civil Aeronautics Board is a classic case of denying the public the kind of air service Congress wanted but which the staff, blindly devoted to Pan American, a disease which Mr. Laker calls Panamania, effectively blocked.

I might tell you that neither Pan American nor any other American carrier wanted to provide a similar service. The first line of defense was the aviation division of the State Department. These people have a totally irreversible and terminal case of "Panamania." I never heard any of them even mutter the term "public interest."

The British gave notice of their intention to designate Laker in December 1972. The idea was to have the service in operation for the summer season 1973. I assure that that in the normal course, under the procedures set forth in the law, the service could have been operational by that time.

The battle plan was delay. If the hearing could be held up long enough, circumstances could change. There could be a new government in England, anything could happen. And the awful horror of a low fare service enabling some people of limited means to visit America or Americans who could not afford to pay Pan American's prices of $600 to $700 per person round trip, might actually fly to Europe.

Step No. 1 was to request consultations with the British. This chewed up 2 months. The "consultation" was a farce. All the U.S. staffers did was ask questions on what skytrain was, which they already knew.

The consultation gambit ran out and the British sent Laker's application to the State Department for onward transmission to the CAB. This is essentially a protocol exercise and normally takes a few days.

Bless the Aviation Division of the State Department. They sat on the application for most of the spring of 1973. They just did not transmit the application. They needed clarification from the British.

Finally, that gambit ran out, so the State Department handed the ball to the staff on the CAB. They were equal to the task.

They succeeded in holding up a hearing until December 1973. A whole year until we could get a hearing.

What an achievement for America. They had succeeded in keeping this awful low fare service out of the market in 1973 and had a good start on keeping it out in 1974.

Further procedures by the administrative law judge—who I might tell you would not play the delay game and promptly issued a decision recommending issuance of a permit to Laker—and the Board in hearing oral argument on appeals from the administrative law judge's decision, chewed up the spring of 1974.

Back to the State Department's Aviation Division which now had the ball as adviser to the President. They needed to know if the Labour Government which had taken over in the spring of 1974 from the conservatives in England, still supported skytrain. The British Government said "Yes." The State Department said, "Do you mean 'yes'?" The British said "yes; we mean yes." These are notes going back and forth for weeks at a time. The State Department said, "Cross your heart?" The British said, "Cross our heart."

This lovely game went on all last winter and, can you believe it, until the summer of 1975. Finally, the Lord be praised, the Labour Government said that initiation of skytrain should be deferred until 1976, but he did not withdraw Laker's request. The CAB said to the White House, "Quick, send our decision back to us." You see, President Ford has shown too much interest in lower air fares and competitive air service for the CAB to trust the White House with the skytrain decision. They might approve it.

After a while, those opposed to skytrain prevailed, and the case went to the CAB to moulder.

If I sound bitter, you should hear Mr. Laker. He has lost over $15 million getting ready to operate skytrain.

This is an interesting but not unique case. It shows what are, in my judgment, the basic problems which face this committee in its formidable task.

First, those parts of the process which worked reasonably well were the parts in the Federal Aviation Act. The hearing itself, the judge's decision, and the Board members decision took only a few months.

The rest of the time was taken up with delaying tactics by staff officials in the State Department and at the CAB. They exercised their stranglehold control over the hearing process behind the scenes. This was not what Congress intended.

The first real problems this committee must come to grips with, in my submission, are the secret actions by faceless but all-powerful staff officials who can and frequently do frustrate the congressionally mandated objectives of our laws.

We have not had a thorough legislative oversight hearing of the type this committee plans for almost 20 years. I respectfully submit that one is long overdue and I thank this committee for undertaking the difficult and important task.

In my judgment, the CAB has stultified competition, allowed service deterioration, and encouraged cartelization with high fares. The CAB is the arm of the Congress. If your investigation confirms what I have told you, I am confident that appropriate legislation will be forthcoming to put the CAB back in the public interest business.

Chairman RIBICOFF. Thank you very much, sir. Let me ask you: What would be the savings to a person flying round trip to Europe on Laker Airways skytrain as opposed to current services?

Mr. BECKMAN. He would save between $300 and $400, depending on what fare he was able to take on the IATA carriers.

Chairman RIBICOFF. Are you aware of any organized effort by the major domestic carriers to prevent Laker from getting its transatlantic route?

Mr. BECKMAN. Oh, yes, sir. This was all very clear. In fact, they actually made an agreement, and we brought suit under the antitrust laws and under the pressure of that complaint they withdrew the agreement.

I could document that. It has been documented fully.

Chairman RIBICOFF. Do you think the CAB and State Department were in cahoots to stall and frustrate Laker's application?

Mr. BECKMAN. Yes, sir, no doubt about it.

Chairman RIBICOFF. When you say, "no doubt about it," how do you know that?

Mr. BECKMAN. That is one of the most interesting questions of the day, Mr. Chairman. As Mr. Nader said, and as you have heard me definitely support his view, public accountability, public information to find out what is going on is one of the most important aspects of sound government. How do you find out what is going on? Well, you have spies. You do your best. You trade information. How one finds out is very difficult, but very important. Obviously, one of Mr. Nader's suggestions and one I expect to lay before the committee as part of its task is to devise ways to make it simpler for us all to know what is going on.

Chairman RIBICOFF. I would gather from your testimony that you feel very strongly that the CAB and its staff really represent the airline industry and not the public which it is supposed to represent?

Mr. BECKMAN. That is correct. There is no question about that.

Chairman RIBICOFF. What kinds of reform would you suggest to insure that an agency like CAB actually represents the public?

Mr. BECKMAN. That, of course, is a marvelous question, Senator. In truth, reform is unnecessary because the statute that this Congress passed in 1938 and retained virtually unchanged in the reenactment of the Federal Aviation in 1958 is an excellent, indeed, brilliant piece of legislation. That statute said that there shall be hearings, public hearings, on all applications. And the CAB was directed to dispose of all applications as speedily as possible. The CAB does not set matters for hearing. It controls and limits what new ideas will see the light of day in a hearing room by not following the law as written.

The law has a most unusual feature in transportation regulation. In addition to rights conferred by a certificate of public convenience and necessity, there are responsibilities. A carrier is required to perform the service set forth in a certificate and more. Congress says there must be adequate service, equipment, and facilities. The CAB has written those provisions out of the act 15 years ago. They have never held an adequacy of service case since before 1960. This statute says there must be competition. The CAB is encouraging capacity limitation agreements. The statute says there must be the lowest possible fares. The CAB and its staff have been a bulwark for high fares. We do not really need reform because the 1938 statute was a marvelous reform. What we do need is for the Congress to assure itself that its arm, its extension, its servants, the Civil Aeronautics Board, carry out the law as written and intended by the Congress.

Chairman RIBICOFF. Let me ask you, is Laker through? Has it been destroyed by these delaying tactics?

Mr. BECKMAN. No, sir. The British license is valid. The designation is still before the United States and the British Governments, as far as I know, is still actively requesting the United States to comply with the U.S. solemn agreement to honor the designation and grant the license.

Chairman RIBICOFF. What remains to be done by CAB, one way or the other?

Mr. BECKMAN. We don't know. That is lovely. I find out through my spies that the decision, which was in the White House for approval, has been taken back to the CAB. Where is it? What is it doing? There is no public announcement. That is a very good question.

Your committee, Mr. Chairman, has the resources to find out, They are beyond my resources to find out.

Senator PERCY. I would suggest, Mr. Chairman, that we join together in sending this testimony to CAB and to the State Department and request that they comment on it and explain what happened in the process of these delays.

Mr. BECKMAN. Thank you, Senator.

Chairman RIBICOFF. Your testimony will be forwarded to the CAB and the State Department to provide an opportunity to respond.

Senator Percy?

Senator PERCY. I was very much interested in your comments on our domestic air service. I think when you are coming in as a critic, I think it is balanced testimony to point out we do have the best air transportation system. It is expensive, and we are trying to figure out ways to reduce that expense. I suppose the airlines are trying to figure out ways to reduce costs under an inflationary period. Compared with any other place in the world, we have the best.

Mr. BECKMAN. No doubt about it.

Senator PERCY. Well, we ought to keep trying to improve it. We feel we have to stay ahead in this field.

I was also interested, on page 2, that you mention there, Mr. Beckman, that the Civil Aeronautics Board has a negative attitude toward new entrants. I imagine you can say, if it plays in Peoria, it will play some place else. But I can tell you Peoria's problem. It is a major city, It is the headquarters of the Caterpillar Co., a long way from Chicago and a long drive. They have a beautiful airport, but just one airline. You fly when Ozark wants to fly. And if they are on strike, you don't fly at all. That city wants a second airline, they have been trying to get a second airline. We think the market is there, we just cannot get another airline there. We are going to find out why. Because maybe as it is playing in Peoria, maybe that is the way it is playing in other parts of the country.

Our job ought to be to provide service to the people, not just to see what we can do to make a very comfortable situation for the airlines. I have always wanted to make a product that costs a dime and sells for a dollar and is habit forming in the best sense. I suppose the airlines have the same sort of feeling, but it is not good for the consuming public and it is our purpose to find out better ways to provide better service to the public at more reasonable prices.

I find it rather incredible that Laker Airways could afford to offer transatlantic flights as low as you indicate and fly a DC-10 at a rate one-third of what the going rate is for other flights. If they could afford it, we ask the question, why are other airline fares so high and how can Laker afford to fly transatlantic flights at such a low fare?

Mr. BECKMAN. Very briefly, it lies in the lower cost structure of an airline such as this, which is essentially a charter type airline. If you will open up a register of Pan American's offices and officers, it goes for pages. They have vice presidents after vice presidents and staffs and offices all over. Laker can hold his meetings of his management for the whole airline and sit around this table.

Senator PERCY. But the equipment is the same or comparable?

Mr. BECKMAN. The same.

Senator PERCY. Pilots, no question about their experience?

Mr. BECKMAN. But they don't get paid as much. After all, a Pan Am pilot makes $60,000 a year. A top pilot flying for a British airline makes $20,000. There is quite a difference.

Senator PERCY. But they have the authorized number of personnel?

Mr. BECKMAN. Oh, yes.

Senator PERCY. Where they start saving money then is in stewardesses and in-flight services?

Mr. BECKMAN. No, no. All the quality of the service is there, but it costs less to hire them. That is point one. The overhead and cost structure is lower. And two, the theory of this type of service is, you fill up the airplane. They believe the airplane will fill up with a lot of people who want to fly cheap. The regular scheduled airlines price their service so as to keep an empty seat beside you, Senator. You see, you are paying for two seats every time you fly on the regular IATA or domestic airlines. They program their fares for about a half-full airplane.

Laker's fares are immediately cut in half because he is programing for a full airplane.

Senator PERCY. The Civil Aeronautics Board claimed it turned down Laker Airways bid to fly low-cost transatlantic flights because the Board was afraid a disastrous price war might result if they granted the request. What is your own judgment as to what actually would have happened if the Board had gone ahead and approved the request? Can you project ahead and see whether or not a destructive cutthroat competition would have resulted that would have ultimately done injury to the consumer?

Mr. BECKMAN. No, sir. This, of course, has always been the complaint. In fact, it would be interesting to replay the hearings held before Congress in the late 1940's when those awful nonscheduled airlines introduced a new concept, you may remember after World War II offered a new concept, which is coach service, cheap fare, to try to develop a mass market, to the great horror of the established airlines who made the same predictions of disaster and doom we hear today.

There will not be a war because, as Pan American and TWA and the other carriers know, their cost structure does not permit them to operate, to offer such service. What they have done, Senator, is they have put a gun at their own temple and said, "If you authorize Laker service, we are going to blow our own brains out by matching it." They don't have to. There are plenty of services, like Icelandic, who operates today at a lower fare. They carry people who are willing to experience some inconvenience, but Pan Am and TWA and British Airways are not going to self-destroy. That is a threat that should be given no credence whatsoever.

Senator PERCY. Could you position yourself about the arguments on CAB? Some people say it is a love affair between the airlines and the CAB, that the airlines want to be regulated, that they would be in the forefronts of those fighting to prevent any change in the CAB. Others have said really that Civil Aeronautics Board has actually hurt the airline industry as a whole. Where do you put yourself on that?

Mr. BECKMAN. I think there is no doubt that history tells us that the Civil Aeronautics Act of 1938 was written by the industry. It was written in a hotel suite, the Statler Hilton Hotel, by the Air Transport Association. Colonel Gorrell and Howard Westwood did a brilliant job. It was designed to provide a protected environment and hand out Federal subsidies at that time which were vital to the industry in a way that would be free of the political scandals that had bothered the post office contracts in the early 1930's.

The criticism you hear is in fact criticism from the same airlines. I think it is sort of a brainwashing technique. They keep castigating the CAB for not doing enough for them. But I think, Senator, you have seen that when the first cries of deregulation were heard dimly from the White House, the administration, the Air Transport Association geared itself up for a massive lobbying effort. They do not want to see the end of regulation.

Senator PERCY. What is your feeling about abolition of the CAB, or moving in the direction that the President is and John Robson seems to be, as the new Chairman, just removing regulation, providing for greater freedom to adjust rates and set rates and go into competition, and so forth? What would be the preferable route in your judgment?

Mr. BECKMAN. I think we cannot seriously entertain the idea of abolishing regulation. Air transportation is perhaps the basic infrastructure for our commerce industry and way of life today. It is the principal means of intercity transportation. It is vested with a deep, important public interest. It must be regulated. What we are saying in the calls for deregulation are, in my judgment, really the reaction to the policy of the Civil Aeronautics Board which are contrary to what the Congress has told the Board it wants them to do in the statute.

What Chairman Robson is doing is leading the Board back into the path set for them by the Congress in the act.

Senator PERCY. Lastly, price should be a major factor in any purchase of any goods or services. It is one of the main ingredients along with quality. It does seem the airline industry almost appears to be competing with the Playboy Clubs. You get the sensuous stewardesses advertised, movies, blankets, foot warmers, magazines, alcohol, you name it, you can have it, practically. But it all costs money. Is it your main point that the emphasis is too much at the end of the spectrum, that competition is too much there to advertise all these exotic services where there ought to be more emphasis for those who just want safe, efficient, but low-cost transportation? Not abolishing first class, you can have first class, but also taking into account that an awful lot of people cannot go first class, and that you ought to have a wide variety of services and enough frequency of flights at not just the midnight ready special lines that are appealing for low cost. Is that the main thrust of your thought?

Mr. BECKMAN. You are absolutely right, Senator. We are so starved for merely an opportunity for an innovative new idea to be heard. You used the word emphasis. I think I and others who feel the same way would settle for just the hearing of the application, just let it see the light of day of a hearing room. We are that starved for the kind of thing you describe.

Senator PERCY. If we accomplish nothing else in these hearings, I think we can see that there will be a useful exchange of facts and ideas. I think these new ideas and innovative thoughts about Government regulation ought to be brought to light and heard. Maybe they are not good. We ought to have that chance to at least hear them and hear them expeditiously.

Chairman RIBICOFF. Thank you very much, Mr. Beckman.

John Ingram, please, and Anthony Haswell.

Senator PERCY. Mr. Haswell, we appreciate your patience. We were trying to adjourn these at 12:30. It is 12:25 and we will not make that. Certainly, all your testimony will be incorporated into the record. You can summarize it if you wish. Proceed as you see fit.

Rock Island Railroad

Anthony Haswell, an official of Rock Island Railroad, testified before the Senate Government Operations Committee in 1975. Rock Island, a small rail company, has had financial difficulties for some time and has sought ICC permission to merge with the stronger and more solvent Union Pacific line. By the time Haswell appeared before the committee, Rock Island had endured almost ten years of regulatory delay and inaction. Haswell was questioned first by Senator Charles Percy, whose constituents are served by the Rock Island line.

Mr. HASWELL. Thank you very much, Senator.

First off, I apologize for Mr. Ingram's not being here today. I am Anthony Haswell, manager of passenger service at Rock Island, and I am representing John Ingram, our president and chief executive officer. He had planned to be here up until yesterday, but he has been asked to be ready on short notice to testify before the U.S. district court in Chicago concerning the proposed sale of $19 million of trustee certificates to raise vitally needed funds for normalized maintenance of our railroad.

This matter is very pressing, as yesterday the Secretary of Transportation announced that he would guarantee the repayment of these certificates. We are very grateful.

Senator PERCY. Inasmuch as the chairman has had to go over to a consumer group and I will have to join them, maybe you would like to, and I have read your testimony, maybe you would like to read the summary on page 5. Then I would like to ask some questions of you.

Mr. HASWELL. I would be pleased to do so. The essence of the testimony, of course, is to describe to the committee the consequences flowing from the almost 10-year period, or more than 10-year period, depending upon when you want to call the start, consumed by the proceedings before the Interstate Commerce Commission, involving the proposal by the Union Pacific Railroad to merge with the Rock Island.

As a result, our railroad, perhaps understandably so, went downhill to the point where, when the new management took over, bankruptcy was unavoidable. We are now very hopeful of a comeback. We have accomplished a great amount of progress. The battle is not over, but with some reasonable amount of assistance and the support of our shippers and the public along our lines, we are confident that we can make it. But with regard to the subject in front of your committee today, we see three areas of improvement that the committee could consider. First, there must be a determination that the laws under which our regulatory agencies operate be updated on a regular basis. Second, the agencies themselves are in the best position to know what their statutory recommending limitations and strictures are and should play a key role in recommending constructive changes. Third, the Congress should guard assiduously against the layering of new bureaucracies atop old ones.

New brooms don't always sweep clean; sometimes they just clutter up the broom closet. The ICC and the Department of Transportation are sufficiently capable of handling railroad problems in this country, working in concert with a Congress that cares. Sometimes it is better to do more with less, and a good example might be our experience on the Rock Island during the very difficult summer just past. We were forced as an economy measure to get rid of almost half of the railroad's management personnel, and we have found that we have suffered no loss whatsoever in managerial efficiency.

Senator PERCY. Thank you very much, indeed. I will ask a few questions, and if you could respond briefly to them, then, if you would like to expand on your answers at all, we will keep the record open for several days for you to do so.

Mr. HASWELL. Thank you.

Senator PERCY. I am sure the committee members will want to read the record. Regretfully, there were conflicts in committee hearings this morning.

You have had a harrowing experience with the Interstate Commerce Commission. You are not alone in this regard. I wonder if you could give us some other examples of problems that railroad lines in the Midwest or elsewhere have had with the ICC and how these problems have affected overall rail freight and passenger service?

Mr. HASWELL. One example that comes immediately to mind is the inordinate delays that used to be the case when the ICC considered freight rate increases. Understandably, no one likes to pay higher prices, but regulated industries like railroads are not immune from the operation of inflation. They simply have to raise their rates to cover cost increases like anybody else does.

In past years, however, there would be a delay of a year, 2 years and more whenever a rate increase was asked for. In fairness to the Commission, recently they have attempted, and have succeeded to some extent, in speeding up this process.

Another example in the rate area which is fairly well known is in the other direction. About 10 years ago the Southern Railway, which is based here in Washington, came up with a proposal for a substantial reduction in grain rates through the use of a much larger type of covered hopper car, known as the Big John. This was an obvious benefit to consumers. Because of the technology and operating techniques that the Southern had designed for the service, it was intended to be very profitable to the company. In other words, everybody would be a winner. However, that proceeding was tied up for a period of, as I recall, 4 to 6 years by the Interstate Commerce Commission and the courts before the public and railroad could reap those benefits.

Before I went to work for the Rock Island and was an advocate for rail passenger service with the National Association of Railroad Passengers, we were very interested in getting the Interstate Commerce Commission to require adequate standards of service on passenger trains. In early 1966, a case was brought before the ICC. Very extensive hearings were held. Arguments were presented. However, more than 3 years after the case was initiated, the ICC suddenly figured out that they did not have jurisdiction and they dismissed the case.

After the advent of Amtrak, the Commission took an equally long time to formulate adequacy regulations under the specific mandate of Congress under that particular act.

Unfortunately, delay seems to be a basic hallmark of the Interstate Commerce Commission. I do not mean to imply that this is necessarily the fault of the people at the Commission. As indicated in Mr. Ingram's testimony, the basic problem is more likely the laws under which the people operate.

Senator PERCY. Could you describe to us the problem that you have of holding good management personnel on a railroad? I realize you are only recently with the Rock Island, but what kind of problems have you heard? When there is 11 years of indecision as to which way the railroad is going to go, how do you hold people under conditions like that, good people, that is?

Mr. HASWELL. I think it is very difficult. Let's face it. If a company is facing a merger, a lot of people within the company, certainly a majority of management people, wonder what their future is going to be when the merger comes about. Who is going to dominate the new management? How much management will they need? After all, one of the objectives of mergers, quite frankly, is to streamline efficiency and streamline management structure. Who is going to be streamlined out?

So, that kind of a climate is a very serious impediment to hiring talent. A person figures, "Well, I will be new around here. When the merger comes along they will favor the people that have put in their time. So, why should I delay my career by hiring on here?" I think that is the essence of it.

Senator PERCY. The Interstate Commerce Commission has, through the years, been given a certain amount of responsibility for the downfall of the railroads in the country. How much do you feel the Commission, itself, and the whole concept of the Commission as created by Congress, has been responsible for the sorry state of the railroads in this country?

Mr. HASWELL. I think regulatory rigidity has made an important contribution. However, in all honesty, I cannot say that this is the sole cause or the overwhelmingly important cause. From my personal point of view, the conclusion is irresistible that at least an important a cause, and perhaps an even more important cause, has been the gross imbalance in governmental financing between railroads on the one hand, which are privately financed and taxed on their property, and other modes of transportation which are publicly financed, which pay only partial and in some cases no user charges, and whose property is exempt from tax. This issue must be dealt with at least as vigorously as the regulatory problems which we are facing.

Senator PERCY. Do you associate yourself with the position that the ICC ought to be abolished entirely, or that its responsibilities merely should be curbed or curtailed?

Mr. HASWELL. Our position would be that the ICC's functioning should be substantially improved. Perhaps some areas of its regulation could be reduced, and, therefore, its total scope reduced in size. But I think that the country would be worse off with no regulation whatsoever than it is now; we have got to improve the process. We must make it faster, more responsive, more sensitive to innovation, more conducive to encouraging imagination and creativity on the part of the managements of the companies that are regulated rather than constantly being a threat to stifle such innovation.

REGULATED COMMERCE AND CONSUMER INTEREST
([74], pp. 255–271)

Commerce is, in effect, regulated by any government office in a position to approve or disapprove a commercial activity, and the list of such offices is indeed long. There are more than 67 units of government that engage in some form of regulation, according to hearings before the Subcommittee on Administrative Law and Governmental Relations of the House Committee on the Judiciary (94th Congress, 1st Session, October and November 1975).

All regulated activities which take place in a competitive environment involve a degree of regulated competition, but some regulatory agencies have been created with the explicit mandate to regulate commerce in order to foster and preserve competition. They have their genesis in the late nineteenth century when the laissez-faire notions of Adam Smith's economics (in the *Wealth of Nations*) began to be questioned by a Congress outraged over the growth of huge trusts.

Transportation, communications, and banking are three heavily regulated industries. In recent years, especially, the performance of the Civil Aeronautics Board, Federal Communications Commission, Interstate Commerce Commission, and several financial regulatory bodies, has been challenged by representatives of industries and consumers. They have expressed concern that these federal agencies, and others, actually impede free competition in the marketplace by placing unnecessary rate restrictions on potential competitors, by inundating them with red tape and delays in decision-makings, and by favoring established concerns in denying permissions to new competitors. This has given rise to an unusual coalition of laissez-faire business economists and consumer activists, joining forces in favor of deregulation.

In the following excerpt, James Turner, testifying as an expert on the subject of food and its regulation, articulated a pro-competition, pro-consumer view before the Senate Government Operations Committee. An attorney specializing in consumer affairs, Turner was formerly a consultant to Ralph Nader's Center for the Study of Responsive Law. He wrote the Nader report on the Food and Drug Administration, called *The Chemical Feast,* published in 1970.

STATEMENT OF JAMES S. TURNER, ESQ.

We are examining regulatory agencies today because our economy is functioning badly and some people have suggested that regulatory agencies are part of the cause of this problem. Any assessment of the soundness of this suggestion should begin with certain fundamentals.

First, a good deal of what we have come to know as regulation is not carried out by the well-known "independent" regulatory agencies or even by the more obscure regulatory agencies which are a part of the various departments of government. Rather it is carried out by boards and commissions such as those that determine the marketing practices for dozens of kinds of agricultural commodities within the United States. No effort to examine, understand or alter the impact of regulation on the economy can be positive in its effects unless these relatively obscure agencies of policy are included along with "dependent" and "independent" regulatory agencies in any study of the impact of regulation on the economy.

Second, regulatory agencies will function effectively only if they are used to enhance rather than replace the interaction of a dynamic marketplace based on competition between producers and consumers. Thus, whenever a study of the effect of regulation on the economy is undertaken, the measure of successful regulatory action should be the degree to which it enhances competition.

Third, regulatory agencies must act as umpires regulating the dynamic interactions between consumers and producers which give the nation its economic vitality. Unless consumer power equal to producer power can be made an effective economic force, tinkering with the regulatory agencies will do little to help the economy.

1. LACK OF MARKET COMPETITION

The way agricultural commodities are regulated gives an insight into the problems posed to the economy by regulatory action. The distribution of California navel oranges is under the control of a commodity board. This board is made up of California navel orange producers who determine by board policy how many of their oranges will be allowed to leave the state.

When the Cost of Living Council was operating with strong price control authorities, they noticed that the price of oranges was being kept high by keeping the number of oranges leaving California low. The board took action to increase the number of oranges leaving California and claimed to have found a direct lower of price in the Eastern market as supermarkets began to have specials on oranges.

Commodity boards such as this one operate in dozens of commodity markets from prunes to walnuts to tomatoes. Similar promotional boards operate in the meat and egg areas. There are also the milk marketing boards and their satellites, the milk marketing cooperatives, which have virtually stifled competition in the milk market and have brought heavy pressure on independent milk producers. As these mechanisms cut the amount of competition inflationary practices—reducing quality and/or raising prices—begin to replace dynamic business practices and first the consumer and then the entire economy suffers.

Examining how these commodity boards work gives some insight into how these defacto regulatory agencies can be made to function more soundly. Currently the producers of a commodity in which a board operates, on either a state or national level, is assessed a returnable fee which, to the extent it is not sought for refund, become the working budget of the board. These funds then become the operating money for education, information, advertising and promotional functions of the board. Since the money all comes from producers and since the members of the board are predominately if not solely producer, it is rare that any interest other than the producer's is ever seriously attended to. In such a situation it makes relatively very little difference whether the parties at interest (the producer) get a high price for a few items or a low price for a lot of items. As a result, situations like that described in navel orange board occur frequently and are spotted with relative ease by economists.

This organizational structure suggest one possible remedy for the inequitable operation of the commodity marketing boards. It might be possible to create a comparable set of commodity consumption boards. Or better yet turn the existing marketing boards into marketing and consumption boards in which there was an equal balance of consumer and producer power. The consumer function—whether a new board or made a part of the old boards—could be funded by a voluntary refundable consumer checkoff system at the food store checkout counter. With a funding base and equal consumer representation in the marketing decision making, the one-sidedness of the current regulations would be altered.

This idea is sketchy and is offered primarily for its illustrative value rather than its details. However, any serious study and evaluation of the economic effect of regulations and regulatory function would be severely flawed if it overlooked the impact of regulatory actions that occur outside the traditional regulatory sectors. It would also be seriously flawed if it failed to examine regulation and regulatory action inside the larger contest of the interaction between consumer and producer power.

Similar efforts should be directed at the milk marketing boards where the near total power of milk producer cooperatives should be balanced by the equal power of organized consumers with representatives on the marketing boards. In fact a good deal of the regulatory process could be better understood and possibly improved if a study of it included efforts to determine if and how the power producers have over the process could be balanced by power to consumers.

2. COMPETITION BETWEEN PRODUCERS AND CONSUMERS

One of the major misconceptions of modern American economic thinking rests on the belief that vigorous antitrust policy is the primary tool for the restoration of Adam Smith's free market competitive Capitalism. In fact, antitrust policy is an essential but secondary method for bringing about Adam Smith's type of Capitalism.

Antitrust policy is designed to ensure that there are sufficient number of sellers to offer the consumer a choice so that only the best buys (the highest quality for the fairest price) will be made by the consumer. Such effective choices by the consumer are the primary discipline on the market and the major source of competitive activity according to Adam Smith. But once the primary role of consumer power in the marketplace is recognized as the essential engine of competitive, capitalism's many alternatives or supplements to antitrust policy suggest themselves as appropriate ways to restore vitality and balance to both the economy and the role of the regulatory agency. The very basis of the American economic system demand equal power for consumers and producers.

Adam Smith assigned consumerism a central place in his theory of a free market economy and the wealth of nations. In describing the plan of work for his revolutionary book, "The Wealth of Nations," Smith argued that a nation's wealth depends on the percentage of its population which has enough real per capita income to consume the necessities and conveniences of life.

"Consumption," he wrote in the book itself, "is the sole end and purpose of all production; and the interest of the producer ought to be attended to, only so far as it may be necessary for promoting that of the consumer." As his central thrust, Smith vigorously attacked mercantilism, the then predominant economic system, for inverting this natural and proper economic state.

"In the mercantile system," he argued, "the interest of the consumer is almost constantly sacrificed to that of the producer; and it seems to consider production and not consumption, as the ultimate end and object of all industry and commerce."

Smith laid precise blame for this destructive situation on the nation's producers. "It cannot be very difficult to determine who have been the contrivers of this whole mercantile system; not the consumers, we may believe, whose interest has been entirely neglected; but the producers, whose interest has been so carefully attended to; and among this latter class our merchants and manufacturers have been by far the principal architects."

Without an understanding of the role Adam Smith assigned to consumerism, the free market system cannot be made to work. Unfortunately, many twentieth century spokesmen who rely on the arguments for a free economy, use them to justify practices which Adams Smith sought to condemn. As a result "free enterprise" and the existence of "corporate economy" have come to be viewed as synonymous. Actually Smith viewed them as opposites.

In fact he directed much of the attack contained in "The Wealth of Nations" against corporations. "Increase or competition," he wrote defending the competition, "would reduce the profits of the masters as well as the wages of the workman. The trades, and crafts, the mysteries would be losers. But the public would be the gainer, the work of all artificers coming in this way much cheaper to the market. It is to prevent this reduction of price and consequently of wages and profit, by restraining that free competition which would most certainly occasion it, that corporations and the greater part of corporation law have been established."

Smith condemned "the clamor and sophistry of merchants and manufacturers (which) easily persuade(s) * * * that the private interest of a part, and of a subordinate part of the society, is in the general interest of the whole." He attacked as "without foundation" the pretense that corporations are necessary for the better government of trade." "The real and effectual discipline which is exercised over a workman, is not that of his corporation, but that of his customers. It is the fear of losing their employment which restrains his fraud and corrects his negligence."

Since Americans, at least rhetorically, trace their economic roots to Adam Smith's capitalism, they should remember that much of its thrust was against the intricately constructed corporate protectionism of late eighteenth century England's government-industrial complex of which "the merchants and manufacturers have been by far the principal architects." To the extent that an analogy can be drawn between then and now, Adam Smith would be critical of many practices which his writings are often called upon to defend.

Recognizing the insights of Adam Smith's capitalism gives a beginning point to consider the future role of the regulatory agency. Specifically, if it is to have a role at all, it must be as the regulator between consuming and producing sectors of the economy which are of roughly equal economic power. Any effort to substitute the judgment of the regulatory agency for the interactive judgments reached by the competition between consumer and producer will continue the trend toward distortion and disintegration of the American marketplace.

The current nature of the American corporation and corporate law operating much as Adam Smith described their 18th century counterparts is the single most significant barrier to the creation of the balanced competitive free market economy on which the economic future of America and probably the world depends. Nothing so sharply captures the delay of corporate self-reliance or the drift toward a government/business complex as the comment of the Treasury Secretary, John Connally to Senator Proxmire during hearings on the Lockheed Loans. "Let's face it," he suggested, "we no longer live in a free market economy."

3. REGULATORS AS UMPIRES

James Madison, writing during the constitutional crisis of 1787, set out a fundamental guideline for the activities of government as he saw them and as they came to be in early America, thinking largely under his guidance and tutelage.

"The great desideratum in Government is such a modification of the sovereignty as will render it sufficiently neutral between the different interests and factions, to control one part of the society from invading the rights of another, and at the same time sufficiently controlled itself, from settling up an interest adverse to that of the whole society."

This neutral sovereignty properly conceived and executed serves as the regulator of the society. Twentieth Century regulatory agency inside the American government stepped into Madison's concept of the neutral governmental function. This concept gave the regulatory agency its theoretical legitimacy.

Two years after setting out the neutral government concept, Madison stated his proposition even more boldly: "The best provision for a stable and free government is not a balance in the powers of the Government though that is not to be neglected, but an equilibrium in the interests and passions of the society itself, which cannot be attained in a small society. Much has been said on the first. The last deserves a thorough investigation."

Applying this principle of Madison's to the regulatory sector of government helps that sector make some sense. If the marketplace is looked at as a football game, the referee role of the regulators begins to take shape. If one football game appears to be too simple an analogy, then the permutations and combinations that develop inside a division, a conference, or a league can be used as a more fitting model. In any case, the whole composition depends on the competence skill and incorruptability of the officials.

If a football game is used as an analogy, then following the premise of Adam Smith, one team is the producers and the other is the consumers. If there are not two teams of relatively equal power, then the game will be a bore. If there are two teams of equal power, the game will be a bloody mess unless the referee/regulators do their job effectively.

Currently, the major problem is that the producers field an immensely more powerful team than consumers field. In addition, there is a tendency for regulators to play right guard, quarterback or end on the producers' team, blocking (withholding information), running the ends (subsidizing the market) or catching passes (working out problems in endless closed meetings). The result is that the regulatory/corporate complex administers the marketplace in an effort to anticipate, plan for and overcome its irrationalities. Such an effort removes the vitality from economics and begins to sap the wealth of the nation.

Thus the real future for the regulatory agency depends on modifying corporate law and corporations so that regulatory agencies have producer and consumer sectors of relatively equal power to regulate.

4. SUMMARY

Competition between various producers is an essential but secondary need in preserving the economic vitality of a society. Such competition is meant to serve as a tool to aid in the primary competition between producers and consumers that makes the system function.

The structure of the Twentieth Century American corporation is flawed. It has become insensitive to the marketplace, reliant upon government and uncomfortable with competition. As a result, it has lost its ability to respond to the consumer. The regulatory agency has served as the crutch for this decline.

Regulators who can only be effective as neutral arbitrators of economic confict find it difficult, if not impossible, to resist the pressure brought to bear on them by large corporate power centers. They cannot be made to function effectively unless and until the pressure on them is relieved by the building of strong consumer pressure to counter the pressure of producers. Future regulatory agencies need to be part of a general economic renaissance which will place the principles of competition between producers and consumers back as the central function of the American marketplace. Succeeding in such an effort might well restore the economic vigor and dynamism that along with American ingenuity and abundance of resources has allowed Americans and unparalleled productive capacity. Harnessing that capacity might well be part of, if not the only answer to meeting the growing pressure on world resources. Properly structured the regulatory agency can be a useful tool in such an effort.

Mr. JAMES TURNER. As the witness preceding me said, we are at a watershed period in the question of regulation. I think it is really a conceptual watershed. We are actually facing two basic questions that I think should be addressed by this committee and then by any subsequent investigation of regulation that may be carried on.

They are first of all the nature and purpose of regulation, and secondly the nature and purpose of competition.

I would like to begin with the first and do that by picking up Mr. Statler's question about why agencies such as the Department of Agriculture and the Food and Drug Administration should be excluded from the kind of investigation that is being proposed in legislation before you today.

I would suggest that all of the reasons that I have heard are fallacious, and nothing could do us more disservice than to conduct a series of investigations on the subject of regulation that were not coordinated, indeed, were not a single investigation. The rationale presented this morning was that those that are involved on the executive side are involved in safety and health, where those involved in the independent area are involved in questions of regulation of the economy.

There is no such distinction that exists. For example, one of the agencies listed as an independent regulatory agency in the administration proposal is in fact the Consumer Product Safety Commission, which is not charged with any regulation in the economic area, but indeed does have major economic impact.

Conversely, the Food and Drug Administration, which was excluded in this morning's testimony because it was inadvertently or accidentally an impacter on the economy, maintains within its own structure a division to look into the impact of its decisions on the economy. It has a staff of people who produce reports about how a particular regulation will affect the economy, and indeed, it has statutory authority to work on economic fraud questions. Indeed, it maintains a series of interagency arrangements with the Federal Trade Commission with input on economic questions, and indeed, it is the maintainer of a series of food standard systems that are designed purely and simply for their economic impact aside from all safety activities.

So I would suggest that the question of whether independent or nonindependent agencies should be mixed together cannot turn on whether they investigate safety or nonsafety items. Both kinds of agencies do both things. Indeed, in the Agriculture Department you have a series of marketing order and other boards that regulate purely economic questions. It is in these areas that it would be extremely important for some investigation to be undertaken.

And this raises, by the way, a third serious area of focus that has not even come up in the hearings. We had discussion about independent regulatory agencies and about dependent regulatory agencies. In fact, the Agriculture Department regulators are neither of those, but are in fact independent boards in the sense that they bring competing interests to sit down and establish the framework of a market.

So not only should all regulatory agencies be included in any review of the nature and purpose of regulation, but there are some institutions that are not even regulatory agencies which should be included in such a study.

For example, you have the entire milk marketing order system which is not a regulatory system, but which is operated in such a way that it does have tremendous impact on the price of milk. Indeed, it has been estimated that the operation of those boards at the current time is operating ineffectively to the extent that perhaps as much as $4 billion has been lost to the American consumer over the last decade.

In addition to those kinds of boards, the milk marketing boards, there are fruits and vegetable boards. There is, for example, a board known as the California Navel Orange Board. This board during the operations of the wage and price control system 2 years ago was noticed to be limiting the transport of oranges from the area by administrative decisions.

The wage and price controls regulators went to that board directly and using their legal authority, forced more oranges to be released from California in the eastern domestic market, with the direct result that the price of oranges on the wholesale level to supermarkets dropped 15 percent.

This is a clear situation in which a regulatory activity outside of regulatory agencies was in fact impacting on the economy in such a way as to lead to inflation.

I would suggest that the question of the nature and purpose of regulation has been misunderstood by those who are trying to separate out certain kinds of regulatory activities. Senator Allen last week asked Mr. Ash when did we get into this mess? How recently was it that the problem occurred that we are all talking about? Mr. Ash said, well, I was not around at that time, but I would suspect that back around a year after the Interstate Commerce Commission was created we started getting into this mess.

I would suggest that there is on the historical record evidence that our problem began before the Interstate Commerce Commission was created. Indeed, the historical analysis of the creation of the ICC by the historian Gabriel Kolko who is widely respected and whose work on the ICC is considered to be a historical classic, points out that the legislation was drafted by railroad lawyers working on behalf of the railroads, that the passage of the legislation was urged by the chambers of commerce in existence at that time. Going back and looking at the historical and contemporary newspaper record, you find a great deal of support for the Interstate Commerce Commission coming from the industry itself. Indeed, the bill languished for almost 11 years, until industry embraced it. Then it passed.

I would suggest to those who say regulatory agencies soon become captured by those that they regulate, that there is strong evidence that they are born captured. They do not come into existence until such time that the industry to be regulated finds that it needs them. Indeed, prior to the creation of the Interstate Commerce Commission there were many efforts on the part of the industry to set up private, voluntary systems very much like the Interstate Commerce Commission. These systems were set up to manage price, to manage markets. They were called railroad pools. Every member of the railroad industry signed an agreement that he would only charge a certain price. Remember, there were no antitrust laws at this time. They agreed to charge a certain price. They agreed to market only in certain areas.

There was a pool administrator that was appointed whose job it was to insure compliance on a voluntary basis with this system. It was only after the collapse of this system on several different occasions that finally the railroad industry used its support to bring about the creation of a Federal Interstate Commerce Commission. In essence this put into legislation the kind of voluntary system that could not be enforced privately. But it also brought into the framework the arm of the Federal Government to enforce what could not be enforced privately.

Indeed, shortly after the passage of this statute, J. P. Morgan and other railroad interests met and made as their first priority of business enforcement of the Interstate Commerce Commission against their competitors who would not comply with it.

I would suggest then in the Interstate Commerce model, we have a framework in which institutions have come into being to help industry people, but have come down to us in history as if they were meant to help the consumer. They were not necessarily meant to help consumers. The Food and Drug Administration did not come into existence while it languished—for 30 years—in the U.S. Congress until the National Canners Association, the biggest trade association in the food industry at that time, endorsed its creation.

For the moment I just would want to make one small aside and say that by saying that these institutions were created to serve the industries that they were designed to regulate, I do not mean at that time in history that was necessarily a bad policy. We had a serious problem with railroad pirating, with cutthroat competition, and other kinds of destructive activity that were going on.

This may very well have been a reasonable system to incorporate. It may well not have been. Nonetheless, the point is these institutions were created to work out the warring conflicts between various segments of the industry that were causing serious economic problems. They were not designed as consumer protection institutions.

I would suggest with that point in mind that the second conceptual problem that we must address is the nature and scope of competition. What is competition supposed to be in the framework of what we call a capitalistic or a free market economy?

Adam Smith, of course, was the father of the concepts that make up the free market system, and he identified the central force in his free market system as the consumer. He said:

Consumption is the sole purpose of all production, and the interests of the producer ought to be attended to only so far as it may be necessary for promoting that of the consumer.

His argument was that primary to the development of a free economic system is the placing in the hands of the consumer the kind of economic power that will make it possible for that individual to act as the disciplinary force on those who are the sellers.

Indeed, the antitrust concepts that have grown up around the idea of free marketing have grown up as a secondary effort to support the economy. They have grown up in an effort to provide enough sellers so that the consumers' discipline would have someplace to be expressed.

The primary force in the free market system was the force of having consumer power. Adam Smith went on to say that in the system that he was attacking, which was called mercantilism:

The interest of the consumer is almost constantly sacrificed to that of the producer, and it seems to consider production and not consumption as the ultimate end and object of all industry and commerce.

I would suggest to you as you are given arguments about efficiency and cost of producing and so forth, we tend to move into an area where the producers' interests get focused on more effectively than consumers' interests. The point that Adam Smith made over and over in the "Wealth of Nations" was we have major corporations that have been created like the East India Co., and whenever they run into economic problems, they go to the Parliament for a subsidy, as the East India Co. did. When the subsidy does not save them economically, they ask for special trading privileges which the East India Co. did. In one instance, the trading privilege was to sell tea to the United States without the duty that would be required on other people selling tea, giving them a market advantage.

We met that particular challenge to the United States by having the Boston Tea Party, and it was the East India Co.'s tea that went in the water, not the King's tea.

The point is, the arguments that Adam Smith made, the arguments that support our free market system, placed the consumer at the center of the whole competitive structure. Smith went on to describe the laws that had been created to support and protect corporations in mercantile England, which I think are very similar to laws that we now have, and said:

> It cannot be very difficult to determine who have been the contrivers of this whole system, not the consumers, we may believe, whose interests have been entirely neglected, but the producers, whose interests have been so carefully attended to, and among this latter class are merchants and manufacturers who have been by far the principal architects.

I would suggest to you that the whole concept of the free market system as designed by Adam Smith was to provide an opportunity for those who were the consumers, the buyers in the market place, to exercise force in that market place equal to that exercised by the producers. I would suggest to you, as the economic situation in the United States began to become more and more corporatized, at the turn of the last century, we as a society began to think up a series of ideas about how to remove power from the corporate sector, and as a counter to those ideas, the regulatory agency concept was planted to allow the managers of the corporate economy a forum in which they could work out their problems which would not disrupt the rest of the economy drawing down on their heads all the wrath of the society.

I would suggest in 1974 it is untangling that kind of a problem that we face. Given this kind of conceptual framework, it seems to me that we face a question of rationale as the last speaker talked about, and as the counsel mentioned. A question of whether the real choices are returning to a free market system or continuing in a regulated system. I would suggest there is a third alternative, to design legislation for institutions, to allow consumers to express their power in the marketplace as the theory of the marketplace demands, if it is going to work.

This would mean, for example, the creation of institutions that will bring consumer input directly into the operation of the regulatory system. This would mean taking the area that has been exclusively occupied by the industry being regulated, and bringing consumer input directly into that framework.

Without such structural change, you will not seriously address the problem of regulation and its impact on the economy.

Specifically in regard to the legislation that is before you today, I suggest that the Commission that has been proposed must, if it is going to be effective, include as members of the Commission, people who are representative of both the consumer interests and the producer interests. This would mean that the kinds of issues that I am discussing would become a serious focus of any kind of regulatory investigation. Without that kind of focus, we would merely get a replay of things such as the Landis report, the Ash report, and the others cited by the witness earlier today. Such a replay would lead us not to a reform of the system, but to digging ourselves in deeper by excluding those activities which are effective in regulating the corporate economy and including those which are not effective. It will allow us to make exactly the same choices we made each other time that we have looked at the regulatory agencies; that is, enhancing the power of the regulated industries within regulatory agencies and minimizing the power of the consumer.

I have given you the general framework that I think should be used to look at the kind of legislation before you.

Senator HUDDLESTON. You mentioned that the ICC and the FDA, and mentioned that they are captive of those that they are supposed to regulate. What other agencies do you put in this category? All of them?

Mr. JAMES TURNER. Dr. Kolko has gone on and examined other agencies. He did a more thorough examination of the Interstate Commerce Commission. But he has examined all others. I would suggest they are all in a power situation, where their contemporary peer group activities revolve around the industries that they regulate. You have a series of very real problems. First of all, all of them. Then, you have very serious, real problems that caused this to occur. In the Food and Drug Administration, when it came time to appoint a new general counsel to replace one that had been there since creation of the agency, there was only a small community available from which to draw someone who could work in that office. The person came from one of the major food and drug law firms, with a series of food and drug clients.

Senator HUDDLESTON. You emphasized the need to have consumer interest represented, to paraphrase, in the proper proportion to their power and interest. Is there an area where the interest of the producer has to be taken into account particularly in the long term if the interest of the consumer is to be protected? There is a question of competitiveness in keeping production at a level where the consumer can use his power.

Mr. JAMES TURNER. Yes, there is definitely that and in quotation from Adam Smith, he says: "The interests of the producer are to be attended to only insofar as it may be necessary in promoting that of the consumer," which is exactly what you said. Certainly, it is important to be sure that the producer is not overburdened, not unnecessarily overburdened or overburdened period; because overburdening is not necessary. It is a part of the argument today, we are concerned about your interests, because your interest is important in advancing the consumer's interest.

Senator HUDDLESTON. The lowest possible price immediately might not always be the total criterion for determining whether the consumer's interest is going to be served over the long term.

Mr. JAMES TURNER. Not only will it not always be, but it will never be. The lowest possible price is never the proper criterion to utilize. There has got to be the highest possible quality for the lowest possible price, but the lowest possible price itself used as a measure, will only lead to the depreciation of quality. This in turn would lead to a serious disruption of the whole situation, and become inflationary.

Senator HUDDLESTON. Availability of supply?

Mr. JAMES TURNER. Exactly.

Senator HUDDLESTON. From your study of the FDA, what extent has its policies been inflationary and increased the cost, without regard to quality control and the other type of things that they may be concerned with?

Mr. JAMES TURNER. I cannot put a dollar figure on the FDA. The FDA regulates a marketplace that includes $250 billion worth of retail products. It has a tremendous impact. There are indications of the kinds of problems that need to be looked at. I would argue that the depreciation of quality is an inflationary factor, if you are paying the same price for a lower quality goods, you have actually had your dollar inflated. You are not able to buy as much with it as you have in the past.

The FDA has tended to overlook this impact in such instances as setting the standard for orange juice. In that orange juice product area, there was a tremendous debate between consumer groups and the FDA about how to label orange juice products. They wanted to say, all orange juice products that contained between 25 percent and 75 percent orange juice should be labeled the same way, as orange juice products. The problem with that is you immediately depreciate the quality of every one of the products that was above 25 percent down to 25 percent. That is a direct cost to consumers—how much of a cost, I cannot tell you—but I can say that the FDA has an economic bureau—or economic activity. They ought to be looking into these activities.

We have a problem—that is enough. There are others in the agriculture area. You can find at least four marketing areas in which the Cost of Living Council projected a problem in costs to consumers. Cling peaches, nuts, oranges—I do not remember the fourth—those could add up to several million dollars, if not $100 million, collectively. And in the milk market area, as I say, a very conservative estimate is $4 billion over the past 10 years.

I should mention one other thing about regulatory agencies in the cost area which is often overlooked. When you are talking about excess profits as being a result of these activities, you may not be taking into consideration the entire price rise. The Federal Trade Commission did a study several years ago on the outdoor bleacher industry, and in that industry, it was projected by the FTC that there was a 15-percent excess profit situation which suggested collusion. They went to the industry, got a consent decree against collusion, and that led to a price drop of almost 30 percent in the marketing price. This happened because the FTC was squeezing out excess administrative costs, which included corporate jets and fancy offices, and high, inflated expense accounts, and so forth, as well as excess profits. When you think about this, you have a lot of different ways that you can make the economy less inflationary, by the way regulatory action is used.

Senator HUDDLESTON. In determining the potential of the cost of the milk marketing situation, your estimate was $4 billion. How do you determine that? Is that $4 billion above what the consumer could have bought the same quantity of milk for?

Mr. JAMES TURNER. That is an extremely important point, and I would like to take a moment to address it because of the way that the hearings have proceeded while I have been here. When, I say the milk marketing has led to, perhaps, by conservative estimate (and that was done by a former Department of Agriculture official), to a $4 billion cost to the consumer, I do not juxtapose to that the concept that we should eliminate milk marketing orders. Eliminating milk marketing orders could lead to a situation far worse than that cost. The problem is, how to make those marketing orders operate in such a way that they will take into consideration the entire marketplace, both producers and buyers, when they come up with a regulatory activity or the regulatory impact.

In that particular instance, that money was taken from premium charges, and what is considered to be excess premium charges. It might well be possible to restructure the marketing order system, having a framework within which the consumer interest and the producer interest are both represented in a price-setting situation, to maintain supplies—that they were designed for—maintain producer market power opposed to retail market power—which they were designed for—and at the same time, not allowing that power to be so all-pervasive that it goes beyond the power of the other parts of the marketplace, to the extent that it is bringing in excess money. That is the framework that I believe any study of regulation in regard to the economy should be conducted in. If it is conducted in the framework, should we have regulation, and regulation costs a lot, therefore we ought to get rid of it—then we are moving back to a situation that we had at the turn of the century, where practices that are now under regulation that we have forgotten about would again become rampant; the least of which is what Nicholas Johnson has suggested. Incidently, I would point out that the previous witness did not say that in all cases, you will not have an oligopolic situation. If you go to a situation where there is no regulation, and end up in an oligopoly situation, it is very problematic even if the Justice Department would have the authority to break up oligopolies at this point. You could move yourself into a very serious problem if it was juxtoposed as a free market versus the regulated market.

Senator HUDDLESTON. You say regulation is necessary?

Mr. JAMES TURNER. Yes. But it ought to be done properly, and properly means bringing the consumer interest in the framework.

Senator HUDDLESTON. Let me quote from your book, "The Chemical Feast," that was published in 1970. Page 17, and I quote:

If the food industry can use that questionable additive until it is conclusively proven to be unsafe, people will be injured. The processing provisions of the food additive law are designed to avoid this kind of entry. But FDA has failed to protect the public interest against such injury.

Could you expand on that charge?

Mr. JAMES TURNER. Yes.

We are talking about one of the laws that the Food and Drug Administration enforces, the food additive law. I will give you a specific example that we are involved in at the present time at the Food and Drug Administration. It will give you also, I think, an insight into the regulatory question that I was talking about earlier.

In 1970, as that book was being prepared, a number of food additives were under very serious criticism. Cyclamates had just been removed—incidentally, we had had meetings with HEW, with Secretary Finch, on the question of cyclamates, and I believe that had a great deal to do with this action. In addition, monosodium glutimate had been voluntarily removed from baby food. In addition to that, you had had other additives such as brominated vegetable oil and other substances changed in status to require further testing.

At that very time, the Serle Co. began development of a new artificial sweetener called asnevtome. We began to ask the Serle Co.— we representing the interests of consumers, and being concerned about the potential safety of that substance—whether we could be involved in some way, by raising questions as that substance was developed. We were not allowed to be involved in any way.

Two years ago, the Serle Co. filed a series of safety test results with the Food and Drug Administration, and we asked at that time, could we be involved now in reviewing those tests to see if the law had been followed. And we were told that we could not' the law did not permit it, because this was commercial data which is excluded under the Freedom of Information Act. By the way, we went to court to receive this kind of data in another case, and we got an indeterminate opinion saying in that particular case, no; but bring it back in another case.

For 2 years, this substance resided in the FDA which it issued through the studies. We sought both through the companies involved and through the FDA, to bring the consumer input in, discussing the safety of that additive. Subsequently, 4 months ago, the FDA announced that they would permit the marketing of chemical in food. At that time, for the first time, myself and our scientific advisers had the opportunity to go to the FDA hearing clerk's office, and look at that data. I want to mention that that was a very unique situation. It was only the first time that, in granting a food additive—the first time in the history of the law—in granting a food additive petition, the FDA had allowed the safety data to be looked at. We went and looked at that data.

The reason they did allow access is that we pressured them to do so, by repeatedly asking what they base their decision on. We looked at that data, and found that there had been a study done on monkeys in which monkeys had eaten this particular substance in medium to higher doses, and all of them had gotten epileptic seizures. Our argument was, that this posed a very serious question about whether or not that substance should be on the market. Our argument was, we should have been allowed to ask that question much earlier in the process. Our argument was that, since we had not been, we demanded a hearing from the Food and Drug Administration, which was our right under the law. We now have a hearing which is being developed. We will be holding a hearing on that substance.

Incidentally, the whole time that we are trying to get this hearing, and so forth, the FDA has legally allowed the marketing of that substance. It has not yet been marketed, but there is not a legal restriction on marketing. My suggestion is that here is a specific example where the FDA has allowed something to come on the market that poses a potential hazard, where the consumer was excluded completely from the regulatory process all the way up to the very last minute, while for 2 years the FDA met, on an ongoing basis, with both the food company, General Foods, that wished to market this under contract from Serle, and the Serle Co., the company that manufactured it.

My suggestion is, on these kinds of issues, the absence of the consumer input early in the process is a serious problem from the policy point of view.

Senator HUDDLESTON. Has the situation improved any since 1970?

Mr. JAMES TURNER. I gave you the major improvement. Under pressure, they filed the documents that showed that they were, in our opinion, making a mistake. That is an improvement; I would not say it is not. On the other hand, from the standpoint of protecting the American public, it poses some very serious questions about how that process operates.

Senator HUDDLESTON. Your testimony describes how a commodity board in California controlled the supply of navel oranges in this country. Who actually selected the members of that particular board?

Mr. James Turner. The board—I am not clear exactly who selects them. They are certified by the Secretary of Agriculture. They report under his authority, and they are almost exclusively representatives of the industries involved. There is now a tremendous effort on the part of consumer groups in the California area to include consumer representation on all commodity boards, starting right now, and that is beginning to gain momentum.

Senator Huddleston. Are they responsible to the Department of Agriculture?

Mr. James Turner. It is the Federal marketing order, and their activities are regulated under the Department of Agriculture rules.

Senator Huddleston. Do you have any statistics as to what proportion of food the housewife buys is controlled by such a board?

Mr. James Turner. There are over 70 of both kinds of boards. Then there are the milk boards, and you end up with a very high percentage—maybe 25 to 30 percent—clearly under their control, perhaps some peripheral control. Let me suggest, in regard to these last two questions, perhaps you can understand more clearly what my concern is about consumer interests if I explain how they work.

These boards levy a tariff on the sale of the commodity that they are regulating. Let us take an Ohio board, for an example. These are both State and Federal, and they work in roughly the same way. Ohio has a beef marketing board which levies a tariff, essentially, on the sale of beef. So for every head of cattle that is sold that is raised in Ohio, the seller pays in a dime—I think that is the present rate—to a general fund that is managed by the Ohio Department of Agriculture. The management is purely fiscal. The people who raise cattle in the State of Ohio elect the membership of the board that sets policy. That board then sets the policy of how to use this money, and it operates at about $100,000 to $150,000 a year. Any member of the group can write to the Department of Agriculture and ask for his money back. That makes it a voluntary process.

The result of this is, you have a producer-controlled, producer-financed institution, whose primary purpose is to provide information, education, and publicity for the sale of the commodity involved, in this case beef. They have it for apples, or any other area that you may want. What we are arguing is that there should be a comparable framework for the people who consume food. There ought to be an agricultural consumers' board, or there ought to be the two married together. Conceptually, we would argue that a similar voluntary checkout system could be instituted. For example, the supermarket checkout counter, where a person is asked to voluntarily donate 1 mill of their purchase to the consumer marketing board. This would raise in the food area $125 million annually nationwide, if everybody gave their 1 mill.

What we are suggesting is the creation of that kind of an institution to counterbalance the kind of marketing institution on the producers' side would lead to an interaction between what we call competitive, in the classic Adam Smith free market sense, for the setting of policy and the selling and buying of food. For example, the advertisements of such institutions that go on television, that says buy prunes, buy peaches, et cetera, would be able to be subjected to the kind of review that now the FTC is demanding they be subjected to by law. The question of how much should be released or not released, as in the case of the navel orange board, would be subject to a much different kind of discussion, not only preserving the producer's marketplace, but also having consumer input; saying, look, you put this many oranges at a lower price, you are going to make even more money. So just do not focus on raising the price of the commodity you have, but also focus on the possibility of creating a larger market. If you can create a larger market at a lower price, you will make more money in the long run than if you create a smaller market at a higher price. These kind of arguments could be carried out in the framework of such an interaction.

That is the kind of question that I think the Review Commission N1 that we are talking about in this legislation should undertake. Any tinkering with the way the process is, trying to improve this part or get rid of that part, would really be counterproductive.

Senator HUDDLESTON. In absence of consumer input, is it your judgment that these boards ought to be limited or eliminated?

Mr. JAMES TURNER. You would have to look at each of the boards specifically to decide that question. As soon as you begin doing that, you are in a situation where what you really need as an ongoing review N2 process. The Cost of Living Council began that. They were going down the boards one at a time, looking at those where objective economic data suggested a serious market manipulation problem. They had already identified four; and then, as we all know, they went out of business.

I am suggesting that that kind of ongoing process can be extremely useful in creating a much more effective economy, that puts more supply of food, in this case, in the marketplace at a better price for the consumer, and a better return for the producer. I do not believe we are going to be able to market agriculturally without some kind of a management system, of which this is the very rudimentary beginnings. I am suggesting that the next addition that should be made is the putting in of the kind of inputs I am talking about.

Senator HUDDLESTON. I am wondering whether there is any danger here of an oversimplification when you refer to producers and consumers as two separate, distinct, monolithic-type groups. The interests of consumers are so varied, and certainly the interests of the producers are quite varied. It is almost begging the point to refer to them just as separate, with separate interests that are easily defined and described.

Mr. JAMES TURNER. Let me answer that this way. In trying to develop this concept, and speaking to others about it, I used the analogy of the football game. In the football game, we have the producer—in my analogy, you have a producer team and you have a consumer team, and you have all the officials who are the regulators. Our biggest problem in our society, in terms of regulation and so forth, and one which is getting a great deal of support from the public, is that the head linesman and field judge and so forth have started playing right guard and quarterback on the producer's team. We do not want that; we think that is bad. But we are not arguing that they should play left guard or quarterback on the consumer team. They should be regulating equal forces in the marketplace. That is an over-simplification. But to understand how that analogy can be carried further, we can say, let us then, instead of thinking of a football game, think of the central division of the NFL, so we make it a little more complicated; several different producer teams and several different consumer teams. Then we can put it in the three divisions, then the AFL, and then the whole concept of the football structure.

All I am suggesting to you is, the oversimplification that has occurred up to now is the oversimplification that our only problems are on the production side, and that there is a clear and distinct consumption side. That does not mean that the interest of the producer is always opposed to that of the consumer. It is quite clear that they are not always the same, and we have continuously had a presentation and analysis of regulation of our economy. If only we can work out the differences between all the different producers, and provide enough of that in the ball game, then everything will be all right. And we have completely overlooked the development of the consumers' skill in making the economy work.

Senator HUDDLESTON. The only fault I find with your analogy is it does imply that there is a continual conflict between consumer interests and producer interests, and in some cases, they may be traveling along the same road, going in the same direction. What about agencies like FDA and USDA that are not directly subject to Presidential direction? Do you think they would better represent interests of the public less susceptible to the judicial pressure than the independent regulatory agencies?

Mr. JAMES TURNER. It is perhaps more likely that the opposite is true, and indeed, that is why independent regulatory agencies were created; to avoid that kind of influence from the elected administrative personnel. I believe, actually, from looking at the situation, and the way that regulation has developed as the dynamic in this society, it makes little difference where the regulatory agency is placed. Indeed, the Food and Drug Administration is a dependent regulatory agency, merely by the historical accident that the man who drafted the legislation happened to be an employee of the Department of Agriculture, and asked that the authority be placed in the Department of Agriculture, in his Department. That is why it is there; there is no other reason. The fact that it has been moved from department to department over the years shows that there is no particular reason why it should have been put where it was in the first place, other than historical accident.

I am suggesting that the dynamic of the framework, the dynamic of the constant input of one side of the economic argument, is what has created the situation that leads regulation down roads that are not the most productive. It does not matter whether it is the independent or dependent.

Senator HUDDLESTON. Does counsel have any questions?

Mr. TURNER. I do have several questions, but I am going to cut it short, and get to a specific example, and maybe get your response to it, Mr. Turner.

Am I correct that you are favoring, in your recommendations, a return to the free market system wherever possible?

Mr. JAMES TURNER. Yes, definitely that, and more. That is, a return to the principles of the free market system, we cannot go back to the village marketplace that Adam Smith had. But we can restore the principles of the free market system. That is what I am relying on.

Mr. TURNER. Is it not a fact that the sugar market today in the United States is operating unregulated and is a free market, other than the import quotas?

Mr. JAMES TURNER. Yes, that is correct.

Mr. TURNER. Is it also not a fact that the price of sugar has skyrocketed in this country over the past several months?

Mr. James Turner. Correct.

Mr. Turner. Is it also not a fact that the sugar industry is dominated by a concentrated group of sellers, no more than four, who hold the power to control the price and the allocation of supply of sugar?

Mr. James Turner. I would agree with that, definitely.

Mr. Turner. Then this would be an example of a free market operating. What is your response to that?

Mr. James Turner. My response was, first of all, it is not an example of a free market operating. It is an example of an oligopoly operating. The point I made earlier, and I join with the kind of concern that Nicholas Johnson expressed—if you move to a nonregulated economy, you are going to end up with a very serious problem. The real functional problem in sugar, as nearly as we can tell from looking at it, is we have dropped from a 20-week to 15-week supply in the pipeline, or in the pipeline framework, which is merely the result of, apparently, the Russian agriculture policy, planning to go on the world market rather than staying out of it. It is the relatively small dislocation, but enough to set off the forces of the managed sugar economy to run prices up.

Mr. Turner. You would agree that we would not be able to rely on the antitrust Division to solve the problem?

Mr. James Turner. That is correct.

Mr. Turner. Then what kind of regulatory mechanism should this study commission be looking at as a means of resolving this problem of concentrated sellers in a market?

Mr. James Turner. Incidentally, I would suggest the intervention of the American Government in the sugar market was greater before consumers proposed the legislation than it is now, and the prices were still going up. It was a serious problem, unrelated to the Sugar Act activities. What I am suggesting, as a general principle, a philosophy, is that a regulatory framework should be established in these kinds of situations. It does not mean it only has to be regulation that would bring the consumer interest directly in impact with the policy planners. I, for example, believe——

Mr. Turner. Excuse me, I am only looking for potential mechanisms. How can consumers be brought together with this concentrated group of four, to cause them to change their planning with respect to price?

Mr. James Turner. The sugar marketing board, in that kind of instance, would be a good thing, if it was made up of 50 percent of consumers and 50 percent of producers, with the Government controlling it, as the regulators of that interaction; and sitting down with money for the consumer people to do research in the marketing framework, and so on, and money for the sugar people, which they already have—which we do not have—to begin to bring into the decisionmaking the design for a planning of the sugar market, the other side of the point of view.

I want to go back and say, this does not mean when they sit down and talk, they are not going to agree on perhaps, most of what they talk about. But there are those points where they do not agree which now exclude completely the point of view of the consumer from the planning process. There is only the point of view of the producer in that process. That is the kind of regulatory mechanism I would see operate.

Mr. Turner. I would suggest such agreement may be in direct violation of the antitrust laws.

Mr. James Turner. That is a serious problem that has to be looked at by the Commission that is doing the regulating. For example, there are serious questions about the antitrust implications of milk marketing. I believe the kind of framework we are talking about, if a Commission is going to look at regulation, and come out with some kind of recommendation, and the kind of approach I am talking about is part of that. Quite clearly, they must look at the antitrust regulations to determine how they can be effectively utilized, and where they have been counterproductive.

Mr. Turner. Do you support breaking up these large companies, these concentrated markets, into small units?

Mr. James Turner. My personal feeling on that question; any company that is beyond the point of efficiency in terms of market activity should be brought back to efficiency. That does not mean breaking down companies just because they are large. Almost every issue where there has been a question of size will feature a company or a pair of companies that are larger than the point of market efficiency. Just raw economic data indicates points of diminishing returns, the next increment of production costs more than mere preceding.

Quite clearly, by antitrust action, all companies of that size should be broken back to the point of diminishing return, or whatever standard that was determined that would be the most efficient objective economic standard.

On the other hand, there are many companies operating today that are large but efficient because they have been able to make use of economies of scale. I do not believe those should necessarily be broken up if you can bring alternate power for decisionmaking into their structures.

Mr. Turner. Do you feel the Antitrust Division of the Department of Justice is ineffective in doing its job?

Mr. James Turner. I do not think it is effective. For structural reasons it does not have the money, it does not have the resources or legal conceptions. There is serious question whether they can really go after an oligopoly. The fact that a serious question exists in such a framework creates tremendous legal problems. That is where most of the delay comes from when there is a serious legal question, even if all the scholars in the world accept one agree you are going to have serious legal delays.

Mr. Turner. I have no further question.

PERSPECTIVES OF PAST REGULATORS: A PANEL DISCUSSION ([76], pp. 58–82)

Former officials of regulatory agencies appeared before the Senate Committee on Government Operations in 1975, and engaged in a panel discussion with Senators Abraham Ribicoff, Charles Percy, Lee Metcalf, and Jacob Javits. While testifying in favor of reform efforts, they cited specific experiences to illustrate the difficulties inherent in any attempt to overhaul the regulatory agencies. Those testifying were: Lee White, former chairman of the Federal Power Commission; Peter Hutt, former general counsel for the Food and Drug Administration; Harry McPherson, former special counsel to President Johnson; Roger Noll, professor of Economics, California Institute of Technology; Merton Peck, professor of Economics, Yale University, and former member of the Council of Economic Advisers; Robert Pitofsky, former director of the Bureau of Consumer Protection and the Federal Trade Commission, and professor of law, Georgetown University Law Center.

Mr. WHITE. Thank you, Mr. Chairman.

I have no prepared comments. I share your lack of enthusiasm for Presidential commissions and the concept of having sort of a special assignment by one of the committees capable of writing legislation, or at least recommending it to other substantive committees could indeed be a short circuit if we are able, through the process, to develop any ideas that are worthy of implementation.

Obviously, it does not have to filter through an extra two or three layers and sets of people. I don't think you misunderstand the difficult nature of the assignment. Just about everybody is in favor of regulatory reform in the abstract. It gets a little sticky when you get it down to the specific and concrete. One person's reform is another's pain in the neck, and worse obstacles to achieving goals.

We have had one session with the committee staff. I guess I should not talk about it other than to tell you my view. That is that one of the greater needs is beyond the scope of this committee and I guess anyone else. That is to improve the selection process at both the operating head level, and the top staff and the middle staff level. Having said that, I don't know how useful that is, but I think my own experience and my own observations tell me that, regardless of what tables of organization are prepared, or how the process and structure is set up, the most important considerations are the women and men that are selected to implement those jobs, and they are tough.

There is no sort of ready made check list that I am aware of that lets somebody judge whether a regulatory agency or individual has done a particularly good or bad job, so that so much of it is subjective. That is perhaps a truism, but also a very discouraging thing to have to accept, as you undertake this particular assignment. Within that framework, however, I think able people would be able to do a better job to the extent that the procedures and processes and substantive assignments are more thoughtfully set out in the structure. I do not mean to be totally discouraging and negative. As you may know from our prior experience every once in a while my boundless optimism grabs hold and we begin to think you can do things. Here there is an opportunity.

I have never seen such a mood as long as I have been watching Washington that says we have to make some changes. With that kind of an impetus behind it, there is reason to be optimistic that something worthwhile and constructive can be accomplished. I gather that is one of our roles here, to assist the committee and the committee staff in sorting its way through these various ideas and recommendations.

Chairman RIBICOFF. Mr. McPherson.

Mr. McPHERSON. Thank you, Mr. Chairman. Just to pick up on something Lee White said, as far as the quality of the people who are in the regulatory agencies is concerned, this is where Jim Landis came out in 1960 and 1961 when President Kennedy asked him to make a study of the regulatory agencies. He came out believing that the biggest reform would be improving the quality of personnel. That seems to be a fairly generally accepted idea.

From my observation of the regulatory agencies, which is certainly not as broad as I wish it were, I would judge that there are fashions in agencies. One agency is attractive to first rate people at a given time, and then that fashion passes. At one time the CAB, for example, attracted some of the ablest people in Washington. It still has some able people but it perhaps is not as magnetic to first-rank law students and economists as it once was.

The FPC may be another case of that. The SEC and the FTC at the moment are lively places and they are places that bright young people are attracted to because they offer lots of action and perhaps the potential for a future career in private life in that field.

So you do have a certain modishness that attracts people to different agencies.

One thing, though, is fairly clear. In an environment where an administration is saying that regulation is bad, per se, I think it is unlikely that a great many bright people would be attracted to agencies, where you have the Government, in effect, discrediting its own regula tors. It has a certain chilling effect on the attractiveness of that work to bright young people.

Let me make one or two other statements very briefly. As I said in meeting with the staff, I think there are really two drives for regulatory reform that are going on right now, and they are rather distinct. Perhaps the committee ought to consider those. One is the general "get the Government off my back" drive, and that affects every Senator and every Congressman. I am sure you get a lot of mail about OSHA and about the Consumer Products Safety Commission and about the hangups in the Federal Energy Administration. The enormous number of filings and reports, many of them contradictory, many of them impenetrable, particularly for smaller businesses who simply don't know how to comply with OSHA's requirements or many other agency requirements. When a President goes out and talks about getting the Government monkey off peoples' back, that is really what he is talking about. That is the sympathetic response that he invokes, having to do simply with paperwork and requirements, forms, new loads put on business and individuals. The EEOC is another example.

These are chiefly requirements put on as a result of congressional desires to achieve some social goals—health, safety, equity in hiring, and employment. They are things people haven't had to cope with before. Suddenly, having a load of new Government agencies instructing them to fill out forms, to make changes to operate differently in their business lives, is a pain in the neck.

The other drive is an economist's drive. That is to free up trucking and railroading and airlines and electric utilities, natural gas pipelines, and so on, from economic regulation. These two drives have points of intersection. There is heavy paperwork, tremendous procedural requirements, and so on, on both sides. But they are rather distinct. So I think the committee should be aware as it goes into this field that there are really two motivations that are driving the regulatory reform movement at the moment.

I would recommend strongly that the committee ask the regulatory agencies, the economic regulatory agencies to tell it in as specific detail as possible what they are doing, what they are spending their time on, what their staffs are devoted to, how many man-hours are given over, say, to entry regulations of irregular route carriers in the ICC. I think that perhaps more than half the ICC staff is involved in regulating the entry of irregular route carriers. These are very small carriers, whether or not they are in the market really doesn't matter that much. It is a very complicated open proceeding that takes up a tremendous amount of the Commission's time.

One function you might perform is helping the agencies see whether they are spending their time on relatively unimportant matters to the detriment of more important things.

Chairman RIBICOFF. Mr. Noll.

Mr. NOLL. Thank you.

In characteristic fashion I, perhaps, overestimated the intent of Dick Wegman's statement that we prepare some remarks for today. I actually wrote something which is in the hands of the committee staff.

I am honored that you have selected me to serve on the Advisory Panel on Regulatory Reform, and pleased to have this opportunity today to express my preliminary views about the significance of the investigation you are undertaking.

This investigation is the most important manifestation to date of a profound change in the politics of regulation that has taken place in the past few years. It is symbolic of the ascendancy of the issue of regulatory reform from a largely polemical debate between competing ideologies to a serious consideration of the proper form and scope of governmental intervention into private markets. As a resident of the Los Angeles air shed, it is apparent to me that Government intervention is both necessary and desirable to deal with some pervasive undesirable consequences of private market decisions. At the same time a reading of the scholarly studies of the effect of regulation leaves no room for serious doubt that in some instances regulation imposes significant costs on society without generating offsetting benefits.

The task of evaluating regulatory activities involves several difficult, discrete steps. First, while general conceptual models of the regulatory process and the behavior of regulated entities are a useful starting point for organizing thoughts and raising relevant questions, the evaluation must be on a case-by-case basis. Regulation is neither intrinsically evil nor obviously beneficial; it is instead one alternative mechanism for implementing public policy that automatically entails certain social costs. Thus, after stating certain general principles about regulation, the second step is to investigate the details of each regulatory activity: what, specifically, is the policy objective of the regulatory activity, and what, precisely, is the form of the market failure that gave rise to it?

The third step is to examine the effects—usually undesirable—of the regulatory activity that are not part of its policy objective. What, approximately, is the magnitude of these costs; are they endemic to the particular regulatory process under examination, or can they be significantly ameliorated through changes in the methods and process of regulation?

Finally, the alternatives to regulation should be explored. The range of Government responses to social and economic problems is broader than the presence or lack of regulatory intervention, yet often the debate over regulatory policy focuses only on the choice between maintaining a conventional regulatory agency or doing nothing.

Casting the problem of the design society's institutions in terms of benefit-cost analysis is a significant methodological innovation. This approach cannot, of course, ultimately resolve the issue, for that requires incorporating values with regard to the consequencess of government actions with respect to income distribution and procedural justice that are best left to political determination. It can, however, make explicit the relative economic benefits and costs of various forms of governmental intervention into private market behavior, and thereby implicitly place price tags on decisions to opt for more costly but, in the minds of some, more equitable methods of policy implementation.

In this framework, the role of studies of the procedural details of the regulatory process, such as the extent and causes of delay in decisionmaking or the mechanism for selecting regulatory commissioners and bureau chiefs—is somewhat more subtle than is conventionally recognized. These studies are attempts to uncover cost-reducing innovations in the technology of regulation. If successful, they will assuredly reduce the economic costs of existing regulatory activities. But less obvious is the point that they will increase the socially desirable scope of regulation—they will improve the cost-effectiveness of regulatory intervention in comparison with other alternatives, including the alternatives of doing nothing.

This last point leads to a final observation on the appropriateness of regulatory intervention. The benefits and costs of regulation depend on numerous factors, such as the organizational efficiency of regulatory agencies, which change with time. Other examples include the technology of the regulated industries, the viability of competition, and the pattern of consumer demand. As a result, it is inappropriate to believe that any assessment of the proper scope of regulation is timeless. While this investigation can provide useful information on what regulatory activities are appropriate for the coming few years, it can do no more than provide a methodological framework and a few good guesses about the proper scope of regulation a decade or two from now. Regulation needs continuing oversight in a more fundamental sense than the review of its current decisions for consistency with reasonable policy objectives that most of us—academics and politicians—normally give it. At regular intervals the more fundamental questions need to be asked: Is regulation still appropriate in the arenas in which it was appropriate in the past? Are better policy instruments than regulation available now that were not available in the past? Are there some activities which were well carried out in unregulated markets in the past now good candidates for some form of Government intervention?

None of us should ever believe that the issue of regulatory reform will now or in the future reach ultimate resolution. This recognition gives us an important perspective to the nature of the current investigation. It is important because it will shed light on which regulatory activities are outdated, and which need substantial revision to be made relevant to today's world. And it is also important because, if we take the appropriate long-term view, it can contribute to the development of a conceptual approach to regulation that will enable better continuing evaluations of regulation in the future.

Chairman RIBICOFF. Thank you, Mr. Noll.

Mr. Peck.

Mr. PECK. I want to pick up on the remark of my colleague, Mr. McPherson, who pointed out that the drive for regulatory reform comes in part from economists. He mentioned several industries. I doubt economists are that influential, even though there have been a substantial set of studies of regulation. These studies suggest that the kinds of situations in which regulation is applied are extremely diverse. I think that one of the concerns I have on the current emphasis on regulatory reform is that as the notions about deregulations are applied to varying situations, that diversity is not well recognized. So that one of the things that the advisory committee could do is to recognize the diversity of regulatory situations.

That is why I am particularly pleased to see your remarks that we would not wait until we had one massive study, but rather proceed area by area and topic by topic. I think it is particularly important to recognize the distinction between what one might characterize very crudely as old and new regulation. Old regulation in my mind is the ICC, the FCC, the economic regulation of the traditional regulatory commission. The new regulation is related to safe jobs, safe products, safe environment.

I think the questions the two kinds of regulation present are really quite different. It worries me if we merge them, and I am glad to see we are making a distinction.

The second thing I would say is that I am glad our study includes all the three important areas. First, we plan to look at the appropriateness of regulation. That is an extremely important question and perhaps a fundamental question, because it has to be rethought from each decade, each industry. I think that is the import of the remarks of Roger Noll.

Second, the proposed study plan includes the question of congressional oversight. One thing my own studies and experience with regulatory agencies suggests is that they seem to be a free-floating form of government. There is a very general statute that speaks to the public interest; such as sound transportation systems, but there is not a close link between the objectives of regulation and broader questions of economic and social policy. And we sometimes speak of the regulatory commissions as the fourth branch of Government. That has its advantages, it gives some freedom to the Commissions. But also, it seems to me, it raises questions of how to fit the regulatory agencies into the wider scheme of Government and social objectives, and I doubt whether we want regulatory commissioners really legislating. So I am glad to see there is attention paid to the question of congressional oversight. It is a question that has to be thought about, whether it is the right amount, whether it is the right form.

The third thing the study group is concerned with is the question of procedure. I think that is important. In my own mind and my own interests, I don't put that quite on a parallel of importance with the other two topics. But I think procedure is important because there are going to be areas we will want to regulate and we want to regulate for the next decade and do it well.

Thank you.

Chairman RIBICOFF. Mr. Hutt.

Mr. HUTT. I think I would agree with everything that has been said about the need to isolate different issues and different areas, and to proceed seriatim rather than to try to cover the entire problem of regulatory reform in one massive report.

I would, however, disagree with Mr. Peck slightly in terms of priorities. I think that the first order of business for the committee is to set priorities, because if we are to proceed step by step, we must know which step to take first.

In reviewing the seven areas that Mr. Wegman went over with you, I understand, yesterday. I have tried to come to some idea as to where to begin. In doing so, I attempted to assess what would have the largest impact and the greatest possibility of success, combined, because one without the other is not terribly useful.

My assessment as to what would have the greatest impact and be most feasible is in the area of reducing delay in the regulatory process, wherever it might occur. This is an issue that cuts across all agencies and is not unique to any particular agency. Therefore, it would have a huge impact. It is my belief that useful things could be done by amending the Administrative Procedures Act, to cut down some of the redtape and delay what occurs now, and that it could be done relatively quickly and, perhaps, with the greatest possibility of agreement in Congress.

I will come back to that in a moment because I am more concerned about getting agreement in Congress than I am concerned about getting agreement among this panel or, indeed, the public as a whole.

Chairman RIBICOFF. What you are saying has great significance. We must achieve successes in the early stages of the study. The more complex problems will take longer.

From a practical standpoint it is important that initially we look into problems with positive solutions.

Mr. HUTT. I certainly agree with that, Senator.

Chairman RIBICOFF. I just wonder how the other members of the panel react to Mr. Hutt's suggestion. Do you agree or disagree with that general type of approach? OK. Go ahead, Mr. Hutt.

Mr. HUTT. My second category is where there would be a major impact, but relatively lower possibility, or perhaps no possibility, of success. I put two of these study areas in that category. This is not to say they should not be studied, but one has to be very realistic about what the outcome might be.

The first is elimination of duplicative regulation. Just to give you an example, there has existed since 1906 duplicate regulation over food between the Department of Agriculture and the Food and Drug Administration, as well as at the State level in every State, and the Federal Trade Commission, the Treasury Department, and more recently, EPA. I find a little possibility, however, that Congress will now undo that, because I find enormous political considerations and great constituencies battling each other to keep it the way it is. Therefore, while this would have a huge impact, the feasibility of actually untangling this mess which, I might add, has been recommended by every commission that has studied it in the last 70 years, I find at a very low level.

Chairman RIBICOFF. From your experience, has there ever been a President who has tried to eliminate this duplication?

Mr. HUTT. Going back to the Hoover Commission, every person I know who has looked at it has recommended it.

Chairman RIBICOFF. Not commissions. Has there ever been a President who has been willing to carry that ball?

Mr. HUTT. Yes; my recollection is that it was in the Ash recommendation and that it was in a message sent to Congress with legislation that would have, for example, moved the food regulatory mechanism in USDA to the Food and Drug Administration.

Chairman RIBICOFF. But after the message was sent, what did the President do about it ?

Mr. HUTT. I must confess, probably very little. I think he may also have been reading the tea leaves in Congress and realized that it was not going to happen anyway. I think it would have a huge impact, Senator, and it would be a tremendously great step forward for the country if it were to happen. I do not think politically that I see it in the near future unless someone like the President and Congress got together and really decided to do it in spite of all the factions who would oppose it.

The second area where there would be a big impact but, I think, reform is probably not feasible, is the very issue that Harry McPherson raised, the quality of both leadership and, in my judgment more important, the career civil servants.

Chairman RIBICOFF. May I say, Senator Metcalf, any time you want to interrupt, please feel free to do so.

Senator METCALF. Thank you.

Mr. HUTT. I see very little possibility that the way that the civil service has grown in this country will be radically changed, which would be needed if there were to be a major impact made in this area. So here again, while it should be studied and perhaps new ideas sought—

Chairman RIBICOFF. Which way does the civil service as it is set up frustrate this?

Mr. HUTT. I think that there is general recognition that the possibility of firing an incompetent person in Government is far, far less than the possibility of doing that in private enterprise, with the result that, with the best of administrators, one can be left with people who can frustrate needed reform within an agency because they will continue to do things the way they have always been doing them, with little possibility of impacting them.

Chairman RIBICOFF. Many of you men have had governmental experience with agencies. What percentage of Federal employees would you say are incompetent? [Laughter.]

Mr. HUTT. According to the recent survey, 20 percent of all of us are incompetent, so one would have to factor it against that.

Chairman RIBICOFF. Is anyone brave enough to estimate the percentage of Federal employees who are incompetent or dispensible?

Mr. HUTT. I do not think anyone would wish to comment.

Mr. NOLL. In comparison to Senators, or professors?

Chairman RIBICOFF. All; the difference is, the Senators have to go to the electorate, you know. The electorate makes a decision, whether they put in a competent or incompetent man. The others don't have to go through the electorate every 2 or every 6 years.

Senator METCALF. And teachers and so forth and professors have tenure, Mr. Chairman.

Mr. PECK. That is the reason professors on tenure always advocate competition.

Mr. HUTT. I would prefer to answer your question in a very indirect way. In private enterprise there is an economic motive that moves people to do things quickly and as efficiently as they can and to get problems solved in a much more diligent way than there is in the Government. There is a counterveiling force in the Government that, if you take no action, you certainly are making no mistakes and no one can criticize you. So that the same forces that lead toward action in the private sector lead toward delay and inaction in the Government. Therefore, you need to encourage, in the Government, recruitment and retention of the best possible people at middle- and low-levels, and in my judgment more so than at high levels because I think we are doing a pretty good job there. But you need the middle level people to be, if anything, far more competent than in private enterprise because they have to take more risks in the Government, in making decisions. Their decisions are likely to be second guessed, not just by the courts, but by Congressmen and the newspapers and consumer advocates and everyone else. That does not happen very often in private enterprise.

Mr. WHITE. If I may, Mr. Chairman, at that point, I do not think I quite share Peter Hutt's view on that from my own personal experience. It is really more a case of emphasis than flat out disagreement. But if there is strong leadership, or apparent leadership at the top of the staff, I have a hunch that that does tend to permeate into the middle levels.

In 1961, when the Kennedy administration came in, there were an awful lot of middle level bureaucrats who seemed to have been kind of just waiting for that happy moment. And more ideas came bursting out of the bureaucracy than all of the task forces that had been created by candidate Kennedy. To some extent, and I would admit it is very discouraging and the time you have to spend getting rid of people simply doesn't warrant administrative time, so what the tendency is, and I am not sure how different it is in private life, is to simply leave them there and work around them. But again, I guess I am going to have one recurring theme through all of this, and that is the tone and mood and the atmosphere of leadership can make a difference, even at the middle levels, although I share a little of Peter's thought that sometimes it is disheartening to think that things don't get done there. But there are techniques other than firing and other than compensation by dramatic increases in compensation. And that is a job well done and the recognition and the encouragement of an attitude of coming forth with results and conclusions.

All of us hate to make mistakes, and we don't like to have people point them out. So there is that natural tendency. I think it is not fixed and so solid that it can't be shaken a little bit. So I want to temper Peter's views with mine.

Chairman RIBICOFF. I am just wondering if you gentlemen feel, that regulatory leadership has to emanate from the President of the United States. Or, do you think that this spirit can evolve without Presidential leadership and interest?

Mr. McPHERSON. Oh, yes, very much, there are esprits in agencies, and among the ones I have worked with; the highest esprit was in the military. It has its own history, going back hundreds of years. It doesn't take a President, it didn't even take a victorious and magnetic Chief of Staff of the Army to provide that high morale. People have it in very great amounts. They are hard-working, decisionmaking people, despite all the paper work of the Pentagon. The same thing can occur in other agencies. It might embarrass Lee to say it but I have been told that there was a very high espirit in the Federal Power Commission when Lee White was chairman.

Mr. WHITE. It doesn't embarrass me at all, Mr. Chairman.

[Laughter.]

Mr. McPHERSON. He can take it. But it doesn't have to come all the way from the President, no. It can come within the agency. I think at times it comes because of the nature of the problems.

The SEC, certainly in the 1930's, and even to some degree now, has been an agency where really first rate people have gone.

Chairman RIBICOFF. In other words, you feel that if an agency has leadership character and imagination it will have enough momentum to generate public support even in the absence of the President or the Congress.

Mr. HUTT. Absolutely.

Chairman RIBICOFF. The agency can be effective without the support of the President, Congress or self interest groups?

Mr. PITOFSKY. Senator, let me add something on this question of the impermeability of the bureaucracy to change; the standard change is that reform panels and commissions will come and go, reform chairmen will come and go but the bureaucracy will remain. I really think that is utterly untrue. One point to recognize is that turnover in administrative agencies is very considerable. The standard turnover may be 10, 15, 20 percent a year. It is also true that if an agency gives off a sense of mission and quality, that the best young people coming out of law schools and other professional schools, out of economic disciplines, are attracted to Government service early in their career. The result is that you can turn an agency around very, very quickly. The statistics, for example, on the Federal Trade Commission, which is an agency I was associated with, is that during a period of alleged reform, that is, after the Nader and the American Bar Association Commission critiques and then the Kirkpatrick attempts at reform, something approaching 50 percent of the staff turned over in a period of 2 to 3 years.

So the fact of the matter is that the bureaucracy is not impermeable to change. Indeed, personnel that are there, a point touched upon previously, like all good bureaucrats, appreciate the way the winds are blowing. If they see that the sense of the agency is innovation and activism, personnel at the agency will pick that up as well and will become more innovative and more active.

Chairman RIBICOFF. That is an interesting point. Would the Civil Service Commission be able to give you some figures as to the turnover rate in the agencies; do you think the Civil Service Commission would have that, Mr. Wegman? Would you get that for the committee's use?

With such an extensive turnover, a vibrant agency will have the opportunity to fill these slots with good people.

Mr. HUTT. Senator, perhaps I can clarify my comment. I was not trying to paint this as a black and white situation. I have no major disagreement with what Lee or Bob have said. But what does concern me is, as Bob points out, while there is sometimes in some agencies a high turnover, in other agencies there is a much lower turnover. And certainly, among the lowest staff there is a low turnover. Moreover, with the way the Government currently runs, the incentive is for the brightest and most capable people to leave and go on to additional careers because they can attract much higher salaries and get much greater economic reward outside of Government. Those are the people you are most likely to lose.

The people who are least likely to leave are those who cannot receive those kinds of rewards outside of Government.

Chairman RIBCOFF. Do you other gentlemen agree with that statement?

Mr. PECK. Senator, my experience has been limited in Government to 4 years. However, I have never found the civil service restrictions to be particularly onerous. It is true that occasionally you had an individual whom you would prefer to see leave, and he stayed. But since I was from a university I was used to that. But in fact the turnover was high and the flexibility was such that except for the low salaries in supergrades, I do not think the civil service restrictions are, or were, important.

My experience however is limited, there may be exceptions. I do think one can change an agency rather quickly with the right set of Commissioners, and so it is crucial that the President appoints able Commissioners. That may be the most key thing in the area of personnel.

The final point that was raised here is the question which Mr. McPherson introduced about the effect of controversy over regulation or recruitment of Commission staff.

My experience is controversy helps recruitment. If you criticize an agency, it actually attracts people. Maybe it offends career people who have a heavy investment but when the FPC was criticized, I think it helped the recruiting.

Similarly, current criticism of the CAB has raised interest among economists in going there.

Chairman RIBICOFF. It might have raised interest of economists but, on the outside, or together to work for the CAB?

Mr. PECK. To go to work for the CAB, because there is a sense that here is controversey and here is where things are changing. I think that does attract able people. Controversy is attractive in recruiting, even though people are saying bad things about your agency.

Mr. NOLL. One footnote to add to that would be that it doesn't really make sense to worry about the competence of people carrying out idiotic policies. One of the ways to make an agency more attractive to competent people is to give it something worthwhile to do. I think that in large measure, some of the reasons for observing not so much incompetent as lethargic people in regulatory agencies or any other part of the executive branch is that in some instances what they are told to do is silly. It is no fun to be doing silly things if you are competent and could be doing something that isn't silly.

There is much to be said for having incompetent people carry out idiotic policies because they will do less damage than competent people would do carrying them out. So I think the issue of the competency of Commissioners, their staffs, and the middle level bureaucrats, is one that is important only after you have decided what is appropriate for the agency to do and what is a realistic expectation for the agency's accomplishments. Once that is done, then I think the competency pretty much solves itself. I think it is important that Lee White was with the FPC at a time when exciting things were happening in the power industry that made the FPC an exciting place to be. In the electrical industry, owing to the increasing size of generating equipment, the importance of Federal regulation was growing because regional power pools were coming into existence and natural gas field price regulation had really just begun. A whole set of new policies were being developed, some of which were probably good ideas and some bad, but no one knew at the time how things would turn out. So a man of Lee White's competence was interested in becoming a Federal Power Commissioner and the staff that he was able to attract to him was interested in helping out because of the exciting nature of the job, rather than because of any accident of fate.

Chairman RIBICOFF. Any other comments?

Mr. Pitofsky, I think you are the only one that hasn't made a general statement.

Mr. PITOFSKY. Much of what I intended to say has been touched upon. I share Lee White's sense of optimism that there is an unusual opportunity to achieve some things in the regulatory process now that was not present in the past. In particular, it seems to me there is a consensus, not only of those who are the traditional critics of the regulatory process, but many who represent consumer and public interests, that regulatory process to a certain extent has been counterproductive. People are prepared to see some real changes take place now.

I have in mind particularly two areas, one substantive and the other procedural. In the substantive area there is a body of literature now that certain kinds of regulation, particularly of rate and entry, has disserved the public interest by uselessly, unnecessarily interfering with the free market. While I appreciate what was said earlier about the advisability of doing those things that are feasible, I hope the opportunity will not be missed at this particular time to reconsider the worth of certain kinds of regulation, surface transportation, airlines, natural gas, and so on. I think a case, quite a plausible and solid case, can be made that some of that regulation would be best discontinued.

Two caveats on that, however. One, I think some who would prefer to dismantle a good deal of all regulation are using the case against rate and entry regulation as a kind of camouflage to challenge other kinds of regulation. I think it is important to appreciate that much that has been achieved by regulation in the fields of auto safety, advertising regulation and environmental control does not share the deficiencies of rate and entry regulation.

Second, as to those projects that the committee does undertake, I think it is time to leave the high road of theory and begin to become very solid, pragmatic and concrete about exactly what kind of deregulation ought to take place. I think of such questions as timing and other transitional problems, the scope of deregulation, the necessity of deregulating other competitive products, fairness to share holders and so on.

In other words, I think it is time to get down and write a draft statute on deregulation rather than to continue to debate on the theoretical level free market laissez faire concepts as opposed to regulation.

Chairman RIBICOFF. When you say writing a draft statute, are you talking about an omnibus statute or would you take one agency at a time?

Mr. PITOFSKY. One agency, one industry, one area at a time. I mean to emphasize the specificity of the project.

Chairman RIBICOFF. Would there be a general consensus among you gentlemen as to where the priorities ought to be in the area of deregulation? What is your sense of the priorities? Is it the ICC, the CAB, the FPC? Have you any thoughts about this?

Mr. PITOFSKY. I do. We haven't had a chance to discuss it, but it seems to me——

Chairman RIBICOFF. I mean while you are here off the top of your head, would you indicate where you think the priorities ought to be?

Mr. PITOFSKY. I would think the case has been fairly well made that deconcentration ought to be considered and implemented with respect to specific airline transportation patterns now regulated by the CAB, surface transportation—I have in mind trucking and railroads—and natural gas. As to natural gas, I have in mind current regulation by the FPC. I think those are places where we ought to start.

Chairman RIBICOFF. Does anybody else have any comment?

Mr. PECK. Probably this comment only reflects my own personal experience. I think questions about the appropriateness of regulation should be directed first at the airlines, and then at surface transportation. I am not so sure about natural gas for that may be a special problem. But I think one of the most difficult problems is the one you mentioned; the question of transition from regulation to competition. We have industries that have been built up and are used to doing business under regulation. There is a question of how to make a change that is equitable, a change that is economically efficient. That is a difficult question which, frankly, I don't think people in or outside of Government are addressing with the detail it deserves.

Chairman RIBICOFF. In other words, you have a problem of transition. I guess, almost all of them are up against the wall economically.

What would happen to them, if you subjected the airlines to wide open competition? What would happen to the airline industry as a whole? Is this what you are driving at?

Mr. Peck. It also turns out there is never a right time to make a change of anything. But with the airline industry, for example, I think there is a quite persuasive case for considerably less CAB regulation.

On the other hand, the airline industry is used to and has made its investments on a basis of regulation. Furthermore, currently the industry itself is in a difficult financial position for reasons I think apart from regulation. Therefore, the question of how to move from the present situation to a situation of less regulation is a question of extreme difficulty, I think, and of extreme complexity.

I don't think, however, one should admit defeat and say one never wants to move. But I am trying to point out I think it is an extremely difficult question and one that is really not addressed. People argue a great deal that you should move to deregulation, but they do not worry enough about how to get there.

Chairman Ribicoff. Mr. White, on the question of deregulation of natural gas. That has been a tough running battle, with very close divisions in the Congress. That fight has been going on for a long, long time.

Mr. Noll. I would like to interject a point on the natural gas issue. I think that the interesting thing about the natural gas argument, despite the fact of the division of opinion on what to do, is a more widespread agreement on what the purpose of natural gas regulation is and what you would like to have as the outcome.

I was intrigued by the bill the Senate passed 10 days or so ago that would not have deregulated existing pools, but would have allowed firms to pay intrastate prices for additional gas. This is a stab at what Joe was talking about as the transition problem.

On the one hand there is no particularly useful social purpose to having windfall gains to existing pool owners. There is no point in redistributing a few billion dollars of national wealth to people who are already signed up to sell it.

On the other hand, it is quite apparent that we are misusing natural gas and that there is no really sensible way to allocate it bureaucratically. For example, in the Los Angeles air shed, people are now breathing sulfates and sulfur dioxide in enormous proportions because of the inability to get natural gas instead of fuel oil. Yet in Texas, localities without serious air pollution problems are burning gas when oil would do as well.

I think it is obvious that in industries like the airlines, surface transportation and natural gas, a change must take place. But we must keep our eye on the ball. That is to say, the point of natural gas regulation is to prevent windfall gains. We have to figure out a way to deregulate without having the windfall gains.

The second point relates to another priority. I don't think we should bother with the basic question of whether we should regulate airlines. One of the issues I would like to see given a high priority is a study of regulatory activities that most people agree cannot be totally dispensed with but that simply don't work.

In December of 1972 the FCC in an incredibly melancholy event voted 4 to 3 to terminate a rate hearing of A.T. & T. Although the vote was 4 to 3 and later overturned by the courts, all seven of the Commissioners agreed to the point that the Federal Communications Commission was completely incapable of digesting all of the information being supplied to them by the telephone company and reaching a sensible determination about what the rates of the telephone company ought to be.

I don't think anybody would propose that a monopoly with 85 percent of something as important as communication services can go totally without any policy intervention at all.

On the other hand, the Commission that is given the responsibility to perform this public policy service is just incapable of dealing with it. I would like to try to give some attention to the problem of how you deal with those areas where monopoly regulation is necessary, because the very fact that it is necessary; that is, that there is a real, honest-to-goodness powerful monopoly out there, makes it incredibly difficult to get sufficient information to do a good job of regulating it.

I would like to see us come to grips with what is to be done in terms of staffing and in terms of the objectives of regulation to make it possible to regulate things like the telephone company.

Mr. WHITE. If I may, could we have a general understanding that just because we don't comment on something that is said by somebody else, it doesn't imply acquiescence, agreement, et cetera.

Chairman RIBICOFF. No, no. What is happening today is exactly what I would hope would happen with the panel. I don't expect unanimity here. We are trying to make up our own minds where we are going. I don't think any of us on this committee come with any preconceived thoughts. We are groping ourselves.

We know where we want to go, and we have you because we feel you are competent, and we are being educated too. What you are doing is very valuable. We understand that.

Mr. MCPHERSON. Mr. Chairman, following up something Mr. Noll just said and going back to my original statement, I really do think one of the biggest problems the regulatory agencies have got is that through a Parkinson's law syndrome they are continuing to proliferate in areas that do not matter very much, to the cost of areas that do matter.

Chairman RIBICOFF. I think that is a very important point. I think here you could get a set of priority recommendations that would immediately receive a positive reaction in the Congress and the public and the executive branch, if they were implemented.

In other words, I have been insisting that we evaluate each program to determine if it is necessary, if it is working, should it be dispensed with—especially in a time when you have a shortage of money, where do we address our priorities? This is very important.

If agencies are just grinding their wheels and regulating things and are in fields that do not matter any more, it is ridiculous to continue.

Mr. MCPHERSON. One of the reasons why the FCC might not have been in a position to examine A.T. & T. is because the FCC was deciding whether WMOX out in Sioux Falls ought to have its license renewed. We just went through something like this in representing the new owner of the Washington Star. He filed before the FCC 9 months ago, now almost a year ago, for approval of his acquisition of the TV station, WMAL; 8 months passed by with no word from the Commission, until the Commission finally said we are going to have to set it down for a hearing. That would put a decision a year away, in which time the Washington Star would go down the drain. That is because it took its place in the chronological line of FCC matters to be determined. A matter of that consequence and significance to Washington could not be pushed up ahead and considered first.

Chairman RIBICOFF. This is important. Every television station is a priority in that community, yet there are overall priorities. It is obviously a matter of great importance whether a television station, would exist in the Nation's capital. How do you jump one proceeding over others that are piled up? Who makes the decision?

Mr. McPHERSON. We urged that it be done but I don't know how the FCC will handle it.

Mr. WHITE. If I can help Harry on that, it is made by human beings who have the right to change their own rules. A court has no difficulty, especially here in the District of Columbia circuit, in understanding what is important and has to be done immediately. We have seen courts take such matters as the handling of nerve gas off the coast of Florida, where it is obvious that you can't sit around and take the normal process. Somebody is bright enough and sensitive enough to make those decisions. That is where we come back, again.

Chairman RIBICOFF. Are you aware of a procedure whereby a majority of commissioners can sit down and make a determination of what comes first?

Mr. WHITE. Absolutely.

Chairman RIBICOFF. Do they do it?

Mr. HUTT. Yes.

Chairman RIBICOFF. It is done.

Mr. McPHERSON. It can be done, certainly.

Mr. PITOFSKY. I think there are two different issues here.

Chairman RIBICOFF. May I say to my colleagues, please don't hesitate to interrupt. There is no set procedure, no time limit. Senator Percy, Senator Metcalf. Any time you want to comment.

Senator PERCY. Maybe this would be a good time. I am very sorry, but we have a Government Operations bill on the floor and I have to be there.

I have several questions that I would like to address to this very distinguished panel. If it would not interrupt the continuity of your conversation too much, I would like to interject them now and then hopefully come back just as soon as the vote is over on an amendment we have on the floor.

I would like to first ask about a recommendation the Ash Council made. It addressed some of the overlapping and inconsistent policies that have been blamed for some of the regulatory inefficiency and delay. The Ash Council recommended that the three major commissions now responsible for transportation regulation—the ICC, the CAB, and the FMC—be merged into one superagency.

Do you think that such a merger of functions would help the country to develop and implement a more consistent and coherent national transportation policy? Maybe a one-word answer from each of you, yes or no, or you haven't made up your mind would help us get everyone's opinion.

Mr. WHITE. I have never been able to say things yes or no, Senator. But the answer is yes. For your historical benefit, in 1965 when the Johnson administration proposed the creation of the Department of Transportation, there was lurking around in those high quarters another proposal to consolidate the regulatory functions. With the wisdom that President Johnson had about how to get legislation, he said let's get the first one first. But that idea is long overdue.

I have a hunch it is one, since before you came in the chairman was wondering if there is not some way to show progress. I think that is probably one that can more easily be achieved than any other one. That would be a worthwhile one. I am sure you will have to cooperate, as you will, with the Commerce Committee.

Chairman RIBICOFF. We have invited the Commerce Committee to sit with us today. So far they have been tied up and could not do it. I would suggest, Mr. Wegman, that, with the chief of the minority staff, you talk to the staff of the majority and minority of the Commerce Committee staff and sound them out about their reaction to this proposal.

Senator PERCY. Mr. McPherson?

Mr. McPHERSON. We even went further in 1965 and tried to sound that out on the Hill and ran into an absolute storm of political opposition. It makes some sense but it really does raise a lot of problems.

Senator PERCY. Does the resistance mainly come from those who are regulated by these agencies, who don't want to change the pattern of regulation?

Mr. McPHERSON. Yes. I don't know what the docket is like at the Maritime Commission but I would hate to saddle it with the docket at the ICC. If you can get some synergistic effect from it, it would be good.

Senator PERCY. Mr. Noll, again, I have several questions here and if you could give us a simple yes or no we would be able to tell if we are on the right track.

Mr. NOLL. Yes.

Senator PERCY. Thank you, sir.

Mr. Peck?

Mr. PECK. Yes.

Senator PERCY. Mr. Hutt?

Mr. HUTT. It is outside my area of expertise. I simply could not comment.

Mr. PITOFSKY. That couldn't stop me. [Laughter.]

Let me just say first, yes, and second, the instance you mentioned is just one example of what I think is a more general problem that might very well be treated by the committee in this broad framework—that is, complex, national problems that range beyond the jurisdiction of any particular agency. It is true of transportation, health, energy, and so on. I am not sure that in the long run the best answer is realignment and merger and reconsolidation of different agencies. It may be that with respect to every one of these problems, some overriding kind of committee or commission operating out of the White House or out of the Congress would be a better answer.

Senator PERCY. Thank you very much. The next question has been debated by scholars, politicians, and everyone else: the question of whether the regulatory structure really has a built-in mechanism for delay, procrastination, not making decisions, not biting the bullets. Most of our commissions have a chairperson and one or more commissioners. ICC is the biggest with 11 members all told. I have often wondered how a business would run if every decision had to be made by majority vote of 3, or 7, or even 11 people. But, of course, government is not a business and you cannot run it just exactly like a business. Some people have suggested however, and I think some studies have found this to be true that a single administrative structure would make for more effective regulation. It enables the commission to attract better talent, focuses the decisionmaking process, shows everybody just where the buck stops, and makes Federal regulators accountable to the Congress and executive branch.

Would you agree that a single administrator form of organization would improve the quality of regulation? Mr. Pitofsky?

Mr. Pitosky. I would be inclined to be skeptical of that as a solution, especially in agencies with judicial authority, that are not just administrative, but adjudicatory as well. I think there are virtues in a multicommissioner system in terms of representing different viewpoints, staggered terms, representing different political parties and the general virtues of a collegial approach.

In general, I would say that while delays are an enormous problem, I don't think any single solution can be devised. Delay at the ICC is a quite different matter than delay problems at the FTC or CAB. I think the delay problem can only be examined on an agency-by-agency basis.

Mr. Hutt. Senator, I would disagree with Bob on this. I believe very, very strongly that a single administrator is essential for a number of reasons. You are not going to attract as high quality people to any position other than the chairman of the commission. In our discussion with the staff, each of us admitted that, if asked to serve on a regulatory commission, we probably would not serve unless we were to be selected as the chairman, because the chairman is the most important position, and the other positions are quite frequently not only unimportant, but, indeed, almost impotent.

Senator Percy. You probably feel like the minority does in the Senate.

Mr. Hutt. That might be. Perhaps the reason Bob and I might disagree is that for the past 4 years I have worked with an agency where there is a single Administrator, the FDA. His experience was with the FTC where there were five commissioners. I do think it is fair to say that the decisions at FDA were made far more promptly than would have been possible if there had been five commissioners. The issue, for example, of priority, of what comes up first, and of taking things out of order, which seems to be a problem in other agencies with multi-member commissions, and deciding things literally, if necessary, at 11 o'clock at night without having to check with eleven people, those are done very, very quickly, which, of course, is necessary in the health and safety area.

Senator Percy. Mr. Peck?

Mr. Peck. I am unsympathetic to the single administrator idea generally, because it seems to me much of what regulatory agencies do is, perhaps unfortunately, choose between two applicants who will get an airline route certificate, and I think that is a more judicial function. There may be areas, however, where a single administrator makes a great deal of sense, perhaps in the Food and Drug Administration. So one should not impose a rigid cast or give a "Yes" or "No" answer. I think it varies with the type of regulation involved.

I don't think a single administrator is always preferable.

Mr. Hutt. I would just interject one comment. I would solve that problem by taking the judicial functions in the FTC and other agencies and handling them in a separate way from the administrative functions. I do not think it necessarily makes much sense to have them in the same group.

Senator PERCY. A valuable addition.

Mr. NOLL. I think that the issue of a single administrator also is vastly overrated in importance. This is based on several observations. The first is the fact that lots of agencies, which do, in fact, have single administrators do not perform particularly efficiently or effectively. The Food and Drug Administration is, in my opinion, one example. For instance, the FDA never really responded to the Toy Safety Act, which the Congress passed in the late 1960's. It went into long thought for several years and breathed a sigh of relief when the responsibility was transferred to the Consumer Product Safety Commission. It simply didn't want to get involved in that particular activity and managed not to do anything for a long period of time.

I think there is a distinction to be made between something like the Antitrust Division and the FTC. It probably doesn't make sense to make an agency which has an adversary or advocacy function take orders from a multiheaded group. I think it would be really silly to have the Antitrust Division in the Justice Department have several coequal assistant attorneys general to carry out antitrust policy. And, equally obvious, an 11-man ICC is out of the question for reasons given. There is very little incentive to have one-eleventh of the vote in ICC matters because it is just so rare that you have anything to say about anything that there is no reason that anybody would want that kind of job. But matters can be different once you get down to the size of the FTC or even the FCC. The FCC, with its broad responsibilities, has a formal division of responsibilities among its commissioners. The activities of the agency are so widespread that no single person can be completely expert on all of them. So they divide it up among such issues as educational broadcasting, commercial broadcasting, specialized common carriers, et cetera, down the line.

I believe that the issue of delay is a far more fundamental one. I think it is at the very heart of the structure of the regulatory process, vis-a-vis its relationship to the other parts of government. As was pointed out a while ago, regulatory agencies get it from all sides. Usually there are three or four very well represented and conflicting groups that are powerful politically and economically that the agencies have to ameliorate conflicts among. The deal with all three of the branches of Government—the courts, the Congress, the executive. They can all do the agency in—the Congress with legislation and appropriations, the executive by appointments and OMB, and the courts through appeals. They really have an enormously difficult task as they perceive it, which is to get a policy through without someone knocking them in the jaw. I think that is what causes delay. The kind of responsibility they are given is not one which for all cases you can reach a conclusion with dispatch. I agree that the *Washington Star* case probably could have been decided quite quickly or moved up on the docket list. But the basic point is that they have an impossible task. You have to expect on the average that to make decisions in those cases is going to take a long time if those decisions are to withstand all the pressure brought to them.

Senator PERCY. Thank you.

Mr. McPherson?

Mr. McPHERSON. I agree with Pitofsky and Peck and Noll.

Mr. WHITE. I do, too. The only point I would add, or two points, first, the collegial system does provide a different viewpoint. It may be a little slower but it is nice to have that. Most important of all is the ability to have a written dissent. If you want to carry it to the minority in Congress, it is pretty useful to have people justify their actions and decisions in the face of dissent. The classic case in environmental matters is *Scenic Hudson*. As Senator Javits will remember that is the project that still is not even certificated on the Hudson River near West Point. One of the reasons is that one member of five, and not the chairman, dissented on the grounds that not an adequate job had been done on the environmental considerations. So one man did make an enormous difference.

I think it would be a shame to lose that in the interest of having just one person. If you are going to have only one person, you better make sure you get absolutely the right one then.

Senator PERCY. I would like to ask for a vote on three different propositions. Pretend you are the head of personnel for the White House. You have a good friend who you wouldn't misguide or mislead, a top executive, and you think he is the kind of man who ought to serve in Government. How many of you, if you were given the responsibility by the President to find the head of a regulatory agency run by a single administrator, how many of you would go to your good friend and implore him to come into Government?

[Show of six hands.]

Senator PERCY. How many of you would do so if you could offer him the chairmanship of a commission with seven or eight commissioners?

[Show of four hands.]

Senator PERCY. How many of you would do it if he would just be a member of a commission with seven or eight commissioners?

Mr. WHITE. That depends. It is very hard to say "Yes" or "No" to that, Senator, without knowing who is the chairman, who is the track record, what have they done, how interesting is it.

Senator PERCY. Let's say you have a reasonable chairman. It is the usual kind of commission.

Mr. McPHERSON. Certainly not to be 1 of the 11 ICC Commissioners. That is ridiculous.

Senator JAVITS. Could I ask that a different way? Perhaps we could get a better answer.

Suppose we limited the commission to five. We are a commission of five. Would you advise your friend to take the job?

Mr. WHITE. Once again, Senator, it depends.

Senator JAVITS. Let's get the vote. We will find out in a minute. Let's say five.

[Show of no hands.]

Senator JAVITS. Suppose it were three.

[Show of 3 hands.]

Senator JAVITS. Those three, anybody added if it were three?

Senator PERCY. As long as we are voting, how many of you would accept a job as the sole head of a regulatory agency?

[Show of six hands.]

Senator PERCY. How many would accept the chairmanship of a commission with six commissioners, if the President asked you to do it?

[Show of five hands.]

Senator PERCY. How many would accept a job as a non-chairman commissioner on a commission?

[Show of no hands.]

That helps.

Mr. WHITE. You caught some of us in the wrong stage of our lives, Senator.

Senator PERCY. I am going to yield to Senator Javits. The chairman has wisely structured this forum in a very open-ended way. All of you on this panel have a broad knowledge of the economy and how it is functioning, and specifically what areas of the economy seem most in need of deregulation and what areas of the economy, conversely, would not lend themselves to substantial increased competition? As the spirit moves you, any of you may respond.

Chairman RIBICOFF. I think, Senator Percy, just to help, this was discussed before you came, to quite an extent. The comment was made generally that, while this was very advisable, it should be kept in mind that there would have to be a transition period for certain activities that had been under regulation for many, many years. While it would be advisable, we would have to figure out a transition mechanism. But if there are any further comments you might have.

Mr. HUTT. I think it well to keep in mind that we must constantly distinguish between what I would call the health and safety regulation, and the economic regulation. When you talk about deregulation in economics area, you are talking about what our economists were talking about; namely, removing regulation in large portions. When you talk about it in the health and safety field, you may be talking about tinkering with the regulatory process, but you are not talking about removing the current forms of regulation. At least, I do not think anyone in our group is.

Senator PERCY. I thank you very much indeed. I have to go over to the floor. But we are very grateful for your time. You are a very distinguished panel.

Chairman RIBICOFF. We have been covering this today very well. Both Senator Metcalf and Senator Percy have introduced Senate 363 which would seek to increase the independence of the independent regulatory agencies. Under present law and practice, budget requests or legislative comments are submitted by the independent regulatory commissions to OMB. Their bill would require the commission to submit concurrently to the Congress and to the OMB their budget estimates and requests and also their legislative recommendations, testimony and comments on legislation.

Generally, commissions are required to clear all requests for certiorari to the Supreme Court through the Solicitor General of the United States. In addition, commissions are not given the discretion to conduct civil litigation through their own name or through their own attorneys. The Metcalf-Percy bill would authorize the commissions to supervise and, at their discretion, conduct any civil litigation in their own name through their own attorneys.

I would like to get your reaction to the basic premise of the Metcalf-Percy legislation, any of you.

Mr. WHITE. I am very positive toward it, Mr. Chairman. I think all of those points are valid and useful.

Chairman RIBICOFF. Anybody agree or disagree?

Mr. PITOFSKY. I agree that they are useful reforms. However, I don't think the significance of the reforms should be exaggerated. As to the opportunity of agencies to submit their own budget to Congress, my experience with the FTC was that even though the FTC had to submit its budget through OMB, the fact of the matter was, soon after appropriations hearings were initiated, one of the members of the congressional committee would ask whether the agency's budget was consistent with the budget they had received from OMB. The answer was often no. Then the budget that the agency had proposed in the first place was discussed, so that I think it is a formal change, a useful one, but of modest significance.

Mr. NOLL. I have one question that could be answered by Lee White. It relates to the potential cost of this legislation. When Lee White went to the FPC, he did so because the Administration decided that one of the things it wanted to do was to perform better in the regulatory arena. Besides appointing Lee White, they also substantially increased the budget of the FPC and advocated in Congress that more resources be allocated to the regulatory process. Whereas you lose the influence of the Executive to control your policy through this kind of legislation, you also lose the potentiality of advocacy of your position by the Executive in formulating your budgetary prgrams. Apparently Lee is not concerned about that, and maybe it would be interesting to find out why.

Mr. WHITE. That is a fairly easy question in my view because if I understand the proposition, it is not to exclude OMB or the President from the situation, but simply to give the Agency both opportunities.

One, to get Administration support, and the other, to make some progress if it is unsuccessful in getting OMB or the President to accept. So I don't think you really have to give up a thing. It is an open option.

Mr. HUTT. I believe this would have even less impact than Bob thinks. There are few agencies who do not make known informally to Congress their views on legislation and on budget long before it even goes through the OMB process.

All you would be doing by this kind of legislation would be legitimizing what is currently taking place. I don't think anyone could oppose it, but it would not have, in my judgment, a major impact.

Chairman RIBICOFF. If you gentlemen would yield, there will be a vote at 11:30, and I do not want to prevent Senator Javits, who usually has a lot of good questions, from having an opportunity of at least asking a few.

Senator JAVITS. Thank you.

Gentlemen, I was interested in one thing. I am sorry I am late. But you know what we do up here. We run four committees in a morning, especially when you are as old as I am. But I was very interested in one statement of Professor Noll, being the only written statement before us. May I read it to you and get a comment.

"Finally, the alternatives to regulation should be explored." That to me is a very critical point. Do you feel that in this study of the regulatory process we should also determine in given cases, case by case, whether we are better off without regulation, whether we simply would leave it to the multitudinous transactions theory, transferring that economic concept to this particular domain.

For example, there is a lot of feeling that we should allow competition in the transportation field, free and open competition, at least a much more loosely structured regulatory scheme. That would be the way to deal with the problem of rate and routes much more effectively than we are dealing with, it, with restraints and prohibitions and so on, and just let them fight it out. Or to modify that concept by simply taking broad issues out of the public domain, for example, fares, let the airlines simply fight it out on fares and see who can do the most economical job and make the most money and prohibit the Agency from regulating fares. Regulate safety and everything else, but if you meet safety standards and whatever is the Federal interest in reserve availability in case of emergency or schedule, even if you want that, just leave them free to charge whatever fare they can make a profit on. Are there any thoughts on that?

Mr. NOLL. You are obviously right, that we can think of a certain number of examples where there is no reason to believe that competitive activity would not produce a reasonable result. I think the airline case is one.

The point I was referring to in that comment was the fact that I think it is a poverty stricken set of alternatives when you consider regulation or nothing.

For example, at the local level, government performs functions that are like regulatory functions but that are usually done through city ordinances and statutes. The legislative body writes a law defining specifically what performance characteristics and standards for the industry will be.

Zoning is an example. Building codes are an example. These admittedly have problems but they seem to be more flexible than regulation by commission. City governments do change zoning and building codes more frequently than I think regulatory agencies change policy.

One idea would be to make certain kinds of regulatory activities be like criminal statutes where enforcement is done by something more like a police force and less like an adjudicatory and legislative body.

The FCC has some responsibilities like that with regard to spectrum management. They do a remarkably good job. In a few places it is impossible because there are so many users. But in general they do a good job of enforcing spectrum rights and allocations.

One alternative is to have the specific standard setting activity be done by Congress in the way that city councils do specific building codes. Another alternative is using taxes and subsidies, again putting the onus on Congress to decide the amount and the incidence, in areas like standard setting, more possibilities than simply the commissioner form of regulation should be considered.

Mr. McPHERSON. Senator, the more you pursue this question, you are going to end up like Pogo, who said "We have met the enemy, and he is us." Because you are the guys who created this regulatory maze with the best will in the world, by intending to protect the health and safety of American citizens, by intending to provide for transportation in small communities, to make sure that small cities were served just as well as the great big markets, and to make sure that shippers were served in smaller markets.

That is what the Interstate Commerce Act does. So you create, through various economic and social purposes, which you express up here in the form of legislation, the groundwork for this enormous regulatory maze. When you ask whether these regulations are good you really have to go back to the first questions: Ought we to have legislated it? Ought the Congress to have gotten into it? Those are all substantive questions, in which committees here have great interest.

That is why I suggest that in the beginning you ask the agencies to tell you in great detail what they are doing, how many people and how many man-hours they are devoting to various subjects within their jurisdiction. Why should the ICC give half its time to the irregular route carrier entry question? That doesn't matter. It is a guy with two or three trucks that he leases from someone else.

The big questions, the Rock Island acquisition, took 11 years, probably because half the ICC staff was worrying about two or three truck entry regulations. That is nuts. So if you started on a kind of a cost-benefit basis, looking at these agencies, what they are doing, where they are spending their time, you might be more successful in the long run than addressing the huge question of regulation or none.

Mr. Peck. Senator, your question about deregulation is, I think, the controversial issue today in the regulatory area. I am very glad that we have among our seven topics for the study agenda the question about the appropriateness of regulation, because to me that encompasses the question of whether we are regulating in the right areas and is regulation necessary. It is a very important question.

In fact, I would say it really is not one of the seven questions. It may be one of three or four. What concerns me is that we distinguish two things. One is the diversity of situations. I think the question about deregulation is generally addressed to old regulation, CAB regulations, ICC regulations. I think it is a quite different question when you deal with what I call new regulations, safe job, safe environment, safe products. I hope we would be able to distinguish between different regulatory situations.

Second, I hope we could worry about transition when we talk about deregulation as the major change.

Senator Javits. Any other comments? I have just one other question. That would be addressed specifically to Mr. White, as former Chairman of the Federal Power Commission.

I have been against the deregulation of natural gas. But one of the things that has deeply troubled me and why I am so interested in what you gentlemen are commenting on and the fine initiative of our chairman, Senator Ribicoff, in this field, is why it is that they seem, I strongly emphasize that, to have made decisions heavily influenced by political factors in setting the price of natural gas.

For example, instead of being 50 odd cents, if this price has been allowed to rise on economic levels because we need the gas, and to bring it out, certain incentives are required in a capitalist society to x cents. dollars, whatever.

I don't think we would have had this terrible pressure for absolute deregulation; that the regulatory process doesn't work. It inhibits production and so on. I have the instinct as a politician that that price was artificially held down for political reasons. Can you enlighten us in any way on that?

Mr. White. I certainly can, but Senator, you will forgive me if I don't even claim to have any objectivity or detachment about it. I am in the center of it.

All I can tell you is that I think it was set without regard to politics because, as Harry McPherson suggested, there was a magic phrase woven into the Natural Gas Act in 1938. It said the responsibility, and of course, it took the Supreme Court by a vote of 5 to 4 in 1954 to make it clear to the Commission what the Congress meant, that you have to find it a "just and reasonable," price. And through judicial interpretation that has come to mean the lowest price consistent with the consumer's interest that will preserve and maintain the industry and keep it going.

The Power Commission has struggled initially on a company-by-company basis and abandoned that in 1960 as unworkable and went to an area-rate basis where it took offering cost production and then allowed a rate of return, which is somewhere on the order of 15 percent, which is in view of people with my prejudices, quite reasonable.

So I don't think there was a political motivation to keep it low. I think it was a design to live within the understanding of the Commission's view of what just and reasonable meant as interpreted by courts and using their own instincts. I think probably since I left the Commission in 1969, and I have not agreed with what the Commission has done, they have done what you have suggested. They have moved away from the concept of just and reasonable, or the cost of production plus a reasonable rate of return, to what they thought was politically acceptable and moved the price up.

If you believe in regulation with a commodity whose character is such that you really can't have head to head competition, you have to move gas through very expensive pipelines, then the regulation takes the place of the competitive forces.

So we have that concept of giving a guaranteed reasonable return on investment as distinguished from the possibility of having excessive windfall profits on the one hand, or minimal profits on the other. So I guess in a long-winded way I am saying I do not think it was political motivation on the part of the members of the Commission who made these votes. For the most part they were unanimous, people who were Republicans and Democrats.

The complexity of the question rests in the view that I and others hold, that it was not the price that held down investment. It was the two events that took place in 1968. The first was a sharp increase in the growth of consumption. Whereas previously it had been about 4 percent annually, the increase in consumption of natural gas in this country, in 1968, New York City, St. Louis, Los Angeles, prohibited the use of fuels that had sulfur in it for air quality reasons. So there was a big jump.

The second thing that happened was that President Nixon was elected on a platform which said in part, if I am elected, we are going to have a different attitude toward regulation. So a prudent businessman in 1969 is waiting, he has been waiting now for about 6 years, for the day that the President signs deregulation. Why in the world should he make investments, Senator, if he believes that if he hangs on a little bit longer that wonderful day will come to pass when there aren't any controls. Then this stuff will be worth what the market will pay for it.

Senator JAVITS. Thank you, Mr. White.

The only thing you teach me is that the one line directive, which is the basic criterion for each commission, is decisive.

Mr. WHITE. It really is.

Chairman RIBICOFF. Gentlemen, I am convinced the committee has a great panel. My gratitude and thanks to each and every one of you.

We will be in touch with you frequently and consistently. We have to go to a vote upholding this committee.

The committee will stand adjourned until further call of the Chair.

Senator JAVITS. I would like the record to show that I join in satisfaction with the panel.

[Whereupon, the committee was adjourned at 11:25 a.m.]

THE CASE FOR REGULATION: A SYMPOSIUM ON REGULATORY MYTHS ([66], pp. 1–14, 21–37)

There has been dramatic testimony presented in congressional hearings on the failures of regulatory programs. Nevertheless, there is a view that, by and large, the federal programs are well conceived and provide important benefits to the economy and to the individual. There are, however, regulations that tend to be taken for granted. Child labor laws, highway safety, mandatory milk pasteurization and water purification, labeling of dangerous drugs, and control of aviation traffic all represent regulation and are generally accepted by the public.

As the hearings on regulatory reform progressed, several members of Congress feared that an antiregulation mood was gaining political momentum. In June 1975, Representatives John Moss and Senator Frank Moss chaired a joint hearing, referred to as a symposium on "regulatory myths." The hearing was designed, in part, to restore some balance to the debate over deregulation. Testimony was taken from consumer advocates, representatives of industry, and safety experts, pointing out what was at stake for the public in the act of deregulating agencies.

Senator Moss. The symposium will come to order.

This is a symposium on regulatory myths.

We have been delayed a little bit because I had hoped Congressman John Moss would be here, but apparently he has been tied up. So we will now begin.

Our subject is regulatory reform. It is one of those phrases that has been bantered about by so many and in such a broad variety of contexts that its meaning has become obscured. What is one person's concept of "regulatory reform" is another's rape of the environment, exploitation of the consumer, or return to the robber barons of yesteryear.

The regulatory framework that has emerged today is multifaceted and multipurposed. There is economic regulation designed to foster and promote industries, there is economic regulation designed to prevent fraud and assure a freely operating free marketplace, and there is health and safety regulation designed to protect the American consumer in a complex and technological surrounding in which he lives.

Surely, some of this regulatory activity, particularly in the area of regulation establishing rates and limiting competition without assuring adequate service, needs to be reexamined and in some cases overhauled. But before we cast away our regulatory accomplishments of the past, let us be sure we know where we want to go. Regulatory activity should be refined so as not to saddle the small businessman with a myriad of Federal forms to file, but does it follow that great drug companies should be free to market drugs that are inadequately tested and in some cases are potentially dangerous, such as thalidomide?

Our purpose this morning is to focus attention on the issues raised by the President and by prominent business leaders that seek to lay the blame for the recession on the doorstep of overzealous or misguided safety, health, environmental, and commercial practices regulation. Just last week the President himself, somewhat carelessly, characterized all regulation as "radical social theories that would collectivize American society and American life." He addressed his remarks to those who have a "disdain for profits and distaste for free competition," and he promised businessmen that he will work to "get Government off your back."

It is absurd to think that regulation is nothing more than a plot against General Motors or Bristol-Myers. It is ridiculous to believe that is is merely a gratuitous burden designed to wreak havoc with a profit-and-loss statement. Is the Interstate Commerce Act, legislation which is over 90 years old and defended vigorously by business, the type of radical collectivism to which the President was referring?

When a small child is burned and permanently scarred by pajamas which burst into uncontrollable flames, do we really want Government off business' back?

What kind of "radical social theory" and "disdain for profits" is it that strives to prevent a workingman from being struck down in the prime of life by a mysterious cancer emanating from chemicals with which he works and about which his employer is aware?

Is it "un-American" to insist that advertising on television be honest?

Is it really "collectivizing American life" to ask a great steel company to dedicate a modest share of its profits to keep its contaminants out of a mighty river; to be concerned about the decontrol of oil and gas prices which may cost consumers billions of dollars, which will heat up the economy with another intolerable round of inflation, all without the slightest assurance against significantly higher gasoline supplies; to reexamine the current tort system which offers consumers escalating insurance premiums and only compensates them for half of their losses?

Of course we, like most people, favor regulatory reform. The Senate Commerce Committee is prepared and committed to a reassessment and a constant review of the regulatory programs, both old and new, economic as well as safety related, that are within our jurisdiction. In reviewing individual programs, however, we must remain cognizant of the fact that in almost every instance these programs were adopted to fill a felt need to protect consumer and legitimate businessmen alike. Perhaps in some instances that needs to be changed. But we must strive not to take actions which would return us to the intolerable conditions which brought on regulation in the first place or cause new equally undesirable conditions.

On Wednesday, when we meet the President at the first of his regulatory summits, we will be prepared to join with him enthusiastically in developing priorities for a legislative program for regulatory reform. This morning, our purpose is to help define the public interest goals of regulatory reform in the consumer health, environmental, safety, and commercial practices area. We will want to explore some of the charges and some of the myths that have been hurled at regulation in the name of reform, and we will want to discriminate between those which identify real needs from those which are nothing more than the rhetoric of reaction.

What we learn today will facilitate our consultations Wednesday and in the months ahead.

We have several very knowledgeable persons who have come to participate with us this morning in this symposium, and we appreciate the attendance of all of those who have come.

I am going to change the listing a little bit from what appears on the mimeographed sheet, and I think I will call as our first witness Prof. Robert Pitofsky of Georgetown University Law Center, to have him set forth some of his studies and writings in this field of regulation and regulatory reform.

Professor Pitofsky.

STATEMENT OF ROBERT PITOFSKY, PROFESSOR OF LAW, GEORGE-TOWN UNIVERSITY LAW CENTER, WASHINGTON, D.C.

Mr. PITOFSKY. Thank you, Senator. I have a short statement that I will read in part and summarize in part.

This year's fashion in criticism of Government agencies is to blame Government regulation itself for a wide range of current ills.

According to those views, Government regulation is responsible for wasteful inefficiency by preventing the free market from organizing industrial units in optimal fashion. At the same time, it is responsible for inflation by adding unnecessary costs, generated by producing safer products or nondeceptive marketing programs, to the retail price of products.

And if there are any price fixing or production control conspiracies in the American economy, these are now said to be more often the fault of Government regulation than illegal conduct by businessmen.

The truth is that those who have turned the spotlight on Government regulation and asked probing questions—about whether the benefits of particular Government programs outweigh the costs—have performed a valuable service.

Certainly much Federal regulation does displace vigorous competition, and the performance of regulatory agencies over the past 50 years demonstrates that many of those agencies are more concerned with the welfare of the industry they regulate than of consumers. But like many faddish ideas, this challenge to Federal regulation can go too far.

When Government agencies begin to eliminate programs designed to check consumer fraud and deception—on grounds that consumers are adequately protected by free competition in the marketplace or that they are capable of vindicating their own rights in private suits—one might understandably become apprehensive that the progress that has been achieved in the last decade or so in terms of augmented consumer protection is in serious danger.

Where free market competition is effective in providing consumers with safe, quality products at reasonable prices, there is usually no reason for Government intervention.

Despite what economic models may predict, however, the markets that consumers actually find in the real world are often far from competitive.

Consumers may face monopolies or near monopolies in many situations—for example, in their dealings with the telephone company or public utilities—and it is hardly sensible in those situations to ask consumers to depend upon the competitive process to protect their interests.

Even where there are a large number of sellers, companies may find it in their own best interests to avoid competition. For example, whole industries may operate on an essentially fraudulent base, and therefore, competition among them is unlikely. Many people believe that door-to-door marketing of encyclopedias and home improvement services in the 1950's and 1960's was characterized by deceptive and unfair practices by most or all sellers; the same may be said for pyramid sales or land fraud schemes that until recently fleeced so many people out of their savings.

The second principal argument of the antiregulators is that consumers are better off vindicating their own rights in court than asking the Government to intervene on their behalf.

Again, the reality of the world consumers live in is far removed from thetry.

Soated simply, existing dispute settlement techniques rarely permit consumers to vindicate their own rights in courts because the characteristic consumer injury is too small in dollar amount to justify resort to expensive legal processes.

As a result, sellers often are undeterred from engaging in illegal practices, and those few sellers prepared to break the law put powerful pressure on others to engage in similar tactics; consumers knowing they have been treated illegally or unfairly suffer the frustration of a known wrong for which there is no recourse.

The present unfortunate situation could, of course, be changed if consumers were permitted to aggregate their claims in class actions against sellers or lenders engaged in illegal practices, or if substitute complaint settlement techniques were devised that would permit speedy, efficient, and low-cost relief.

Unless and until such remedies are devised, it will remain for Government, through regulatory agencies, to intervene on behalf of the consumer interest.

Examples of situations in which Government regulation is essential are commonplace. For example, it is widely accepted that the free market currently fails to generate with respect to many product categories essential information that consumers need to make rational choices among competing brands.

Until Government agencies—and particularly the Federal Trade Commission—intervened, there was no effective way for consumers to compare competing gasolines in terms of octane ratings, cigarettes in terms of tar and nicotine content, light bulbs and many other products in terms of durability, or wearing apparel in terms of care labeling instructions.

Currently there are pending projects which would make available nutritional information for foods and price information with respect to drug products.

As a result of Government-required disclosure of strategic product information, one would hope that free competitive markets—that ideal the antiregulators so warmly espouse—will operate more effectively than would otherwise be the case.

Government regulation of advertising is another area where the antiregulation argument is weak. In many situations, consumers are in no position to evaluate for themselves the truth of product claims— for example, nutritional content of food or auto tire safety—particularly where the targeted group is especially "vulnerable," such as children or the illiterate.

If Government agencies do not intervene and demand substantiation, advertisers will be tempted to dream up wilder and more fanciful advertising claims.

Indeed, it is precisely because advertising remedies in the 1950's and 1960's were so mild that a virtual free-fire zone developed during those years, and why current congressional and FTC efforts to develop an arsenal of effective remedies against false advertising, including restitution and corrective advertising, are so necessary.

Finally, there are the run-of-the-mill quick money schemes of con artists: pyramid sales and land frauds, phony condominium and franchise schemes, home improvement frauds, and so forth.

The position of those who would dispense with regulation in those circumstances is that people should watch out for their own interests, and that if they are the victims of such frauds it is largely their own fault.

It is hard to understand in a society otherwise so concerned with problems of law and order why these white-collar deceptions are not a matter of considerable concern.

And as I have tried to make clear, unless the Government is prepared to intervene on behalf of consumers, there is no present way for many consumers to protect themselves against such schemes. Thank you.

Senator Moss. Thank you very much, Professor Pitofsky.

I think that the way we probably should proceed in this symposium is to hear from each of the people who have come here and if each would feel free to make comments on what has been said by the others.

We are not measuring this against the language of any bill. We are surveying the field to determine what we ought to be doing in the field of regulation, and trying to identify needs or areas where there should be reform, if there are any, and also whether regulation is useful or whether there is some other alternative.

So I will ask Commissioner Pittle if he would go ahead. He is Commissioner of the Consumer Product Safety Commission.

We are very glad to have you, Commissioner Pittle. Please proceed with your opening statement.

STATEMENT OF DAVID PITTLE, COMMISSIONER, CONSUMER PRODUCT SAFETY COMMISSION

Mr. Pittle. Thank you, Mr. Chairman.

I brought a prepared statement that I would like to read. I appreciate the opportunity to address this committee regarding the effectiveness of Government regulation in this country.

At the outset, let me state that while I do not for a moment think that poor Government regulation should be spared criticism, I do think that the efforts of regulatory agencies overall have advanced the public interest significantly.

My perspective is as one of five Commissioners of an agency set up to regulate consumer product safety. I do not speak to you as one who regulates rates, markets, or competitive practices. I emphasize this point because I sharply distinguish—as I believe President Ford does—between the regulatory goals and problems associated with agencies that regulate competitive economic behavior in the marketplace and those that regulate health, safety, and the environment.

While it is true that agencies such as the Consumer Product Safety Commission probably do affect markets and competition, I do not believe that our impact is as direct or as powerful as that of the "economic" regulators. Our mission is to reduce unreasonable hazards to health and safety as effectively and cheaply as possible, not to guarantee companies a minimum rate of return on investments or to insulate companies from fluctuating business cycles.

As you earlier stated, Mr. Chairman, many people now are hotly debating the need for regulatory agencies. It is argued that some agencies have outlasted their function, and that others never performed even minimally. These arguments may in many instances have merit, but I cannot believe that the solution to the economic problems facing the United States in 1975 lies either in abolishing regulatory agencies or in sharply curtailing their powers.

I shudder to think of a return to some of the abuses which led to the establishment of Government regulation in the first place.

Let me cite just a few examples. At the turn of the century, in spite of constant pleas from many physicians, manufacturers refused to voluntarily label even pure lye as a poison or to list treatments for the excruciatingly painful burns to the eye, throat, or skin caused by ingesting or handling lye.

Not only did manufacturers refuse to warn the public; some even lied about the dangers. I have read that one manufacturer claimed that his lye preparation would "not injure the skin or the most delicate fabrics."

Painful throat injuries were especially common in children who, after seeing the white sugarlike powder in unmarked tins, often ingested it. Some children died of thirst because they could not swallow after eating lye. Their tragic plight finally moved many State legislators and ultimately the Federal Government to pass labeling laws that required manufacturers to publish the contents and dangers of products containing lye and caustic acids.

The safety of our food is another example. Upton Sinclair's book, "The Jungle," graphically described the filthy conditions under which this country's meat was packed at the turn of the century. The protests of horrified consumers quickly led to the Meat Inspection Act of 1906. I, for one, am not ready to let groups such as the meatpackers regulate themselves.

Yesterday's New York Times reported a current example of the need for regulation. Approximately 2½ years ago, 23 infants died in France from poisoning after having been dabbed with a certain dangerous type of talcum powder. Until now, the French cosmetic industry has been virtually unregulated. As a result of this tragic occurrence, new regulation for cosmetics is virtually assured passage in that country.

This country has recently seen the passage of several laws relating to health and safety, in addition to the Food, Drug, and Cosmetic Act. I do not pretend to be an expert with respect to the FDA, or any of the other agencies that administer these laws, but I have checked some of their statistics and would like to share them with you. I believe that a few highlights of their work inescapably leads to the conclusion that Government regulation has been essential.

Anyone who questions the need for regulation of cosmetics and drugs in this country need only recall the cure-all claims of products like "Kick-a-Poo Indian Sagwa," "Warner's Safe Cure for Diabetes," and thousands of other patent medicines marketed to trusting consumers at the turn of the century.

The unceasing claims for worthless and dangerous tonics and the use of poisonous preservatives and dyes in foods prompted Congress to pass the Food and Drugs Act of 1906.

Today's "cure-alls" are more sophisticated and subtle. They range from potentially unsafe drugs and food additives to faulty medical devices and electronic radiation from appliances.

Through regular FDA inspections of food warehouses, the number out of compliance with federal sanitation standards dropped from about 60 percent in 1971 to 14 percent in fiscal year 1974.

Recent FDA actions have included—

The prevention of human consumption of some 6.5 million contaminated chickens which had been given feed containing a cancer-causing pesticide;

Clearance from the marketplace of more than 1.7 million cans of mushrooms suspected of containing botulism toxins;

The prevention of 3 million pounds of adulterated food ingredients from reaching the marketplace; and

An FDA-prompted industry program to correct more than 400,000 color television sets suspected of containing a radiation hazard.

No consumer could have protected himself or herself from these hazards.

Another area requiring nationwide regulation is transportation by automobiles. Since the National Highway Traffic Safety Administration (NHTSA) was created in 1966, traffic fatalities per 100 million vehicle miles have declined from 5.7 deaths in 1966 to 4.29 deaths in 1973, the last reported year. That drop came despite a steady rise in the total number of miles driven. Preliminary statistics for 1974 show a still further reduction of some 20 percent in highway fatalities, from about 56,000 in 1973 to fewer than 45,000 last year.

Of course, many factors have contributed to this decline, including the 55-mile-an-hour speed limit mandated by Congress. But we cannot underestimate the role of the NHTSA and its companion agencies in educating the public about auto safety risks, in establishing more stringent standards for auto crashworthiness, and in establishing procedures for the recall of defective vehicles.

The Center for Auto Safety, a consumer organization, recently calculated the cost to automakers of adding mandatory safety equipment. Their calculations were based on data supplied to the Department of Labor by the auto manufacturers themselves. For the model year 1974, the highest ever, the figure was $107.60, mostly the result of the bumper standard. However, the figure for model year 1975 was $10.70, of which only $1 was the result of a mandatory standard. The remainder, I understand, was in anticipation of further standards.

The auto industry's campaign to imply governmental regulation of safety and pollution has caused most of their current price increases, seems somewhat hard to believe. Safety and emission control standards mandated for 1975 cars cost manufacturers an average of $120. Compare this figure with the average price increase of $386—more than three times the cost increase.

More importantly, this price increase is a small burden for the potential saving of thousands of lives per year.

Among the most visible of NHTSA's activities are the defect investigations that have acted as a spur to industry in speeding the recall of potentially hazardous cars. The most extensive of these efforts involved 7 million automobiles with defective motor mounts that could fail and lead to uncontrolled acceleration.

In the last year alone, some 3 million foreign and domestic cars were recalled under section 113 of the NHTSA Act of 1966.

I turn now to consumer product safety, an area with which I am more familiar. Statistics compiled by the National Commission on Product Safety, clearly indicate the depth of the problem:

(A) Every hour of the day, three Americans are killed using one of 10,000 household consumer products.

(B) During the same period, more than 3,000 product-related injuries occur which restrict the activities of about half of the victims and force a third of them to take to bed to recover.

(C) The total number of Americans injured each year by consumer products is at least 20 million. Of the total, 110,000 are permanently disabled and 30,000 are killed at an annual cost to the Nation of more than $5.5 billion.

The CPSC was established in May 1973, and one of its first regulatory actions was an illustration of the clear need for Government regulation in the product safety area. I brought one of them along with me, Mr. Chairman, to point this out to you. This is a TV antenna that was—that is comprised of a plug at one end, connected to a piece of TV lead-in wire, and at the other end of the lead-in wire are two little clips.

The idea is, if you clip this on to the back of your television set, the two little screws that are connected to the rabbit ears, and plug the other end of it into the wall, this is supposed to use the wiring system in your house as a big antenna.

Now, the problem with this design was that the little clips that were connected to the rabbit ears also were directly connected to the power-line in the house. That means that through these blades on the plug, 110 volts went right up to the two rabbit ears on your TV set. If a consumer were to grab one of the rabbit ears and at the same time touch a radiator or some other grounded appliance in the house, he or she would get the "big picture" in a hurry.

This was brought to our attention shortly after the Commission was established, and the "antenna" was pulled off the market immediately. Prior to the establishment of the Consumer Product Safety Commission, there was no authority anywhere in the Federal Government to get this dangerous product out of the marketplace.

Many injuries must have been prevented as a result of the Commission's action

I would like to share with you four other Commission experiences with product safety.

Toys have always been an area of special concern in the regulation of safety. Children generally are involuntary risk takers. They often cannot read or understand warning instructions. They are unpredictable in their use of products. And they do not have the experience to evaluate adequately the hazards associated with most consumer products.

Because children are so vulnerable to injuries from toys, the Commission has engaged in a comprehensive toy safety program consisting of both enforcement and education efforts.

Since July 1, 1974, approximately 1,000 toy products have been placed on a banned products list circulated nationwide. After several surveys were made using this list, we went back to the hospital emergency rooms and counted the number of injuries involving toys.

We found that the number of injuries associated with toys on that list dropped by 20 percent in 1 year. I think there is no question that this significant decrease was well worth our regulatory effort.

Bicycles have consistently ranked No. 1 on the Commission's product hazard index. Our staff estimated that in 1973 nearly 419,000 bicycle-related injuries were serious enough to require hospital emergency room treatment. Children 14 years and younger suffered more than 75 percent of these injuries. Bicycle-motor vehicle accidents claimed the lives of an estimated 1,100 bicyclists.

Last January 3d, the Commission proposed mandatory safety standards for bicycles to include such fundamental requirements as illumination, strength and performance of the bike frame, steering system performance and brake performance.

The bike standard serves, I believe, as an example of the way that government safety standards can reduce substantial numbers of injuries [1] at minimal cost and inconvenience to both industry and consumers.

The regulations have caused some concern to consumers. Many bicycle enthusiasts feared that our standard would effectively ban light, 10-speed bicycles or make them so costly that only a few could afford them. According to our estimates, however, the proposed standard will, at most, add a few ounces and a few dollars to complying bikes. Yet it is expected to reduce injuries by the thousands.

As you pointed out, Mr. Chairman, a most serious area of product hazard is children's sleepwear and flammable fabrics. Each year there are 3,000 to 5,000 deaths and 150,000 to 250,000 injuries associated with flammable fabrics in the United States. A large percentage of these injuries are to young children wearing flammable sleepwear.

To reduce this devastating number of injuries, the Commission issued regulations requiring sleepwear to be flame-retardant in sizes 0–6 as of June 29, 1973, and in sizes 7–14 as of May 1, 1975.

I have welcomed these standards as much as any safety standard worked on by this Commission. Few forms of injury that can befall a child are as painful, traumatic or gruesome as a serious burn.

Recently, I checked with our staff to see if they could determine the effect of our standards on burn statistics. They could not give me what they considered to be reasonably accurate figures because many burn victims are taken directly to burn centers and therefore are not counted as part of our emergency room data. However, I can report about two specific incidents, and there are others in which children benefited from flame-retardant sleepwear:

(A) A 6-year-old Seattle girl, was playing with a candle when her untreated terrycloth robe burst into flame. Fortunately, beneath her robe she was wearing flame-retardant pajamas which held her injury to minor burns.

According to a newspaper account, Dr. Robert Schaller, chief of the burn unit at Children's Orthopedic Hospital, said she avoided "what could have been a disaster for a lifetime" because she was wearing the specially treated pajamas. And because of the May 1, 1975, regulation, children's robes (sizes 7–14) now are required to be flame-retardant.

(B) A 6-year-old Milwaukee boy was playing with matches when his bed caught fire. The frightened boy then crawled under the burning

---

[1] CPSC staff analysis indicates that defective bicycles cause about 20 percent of the injuries.

bed and was rescued by his parents when he screamed for help. The boy was wearing flame-retardant pajamas.

According to Fred Bolzinger, the local fire chief, had the boy been wearing untreated pajamas, they undoubtedly would have caught fire. As it was, he suffered only some singed hair.

Aspirin ingestion by children is another hazard the Commission has reduced. Some consumers complain that they now have problems opening medicine bottles because of the safety closures required by the Commission. But these same caps already have dramatically reduced the number of child poisonings—and at a cost of only a penny a bottle.

In 1973, the first year that aspirin was required to have child-resistant closures, aspirin ingestions by children under the age of 5 dropped a dramatic 20 percent. Although the 1974 figures are not yet available, I am confident that they will show a continuing decline in the rate of poisoning from aspirin and other hazardous substances for which the new caps are required.

I would like to end my remarks by sharing several conclusions I have reached from my experiences as a regulator.

First and foremost, I believe that Government regulation is essential to maintaining an adequate level of health and safety for the American public. The success of the free-market system depends on participants whose strengths are similar and whose powers are balanced. Because an individual consumer is generally on the low side of an imbalance favoring the more knowledgeable, resourceful producer, there is a critical need for Government to provide support to insure that the system operates fairly.

Second, I strongly disagree with the argument that the marketplace can police itself in the sense that unsafe products will be driven from the marketplace by lack of consumer acceptance. I wish that this were true. Sadly, it is not. The problem is that safety in any consumer product or service is generally a dimension which is invisible to the untrained consumer. It cannot be seen, tasted, listened to, or driven 40,000 miles.

However, safety is in fact as vital a component of the product as other more tangible aspects such as materials, color, or taste. But because it is so hidden, in the absence of regulation many producers will ignore safety in order to reduce price. To my mind, this is an incredibly unfair method of competition because the consumer generally cannot tell the difference between a potentially hazardous product and a safer competing product.

Finally, the argument that the costs from safety regulations too often outweigh the benefits should be closely examined. We cannot overlook the cost increases that may result from safety regulation, but benefits are not always so easy to calculate. In a cost-benefit analysis of regulation, one must include not only the decrease in the number or severity of injuries but also the decrease in medical and rehabilitation costs, lost earning power and other societal costs.

And, of course, there is one benefit that can never be measured completely—the benefit of not being sickened, maimed or killed.

Consumer safety is not a luxury. It is a consumer right. I do not feel that government regulators have done a flawless job, but I am convinced they have done a necessary one.

Thank you.

Senator Moss. Thank you, Commissioner Pittle, for your contribution to the symposium.

Mr. Mike Lemov, the chief counsel of the Subcommittee on Oversight and Investigations of the House Interstate and Foreign Commerce is here as a stand-in for his boss, John E. Moss, the chairman of that subcommittee. I would like to have Mr. Lemov make his presentation.

STATEMENT OF HON. JOHN E. MOSS, U.S. REPRESENTATIVE FROM CALIFORNIA, AS PRESENTED BY MICHAEL R. LEMOV

Mr. LEMOV. I would like to express Congressman Moss' regrets for not being here this morning. A meeting of the House Commerce Committee dealing with energy legislation kept him away.

Congressman Moss' statement is as follows:

I commend the decision of the Senate Subcommittee on the Consumer to hold this hearing on regulatory reform. Since the regulatory agencies were set up by Congress to carry out policies set by Congress, it is fitting that Congress take the lead in examining the strengths and weaknesses of existing legislation and in recommending appropriate reform.

The key word is appropriate. In a recent speech in New Hampshire, President Ford said that reform of the regulatory agencies must be based on less dependence on Government and more reliance on the citizen as producer and consumer. Mr. Ford has proposed a lower profile for the agencies regulating the transportation industries. The theory is that lower control will foster wider competition and lower costs to consumers. This may be a good approach to reform of price-regulating agencies like the CAB and the ICC, which have sometimes kept fares and rates artificially high and imposed unnecessary barriers to entry, but it is not a good approach to safety-regulating agencies such as the Consumer Product Safety Commission and the National Highway Traffic Safety Administration, to an environment protecting agency like EPA or to the FTC, with its consumer protection and antitrust responsibilities.

It is somewhat misleading for the President to generalize from examples of poor regulation, like the CAB and ICC, to say that the private sector is overly burdened by safety standards, environmental standards or consumer information standards and that these should be removed, lightened, or postponed.

There is no foundation for Mr. Ford's contention that looser federal control should be the pattern of reform for other regulatory agencies. A sounder approach is the one taken by Congress in amending the Securities and Exchange Act to streamline and rationalize securities regulation and insure better protection of public investors by imposing standards of professional competence, standards of financial responsibility, and by policing compliance with those standards.

Congress and the Executive had been deficient in not paying enough attention to the regulatory agencies. There was no reason to assume when the regulatory agencies were set up that their regulations and operating procedures would be forever valid. It was just the opposite. There was every reason to assume that their regulations and operating procedures would be revised to respond to changing market conditions. In fact, precious little revision has taken place.

The regulatory agencies are far from perfect, but is the President's proposal for looser federal control a better idea? Let's not forget why these agencies were set up. They have been established over the past century to correct corporate abuses and to respond to ordinary citizens' appeals for help against the emerging industrial giants.

Business abuses in 1975 may be less obvious than business abuses in the 20s and 30s, but they still abound. To cite just a few, they include illegal corporate campaign contributions, tax dodges, mishandling of pension funds and, all too often, lack of concern for worker health and safety. A Justice Department suit against IBM for attempting to illegally dominate the market, the SEC suit against Equity Funding for stop manipulation, and the recent FTC staff complaint against eleven oil and gas majors for a system of reserve reporting "tantamount to collusive price-rigging," raise serious questions about the ethics of some corporate officials.

If this Administration needs any more evidence of businesses abuses, let the President and his regulatory reform advisors take a look at the 1974 report entitled "White Collar Crime" published by none other than the U.S. Chamber of Commerce. In a section headed "Consumer Fraud, Illegal Competition and Deceptive Practices," the report says, and I quote, "The financial impact of this category of white-collar crime is staggering. With regard to consumer fraud alone, a district attorney estimates that there is more crime committed against consumers every day than there is crime in the streets. The public is constantly being fleeced . . . ."

It is obvious to me, and it should be obvious to the President, that effective regulation is still very necessary. All of our experience indicates that self-policing by industry does not give the public adequate protection. Only sound and independent regulatory action will do that.

There are at least six fundamental problems with the regulatory agencies as they currently stand. These include (1) inadequate legislative authority; (2) miniscule budgets in relation to the industries they are supposed to regulate; (3) antiquated procedures; (4) lack of quality appointments; (5) too close an identification with the industries being regulated; and (6) insufficient consumer representation in regulatory proceedings.

Now let's examine each of these problem areas in turn. First, inadequate legislative authority. An example: forcing the regulatory agencies to work through the Justice Department for both civil and criminal matters leaves too much time for political interference and unreasonable delays. Congress should consider giving the regulatory agencies authority to prosecute their own civil cases. There has been powerful little support from the Administration thus far for this proposal.

Second, the miniscule budgets of these agencies in view of the size and economic strength of the industries they are supposed to be regulating. The President's recommended appropriation (FY 1976) for all the regulatory agencies except EPA was $256 million, much less than one percent of the federal budget. If $256 million is compared with the $3.1 billion in net income enjoyed by Exxon Corporation alone in a single year, the mismatch in economic muscle is all too apparent.

Slashes by OMB in the regulatory agencies' appropriation requests have deprived these agencies of sufficient staff to handle their workloads and prevented them from attracting top talent.

The Appropriation Committees of the Congress are partially to blame for failing to provide enought money and manpower to do the regulatory job right. The Executive and Congress have tended to underbudget the regulatory agencies so that they have inadequate personnel for long-range policy planning.

Besides significantly increasing the appropriations for these agencies, Congress should prevent OMB from interfering with their money requests to Congress. One way to do this is to require the agencies, when submitting budget requests to the Executive, to concurrently submit all estimates or requests to Congress. The regulatory agencies were invited to comment on this section in H.R. 3458, and they all gave this provision very strong support. No support has been forthcoming from the Administration.

Third, the antiquated procedures being followed by these agencies. It took the ICC 11 years to rule on the Rock Island Railroad merger, and in the meantime the railroad went bankrupt. It took the same agency about three years to rule on whether Southern Railways could introduce the technologically-advanced and cost-saving freight car, "Big John." Ironically, by the time the FCC got a decision against WHDH, Boston for broadcasting contrary to the public interest, the station had changed its ways and was acknowledged to be operating in the public interest. A streamlining of regulatory agency procedures is clearly necessary to avoid such unconscionable delays.

Fourth, the lack of quality appointments by Presidents of both Parties. It is imperative that occupants of the White House consider the regulatory agencies guardians of the public trust—not as depositories for defeated politicians or as platforms for expressing industries' viewpoints. Successive Presidents of both Parties have appointed as Commissioners men and women with close ties to the industries they are supposed to be regulating.

A Washington Post investigation last April revealed that more than 100 former oil industry employees are employed by the FEA. Fifty-one of them hold key positions, and ten are in top-grade policy jobs. The FEA could easily have found academicians and competent economists and specialists to fill those jobs without turning to the very industry that is being regulated.

Let's take a look at one specific example of this widespread practice—the appointment of Melvin Conant as director of FEA's international trade office. Conant, you may remember, was government relations counsellor for Exxon before being named to the FEA job. During his confirmation hearings it was revealed that Conant had accepted a discretionary bonus of $90,000 from Exxon for past services. He admitted that without this bonus he might not have accepted government employment and acknowledged the strong possibility of his returning to the oil industry. Was this appointment necessary or prudent? In my opinion, the answer is "No."

Many of those appointed as Commissioners hope to retire to high-paying jobs in the industries they now oversee. That discourages them from either proposing or supporting tough regulation. Unquestionably, expertise is necessary, but the problem of conflict of interest deserves much more attention than it has received from the President or the Congress. There may be no totally satisfactory way of resolving the conflict of interest problem, but a partial solution would be to prohibit an official of an agency who makes or influences regulatory policy from accepting employment or compensation from an entity subject to any regulatory act administered by the agency for at least 24 months after his departure. Such a provision was incorporated in the Consumer Product Safety legislation, and it ought to be incorporated in legislative amendments covering other regulatory agencies as well.

The problems encountered by the Consumer Product Safety Commission with both the Nixon and Ford Administrations regarding appointments have convinced me that Congress must prohibit political clearances for regulatory appointments. Legislation for these agencies should be amended so that the appointment of any person to the staff of an independent regulatory agency shall not be subject to approval by the Office of the President, OMB or any other office or agency other than the Commission.

The sixth problem is insufficient consumer representation in regulatory proceedings. This is another extremely important reason for industries' undue influence over regulatory agencies. For far too long, a serious imbalance has existed in regulatory proceedings. Business-financed trade organizations are always able to present their viewpoints, but there is no assurance there will be a presentation of comparable quality regarding how the decisions in question would effect consumers.

Corporations or trade organizations can detail one or more employees full-time to participate in these proceedings and deduct the costs as a business expense, while consumer groups that engage in lobbying are denied tax-exempt status.

One important exception to the lack of provision for consumer input in regulatory proceedings is contained in the recent Consumer Product Warranty Bill sponsored by you, Mr. Moss, and Senator Magnuson, as well as Congressman Moss. This new law gives the FTC up to $1 million a year to finance participation in rule-making proceedings by consumer groups or small businesses that otherwise could not afford to take part.

The Product Safety Act also empowers the Commission to subsidize offerers or participants in the standards-setting process, and the Commission ought to implement that provision, not rely on volunteers. In most cases, the number of experts who could serve without pay would be few in number and unrepresentative of broad consumer interests. Not to implement this provision would be shortsighted economizing on the part of the Commission.

Since other agencies have no provision for consumer participation in regulatory proceedings, the proposed Agency for Consumer Advocacy is clearly needed.

Any piece of legislation that has the Grocery Manufacturers of America, the National Association of Manufacturers, the U.S. Chamber of Commerce, and James J. Kilpatrick lined up against it, can not be all bad. The Agency for Consumer Advocacy would have no regulatory power itself, but would act as a consumer advocate before federal regulatory agencies and the courts. It would be empowered to intervene in both formal and informal proceedings before such agencies as the FTC, FPC, FCC and would be able to appeal agency decisions to the courts.

While the Agency for Consumer Advocacy would be able to obtain internal information from businesses through written, court-enforced questionnaires and discovery proceedings, it is not designed to have an antibusiness bias, pry into trade secrets, or tie-up firms in government-financed litigation, as opponents contend—and enlightened corporate officials know it. Montgomery Ward, Zenith, Motorola, Kimberly-Clark, Polaroid and Connecticut General have all gone on record in support of ACA, in part, because it will restore consumer confidence in business.

If the ACA had been in existence last fall, it could have intervened on behalf of consumers before the CAB during the Board's consideration of fare increases and saved consumers millions through lower air fares. It might even have saved the airlines from themselves since the fare increases only produced more empty seats.

In short, ACA would give consumers no more power in regulatory proceedings than business already has. Yet, the President, who says he favors regulatory reform, threatens a veto. In its stead, he proposes that the Departments "beef up agencies within their own branches to monitor consumer matters and be concerned about the interests of consumers in their bailiwicks." That is no solution.

Since the Departments are political arms of the Executive which may, under either political party, have an overly close relationship with the regulated industry, that approach would afford consumers little or no additional protection.

For purposes of comparison, let me give you a few examples of what I consider good independent regulation:

One striking example concerns the cost-effective five-mile-an-hour bumper standard. Despite extraordinary pressure from the automobile industry to lower the standard, the Administrator of the National Highway Traffic Administration, Dr. James Gregory, recently held firm and refused to change it.

The Federal Trade Commission recently proposed rules that would allow the nation's 50,000 drug stores to advertise retail prices for prescription drugs—a step that could save consumers millions of dollars a year.

The recently enacted Consumer Warranty and Federal Trade Commission Improvement Act may not sound very dramatic but it is of monumental importance. It gives the FTC remedies it never had before for dealing with fraudulent advertising and marketing practices. Most were vigorously opposed by this Administration.

Now, with passage of that bill, the FTC may go to court to force a company that has sold shoddy or worthless merchandise to make restitution to victimized consumers. Under this provision, which has been in effect only five months, the FTC is already seeking more than $40 million in refunds to consumers.

These examples demonstrate the difference between what the Administration considers good regulation and what I consider good regulation.

In summary, the major problem with the Administration's approach to regulatory reform is that it is heavily weighted in favor of industry and tends to ignore legitimate consumer needs. It is incumbent on Congress, to right the balance by legislating real reforms that will give equal protection to consumer interests. . . .

STATEMENT OF RALPH NADER

Mr. Chairman, a consumer fraud is sweeping the business community and its indentured servants in Washington. There is a well-orchestrated publicity campaign, in which President Gerald Ford is a willing cheerleader, to confuse wasteful *cartel regulation* with life-saving *consumer regulation*. Aiming their shotgun indiscriminately at "government regulation," business proponents invariably confuse the two and invariably conclude that it is consumer regulation which must be curtailed.

The American Enterprise Institute and its consultant, Murry Weidenbaum, spread this gospel prolifically. An editorial in *Industry Week* call people "antipreneurs" who "create the punitive business proposals, laws, and regulations that make the entrepreneurs an endangered species. Under the guise of progress, quality of life, equal rights, environmental improvement, or whatever, they create such a hostile business climate that the entrepreneur has no choice but to back off." NAM president E. Douglas Kenna announces that government regulatory actions have become a "major inflation bias in the nation's economy, adding untold cost to every product." President Ford tells the National Federation of Independent Business Conference that "I want small business released from the shackles of Federal red tape. Your tremendous efforts are stifled by unnecessary, unfair and unclear rules and regulations."

It is certainly true that government regulation which fixes price far above competitive levels can inefficiently and irrationally worsen inflation, as our book, *The Monopoly Makers*, explained in 1973. That book carefully documented how rate-setting, entry restrictions, merger permissiveness, technology frustration, political interference, delays, data deprivation and incessant business pressure at such agencies as the Civil Aeronautics Board, Federal Communications Commission and Interstate Commerce Commission cost consumers between $16 and $24.2 billion annually in waste and overcharges. This is why my associate, Mark Green, and I wrote to seven business trade groups to ask them to join us in an effort to restore competition and deregulate cartel regulation; only one even replied and none shared our concern for this violation of their much-touted free enterprise system.

It is, however, not such cartel regulation but consumer-benefit regulation which businessmen today attack—although the distinction between the two could not be more clear. Cartel regulation replaces workable competition with government-approved price-fixing; unless there are bona fide natural monopolies present, economic competition should be allowed to work where it can work. Consumer regulation, on the other hand, protects the consumer where the marketplace either cannot or will not. A traveler can compare the prices of taking a plane or bus between Washington and New York City, and arrive at a choice without the need of a CAB or ICC. But can consumers smell carbon monoxide seeping into their car's compartment, detect that the drug they are giving their children is mutagenic, taste the cancerous pesticides that went into the production of their food, or not "buy" the air pollution given off by local steel mills? Hence, a National Highway Traffic Safety Administration, Food and Drug Administration and Environmental Protection Agency establish health and safety standards to control such product defects and what economists call "externalities"—costs of production imposed on society but not reflected in product price.

The failure to understand or articulate this distinction can perhaps be traced to the fact that cartel regulation profits producers while consumer regulation benefits consumers. However adroitly business deregulators drape their arguments with the public interest, theirs is patent vested-interest advocacy. And given the well-documented insensitivity of business to consumer health and safety, their suggestions about consumer regulation are ironic if not presumptuous.

To fully appreciate business propaganda against necessary consumer regulation, we should look more closely at three sectors especially vocal on this issue: autos, energy and drugs.

Autos.—General Motor's annual report urged reexamination of safety and emission control regulations "in the harsher light of economic recession and the now critical need for energy conservation." And the Automobile Dealers Association of Trenton, N.J. signed a full page advertisement in the *New York Times* which said, "Pennsylvania Avenue must stop forcefeeding expensive boondoggle doodads onto Main Street's car bill . . . without giving the buyer the option of saying yes or no."

It is perhaps predictable that the auto industry would point its finger elsewhere for its self-inflicted problems—it was the industry's own insistence on large, expensive, fuelish cars that allowed foreign models to garner 22 percent of the market—but the facts contradict their arguments.

In a March, 1975 interview in *Nation's Business*, Edward Cole, former president of General Motors, said that the automobile industry cannot increase cars' average gas mileage 40 percent over the next four years unless the "government changes some of its current emission and safety standards." Yet three different government reports, one each from the Federal Energy Administration, the Environmental Protection Agency, and a joint EPA-Department of Transportation study all indicate that a 40-60 percent gain in fuel economy can be achieved by 1980 *without* a relaxation in auto emission and safety standards scheduled for implementation by 1980, including the lifesaving passive restraints. Such significant gains can be achieved because the fuel economy of the large domestic manufacturers is so poor.

Cole also attributes $800-900 increases in price on "inflation and the large costs of government mandated equipment," noting that "as a result of the costs of product improvement—items required by government, such as emission controls and safety features—from 1972 to 1975, the average net price of the dealer has gone up $867, and the cost to the manufacturer has gone up $1,277." Yet even self-serving auto industry price data supplied to and uncritically accepted by the Bureau of Labor Statistics show the cost of all federal auto regulations for a nine year period, 1967-1975, to be only $408, and, excluding profit, probably near $250. This discrepancy should hardly be surprising, since it has been standard practice in the industry to exaggerate the cost of regulatory programs. Auto executives warned that 1970 pollution standards would cost the public $150 per car. The actual cost, according to GM publications, was $8. Volvo, in a letter to the GAO last spring, noted that most of the data released by U.S. automobile manufacturers on the cost of federal regulation has been biased and "aimed purely at resisting regulation." [1]

Like most other auto company spokesmen, Mr. Cole criticizes the 5 mph frontal crash bumper standard, asserting that "there's no way the increased bumper cost can be recovered by the buyer in terms of insurance price reduction." Yet he neglects to notice the potential billions in savings to car owners in reduced repair expenses: the Insurance Institute for Highway Safety has found that while 32 percent of 1972 model year cars had unrepaired damage in 1972, after bumper

---

[1] It is more the rule than the contrary that an industry fighting off health and safety regulation will exaggerate the costs. Consider, for one more example, flammable fabrics. During hearings held by the Department of Commerce in 1971, Sears, Roebuck & Company testified "that the total cost of flame retardant cotton nightwear was over 50% higher than for comparable ordinary sleepwear." However, once the standard went into effect, Sears actually charged only about 30 percent more for sleepwear that met the standard, and according to Commissioner Barbara Franklin at the Consumer Product Safety Commission, "only half of the actual increases can be attributed to the flame-retardant treatment added to the fabric." Another garment manufacturer, responding to my inquiry in 1971, anticipated a $1.70 price differential between flame retardant and regular pajamas; it turned out to be only 55¢.

standards went into effect only 14–20 percent of 1974 model cars had unrepaired damage. If anything, Cole should blame the domestic auto manufacturers, not Washington, for the 150 pounds added to the weight of American cars due to bumper standards, for foreign cars like Volvo, Opel (a GM import), Toyota and Datsun are meeting these standards at one-third to one-half this weight. As an Insurance Institute for Highway Safety report appropriately emphasizes:

> A motor vehicle safety performance standard has no costs per se and there-fore it cannot be evaluated either in cost-benefit or cost-effectiveness terms. A performance standard is a minimum goal, and must not be confused with the manes for achieving the goal. It is the particular design chosen by a manu-facturer to satisfy the objectives of the standard that has costs.

All of which makes understandable the NHTSA's recent decision, after extensive hearings, to reaffirm the bumper standard.

General Motors devoted a considerable portion of its First Quarter Report, 1975 to the issue of regulation. It states quite categorically that the 1975 interim automotive emissions standards are adequate to achieve Federal air quality goals if given time to make their full contribution; but the National Academy of Science, in a June 5, 1975 report summarizing four years of investigation into auto emissions and air quality, found that the interim 1975 standards were insufficient to protect public health. The GM report also leads the reader to believe that the government has mandated the elimination of large cars when in fact the Congress is only now considering fuel economy legislation. The Big Three have doomed the large car by not producing vehicles with reduced weight and engine sizes (increasing fuel economy and simplifying emission control) while retaining the same interior passenger space (the Volvo 245 is capable of carrying 8 passengers and gets 25 mpg).

Ford Motor Company spokesmen have made comparable arguments in the auto safety area. Company President Lee Iacocca blames the federal government for the $500 million cost to consumers for the now defunct interlock system—conveniently omitting to mention that the interlock system was "one of Ford's better ideas," in the admission of company lawyer Lloyd Cutler. It seems that Chairman Henry Ford II himself suggested the interlock system as an alternative to air bags. The chairman attacked the passive restraint air bag system in full page advertisements entitled "An Up-To-Date Report on Air Bags"—which were so erroneous that the NHTSA felt obligated to deflate them in a point by point rebuttal.

Ford conveniently ignored the life-saving potential of passive restraints. Yet conservative estimates by the NHTSA show annual savings in lives range from 15,000 to 19,600 with about a half million injuries prevented or diminished. And, as expected, the auto companies have greatly exaggerated the cost figures for passive restraints as the NHTSA and John Delorean, former General Motors Vice-President and engineer, have shown.

For all its propaganda, the auto industry has neglected three salient facts. First, although the motor vehicle safety program has far to go, it has helped reduce auto fatalities about 25 percent per vehicle mile driven between 1966 and 1973. Second, the car manufacturers are noticeably silent about the extent of increased costs due to unnecessary and expensive styling changes and items such as opera windows, digital clocks, hood ornaments, rectangular headlights, wood-grain molded dashboard inserts, luxury trunk interiors, cut pile carpeting, day-night mirrors, bumper guards, radial tires, cigarette lighters, chrome stripping, and mandatory option luxury-type features such as vinyl roofs, power seats, power windows, and air conditioners. And third, there is no mention of the increased price to car customers due to the oligopolistic structure of the industry. One internal study by the Federal Trade Commission published in 1972 put a $230 price tag (it would be higher today) per car on this structural economic defect.

Energy.—Spearheaded by Mobil's $5 million yearly campaign in at least 25 major newspapers and several national magazines, the energy industry is waging a massive advertising campaign singling out the government as a major factor in the current energy "shortage."

The Mobil campaign contains comments like "What's needed is to develop more energy right here at home. That means cutting the red tape that's been tying up offshore drilling for oil and gas," or more straight-forward assaults on the FPC such as "the present shortage of gas to residential consumers has risen largely because of obsolete and harmful price regulations imposed by the federal government." A Texaco advertisement features a professional type sitting with a bunsen burner, originally burning smoothly. He comments that natural gas reserves are becoming short, and that proposals in Congress would cut them even shorter. The flame reduces to barely a flicker to emphasize his point. Then he notes that if we can get more money pumped into the natural gas industry, our energy problems will be lessened. All of a sudden two bunson burners are flaming strongly. Finally, in public relations materials prepared by the American Gas Association, the claim is made that "if gas is not deregulated, a national shortage of 9 tcf could exist by 1985." This would cost consumers $20 billion in extra energy costs compared to the price of deregulated natural gas, according to the materials

Advertising by oil companies has been so intense that the periodical *Environmental Action* was prompted to do a special story on the subject last year. The magazine reported that it "could not find a single advertisement in a major newspaper or magazine which attempted to counter the energy company line. Groups contacted who have charged the companies with misrepresentation or falsehoods said they simply did not have the money to answer the company claims through advertisements." In addition, the *Columbia Journalism Review, Consumer Reports*, the Media Access Project, and the Federal Trade Commission have all examined industry non-product advertising and found many examples of false or misleading use of facts and arguments.

For example, a Mobil advertisement in the *New York Times* on January 24, 1973 claimed that "law suits and regulations stemming from exaggerated environmental fears have blocked the construction of new refineries." As the *Columbia Journalism Review* notes, "to say that the current shortage of refining capacity resulted simply from environmental opposition is, charitably, half truth." The full truth is that the major oil companies have resisted efforts by smaller independent oil companies to build new refineries in this country. To this end, they supported an oil import quota system during the 1960s, which discouraged construction of new refineries by potential competitors who could not be sure of enough imported oil to justify investing hundreds of millions of dollars in new refineries. The decline in domestic oil development is also traceable to a handshake agreement between the oil industry and the federal government in the early 1950s which subsidized the export of oil production capital for the past 20 years. That agreement permitted the oil companies to pretend that the royalties they paid for foreign oil were really foreign income taxes and therefore deductible from their American income taxes rather than simply deductible from their income before taxes. This multi-billion dollar tax subsidy, not government regulation, discouraged investment in domestic oil production.

Another industry argument is that the government should get out of the way and let the free market in the oil industry operate. Thus, Z. D. Bonner of Gulf Oil has written in favor of "the option of adopting a policy of de-regulation, of freeing the market from disabling controls and replacing bureaucratic with consumer choice." For persons familiar with the history of the oil industry, this argument is, to say the least, a refreshing novelty. If we take Mr. Bonner at his word, the oil industry is finally willing to resect its history of corporate socialism (state production quotas, import quotas, tax subsidies and other barriers to market risks) and "go on the wagon" of a competitive free enterprise sobriety. But Bonner is not really asking for more competition. Rather, he is asking the U.S. government to step aside and allow his company and others to charge American consumers a monopoly price for oil set by a cartel of foreign governments. The oil companies are eager to forego price regulation by *our* government only because they can get a higher price through regulation by the governments of the OPEC cartel, or, more regulation by the governments of the OPEC cartel, or, more accurately, the Exxon Opec cartel. The spectre of regulation then offers the choice between a monopoly price set abroad or a reasonable incentive price set by our government.

Energy industry criticism of Federal Power Commission regulation of the wholesale price of natural gas is as self-interested and spurious as the other content of oil industry criticism.

In reality, our present production shortage of gas is not caused by cost-based prices which provide for a tidy 15 percent rate of return above costs, but by producer expectation, induced and confirmed by FPC price policies which reward producers for keeping gas in the ground by giving ever higher natural gas prices when shortages occur. The sequence of events which has induced this shortage is worth recounting. The concentrated industry under reports its reserves as the Federal Trade Commission, for one, has shown, The FFC responds by raising prices. These rising prices induce the producers to cut back on production and exploration because they are hoping for higher future prices. And then these "shortages" are used as a justification for deregulation.

Regulation of natural gas prices must be continued because, despite contentions by the industry to the contrary, the natural gas industry is not workably competitive. Although there are over several thousand small producers, an FPC Economics Division study has found that the eight largest natural gas companies control between 62 percent and 99 percent of the new reserves, depending on the gas field involved. Besides this horizontal lack of competition, the natural gas is tied together by a web of inter-locking arrangements and joint ventures. Not only is the natural gas production market not competitive, but the natural gas consumer is in a uniquely weak bargaining position. He has no choice but to buy from the local utility, which in turn is usually limited to choosing between one or two long-distance pipeline.

Instead of deregulation, the energy industry needs to be baptized in the cold waters of more competition and more economic disclosure. If the Z. D. Bonners really mean what they say about the free enterprise system, they would support proposals to make this industry less monopolistic by a) divesting major oil firms of their interests in competing energy sources like coal, uranium, geothermal and solar, and b) divesting major oil firms into their four separate functions—production, refining, transportation and marketing. And to devise intelligent public policy on energy requires more accurate data on our energy resources. To date, however, government policymakers have relied almost exclusively on unverified data volunteered by oil companies and their trade associations. In the few cases where the validity of this data has been tested by government investigators, major flaws and misstatements have been discovered. As a result, the House Commerce Subcommittee on Oversight and Legislation recently served subpoenas on seven of the nation's largest oil companies to produce data on their natural gas reserves. And Representative John Moss has recently placed on public record FTC documents indicating that the staff.had recommended the FTC sue 11 major oil companies and the American Gas Association for consistenly underreporting natural gas reserves used by the government to set prices.

Drugs.—I would like to mention, far more briefly, regulatory issues raised in the drug industry. One would understand why the federal government would be keenly interested in drugs which (a) cause 1.5 million adverse reactions annually, (b) lead to at least 30,000 hospital deaths annually, and (c) can support their therapeutic claims only one-fifth of the time, according to a National Academy of Sciences-National Research Council study. This industry also spends four times as much on advertising as on research and development and can earn astronomical profits due to an unique system of patent restrictions and brand, rather than generic, pricing.

Still, as if the 10 percent elixir sulfanimide deaths in 1937 and thalidomide horror of 1962 were mere historical aberrations, a small group of reactionary academicians are attempting to include pre-market testing of drugs in the deregulation movement. Their sole asserted support is a study by economist Sam Peltzman entitled *The Benefits and Costs of New Drug Regulation.* That study purports to demonstrate that the FDA requirement that new drugs be proven safe before being allowed on the market frustrates beneficial as well as harmful drugs from entering the market. It has been thoroughly discredited by medical authorities, who concur that while the FDA has of course blocked some dangerous drugs, it has not thwarted any safe and substantial ones.[2]

Nevertheless, necessitous philosophic sympathizers like Professor Milton Friedman have seized upon this "study" to actually argue for the abolition of the FDA. Though the first amendment permits such nonsense, there is little more to commend it. It is, to put it candidly, intellectual butchery—which would blithely consign thousands of patients to death in the name of ideological purity. But coming from an academician like Professor Friedman—who has argued that the state should not even license doctors; after all, we could find out who the bad ones were when they botch things up—perhaps these views should not be taken seriously.

---

[2] Peltzman shows that the number of "new chemical entities" in drugs declined from 43.5 per year during the pre-regulation 1956–1962 period to 16.2 per year during the 1963–1970 period; he attributes the decline to the effects of mandatory pre-market safety clearance. The number of "new chemical entities" introduced, however, bears no relation to significant advances in medicine. Any slight molecular modification of an existing compound qualifies as a "new chemical entity." Actually, the number of *significant* therapeutic advances in new drugs has been about the same during the period of regulation as before. H. Dowling, *Medicines for Man* (1970) places the number of important therapeutic advances at three to four per year for both the regulation and pre-regulation periods. The analysis of Dr. Henry E. Simmons, Director of the FDA's Bureau of Drugs, indicates that the average yearly number of important therapeutic advances was 6.8 during the 1950–1963 pre-regulation period and 5.7 during the 1964–1971 period. The "new chemical entities" statistic on which Peltzman relies thus reflects drug firms' successes in differentiating their products and in carving out new patent monopolies, not in reducing the toll of illness.

Rather than confuse CAB deregulation with FDA deregulation, government and business leaders should be pressing for far more effective drug regulation and testing. Indeed, FDA has delayed or opposed the implementation of the 1962 Drug Efficacy amendments, which require most drugs marketed after 1938 to be proven effective. Over ten years after passage of the Act, FDA has taken no action on 2,300 out of 2,800 drugs which the National Academy of Sciences found to be ineffective.

Not only should the government maintain vigilant regulation in the areas of autos, oil and drugs, but regulation should expand into important but neglected areas of consumer health and safety. I will briefly list four as examples:

Food Sanitation—A 1972 General Accounting Office Study found that about 40 percent of food manufacturing plants were operating under conditions that were unsanitary or worse. The report documented such conditions as:

Rodent excreta and urine, cockroach and other insect infestation, and non-edible materials found in or around raw materials, finished products and processing equipment.

Improper use of pesticides in close proximity to food-processing areas.

Use of insanitary equipment.

Dirty and poorly maintained areas over and around food-processing locations.

The GAO report, together with FDA's own inspection records showing a general decline in food industry sanitation practices, indicates that the consumer expectation of clean food has been seriously undermined by the food indsutry, and, that the Food, Drug and Cosmetic Act has been flagrantly disobeyed.

Food plants are only rarely inspected by FDA. Former Commissioner Edwards testified in 1971 that FDA inspections occurred only once every five to seven years. Kenton L. Harris, a former FDA official, has stated that FDA is making less seizures and prosecutions throughout the entire country than it used to make in one district alone.

There are two important contributing factors to this situation: First, the FDA relies on "voluntary compliance" by industry and shies away from the policing function that Congress intended it to take. FDA Commissioner Schmidt lauds the voluntary compliance approach:

[Voluntary compliance] takes us out of the traditional game of cops and robbers. The program relies not on surprise inspections but on advance notice. It fits in perfectly with my personal choice of communications in preference to the club . . .

A recent FDA innovation is the "industry self-certification" program whereby federal inspectors cease to appear on the premises at all, except in an infrequent, advisory capacity, after the industry promises to keep itself clean—which, given the record of many of these firms, is naive reliance at best.

Second, even if the FDA had the will to police, it lacks the tools. Inspectors may enter factories and examine equipment and storerooms, but they have no access to plant records that may show illegal chemicals in the products, or other records showing routine health-related problems in the plant. S. 641, which is now pending, would give FDA better enforcement tools by allowing inspectors access to factory records and by granting the FDA authority to seize and recall contaminated foods on a wide spread basis.

Toxic Substances.—The scope of the public health and environmental problem presented by toxic substances was clearly stated by the Council on Environmental Quality in its April 1971 report entitled "Toxic Substances."

About two million chemical compounds are known and several thousands new chemicals are discovered each year.

Most new compounds are laboratory curiosities that will never be produced commercially. However, several hundred of these new chemicals are introduced into commercial use annually. Testing has largely been confined to their acute effects, and knowledge of the chronic, long-term effects, such as genetic mutation, is inadequate. Although far from complete, available data indicate the potential or actual danger of a number of these substances.

Generally, safety testing does not occur on these chemicals before sale, no matter how large the volume released to the marketplace or environment. Typical of the adverse results are these: PCBs, a highly toxic chemical used to fireproof industrial machinery, has contaminated poultry and the water supply; lead added to gasoline pervades roadside dust as well as the air; phosphates in detergents have contributed to overgrowth of algae and plants in rivers and lakes, helping choke off other life; mercury from scores of consumer products such as batteries, thermometers and newsprint make fish by the thousands inedible;

workers die from liver cancer induced by vinyl chloride, from cancer of the lung lining induced by asbestos, from lung cancer induced by bis-chloromethyl ether.

In short, for want of proper testing and controls, the chemical industry is using our globe and our lives as a vast uncontrolled laboratory for their products.

Needed is Toxic Substances legislation to require safety testing and to give EPA authority to control chemicals if danger is demonstrated. Industry has opposed the bill on the basis that testing will be "inflationary." Testing may add somewhat to the costs of manufacturers who do not test their products thoroughly now. Dow Chemical estimates that a Toxic Substances bill would cost it $82 million, which should be viewed as a self-serving assertion. Even if it *were* accurate, testing costs are a tiny fraction of the potential billions in savings from reducing by some fraction our $100 billion plus annual medical bill, a sum which includes the cost of chemically caused diseases, not to mention the deferred costs and casualties to be paid by present and future generations.

Cosmetics.—Cosmetics have gone untested and unregulated over the years because everyone wrongly assumed that the skin was an impenetrable barrier which would protect the body no matter what the chemical. The prevailing view was that the worst harm a cosmetic could wreak was skin irritation. Today we know better.

There is a very high absorption into the bloodstream of chemicals applied to the skin. Once beyond the skin, cosmetics have as much likelihood of damaging the body as chemicals which are eaten or injected. Moreover, cosmetics also enter the body through the eye or lung. Here are a few examples of cosmetics hazards to health:

Animal studies have shown that zirconium, contained in Super Dry Sure deodorant, presents a risk of lung disease.

Hexachlorophene in talcum powder was responsible for the deaths of dozens of infants, and is associated with neurological damage in animals and in premature infants washed with hexachlorophene soaps.

An ingredient in Mennen deodorant caused frequent rashes, in some cases over the whole body.

"Long Nails" plastic nail lengthener contained methyl methacrylate, a chemical known to repress respiration and lower blood pressure.

Some coal tar hair dyes may cause cancer.

For cosmetics, except hair dyes which are excluded, the FDA has authority to ban only if it has the evidence in hand that a product is hazardous. The problem is, of course, that no one is required to test these products. If a product causes a delayed reaction or a reaction in a relatively low proportion of users—such as death in 1 in 500 premature infants—the product would probably not be identified. In the hexachlorophene case, for example, the human deaths and brain lesions would probably not have been identified as hexachlorophene-related, except that animal tests on hexachlorophene had already identified the potential for that type of injury.

Cosmetics have annual sales of $7 billion, projected to double by 1980. The National Commission on Product Safety estimated in 1970 that cosmetics caused 60,000 injuries annually. For this industry, like the chemical industry generally, there is a small cost for manufacturers to test products for safety, but it is much cheaper for society as a whole.

Government Purchases of Generic Drugs.—Last fall, finally, HEW decided to reimburse federal and local agencies in their drug buying under federal programs only up to the lowest widely available cost as determined by HEW for that community. This proposal, in process for at least six years, has been opposed by the large drug manufacturers, who fear any system which threatens the profitability of brand name sales. Their trade association, The Pharmaceutical Manufacturers Association, has conducted a massive advertising campaign in medical and lay periodicals opposing the program. The PMA has also sued the state of California to prevent the state generic buying program from operating.

Brand name drugs have long been more expensive than chemically-identical drugs sold by chemical or "generic" name. For example, in 1961 Senator Kefauver noted that the drug prednisone was sold to retailers under its chemical or generic name for 1.7¢ a tablet; while Merck, Upjohn Schering and Parke, Davis were selling brand-name versions that were chemically equivalent for about 100 times more. This magnitude of price differential has been redocumented in the 1967 hearings by Senator Nelson and in numerous other sources.

Based on such differentials HEW conservatively estimates that the government can save $89 million a year, in the first stage alone, of the generic-buying program. Much more will be saved as the program expands. There is no reason why the government should pay for the high profits of the large, brand-name manufacturers.

In conclusion, as the debate over regulation widens and develops, it is essential to avoid the conceptual confusion between regulation which should end, regulation which should continue and be improved or enforced and new regulation which is now needed. Where the competitive market can provide diverse and competitively priced products, economic regulation should end. But where the consumer stands exposed to the kind of technological violence that the marketplace alone cannot contain—sharp protrusions on dashboards, DDT, radioactive materials, asbestos fibers dumpted into our lakes—then government regulation is a humane last resort for the public.

Such consumer regulation must continue and improve. The problem with agencies like the NHTSA and EPA is not that they exist at all but that they don't perform their missions well enough. For them to perform up to their potential requires the creation of a Consumer Protection Agency to ensure that existing regulators at least hears both sides of important business and consumer issues.

And it requires a zealous commitment to basic principles of fairness and honesty which benefit not only consumers but also honest businesspeople. The essence of regulatory reform for any agency is citizen access rights and their prerequisites as follows:

Openness of proceedings, avoidance of *ex parte* contacts at the Commissioner level or the logging of outside contacts.

Citizen standing to file lawsuits, and the provision of attorneys fees when successful, to compel fulfillment of statutory requirements by ineffective agencies.

Funding systems, such as the $1 milion FTC authorization, to encourage interested citizens to participate in regulatory activities.

Adequate and innovative sanctions for violation of agency rules or regulations, and personal sanctions on regulators who themselves demonstrably neglect or flout their statutory obligations.

Strict deadlines, with appropriate penalties, for lawyers and their respondents who often have an incentive to systematically slow down proceedings.

Compliance reports every year by regulatory agencies.

The provision of adequate powers (e.g., subpoena power) for an agency to conduct its assigned business.

Disclosure of the economic interests of Commissioners and higher level staff, as well as a prohibition on employment by an agency-regulated firm within three years of departure from government.

Gerald Ford's speeches, invariably to business groups, do not allude to these citizen access rights to their government. He has never addressed a consumer group to tell them he will do everything he can as President to help make products and services safer or more reasonably priced for consumers and their children. But last week he told businessmen that he will work hard to make them bigger. I suppose that sums up where our unelected President's mindset is at. Let us see what Congress does in response.

Thank you.

Senator Moss. Next we will hear from Dr. Nicholas A. Ashford, senior staff member, center for policy alternatives, MIT.

STATEMENT OF NICHOLAS A. ASHFORD, SENIOR STAFF MEMBER, CENTER FOR POLICY ALTERNATIVES, MASSACHUSETTS INSTITUTE OF TECHNOLOGY, CAMBRIDGE, MASS.

Mr. Ashford. Thank you, Mr. Chairman. I want to read in part from my prepared statement and summarize in the interest of time.

Senator Moss. You may do so. Thank you.

Mr. Ashford. The disadvantage of going last, is I think, inevitable that someone else says more eloquently what you intended to say, but I will proceed in any event.

Senator Moss. We are very glad to have your point of view, and even though it coincides with something we have heard, it would strengthen it to hear you say it again.

Mr. Ashford. Thank you.

In difficult economic times, it is to be expected that a society reexamine the question of whether the longer-range benefits that are likely to accrue from environmental/safety regulations are justified by potentially high shorter-range costs. This is the simplest way to state the problem; it can also be the most deceptive. Let me instead address four other interrelated questions whose answers illustrate the true complexity of the regulation issue:

One: Are there important distinctions in the justification of Government intervention in environmental safety matters as compared to economic regulation such as that found in antitrust or utility regulation?

Two: How appropriate are traditional cost-benefit techniques for making social decisions?

Three: What are the problems inherent in evaluating and comparing the costs and benefits of a particular environmental-safety regulation?

Four: What evidence do we have as to the effects of regulation on technological innovation?

This last question is important not because technological innovation is a surrogate for industrial growth, measured in GNP or productivity terms—but because technological innovation is a measure of the ability of a society to change and to ameliorate in some sense the problems created by technology itself. This is especially important since many of a society's problems, though real, are primarily adjustment problems—transient problems—like the oil crisis.

THE JUSTIFICATION FOR GOVERNMENT INTERVENTION IN ENVIRONMENTAL-SAFETY MATTERS

The rationale for Government intervention in the marketplace is usually expressed in terms of two purposes; either (1) to improve the working of the market for goods and services by encouraging competition, economic efficiency and the diversity of available goods and services, or (2) to ameliorate the adverse consequences of market activities and technology in general by reducing the attendant social costs.

The underlying reason for pursuing these goals is not to improve the efficiency of the market for its own sake, but to optimize social welfare. Economic regulation generally addresses itself to the first purpose by attempting to ensure that the price mechanism operates efficiently to properly allocate goods and services between economic sectors and between producers and consumers, but also to properly allocate resources between generations.

Economic regulation, properly carried out, thereby is generally expected to reduce the prices of the goods and services it seeks to regulate.

Environmental safety regulation, on the other hand, attempts to internalize the social costs attending market activities—especially those associated with technology—and it does this by making sure that the prices of goods and services reflect the true costs to the consumer. Thus, it might be expected that prices increase in some cases. Including the costs of minimizing adverse health or safety consequences from technology in the price of goods and services represents a shift in the way the costs are accounted for and not necessarily a true increase in the cost to society.

Furthermore, for reasons to be explained a little later, environmental or safety regulation may not only decrease the total cost to the society but may reduce prices as well.

Thus, we can see that the two kinds of regulation, economic and environmental safety, are expected to operate somewhat differently because they address different apsects of market activity.

There is, however, one further critical distinction: environmental safety regulation also may have as a fundamental purpose the protection of certain groups of people—for example, children, workers in an asbestos plant, or the less educated. This is justified under the principle of equity or fairness whereby some economic efficiency is said to be sacrificed for the health or safety of those special groups.

Price increases which result from internalizing the health or safety costs, for example in making products safe, do not necessarily result in a reduction of real economic efficiency, but protecting a group of workers may. Optimizing the social welfare should not be confused with maximizing the social welfare. To the extent that a regulatory decision seeks to protect a select group of people, additional costs—and benefits—arise above what might be expected if the only concern were to protect as many lives as possible, regardless of their distribution.

For example, it is conceivable that asbestos might be banned from use as a brake lining with the result that more lives are lost on the highway, due to less efficient brakes, than are saved in asbestos manufacturing operations. These additional costs might be justified or even demanded by consideration of equity, since it is selected workers in those plants that pay for it with their lives.

The fact that economic efficiency is sometimes treated for equity considerations should not be disturbing unless it is either unnecessary for the result or one forgets that economic efficiency is a measure of maximizing rather than optimizing social welfare.

In fact, it should be remembered that we do pay special attention to small business in formulating our economic regulatory strategies, and we do this with a conscious tradeoff between economic efficiency and equity considerations in maintaining the viability of the small firm. Regulatory policies aimed at fairness to the consumer or worker are no less justified.

Lest one is left with the impression that environmental safety regulations either contribute to economic inefficiency or at most do not improve economic efficiency, a further observation is helpful.

The price mechanism is theoretically supposed to allocate resources properly between this generation and the next. If the price today does not reflect all the real economic costs, the commodity may be underpriced and too much is consumed. This has been made fairly clear to us in the case of oil. Difficulties arise from both the fact that the economy is operating some distance from efficiency and also because a rapid attempt to bring the market into equilibrium may cause immense adjustment and transient costs.

If, in fact, the prices of goods and services today similarly do not reflect the attendant social costs, and especially if these costs are increasing rapidly—like pollution—or will be included in the price at an increasing rate, because of consumer action, we are also using material resources too rapidly because they are underpriced. In the language of the economist, we are made economically inefficient by not internalizing the externalities. Having reviewed some of the distinctive justifications for environmental safety regulation, we might ask how appropriate are traditional cost-benefit techniques for making social decisions?

THE APPROPRIATENESS OF COST-BENEFIT ANALYSIS FOR MAKING SOCIAL DECISIONS

Economic analysis not only helps to describe many issues in environmental safety regulation, it also provides tools such as cost-benefit analysis for helping to evaluate the consequences of decisions.

There are seen to be several levels of application for cost-benefit analysis: (1) cost-benefit analysis can be used to estimate the immediate economic consequences of a project which have established market values; (2) theoretically it can also include monetarily quantifiable costs that the market does not normally capture—because of imperfections, lack of information and so forth; (3) at yet a more sophisticated level, cost-benefit analysis theoretically can attempt to include even those effects with no established market value, but which are clearly part of the entire social cost of the project.

Some of the major problems arise at this third level. Health and safety benefits are not easily compared to dollar costs. The market value of human life is not adequately represented in the traditional measures of lost wages, awards for pain and suffering, or willingness to trade off risk of harm for lower prices in the marketplace. It is extremely difficult for one to relate to long-range, low-probability risks of harm or, to put it another way, it is difficult to value benefits likely to accrue in the future, if at all. Furthermore, since the costs and benefits of regulation occur in different time frames, one is faced with the inevitable difficulty of applying an appropriate discount rate to items difficult if not impossible to quantify monetarily in the first place.

The situation is further complicated by the fact that often too little is known about adverse health effects of environmental pollutants and decisions and valuation of these effects must nonetheless be made.

Often, decisionmaking has economic efficiency as its only objective. However, the question of who pays the cost and who reaps the benefit is also important. Minimizing nonrandom victimization through a concern for individual justice is a legitimate social goal which may at times conflict with attainment of economic efficiency. Society may prefer to move away from an economically efficient point in order to have a fairer distribution of costs and benefits. Of course, different people view what is fair differently, but this fact makes the consideration of equity no less important. Whatever the alternative value judgments are as to what is fair, we should know what the costs are for those alternatives we wish to consider. This fourth level of applying cost-benefit analysis is rarely considered and differs from the previous level because it recognizes that one person's cost cannot simply be evenly traded for another person's benefit if the risk of harm falls on a selected group of people.

In short, cost-benefit analysis takes no special notice of the fact that the cost and benefit streams accrue to different elements of society. To what extent then is cost-benefit useful as a rational basis for action?

Expert consultants, economists or otherwise, have little more to contribute than other citizens to the evaluation of equity effects or regulatory decisions. Such an evaluation should be made collectively by an informed public and be a reflection of the societal values. The value put on equity consideration is in practice assessed—usually implicitly—by the public's elected and appointed representatives.

One of a public official's responsibilities is, in fact, to protect minority interests and the disadvantaged. What economists can do is specify the equity effects, as well as allocative effects, of regulatory decisions. The nature and distribution of these effects among the population are important considerations in society's evaluation of regulatory decisions, for which expert opinion cannot substitute.

One word of caution: despite its implications and the methodological problems associated with its use, one might think that cost-benefit analysis is at least employed in good faith, solely as a technical aid to decisionmakers.

In practice, unfortunately, this description is often not the case. Cost-benefit analysis is too often used in an attempt to convince other parties that a course of action—predetermined on other grounds—is justified. Value judgments are often hidden in the assumptions on which the calculation is based.

It should be clear that what is needed is a procedure which will present the uncertain costs and benefits in a scheme which will allow comparison of alternative regulatory strategies, setting out separately the monetarily quantifiable elements, other quantifiables, nonquantifiables, equity consequences, and so forth. In other words, what tradeoffs—dollars, health, equity—are in fact made by the regulator should be made obvious since no attempt should be made to reduce the analysis to a cost-benefit analysis with a single normative value—i.e. dollars.

In practice, the uncertainty of the many factors important for making regulatory decisions may not be reduced significantly for a variety of reasons. Especially if that is the case, the setting of immediate and subsequent requirements and the timing for compliance are crucial elements of a dynamic and continually responsive regulatory scheme.

The word responsive is key here. Regulation in the last analysis is a political process. If the decisionmaking process is equally accessible to all affected parties, if minority interests are not weighted away, and if the regulator is held accountable for stating explicitly the tradeoffs he or she is making, then more responsive—and responsible—environmental safety decisions may be made.

EVIDENCE OF THE EFFECTS OF NEGOTIATIONS ON TECHNOLOGICAL INNOVATION [1]

I would like to end with a brief discussion of the evidence we do have of the effects of regulation on technological innovation.

Some analysts have expressed concern that governmental regulation of economic activity tends to inhibit innovation. Others argue, however, that regulation may stimulate innovative activity by focusing attention on hitherto overlooked problems and possibilities.

With respect to chemicals, the issue of the impact of regulation on innovation has been investigated in perhaps the greatest detail

---

[1] Some of the material presented here has been excerpted from the National Science Foundation study on innovation entitled, "National Support of Science and Technology: An Evaluation of Foreign Experiences," conducted by the Center for Policy Alternatives at M.I.T., soon to be completed. Material has also been borrowed from the interim report of a study sponsored by the Council on Environmental Quality and the Environmental Protection Agency entitled, "The Impact of Governmental Restrictions on the Production and Use of Chemicals," also conducted at the Center for Policy Alternatives.

in the case of the pharmaceuticals industry. Peltzman argues that the 1962 Kefauver amendments, establishing an efficacy requirement for newly introduced prescription drugs, resulted in a reduced rate of introduction of new drugs, and a much higher R. & D. cost per drug introduced. The net effect of this governmental regulation, according to Peltzman, was to increase the cost and reduce the therapeutic value of drugs available to consumers. In a similar vein, another researcher has found that the 1962 regulations had the effect of increasing the tendency toward concentration in the pharmaceuticals industry, presumably by raising the minimum efficient scale of corporate R. & D. activity.

A third researcher, comparing the United States and Britain, finds evidence of a drug lag—delayed introduction into the United States of new drugs of proven therapeutic value—which he attributes to the greater stringency of U.S. regulation.

Others have disputed some of these findings, arguing that the number of new drugs is a poor index of the rate of therapeutic advance. Moreover, the decrease in the rate of introduction of new drugs preceded the Kefauver amendment and could have been attributable to diminishing returns. It would not be expected that continued expenditure of a given amount of resources would yield equal increments of therapeutic advance forever—having spent a certain sum on development of aspirin, for example, it is not likely that an additional R. & D. investment of the same magnitude for development of new headache remedies will result in the same degree of therapeutic advance over aspirin as aspirin represented over its predecessors.

In sum, the issue remains unsettled, and presumably would benefit from additional research through here, as elsewhere, the ubiquitous phenomenon of diminishing returns might quickly set in.

In addition to possible negative implications of regulation for innovative activity, there may also be beneficial consequences which should be considered. Regulation may stimulate recovery of hitherto discarded, economically useful byproducts of manufacturing processes. Effluent controls, for example, may be partly responsible for recent, substantial increases in chemical recycling and recovery activities in the paper industry.

It should be noted that the National Science Foundation recently sponsored a comprehensive survey of the literature on the impact of regulation on innovation in the chemical industry. The study concludes that:

Environmental regulations which are designed to internalize external costs of the production or use of chemicals or other products will nearly always raise the costs of production or reduce output in the short run. These increased costs may provide a stimulus toward innovative activity. In fact, innovation may be necessary if firms are to meet environmental regulations at all. Much concern has been expressed about the impact of such costs on profitability and on funds available for innovative activity in the longer run. However, new environmental regulations have opened up large markets for new pollution monitoring and control devices as well as new opportunities for creative process engineering.

Unfortunately, almost no work has appeared in the literature which has attempted to measure or even to model in a rigorous way the impacts of environmental regulation on technological innovation. There is a clear need for careful research in this area.

In a study conducted for the National Science Foundation, now in its final stages, the Center for Policy Alternatives has investigated the characteristics of innovation in five industries in France, Germany, Holland, the United Kingdom, and Japan.

On the basis of interviews of 164 successful, unsuccessful, and ongoing projects conducted in the firms, the relative importance of various governmental programs for stimulating innovation was assessed. The Government programs studied include those designed to enhance technological change and those intended to ameliorate its adverse consequences.

Much discussion of regulation focuses on how environmental programs function when seen from a governmental perspective. It is also necessary to view them as a firm would in order to perceive fully their influence on technological change. Broadly speaking, there are three basic kinds of effects the environmental laws have been seen to have on firm activity.

The first type of impact is the one which is most generally perceived and discussed—it is also the one most bemoaned by corporate spokesmen. This is the essentially restrictive influence environmental regulations have on corporate activity. It may legitimately be termed restrictive since one can assume that without legislation or other legal sanctions environmental concerns would not enter into corporate decisionmaking to as great an extent, and that therefore the resources which after regulation are devoted to environmental amelioration must be diverted to some degree from what would have otherwise been their uses. This imposes certain additional production costs, especially in the case of heavily polluting firms, and constrains the choice of product and process technology. Similarly, but more indirectly, the new restrictions may change the pattern of resource availability, increasing or decreasing raw materials costs and altering sources of supply, and thereby modifying methods of production.

Lastly, the environmental programs may also be costly in terms of time. Not only is additional time required to plan for and implement environmental regulations, but also one sees the recent record of new corporate development replete with instances of lawsuits, protests, and administrative proceedings delaying and halting efforts toward expansion.

But this is not the entire story. A second type of general impact from environmental regulation is expansive in that it tends to encourage technological innovation in firms. The existence of this effect is a very important part of the findings of our study and one which will he documented to a fuller extent below, and completely when the report is released. What has been seen is that environmental regulation, by forcing firms to implement product or process changes, oftentimes incidentally, shocks them out of a rather inflexible production system and thereby provides the catalyst which is necessary for innovation to occur.

In short, we see that firms, especially large firms and older firms, become caught in an inertial circle which hampers their innovative potential, and from which governmental regulation may extricate them. The prototypical example of this salutary effect is that a firm, forced by antipollution regulations to abandon or modify a long-used product or process, in so doing is able to improve greatly upon that product or process. The improvements generated in this manner go far beyond the changes mandated by regulation, but they are in large part derived from the reassessment which is necessitated and stimulated by regulation in the first place.

A third type of effect, also expansive, is more particularized in that it centers on the products and processes which actually control environmental pollution. Regulation here has virtually created a whole new source of demand for industry to satisfy—not only through increased production of existing abatement technologies, but also through development of new and improved techniques. Moreover, it seems reasonably certain that this demand will continue at about the same or greater magnitude for the foreseeable future: In spite of the energy crisis and difficult economic times, most of the industrialized nations have made long-term commitments to environmental programs which are only now beginning to operate at full steam.

The above discussion outlines in broad terms the quality of the effects environmental regulation has on industrial firms. It neglects to deal directly with the issues of where and by whom such effects are felt. Yet, the distributional problem is a very important part of any consideration of environmental regulation, and one which has significant implications for the pattern of innovation.

Pollution may be said to be a sectoral phenomenon in many respects: Certain industrial sectors produce the bulk of it, that is chemicals, automobiles, energy production; certain geographic sectors are heavily beset by it, while others suffer hardly at all, and certain industry groups are reaping most of the profits from its control. As a consequence, the restrictive effect of environmental regulation is felt strongly only in a few industries. In our sample, for instance, chemicals and automobiles were greatly effected, textiles to some degree, and computers and consumer electronics almost not at all. This pattern of impacts was uniform across the five countries. Similarly, the incidentally expansive effect of regulation will be felt only in certain industries, as well the more directly expansive demand for pollution control technologies.

In response to this last phenomenon, we have seen a pollution control industry arise throughout the five countries and the United States. This industry has experienced a period of incredible growth and prosperity during the last 5 years, suggesting the conclusion that whatever flagging profits may result from environmental constraints elsewhere are being absorbed by the pollution control sector. One sees, therefore, that regulatory costs, far from being a net drain on society, actually are a transference of wealth from one sector to another. The emergence of this new sector is a significant phenomenon since it shows governmentally-stimulated innovation on a large scale. The contours of this new industry have not yet been charted, although this is an important area for futher study. Our study, in any case, confirms itself to the forementioned industry groups, which are not, generally speaking, part of the pollution control industry itself.

We noted for each of the projects studied whether the degree of regulatory constraints involved was perceived to be of marginal, moderate, or great significance for the project. Table 6.18 shows that the expected relationship indeed exists and is highly significant [p< .006]. Regulatory constraints are perceived to be of moderate or great significance in only 9.5 percent and 13.0 percent of the computer and consumer electronics projects in contrast to textiles [17.2 percent], industrial chemicals [31.7 percent] and automotive projects [57.2 percent].

TABLE 6.18.—FIRMS' PERCEPTION OF REGULATORY CONSTRAINTS IN EACH OF THE INDUSTRIES (MOSTLY ENVIRONMENTAL AND SAFETY)

Perception of regulatory constraints	Computer	Consumer electronics	Textiles	Industrial chemical	Automotive	Total
Marginal	19	20	24	28	12	103
Percent	90.5	87.0	82.8	68.3	42.9	72.5
Moderate	0	1	1	6	5	13
Percent	0	4.3	3.4	14.6	17.9	9.2
Very significant	2	2	4	7	11	26
Percent	9.5	8.7	13.8	17.1	39.3	18.3
n	21	23	29	41	28	142
Percent	100.0	100.0	100.0	100.0	100.0	100.0

Note: Chi square=21,83850 with 8 degrees of freedom. Significance=0.0052. Number of missing observations=22.

Interviewers were asked to indicate whether a project was: (1) a direct response to a Government action, (2) an indirect response, or (3) conducted any differently because of regulatory constraints. Here we find that it makes no difference whether a project is initiated in either direct or indirect response to Government action. But Government regulatory constraints are more likely to be found in association with successful projects.

This may come as a bit of a surprise. None of the policies directly aimed at stimulating innovative performance shows any relation to performance, while regulatory constraints not directly aimed at stimulating innovation—mostly environmental and safety—are related to performance. One way of viewing environmental/safety regulatory constraints is that they add critical performance dimensions to the problem space faced by the engineer. An engineer faced with a technical problem attempts to fit a solution into an envelope defined along a number of critical dimensions, for example cost, weight, energy consumption, resolution, channel isolation, et cetera. The introduction of regulatory constraints increases the number of critical dimensions, making the problem space that much more complex.

The technology for accomplishing product safety improvements, reducing pollutants, et cetera, is often readily available. The only reason these improvements had not been introduced is because the dimension of safety or reduced pollution was not seen by the engineer as a critical dimension in his problem space, or was given a low rating relative to other dimensions. Once these dimensions are given some importance, however, a reservoir of technology can be tapped, which will allow relatively easy improvement.

Furthermore, since Government regulations are often stated in terms of fairly precise specifications, the problem solver is allowed, indeed tempted, to place these fixed requirements on the critical dimensions. There is no payoff for optimizing along the dimensions. One need only meet the specification. When this is the case, it has been argued in the literature that such dimensions operate as a filter, through which each potential solution is passed with a go/no-go decision on each dimension. Such dimensions are viewed as more important than those along which there is some freedom of movement. Consequently, greater resources are applied to meeting the fixed requirements, and this coupled with the availability of untapped technology increases the likelihood of successful accomplishments.

On the other hand, performance rather than specification standards would encourage technological innovation along the dimensions demanded by regulation since no predetermined compliance method is mandated.

These preliminary but statistically significant results in the industry interviews give persuasive evidence that regulatory demands stimulate technological innovation in a beneficial way and suggest that more indepth, especially long-range, planning be formulated to further optimize the firm's positive response.

Let me summarize what the results of those studies are. We see very few examples of adverse effects on innovation, and a sizable number of projects where positive effects or no effects on technology were evidenced.

Environmental regulation is found to be positively correlated with project success. Thus we can assert with certainty that our data shows environmental regulation often to be a positive influence on innovation.

This would be more strongly the case if the pollution control industry had comprised part of our interview sample. Where regulation was seen to have very little positive or negative stimulation effect, it was nevertheless often present as part of the innovation planning process.

This suggests that in many instances it may be fairly easy for environmental ameliorative devices to be incorporated into new products and processes, especially if this incorporation is accomplished at an early stage.

THE INDEPENDENCE OF REGULATORS

Critics of the regulatory bodies frequently charge that they are presided over by insensitive captives of the industries they regulate or by apostles of bureaucratic self-perpetuation and empire building. In 1975, the General Accounting Office conducted a study of the origins and orientation of regulatory officials, which provided a factual perspective on these charges. The GAO is an official oversight and investigatory unit of the Congress and is headed by the Comptroller General of the United States.

Government Accounting Office Study ([35], pp. 46–51)

Mr. RIEGER. My name is James H. Rieger.

I have been an auditor with the U.S. General Accounting Office— GAO—for 14 years and am currently assigned to the subcommittee staff to assist them with their work on regulatory reform. I am on a temporary assignment with the subcommittee and thus do not represent GAO today. With me is Robert Clarke Brown, a counsel to the subcommittee staff.

As part of the subcommittee's study of the "Quality of Regulators", the staff has examined recent high-level appointments to the nine agencies under review: Interstate Commerce Commission; Federal Communications Commission; Federal Power Commission; Securities and Exchange Commission; Federal Trade Commission; Consumer Product Safety Commission; Environmental Protection Agency; Food and Drug Administration; and National Highway Traffic Safety Administration.

The professional experience of those receiving appointments as commissioners or administrators and as noncareer executives (NEA's)[1] was analyzed with a view to developing information which would be useful to the subcommittee in determining whether these persons as a group have brought to the agencies both the technical competence and the balance of viewpoints which are prerequisites of good regulation.

SUMMARY OF FINDINGS

In summary form, the subcommittee staff's findings are these:

One: Only a tiny minority of commissioners, administrators, and NEA's appointed during the period studied have, prior to their appointment, demonstrated a significant sensitivity to the interests of consumers.

Two: A sizable percentage of those appointed commissioners and administrators during the last 15 years have been persons from the regulated industries, and this percentage has increased dramatically in recent years.

Three: Substantial numbers of commissioners and administrators have taken positions in the industries they regulated at the conclusion of their service.

Four: The bulk of those appointed commissioners, administrators, and NEA's were public officials of one sort or another prior to their appointment.

METHODOLOGY

The subcommittee obtained from the nine agencies biographical data on all of the 120 commissioners and administrators who have been appointed and confirmed since 1960. This data covers 15 years almost evenly divided between Democratic and Republican administrations. The subcommittee also obtained biographical data from seven of the nine agencies on the persons appointed to NEA positions during the last 3 to 5 years. In analyzing this data, the staff used the following guidelines:

(a) The official was considered to have "demonstrated a significant sensitivity to the interests of consumers" if he—

had participated, in either a full-time or part-time capacity, in any activity or organization promoting a consumer, environmental, or conservationist cause. This criterion contemplates Government service as well as private-sector activities;

described himself as expert or deeply interested in the goals of a consumer. environmental, or conservationist cause; or

had published any article pertaining to consumer, environmental, or conservationist affairs.

(b) Employment in the "regulated industry" was considered to include not only employment directly by firms engaged in the producing activity itself but also employment in enterprises which worked to further industry interests, such as law firms and consulting companies. The latter is referred to as "indirect" employment in the regulated industry.

---

[1] NEA positions differ from career civil service assignments in that they are filled by persons who will participate significantly in formulating administration political policies, advocate administraton programs or serve principally as personnel assistants to Presidential appointees or key political figures.

(c) In characterizing the prior employment of those individuals who had served in a variety of occupations before appointment, a judgment was made based on the length of time spent in the various occupations, with greater weight given to time spent in the more recent occupations.

Most of the information I am presenting today has been developed from the subcommittee staff's analysis of the biographical data provided by the agencies. In some cases, however, the staff has relied on the agencies' own determinations, as reported in their replies to the subcommittee's questionnaire last summer. Where the questionnaire responses are the source of the information, it has been so noted in the exhibits.

Before presenting the staff's findings I would like to state that our purpose has been only to determine the kind of professional experience that regulators have had prior to appointment. We have not attempted to link the prior professional experience of individual regulators with their subsequent performance with the agencies. Nor have we intended to imply that professional experience of itself is necessarily an accurate indicator of whether the regulator is pro consumer or pro industry. Second, the information which we have used has been obtained from documents provided by the agencies. Although we have no reason to doubt the accuracy of this information, we have not independently verified it.

FINDINGS

I. CONSUMER REPRESENTATION

During the past 15 years, fewer than 10 percent of the 120 persons appointed as commissioners or administrators of the nine subject agencies had, prior to their appointments, demonstrated a significant sensitivity to the interests of consumers, either as public officials or in private-sector activities. Only the newly created Consumer Product Safety Commission has had a majority of its commissioners sensitive to consumer interests, and four of the nine agencies have had no such appointees during the entire 15-year period. These data are presented in exhibit 1. Only one commission chairman, the Chairman of the Consumer Product Safety Commission, had prior significant experience in consumer activities. See exhibit 2. Virtually all the consumer-sensitive regulators have been appointed to the executive agencies. See exhibits 1 and 2.

During the 3- to 5-year periods for which NEA appointments were studied, 18 percent of the appointments went to persons who had demonstrated a significant sensitivity to the interests of consumers.[1]

II. REGULATED INDUSTRY REPRESENTATION

For the same 15-year period during which less than 10 percent of the commissioner and administrator appointments have been to persons with demonstrated sensitivity to consumer interests, nearly 30 percent came from the regulated industry. See exhibit 3. This percentage has not been constant during these 15 years, however. Recently, it appears to have been increasing dramatically. Of the forty-five persons appointed in the last 5 years, twenty-four—more than half—came from regulated industry. See exhibit 3. On the other hand, only 7 per-

---

[1] Findings pertaining to NEA's are based on data obtained from only seven of the nine agencies: FCC, ICC, NHTSA, CPSC, FPC, FDA, and EPA. It should also be noted that nearly half of the samples studied, 26 of 55, consisted of NEA's from one agency, EPA.

cent of the NEA appointments examined were persons from regulated industry. By comparison, 14 percent of upper-level, GS–15 and above, agency civil service personnel have come from regulated industry. See exhibit 4.

III. SUBSEQUENT EMPLOYMENT

Upon leaving the Government, substantial numbers of commissioners and administrators during the 15-year period studied became employed, either directly or indirectly, by the industry they had regulated. Of the 85 persons who have left the agencies during that period, 32 have, at some time during the immediately subsequent 5 years, been employed in the regulated industry. See exhibit 5. We based the analysis on positions held over a 5-year period rather than simply the first job subsequent to departure from the Government because many persons, often for ethical reasons, do not accept employment immediately with the regulated industry. It should be noted that not all agencies compile information on subsequent employment. Thus, since this aspect of the subcommittee staff's study is based on information provided by the agencies, it may not represent the complete picture. That is, there may be additional persons, unknown to the agencies, who are currently employed by the regulated industry.

IV. THE GOVERNMENT AS A SOURCE OF REGULATORS

During the periods studied, more than half of both the commissioners and administrators and the NEA's have been persons of substantial Government experience. As exhibit 6 shows, just over half of those appointed as commissioners and administrators have been career civil servants or other Government staff, State or local government officials, or former Members of Congress. Similarly, almost half of the heads of agencies—administrators and commission chairmen—were from the Government. See exhibit 7. Of the NEA's, approximately 60 percent were previously career civil servants.

I hope that these data and findings will aid the subcommittee in its assessment of the quality of high level officials in Federal regulatory agencies.

Thank you, Mr. Chairman.

That concludes my prepared testimony.

[The exhibits attached to Mr. Rieger's prepared statement follow:]

EXHIBIT 1

COMMISSIONERS OR ADMINISTRATORS OF REGULATORY AGENCIES WITH DEMONSTRATED CONSUMER SENSITIVITY, 1960–75

Agency	Number	Total regulators appointed
CPSC	1	5
FCC	0	24
FPC	0	18
FTC	2	20
ICC	0	21
SEC	0	19
EPA	2	2
FDA	1	6
NHTSA	3	5
Total	9	120

Source: Biographical data provided to the subcommittee by the agencies.

EXHIBIT 2

CHAIRMEN OR ADMINISTRATORS OF REGULATORY AGENCIES WITH DEMONSTRATED
CONSUMER SENSITIVITY, 1960-75

Agency	Number	Total regulators appointed
CPSC	1	1
FCC	0	4
FPC	0	3
FTC	0	4
ICC	0	6
SEC	0	4
EPA	2	2
FDA	1	4
NHTSA	3	5
Total	7	33

Source: Biographical data provided to the subcommittee by the agencies.

EXHIBIT 3

NUMBER OF COMMISSIONERS AND ADMINISTRATORS APPOINTED WITH PRIOR DIRECT OR INDIRECT
EMPLOYMENT IN REGULATED INDUSTRY

Agency	Employment in regulated industry		Total regulators appointed
	Number in last 5 yr	Number in last 15 yr	
CPSC	0	0	5
FCC	8	12	24
FPC	1	1	18
FTC	7	8	20
ICC	2	3	21
SEC	4	9	19
EPA	0	0	2
FDA	2	2	6
NHTSA	0	0	5
Total	24	35	120

Source: Replies to the subcommittee questionnaire of June 1975.

EXHIBIT 4

PRIOR EMPLOYMENT UPPER LEVEL CIVIL SERVICE [1] PERSONNEL IN REGULATED AGENCIES

Agency	Number having prior employment in regulated industry	Total number upper level personnel	Percent total from regulated industry
CPSC	0	77	0
FCC	24	179	13
FPC	29	140	21
FTC	64	178	36
ICC	15	266	6
SEC	42	116	36
EPA	51	524	10
FDA	15	272	6
NHTSA	22	165	13
Total	262	1,917	14

[1] GS-15 and above.

Source: Replies to the subcommittee questionnaire of June 1975.

EXHIBIT 5

SUBSEQUENT EMPLOYMENT OF COMMISSIONERS OR ADMINISTRATORS DIRECTLY OR INDIRECTLY IN
REGULATED INDUSTRY

Agency	Employment in regulated industry			Total leaving agency
	Direct	Indirect	Total	
CPSC	0	0	0	0
FCC	3	1	4	19
FPC	0	2	2	13
FTC	0	6	6	13
ICC	2	0	2	10
SEC	3	10	13	20
EPA	0	1	1	1
FDA	2	1	3	5
NHTSA	1	0	1	4
Total	11	21	32	85

Source: Replies to the subcommittee questionnaire of June 1975.

EXHIBIT 6

PRIOR EMPLOYMENT OF INDIVIDUALS APPOINTED COMMISSIONERS OR ADMINISTRATORS OF REGULATORY
AGENCIES 1960–75

Agency	Private sector (total 58)						Public sector (total 62)				Total
	Regulated industry	Industry	Law practicing before Commissions	Other private practice of law	Certified public accountant	Educator	Career Federal service	Professional staff of the Congress	Member of Congress	State government	
CPSC		2				1	2		1		5
FCC	4		8	2			6	2	1	1	24
FPC	1	1		3		1	2	4	2	4	18
FTC			8	3			6		1	2	20
ICC	2		3	5			2	5	1	3	21
SEC			8		1		6	1	3		19
EPA							1		1	1	2
FDA	2					1	3				6
NHTSA		1				1				3	5
Total	7	6	27	13	1	4	28	12	8	14	120

Source: Biographical data provided to the subcommittee by the agencies.

EXHIBIT 7

PRIOR EMPLOYMENT CHAIRMEN AND ADMINISTRATORS OF REGULATORY AGENCIES, 1960–75

Agency	Private sector (total 18)					Public sector (total 15)			
	Lawyers practicing before commissions	Other private practice of law	Regulated industry	Industry	Educators	Career Federal service	State government	Member of Congress	Professional staff of the Congress
CPSC			1						
FCC	1	3							
FPC	1					1			1
FTC	1	1				2			
ICC [1]	2					1	1	1	1
SEC	2				1			1	
EPA						1	1		
FDA			2		1	1			
NHTSA				1	1		3		
Total	7	4	3	1	3	6	5	2	2

[1] Until 1969, the Chairman of ICC was elected by the members of the Commission; after 1969 the Chairman was appointed by the President.

Source: Biographical data provided to the subcommittee by the agencies.

Common Cause Perspectives on Conflict of Interest ([35], pp. 77–81, 85–90)

The conflict between financial interest and public responsibility will be a source of continuing concern as long as government officials are recruited from, depart to, or retain ties with private enterprise. Because the use of public position as a means to enrich one's estate is repugnant to the American values, the issue of conflict-of-interest should be considered. It is certainly a matter to be examined as part of the process of selecting and confirming public officials.

In 1971, President Nixon appointed William Casey as Chairman of the Securities and Exchange Commission. Casey, a corporate tax lawyer with varied corporate holdings, was eventually confirmed after agreeing to put his holdings in trust. (Senator William Proxmire's views on the Casey matter are contained in the Congressional Record of March 25, 1971, p. S 3905.) This controversy not only brought to light the limited extent to which the White House investigated this dimension of its appointee's fitness for a position of public trust, but it also had an impact upon selection procedures. The White House Legal Counsel subsequently issued a "Personal Data Statement," requiring appointees to disclose their financial holdings in considerable detail. President Ford's administration continued that practice and President Carter has vowed to further strengthen conflict-of-interest scrutiny in making his appointments.

A public affairs lobbying group called Common Cause was founded in 1970 by John Gardner, Secretary of HEW during the Johnson administration. Common Cause has set forth a model conflict-of-interest Executive order and has proposed its adoption. In the testimony which follows, Common Cause Executive Director David Cohen discusses the problem of selecting regulatory agency officials and presents his organization's proposal on conflict-of-interest restrictions.

Mr. COHEN. First of all, thank you, Mr. Chairman. I think it is terrific that you are having these joint hearings, that you are doing it for the purpose of getting information because I think all of us are troubled by both the selection process as it relates to the regulatory commissioners and how regulation itself works. So it is just really good that you are conducting these hearings. . . .

I think one of the problems we are trying to get at here is how to attract capable people to public service. I think that one major point is the recognition that the selection of our regulators has become increasingly dominated by political patronage. The overriding consideration is often political loyalty rather than merit and expertise. Too often regulatory posts have been parceled out as rewards for party service, personal allegiance to the President, or legislator, or assistance during campaigns.

Now the problem as far as we can tell has grown more acute since 1950 when Congress accepted President Truman's plan to have the chairmen of regulatory commissions designated by the President in office. Most chairmen now serve at the President's pleasure, and each time the White House changes party hands the chairmanship also changes party hands. While this serves to strengthen accountability for regulatory decisions, it has also increased political patronage.

The point I want to make is not that Presidents should not be able to choose who is the chairman of the commission. The President should. The problem is with the selection process that Presidents engage in.

We believe the White House Personnel Office has done a poor job in actively recruiting and searching for the most capable nominees. It remains too often a clearinghouse to insure that appointees have had the proper political coloring. A national network of qualified individuals should be established and incorporated and put into a talent bank. However, the recruiting process remains subject to political pressures and the situation has deteriorated even since the computerized talent bank was developed.

Today there is no systematic or uniform process for finding highly qualified regulators. Outside referrals are simply programed into the office's computer with no independent check of their background, views, or expertise.

Too often the industry regulated by an agency plays a major role in approving nominees suggested by the White House. This is well documented in books like Louis Kohlmeier's book on the regulatory agencies.

Kohlmeier writes:

> The test of competence to which a candidate for initial appointment is subjected consists of the submission by the White House of his or her name to industry before sending it on to the Senate for confirmation. CAB appointees are cleared with airline executives, FPC appointees with gas and electric companies, ICC appointees with railroad officials, and usually truckers, too.

There are several reasons for this practice. Most Presidents regard regulation as industry's preserve; they want to avoid industry opposition during confirmation hearings; they have many leading industrialists as personal friends, and if you look, as I had a chance to look, at the list of secret contributors to the Nixon campaign between March 10 and April 7, which was that period in controversy which Common Cause litigated and forced the disclosure of that campaign, it read as a Who's Who of American Industry. I am sure it was not true just for the Nixon campaign. I am sure it was true for early campaigns, including campaigns for Democratic Presidents.

Although we have regulated and changed our method of campaign financing at the Presidential level, we still haven't really changed the process of that consultation between the President and industry, or the agency regulated and the effect is devastating. It transforms regulatory agencies into special interest protectorates, and the public pays.

The Senate has traditionally failed to scrutinize regulatory appointees or evaluate their qualifications on the basis of well-defined standards. The Senate Commerce Committee is the single outstanding exception to this trend. Too often the confirmation hearings are perfunctory, they are superfluous rituals. They result in hasty and sometimes mindless ratification of White House nominees. Little attention is usually given to a nominee's background, views, or expertise. The committees, with the exception of the Senate Commerce Committee, and perhaps the beginning of a trend in the Senate Interior Committee, simply do not take their constitutional responsibilities seriously when it comes to evaluating Presidential appointees.

We think that there are some ways that we can reform the process, recognizing that nothing is ever perfect, but we think that things can be done that would make the appointment process more open, and the confirmation process more precise.

First, we think that it is perfectly appropriate for the committees of Congress to suggest standards for appointments. Among the kinds of standards that Common Cause would suggest is that regulatory nominees should be individuals of high personal and professional integrity. This means that a nominee's past record as a Government official or in private enterprise should demonstrate that he or she has conducted his or her affairs honestly and fairly, and that they have consciously complied with the law, and that any previous Government service was never used for personal financial gain.

In other words, don't reward people who have problems in this area. Let us try to attract people who at least as a minimum have high standards of professional and personal integrity.

Second, nominees should have the administrative competency to responsibly exercise the duties of the regulatory posts to which they are appointed. In addition to the necessary experience their records should demonstrate sound judgment, compliance with proper administrative procedures, and skills which would be relevant to their roles as regulators.

Third, nominees should be fairly committed to the basic principles of accountability in regulatory agencies. These include strong conflict of interest regulations and enforcement of antisecrecy measures, public personal financial disclosure, public participation in administrative procedures, and checks on the inordinate influence by regulated interests over regulatory policy.

These are fundamental elements of administrative responsiveness to public interest and concerns.

It is the duty of the Senate to see if nominees support these principles, and if they do not, then the Senate has to really look with great care as to which of such people ought to be confirmed.

Fourth, a nominee should have a clear commitment to enforce and implement the major laws and programs under the jurisdiction of the agency to which the nominees would be appointed. Put negatively, this means that the person should not be hostile to any of the major regulatory missions of the agency. In many cases this will require that a nominee demonstrate a sensitivity to the conflicting interests and needs to which the agency must be responsive such as conflicts between industry and consumer interests.

We are talking about judgment. We are talking about balance here. We are talking about an ability to weigh those competing and conflicting concerns, and not just be a representative for one concern to the exclusion of other concerns.

Nominees who have an inability or unwillingness to show this balance really jeopardize the agency mandate.

Now we believe that in order to thoroughly evaluate nominees on such standards that Senate oversight committees and the Senate standing committee should adhere to the following guidelines in conducting confirmation hearings:

One, they should engage in broad and extensive questioning of the nominee's expertise and views and should carefully investigate his past record.

Two, they should require nominees to submit a public financial disclosure statement and examine it for any conflict of interest problems, and demand resolution of any such conflicts.

What has happened in the Commerce Committee recently in the last 2 years is really a wholesome thing. What has happened in the Senate Interior Committee at the time of Hathaway and Kleppe nominations is very constructive. Those are the only places where that start is really ingrained.

Three, they should postpone voting on nominees for at least 2 weeks after the hearings to allow time to study the hearing record. There should not be any instant rush. You just never know what might turn up in that hearing record that you might want to pursue further. That instant ratification process just has to go.

Fourth, a report should be issued to the Senate on all nominees at least 3 full days prior to a Senate vote. Often confirmation hearings are held but no report is made.

On October 9 the Senate confirmed Mr. Kleppe. On October 10 the report was available. There is something backwards about that kind of process, and it ought to stop.

Fifth, I would hope that both the Senate and House committees are not bashful about calling regulators back after they have been in office to report on the actions taken with respect to issues raised during the hearings.

Just let me discuss the Kleppe matter. Mr. Kleppe made it clear at least on the basis of a committee report, that he would at least look at whether he ought to have resolution on conflict of interest, on logging of outside contacts. I would hope in that instance the Senate Interior Committee and over here on the House side, the House Interior Committee, would be quite aggressive about asking Mr. Kleppe what progress he is making, what his thoughts are, and what is happening in the administration on it. He should not have to do it during the first weeks, but before 6 months are gone.

I realize I am taking some time, Mr. Chairman. I will only say several things in summary, that I think logging of contacts on outside nominees by the White House and appointing bodies should be maintained. It is very important that logging be public.

When the Senate committees hear a nominee you should have before you the record of all the efforts at trying to influence who that nominee is, not solely for the purpose of wrongdoing because a lot of the influence can be quite healthy, especially if it is broad gaged and the consultative process is wide.

But the outside logging of contacts would let us know, both the public and the Senate, as to whether or not consulting was broad gaged or narrowly based.

I think the efforts made by the Commission for the Advancement of Public Interest Organizations in developing the talent bank are really worthy, and that Common Cause urges Senate oversight committees and the White House to develop procedures for using such resources.

I would hope that one of the places we would look to in addition to all the traditional spots is State government. We are going through an innovative period in State government. It is the best aspect of creative federalism. There are outstanding people, and that should be one of the places that we look for getting talent for the regulatory agencies. The other is that public interest representatives should be an integral part of every regulatory commission.

Second, I think the review process should be more extended than it is. There is an advantage if the President could establish panels for selecting candidates to regulatory posts and voluntarily agree to choose his appointees from these candidates.

There are many examples of that process being used. Senator Chiles and Senator Stone are using it in the Federal Judicial Selection Commission. Governor Gilligan, as Governor of Ohio, used it in his appointment process for judges. Down at the common pleas, county level, he used nonlawyers for it as well as lawyers, and that in itself is healthy.

Governor McCall did it in the State of Oregon. The point is that it is a recognition on the part of the appointing official that if you have 3,000 appointments to make, as Mr. Flanigan said earlier, that you need some help, and no one should be compelled to take one nominee, or even three nominees, but there ought to be a chance at showing that if three or five people are taken the burden then is on the appointer to show why he wouldn't choose from one of those three or five. That would help open up the process.

Third, there ought to be an advisory committee on personnel which at least should be looked at by this committee that would include a variety of interest groups, including the various gamuts of the public interest groups such as environmental, consumer, reform minded groups such as Common Cause. At least that committee could serve to evaluate referrals and actively search for qualified regulators.

We believe that these proposals will help improve the process for selecting regulators. We would hope that this whole process that this committee has started in both the House and the Senate would help continue the public dialog and would help get a sense from Presidents and Presidential candidates what steps they will take in improving the selection process on those 3,000 appointments that they have.

One final item, Mr. Chairman: Common Cause has submitted a model executive order on conflict of interest to the executive branch and one on the logging of outside contacts. It sets up some ground rules and procedures on how to deal with some of the difficult questions of postemployment. If I may, I would like to have these model executive orders be made part of the record.

Senator Moss. We will be pleased to make them part of the record. I think they should be there. . . .

MODEL EXECUTIVE ORDER ON CONFLICT OF INTEREST

By virtue of the authority vested in me by Section 301 of Title 3 of the United States Code, and as President of the United States, it is hereby ordered as follows:

DEFINITIONS

Section 1. As used in this Order, the term—

(1) "agency" means agency as defined in 5 U.S.C. 551;

(2) "Presidential appointee" means the head of any agency, each official in the Executive Office of the President who is appointed by the President and not subordinate to the head of an agency in that Office, and each full-time member of a committee, board, or commission appointed by the President;

(3) "agency employee" means any officer or employee of an agency, including special government employees as defined in 18 U.S.C. 202, in grade GS-15 or above in the General Schedule, in pay grade O-6 or above under 37 U.S.C. 201, or in any of the executive levels under 5 U.S.C., chapter 53, subchapter II, but does not include Presidential appointees;

(4) "agency counselor" means a counselor or deputy counselor designated by an agency head under 5 C.F.R. 735.105;

(5) "Department counselor" means an agency counselor who has been designated as the chief counselor for an Executive department;

(6) "person" includes a corporation, company, association, firm, partnership, society, or joint stock company, as well as an individual;

(7) "adjudication" means adjudication as defined in 5 U.S.C. 551(7), including the process of recommending, initiating, or participating in suits to enforce Federal laws or regulations;

(8) "licensing" means licensing as defined in 5 U.S.C. 551(9);

(9) "contracting" means the process of granting, awarding, or administering of any contract, grant, or procurement authorization issued by an agency;

(10) "rule-making" means rule-making as defined in 5 U.S.C. 551(5);

(11) "agency proceeding" means any adjudication, licensing, contracting or rule-making, insofar as such rule-making involves a rule of particular applicability which directly affects a party to the proceeding;

(12) "immediate family" means a person required to file financial statements under Section 2 of this Order, his spouse, and their dependents.

FINANCIAL DISCLOSURE

Section 2. (a) Each Presidential appointee shall submit to the Chairman of the Civil Service Commission, and each agency employee shall submit to the agency counsel designated by such agency's regulations to advise him on questions of conflicts of interest, a financial statement containing the following information:

(1) each source of income received by any member of the immediate family if that source yielded income in excess of $100 in amount or value, including a description of the nature, purpose, and amount of such income;

(2) the names of each person or organization—

(A) with which he is associated as an employee, officer, owner, director, trustee, partner, advisor, or consultant,

(B) in which he has any continuing financial interest, through a pension or retirement plan, shared income, or other arrangement, as a result of any current or prior employment or business or professional association, or

(C) in which any member of the immediate family has any financial interest through the ownership of stocks, bonds, or other securities, including the amount and value of such interest;

(3) the identity and value each real property holding, rights of land, or other assets held by any member of the immediate family, other than those identified under paragraph (2) of this section, which exceed $1,000 in amount or value;

(4) the identity and value of each liability owed by any member of the immediate family which exceed $1,000, including the name and address of each creditor, whether the loan is secured and by whom and the terms of repayment;

(5) the identity of all transactions in securities, commodities, or real or personal property by or in behalf of any member of the immediate family which exceed $1,000, including the monetary value or amounts involved, the number of securities or volume of commodities when applicable, and the terms of each such transaction and;

(6) the identity of each gift, gratuity, honorarium, fee, service, or other thing of value received by any member of the immediate family from a nonrelative which exceeds $25, including the source, purpose, and monetary value or amount.

(b) Each Presidential appointee shall submit the statements required under subsection (a) of this section within ten days of being nominated by the President, and not later than July 31st of each year thereafter. The initial statements shall cover the 12-month period prior to the date of such nomination, and the subsequent statements shall cover the preceding 12-month period up to June 30th. The statements must be reviewed within 30 days by the Chairman of the Civil Service Commission for any real or potential conflicts of interest. During this 30-day period, the Chairman must notify, in writing, each Presidential appointee of the results of this review, specifying appropriate remedial action to resolve any such conflicts. Copies of such statements and review notifications must be submitted to the agency counselor of the agency to which such appointee has been named.

(c) Each agency employee shall submit the statements required under subsection (a) of this section within ten days of becoming an agency employee, and not later than July 31st of each year thereafter. The initial statements shall cover the 12-month period prior to becoming an agency employee, and the subsequent statements shall cover the preceding 12-month period up to June 30th. The statements must be reviewed within 30 days by the agency counselor to whom they are submitted for any real or potential conflicts of interest. During this 30-day period, each counselor must notify each agency employee under his jurisdiction of the results of this review, specifying appropriate remedial action to resolve any such conflicts. Such notification must be in writing, and copies must be submitted, when applicable, to the Department counselor.

(d) The statements submitted by Presidential appointees under this section, together with copies of the review notifications required under subsection (b) above, shall be maintained by the Chairman of the Civil Service Commission and the counselor's office of the agency to which such appointee has been named for a period of five years from the date filed. The statements submitted by agency employees under this section, together with copies of the review notifications required under subsection (c) above, shall be maintained by the counselor's office with whom they are submitted for a period of five years from the date filed. All such statements and notifications shall be made available for inspection in a convenient location by any person after 45 days of the date filed, and copies shall be made available upon payment of a fee not to exceed the actual cost of making such copies.

DIVESTITURE

Section 3. (a) Each Presidential appointee and each agency employee who participates personally and substantially in an agency proceeding must divest of all financial interests in any person directly affected as a party to such proceeding.

(b) Each Presidential appointee and each agency employee who participates personally and substantially in an agency rule-making must divest of all financial interests in any person affected by such rule-making, provided a substantial part of such person's activities are regulated by the agency in question.

(c) The divestiture required in this section shall be made by such Presidential appointees and agency employees prior to their participation in the agency proceeding or rule-making in question.

POST-EMPLOYMENT RESTRICTIONS

Section 4. Each Presidential appointee must, as a condition of assuming or maintaining a position designated under Section 1 (2) of this Order, enter into a legally binding contract with the Chairman of the Civil Service Commission. Each agency employee must, as a condition of assuming or maintaining employment with an agency in a level designated under Section 1(3) of this Order, enter into a legally binding contract with such agency. The terms of such contracts shall prohibit the Presidential appointee and agency employee, for a period of two years following the termination of his employment with the agency in question, from—

(1) accepting employment or compensation from any person directly affected as a party to an agency proceeding in which such appointee or employee participated personally and substantially;

(2) accepting employment or compensation from any person affected by an agency rule-making in which such appointee or employee participated personally and substantially, provided a substantial part of such person's activities are regulated by the agency in question; and

(3) representing any person before such agency in any legal, lobbying, or other professional capacity.

REPORTING OF EMPLOYMENT

Section 5. (a) Each Presidential appointee must submit, within 10 days of becoming a Presidential appointee or, with respect to those who are such appointees at the time this Order is implemented, within 10 days of such implementation, and each agency employee must submit, within 10 days of becoming an agency employee or, with respect to those who are agency employees at the time this Order is implemented, within 10 days of such implementation, a statement to the Chairman of the Civil Service Commission or the appropriate agency counselor respectively containing the following information:

(1) his occupation(s) and place(s) of employment during the 24 months prior to the date he became employed by the Federal government; and

(2) his occupation(s) and place(s) of employment, when applicable, during any period subsequent to his initial employment with the Federal government during which he accepted non-governmental employment or compensation.

(b) The contract with the Civil Service Commission or the agency which each Presidential appointee and agency employee, respectively, must enter under section 4 of this Order shall require such appointee and employee to submit, during the 24 months following the termination of his employment with the agency in question, statements to the Chairman of the Civil Service Commission or appropriate agency counselor, respectively, identifying his current occupation and place of employment. An initial statement must be submitted within 10 days of terminating employment with the agency, and subsequent statements must be submitted within 10 days of changing his occupation or place of employment during the 24-month period.

(c) Each Presidential appointee and each agency employee must submit, upon the arrangement of future employment with a non-governmental person, a statement to the Chairman of the Civil Service Commission or appropriate agency counselor, respectively, identifying the person with whom such employment has been arranged. Such appointees and employees shall not participate personally or substantially in any agency proceeding which affects such person as a party to the proceeding.

(d) The statements submitted by Presidential appointees under this section shall be filed with the agency counselor of the agency to which such appointee has been named and shall be maintained by the Chairman of the Civil Service Commission and such counselor's office for a period of three years following the termination of such appointee's employment with the agency in question. The statements submitted by agency employees under this section shall be maintained by the counselor's office with whom they are submitted for a period of three years following the termination of such employee's tenure with the agency in question. All such statements shall be made available for public inspection in a convenient location by any person within 10 days of the date filed, and copies shall be made available upon payment of a fee not to exceed the actual cost of making such copies. Each agency counselor shall submit, when applicable, copies of such statements filed with him to the Department counselor within 10 days of the date filed.

ADVISORY OPINIONS AND REPORTS

Section 6. (a) The Chairman of the Civil Service Commission and each agency counselor shall, upon request from any Presidential appointee or agency employee respectively or at their own initiative, issue written advisory opinions which clarify the requirements and restrictions of this Order and recommend appropriate action in specific cases. Such advisory opinions shall be maintained by the Civil Service Commission or the counselor's office which issued them and shall be made available for inspection in a convenient location by any person within 10 days of the date issued. Copies of such opinions shall be available to any person upon payment of a fee not to exceed the actual cost of making such copies. Each agency counselor shall submit, when applicable, copies of such opinions issued by him to the Department counselor within 10 days of the date issued.

(b) The Chairman of the Civil Service Commission and each agency counselor, other than those within Executive departments, shall issue a report not later than September 30 of each year which summarizes his activities and findings in the implementation and enforcement of this Order during the preceding 12-month period up to September 15th. Such report shall include an explanation of his procedures for reviewing statements submitted to him under this Order and a summary of the results of such reviews and any recommendations for remedial action, and shall be published in the *Federal Register* within 10 days of the date issued.

(c) Each Department Counselor shall issue a report not later than September 30th of each year which summarizes his activities and findings, and those of each agency counselor within his Department, in the implementation and enforcement of this Order during the preceding 12-month period up to September 15th. Such reports shall include an explanation of his and each agency counselor's procedures for reviewing statements submitted to them under this Order and a summary of the results of such reviews and any recommendations for remedial action, and shall be published in the *Federal Register* within 10 days of date issued.

SANCTIONS

Section 7. (a) Any Presidential appointee who knowingly and willfully violates any provision of this Order shall, upon recommendation by the Chairman of the Civil Service Commission, be subject to disciplinary action as the President shall deem appropriate.

(b) Any agency employee who knowingly and willfully falsifies, forges, or fails to submit any statement as required by section 2 or subsection 5(a) and 5(c) of this order shall be terminated or suspended from such agency for such period as the agency counselor or, if such agency is within an Executive department, the Department counselor shall deem appropriate, but for not less than 30 days. Those suspended shall be allowed to resume employment with such agency only upon full and accurate compliance with the reporting requirements of such section or subsections.

(c) Any agency employee who knowingly and willfully violates section 3 of this order shall be terminated or suspended from such agency for such period as the agency counselor or, if such agency is in an Executive department, the Department counselor shall deem appropriate, but for not less than 30 days. Those suspended shall be allowed to resume employment with such agency only upon full compliance with the divestiture requirements of such section or upon appropriate reassignment of duties within the agency.

(d) The Chairman of the Civil Service Commission, each agency counselor other than those of agencies within an Executive department, and each Department counselor shall initiate civil proceedings to enjoin any former Presidential appointee or agency employee from violating the terms of the contract entered into pursuant to section 4 and subsection 5(b) of this Order.

MODEL EXECUTIVE ORDER ON LOGGING OF OUTSIDE CONTACTS

By virtue of the authority vested in me by Section 301 of Title 3 of the United States Code, and as President of the United States, it is hereby ordered as follows:

DEFINITIONS

Section 1. As used in this Order, the term—

(1) "agency" means agency as defined in 5 U.S.C. 105;

(2) "agency employee" means any officer or employee of an agency, including special government employees as defined in 18 U.S.C. 202, in grades GS–15 or above in the General Schedule or in any of the executive levels under 5 U.S.C., chapter 53, subchapter II;

(3) "person" includes an individual, partnership, corporation, association, firm, society, joint stock company, Members of Congress, officer or employee of the executive branch, or any party to a proceeding;

(4) "informant" means any person who offers incriminating information, under an assurance of confidentiality, to an agency employee for use in a civil or criminal enforcement proceeding;

(5) "pre-adjudicative stages of a proceeding" means agency activities prior to the commencement of an administrative or judicial enforcement proceeding held to determine punishment for or to prevent the violation of Federal law or agency regulation;

(6) "record of communications maintained for internal disclosure" means a record of communications received by an agency employee which shall contain—

(A) the name and position of the employee who received the communication;

(B) the date upon which the communication was received;

(C) an identification, so far as possible, of the person from whom the communication was received and of the person on whose behalf such person was acting in making the communication;

(D) in the case of communications through letters, documents, briefs, and other written material, copies of such material in its original form;

(7) "record of communications maintained for summary disclosure" means a record of communications received by an agency employee which shall contain—

(A) the name and position of the employee who received the communication;

(B) the date upon which the communication was received;

(C) an identification, so far as possible, of the person from whom the communication was received and of the person on whose behalf such person was acting in making the communication;

(D) a brief characterization of the subject matter under discussion;

(E) in the case of communications through letters, documents, briefs, and other written material, copies of such material in its original form. In the case of materials which fall under 5 U.S.C. 552(b), a summary of the communication or a copy of such material with suitable deletions will suffice in lieu of the original;

(8) "record of communications maintained for full disclosure" means a record of communications received by an agency employee which shall contain—

(A) the name and position of the employee who received the communication;

(B) the date upon which the communication was received;

(C) an identification, so far as possible, of the person from whom the communication was received and of the person on whose behalf such person was acting in making the communication;

(D) a brief summary of the subject matter or matters of the communication, including relevant docket numbers if known;

(E) in the case of communications through letters, documents, briefs, and other written material, copies of such material in its original form. In the case of materials which fall under 5 U.S.C. 552(b), a summary of the communication or a copy of such material with suitable deletions will suffice in lieu of the original;

(F) a brief description, when applicable, of any action taken by the employee in response to the communication.

RECORD-KEEPING REQUIREMENTS

Section 2. (a) Each agency employee shall prepare a record of communications maintained for summary disclosure for each oral or written communication initiated by persons outside the agency, pertaining to a substantive policy matter before the agency, except any such communication from informants or members of the working press. For the purpose of this paragraph, a "substantive policy matter" means any important agency action or policy issue as prescribed in regulations promulgated by the agency, except that no such regulation shall apply to agency proceedings as defined in 5 U.S.C. 551 (12).

(b) Each agency employee shall prepare a record of communications maintained for full disclosure for each oral or written communication, initiated by persons outside the agency, during the pre-adjudicative stages of a proceeding or pertaining to a pending agency proceeding, except (i) any such communication from informants or members of the working press and (ii) any such communication initiated by the party to an enforcement proceeding during the pre-adjudicative stage. With respect to communications initiated by the party to an enforcement proceeding during the pre-adjudicative stage, the agency employee shall prepare a record of communications maintained for internal disclosure.

PUBLIC FILING

Section 3. (a) Each agency head shall assure that records of communications maintained for summary disclosure and records of communications maintained for full disclosure which are prepared by the agency employees under their jurisdiction shall be furnished for inclusion in a public file within five working days of the receipt of the communication. Public files containing such records shall be located in the public reading room of the agency. Such records for which no public file already exists shall be placed in public files located in the public reading room, appropriately indexed pursuant to regulations promulgated by the agency. All public files shall be maintained for a period of five years, and shall be available for public inspection and copying.

(b) Each agency head shall assure that records of communications maintained for internal disclosure prepared by the agency employees under their jurisdiction shall be furnished for permanent inclusion in the case or other appropriate file and that a copy of such record shall be furnished for inclusion in a centrally located file in the agency within five working days of the receipt of the communication.

(c) Each agency employee who is compensated under 5 U.S.C., chapter 53, subchapter II, shall provide for the maintenance of his prospective and retrospective calendars for public inspection in the public reading room of the agency. Such materials shall be submitted, and updated, the first working day of each week.

SANCTIONS

Section 4. Any agency employee who knowingly and willfully falsifies, forges, or fails to file any record required by these regulations shall be terminated or suspended from the agency for such period as the agency head shall deem appropriate, but for not less than 30 days.

SELECTING THE REGULATORS: A PANEL DISCUSSION ([35], pp. 53–74)

Even with structural and statutory changes, the quality of regulation is still subject to the integrity and skill of the regulators. In late 1975, the Senate Committee on Government Operations considered the matter of the selection of regulators and their qualifications. Some very practical questions were addressed, among them: If the regulator has never worked in the industry he or she is to regulate, how is it possible to have the technical qualifications needed to understand that industry? If the regulator has had such experience, how can it be assured that he or she is free of industry bias? Testifying on these matters were three former White House aides from the Kennedy, Johnson, and Nixon administrations. They were: Peter Flanigan, Director of Dillon, Reed, an investment banking firm; Lee White, an attorney; and Ralph Dungan, New Jersey Chancellor of Higher Education, and former Ambassador to Chile.

Senator Moss. The hearing will come to order.

I first apologize for being a little tardy arriving this morning. I had two or three other assignments this morning that took a little of my time and I apologize to my colleagues, as well as the witnesses for the delay.

I am pleased to represent the Senate Commerce Committee at this second day of our symposium on the quality of appointments to regulatory agencies. I firmly believe that one of the most debilitating flaws in our regulatory system has been the chronic failure of Presidents to name—and the Senate to insist upon the naming of—outstanding public servants qualified by training and commitment to implement our regulatory statutes. All too often, these posts have been parceled out as rewards for political service to President or party, as tokens of appreciation to favored segments of industry, or as booby prizes for inadequate officials ousted from other jobs or political candidates rejected by the voters.

I believe that we have a leadership gap of a sort, in our regulatory agencies and that this may be largely responsible for many of our regulatory failures. As Professor Edwards so aptly pointed out yesterday, we demand a lot from our regulatory leaders and it requires individuals of unique talent, foresight, and intelligence to keep those agencies on an even keel. The question to which we are seeking an answer during this symposium is how do we locate and recruit such individuals to the public service?

We are fortunate this morning to have with us a distinguished panel of former White House staff officials who were directly responsible for recruiting Presidential nominees.

Our three panelists—Ralph Dungan from the Kennedy administration; Lee White from the Johnson era; and Peter Flanigan of the Nixon administration—afford us a unique opportunity to review the selection process of three administrations and both parties. I should note here that we had invited the current incumbent to designate a member of his staff to participate in these proceedings but the invitation was declined.

We are also fortunate this morning to have two additional witnesses, Dr. Carl Clark of the Commission for the Advancement of Public Interest Organizations and Mr. David Cohen of Common Cause. These gentlemen will evaluate problems with the selection process and then proceed to offer suggestions for remedying these defects.

Fifteen years ago, James M. Landis reported to President-elect Kennedy that—

The prime key to the improvement of the administrative process is the selection of qualified personnel. Good men can make poor laws workable; poor men will wreak havoc with good laws. As long as the selection of men for key administrative posts is based upon political reward rather than competency, little else that is done will really matter.

That was as true then as it is now.

I am hopeful that as a result of our deliberations, the action that we take in the future, and the procedures which Chairman Magnuson outlined at yesterday's session, we will finally see the upgrading and increased responsibility on the part of both the legislative and executive branches which is needed if these agencies are to fulfill the responsibilities for which they were created.

In pointing this out, I stress that we are looking at what we think are the weaknesses in the system. By this, I do not mean to imply that we do not have good service and very excellent regulators. It is just that the whole system, itself, needs to be reexamined so that we can select superlative regulators to man our regulatory agencies.

My colleague from the House, Mr. Moss, do you have any opening remarks to make?

Mr. Moss. Senator, I have no opening statement, other than to express my appreciation to the members of the panel who are appearing here today. I look forward to hearing their views.

Senator Moss. Thank you very much.

Mr. Lent, do you have any statement?

Mr. LENT. No comment, Mr. Chairman.

Senator Moss. Are there any other members of the panel who would like to have opening comments at this time?

I appreciate your being here.

Of course, we will have questions when the witnesses have completed their opening statements which we hope will be brief so that we can get into the questioning period.

Mr. SCHEUER. May I say a word?

Senator Moss. Yes; you are recognized.

Mr. SCHEUER. I don't have any prepared statement but I want to congratulate you, Mr. Chairman, on this marvelous cooperation that we are getting. A joint probe by the Senate and the House, I think, in this day and age, shows people that this institution can work, that these two great bodies can work together to face up to this national problem in an intelligent way.

If the House had confronted the problem of energy the way you have cooperated in confronting this problem, we would have a lot more credibility with the public than we have now.

There was a promise common to all the campaigns of the 75 freshmen Democrats; you must remember that the preponderance of these young men and women came from areas that are overwhelmingly Republican, where there had not been a Democratic Representative in this century, or ever.

They did not run as New Deal Democrats or Fair Deal Democrats. They ran on one common promise, to make Government work better; to make Government more honest; to make Government more responsive; to make Government more responsible.

I cannot think of any congressional action this year, more relevant to that common promise, than these hearings.

There is a sense of enormous frustration in the public at large that the regulatory agencies, instead of serving the public, have become the protectors and coddlers of the very industries they were supposed to regulate and have actually interposed a silken veil between these industries and the public.

Instead of subjecting the activities of the industries that they are supposed to regulate to public scrutiny, the agencies have actually protected these industries from public scrutiny. The public feeling is that both agencies and industry should become more responsive.

So, I congratulate you, Senator.

I congratulate Congressman Moss.

I welcome you all here today.

Senator Moss. Thank you very much.

Mr. Moss. Mr. Chairman, may I briefly observe that we seem to have the class of 1923 before us, all members of the panel having been born in that year.

I should say, welcome youngsters. It is nice to have you aboard.

Senator Moss. Now we will hear from the vintage year of 1923.

I will ask the witnesses here if they will give us a 10-minute opening statement, a general statement, and then we will get this session moving as a symposium.

I will ask Peter Flanigan, who is a director of Dillon, Reed, an investment banking firm, if he will proceed.

STATEMENTS OF PETER FLANIGAN, DIRECTOR, DILLON, REED; LEE WHITE, ATTORNEY, WASHINGTON, D.C.; AND RALPH A. DUNGAN, NEW JERSEY CHANCELLOR OF HIGHER EDUCATION

Mr. FLANIGAN. Thank you, Mr. Chairman.

In regard to my service in this particular area, I started in 1968, right after the election, looking for personnel for the Nixon administration and continued that through 1971, with particular responsibility for not only staffing but also relationship between the White House and the regulatory agencies.

Therefore, I spent a good deal of time and feel strongly about the subject which the committee is considering today, and I appreciate the opportunity to express those feelings.

I was asked to break my comments down into, first, some comments with regard to the qualifications and characteristics of the nominees that we sought; what the search methods and clearance procedures were; did we have any problems in getting affirmative responses and then getting some recommendations?

Going first to qualifications and characteristics.

The first qualification which we considered was expertise. If a regulatory commission member was to deal with the difficult regulatory subjects regarding an industry, we thought he ought to know something about that industry. He ought to be a qualified expert in the area. If we were looking for someone to be a chairman, we looked for leadership characteristics. We tried to find somebody who had proven he could lead a diverse group of people who by legislation would have different political commitments.

Finally, and very importantly, we also looked for people who were comfortable with the enunciated philosophy of the President.

We perceived it to be our task to man these agencies with individuals who would regulate in accord with the stated principles of the President.

In carrying out the search, we obviously looked at all of the names that had been sent to us by various individuals, whether in the Congress or throughout the land, but clearly we did not think that was a broad enough search.

So, we asked interested parties, we asked the bar association when it came to agencies such as the Trade Commission, we asked other people in the administration who had some knowledge in the field. I would ask people whose judgment and integrity I held in high regard. From those many people, we tried to find the individual who best fitted those qualifications I enunciated.

The clearance procedure was a normal one: FBI, discussion with the individual's peers, and, of course particularly important, discussion with the congressional delegation.

The problem of response was, if I remember correctly, with one exception, a nonproblem. With one exception, we never asked a person that we sought to come to Washington and join the Commission and were turned down by virtue of disinterest.

So, I am personally convinced that that should not limit the range from which you can draw people to staff the regulatory Commissions.

But there are other matters that very clearly limited our ability to follow the injunctions that Judge Landis laid down which you read, Mr. Chairman, and which indeed I read when I started this task. I subscribed to it then, and I subscribe to it even more deeply now.

First, I think it is important that the Congress keep reviewing the agencies and their structures to make sure that they are effective mechanisms.

While Judge Landis may have been right in saying good people can make bad laws work, it is a lot harder.

I recall that the first reorganization bill, Reorganization Bill No. 1, that President Nixon sent to the Congress, had to do with reorganizing the Interstate Commerce Commission. As perhaps you recall, at that time it had what was known as, categorically defined the post and not the individual, a weak Chairman, that is, a Chairman who did not have the authority to lead, and that Commission had 11 members.

We soon got the word back through to the White House Congressional Relations Office that we could perhaps change the nature of the chairmanship but under no circumstances would the Congress agree to cut down the number of commissioners, that being the number of attractive jobs that were available in a regulatory agency.

So, we amended Reorganization Bill No. 1 and did indeed change the nature of the chairmanship. It became a strong Chairmanship, but we still have 11 members on that Commission.

The second recommendation that I would make is the same as yours, Mr. Chairman, that these very important posts, in managing what is known as the fourth branch of government should not be given out as a reward for past political favors or activities.

Neither branch in my time in finding appointees to these commissions, neither the executive nor the legislative branch, had a monopoly on urging or insisting on political appointees. But inasmuch as the regulatory agencies are a creature of the Congress, and inasmuch as they did the job which the Congress previously had done, in all candor I must say that I felt more pressure for appointees, political appointees, from the Congress than I did from our own executive branch.

It was clear to me that often a worthy member of the staff was urged on the President in the strongest possible terms, often in terms that he could not resist.

But I have to say again that on occasion that same unsatisfactory practice originated downtown.

It is also very fair to say that neither side of the aisle has any monopoly on that practice, and therefore I would like to urge on both sides of the aisle that they consider very carefully the real qualifications of the individual whom they are recommending for appointment.

I think that the requirements for a good regulatory agency commissioner are different than the requirements for a good staff man here on the Hill.

The analytical approach that we would like to see, the nonpartisan approach that we would like to see practiced in those agencies, is by its nature different from the appropriate political partisan approach that seems to me is often practiced and should be practiced on the Hill.

Finally, I would urge that we stop disqualifying anyone related to the activity which the commission is supposed to regulate, on a presumption of guilt.

Businessmen and lawyers and accountants who have spent a lifetime in some relation to an industry and therefore are the experts in that industry are Americans first and businessmen or lawyers or accountants second, and their primary desire is to serve their country, and not their industry.

I will agree that their past and their interests should be very carefully looked into, as well as their continuing financial interest.

But I do not think that the immediate assumption of inability to act on an objective basis is good for the agencies or good for the country.

I think another side of that argument goes to the impression that Mr. Scheuer very properly described, that the industries have been co-opted by the agencies that were designated to regulate them.

Certainly the airlines, which are struggling and losing money because they feel they have inadequate rates, do not feel they have co-opted the CAB.

Certainly the gas producers who are not producing at what they consider to be the market price don't feel they have co-opted the FPC.

My own experience, now that I am back in the securities industry, leads me to say with some fervor that we don't feel we have co-opted the SEC. That is not to say that we don't think that their regulatory activities are correct. I do.

But I think that that opinion which Congressman Scheuer has so properly described is more myth than reality.

It is my belief, Mr. Chairman, that if we have well-structured agencies, if we remove political preference from the appointment process, uptown and down, both sides of the aisle, and if we will look more objectively for experts in the areas that the agencies regulate, that we can make this fourth branch of government a more effective part of our Government.

Thank you.

Senator Moss. Thank you very much, Mr. Flanigan.

We would like to hear from the others and then begin our symposium.

Mr. Lee White, who was former chairman of a regulatory agency, is now a practicing attorney, here in the city.

We will hear from you, Lee.

STATEMENT OF LEE WHITE

Mr. White. Thank you, Mr. Chairman.

I spent a little time while a member of the White House staff under President Johnson in this field and yet I would say it was not much of an assignment for me.

President Johnson used the Chairman of the Civil Service Commission at the time, John Macy, as his head hunter. I had some opportunities.

I know that when President Johnson first took over, he looked at this particular problem and came up with an idea, and I know that my views were rather strong on it. I know my colleague, Ralph Dungan, also had something to say about it at the time. Maybe if I misstate it, he will straighten it out.

The President thought it would be a good idea if there were some kind of panel equivalent to the American Bar Association's Review of Judges that would take a look at potential appointments that he planned to make to regulatory agencies.

We thought it was a pretty difficult thing to do and, in short, kind of a bad idea for the simple reason that, and I hope nobody misunderstands this, it is very difficult to figure out what the criteria are that you are going to use to find a good person.

If you are looking for a judge, I presume you have some indicators, such as whether somebody has practiced law for a long time, is held in high esteem by his colleagues, has never been in any difficulty and is generally regarded as having been a good student at college and all that.

But, when you are looking for somebody to serve on a regulatory body, where indeed do you find that check list of criteria that makes you believe that you have the right individual? It is very nearly impossible.

For a President to kind of stick himself in the box of having somebody else make his choice or even restrict his choice seemed to me at that time, and I haven't changed my mind since, to be inappropriate. What that argues for is that the President, himself, and the staff people who work with him have a serious responsibility. I think that also applies, certainly insofar as the Senate is concerned, to its confirming role and insofar as both the House and the Senate are concerned, to their roles in oversight of those people who wind up in those spots.

Of course, there is no one who would not like to see these agencies studded with great stars.

I went to the Power Commission and, after having been there for a while, I visited my old buddy, John Macy. He said, "Now you are there, what do you think about it?"

I told him, "John, it is kind of simple. The first thing you do when you are looking for important people at commissions, is to find somebody who is ruthless as hell. Second, you find somebody who knows something about the subject. Third, you ought to get somebody who works nicely with people. Fourth, you ought to get somebody who goes along with the Chairman. If the first three don't work, that fourth one is the one that makes all the difference."

I don't know how you can be much more precise, frankly.

If you believe that you are going to adopt some procedures that are going to require the President of the United States and his people who assist him to select the right individuals, I don't think it is possible. That does not mean that we should not explore it and I think these hearings are very useful.

One of the ways, frankly, is to make the assignment as attractive as possible so that there are good applicants. Now, sometimes you go seeking the individual. In the real, every day, kind of routine world, it is the other way around. If there are vacancies, there are people coming around suggesting that they know an absolutely spectacular fellow.

Peter Flanigan and Ralph and people like myself will have an awful lot of volunteers, either individuals volunteering themselves or their close, dear friends they know well and sometimes it will be political.

I can't remember exactly the person involved, but I do remember President Johnson intending to appoint a couple of people to regulatory agencies and changing his mind because he had a visit from an old friend of his in the Senate or the House or some other place.

I don't think anybody is going to expect that politics will stop being played by politicians, and Presidents are politicians.

If the jobs can be made attractive in the sense that there is recognition given by their colleagues and by others in the field, if there are satisfactory substantive acts to enforce and implement, if there is a sensitivity to the kind of loneliness, if you will, of the people who come from across the country to fill these jobs—I have a little fantasy I frequently go through. There is a guy from Indianapolis who runs for office and he doesn't make it but he is a hell of a good guy.

So, somebody says he will make a superb commissioner on some commission. He is checked out and indeed he did run a good race and indeed he is a very able fellow. He is about to leave and the people back home have a going-away dinner for him and they tell him and his wife, "Be sure when you see the President, tell him hello," and they are sort of joking.

But he thinks to himself when he gets to Washington that he and his wife will be pretty important. They pack up the station wagon and they get here and, by God, there is not anybody really paying any attention to him. He thought he would be at least a little frog in the big pond. But he is not even a little one.

But there is a group who recognizes his ability. If he happens to be on the Communications Commission, the National Association of Broadcasters or some other group will have a reception to introduce him to the community and indeed there will be some fine people who will welcome him.

So, I suggested to Macy and subsequently to my good friend, Peter Flanigan, because our service in government overlapped briefly, that somebody ought to get these people and make them know that they do have other friends and that their colleagues in this whole regulatory world, for example, might be a source of the social life and professional life that blends. I don't know how important it is, but at least I throw it out.

I hope that there is some other effort to take into account different disciplines.

I am trained as an attorney and I think most of us believe that part of the problem of regulatory agencies is the overjudicialization. But there ought to be a broadening.

We had on the Power Commission when I was there an accountant by the name of Larry O'Connor. Larry and I did not vote together on a lot of issues. He was somewhat more conservative than I, it seems, but he was a very good accountant. The Federal Power Commission has a lot of things involved in accounting. I could easily recommend to President Johnson that he be reappointed because I thought it was useful to have somebody like that.

We never had an economist at the FPC, so far as I know, while I was there. I think Pinky Walker came along afterward as an economist. I think it was a good idea. I don't know that I would have selected Pinky, but I would have had at least an economist on the Commission.

One other point, and the subject can go on and on and on, has to do with what happens to the individual when he is in office.

President Johnson signed an Executive order having to do with the conduct and the ethical requirements for Federal officials, including those who were appointees of his that served on regulatory agencies. He was very reluctant to sign the thing. It is kind of interesting. Macy and I worked on that order. Johnson said, "If I sign that thing, it will bring up all the Bobby Baker stuff again." So, he was scared to death he would bring up the Bobby Baker stuff again.

He signed it. Lo and behold, it is now incumbent on all members of regulatory agencies to live with that code of ethics. Basically, it says you can't take any gratuities and that you are expected not to act like a fool. We recognized that if two members of the Federal Power Commission are out checking on a platform in the Gulf of Mexico that they are not going to get back in a helicopter and go get lunch some place. You can't be a fool about it. At least, it offered some standards and, above all, it offered to members of those agencies a shield if they wanted it.

Nobody believes he can be bought for a lunch or that he can be compromised for a reception or a dinner. But if he doesn't want to do it, it is very nice to be able to say that some other individual made that decision; you have to live with it. By that technique you do not offend people.

Selection is important but it is a relatively blind item. Of far more significance is what happens after you get there.

If I may suggest, the House Commerce Committee is a very busy animal and the Senate Commerce Committee is a very busy animal and it has a hard time finding the time to do its oversight responsibilities.

But, the most important period while I was at the Commission was preparing for the two oversight hearings we had, and we did more shaping up in understanding what was going on in preparation for those than for anything else.

So, I would urge you here to press that, and hopefully, it will be useful to the agencies downtown.

Senator Moss. Thank you very much, Mr. White.

We appreciate your contribution.

We will now turn to Ralph Dungan, who is the chancellor of higher education for the State of New Jersey, and a former Ambassador. He will give a viewpoint from the Kennedy administration.

STATEMENT OF RALPH A. DUNGAN

Mr. DUNGAN. Thank you, Mr. Chairman.

First, if I might digress, I would like to observe to the members of this committee that for a person from the hinterland, the very fact that you are jointly holding an oversight hearing on the regulatory process, one aspect of it, to me is extremely heartening.

We personally think that we would have many fewer problems in government if legislators at all levels, State and Federal, performed the oversight functions with more precision and more regularity than they actually do.

I want to compliment all concerned with this matter.

I would also like to quickly assert at the outset of the thing, a kind of bottom line of my few comments, that I don't think that you ought to be tempted into legislating in this field.

I would suggest that the proper execution of the responsibilities of the President in the first instance, any President, and the responsibilities of the Senate in the confirmation aspect of the process, plus the oversight function, are all that is needed.

I am getting conservative as I advance in years and I do not believe that the most critical aspect of the legislative function in contemporary society is to legislate but, rather, to monitor the activities of the executive.

I think that the monitoring function is an appropriate and proper responsibility in our society, particularly as we are in a transition where the old systems don't seem to be working as well as we thought they did in the regulatory field at the turn of the century.

Let me take as a corollary to Judge Landis' assertion that the most important aspect of the regulatory process is the selection of the regulators and say that if that is true, then the corollary of that principle is that the President has to be concerned in an informed and intelligent way and somewhat knowledgeable about the areas in which he is appointing regulators. I think in recent years—and I would be pleased obviously if history said somewhere around 1960—Presidents began to be more concerned, more specifically concerned, with this.

I think we are well on our way in this country to kind of institutionalizing Presidential concern for top-level appointees, both in the regulatory fields and the other elements of the executive branch.

Not to go into any cookbook- or textbook-type prescription, the obvious thing for anybody assisting the President, or the President, himself, in deciding on an appointee to a regulatory commission is an acknowledgment that the situations in that commission are not all the same. The only thing that one can generalize about, it seems to me, with regard to the characteristics that a good regulator should have is that the person be a man or woman of intelligence and intellectual integrity. That is all.

I would not place, for example, as heavy a stress as Peter Flanigan does on knowledge of the industry. But I would also assert as he does that the fact that the person knows something about the industry ought not to be an automatic bar. It depends on the kind of person he is. Is he slave to a particular corporation or element or is he biased tremendously in his views on one issue or another in the industry? If he is, he is not a good prospect, I would say.

But if he is knowledgeable and honest then he, it seems to me, has two of the most important requisites for appointment to a regulatory commission.

I don't think it profits us very much to describe the details of the headhunting process used during the Kennedy administration, although I would be happy in the colloquy to describe any aspect that the members may wish of the so-called Kennedy process. I think that any selection and appointment process will change very, very much with the style of the President sitting at 1600 Pennsylvania Avenue. He or she, as the case may be, will adopt a style, a mode of operation, which will be unique to his personality and to the people that he has helping him.

Having served briefly under President Johnson and for a few years with President Kennedy, I can tell you their styles, as all of you know, were distinctly different. I wouldn't mind telling you the ways in which they were different. I don't think it is particularly relevant.

What is relevant is that it is not useful to think of any particular pattern as being best or ideal. What you ought to be sure of—or the Senate particularly in its confirmation responsibilities ought to be sure of—is that there is some sort of rational process in place down there and if there isn't somebody ought to take the time to say to the President: "Mr. President,"—quietly, I would suggest, not publicly— "You had better get your headhunting operation"—to use a shorthand term—"in shape because you are sending up people who are neither competent nor trustworthy," if that is the case.

It is hardly ever that way, as you all know.

Let me make one final comment and then stop.

I think there is one aspect which has been on the whole neglected over the years. I think we see it as neglect now because we are very sensitive to the consumer interest.

I am all for representing the consumer, whoever he or she may be. The problem is that he is difficult to identify. Not every group which puts on the label of consumer actually represents the consumer's viewpoint, as you very well know.

However, again I think this is something one ought not to try to formalize. I think one ought to be concerned as to how sensitive the appointing process is to the consumer's point of view as distinguished from the industry point of view.

Lastly, I think one has to comment on the amount of interference, untoward interference, that characterizes the process.

I am a political animal, as all of you are, and we all recognize that that is what makes the process work. But the political process, in my opinion, operating at its best is characterized by restraint where people do not press the power that they may have all of the way.

I am suggesting here strongly that the Congress ought to lay off a little bit.

I agree with Peter Flanigan—in my years of involvement in the appointing process, the most untoward, unconscionable, immoral, I would say, pressures came from this end of the avenue, not in terms of maintaining high standards but in terms of getting "my friend" appointed to such-and-such a commission representing this, that, or the other industry.

So I think, with all due respect to the Members of Congress, I believe that may be one of the more serious problems that we have had over the years. You can't legislate that away.

I think what we can do is to put it out in the open and hope that that will induce the kind of restraint which I think is appropriate.

Mr. Chairman, thank you very much for the opportunity to testify.

Senator Moss. Thank you, Ralph, for your contribution.

We have now had three different presentations. You are much in agreement, I would say, and each with a little bit of flavor to it.

We want to start the symposium.

I propose to do something which is something that could never occur in the Senate. We are going to impose the 5-minute rule, showing that we do learn from time to time. We will try to do that so that we can keep the questions revolving. It does not mean however, that we are going to be limited to only one 5-minute period but at that point we must pass on until each has had an opportunity to ask his questions.

I was intrigued particularly by what Mr. Dungan was saying in his presentation, that the Congress perhaps is more at fault in many respects than the executive branch in some of the appointments because of pressures put on them for nominations of certain individuals.

I wanted to test what has been said by some, on the Senate side at least, and that is that the President is entitled to his appointment and as long as he is not a scoundrel, doesn't have a criminal record, and is what we think is relatively honest, we should not dig deeper than that.

Is that a lazy copout or is that essentially all we should look at? Should these disabilities which obviously should rule them out and have been overlooked in the selection by the White House be ignored?

Could each of you spend a minute or two on that?

Mr. Dungan. I think it is a bit of a copout. The presumption should generally be that the President as the Chief Executive ought to have the opportunity to put forward a name and unless this fellow or a person is a scoundrel, he or she ought to receive the approbation of the Senate.

On the other hand, suppose he or she is just a blah, a nothing. It does seem to me that the Senate has a responsibility to discuss it at some length so that it then becomes so apparent to the Senate as a whole and to the public that the President may be brought to the point where he or she, as the case may be, will want to reconsider the appointment. I don't think you ought to automatically pass them.

On the other hand, I do think the President ought to be accorded some benefit of the doubt.

Senator Moss. Lee?

Mr. White. I would point out one distinction, Mr. Chairman.

Most of these regulatory positions are for a fixed term. So, I think there is a slightly different obligation on the Senate than in the case of people who serve at the pleasure of the President who could be fired tomorrow—or maybe Sunday. You know, those things happen.

As far as the confirming process, though, in addition to giving the President the benefit of the doubt, those are extremely educational experiences for members of the regulatory bodies who are there. It is part of their learning process.

Secretary Hickel turned out to be quite a different Secretary of the Interior, Mr. Chairman, in large measure because of what you people in the Interior Committee did to him in bringing him into the real world where these pressures are.

So, the confirmation hearings can be extraordinarily valuable.

Just to take one extra point, the Senate very recently by a vote of 47 to 44 rejected a nominee for the Federal Power Commission. The basic reason is that he had come from a law firm where he had represented industries practicing before the Commission. I agree with Peter and Ralph that this should not be an absolute bar.

It just so happens that that commission at that time was perceived to have nothing but people who were sympathetic to the industry. So that I think that the selection, and I think the man was a great deal better than that vote, but the selection put him in an awkward spot because at that moment the Federal Power Commission, like every other commission at every other moment, was not living in a vacuum. There are other things happening.

So, it argues again for good advice and counsel to the President and good action on his part.

The confirming process is very important.

Senator Moss. I would say that if the President has overlooked what we might call the philosophical spectrum of the commission then it is the duty of the Senate in the confirmatory process to look at that and to point it out the instant it is sent up.

Mr. White. Yes.

I think really the experience in the last 2 years since that time has been salutary, a Republican administration and Democratic-controlled Senate. Yet, I think there is now a much easier, smoother operation, that people on that committee staff, Commerce Committee and other committees, that have nominees come to them, are checking them out a bit.

The President is not abandoning his appointment power but he wants to have an idea of what will happen. I think it is constructive and useful.

Senator Moss. Peter.

Mr. Flanigan. Mr. Chairman, I think we can properly, as Lee suggests, distinguish betwen appointments or nominations to these regulatory commissions and the other nominees to executive positions that need confirmation. That is because of the nature of the commissions being creatures of the Congress, and because, as Lee says, the term of the appointments.

I do think that there is a difference in the attitude that should be taken by a Senator when he considers an appointment or recommendation, a nominee from the President, and when he undertakes to present a nominee of his own. I think it is incumbent on the President to get an intelligent, honest, hopefully knowledgeable individual, and that same set of requirements rests on Members of the Congress if they wish to make a suggestion for a nominee.

Now I don't think that the confirmation process should be as stringent in accepting the President's nominees as they would be on coming downtown and saying, "Here is a fellow I think should be considered for the job." I think that stringency would be equally between the President when he sends the name to you, and you when you send the suggestion to him.

Senator Moss. Thank you.

Congressman Sharp.

Mr. Sharp. Thank you, Mr. Chairman.

Yesterday we heard testimony in which two suggestions came up. One was the substantive question which obviously most of you disagree with, which is that somehow we could set general standards as to who is qualified to be a commissioner. I gather in your testimony that none of you thinks that can be done in any kind of precise way that would really be helpful.

The second suggestion for change was procedural, that maybe there were some changes we could make like making the appointment process more public prior to the confirmation hearing. I get the impression from all of you this morning that you actually see no specific changes in that area.

I was just wondering if perhaps the suggestion of Mr. Dungan is an approach you all tend to agree with, where we might be more effective if we had, certainly at the beginning of a Presidency, if not once or twice during that Presidency, a review of the actual headhunting process.

Do you have any comment on that? Is that a direction you think is most useful, or do you think we should not involve ourselves?

Mr. Dungan. Let me try that.

I would say you shouldn't. If I were advising a President and you attempted to, I would tell you to go to the Committee on Administration and worry about your own problems.

You ought to understand that both Lee and I worked on the Hill as well as in the executive branch, and I am a great believer in the separation of powers. I think how the President conducts his affairs in the headhunting ought to be his choice. You can learn enough about that process without formally reviewing it.

Mr. White. I would only add that you really don't have to ask for a precise description, because the press, the media, that follow every action of the President, pick up areas of specialty, and some of them will zero in on this aspect of the Presidency. Some reporters may, for example, report or misinterpret the fact that Peter Flanigan is the czar for appointment purposes and the President may be compelled to explain that is not the case, or he may believe it is not important enough to straighten out.

The point is, there is some public discussion about the function and Congress need not prod him.

Mr. Flanigan. Even if the executive privilege were breached I don't think you would learn much because the process need not be in fact the substance. It would be very difficult to get a meaningful review.

Mr. Dungan. Could I flip something in here, if I may, Mr. Chairman?

I think the point of opening up the nominations and appointments process is a good idea on the whole. I would say that if I had the responsibility for headhunting, mainly because, and I think Peter and Lee would both agree with this, it is very difficult, even operating from the White House switchboard, to comprehend the total universe of potential appointees; a more formal way to flush names up, if you will, than the old boy network, or the industry, or whatever, might not be bad.

For example, a formal announcement in the Register, the Federal Register. The consumer groups, the industries, obviously the Members of Congress know when appointments are opening up. But folks in the hinterland might not and there might be ways that we could elicit suggestions from a broader range of people than we now do to build that inventory of potential candidates.

Mr. White. If I may add to that, Mr. Chairman, it brings to mind something that had not occurred to me before.

Anybody who was in Washington at the time President Johnson was in office knew his great penchant, almost an obsession, for secrecy. He would sit back with these damn names held right close to his vest, and at the right moment he would drop them out.

Happily Dungan did not do that, but I lived through it. When Peter Flanigan came along I said to him, "You know, there is an enormous technique around here, such as trial balloons. If you will send up a name, or let somebody else send up a name and let it float a bit, you will perhaps pick up something that no FBI examination or anything else has picked up, and you will spare yourself enormous embarassment, and there can be a little of that."

I am delighted to say that with all the other criticisms you might have, President Nixon on that score was quite good, of letting names float a little bit. I assume and presume that there were a few that may have been in the President's mind that turned out not to be in the President's mind when some reaction came in, whether public or private.

There is no way I can see that the Congress or anyone else can say to the President, "Mr. President, this is the way you ought to operate." It is very, very difficult.

What it means is that we have to be very careful about whom we select to be President.

Mr. Flanigan. Mr. Chairman, I want to confess I did learn a lot from Lee White. We even took the regulatory agencies on the Sequoia at his suggestion.

Senator Moss. Mr. Collins.

Mr. Collins. Thank you, Senator Moss.

In evaluating this appointment process I want to go back and put in the picture of civil service and what we have here. We have about 3 million people that are a self-perpetuating bureaucracy, of which so far as I know last year none of the top echelon was fired for incompetence, laziness, lack of ability, or anything.

In other words, we have a Government that is based on a completely independent organization. Now when an executive gets into power he has about 3,000 appointments that we are talking about out of 3 million people to control. If he does not pick people first, and we named these different characteristics, you said No. 4 is to be responsive to the chairman, I thought you really hit it on the head, if we don't have people who are responsive to the President, and who believe in his policies, and also who are strong individuals, I don't see how it is going to be possible to deal with a bureaucracy, or to come in with any innovative programs or anything else.

As you know, we write the laws in Congress, but it doesn't mean a thing until those bureaucrats sit and interpret them and put them into effect. What I am saying is should the Presidential prerogative of picking a strong man who is completely sympathetic and in line with his own policies be the primary influence? I cannot help but think that the President had a lot of confidence in you in each case when he brought you in. In my opinion, that should be the dominant characteristic.

Mr. DUNGAN. I would say most emphatically that he should, Congressman. As an old bureaucrat, I don't think that the bureaucracy is as hardheaded and obstinate and stupid as many do. It is malleable. It does take direction. But where it is hardheaded, and obstreperous, and obtuse, and not subject to Presidential, or Presidential appointee direction, I think we do have to find devices to permit more effective Presidential control. One device which has been discussed from time to time is the designation of a certain upper level policymaking position held by civil servants. Persons moving into such positions could be moved out of them on the initiative of the department or agency head. If removed such a person would move into the highest permanent grade in the civil service which they held prior to entry into the policy executive position. In other words tenure would be in the grade, not necessarily in the position, and individuals could elect or not to move into what I call the "executive zone" where tenure would be subject to administrative discretion.

I think there are devices like this which one can work with that will solve the problem to the extent that it exists. I personally don't feel it is as bad as many have believed in the past.

Mr. WHITE. I can even give you one example, Congressman. Out of a spirit of charity I will pick the best one I know. When President Nixon selected a guy by the name of Miles Kirkpatrick to be the Chairman of the Trade Commission I thought it was the worst choice in the world. He picked a fellow, a lawyer representing antitrust clients, who had been head of the American Bar Association Review Committee. He went into that job. I must say I think he did a superb job. It was already moving by virtue of an earlier good appointment by President Nixon, Caspar Weinberger. I think he was a much better Federal Trade Chairman than Secretary of HEW, but that is irrelevant. He was doing a good job.

Lo and behold, in a matter of 2 years there was a turnover, a 50-percent turnover in that agency, all to the good, using my own biases. So we are talking about a very important function. That is to get people who are able and inspiring and have leadership.

I don't have quite that same belief that Civil Service, that whole, faceless, shapeless mass, can't be moved. I think it can be moved if you are working correctly at the top.

Mr. FLANIGAN. Mr. Congressman, I join with my colleagues here in believing that the Civil Service, after watching them work and working with them for some years, is, by and large, competent, and that they will respond to leadership.

In describing the qualifications of members of the Commission I said, after describing some others, and very importantly, that they be philosophically in tune with the President. I agree with you entirely, and I did not interject, but I will now, when the Chairman suggested, and Mr. White agreed, that it is part of the confirmation responsibility and process to decide whether or not any more of that philosophy is appropriate on the Commission, and if they don't think it is appropriate that they should refuse to confirm. It seems to me that that problem only exists with the President of one party and a Congress of another, but it seems to me that a President, having been elected on the basis of a stated philosophy, particularly with regard to Commissions where by law no more than a majority of one can be of his party, and where inevitably appointees of his predecessor will be in office, but he properly should send up to the Senate for confirmation nominees that reflect his philosohpy and the philosophy that he presented when he presented himself to the country for election.

As long as those people are honest, capable individuals, then I think that the Congress should not reject them because they don't happen to reflect a philosophy that they prefer over that of the President.

Mr. COLLINS. Thank you, sir.

Mr. WHITE. Mr. Chairman, I can't resist. There is a great tag line. I don't know if you were present at the time in the Commerce Committee, but the question was raised as to whether an appointee of President Nixon to a regulatory agency was really a Democrat on the basis of what he had done. The guy had an absolute perfect answer. He said, "Why, of course, he was chairman of the Tennessee Democrats for Nixon." So he had obviously been a Democrat.

Senator Moss. I remember the sequel of that. He was rejected for confirmation by reason of being not a Democrat to fill a Democratic slot, whereupon he was renominated as an independent, and he had to be confirmed.

The gentleman from New York.

Mr. SCHEUER. To continue on this question, how do you find the men who are honest and able and who also are going to do a job for the consumers, for the public? You are in sort of a judgment-making process here. Out of the many suggestions that were made, how do you think that we could struggle the decision-making processes toward doing a better job of finding able men and honest men who are not admittedly proponents of the industry from which they have emerged?

The committee staff, with the help of a very able gentleman from the General Accounting Office, did a study. We studied 120 appointments of regulators. Of 85 who recently left, 32 of them, within the next 5 years, took jobs in an industry which had been subject to their regulation. Thirty-five of the one hundred and twenty came from an industry which they were to regulate. Only nine of them had any prior identification with consumer causes of any kind.

One has the feeling that they left the industry to do a short stint in an agency, with all the time intending to return to the industry. It is quite possible that they did an excellent and fair-minded job while they were on the regulatory commission. Nevertheless, one has the underlying feeling that their perception of themselves is that they were industry men. The question then arises whether they were not consciously or unconsciously serving the industry while in the regulatory agency. That is the problem.

David Cohen of Common Cause is going to testify, recommending that Presidential appointees be reviewed by nonpartisan qualification boards. That is one possible approach.

N4

Another approach might be to formalize the role of the Civil Service Commission. We might scrutinize these men and women who are up for appointment to determine their points of view and their biases.

We might also accomplish this formalization by creating an Office of Regulatory Appointments in the White House that would make a formal search for men and women whose backgrounds were consumer and public protection oriented.

Another idea that we have heard, recommends one term appointments for 10 or 15 years followed by a long timespan during which, appointees could not return to an industry they had regulated.

You and I, Peter, could disagree with whether the regulatory agencies have become industry patsies. However, the public perception is that many of them are. Whether or not that is the case, the perception has a reality of its own, and must be dealt with as such.

The big question is, can we formalize the selection processes in order to find men and women with knowledge of the industry, with intelligence, and with basic integrity, who would be responsible to their Chairman as well as responsible to the public interest.

Must decisions be made based on character judgments, or is there any way that we can formalize the process? Certainly no President can make judgmental decisions about 3,000 appointments.

Does this always have to be a sort of a hit or miss process; it works pretty well when people of your caliber are doing it, but, when others of a lesser caliber are involved, all sorts of abuses and ripoffs of the public interest occur with which we are all familiar?

Mr. DUNGAN. I would like to take a shot at it if I may.

Jim, just taking off from your last point. One of the problems, it seems to me, to be philosophic about the democratic processes, is that it is not surefire any more than directed or structured governmental processes are or claim to be.

I would maintain that there are no panaceas and never have been, even looking at the regulatory process itself, from the beginning of this century when it was prescribed by the reformers of the late 19th and early 20th centuries as the panacea. The idea of taking the regulation of industry out of the hands of the politicians and putting it in the hands of quasi-judicial people who are removed from all those pernicious political forces—I submit one can make a very good case that that has not been the best way to do it. We are stuck with it historically and culturally. I think we have to do the best we can do with it.

On your precise question, yes, there are some things that one might do. For example, restricting a person who is on a regulatory commission from going back into certain kinds of positions in that industry. I would submit, however, that that kind of restriction has not worked very well with respect to military officers coming out of the Defense Department and moving into defense industries.

You know, historically, you get good years and bad years. We just hope there are more good ones than bad ones. In fact, I would say personally that the more you fiddle around with it, the less likely you are to attain the desired goal—that is, by way of prescription of some kinds of techniques—and I say this with all deference to the interests of many in the consumer movement. May I suggest a test on this point. The next time you get a consumer representative up before you, ask him the last time it was that he put forward a viable candidate for anything. It is much easier to be a critic than to find a person who has the variety of capabilities—technical, personal, et cetera—to perform capably in any kind of position. The critics are much better at telling you how you have fallen down. It is not personal at all, but I think it is true of Congress, the executive branch, or anybody else.

Senator Moss. Does anybody else wish to respond to that?

Mr. FLANIGAN. Mr. Chairman, I would like to agree with my colleague that to the extent you seem to relieve the judgmental factor, I think you do a disservice to the proposed process because the judgmental factor is going to be eventually the one on which the choice is going to be made, and you should not leave it out as the key operating decisionmaking entity.

I don't see any way around it. Though if the system could be improved, I would like it.

Mr. Chairman, when I accepted this invitation, it was subject to the fact I catch a 1:30 airplane. Would you and the committee excuse me?

Senator Moss. Yes; but first let me express our appreciation for your coming. I realize you had to travel down here, but we did expect to be through in time. We hope you can still catch your airplane.

Thank you again, Peter; we will have a few more moments with the other two gentlemen if they will remain, but you are excused.

Mr. FLANIGAN. Thank you, sir.

Senator Moss. I would like to expand on what Mr. Scheuer said. Isn't there really quite a bit of pressure on the President in wanting to name people who will succeed in the agencies—if indeed his nominee turns out to be a dud or scoundrel, wouldn't this be a reflection on him and his administration? Exactly what kind of pressure does that exert on the President to want to have his nominees succeed?

Mr. WHITE. Obviously, my experience is limited, but with Presidents I have had anything to do with, I am sure that has to be a factor. For those you haven't worked for, you just assume that logic dictates that they, too, want to have their appointees distinguished.

Unfortunately, though, as important and as prominent as that factor is, sometimes it really has to yield to a political reality of the moment. I don't think it is shocking that a President who might have wanted to pick absolutely the best individual to be the 11th member of the ICC, may decide that if he can persuade a committee chairman to do something by choosing another man, well, what the hell, there are 10 others. It is that tough.

Mr. DUNGAN. I think that is something of a factor, but I don't think it is the one that one can rely on all the time, that is his concern with how he looks as the appointing authority. It gets back to what I was really saying, that is the corollary to the Landis dictum, and that is that the key of it is how sensitive the President is or the people who work with him are to the importance of the regulatory process in that sector of the economy.

In some cases, the case of some commissions, I will be frank with you without discussing them—at the time I was active we practically wrote it off because the law and the tradition and the method of regulation that was peculiar to the Commission did not make it a very useful instrument. There were Commissions that were right smack dab into very important parts of the flow of commerce, or influenced decisively the behavior of the industry. FPC was certainly one of them, where we were concerned with balance, with quality of people, and frankly to the extent that we could resist it, try to resist external pressures, either from the industry or from the Hill.

Now, as Lee points out, there are some times when one's best instincts and motivations tend to get subordinated to lesser principles or objectives.

Senator Moss. To get back to this question about returning to the industry, in the Consumer Product Safety Act we wrote a provision that prohibits a Commissioner or senior staff member working directly or indirectly for a manufacturer subject to the act for 12 months after leaving the Commission.

Is this a desirable prohibition? Will it make recruitment more difficult for service on that Commission?

Mr. Dungan. I would not say so, because anybody who was not sensitive enough to get the spirit of such an amendment and abide by it could find other ways to connect himself, as a consultant, for example, where he would not be a direct employee, or something.

There are oodles of ways, as we have seen. I think the best example of it is the way the military has evaded this over the years. I don't think it is bad. I think it is a good idea; it is a formalization of an ethical principle.

Mr. White. If I may, Mr. Chairman, you happen to hit upon an area where I have an ax to grind. Being very perceptive, I noticed that as people were coming to the end of their term and they didn't know whether the President was going to appoint them or not, there was a subliminal process at work. Some of them, believe it or not, began dickering as to how they ought to be voting on some issues. So it occurred to me that that last period is especially tender and sensitive, and that the worst thing in the world is to be looking for a job when you know that your term is going to end, say, on June 30, and you are making decisions all through January and June of that year.

So I suggested, first to outside groups such as Brookings Institution and colleges, it would be a very nice idea to have what might be called a halfway house for regulators so that they ought to be assured that they could continue for a fixed period, maybe 12 months, same salary, and during that 12 months they can write their memoirs or expand on items that they weren't able to take care of while they were busy members of the commission, and above all look for a job.

If you think of where we put these people, sometimes they honestly don't know until the last minute whether the President is going to appoint them. If you haven't married a wealthy woman and acquired money, or a wealthy husband, all of a sudden the payroll stops, those salary checks stop.

So, if you have kids that are going to college, or a maid, or anything, you are going to figure out what you are going to do. It is especially useful for people whose terms go like that to provide them with some protection.

May I say that as good as the idea seems to me, nobody else has thought it was that good. If the committee would like I will submit it in a formal fashion. It is very useful. So much of it is perception.

I was very fortunate when I left the Federal Power Commission. I took a quiet vow to myself I would not practice before that Commission, at least for a long time. It wasn't because I thought there were some statutory prohibitions against cases that were before the Commission I was personally involved in. I simply didn't want to.

I thought it would be demeaning. Frankly, my idea of heaven was not to spend 3 weeks in a hearing on some damn rate case anyhow.

Don't forget what you do to people who have spent a lot of time in a field if you are going to say they can't do it. It does have some impact, and the problem I think is to do it on the individual's part in a fashion that makes sense, and I think you do have to have some rules, conflict of interest statutes, and some prohibitions.

I don't think you can kid yourself. As Ralph says, it is pretty hard to legislate morality, ethics and commonsense, but you ought to have some standards if for no other reason than to reassure the public.

Right now the public believes, as Congressman Scheuer says, that the agencies are sort of dominated by people who have industry leanings, and if they come there neutral that is the way they leave. They go into the industry, and we who believe they are protecting or supposed to protect the public interest simply don't have confidence in them. Anything that can be done to lift that confidence obviously is all to the good.

Senator Moss. Should Congress be eligible for that halfway house too?

Mr. Scheuer.

Mr. Scheuer. I think it all does come down to morality, decency, and ethics.

As I remember, you two gentlemen span the Kennedy and Johnson years. Were different routes to the selection process tried during that time and if so, might they give us clues as to what works well and what does not?

Mr. Dungan. Mr. Chairman, and Congressman, the styles were completely different. I don't think it profits very much—let me say that it is useful history sometime, but I don't think it is the kind of thing that is appropriate for the public record. Nothing secret about it, I don't mean that, but I simply mean that the style, at least in my experience, of the two gentlemen and their attitudes toward the governmental process were so significantly different that I do think that it influenced to a significant extent the way these appointments were made.

In some particulars they were very much the same. John Macy took over a very crude system of recruitment, if you will that we developed. It was so crude I am almost embarrassed to talk about it. But it was at least a step forward toward the systematizing of the headhunting process.

I think John Macy and his colleagues took that system forward to some extent. But the ultimate criteria in my opinion by which one judges any system, any process, is what happens at the Presidential decision point, and what attitudes form those decisions.

I think there was a major difference there, as I think there would be a difference, I imagine, between any two Presidents.

Mr. Scheuer. It is not only whether the President gets what is put on his platter, but also, who serves it.

Mr. Dungan. That is true, and the Presidential assistant who is assisting in that process very soon knows what the rules of the game are. Let me just be plain. President Johnson had a very hard view of the relationship between the member of a commission and the Office of the Presidency or the President, himself. President Kennedy, it seemed to me anyway, seemed to be more in the spirit of the independent regulatory body.

To tell you the truth, I, like Peter and Lee, too, maintained a lot of relationships on a continuing basis with the commissions, particularly with the chairmen. I can't recall anytime when we discussed any substantive matter, a particular matter. General philosophy of regulation in that particular field, yes. The regulatory process, yes. Lee particularly in the Kennedy years was instrumental in beginning a process that later aborted, because we didn't have time, of bringing the regulators together to talk about the process of regulation rather than specific cases.

I think in other administrations there tended to be more direct substantive interest in particular cases than was true in the early 1960's.

Senator Moss. Thank you.

Lee?

Mr. WHITE. I sense the frustration, because you know, you have a couple of guys, to use the term, stonewalling. You are saying, "Can't you guys come up with any process or anything that will help this procedure?" We say, "No, God damn, you have to use commonsense, get good people." I am afraid that is what it comes down to. I know it sounds terrible to you.

Mr. SCHEUER. You have to get good people to get good people.

Mr. WHITE. Why don't you pass a statute saying the President has to have able staff?

Mr. SCHEUER. I guess what you really need is a good President to select good staff.

Senator Moss. It has been fascinating. I know we can visit here all morning long, and I would like to do it because you were both very competent and eloquent witnesses and great friends. What you have told us has been very revealing.

We are just searching around in the field because it does present some dilemmas and problems to us. I first came to the Senate when we didn't really turn down anybody. We just had a hearing and confirmed them. Gradually that has moved up to where we begin to reject selected ones, but we still confirm most who come along.

So, I am searching in this area, as I am sure my colleagues in the Senate are. The regulatory system, as Mr. Dungan said, for good or ill, is the way we are operating now. Since we have that, it behooves us to do our very best to make it work at its maximum efficiency. That is the purpose of this symposium.

We don't have any statute or bill before us. We are just trying to get information. Thank you. You have helped us a great deal both of you.

Mr. DUNGAN. Thank you, Senator.

NOTES AND REFERENCES

1. The "Review Committee" cited in this portion of the text refers to the regulatory reform commissions, which were to review and report on the impact of regulatory agencies on commerce and the public interest. The establishment of such review commissions was provided for in three bills proposed by the Senate: S. 4155, S. 4167, and S.J. 256. In his testimony before the Government Operations Committee, James Turner addressed these bills, as well as bills S. 704, S. 770, and S. 3604; none of them were enacted into law.

2. The Cost of Living Council was authorized by the Economic Stabilization Act of 1970 in an effort to stabilize the economy, reduce inflation, and decrease unemployment. The Council was established on August 15, 1971 by President Nixon's Executive Order 11615 and it was abolished on June 18, 1974 by Nixon's Executive Order 11788.

3. Consumer advocate Ralph Nader participates in a wide variety of public policy debates. His influence is enhanced by his access to a cadre of experts, both volunteers and professionals, who share his concerns. Nader "organizations," as they are known in Washington, are funded in part by Nader himself, who contributes earnings from lectures and books, and in part by foundations. His statement in the text was made when he appeared before the Senate Subcommittees on Consumers and on the Environment during the committees' Symposium on Regulatory Myths.

4. Representative James Scheuer is referring to the testimony of Common Cause's Executive Director, David Cohen, which appeared earlier in this chapter. In this and some of the other documents in the volume, the original order of reprinted testimony has been rearranged to provide a logical rather than chronological sequence.

Chapter 5
Forcing Action on Reform:
Regulatory Reform Act

Two significant measures were introduced into Congress toward the end of the 94th session, both designed to force action reform measures in the regulatory agencies. One was the Agenda for Government Reform (S. 3428), supported by the Ford administration and sponsored by Senate Republican Minority Leader Hugh Scott. The other was the Regulatory Reform Act (S. 2812), sponsored by Senate Majority Whip Robert Byrd and Senator Charles Percy. The bills contained similar provisions for mandatory examination of the regulatory functions of government on a set schedule over four to five years.

The Percy-Byrd bill contained a "sunset" provision whereby, through failure of the Congress and/or the Executive branch to act, the authority of a regulatory body to operate would become null and void. This provision was missing from the administration bill, as was a complicated provision regarding legislative veto, the constitutionality of which was challenged during Senate hearings. The Regulatory Reform Act, as the broader of the two proposals and the only one to progress substantially in the 94th Congress, was selected for treatment in this chapter. Identical or companion bills of the 94th Congress include H.R. 11383, H.R. 11402, H.R. 11450, H.R. 11729, H.R. 11730, H.R. 11731, and H.R. 14671. President Gerald Ford's Agenda for Government Reform is also discussed in this material, and the White House Fact Sheet on the measure is reprinted in the appendix section of this volume.

The President's Agenda for Government Reform was virtually ignored by the 94th Congress, and by the time the Ford administration ended, the initiative on regulatory reform clearly lay with Congress. The extent to which Congress will continue to assert its constitutional prerogative in this field is a matter of conjecture, but the groundwork has already been laid in the Percy-Byrd Regulatory Reform Act. Even if the Executive branch asserted more involvement in the regulatory process, its management procedures would most likely be affected by the action-forcing mechanism associated with the mandatory review of programs, as proposed by the Percy-Byrd bill. The legislative veto provision is an important element of the Regulatory Reform Act, but its significance as a procedure in Legislative-Executive relations (in areas of shared responsibility) transcends the bill itself. For that reason, a substantial portion of this chapter is devoted to the discussion and debate concerning the desirability and constitutionality of the legislative veto—as an element of the Percy-Byrd bill and as an administrative reorganization concept in areas of shared jurisdiction.

STATEMENTS OF PURPOSE ([73], pp. 4–9)

Senator Robert Byrd

I need not recite the litany of costs connected with government regulation, the economic waste and the loss of jobs, the inflationary impact, the delays—these are all well known to anyone who has given the most cursory attention to the Federal regulatory system. The need for reform is immediate and compelling.

314

The only question, Mr. Chairman, is how best to go about it over-hauling the complex mass of government regulation that we have im-posed upon ourselves.

What is needed is a comprehensive plan for the reform of the en-tire range of Federal regulation. It must go beyond individual agen-cies or particular regulations to deal with the full scope of the prob-lem. It is toward that end that my distinguished colleague, Senator Percy, and I have developed S. 2812, the Regulatory Reform Act of 1976.

Briefly stated, this bill mandates the President to submit to the Congress by March 31 of each year, for a 5-year period, a reform plan in a specified sector of the economy. The appropriate congres-sional committees are then mandated to report a reform bill to be-come the pending business in both houses by September 15. If Con-gress has not enacted a plan by December 31, the President's plan automatically becomes law unless specifically disapproved by either House. If there is such a resolution of disapproval, and no compre-hensive reform has been adopted by June 30 of the next year, then those rules of the affected agencis, the major purpose of which is in the preservation of the public health and safety, will be rescinded.

This kind of discipline is patterned after the Budget Reform Act of 1974. Its success there shows that it can work. In the absence of these kinds of action-forcing procedures, reform proposals are likely to fall victim to the potent opposition of special interest groups.

Since these provisions should make it clear that reform will be enacted, it is our hope that all groups will come forward and partici-pate positively in the reform process. And the procedure embodied in S. 2812 provides ample opportunity for this kind of active partici-pation. We would expect the Administration to solicit all relevant viewpoints in the development of its plan, and there would be the usual opportunity for interaction during Congressional consideration. The action-forcing procedures should ensure that this participation will be in good faith, and not merely a self-interested effort to stall reform.

I would like to make a final observation, intended to put this legis-lation into perspective with the many other regulatory reform pro-posals currently under consideration, some of which are quite good. What I think best recommends S. 2812 is that it will provide a pro-cedural framework through which we can more effectively implement the best of these other substantive plans, as well as the recommenda-tions of the current joint study being conducted by the Government Operations and the Commerce Committees. Each year, we can exam-ine the situation in the scheduled area and then use the timetable in S. 2812 to carry out what we find to be the most effective solution for the problems with government regulation in that area. And the defi-nite timetable will allow the maximum coordination of effort—within the Executive branch, the Congress, the academic community, the affected interest groups, and society as a whole.

Of course, if we are ready to institute some reform ahead of the schedule set forth in S. 2812, there is nothing in the bill to prevent that. Rather, the bill gives a latest possible date for the reform of federal regulation in each of various areas subject to regulation.

I would like to take a few more minutes to discuss the advantages of S. 2812 over the President's plan introduced on May 13th.

Senator Percy and I applaud the President's support for regula-tory reform, and his proposal incorporates the underlying concept contained in the Percy-Byrd bill: that there is a need for a comprehensive approach in which government regulations in different areas are dealt with systematically each year over a period of several years. The Administration bill also accepts the proposition set forth in S. 2812 that certain action-forcing measures are needed to ensure that reform plans are submitted by the President and acted on by the Congress.

Here, unfortunately, the Administration bill does not include the "sunset" provisions of the Percy-Byrd proposal which are vital to assure that regulatory reform actually will take place.

Under the provisions of S. 2812 there are four action-forcing mechanisms which guarantees regulatory reform.

First: The President must submit a reform plan to Congress by March 31, or the committee will develop their own plan.

Second: The congressional committees must report reform legislation to become pending business in both Houses by September 15.

Third: If Congress has not enacted reform by December 31, the President's plan automatically becomes law, unless specifically disapproved by either House.

Fourth: If there is such a resolution of disapproval, Congress has until June 30 to enact comprehensive reform, or most of the rules of the affected agencies become null and void.

The administration plan contains provisions similar to the first two of the Percy-Byrd bill's action-forcing mechanisms—the President must submit a reform plan to Congress by January 31 and if no reform is enacted by November 15, the President's plan becomes the pending business in both Houses and remains such until acted upon.

The failure of the administration bill to include the "sunset" provisions of S. 2812's approach is the basic difference between the bills and the critical flaw in the President's approach.

The stronger approach of the Percy-Byrd bill contained in the final two action-forcing mechanisms, or "sunset" provisions, of S. 2812 are essential if regulatory reform is ever going to be effective. By taking the teeth out of the Percy-Byrd approach, the administration plan invites the full-scale opposition of interest groups who would have nothing to lose and everything to gain if they were able to kill the reform plan. Under S. 2812, the interest groups would risk losing everything by opposing reform, for if no comprehensive measure is enacted by June 30, all rules conferring economic benefits to the affected industry would be rendered inoperative.

Again, let me say that Senator Percy and I are pleased that the President has submitted a plan for regulatory reform which accepts the underlying concepts of our bill—but, I hope this committee and the Congress will recognize that without the teeth given S. 2812 by its "sunset" provisions, effective regulatory reform will be very difficult to achieve.

In concluding, let me say that I am pleased that these hearings are underway and that such an outstanding group of witnesses has been scheduled. I think that S. 2812 is an important measure, and I look forward to some insightful testimony and constructive criticism. Speaking for myself, and I know for Senator Percy, our primary concern is to come out of these hearings with the very best regulatory reform agenda that we can. Only then can we hope for truly comprehensive and truly successful reform to be accomplished in this crucial area....

Senator Charles Percy

Fortunately there is growing awareness, both within Congress and throughout the country, of just how serious this problem is. In fact, there are several dozen proposals, now before the Senate alone, designed to deal with the burdens caused by misdirected regulation.

These proposals tend to fall within one or another of nine basic categories. Specifically, there are proposals for: (1) further study; (2) congressional review of agency regulations; (3) creation of a joint congressional regulatory oversight office; (4) eliminating or phasing out designated agencies; (5) organizational and administrative changes; (6) substantive reform in a specific area; (7) cost-benefit analyses of regulations; (8) zero-base budget review of agency N1 effectiveness; and (9) enhanced antitrust enforcement.

Although several of these proposals contain valuable ideas, they generally suffer from certain common flaws. First: Many are not truly comprehensive, in that they deal only with the specific regulations issued by Government agencies (regulatory performance), and do not touch upon the more fundamental questions of appropriate regulatory functions and structures. Second: Many proposals tie themselves exclusively to a single approach to be used in all situations. But just as no one medicine is the best cure for all physical ills, it is unrealistic to think that any one substantive approach will be the best solution to all regulatory problems. And third: Many of the proposals are not politically realistic. The wholesale and arbitrary transformation or elimination of agencies simply will not receive needed support either within or outside the Government.

These flaws are especially distressing because the enactment of inadequate or inappropriate reform holds forth a double danger. Not only will these very serious problems not be solved, but future reform efforts will become even more difficult to accomplish if the current healthy momentum for change is lost.

It is, therefore, essential that any reform effort be comprehensive, flexible, and, above all, successful.

But there are formidable obstacles in the way of such reform. Perhaps foremost among these is the tenacious opposition of certain interest groups tied to the affected agencies. Often these very groups will join the call for reform, but when the rhetoric comes home to roost, when specific proposals are on the line, it becomes disturbingly clear that for many of them regulatory reform means, "Get rid of the regulations I don't like, but keep the regulations I do like." The status quo may not be ideal, but they would rather bear those ills they have than fly to others that they know not of.

Worst of all, the opposition to reform is not confined to outside interests. Not infrequently the agencies themselves, and affected committees of the Congress will close ranks and raise a hue and cry of their own—sometimes more shrill than that of the affected interest groups.

Indeed, Congress has been woefully deficient in pursuing reform. For this reason, a disciplined approach is needed to ensure full-scale reform.

It was to answer this need and to overcome the common pitfalls that we saw in many other reform proposals that Senator Robert

Byrd and I developed and introduced S. 2812, the Regulatory Reform Act of 1976. . . .

Last week, on May 13, President Ford submitted his "Agenda for Government Reform Act" to Congress. This action was an important affirmation of the need to agree upon an agenda for timely and comprehensive action. I am pleased that the administration's bill is so similar to S. 2812. The administration proposal adopts the two key underlying concepts of S. 2812: that there is a need for a comprehensive approach in which Government regulation in a different area is dealt with systematically each year over a period of several years; and that certain "action-forcing" measures are needed to insure that reform plans will be submitted by the President and acted upon by the Congress.

However, there are important differences between the administration proposal and S. 2812. The administration's "sectors of industry" approach reflects some serious internal inconsistencies which are minimized by the "sectors of Government regulation" approach taken in S. 2812. The vital "sunset" provisions of S. 2812 should cause interest groups which might otherwise be tempted to oppose reform to have serious second thoughts about such opposition. This is because S. 2812 mandates that all rules issued by the affected agencies, except those whose principal purpose is to promote health and safety, would be rescinded if no comprehensive reform is adopted. The administration bill has no similar provision, and consequently interest groups risk nothing by trying to scuttle reform plans.

It is, of course, my firm hope that the appearance of an administration bill at this time will not turn regulatory reform into a partisan issue, and that the strong bipartisan support which has been building behind S. 2812 will not fall victim to election year politics.

In conclusion, S. 2812 is comprehensive in scope, going beyond specific regulatory performance to the more fundamental questions of agency functions and structure. At the same, it does not tie itself prematurely to any one approach to reforming federal regulations. Rather, it establishes a disciplined procedure through which the most appropriate solution can be identified and adopted in each situation.

In the effort to reform federal regulation, all interested parties must work together if reform is to be successful. As a starter we must accept the fact that comprehensive reform must be just that—truly comprehensive. For if we give all groups a prior veto on proposed reforms—if we exempt everyone's sacred cows from searching review —we will accomplish nothing.

It is essential, therefore, that we put all our cards upon the table. All regulations must be reviewed. All special arrangements reconsidered. All sweetheart relationships reassessed. Clearly, the unexamined agency simply is not worth keeping.

Admittedly any such effort necessarily involves certain risks on the part of us all. But if we approach the task with perseverance and integrity there are substantial benefits for each of us individually and for society as a whole.

As we shake off the shackles of unnecessary regulation we will regain the dynamism that made America the richest and most powerful nation in the world. This is the challenge with which we are faced, and we must work together to meet this challenge.

PERSPECTIVES OF LEGAL SCHOLARS ([73], pp. 11–16, 41–51, 53–67)

In Support: Lloyd Cutler

Mr. CUTLER. . . .

Mr. Chairman, I am pleased to accept your invitation to appear before the committee on this important subject. By way of background, I have been engaged in practice before a number of the regulatory agencies and before the courts reviewing agency decisions for more than 30 years. For the past 3 years, I have been a visiting lecturer in law at the Yale Law School, where I have been teaching a seminar called "The Limits of Regulation" dealing with the problems now before your committee. Along with my colleague, David Johnson, I am the coauthor of an article that appeared in the June 1975 Yale Law Journal (84 Y.L.J. 1385) entitled "Regulation and the Political Process," which makes a proposal that bears at least a family resemblance to S. 2812, the Percy-Byrd bill. I understand that the committee staff is familiar with this article.

Senator PERCY. Mr. Chairman, I would like to welcome Mr. Cutler. It is very appropriate that he be our first witness from the outside.

Mr. Cutler is one of the most respected lawyers in America today and one of the truly great experts in regulatory agencies and we certainly welcome your testimony today, Mr. Cutler.

Mr. CUTLER. Thank you very much, Senator Percy. I wish I had brought along a set of charts as good as yours.

Senator NUNN. Mr. Cutler, would you pull the microphone up a bit?

Mr. CUTLER. I fully agree with the analysis of the inherent limitations of the regulatory process, as well as the analysis of the shortcomings of our present method of regulation, contained in the chairman's opening statement and Senator Byrd's and Senator Percy's statements and in the preambles of the various bills. Indeed, I cannot think of any other question on which the President of the United States, the Members of Congress, public interest lawyers and the lawyers and executives of regulated industries are in such a consensus as to the nature of the problem, even though this consensus will inevitably break apart in the search for a solution.

I would add only one thought to the analysis—that a very large part of the problem lies in our decision to entrust each of the wide variety of regulatory goals to separate and independent single-mission agency, without adequate consideration of how these goals inevitably conflict with one another and compete for the same resources, and of how these conflicts continually, and I emphasize continually, need to be reconciled as essentially political questions by the elected President and the elected Congress, who are not politically accountable for what the agencies do. I will have more to add on this point later in my statement, along with a suggsted solution that might be included in the Percy-Byrd bill.

As to the bills themselves, I fully support the Percy-Byrd bill and the portion of the Javits-Muskie bill establishing a Congressional Office of Regulatory Policy Oversight. But while I am in sympathy with the objectives of the Brock and Nunn bills and the other half of the Javits-Muskie bill, all providing for legislative vetoes of some or all agency rules and regulations, I think that the veto idea poses serious and self-defeating constitutional and practical problems, at least as applied to all agency regulations.

Let me deal first with the problem of the legislative veto, because it is a common thread running through all the bills.

As all of you know, I am sure, the constitutionality of a legislative veto of Executive or agency action has never been squarely adjudicated, not even in the case of reorganizations that you mentioned, Senator Percy, but the weight of scholarly opinion in the articles published on the subject falls heavily on the unconstitional side of the scale. While Mr. Justice White's recent concurring opinion in the campaign financing case, *Buckley* v. *Valeo*, in which I had the privilege of arguing, would have upheld the one-house veto as applied to Federal Election Commission regulations, the majority opinion expressly left the question open. Most Supreme Court handicappers would probably quote odds that when a case arises in which the issue cannot be avoided, the Supreme Court will hold the legislative veto unconstitutional. I, myself, believe the legislative veto is a practical modern accommodation much as Justice White said, between the Executive's superior ability to apply legislative policy to particular situations and the superior and important ability of the Congress to check an arbitrary or overzealous Executive. For this reason, I believe that whether or not the legislative veto is constitutional, it ought to be. Nevertheless, I would have to agree with the handicappers that the odds are against its survival in a Supreme Court test.

For a reason I will mention later on, I do not think that the veto contained in Percy-Byrd has that practical problem in it.

There is an additional equally important practical objection to the legislative veto as applied to agency regulations.

It is one thing for Congress to disagree with an agency regulation in an area where there has to be some regulation and to put some different regulation in place of the one that is rejected.

But it is entirely destructive and irresponsible, it seems to me, for Congress to strike down a regulation in a needed area and leave only a vacuum remaining.

While the agency can, of course, issue a new regulation, it will have no way of knowing whether the new regulation would itself survive a veto and as a matter of plain political accountability Congress ought not to be, I should think, in the privileged position of disagreeing with one regulatory solution without having to think through the difficult problem of what different solution to put in its place.

In my view a much better way for Congress to exercise a review power over agency regulations would be to add a provision to the Percy-Byrd bill. Percy-Byrd could be amended to provide that when the policies and powers of each agency or cluster of agencies come up in turn for review, the agency's substantive regulations with continuing effect would automatically expire unless Congress enacted and the President signed a specific statutory provision renewing them, with such amendments or deletions as Congress might then legislate. The agency, of course, could subsequently amend and supplement these regulations under its own ongoing powers, in the light of any legislative policy changes reflected in the congressional action. While this would doubtless be a formidable task—I understand, though I have not made the count myself, that every daily issue of the Federal Register contains approximately 300,000 words of new and revised agency regulations—I believe it would improve the accountability of the entire political process if Congress assumed specific responsibility in this way for all the regulations spawned by its children the agencies that Congress does not itself modify or reject.

In my opinion the Percy-Byrd bill itself is a sound and much needed step, particularly if an amendment along the above lines were added. However, I do not believe it takes adequate notice of the problem of coordinating the conflicting goals of independent single-mission agencies that I mentioned earlier above. For example, section 4a of the bill would call up clusters of related and overlapping agencies for review, but in clusters which account for only a portion of the many overlaps and conflicts that inevitably exist as our problems multiply and every problem and its solution interact with every other. For example, subparagraph 2 clusters five energy and environmental agencies; namely, EPA, FEA, FPC, NRC, and the Department of the Interior, and that is certainly a good start.

However, the energy problem alone is in part the responsibility of at least seven additional agencies; namely, the ICC for rail and truck transport, the Federal Maritime Board and Maritime Administration for tankers and other forms of sea transport, OSHA for employee health and safety, which add substantially to energy costs, the Department of Transportation for motor vehicle performance standards, which add substantially to gasoline consumption, the Treasury Department, which makes tax policy on fuels and their producers, the International Trade Commission, which recommends restrictions on fuel and other imports, and ERDA, which coordinates and finances research and development for new energy processes.

Energy, of course, is only one of many major current issues for which numerous agencies have conflicting and overlapping responsibilities. Even a quinquennial review of overlapping agencies, as proposed in Percy-Byrd, cannot by itself provide the necessary coordination and harmonization of our many competing public policy goals, and the conflicting actions of so many single-mission agencies. Moreover, recent congressional attempts to harmonize these goals have been less than successful, no doubt because Congress itself is largely managed by single-mission committees that mirror the single missions of the various agencies. Take, for example, the statute with the high-sounding title of the Energy Supply and Environmental Coordination Act of 1974, Public Law 93–319, 93d Cong., which can fairly be described as the molehill that finally emerged from the Presidential and congressional effort to formulate a balanced and comprehensive program for scaling the mountain we call the energy crisis. Leaving aside the ultimate failure to enact anything remotely resembling a comprehensive program, consider how little was accomplished on the one subject that the final act comprehensively addressed—namely the conversion back to coal of powerplants that EPA had previously ordered to convert from coal to oil. After exhaustive hearings before the energy-oriented House Commerce Committee and the environmentally oriented Senate Public Works Committee, the Congress produced 10 pages of detailed statutory language which boiled down I think to saying that the Federal Energy Administrator and the En-

vironmental Protection Administrator shall consult and, in the event
of disagreement, the Environmental Protection Administrator shall
decide.

It seems to me that the President's proposal now before you im-
proves considerably on Percy-Byrd in this one respect. It focuses not
on named clusters of agencies but on a specific substantive problem
such as transportation, manufacturing or energy and any and all
agencies concerned with that problem.

It requires the President to submit his appraisal of how Goverment
is dealing, Government as a whole, with that substantive problem and
what changes in substantive policies as well as in agency structure he
proposes.

Since the President has come so far to support the principle of
Percy-Byrd, I would urge that his suggested improvement in the approach of Percy-Byrd be adopted. But even the President's proposal,
Mr. Chairman, would not fully solve the problem of harmonizing
our conflicting goals because in the end it would leave the specific decisions on harmonization up to the Congress.

I say that with great deference and respect because while Congress
certainly should be the ultimate policy making body in our Government, Congress itself because of its size and the way it is structured
finds it inherently difficult to reconcile the competing goals of these
single-mission agencies when it comes down to concrete cases such as
what kind of fuel ought to be burned and what kind of emission level
ought to be required in existing or proposed new powerplants in particular places at particular times. Despite our concerns about an im-
perial Presidency, it is still true that only the Executive or an
agency—that is why Congress created agencies in the first place—can
make such a decision and only the President is capable of reconciling
such conflicts.

This is because the Chief Executive officer is not confined to some
special mission such as energy conservation, tax control, or preventing inflation. He is the only one with the broad responsibility for
harmonizing all our competing goals into a single national economic
policy.

For this reason, my colleague, David Johnson and I have proposed
a statutory provision that could readily be added to the Percy-Byrd
bill—one that would authorize the President, on a continuing basis,
to set priorities among competing statutory goals, and to modify or
direct major agency actions, subject to a one-House veto if constitutional, and also subject to expedited judicial review. As we propose it,
such Presidential actions could be taken only by Executive order
openly, based on Presidential findings that an agency action or inaction or a conflict in the actions of various agencies threatened to interfere with or delay the achievement of an important national objective, and stating the reasons for such findings. Before issuing such an
order we suggest the President would have to publish a notice in the
Federal Register stating his intention to do so and inviting written
comments from members of the public. No such orders could be issued
with respect to agency selection among competing applicants for a
grant or renewal of a particular license or privilege, because that
sort of decision has little to do with national economic policy and the
opportunities for abuse would be so great. Agency orders resulting
from such an Executive order would be subject to judicial review for
conformity with the statutory powers governing the agency, except

that the President's determination of relative priority among statutory goals would remain conclusive if a rational basis therefor is set out in the Executive order.

You will note that we have also provided for a legislative veto, just as Percy-Byrd provides for a legislative veto of Presidential proposals for agency reform. While this limited type of legislative veto also raises problems of constitutionality, they may not have serious practical consequence. Unlike the proposals for legislative vetoes of all agency regulations authorized under earlier and entirely separate statutes, these legislative vetoes would be applicable only to Presidential initiatives undertaken under the same statute that confers the Presidential power to intervene and reserves the congressional power to check. The statute could be so written as to make very clear that Congress did not intend to authorize the Presidential initiative unless it were subject to the legislative veto, and that if the exercise of the legislative veto in a particular case were held unconstitutional, the statutory authority for the President to take the initiative in the first place would not be severable and would also fall. Thus, whether or not the legislative veto is constitutional, the President's initiative would be nullified whenever a legislative veto is exercised, even if the veto were successfully challenged in the courts. Interestingly enough, the Attorney General is presently advancing the same argument to the Court of Claims in opposition to the suit filed by several Federal judges who seek a salary increase approved by a congressionally authorized commission, but later nullified by a legislative veto as provided in the statute creating the commission. If the legislative power to veto is not exercised, there is a rational argument that no one has standing to challenge the Presidential initiative, and his action would therefore take effect.

That was true, for example, of all the executive branch reorganizations that had been accomplished under the Reorganization Act. They never were challenged by the Congress when they were not subjected to veto, and when they were subjected to veto, the President simply went along with that.

It is entirely possible that a very limited legislative veto applicable only to the Presidential initiative that is allowed under the very same statute could have practical effect whether or not it is constitutional.

The premise that underlines the proposal is that some increase in the President's ability to intervene openly rather than surreptitiously when he deems the issues sufficiently important will make him chargeable with political responsibility for the agency's action, and will make him more accountable for not intervening when the electorate thinks he should. At the same time, the provision for a one-House congressional veto will require the Congress to assume a similar accountability, even when it is reluctant or unable to take the initiative by enacting a corrective statute. In short, our proposal would make a reality out of Harry Truman's pithy phrase, "The buck stops here." Because of the President's other duties and the political risks of intervention, it seems unlikely that appropriate occasions to exercise this Presidential power might arise more than 5 to 10 times per year. Under our proposal the President, if he persuades Congress not to block his action, would have the power to set and execute a balanced view of the national priorities when he believes that an agency has failed to do so or that the policies set by two or more agencies are in conflict. That is precisely the power that no one possesses under the existing regulatory structure. It is nothing more nor less than the power to govern effectively and accountably in the present age.

Mr. Chairman, I ask leave to attach to this statement a copy of the Yale Law Journal article setting forth our proposal in greater detail, as well as a copy of a much shorter summary paper entitled, "The Fallacy of Regulatory Independence."

N3

[The material referred to above follows:]

THE FALLACY OF REGULATORY INDEPENDENCE

Lloyd N. Cutler

Most of the discussion on regulatory reform focuses on two highly desirable improvements: deregulation in fields such as transportation, where there is good reason to believe more competition will produce better policy results, and procedural and personnel changes intended to help each agency act more rapidly and with greater fairness and effectiveness.

Important as these goals are, a great deal of regulation is bound to continue. No matter how much deregulation we can bring about in fields where market forces can do a better job, we have to recognize that in other fields such as air and water quality, market forces will not work because these are true external costs for which the buyer of steel or chemicals or automobiles will not pay if you give him a choice. Some form of regulation is needed to achieve this kind of social goal.

For this reason, we must not lose sight of a third and even more important weakness in regulation as we know it today. I refer to the independence of each of the scores of federal regulatory agencies from the Executive, from the Congress and from one another.

In an earlier day, it was a deliberate goal of regulatory policy to endow each agency with a single specialized mission, to staff it with non-political experts in that specialty, and to make it independent of political control. But today, this shining vision of what regulation ought to be is the most troublesome aspect of what regulation has actually become.

Even in this wealthy and powerful nation, we are grudgingly beginning to admit to ourselves that many of our social and economic goals conflict with one another, and nearly all compete with each other for the same limited resources. Even Hubert Humphrey now makes this point. Independent, specialized, single-mission agencies, each pursuing its own goal as primary over all others, cannot possibly produce balanced, consistent government policy. It should not surprise us that, faced with one new problem after another, a government consisting largely of independent single-mission agencies seems to be hopelessly paralyzed and endlessly contradicting itself.

One of Government's major roles today, infinitely more difficult than raising an army or running the post office, is to strike the delicate balance between and among the goals of social welfare, economic growth, and we had plenty of time to resolve it. But, of course, the stable prices. Our regulatory agencies exercise a substantial share of the Government's authority in these fields; under their broad statutory authority to act "in the public interest," they make most of the policy decisions. Yet no one of them is solely responsible for all aspects of a particular problem. For example what we call the energy problem is the responsibility of at least twelve different agencies, none of which take orders from any of the others. They are:

1.	Fossil Fuels:	Department of the Interior
2.	Nuclear Power:	Nuclear Regulatory Commission
3.	Pipe and Transmission Lines:	Federal Power Commission
4.	Rail Transport:	Interstate Commerce Commission
5.	Sea Transport:	Federal Maritime Board and Maritime Administration
6.	Employee Health & Safety:	Occupational Safety and Health Administration
7.	Air and Water Quality:	Environmental Protection Administration
8.	Motor Vehicle Performance:	Department of Transportation
9.	Taxes on Fuels and their producers:	Department of the Treasury
10.	Imports:	International Trade Commission
11.	Research and Development:	Energy Resources and Development Administration
12.	Allocation and Price Control:	Federal Energy Administration

Of these twelve agencies, four are within the Executive Departments, four more are so-called independent agencies "within" the Executive Branch, and only four are legally independent agencies outside the Executive Branch. One would think that the President could at least coordinate the agencies within the Executive Branch. But the mystique of regulatory independence is so strong that as a practical matter, the agencies within the Executive Branch are no more amenable to Presidential directives, and the President is no more willing to take the political risk of giving such directives, than is the case for the legally independent agencies.

The truth is that while our elected government is accountable to us for the way it manages the economy, most of the agencies that do the managing are not adequately accountable to the elected government. We expect those we elect to formulate a coordinated policy for the management of the economy, but even if they formulate one they cannot require the regulatory agencies to execute that policy, and we cannot fairly hold them accountable when the policy fails.

It would be bad enough to have twelve separate agencies contradicting one another in balancing our energy needs against our other social and economic policies, if energy were our only major problem and if energy crunch is only one of many major problems, and like all our major problems, its prompt and effective solution involves conflicts with other important economic and social goals.

Indeed, we didn't even know we would have an energy problem as recently as three years ago. It is a hallmark of today's complex interdependent life on this shrinking planet that unsuspected new problems keep coming over the horizon one after the other, and that our time for response is growing shorter and shorter. We have to ask ourselves whether a multitude of independent single-mission regulatory agencies, unaccountable to the elected government or to one another is a luxury we can still afford. When everyone is in charge, no one is in charge, and no one can be blamed when policy or the lack of it fails.

But because we have placed such a high value on agency independence, elected politicians still assume that they need not take responsibility for agency actions, and that any overt attempts by politically accountable officials to influence regulatory policy are improper. The reality that most important agency decisions today have an important political content for which politicians should be held accountable has become completely lost from sight.

Have you noticed how both incumbent legislators and the incumbent President keep telling us about the failures of big Government, in the apparently sincere belief that they are not talking about themselves? It is very comfortable for our elected officials not to feel responsible, or be held accountable by the voters, for the mess that those other fellows we call "bureaucrats" are making. Making choices that prefer one desirable objective over another is a very painful process, and politicians don't like to be put in that position.

Our faith in independence and expertise has created this dilemma, and only our faith in the political process can resolve it. Only elected officials have the power and the duty to provide the requisite overview, coordination, and practical political judgment to weigh competing claims, make the necessary ultimate decisions, and stand accountable at the polls. We need today a mode of economic regulation that is broad enough to consider the impact of regulatory decisions on the society as a whole, and flexible enough to adapt to crises we can rarely foresee much before they are upon us. We need to allow for wider shifts in emphasis and direction within shorter periods of time. To paraphrase Clemenceau, economic regulation has become too important to leave to the regulators.

Under our system of Government, neither the Congress nor the President can fill this vacuum alone. The principle and the practical politics of the separation of powers require a different solution. We need to combine the President's ability to act quickly and to formulate a single consistent policy with the collegiality of Congress and its ability to check an arbitrary and isolated President. Without infringing on the basic value of the separation of powers among the three original branches of government, we need to reduce the present isolation of the hybrid regulatory branch, and the myriad sub-separations within that branch, to a point where government would be better able to perform the functions we demand of it today.

To accomplish this, a series of one-shot statutes to correct and coordinate specific agency policies is

politically unrealistic. The bill proposed by Congressman
Levitas, authorizing a one-house veto of every agency
regulation, raises serious constitutional and practical
problems. In any event, it does not meet what I think is
the central problem. Congress itself is run by single-
mission committees that mirror the single missions of the
agencies, and Congress is unlikely, by itself, to achieve
the degree of balance among desirable but competing
objectives that is required.

A much better idea is embodied in the Percy-Byrd
bill, S. 2812, (and its House counterparts introduced by
John Anderson and Barbara Jordan) which would require the
President to submit proposals for the revision and coordination
of regulatory agencies and their policies according to
a fixed schedule, under which the President's proposals
would take effect unless Congress enacted its own version
or at least one House disapproved the President's version.
The President himself has recently submitted a similar
proposal of his own minus the one-house veto, but with
a provision making the President's proposal the standing
business of each House until it is voted up or down.

In a 1975 Yale Law Journal Article (84 Yale
L.J. 1395), my colleague David Johnson and I had proposed
a similar and, we believe, a more practical reform, which
could be added as an integral feature of the Percy-Byrd
plan, or, if that plan fails of enactment, be substituted
for it. We suggest a statute that would authorize the
President to modify or direct certain agency actions, and
to set priorities among competing statutory goals, subject
to a one-house Congressional veto -- if constitutional --
and to expedited judicial review. Under our proposal:

(1)   The President would be authorized to direct
any regulatory agency (a) to take up and decide a regulatory
issue within a specified period of time, or (b) to modify
or reverse an agency policy, rule, regulation or decision
(with one exception I will come to). Such action could be
taken only by Executive Order published in the Federal
Register, setting forth presidential findings that the
action or inaction of an agency on a regulatory issue
(or a conflict in the actions or policies of various
agencies) threatened to interfere with or delay the
achievement of an important national objective, and stating
the reasons for such findings.

(2)   No such Order could be issued until 30 days
after publication of a notice in the Federal Register
stating the President's intention to consider doing so and
inviting written comments from interested members of the
public thereon. All such comments would be maintained in a
public docket file. No public hearing would be required.
The President and his staff would not be barred from
receiving oral presentations from interested persons
(except where the affected agency's own ex parte rules
would bar such a presentation to the agency itself), but
a public record of those attending any such informal
meeting and a summary of what took place would have to
be kept.

(3)   Any such Executive Order would not take
effect for 60 legislative days, and would not take effect
at all if within such 60-day period either House of Congress
adopted a resolution setting it aside.

(4)   No such Order could be issued with respect
to any agency selection among competing applicants for the
grant or renewal of a particular license or privilege or
any subsequent revocation of such a particular license or
privilege.

(5) Any agency order resulting from such an Executive Order would be subject to judicial review for conformity with the statutory powers governing such agency, except that the President's determination of relative priority among statutory goals of the particular agency and of other government agencies would be deemed conclusive if a rational basis therefor is set out in the Executive Order. Judicial review of agency orders resulting from such Executive Orders would be expedited in accordance with a specified statutory timetable not exceeding 180 days for all proceedings up to and including the filing of appeals or petitions for review in the Supreme Court.

The premise that underlies the proposal is that some increase in the President's ability to intervene openly when he deems the issue sufficiently important will make him chargeable with political responsibility for the agency's action, and will make him more accountable for not intervening when the electorate thinks he should. At the same time, the provision for a one-house congressional veto will require the Congress to assume a similar accountability, even when it is reluctant or unable to take the initiative by enacting a corrective statute. In short, our proposal would make a reality out of Harry Truman's pithy phrase, "The buck stops here." Because of the President's other duties and the political risks of intervention, it seems unlikely that appropriate occasions to exercise this Presidential power might arise more than five to ten times per year. Under our proposal, the President, if he persuades Congress not to block his action, would have the power to set and execute a balanced view of the national priorities when he believes that an agency has failed to do so or that the policies set by two or more agencies are in conflict. That is precisely the power that no one possesses under the existing regulatory structure. It is nothing more nor less than the power to govern effectively and accountably in the present age.

Senator NUNN. Thank you very much, Mr. Cutler.

I think you have posed some very stimulating thoughts and ideas here. Just two or three questions and I will defer to Senator Percy.

You recommend on pages 4 and 5 that the bill introduced by Senator Percy and Senator Byrd be amended so that when each agency comes up for review, under that proposal the regulations, the substantive regulations, of that agency with continuing effect would automatically expire unless Congress enacted and the President signed a specific statutory provision renewing them.

I see certainly the validity of what you are pointing out, but I am just wondering about the awesomeness of that job.

What do you envision as far as Congress and staffing are concerned that would be required to review all these substantive regulations?

Mr. CUTLER. It could, of course, be a 10-word provision in the statute, Senator Nunn, if you were satisfied with the regulations as they stood.

It is really an effort to get at the same thing that the other bills which provide for legislative vetoes and particular regulations get at, but it combines the responsibility for formulating the substitute for what you knock down.

It has always seemed to me one of the greatest problems we have today is that neither the President nor the Congress, none of these elected officials, feel responsible for what the agencies do.

You will hear the President talking about big government, the elected President. You gentlemen are talking about big government. The elected Senators are talking about it and none of you feel that you are talking about yourselves.

You talk about those regulations that some bureaucrat over there put out but you put them there and all of us having elected you and having supported the creation of that agency are responsible for what they do.

We gave them a single mission and we cannot really complain when they are discharging their single mission even when it is in conflict with every other mission that some other agency has.

The idea behind this is that you, the Congress, ought to take accountability for what your children, the agencies, are doing.

If the agencies put out a regulation, then when you call the agency to account to you, you ought to approve or disapprove their regulations.

Senator NUNN. I agree with that completely. I do not disagree with any of that at all, but the question is really what do you do about the regulations that will be issued in the future under the Percy-Byrd bill? Let us say, Congress does it substantively—or the agency—depending on the alternative we come up with and then Congress approves all the regulations under your proposal.

All right then, the agencies are back in business and they start issuing regulation after regulation. The only way to do anything about that is to wait 5 or 6 years until they come back up for review.

How do you handle the new regulations that will come about after you have gone through this?

Mr. CUTLER. Between the 5-year review assuming there is a Percy-Byrd II and a Percy-Byrd III?

Senator NUNN. Yes, sir.

Mr. CUTLER. Under the proposal that Mr. Johnson and I have made we would authorize the President openly, and the whole point is that there is need for a continuing review of what the agencies do, we would authorize the President openly to reverse or modify an agency regulation through this provision of notice in the Federal Register of his intention to do so, followed by an Executive order directing the agency change, followed by judicial review subject to your one-House veto which in this practical context seems to me is workable whether it is constitutional or not.

Senator NUNN. You mean we would be able to veto the Presidential reversal of the regulation?

Mr. CUTLER. Right, if you support it. Of course, if you want to put in something else, you always have the option open to you of a statute.

You can write a statute and either get the President to sign it or override his veto.

Senator NUNN. If agency A, after the review took place and it was recreated with all the regulations, comes out with another regulation and the President decides he does not like that regulation, he would challenge that regulation under your procedure and put it in the Federal Register. There is an automatic court review under your proposal, is that right?

Mr. CUTLER. There would be an opportunity first for a veto by either House within 60 days and then an opportunity for judicial review.

Senator NUNN. Congress would be able to veto the Presidential veto of the agency. It would be a double veto.

Mr. Cutler. In effect, Congress could nullify the Presidential intervention.

Senator Nunn. Again, do you have an alternative?

Your critique of the existing bills is that the Congress should not be able to veto without an alternative, is that right?

Mr. Cutler. Correct.

Senator Nunn. When the President vetoes the regulation under your proposal, does he then propose an alternative?

Mr. Cutler. He could order an alternative or maybe if he thought the whole idea of the regulation was bad, he would simply say do not issue a regulation in this area.

If he thought the substance of the regulation was wrong he would say change it in the following manner.

Senator Nunn. How does Congress react to his substantive change?

Congress has, let us say, regulation 1 of agency A. The President comes in and says I do not like regulation 1 of agency A. I would propose regulation 2 as an alternative.

Now, Congress, as I understand your proposal, could veto regulation 2 as proposed by the President but Congress still would not have any authority to veto regulation 1 as proposed by agency A, would it?

Mr. Cutler. No; it would have authority to enact a statute.

In my judgment, that is all Congress can lawfully have in that situation.

I would not envision, though, that the President under this power would be editing and correcting many agency regulations.

The President would be intervening in the kind of impasse that typically develops between EPA and FEA, let us say, on a matter of coal conversion, or between the NRC and the EPA on a matter of a new nuclear power plant. That is the sort of thing.

Senator Nunn. How do you compare this procedure with the approach of the Muskie bill, S. 2925, if you are familiar with that, which would require periodic reauthorization and zero-based budgeting?

Is your proposal getting at the same thing as the Muskie bill?

Mr. Cutler. Well, I think that is a very healthy proposal. It is a different proposal. It is something like the "sunset" feature of the Percy-Byrd and the separate Sunset bill that Senator Gary Hart has introduced and I think that is a healthy thing.

I also think the notion of an Office of Congressional Agency Oversight or whatever it is called in Senator Javits' bill is a very healthy thing, although I should think the same function could be performed by the Government Operations Committee because we need some specialized staff function in Congress to look at agency actions from an overall point of view rather than from the single-mission point of view that most congressional committees have today. We need something just like the Congressional Budget Office.

Senator Nunn. It may be that we will mark up the Muskie bill first. It would be my intention at the present time to take your thoughts and ideas and others on this question of veto and the procedure and try to amend the Muskie bill with the best proposal we could come up with, the most responsible proposal along this line. That is the reason I am interested in this.

I do not know which bill we will have as a vehicle but it is very likely that that one may come up first.

Mr. CUTLER. If I can be of any assistance to you I shall be delighted.

Senator NUNN. Thank you, sir.

One other question and I think you have already alluded to this. Of course, your proposal would vastly increase Presidential power vis-a-vis the Congress.

You would not disagree with that, would you?

Mr. CUTLER. I would not disagree with that.

I do think that, accepting that there is nothing much we can do about the separation of powers at this point and accepting the great value of the separation of powers as illustrated only 2 years ago, I do think that the Executive has the better talent for initiating the practical execution of policy and that the Congress has the better talent for checking the overambitious or arbitrary President. The worst thing we have done is to complicate that separation which has its obvious values and which we cannot change at this point by the subseparation inherent in creating a whole plethora or complex of agencies that are independent of both of them and also independent of one another, and even the agencies we have put within the executive branch, such as FEA and EPA, which are both styled in your legislation—I do not know what the phrase means—as "independent agencies within the executive branch"—and even though they are administrators that serve at the pleasure of the President, he has, as a practical matter, as little power to interfere with what they do as with the totally independent ICC or the CAB.

In fact, the statutes seem to require that those two administrators operate on a record and they not receive any off-the-record instructions from the President or even on the record as a matter of fact.

Senator NUNN. Let me get away from the theoretical.

What, for instance, if you had to choose and you had had a lot of experience in this area, what area would you say is a priority for Congress to review now?

I know there are a lot of priorities, but what would you put at the top of your list?

Mr. CUTLER. I would put the energy and environmental complex at the top of the list.

The only reason I hesitate about that is you just took a crack at that with so little result. It may be these present policy issues that are so difficult to resolve for elected officials that we had better go to one that we do not feel a sheated about.

Senator NUNN. You are saying there are more competing and conflicting kinds of directives in that area than perhaps any other?

Mr. CUTLER. And I think it is the most urgent one we have and the fact that we have increased rather than decreased our dependence on foreign oil since the beginning of the energy crisis, which indicates some sort of governmental bankruptcy on our part. . . .

Senator JAVITS. The constitutional issue you raise about the legislative veto is a matter of enormous interest to me, the War Powers Resolution, and many other things.

It seems to me and I wish you would check as lawyer to lawyer that we both come close to the situation in your testimony at the bottom of page 9 and the top of page 10. After estimating on the odds that the Supreme Court would generally speaking strike down the legislative veto of an executive action, you say the following, that the statute could be so written as to make very clear that Congress did not intend to authorize the Presidential initiative unless it was subject to the legislative veto and that if the exercise of the legislative veto in a particular case were held unconstitutional, the statutory authority of the President to take the initiative in the first place would not be severable and would also fall. Whether or not the legislative veto is constitutional, the President's initiative would be nullified whenever a legislative veto is exercised even if the veto were successfully challenged in the courts.

Now, let us see if we can refine that. I believe I do not want to pose my views on you. I believe where we give the President a discretionary authority if he finds that the national interest requires he may permit a certain shipment of goods to an embargoed country that there we have the right to retain our discretion just as well as he retains his.

However, where we give him an executive power and he exercises it to administer a law and we do not like the way he does it, then we veto it. Therefore, my question is, is that really what you are telling us here?

Mr. CUTLER. Yes, I think what I am saying is somewhat narrower than the way you just put it, Senator Javits.

If the same statute that permits the President to take an initiative, an initiative which is essentially of a rulemaking or regulatory character, the kind which you could legislate about if you had the time, then it seems to me that you should be able to include in the same bill a veto power, even a one-House veto power and that should you exercise the veto even if it is unconstitutional for you to do that, the statute would be so construed that you never intended to give him the power except with the reserved right to veto.

Senator JAVITS. You would not go one step further, therefore, which is the step I make and to say the use of the power is conditioned upon the fact that he did not veto because it is a completely discretionary power.

Mr. CUTLER. Well, are you speaking of a clear executive power?

Senator JAVITS. Yes, a discretionary executive power, that is if in his judgment that such and such a statement of facts that he may promulgate a set of regulations that says so and so that is the only thing I thought was subject to congressional veto. That is to say where you say to the President, you know, you may not cross this State line with a gun. There is nothing to veto there. We may not like the rules that he issues but that is just too bad, but where we say if the President finds that crossing the State line with a gun is dangerous to a citizen of the United States and the State to which that person is going and therefore we do not like it, we can do it.

Mr. CUTLER. I think myself the line is not so much whether he has a discretionary power as to whether the power falls on the executive side of the line in which case I doubt that you could veto or whether it falls on the delegated legislative side of the line.

We are really operating in a no-man's land.

Senator JAVITS. There is no question about it.

Mr. CUTLER. Once we got over the notion that Congress could not delegate its powers and the delegate it to agencies many times many of which are within the executive branch, the great majority of the regulatory agencies are either part of the cabinet departments, like OSHA, or Food and Drug, or the so-called independent agencies within the Executive branch. There are only about 10 or 12 that are truly independent but once we have delegated that kind of legislative power it may be that in the very statute you can pull back that power subject to a one-House veto.

This is what Justice White thinks you can do.

Senator JAVITS. The question is whether you pull it back alone or whether you pull it back by a law.

Mr. CUTLER. I meant by a veto.

Senator JAVITS. You can always pull it back by law.

Mr. CUTLER. I do point out to you that the Department of Justice is making this very same argument today in the judge's case regarding the salaries.

Senator JAVITS. Now, the last point and my time is up. What if the President can set priorities for the regulatory agencies and the regulatory agencies are delegates of our power, that is the Congress, can we not do the same thing?

Mr. CUTLER. By law, yes. By veto, I am not sure.

Senator JAVITS. By law?

Mr. CUTLER. Yes.

Senator JAVITS. We can then tie both the President and ourselves to the right to participate in setting priorities.

Mr. CUTLER. Absolutely.

Senator NUNN. Senator Percy?

Senator PERCY. Mr. Chairman, while Senator Javits is here, I have one question relating to S. 2878.

Mr. Cutler, in your testimony you do support that portion of S. 2878, the Javits-Muskie bill, establishing a Congressional Office of Regulatory Policy Oversight.

Do you think it need be an entirely new unit, or could some existing body, such as the GAO, the Office of Technology Assessment, or the Congressional Office of the Budget, assume the role of advising Congress on regulatory matters?

Mr. CUTLER. Well, in principle, Senator Percy, I am against any new units. We have too many already and every time we think of a new job, we always want to create some new body to do it.

I should think the Budget Office has a pretty full plate for the next decade or so. I should think it could be an office subsidiary to this committee and your House counterpart.

You do have the broad overview of all government activities as distinguished from the promotion of commerce, or the protection of the environment, or the control of banking or some special single mission.

I do not think you need this one more congressional committee for the oversight of the agencies as distinguished from the oversight of the operations of the Government because they are very much the same thing.

Senator JAVITS. I agree with you about the division of work.

It is a matter of whether you need an agency with the staffing and expertise for this purpose that it could not be effectively carried out the other way. I believe it is so, though, and that is why I did it in this bill.

I will say to you that if we get an Office of Legal Counsel as a result of a Watergate bill, that may give us an opportunity to do two things under one bill.

Mr. CUTLER. That may be. You could just as efficiently give the subcontract to the Brookings Institution or to the Congressional Budget Office.

Senator PERCY. Would you advocate placing these agencies within existing departments as a possible solution short of giving the President the more direct control over the regulatory activities that you have urged?

Mr. CUTLER. I think I would, Senator Percy, if you can reverse history to that extent.

I am sure there would be enormous objection to that.

Also, we now have such a tradition that has grown up that the President and even the Cabinet officers should not interfere with the work of the agencies, even the agencies that theoretically report to them. Unless we make it very clear that he is expected to be responsible, it is not going to work much better.

You notice, for example, that the President does not feel from a general political point of view that he can afford to give a direction to a Cabinet officer on an agency matter. In the case of the Concorde, for example, Mr. Coleman went out of his way to make very clear that he was deciding that on the record before him and he had never discussed it with the President.

Mr. Coleman was protecting the President and the President would not have wanted to spend his capital on that matter.

Senator PERCY. Maybe you could comment on how you see this operating with FDA as a part of HEW. What is the respective role of the Administrator of the FDA and the Secretary of HEW? Does it do any good to have it in HEW?

Mr. CUTLER. As a practical matter, I do not believe the operations of the Food and Drug Administration or its independence have been changed one wit by the fact that it was moved. First, originally, it was under the Department of Agriculture, then it became an independent agency, and then it moved back into HEW. But I do not think it changed anything.

Senator PERCY. In other words, the Secretary of HEW does not exercise a veto over their regulations?

Mr. CUTLER. No, you might put that to your colleague, Senator Ribicoff, but in my experience he never did and none of his successors ever have.

That is quite understandable, Senator Percy. They do have a single mission. Some of us do not agree with everything they have done, of course, and they have never really been subjected to any kind of cost justification.

The point I was making earlier is the difficulty of the President getting agencies even within his own branch to respond. As you know he put out an Executive order more than a year ago requiring the agencies within the executive branch to issue so-called "inflation impact" statements measuring the cost of proposed new regulations.

Most of them still do not do it.

Senator NUNN. We had testimony on that point, I believe, when he issued that directive. I had a similar proposal in a particular bill that would make it a legislative requirement. The executive branch testified it was not needed because it was being done by Executive order. It was removed from the legislation which was later passed.

The order was issued something like November of 1974. I had hearings on that specific subject in May of 1975 and there had not been one single inflation impact statement issued which makes one wonder what power the President does have over the bureaucracy.

Mr. CUTLER. Precisely right. Get Mr. McAvoy over here and ask him how frustrated he is.

Senator NUNN. Excuse me, Senator Percy.

Senator PERCY. That is all right, Mr. Chairman.

You are, as I have indicated and certainly as we all know, one of the most respected lawyers in town on regulatory matters.

How do we go about encouraging the Washington establishment, the lobbyists, the lawyers, the public affairs officials, to take a very active and positive role in the process of reform?

Mr. CUTLER. Well, I think you hit the nail on the head when you were here testifying a few moments ago. They could make a great contribution on reforming the regulatory process in those other agencies that do not affect their clients and their business.

But, Senator Percy, when they get to the agencies that regulate them, we are left with the dilemma that, as bad as most of them think their regulations are, they are terrified about that terra incognita out there beyond the present form of regulation. They do not want to be thrown into that briar patch.

Senator PERCY. Is it possible to develop a climate and an atmosphere that would really call forth the best in our expertise and talent in town here in a very positive role?

Certainly, the U.S. Chamber has now led the way by, in principle, endorsing regulatory reform.

Mr. CUTLER. I wish it were possible.

It has been my experience that those who are regulated, for example, the railroads, and I have served on the board of a railroad, and the airlines —while they think regulation has absolutely ruined them they are really afraid to try that other deregulated world. Even though the case, certainly, the theoretical economic case that we would have been better off to have the free market in those areas—particularly trucks and airlines—and never even think of them as a monopoly, may be entirely valid, and I think it is valid, the question of how you work your way back is a very difficult question. You have to have a certain amount of sympathy with the airlines in how they work their way back, and I would think those bills could be greatly improved by including provisions that would enable them to work their way back in which it would be made easier to merge, for example, for those who could not make it in the tougher environment.

Senator PERCY. In your long experience in this field, is it not rather unusual that we now have at least three heads of regulatory agencies that I can think of that are really trying to move toward greater faith in the market operation—John Robson, Rod Hills and Dick Wiley? They are finding that those who espouse and talk in vague general terms about getting rid of regulations start to scream when reform affects them.

My last question relates to the considerable discussion lately of the need to require agencies to conduct a cost-benefit analysis for proposed regulations.

Could you comment on how practical it actually may be when a regulation is issued, to require a cost-benefit analysis to be issued along with it. And is it desirable for an agency to have this function imposed on it, particularly in areas such as health and safety where specific costs and benefits may be very difficult to quantify?

Mr. CUTLER. It seems to me it is possible, Senator Percy. It is highly desirable.

Certainly, it should be no harder than writing an environmental impact statement.

We had two very recent examples in the health and safety field where the economists on the Council of Wage and Price Stability have stepped in and presented inflation impact critiques first in the case of the air bag, as you know, in which they concluded that the air bag proposal, that is mandatory air bags for all cars by a certain date, was clearly inferior from a cost efficient point of view to, let us say, a prior experiment in which the Government just paid to equip 1 million cars.

Similarly, on the OSHA coke oven standards the Council on Wage and Price Stability, another Government agency has last week issued a critique concluding the proposed standards were going to cost more than the health benefits that might be achieved.

To do it, it is quite true you need a lot of information that is not today supplied to a great extent to the agency and you would need fewer lawyers and more economists on the staff of the agencies.

This is the biggest trouble Mr. McEvoy has is in getting out those statements.

Senator NUNN. An ordinary prudent man who knew nothing about government would assume that someone who was issuing a regulation that would have a major impact on, say, the auto industry would have gone through the minimal process, even without a requirement, of trying to weigh the benefits versus the cost.

Mr. CUTLER. One would think so but it is the natural bias of the single-mission agency.

If you are there to clean up the environment, even though you know there are costs to be incurred, you tend to give those costs a lesser weight than if you are there to control inflation or the price.

It is inevitable and the biggest single gap in the whole process is that there is not anywhere within the Government as a whole that kind of harmonizing is going on. We have conflicting goals and we have so many of them today.

Senator PERCY. Mr. Cutler, thank you very much.

Senator NUNN. Thank you, Mr. Cutler.

Next, we have Dean Ernest Gellhorn and Prof. Harold Broff of the Arizona State University College of Law.

Senator PERCY. Mr. Chairman, I will have to leave for a few minutes to go to the floor in connection with the oversight bill and I will try to be back by 12 o'clock.

Senator NUNN. Do both of you have statements?

In Opposition: Ernest Gellhorn and Harold Bruff

Mr. GELLHORN. Each of us has submitted an outline rather than a statement because we were contacted by the committee staff only recently so that we were not able to prepare a statement.

Senator NUNN. Does this outline serve for both of you then?

Mr. GELLHORN. There are two. There is one for Mr. Bruff and one for myself.

Senator NUNN. You are Ernest Gellhorn?

Mr. GELLHORN. Yes, sir.

Senator NUNN. Who is going to lead off?

Mr. GELLHORN. I will.

Senator NUNN. Go ahead.

Mr. GELLHORN. Mr. Chairman. I am Ernest Gellhorn, Dean of the College of Law of Arizona State University.

I have taught in the field of administrative law for 10 years and written two books on the subject and several articles.

My colleague, Mr. Bruff, has taught in the field of administrative law for 5 years.

We have submitted only an outline because of the shortness of the period of time we had for preparation and the fact that mine at least was prepared on an airplane coming here which may indicate it was a rockier ride than I had hoped.

Senator NUNN. We appreciate your testifying on such short notice and this outline will do fine.

Mr. GELLHORN. What I thought I would do to aid the committee is to focus first on the two proposals or types of proposals that are before the committee, then consider briefly the basis of public discontent with administrative regulation, and finally focus on whether or not these reform proposals are, in fact, responsive to this discontent.

My colleague, Mr. Bruff, will look more closely at the legislative veto proposal in light of the study he and I are conducting for the

N6 Administrative Conference of the United States.

I would suggest that the bills before the committee fit within two categories.

On the one hand, you have a series of bills suggesting that Congress periodically reexamine and reform the administrative process. The major thrust of these bills is to question administrative regulation but they do so only by focusing only on legislative consideration.

There is no effort to address administrative regulation directly or on what the agencies are doing, with the possible exception of the modification suggested this morning by Mr. Cutler.

The technique here is to force the legislature to examine the agencies and to consider proposals for reform.

In other words, this series of legislation does not address the issue of reform itself and I wonder whether it is really necessary.

What Congress requires of itself it may abandon just as easily. It has imposed budgeting requirements on itself as of 1974 and last week appeared to have abandoned that approach, at least in terms of complying with the self-imposed ceiling on budgetary amounts.

Senator NUNN. Would you clarify that point now? I am not familiar with what you are referring to.

Mr. GELLHORN. The Budget Reform Act of 1974, pursuant to which the Congress adopted a budgetary limitation in this Congress, was recently abandoned with the adoption of the Defense Spending bill —or so it appears, at least from my reading of the newspapers.

Senator NUNN. On the House side?

Mr. GELLHORN. I believe so.

Senator NUNN. Well, that is a very good point and I think you have pounded out that last year the House did exactly the same thing.

The House takes the position that an authorization bill does not count which, to me, is an absurd situation and to compound the absurdity in the budget process, the Senate Budget Committee takes exactly the opposite position. The Senate Budget Committee is going to try to mak sure that the armed services bill coming out of the Senate is within the budget limitation.

The House Budget Committee does not do that. I am on both the Budget Committee and the Armed Services Committee. When we get into conference we are faced with the House authorization bill that exceeds the budget limit and a Senate bill that is under it, we have to come back somewhere in between. We have inevitable conflict between the Senate Budget Committee and the Armed Services Committee that has been responsible. I agree with your assessment of that. That is what you are speaking about.

Mr. GELLHORN. Informing ourselves from that experience, I would suggest that even if the Congress were to adopt the proposals made by Senators Percy and Byrd or by the administration, it is under no obligation to follow that timetable. You can ignore it by passing additional legislation obviating it when you find it inconvenient, when you find other matters on your agenda.

Senator NUNN. The only thing I would say, if you do not mind my interrupting, is that it is true that the President has certain authority under this proposal which goes into effect unless Congress vetoes it. It does give the President quite a bit of authority if Congress fails to act, when, of course, the proposals go into effect.

If Congress decides to repeal the authority, it would take a two-thirds vote to override. So there is, perhaps, some imposed discipline.

Mr. GELLHORN. I fear that provisoin more, however.

I find it worrisome because, and this gets to my second point, there is no provision in any of the bills for the establishment of an adequate foundation for administrative reform.

In contrast to the study of administrative regulation in the 1950's by the Hoover Commission, this bill makes no provision for a study and examination.

In contrast to the provisions in the late 1930's and early 1940's of the TNEC, there is no provision here for further examination.

What worries me, in other words, is that the President may be under an obligation to provide a plan of reform, but without adequate study and preparation those proposals may be no improvement.

What I am suggesting, then, is that I do not think the case has been made for this series of bills before you with regard to periodic examination and reform.

I would suggest instead that this legislation, like many proposals for administrative reform, is unnecessary.

The Congress is already empowered to consider specific agency mandates, to request studies, to examine what the agencies are doing, question them and to reform them. So is the administration.

When we get proposals, such as Mr. Cutler makes this morning, of vetoing legislative vetoes or vetoing by legislation Presidential vetoes of legislative vetoes, we compound constitutional questions beyond recognition; these force unnecessary constitutional questions upon us. That is one area of concern.

The second area of concern, it seems to me, that is before this committee is wholly different and that is the suggestion that the legislative exercise increasing oversight and more careful oversight of the administrative agencies.

This proposal, now before the legislature in many forms, is quite dissimilar to other matters which have gotten before the Congress.

Some examples include: The hybrid rulemaking process which has been imposed on the FTC and several agencies; specific directions to the agencies such as contained in the Clean Air Act; the holding of hearings by the Congress on administrative policies such as the oversight hearings in connection with the Federal Communications Commission rulings on fairness and the fairness doctrine; et cetera. The focus in this kind of legislation or hearing is on the need for regulation, on its quality and on its compliance with legislative intent.

This, it seems to me, is more focused on administrative reform. One ought to note parenthetically the technique used here is to impose a negative legislative intervention on the administrative process.

Yet, oddly enough, one of the complaints as reflected earlier this morning by Senator Percy is that the administrative agencies have been often lethargic, have delayed too long, and have been ineffective in their action.

In other words, there is considerable inconsistency in these proposals; indeed somewhat contradictory positions are being taken here by the proponents of the various items of legislation.

Again, one might note this legislation focuses on Congress rather than on the agencies.

On the other hand, it may have a substantial impact on Congress, on the agencies, on public regulation and on the public itself.

To these questions my colleague Mr. Bruff will address some inquiries and some comments.

First, however, I want to pose a question and ask whether or not this latter, proposal, as well as the initial proposal for periodic reexamination, really is responsive to the public concern about administrative regulation.

The reason I raise this question is because Senator Percy's litany of administrative failures is not new.

Every one can be found in the Ash Council study issued in 1971.

Everyone of them is repeated previously in the Hoover Commission report, in the Bronwell report in the 1930's or to the comments of then professor and later Justice Frankfurter in the 1920's.

There is virtually nothing new here. What is new, however, is the political visibility of this issue.

What is new is the public concern and apparently now the legislative reaction.

Let me pose the question "why?" What is this "newness" about it?

I am going to suggest some answers. I am not certain they are right but they reflect my insights gained from my experience.

I have considerable doubt about them and I do not propose them as certainty.

I would suggest, Mr. Chairman, the reason for public concern focuses on really three areas.

First, we have not made a significant impact on living conditions or on the conditions to which administrative regulation was focused despite an increasing amount of administrative regulation (or at least that is the public's perception). Let me give you three examples.

In the 1960's we thought that economic fine tuning would solve the problems of inflation and unemployment.

In the 1960's and early 1970's we thought price restraints and concontrols would control inflation in terms of prices and in terms of wages.

The experience, however, was to the contrary, Mr. Chairman.

Despite these efforts of increasing regulation of the economy, the economy went through wider fluctuations in the early 1970's than they had gone since the 1950's.

The second area included the wars on poverty anc crime, both of which raised public expectations to new highs and neither of which appears to have had a significant impact, at least in terms of the public consciousness, on poverty or crime.

Then there are other regulations which I do not know exactly how to assess, but I want to take two examples.

One was the housing program which, despite substantial moneys to support public and privately financed housing, appears, in part, to have been counterproductive.

Take a look at public housing programs in St. Louis, Mo.: there is less public housing today after a substantial housing program than there was 20 years ago.

There is serious public questioning in other words, about the efficacy of administrative regulation.

On the other hand, some administrative regulation appears to have been too effective.

One illustration is the National Highway Traffic Safety Administration's adoption of a seat belt interlock a few years ago which forced Americans to be seat belted in their cars to their dislike—and very quickly the Congress corrected it.

The second basis for public discontent and policy disagreement with administrative regulation that I would point to is the series of scholarly studies and other investigative efforts raising doubts about the efficacy of administrative regulation, indeed, of its theory.

These attacks upon administrative regulations have come from the political left, the political center, and the political right.

Highly publicized Nader studies raise questions about the effectiveness of regulation. The studies coming out of the University of Chicago raise serious questions about whether or not natural monopoly theories which underlines much regulation really exists.

There are studies questioning the likelihood of efficient administrative behavior.

There are in addition specific studies of administrative regulations such as the Peltzman studies in the last 2 years over drug controls and safety regulations for automobiles suggesting that there was no likelihood that these regulations would be effective. Indeed they purport to show that regulation has only raised the cost of the consumer's use of these products.

The third cause of public dissatisfaction that I would identify for the committee is the shift in the type of administrative regulation that has occurred over the past decade or two.

We have moved from control of monopolies such as the ICC certifications, control of standards such as the SEC certification requirements, control of licensing such as the FCC regulations of radio and television, to new areas. These have involved constraints on conduct such as the Federal Trade Commission's new much-expanded authority in connection with rulemaking and to the establishment of minimum physical standards for products through a wide spectrum of the economy—the EPA, the OSHA regulations, as well as the National Highway Traffic Safety Council and the Consumer Product Safety Committee.

What this shift has meant is that there is no longer in each of these areas an organized constituency supporting the consequences of regulation.

It is important, I would suggest, to the securities industry that there be an effective Securities Exchange Commission maintaining public confidence in the securities market.

That same need for public support and confidence does not apply to the operation of business and its regulation by the Federal Trade Commission.

There is no organized constituency supporting their efforts, Mr. Chairman.

The same would apply, I would suggest, in connection with most of regulation is relatively low in terms of governmental costs and rel-sphere.

Another thing I would point to is the fact that the cost of this kind of regulation is relatively low in terms of governmental costs and relatively high in terms of its impact on the regulated parties.

Third, because its implementation is not narrow and specific, it is inevitably uneven and results in some discrimination. Those who are regulated are not similarly situated. In addition, those who are now regulated are asking questions about the appropriateness of this regulation because what previously had been their right to conduct trade, to engage in business, is now being questioned, controlled, and limited.

What does this suggest?

This suggests to me at least that the causes of public dissatisfaction with administrative regulations are diverse and often inconsistent.

It also suggests to me that these problems are not conducive to a single simple or straightforward solution. Therefore, I question much of the legislation now before this committee because it focuses on a single and I would suggest much too simplistic solution.

In addition, I would suggest that these causes of public dissatisfaction suggest that there is a general feeling that regulation has been imposed without adequate public input and without adequate checks and balances.

Briefly now, looking at the responsiveness of the two reform proposals or the two types of proposals before the committee, I would suggest and reiterate my point that periodic examination purports only to address the effectiveness issue but without I would think adequate foundation.

More importantly, it seems to me that the legislative oversight process appears to be premised on the view at least partly on the view that Congress can do what the agencies had been unable to do and I must wonder about Congress' ability to perform that task.

When the agencies are adopting regulations and take a look, for example, at OSHA's many, many pages of regulations, they are exercising not simply normative judgments where Congress has particular ability and experience. They are also exercising expertise and insight available from the comments of other experts.

They are making combined judgments to determine whether or not it is appropriate to license additional nuclear reactors which is not just a normative judgment of how much electric power should be made available and what kind of a risk is involved, but it also involves an expert judgment as to what those risks are, in fact what the likelihood is of any accident and of what alternatives are available.

To the extent that the complaint being made now focuses on agency regulation because it is effective, then I would suggest that this legislative examination merely informs the legislature rather than controls the agency.

Nevertheless, the legislature oversight aspect of this legislation may contribute to public input and to additional checks on administrative accuracy and therefore to a separability of the administrative judgment.

In this connection the legislative veto idea warrants serious study.

The question here then is whether the legislative veto is likely to be beneficial or worth the cost of that benefit, and how might such cost be minimized?

Professor Bruff now has some comments.

Senator NUNN. Thank you very much.

Mr. Bruff?

Mr. BRUFF. Senator Nunn, the purpose of this testimony is simply to identify some of the principal issues that surround the adoption of a generalized legislative veto statute in order to put them into your consideration in the legislative process.

We have reached in our study no conclusions as yet. The first obvious consideration is that of the simple subject matter applicability of the statute, that is to which rules should a statute apply?

Some of the bills are designed to apply to essentially all agency rulemaking such as S. 2716.

One might observe, however, that the presently-felt needs to achieve better control over the rulemaking process itself may be derived chiefly from rules issued from only a relatively limited number of agencies such as the EPA, OSHA, the NHTSA and perhaps the CPSC.

The question then becomes whether rules that, as these agencies do, set a minimum physical standard may deserve special attention of some sort in the drafting of legislative statutes.

Similarly, there is an extended series of possible exceptions to an otherwise generalized veto provision. The first is an exception such as found in Senate bills 2258 and 2903 for matters involving certain kinds of functions.

It may well be that other kinds of functions or perhaps the rules of particular agencies should also be excepted from the general statute.

Some of the House bills apply only to rules that involve criminal penalties.

One can easily observe the economic burden of compliance with rules that do not have criminal sanctions behind them which may be very high and in practice has as great a criminal penalty.

This does raise the possibility that if a statute is keyed to the present construction of section 553, perhaps the agencies will evade the legislative veto through use of the good cause exception to notice and comment rulemaking.

There does seem to be strong indication of the need for some kind of exception for emergency rules.

The question then arises whether this should be upon an agency finding as present section 553 would have it or should it be by a legislative resolution that allows the immediate effectiveness of the rule?

S. 2878 takes a somewhat unique approach to all of this by providing a veto for only those rules on which there is an agency finding of significance, some dispute in the rulemaking process, or those subjected to the provisions of the statute by other provisions of law.

The existing bills also vary in the extent to which they require that agencies accompany their bills with explanatory submissions of some kind.

This possible requirement raises the issue, I think, of how the Congress can go about reviewing the content of rules that have a heavy expert component, for example, the NRC's safety rules or others of that detailed and expert nature.

The next broad question beyond the subject matter applicability of a veto is the effect on the rulemaking process itself.

I think there are two primary questions about this, the first the extent to which it would have an effect on public participation in agency rulemaking and what that effect would be, whether it would tend to stymie public participation in the agencies in favor of a lobbying effort in the appropriate committees of the Congress.

The second major issue is the question essentially of the probable frequency of use of this kind of a provision.

If, as seems likely, it would be infrequent, the question then arises whether the benefits of its occasional use would override the cost of delay to all rules that have to lie before the Congress awaiting expiration of the period.

One might observe there are probable differences among the rules in terms of their vulnerability to routine delays.

For example, some of the testimony in Mr. Flowers hearings last October indicated that some of the HEW grant rules may be particularly vulnerable because of spending schedule rules.

The broader effect of the veto statutes upon the agencies raises the possibility that the agencies will avoid the rulemaking process entirely in response to a legislative veto statute in favor of increased adjudication, a practice that is presently criticized extensively, in particularly by the Percy-Byrd bill.

Similarly, an overall question is the extent to which agency relations with their oversight committees will change and in what particulars they will change and whether this will be beneficial.

There are differing implications, I think, for the agencies depending upon the way a general legislative veto is structured.

If a resolution of disapproval of one House is sufficient, there is the possibility that policy differences between the two houses of Congress could trap the agencies in a fashion that would make them substantially unable to pass any rule.

There is also the question of the effect of this kind of a statute on judicial review.

The first issue. I think, is whether Congress should state its grounds for a veto both in order to inform the agencies of what went wrong and possibly to constitute a finding of having exceeded legislative intent.

The problem there, I believe, is if Congress states its repeal of the rule is because it was ultra vires perhaps the courts will treat those rules which have not suffered the veto as having been ratified by Congress, essentially a negative implication.

Senator NUNN. You mean there would no longer be a judicial challenge because if Congress had the authority to veto and did not, it would be assumed by the courts that Congress did not think it was beyond question?

Mr. BRUFF. That would be the argument.

I think it might have some force in the sense that perhaps agencies' rules would be harder to overturn as being ultra vires even if they had gotten essentially no consideration by Congress when they went through.

Senator NUNN. You mean the courts would take judicial notice, view each and every regulation within that 60-day period?

Mr. BRUFF. Possibly. It might also depend upon the degree to which a rule received active consideration—at least the subject of a resolution and some committee attention. Then I think you would have that argument with some practical force behind it as opposed to just an argument.

Similarly, I think there is an overall question on how the veto of a particular rule would reflect upon judicial review of related rules.

Would these also be considered quite possibly ultra vires because of Congress veto?

There has been, as I am sure you know, a series of recent Federal statutes that has applied the legislative veto in a number of various forms to a series of agencies.

HEW has several, the FEA, GSA on Presidential tapes, the Election Commission, the NHTSA, even Amtrak and in one particular the Department of Labor.

Our study is going to examine what existing experience there is under these very recently enacted statutes and try to attempt to generalize to the suggestions that can be made in terms of the desirability of a genetic statute.

I might observe also that we have to keep in consideration in judging the desirability of a general veto statute the series of recent statutory devices for oversight of the rulemaking process, simply because the strengths and weaknesses of those approaches and their vulnerability as alternatives should, I think, be before Congress when it chooses whether to enact this kind of statute.

Some examples are recent tendencies of Congress to enact more detailed statutory delegation to confine regulatory power, added procedures for rulemaking, reporting requirements for agencies, recent agency initiatives which I think are hopeful in terms of trying to build in better empirical analyses before rules are adopted and to monitoring their actual effect once they have been adopted.

The Department of Transportation had a policy statement issued just the other day.

The Chairman of the SEC had a statement before the monopoly subcommittee with regard to this in some detail.

We could have increased public intervention or perhaps even Presidential veto—in Mr. Cutler's remarks along that line should be noted.

Senator NUNN. Thank you very much, both of you, for the excellent critique of some of the problems that all of these bills present.

If we set a 5-year timetable, is there a possibility that would cause delay in oversight on the premise of why not just wait until the review period comes around?

Mr. GELLHORN. I think that is a distinct possibility.

On the other hand, when there is pressure for administrative reform that is unlikely to occur.

What worries me is the idea we can find some answers in a cross-agency search now when it has not been available before and when there is no substantial effort at least included within these bills to support careful study and examination.

Senator Percy pointed out in his delightful charts that what we are looking for are three things. First, what are the functions of regulations? I can answer that right now. They are many. I do not think an awful lot can be added to that unless you are going to get specific about a particular agency.

Second, what is the appropriate structure?

A lot of people have written on that. I have contributed some unnecessary work on it myself.

I think the answer again is that there are many different structures. Some agencies appear effective with one structure. Others are effective with another. Others are ineffective with these same structures.

I think the answer is really that the structure is usually irrelevant.

Third, what kind of performance do we want?

On that point, it seems to me, we know the answer already. We want those regulations that are regulating monopoly-type situations, pricing and marketing situations so we have output being sold at marginal cost pricing and are using our resources for their maximum benefit.

Then in other areas we have difficult trade-offs. We want the cleanest environment we can have with the least use of energy, with the highest employment.

Now, unless you are going to adopt some kind of a statutory Phillips curve, which I do not believe we are, I do not think you can be much more specific or helpful.

FORD ADMINISTRATION OPPOSITION ([73], pp. 76–88, 108–110, 121)

To the apparent surprise of Senator Charles Percy, the Ford administration opposed S. 2812. The constitutional objections to the legislative veto are presented and debated in the testimony of Assistant Attorney General Antonin Scalia, the Justice Department witness. In addition to further illuminating the issues posed, the transcript, reprinted here in abridged form, includes passages in which Senators Jacob Javits and Percy engage in heated debate with Scalia as to the constitutionality of the legislative veto provision of S. 2812. These exchanges provide a seldom afforded look at a case in which the White House and the party leadership failed to coordinate their legislative program. The misunderstandings provoked a level of acrimony that may have doomed the administration bill from any consideration whatsoever. The constitutional objections raised by Scalia, plus the crowded congressional calendar and the presence of a broader, sunset–zero-base budget bill effectively killed chances for passage of the Percy-Byrd bill during the 94th Congress. However, S. 2812 is scheduled for reintroduction in the 95th Congress. (Senator Percy's remarks regarding his legislation appear in the *Congressional Record* of October 26, 1976, pp. 18219 ff.) That broader sunset–zero-base budget bill S. 2925, which is the Government Economy and Spending Reform legislation sponsored by Senator Edmund Muskie, is the subject of Chapter 8.

Assistant Attorney General Antonin Scalia

Mr. Scalia. I have with me Herman Marcuse, staff attorney in the Office of Legal Counsel.

Mr. Chairman, and members of the committee, I am happy to appear today to provide the views of the Department of Justice on S. 2258, 2716, 2812, 2878, and 2903. I would like to address first—because I think it most important—that feature contained in each of these bills which would enable action of the President or of executive agencies to be overturned by resolutions or both Houses of Congress, or of a single House of Congress, not presented to the President for his veto. As its presence in each of these proposals indicates, this feature has become very popular in recent legislation. It is no exaggeration to say that we consider its increasingly frequent use a real threat to the carefully constructed system of balances and of assigned responsibilities set forth in the Constitution. Within the past 2 weeks, President Ford's veto of the Foreign Assistance Act, and his signing statement issued with respect to the bill reconstituting the Federal Election Commission, both set forth his view that such a provision is unconstitutional. Those statements do not represent a new position of the executive branch, but to the contrary, as my later testimony will show, echo the strong views of other Chief Executives.

The constitutional impediment to clauses which enable Congress to disapprove Executive action by way of concurrent or one-House resolution rests upon two foundations: First, the general principle of separation of powers, and second, the specific provisions of article I, section 7, clauses 2 and 3 of the Constitution.

The principle of separation of powers—which James Madison described as being more sacred than any other in our Constitution—provides in essence that each of the three branches of our Government must restrict itself to its allocated sphere of activity: Legislating, executing the law, or seeing to its interpretation. This is not to say that every governmental function is inherently and of its very nature either legislative, executive, or judicial. Some activity might be performed by any of the three branches—and in that situation it is up to Congress to allocate the responsibility. See, for example, the statements of Chief Justice Marshall in *Wayman* v. *Southard*, 10 Wheat. 1. 42–43, 46 (1825). Once it has done so, however, once the Congress has so allocated the responsibility, the very essence of separation of powers requires that Congress cannot control the discharge of functions asigned to the executive or the courts, except through the plenary legislative processes of amendment and repeal.

Beginning with a statement by James Madison during the great debate of 1789 concerning the statutes establishing offices, it has been recognized that the power of Congress over the execution and implementation of a statute comes to an end with its enactment.

That quotation is set forth in my text and I will not read it here— I may inject at this point that I will try to abbreviate my comments as much as possible.

Chairman RIBICOFF. The entire text will go into the record as though read following your presentation.

Mr. SCALIA. Thank you.

The foregoing discussion should reveal the flaw in the argument, occasionally made, that the doctrine of separation of powers protects the executive branch only in the areas which are inherently executive, and that Congress may reserve to itself control over activities entrusted to the executive which are not "truly" executive in nature. This reasoning overlooks the basic truth that there are few activities which are inherently executive, legislative, or judicial. The first two categories, in particular, overlap to an enormous extent. Much, if not indeed most, executive action can be the subject of legislative prescription—for example, many aspects of the manner in which the President goes about organizing the executive branch, or even the rules which he lays down to regulate the conduct of executive branch personnel. Another example is the determination of claims against the United States. See *Wiener* v. *United States*, 351 U.S. 349, 355 (1958). To contend, therefore, that Congress can control the Executive whenever the Executive is performing a function which Congress might have undertaken itself is to reduce the doctrine of separation of powers to a mere shadow. The true test is not whether an activity is inherently legislative or executive—a determination which in most cases is impossible to make—but whether the activity has been committed to the Executive by the Constitution or applicable statutes. In other words, the Constitution provides for an enormously broad sweep of possible congressional action; but once a function has been delegated to, or left within, the executive branch, it must be performed totally and entirely there, and cannot be subjected to continuing congressional control except through the ordinary legislative process. Unless the doctrine of separation of powers means this, it means virtually nothing at all.

Having considered the general principles of separation of powers, let me now turn to the text of the Constitution, where we find a provision—the Presidential veto clause—which quite specifically forbids the congressional review devices here involved. Indeed, it is difficult to conceive of language and history which would forbid them more explicitly.

To abbreviate my testimony, there are two separate clauses of this section of the Constitution involved. One clause is the legislative veto clause—and if that were the only provision there might be room for argument that the Presidential veto is only necessary when what is involved is a formal bill, or a formal act of legislation. That is not, however, the only applicable clause. In fact, foreseeing the very situation which these bills raise, James Madison suggested during the debate on the Constitution, that if there were only the legislative veto clause the Congress would avoid the Presidential veto by calling things, as he put it, resolutions or votes instead of acts.

As a result, the final text of the Constitution in addition to the legislative veto clause has the following provision:

Every Order, Resolution, or Vote to which the Concurrence of the Senate and House of Representatives may be necessary (except on a question of Adjournment) shall be presented to the President of the United States; and before the Same shall take Effect, shall be approved by him, or being disapproved by him shall be repassed by two-thirds of the Senate and House of Representatives, according to the Rules and Limitations prescribed in the Case of a Bill."

It should be apparent from the wording of this provision, and from its formulation as a separate clause apart from the clause dealing with legislation, that it was intended to protect the President against all congressional evasions of his veto power, and not merely those that were formally connected with the legislative process. Or to put the point another way, which clarifies its close relationship to the doctrine of separation of powers: The function of the Congress in our system is to legislate, and *all* final congressional action of public effect, whether or not it is formally called a law, must follow the prescribed procedure which includes presentation to the President for his approval or veto.

It will be noted that the constitutional provision just discussed refers only to concurrent resolutions, and not to one-House resolutions. This omission was, of course, not meant to sanction avoidance of the Presidential veto by the latter process. The framers probably never even envisioned that a single House would purport to take any legally effective action on behalf of the entire Congress. In other words, the only reason why a one-House resolution in derogation of Executive action is not in literal violation of article I, section 7, clause 3 of the Constitution is that it contains, in addition to the defect which that provision addresses, the defect of being an unlawful delegation of congressional power to one of its Houses. As one scholar recently stated:

> "It verges on irrationality to maintain that action by concurrent resolution, whereby Congress is at least held in check by its own structure, is invalid because the veto clause so states, but that the invalidity of a simple resolution, wherein a single House acts without check, is more in doubt."

H. L. Watson, *Congress Steps Out: A Look at Congressional Control of the Executive*, 63 Calif. L. Rev. 983, 1066 note 428 (1975).

Proponents of legislative disapproval of Executive action support their position essentially by two considerations. First, they point to a body of legislative precedents which in their view has established a constitutional practice. Second, they argue that this legislative device has become necessary as the result of the current practice of delegating extremely broad discretion to administrative agencies.

The argument that the disapproval of Executive action by Congressional resolutions has acquired the status of a constitutional custom is met at the threshold by the dual warnings in *Powell* v. *McCormack*, 395 U.S. 486, 546–547 (1969), that an action is not any less unconstitutional because it has been taken before, and that the precedential value of a constitutional practice diminishes in direct proportion to its distance from the Constitutional Convention. How recent is the practice we are talking about?

It is very recent indeed. The use of concurrent and one-House resolutions for some purposes—for example, as a condition to the effectiveness of reorganization plans, or as a means of terminating "emergency" legislation—goes back only to the 1930's. Their use to control administrative rules and regulations, which four of these five bills involved, originated only 3 years ago. The earlier constitutional practice, dating back to the formative years of the Republic, was carefully analyzed in 1897 by the Senate Judiciary Committee, which concluded that a distinction must be made between two types of Congressional resolutions: those in which both Houses have a common interest, but which are peculiarly within the province of Congress alone; and those which are of a legislative nature or of concern to the President. The former need not be presented to the President, the latter are subject to his veto power. S. Rept. 1335, 54th Cong., 2nd Sess., pp. 6, 8. A more concise formulation of that traditional test may be found in Congressman Mann's statement that a concurrent resolution not presented to the President has "no force beyond the confines of the Capitol" 42 Cong. Rec. 2661 (1908).

It thus appears that there is indeed a constitutional practice in this field, one which goes back to the beginning of the Republic, and which is fully in accord with the clear text of the Constitution. It requires the presentation to the President of all Congressional resolutions designed to have legal effect outside the confines of the Capitol. This tradition is entitled to far greater weight than the recently evolved practice of providing for the termination of laws or the annulment of agency action by Congressional resolutions not presented to the President.

In addition, it is well-established that resort may be had to constitutional usage only where the constitutional text is in doubt. *United States* v. *Midwest Oil Co.*, 236 U.S. 459, 473 (1915); *Inland*

Waterways Corp. v. *Young*, 309 U.S. 517, 525 (1940). Here the text of article I, section 7, clauses 2 and 3 is unambiguous, and so is the fundamental doctrine of the separation of powers.

There are several other arguments that can be made against the position that we are confronted here with a constitutional practice that must be accepted. Reliance on a constitutional practice is only feasible where that practice has been, first, of long standing and second, generally accepted. As I indicated earlier, the practice in the present case is of recent origin; and it has not been generally accepted. It has been repeatedly challenged by Presidents who objected to its constitutionality, and has been said to be of dubious constitutionality by members of the Congress itself. I will leave further separation of these points to my prepared text. Suffice it to say that there is no way in which any principle based upon constitutional custom can validate such provisions as these.

The second frequently expressed argument in support of nonlegislative congressional control over Presidential or agency action is a pragmatic one: Whatever the pros and cons of ancient constitutional prescription may be, the device is quite simply necessary to run our modern government efficiently. I will discuss later, in connection with my comments specifically directed to S. 2812, that aspect of this pragmatic argument which is addressed to the congressional review of Presidential reorganization determinations, and will limit the balance of my remarks in this general discussion to the asserted practical benefits of legislative veto of agency rulemaking. The argument put forward by the proponents of congressional veto of rule making is that the device is quite simply necessary to maintain the proper balance between the Executive and the Congress in the face of vast delegation of legislative discretion, rendered unavoidable by the inability of Congress to attend to the many complex details of modern regulations. We may first of all question whether the delegation is indeed so unavoidable. In some areas, such as the field of Federal taxation, the Congress has entered into complex detail with regularity and success. But assuming that the premise is correct, what reason is there to believe that the lack of ability or the lack of will to master detail which displays itself in the formal legislative process would somehow disappear when Congress is faced with the task of reviewing agency rules? I suggest that there is none, and that the proposed solution is an attempt to apply a mechanical solution to a much more fundamental problem. While I cannot provide the sum total of all instances in which concurrent resolutions or one-House vetoes of agency action have in fact been applied by the Congress, it is my impression—and the impression of other knowledgeable observers with whom we have consulted—that they have been extremely rare.

What, in the last analysis, is the increased efficiency that is somehow expected to materialize from using the one-House veto or concurrent resolution procedure, instead of formal legislation, to control agency rulemaking. If the matter is handled intelligently, will not a committee have to consider the agency rules just as it would have considered administration legislative proposals on the same subject? And will that committee not have to report its judgment to the full House, just as in the formal legislative process? In fact, the only benefits which I can see to be derived from the procedure are three: First, the avoidance of a Presidential veto. Second (in the case of a one-House resolution), the avoidance of the requirement of concurrence by the other House. And third, the theoretical necessity for the Congress to focus upon the rules which are required by law to be laid before it. Tht first two of these benefits are precisely the simplifications which the Constitution sought to prohibit. The third benefit—based on the expectation of forcing the Congress to get into details when it does not want to do so—is obviously illusory. When the novelty of the new scheme has worn off, review of detailed regulations will be avoided by the Congress to the same degree as enactment of detailed legislation—except, perhaps, for the sort of piecemeal tinkering which may do more harm than good. In short, accepting at face value the argument that Congress must delegate because it has no time or no inclination to consider the details itself, it is inconceivable to me how changing the point at which it is obliged to focus upon details (after, rather than before, the binding provisions are adopted) will remedy the problem.

Finally, I may mention some of the harmful practical effects which a system of congressional review of agency rulemaking must produce. The existing system of rulemaking under the Administrative Procedure Act has been accurately described as an essentially unitary process. The agency makes its decision, which must be based upon rational and analytical factors established with greater or lesser specificity by the Congress; and then the courts review the agency's success in performing that rational and analytic task. Under the new system established by the present bills, the agency will first consider the matter on a rational and analytic basis; the Congress will then decide whether, even though the resulting rule is rationally and analytically correct, it will be thrown away for what may be purely political reasons; but if the rule survives that test the courts will then again review it to see whether it is rationally and analytically correct. A proposed rule concerning pollution emission standards will first be examined by the agency to determine whether it meets specified statutory standards and congressional established societal goals; it will then either be retained or abandoned on the basis of considerations which may—and should—include such factors as whether it would cause the closing of a factory in Connecticut or Georgia, depending perhaps upon the membership of the committee to which it is submitted. If it survives that test, it will once again be scrutinized by the courts to see whether it meets the tests of procedural regularity and analytical correctness. In my view, it is seriously questionable whether the courts can or should continue their present practice of judicial review in this new context. Accepting the very theory of the sponsors of these bills, the courts would be reviewing legislative action rather than executive adherence to the law. The courts have in the past displayed considerable reluctance to review agency decisions which are subject to stringent congressional control or review. *Perkins* v. *Lukens Steel Co.*, 310 U.S. 113, (1940); *Panama Canal Co.* v. *Grace Line, Inc.*, 356 U.S. 309, 318–319 (1958); *Kansas City Power & Light Co.* v. *McKay*, 225 F. 2d 924, 930–931 (CADC, 1955) certiriorari denied 350 U.S. 884. I believe, of course, that the destruction of the principle of judicial review of agency rulemaking would be a great loss to the administrative process.

In a number of respects, congressional review of agency rulemaking will produce quite simply impracticable results. Not infrequently, for example, an issue which is the subject of disagreement between the two Houses in a piece of pending legislation is effectively compromised through the device of statemanlike ambiguity: It is resolved neither one way nor the other in the conference committee report, so that each House approves on the basis of its own interpretation of the ambiguous provision. Under the present bills, what is an agency to do when it comes to the adoption of rules involving such a provision? If it drafts them one way, they will be vetoed by the House; the other way, by the Senate. Is it thereby absolutely prevented from issuing the necessary rules? The dilemma arises directly and unavoidably from the fact that congressional review of rulemaking is inconsistent with the constitutionally established system of final legislative action and subsequent executive responsibility.

The preceding discussion completes my comments on S. 2258, S. 2716 and S. 2903, which are limited to the legislative approval of administrative rules and regulations, and of that portion of S. 2878 which contains a similar provision. I would like to add a few brief comments concerning S. 2812 and that portion of S. 2878 which deals with congressional oversight.

S. 2812

S. 2812 seeks to achieve the difficult and desirable goal of eliminating governmental regulation which has become outmoded and counterproductive. In this laudable purpose, it resembles the President's bill, S 3428, which Mr. Lynn will discuss with you later. I intend to focus my comments not on the respects in which these two bills are similar, but on that distinctive feature of S. 2812 which seeks to compel the reduction or limitation of regulation even where Congress fails— or positively refuses—to enact legislation for that purpose.

I will not describe the procedure by which that is accomplished, except to point out the key provision, which is section 5 (D).

This provides that if the Congress does not act, does not enact either the proposal which the President presents or the revised proposal which a committee can present under the bill by December 31 of the year in which a Presidential plan has been submitted, the Presidential plan as originally submitted shall automatically become effective as of March 15 of the following year unless either House of Congress disapproves the Presidential plan. This, of course, is a form of one-House veto, the constitutional aspects of which I discussed earlier. However, my earlier discussion of practical consequences were directed more narrowly to the rulemaking. With respect to the scheme of legislative veto for Presidential proposals such as set forth in S. 2812, somewhat different practical considerations apply.

I believe the asserted justification for bypassing a normal constitutional procedure with respect to such matters as those covered in S. 2812 is not, as in the case of agency regulations, the general unwillingness of the Congress to focus upon regulatory details, but rather the inability of the Congress—given its existing organizational structure and procedures—to make fundatmental changes which alter significantly the powers or prerogatives of its various committees. Specifically, it is recognized to be a task of considerable difficulty to induce a committee which is charged with oversight of a particular major agency, and which derives significant power and authority in the legislative process from the existence of that agency, to recommend its elimination or any substantial curtailment of its functions. S. 2812 appears to be an attempt to solve this problem by reversing the effect of legislative inertia—that is, by requiring the committee, in order to save a particular agency or program, to convince the full Congress that it is worth saving, rather than (as is the present system) simply to decline recommendation of its elimination.

It is in my view seriously questionable whether the proposed solution would be effective. Particularly where the Presidential proposals have the sweep envisioned by S. 2812, ultimately affecting all major areas of Federal regulation and most of the departments and agencies of the Government, it seems unlikely that those committees of the Congress, if there are any, which would oppose rational reform in the areas within their own jurisdiction, would not make common cause with others similarly inclined so as to defeat the Presidential initiatives in their totality. In short, I would have little hope that the possibility of achieving necessary revisions through this method is substantially higher than the possibility of achieving them through the constitutionally prescribed process of legislation.

Although there is not any constitutional, or for that matter, feasible, method of compelling the Congress to legislate what it does not wish to legislate, one of the problems in this area can be remedied by the use of a "forcing" mechanism. I refer to the fact that under the current procedures of both Houses, a detailed proposal for fundamental reorganization or substantive reduction of Federal regulation can, for all practical purposes, reach the floor only through the very committees which have the paramount interest in retaining the status quo. A mechanical solution can, indeed, solve this mechanical problem—and the administration's proposal, S. 2438, applies such a remedy by amending the rules of each House so that the President's reform proposals, or any substitute proposals developed by the relevant committees, will automatically come to the floor, not having to go through the committees that would have the least interest in any change.

This, it seems to me, is as far as it is either lawful or expedient to go. On both constitutional and pragmatic grounds, we oppose the one-House veto feature of S. 2812.

Finally, and last of all, I wish to suggest to you an additional constitutional defect in S. 2812, which is related to, but nonetheless distinct, from the legislative veto problem common to most of these bills. If we, in the executive, are opposed to improper congressional participation in the function of executing the laws, we are no less opposed to improper executive involvement in the function of legislating. As noted above, we believe that once a function has been properly assigned to the executive branch, it must be left to be performed by that branch alone, without further congressional control except through the process of legislative enactment. There are, however, certain functions which simply cannot properly be assigned to the executive. *Wayman* v. *Southard*, supra, at p. 43, 46. However much the doctrine of unlawful delegation of legislative authority may have been narrowed and eroded in this century, see e.g., *Zemel* v. *Rusk*, 381 U.S. 1, 7–13 (1965), I am confident that it retains sufficient vitality to invalidate the assignment to the President of the "simple" task of designing all the laws that will govern both the organization and the substance of Federal regulation.

Mr. Chairman, I will leave the remainder of my prepared text for your reading and devote myself to any questions which you may have on any of the bills.

Discussion and Debate

Chairman RIBICOFF. You suggest in your testimony that for Congress to assign to the President tasks designing all the laws that govern Federal regulations would violate the constitutional doctrine of lawful declaration.

For policy reasons I tend to agree that it would not be good to give the President the complete responsibility for the initiative in the regulatory reform area.

To what extent do you believe that Congress could give the President responsibility for coming up with reform proposals without overstepping the bounds of the Constitution?

Mr. SCALIA. Well, as I indicated in my testimony, Senator, the doctrine of unlawful delegation, which was once quite vibrant, was thought to have if not died a decent death, at least gone into a coma during the 1920's and 1930's by reason of Supreme Court decisions during that period. I think it is still alive, but what is left of it is doubtlessly very limited.

The Congress can make very broad delegations. You have delegations such as that to the Federal Communications Commission, to regulate communications "in the public interest, convenience and necessity. I nonetheless think that a proposal such as that in S. 2812, to give the President, with virtually no standards, the power to reorganize all regulation—and not only to reorganize it but to change its substance where he thinks that desirable in order to promote competition or for whatever reason—would provoke the courts to say this is too far.

The issue ultimately hangs upon two elements I suppose—how broad the area of authority delegated to the President is, and second, how precise, either through statutory statement or perhaps through prior court decision, the standards for Presidential action are. It seems to me that S. 2812 is not adequate in either of these respects.

I would finally add that the whole way it is designed, to wit, as a means of enabling the President to enact legislation unless the Congress objects, simply increases the probability in my mind that the Supreme Court will look upon it as essentially what it is, an attempt to let the President legislate. . . .

Senator PERCY. So this is the administration's position.

Mr. SCALIA. Yes, Senator. It has been presented to the Congress before, and the President's veto of some legislation has been based upon it, and the President has reserved the point in signing statements pertaining to other regulation.

Senator PERCY. To the best of my knowledge there has never been any administration testimony on S. 2812 at any place before this morning, is that correct?

Mr. SCALIA. I believe that is correct, Senator.

Senator PERCY. I am sure it is correct.

Mr. Scalia. But we have the constitutional point.

Senator Percy. How long has the administration had S. 2812 for study and analysis?

Mr. Scalia. I do not know, Senator.

As I stated, my office at Justice had received the letter on the 10th. Our Office of Legislative Affairs got the referral on the 7th of this month and my office did not get it until he 10th.

Senator Percy. Of this month?

Mr. Scalia. That is all that I know about its progress within the Department of Justice.

Senator Percy. The interdepartmental mail service is worse than the Postal Service.

We sent over a copy to the White House before Senator Byrd and I introduced it.

We introduced it and it was printed in the Congressional Record December 18 of last year.

The administration has had this piece of legislation for some 5 months.

Mr. Scalia. I am sorry, Senator. I was talking about the request from your committee to testify on the legislation.

Senator Percy. If you are testifying on behalf of the administration this morning, then you are aware of the fact that I have met with White House officials on several occasions on this legislation to talk over the field, to talk over how we could work together, and that they have issued public statements of commendation on this legislation?

Why is it then that today, 5 months after it had been introduced, we are notified for the first time that there are fundamental constitutional problems with S. 2812?

Mr. Scalia. Well, Senator, you inserted a statement in the Congressional Record—you did so not so terribly long ago—which I believe expressed an understanding that the administration does favor the objective of your proposal, in fact, heartily endorses it, but does, indeed, disagree with that feature of it that represents what we consider an improper procedure.

I will not bother to get out the excerpt that I brought with me. But I was under the impression you were aware, because of the very difference between the Administration's bill introduced this week and your bill which, in many respects, are similar, that the Administration does not support the one-house veto feature.

Senator Percy. There is a great deal of similarity between the administration's bill and the bill which Senator Byrd and I sent to the administration 5 months ago, and we are pleased with that similarity. We have applauded the President's initiatives in regulatory reform.

We are working toward a common objective.

We are trying to get there, but certainly I would hope that in the spirit in which we have tried to reach out and work together we would have been informed of the possibility of fundamental constitutional problems. We sent it to the administration with the hope of working together.

I will pick up now a few things from your statement that I have just at this moment had a chance to look at because, if what you say in your testimony is true, I am a little worried about some of the agencies that now exist.

For instance, you say on page 25 that "the scheme of the Constitution is that the President may propose and the Congress may enact; not that the President may enact unless the Congress affirmatively objects." You go on then to say, "We do not believe that a statute can alter this basic constitutional prescription."

If this were so then we would have to say that such agencies as the EPA, ACTION, the DEA, the White House Domestic Council and the Office of Management and Budget among a score of others might well be considered unconstitutional.

Senator Ribicoff and I personally dealt with reorganization plans dealing with all of these matters.

Under them, the President proposed and the plan went into existence unless either House of Congress affirmatively objected to it.

That is the reorganization authority that the President and the administration have worked with—in this administration, the last one and the one before it.

Do you mean to say that everything the executive branch sent up to us in all those years and the way we have dealt with them has been unconstitutional and that this is the first we are told about?

How about reorganization authority that has existed since 1932?

Mr. SCALIA. Yes, sir, several points.

First of all, I have a little fear that the agencies will go out of existence if the theory that I have put forward today is adopted. To begin with, there has been clear legislative enactment which, in effect, approves their existence through the ordinary legislative process. Every time an appropriation is made with respect to those agencies there has been clear legislative approval by appropriation through the normal legislative process.

Second: I personally would not distinguish between a reorganization plan and other kinds insofar as the one-house veto feature is concerned, but a distinction can be made.

But apart from the one-house veto feature, I tried to point out in my testimony that S. 2812 not merely says to the President "you may reorganize your Department of Government as you will and then submit it to us and we will veto it" (which is what the reorganization plan legislation said); but it says further that "you can alter the substance of regulation in all of these fields as you will, and it will become the law of the land unless we veto it." This goes much beyond traditional reorganization plans. If one were to adopt the theory that the organization of the executive branch is a matter so inherently Presidential, so close to the proper functions of the President himself, and moreover does not directly affect the public, it is simple to distinguish between reorganization plans and other forms of legislation insofar as any problems of unlawfully broad delegation are concerned.

I therefore do not think that the reorganization plan problem is a real impediment. Those statutes do not go back any earlier than I guess the late 1930's or I should say the early 1930's. If they were wrong, they were wrong.

Senator PERCY. I am just looking at your words, the aim of the Constitution is that the President may propose and the Congress may enact, I repeat, not that the President may enact unless the Congress affirmatively objects.

That is exactly what we do in the reorganization plan.

Mr. SCALIA. You do not disagree with the statement, do you, Senator?

Senator PERCY. Pardon me?

Mr. SCALIA. Are you asserting the statement is inaccurate? Do you disagree with that statement?

Senator PERCY.. I say the reorganization plans that we enacted were reorganization plans sent to us by the executive branch of Government and they went into effect and became law unless either House objected within 60 days.

That is exactly the way we have been carrying them out.

Mr. SCALIA. Senator, I would rather see it done otherwise myself.

Senator PERCY. Are you saying that it is unconstitutional?

You say we do not believe that a statute can alter this basic constitutional prescription.

What you are, in effect, saying is that the reorganization plans that the executive branch has been sending down to us all these years are unconstitutional as I understand it.

Mr. SCALIA. Senator, you can look upon the problem as one of not the plans being unconstitutional, but the provision for a congressional veto being unconstitutional. It is constitutional for the Congress to give the President the power to reorganize the executive branch.

I think the Congress could pass a statute with a one-House veto provision saying the President may restructure his own branch of government as he sees fit—the President could go ahead and do it and it would be lawful.

But, if the Congress then goes on and adds to that, whatever reorganization he performs must be submitted to us for our signing, in my personal view that is a violation of the constitutional rules, just as a provision for congressional veto of rulemaking would be. Some scholars would make a distinction. But the point is what would fall would be the veto provision, and the reorganization would be unaffected.

In any case, the present situation with respect to S. 2812 presents a problem separate and apart from the one-House veto problem. There can be, in my view, no delegation to the President of the sort which S. 2812 would seek to achieve. There is no way in which the Congress could say to the President you may not only reorganize the executive branch, but you may set forth such substantive rules of regulation as seem to you desirable to promote competition or whatever else. I do not think the Congress can make that kind of delegation to the President.

That is the fundamental violation of the separation of powers and of the system of allocated functions that S. 2812 commits. I do not think that the one-House veto cures it. . . .

Senator NUNN. Let me ask you this question, shifting to another point.

N7 Let us assume that Congress enacts the so-called Sunset bill that Senator Muskie sponsored and has a lot of the same provisions that the Percy-Byrd bill does. Do you see any constitutional problems?

That is the first question.

The second requiring each Federal program including the Justice Department be reauthorized from scratch every 4 years including a thorough review, revision, and authorization of regulations of the Department.

Mr. SCALIA. No, sir; I think the Congress can do whatever it wants by legislation—within the limits of the Bill of Rights and other provisions of the Constitution. As long as it is proceeding by legislation, I am not asserting there is any restriction upon the Congress' tinkering with the continued existence of agencies.

Senator NUNN. You do not see any constitutional problem with the provision that says unless reenacted, the program is terminated?

That is clear-cut legislation.

Mr. SCALIA. The Congress can pass a statute which says this statute will last for 5 years, and at the end of 5 years the agency will go out of business. In other words, the purpose of the Senator's bill can be achieved in a constitutional fashion without having to use the concurrent resolution or one-House veto.

Senator NUNN. As I understand it, you are preparing on pages 22 and 23 an alternative. You are saying that the reason Congress is finding it necessary to take this sort of delegation of authority with retention of veto approach is the fact that the committees that control the agencies have vested interest in those agencies and by legislation, Congress is almost practically impotent to change those agencies when it has to pass through the committee that has their authority and power by reason of such supervision of that agency.

I am paraphrasing, but is that what you are saying?

Mr. SCALIA. Yes, sir; though of course that is speculation on my part. It is my attempt to plumb the intent of Senator Percy and those who support the bill.

It seems to me the provision that automatically brings to the floor is intended to avoid one of the major obstacles to fundamental reform legislation—which is that usually you have to get that legislation out of the very committee which has an interest in retaining all of the regulation, within the agency that now exists, because that regulation and that agency are a source of power and influence for the committee.

Senator NUNN. So you are saying you would give the committee 30 days or some definite time to consider the President's proposal and it would automatically go to the floor, whether or not the committee acted, is that right?

Mr. SCALIA. If the committee does not act, the President's action goes to the floor.

I think Senator Percy's bill and the administration bill is similar in that respect. The President's proposal goes to the committees and they have a chance to modify it and report out a modified proposal. If they do so, that is what goes to the floor. If they do nothing, the President's proposal goes to the floor.

Both bills assure that something dealing with the subject matter of the reforms proposals to the Congress does get to the floor. That forcing mechanism is no problem.

Senator NUNN. My time is running out, but I would just close by saying that I think the Justice Department should go look with the President and come up with something. If this is your view and if it is really the administration's view, that not only the Budget Control and Impoundment Act is unconstitutional but the War Powers Act, the veto part of it and all these pending provisions on the reorganization, it seems to me you ought to go to court with some test cases in the immediate future and resolve this because I can foresee some serious constitutional problems, particularly under the War Powers Act or the Budget Control and Impoundment Act to the point of maybe a great crisis.

It seems to me Justice has an obligation, if you think something is unconstitutional, to take action on it so it can be resolved.

Mr. SCALIA. Senator, the War Powers Act was initially vetoed by the President and passed over his veto.

Senator NUNN. That did not make it unconstitutional.

The President vetoes a lot of acts, and he can say it is unconstitutional. The only thing that makes it unconstitutional is that the Supreme Court says so.

Mr. SCALIA. Yes, sir. My point was merely to emphasize that I am not coming forward with a bomb of a disclosure in revealing that the administration thinks a concurrent resolution and a one-House veto presents a grave question of constitutionality. I think that has been the well-known position of the administration.

Senator NUNN. Well, I do not disagree with that.

I am just saying it is important to get it resolved and if that was the point of the administration, I think they have a duty to clarify it by taking the issue to court.

Mr. SCALIA. We have been looking for a case and will continue to do so. They are hard to find.

Senator NUNN. I do not see how they would be hard to find on impoundment.

Thank you, Mr. Chairman.

Chairman RIBICOFF. Senator Javits, I do not know if you have pity on Mr. Scalia, but Mr. Lynn has been sitting back there patiently and chewing his nails trying to testify but I will certainly not cut you off.

Senator JAVITS. Mr. Scalia, is that the right way to pronounce your name?

Mr. SCALIA. Yes, sir.

Senator JAVITS. Is it a fact that in this matter you are the President's lawyer?

Mr. SCALIA. I am the President's lawyer's lawyer. I assist the Attorney General in his advice-giving function to the executive branch.

Senator JAVITS. Well, you are speaking you say, "The administraton has formally taken a position."

Mr. SCALIA. Yes, sir, the views here are approved by the administration.

Senator JAVITS. You are the President's lawyer in your testimony here.

Mr. SCALIA. Yes, sir.

Mr. JAVITS. And this is the President's position?

Mr. SCALIA. Yes, sir.

Senator JAVITS. Now, how is that cleared? Does it go to the President or does it go to the Attorney General to approve this testimony? How are we to know that this represents the President's position?

Mr. SCALIA. Well, I do not know that anything different has been done here than in any testimony. There is a normal Office of Management and Budget clearing process to which testimony concerning pending legislation must be submitted. Administration witnesses are not permitted to go and testify on behalf of the administration unless that process has been completed. . . .

I would like to make one concluding statement. Much of this discussion, Mr. Chairman, has been about the concurrent resolution or one-House veto feature. Apparently, I have at least succeeded in directing the committee's attention to the point.

Senator JAVITS. You have got our attention and there is no doubt about that.

Mr. SCALIA. That is useful.

This problem is one that, as I indicated in my testimony, has been around since 1932. Franklin Roosevelt in the Lend Lease Act accepted a one-House veto provision without saying anything, but he wrote a side letter to then Attorney General Jackson, later Justice Jackson, expressing his view that it was unconstitutional.

A few of these things could be lived with down through the years and have been since the early 1930's. In the last 3 years, however, they have become numerous. The Congress has found that they are, indeed, a very useful device for controlling, to a substantial degree, executive actions. That has happened to such an extent we have felt it is time to make an issue of it. I hope it can be resolved both directly and amicably.

Senator JAVITS. If I may respond to that, Mr. Chairman, that pragmatic consideration, Mr. Scalia, is met by our pragmatic consideration that under modern conditions we have to give so much legislation to the President that we have to find the technique for seeing that it is not uncontrolled.

I think, at the present, that the people will suffer if we cannot find a way out of this morass.

BUSINESS AND CONSUMER VIEWS

Despite the problems the Percy-Byrd measure encountered in the Ford administration, the U.S. Chamber of Commerce and other administration partisans provided qualified support for its action-forcing concepts, including the sunset provision. Such support is offered in the testimony of Roscoe Egger, a partner in Price, Waterhouse & Company, speaking on behalf of the U.S. Chamber of Commerce; and Philip Knox, vice-president of Sears, Roebuck & Company.

Roscoe Egger and Philip Knox ([73], pp. 248–249, 252–263)

Today, the national chamber urges this committee to embark on a new legislative initiative that will bring about an effective beginning in reform of the regulatory process in the Federal Government.

WHY REGULATORY REFORM IS NEEDED

The existence of regulatory agencies dates back to 1863, when the Office of the Comptroller of the Currency was created, and 1887, which marked the creation of the Interstate Commerce Commission.

However, during the seventies we have witnessed an unprecedented and dramatic growth of regulatory agencies, both independent and within the executive branch. Such agencies as the Consumer Product Safety Commission, Environmental Protection Agency, Federal Energy Administration, Mining Enforcement Safety Administration, Occupational Safety and Health Administration, to mention a few, are products of this era.

Prof. Murray Weidenbaum, director of the Center for the Study of American Business at Washington University, has calculated the Federal budget figure for regulators at $3 billion a year, with a workingforce of more than 74,000 individuals. To comply with the various rules and regulations developed by the agencies is an enormous expense for business. For example, Richard L. Terrell, vice chairman of General Motors Corp., has reported that GM's regulatory compliance cost would amount to more than $1.3 billion this year.

An important point to note is that the cost impact of regulation falls not just on business, but ultimately on the consumer. The General Accounting Office has placed this cost at $60 billion annually. In just one item, automobiles, Professor Weidenbaum estimates that the federally mandated cost of a typical 1974 car was $320.

The plain fact is that most businesses must pass along all the cost of Federal regulations to the consumer. It is essential that regulators take into consideration the trade-off between what they seek to accomplish and the criteria that are important to consumers. There is little evidence that any consideration is being given to this question.

It is now time to reexamine the regulatory process. We applaud the fact that this committee, along with the Senate Commerce Committee, has been authorized to study the purposes and effectiveness of the Federal regulatory process. We hope the results of these studies will provide guidance and direction for Congress. At the same time, we feel that action at the individual agency level is essential.

The national chamber is dedicated to a competitive free market economy operating in today's world on a basis consistent with the role of Government in safeguarding the health, safety, and welfare of our fellow citizens. But it is essential that both cost and benefits of Government programs be taken into consideration—and that regulators not lose sight of the fundamental purposes of the programs, what can and should be accomplished and whether the costs, ultimately borne by the public, justify each action. For too long, the regulatory process has gone without this type of fundamental accountability. Senator Percy, in a recent speech recognized the extent of this problem when he said: "It seems that the dynamism of the American economy is matched only by the rigidity and inflexibility of some of the agencies which regulate it."

THE CHAMBER'S GOALS

The national chamber's task force on regulatory reform, recently created, is composed of individuals representing a broad range of professional, business and trade association members of the chamber.

This group sought to develop for the chamber a philosophy of regulatory reform and a set of basic principles to be applied in the process of reform. In brief, we believe that Congress, which passed the legislation creating regulatory agencies and provided their authority, should take the initiative to provide the legislative mandate and the mechanism for reform. What is needed is broad-gaged review of the functions and activities of all agencies having regulatory responsibilities. In conducting such a review, Congress should spell out specific criteria to serve as the basic guidelines in carrying out an effective reform program.

The task of setting standards or criteria for Government regulation is delegated, under our political system, to the legislative branch. Congress has the ability to establish goals and require results from programs created to achieve those goals. And, through its oversight functions, Congress should require accountability from those designated to administer and carry out legislated programs.

We believe it is a proper role of Congress to determine whether, and to what extent, those in a regulatory function, in their zeal, have gone too far, and have perhaps carried regulation to excess. No particular purpose will be served in detailing to this committee a long list of examples of excessive regulations.

The chamber's board of directors, during its February 1976 meeting, considered and endorsed recommendations prepared by the task force. Our board enunciated basic principles which we believe should be written into the law to provide effective regulatory reform:

A competitive free market system should be retained and encouraged to provide an incentive for innovation, and to give consumers the maximum range of choices.

Regulation should be only that essential to the protection of health, safety and the general welfare, and should be revised and administered so as to: (1) Provide that degree of regulation essential to the proper functioning of a competitive free market system, keeping in mind the need for, and the feasibility of, regulation consistent with foregoing principles; (2) Eliminate uneven and inequitable enforcement; (3) Eliminate regulatory duplication and conflict; (4) Provide for prompt regulatory decisions consistent with due process; (5) Assure adequate consideration of costs and benefits; (6) Minimize compliance costs; (7) Provide Federal preemption only in those instances where Federal regulation is essential; and (8) Assure a more orderly development of regulation, with the Congress establishing basic policy, agencies regulating in accord with the intent of Congress, and the Congress reviewing regulatory actions within its oversight function.

We believe these foregoing principles are of the utmost importance. . . .

With those points in mind, the task force reviewed many of the proposals now before this Committee, the Senate Judiciary Committee and their House counterparts. Among the bills that take a sound and beneficial approach to regulatory reform are S. 2812 and S. 3428. . . .

THE RESERVATIONS WE HAVE WITH S. 2812

Our task force has examined S. 2812 in detail. We are in general agreement with the concepts of the bill. However, our analysis suggests several respects in which the proposed legislation could be improved. The following aspects are of particular concern to us.

The findings and Purposes Provisions in Section 2(a), 2(a)(1) and 2(a)(2) contain conclusions which we believe add little to the legislation and may detract from the main thrust of the substantive provisions.

The directions for the plans should be more specific.

There should be more flexibility allowed for the President to designate the subjects to be studied during each year and the agencies and activities which will be incorporated in each year's study.

THE FINDINGS AND PURPOSES ARE OVERSTATED

The Findings and Purposes Provisions, found in section 2(a) detract from the genuine purpose of the bill. S. 2812 should be a positive piece of legislation that seeks better regulation. Although the introductory provision contains language intended to form the basis for, and state the reasons for, the remaining provisions, the language contains excessive overstatements.

Senator PERCY. If you would like to summarize, of course, the whole statement will go into the record, and then we can proceed with the questions.

I might say I have read the full statement.

Mr. EGGER. I would like to comment that we have detailed in the statement here certain basic principles that we believe should get built into this legislation.

I should like to cover those and possibly a few more comments and I would be glad then to just suspend.

Senator PERCY. Fine. These are the principles that you have enunciated on page 4?

Mr. EGGER. Yes. We suggest minimum requirements for each agency's plans, these are the plans that would grow out of the bill's directions. Each agency's plan should include: A definitive statement of the extent to which the plan will enhance competition in the area of commerce and industry involved; cost-benefit analyses for programs; detailed plans for personnel and resource utilization; studies of agency goals and agency ability to accomplish these goals, together with appropriate controls to assure that activities and regulations are consistent with and not in excess of those required to achieve the goals; and offices that will provide the agency head with policy and program evaluation of the agency, we offer the Office of Policy Planning and Evaluation at the Federal Trade Commission as an example.

In general, it is our feeling that the approach which is taken in S. 2812 is a good one in that it offers the opportunity for the President to build on each study with success coming from better results, that is to say, we believe that the plans that develop over the 5-year period will be consistently improved and there will be a great deal of information and knowledge gained from the prior years of study.

Senator Percy, I think if you are satisfied with our statement we might just cover quickly some of our comments on S. 3428 and then we can have your questions.

Senator PERCY. I would appreciate it. I have gone over them and I think they are very perceptive.

Mr. EGGER. We applaud the President's interest in regulatory reform. This is a subject which requires the attention and the involvement of all branches of our Government, and the show of support by the executive branch is especially welcome.

S. 3428 appears to be modeled on the approach taken by Senators Percy and Byrd in S. 2812. It calls for a 4-year program to be conducted starting in 1978. The various agencies would be required to submit reform plans affecting the various industrial sectors of the economy. This is a departure from the Percy-Byrd plan which focuses specifically on the agencies and not the industries affected by the agencies. We have not had enough time to fully consider this approach. Thus, we will defer comment.

The order prescribed in S. 3428 is unique. The schedule calls for transportation and agriculture in 1 year; then mining, heavy manufacturing, and public utilities; light manufacturing and construction; and communications, finance, insurance, real estate, trade and service industries.

One aspect of this ordering is of special significance. There is enough flexibility for the President to add agencies that he deems necessary. As we have just indicated, the National Chamber favors this flexibility.

The plans are to include material in seven areas. We note that the proposal focuses on points of concern to us: enunciation of purposes, focusing on goals, specific cost-benefit information and analysis of expected and realized impacts. These are the type of information we have already characterized as essential. We submit that these points might even be made more specific.

The primary difference between S. 2812 and S. 3428 lies in the action-forcing provisions. The President's bill drops the aspect that deal with congressional failure to act. It does not go beyond requiring the legislation to become the pending order of business in Congress as of a certain date.

Our analysis to date leads us to believe that the action-forcing mechanism may be more effective. Absent is a real opportunity to consider the proposed alternatives. We wish at this time to support the general approach in S. 2812. Some individuals have raised constitutional objections to S. 2812's provision that automatically turn legislative proposals into law and practical objections to agencies losing their powers to promulgate rules, et cetera. On the basis of the national chamber's support of a timetable approach we can accept either approach and ask this committee to adopt the one it finds to be the soundest method for gaining regulatory reform.

Some observations on S. 3428: The tone of this bill is extremely reasonable and takes note of the concerns of business. For instance, the findings and purposes section does not contain the harshness of S. 2812. Rather, it reflects the need for concerted action.

This is especially evident in the educational implications of the bill. We are favorably impressed by the provision that calls for obtaining the views of concerned Americans. We know that there are many members of the national chamber who are ready to assist in gaining regulatory reform.

In sum, we certainly can and do favor the approach taken by S. 3428. We realize that there are certain problems with the bill. For instance, will the Congress be in session on November 15 of each year, and will the new President in 1981 be able to present a plan on January 30? It is the opportunity of this Congress to merge the best parts of S. 2812 and S. 3428 and come up with a bill that can achieve concrete results.

ACTION IS NEEDED

It is now time to act on regulatory reform. We have talked a good deal about the need for reform. Senator Percy has participated in discussion programs at our last two annual meetings in which regulatory reform was the topic. He and others have seen the keen interest on the part of our members for revamping and improving Government. President Ford chose our 1975 annual meeting to give a major address on regulatory reform.

Business, large and small, wants a better, more efficient and effective Government that is responsive to the needs of today in today's economic environment.

SUMMARY

We offer our general approval of S. 2812 and S. 3428. If adopted in a manner which incorporates our suggestions, these bills can accomplish the kind of broadgaged reform of the regulatory process that is so urgently needed.

We urge that this committee follow our suggestions and report these pending regulatory reform bills with the modifications we have recommended.

Actually, we think there are features of S. 3428 which would be merged with S. 2812, and I think S. 3428 comes a little closer to the chamber view that the President should have a great deal of flexibility in selecting the agencies and the subject matters for study.

In other words, we feel that perhaps the real role here for the Congress is to develop a mechanism and have the executive branch actually carry out these studies and then bring them back to the Congress for the Congress to make the final review.

We think that the industry by industry approach in S. 3428 may be helpful if it could somehow be merged with the agency-by-agency approach in S. 2812.

I think we will be happy to have your questions, Senator Percy.

Senator PERCY. Very good. Just quickly running through your testimony on page 1, you have commented on budget reform, and I would like to publicly thank the U.S. Chamber of Commerce.

I think that without the help of the U.S. chamber we could not have accomplished budget reform. There just was not that much interest. But I think that the business community and the U.S. chamber was of immense help.

We had to build our own discipline and certainly your own help and your understanding of what I, for one, was trying to accomplish was immensely appreciated.

On page 4, you outline the chamber's task force principles. I have carefully looked at those principles.

I concur completely with them and we will try to see that the legislation we report out is consistent with them because it is hard to improve on them. You have done a marvelous job.

I think S. 2812 does conform and I think the administration's bill conforms, but I will check it again against them.

On page 6, you comment on the Rock Island Railroad and the years of delay in decisionmaking.

I think from my own industrial experience and my experience on bank boards and in the Government now for a decade, I have seen frustration so great that businesses sometimes say they would rather have a negative decision—they would rather have a ruling against them than have to keep waiting.

Sometimes, it would be far less costly to them if they were ruled against rather than having this constant indecision which benefits only, I might say, the legal profession.

Much of the regulation just carries on and carries on and no one ever comes to grip with it.

I think certain of our chairmen, particularly Dick Wiley, John Robson, and Rod Hills, are trying to face up to this problem. They recognize the terrible cost to the consumer who ultimately is paying all the bill for this delay.

If you have a target, you can aim for it and there ought to be a time schedule in the decisionmaking process.

Mr. KNOX. Senator, may I comment briefly on that Rock Island case because I know that you are familiar with the area there. We made an analysis of the Sears, Roebuck retail facilities and and distribution facilities in the area serviced by that railroad.

Senator PERCY. When you say "we," you mean Sears, Roebuck?

Mr. KNOX. Yes, Sears, Roebuck.

During the period of time that the application was pending before the Interstate Commerce Commission, our company either opened new facilities or changed the location of more than half of its facilities within that market area.

We turned over the products that we sold of more than 50 percent within that same area, so here was the transportation system that services that market, that got the goods from the factory to the stores, unable to make the kind of changes that they were having to make to serve our customers, what they wanted to buy and where they wanted to buy it.

If in the location of our stores and the sale of our products we had needed the same kind of governmental procedures, we would have had the wrong goods in he wrong place.

You commented earlier this morning about the fact that some of us in industry have not always been a part of the process of change and we think that the same thing can be directed to the Government, that that is what this legislation is all about and that is one illustration of the reasons we support such change.

Senator PERCY. I thank you for that example. It does help us a lot. I appreciate your comment.

At the bottom of page 8, you comment that the directions for the reform plans should be more specific in S. 2812.

We very much appreciate any kind of help you can give us on that.

How should we be more specific?

On the top of page 9, you say the language in the findings and the purposes contains excessive overstatements.

I tend to think you are right. We start out by talking about how regulatory agencies have fueled inflation by approving fare, price, and rate increases which are not commensurate with the public interest. And I suppose it is going to be possible for us to find examples where fares have been changed and so forth.

We have not proved that and we should not set out in the findings until we can absolutely demonstrate and prove it.

Mr. EGGER. It is kind of a generalization.

Senator PERCY. When we mark up this legislation, we want to make the statements in such a way that they are absolutely clear and we will take a good look at the way the administration bill is worded to see whether there is some better language there.

I pledge to you we will do that, and when we report out the bill, it will have findings that you can accept.

At the top of page 9, you say the President should be permitted to decide what group of functions would be examined each year, because such decisions will undoubtedly change from time to time as the inquiry progresses.

I would appreciate your task force taking another look at that one in the political context of the real world in which we live.

If you have a Presidential year it is pretty easy to imagine someone in the White House sitting down and saying, oh boy, let's not touch that area this year. You do not dare volunteer yourself to go in and reform the regulation in this area in a Presidential year.

Really, it's better to have that thought through ahead of time and not to put the whole burden on the executive branch but have the burden shared.

This is a mandate, a law. Congress did it and had it done sometime ahead of time so that the requirement is imposed and there cannot be any fast answers about it. We should have all the hearings now, have all the judgments in and make a decision because really we are not going to learn much more.

We are focusing our attention now. We are really concentrating and that is what a piece of legislation does.

It forces us to discipline our thinking in specifics. To leave it to the administration I think is almost unfair to the President.

I would like to see us be realistic about that. Let us take the responsibility now. We can always amend the legislation later. We can always amend it if we find we put something in this year to be done that we are really not quite ready for and that it has to be shoved off another year. But we should have a set timetable.

I really hope you take another look at that.

With a fixed order, all the interest groups, all the groups that are affected by it can then start to think ahead of time.

If, all of a sudden, it is announced to them by the administration that they are next, they may not be ready for it and it may not be fair to them.

Again, we see your objection. Can you let us present some evidence to you that may show that we are really going to be better off fixing a schedule?

Are there any comments now that you have? I would appreciate it.

Mr. EGGER. Senator, the concern we had in the task force when we considered this point was that the series of studies might be too narrow in scope.

We were concerned that some of the regulatory functions in the line agencies might get left out if we simply made a laundry list of agencies and then covered the others by simply saying that the President could add some other agencies if it saw fit to do so.

We will go back and take another look at it, particularly in light of the administration's bill because we think perhaps, this whole problem area can be solved very satisfactorily by a merging of the two approaches, namely, the industry-by-industry approach together with agency-by-agency approach.

We will take another look at it and get back to you.

Senator PERCY. Fine, and the same at the top of page 11 where you are very specific. Certainly there are questions about whether the National Highway Traffic Safety Administration should be in transportation or safety.

We put the NHTSA in the area where it is primarily concerned, that is safety.

Again, I think we can do this thought process now and then give them a time frame and they will at least be on notice.

If any agency objects to where it is, I would rather get that evidence out in testimony now, rather than wait until later and not have them really know when they are going to be reviewed.

The arguments about the indecision and delay that we have discussed before apply equally here. Eventually, we will have to decide, why not now?

The Nuclear Regulation Commission and the NHTSA are not going to change 2 years from now.

Let us think it through now and put them where they belong.

Mr. EGGER. That will be part of our reconsideration.

Senator PERCY. Fine. You defer comment on the order of consideration S. 3428 and S. 2812. Certainly you can take whatever time you need, and we would like to have your comments on that whenever you have them put together.

What I would like to ask is this—we are having a lobbying bill over on the floor this week and the idea is to get more out in the open. There is a little bit of lobbying that is done in private bills and within the administration.

Should the administration lobby you heavily on their bill, would you please advise us of that and let us then come to you?

You know enough about the facts not to be lobbied by us, but if you have a body of evidence presented to you for one bill or the other in the friendly atmosphere in which the administration, Senator Byrd and I are working, and we are working toward the same objective, we would like to know then, because we have thought this through very carefully and feel our way of approaching it would be best. We would like at least to have equal time to present our thinking on it if you would like that.

Could we have your comments that you would let us know?

Mr. EGGER. I certainly will, and we will be getting together with our task force here to go back over our points.

Senator PERCY. I agree with your statement on the top of page 12, that the President's bill drops the provisions that deal with congressional failure to act.

I urged the administration to again realistically look at S. 2812 and see if they cannot support this provision in this bill, and your general support for that approach, I think, is reassuring to us.

Mr. EGGER. We think there is good discipline in that approach.

Senator PERCY. Right. I think that discipline is absolutely essential and necessary given the way the Congress is set up.

I would like to ask Mr. Knox a question along this line. A major problem with many Government actions is there is not a sufficient degree of citizen involvement.

Certainly, Sears Roebuck has always reached out to the community and gotten people involved in things that affect the community.

How can we assure that adequate citizen participation will take place in the reform process?

We know the interest groups will be there. It is their job, and we want them to be there, but how can we get citizenship participation?

Now, it has been suggested that somehow it be supported or subsidized.

Is there some effective incentive you can think of to get citizen input added to the input of business groups, labor representatives, academia and think tanks so that we get the best analysis and best thinking we can in this country on how to go about analyzing and formulating our reform plans?

Mr. KNOX. Senator, we heartily agree with the objective of the broadest possible participation in this process, and in the rulemaking within the agencies and throughout the regulatory process.

I will have to offer the observation that I think citizen participation is at a very high level today and I think it's a very healthy thing when we agree with the point of view being advanced or not.

I am constantly impressed with not only the number but the caliber, ability, and effectiveness of people who spend a great deal of time here on behalf of citizen groups. They are doing so well that I do not know what else needs to be done to encourage it.

If there were any real impediment to this, it ought to be done away with, but I do not know that there is.

There is enormous alertness in the regulatory procedures in commenting on proposed regulations and participation in hearings, and I have found with some of these same groups there are areas in which we have substantial agreement, as we have, for example, on the regulatory reform provisions of the recent railroad legislation. We were impressed with the ability and the talent and the effectiveness of those people we worked with.

Senator PERCY. Mr. Friedman, as the staff director of the task force could resources of the chamber itself be used through its publications, its nationwide network of programs to alert citizens to the fact that now is the time for reform, here is the impact on you as consumers and as taxpayers and that you should become involved in the process now of helping us formulate our reform plans.

Can those resources be put to work to broaden the base of public understanding?

Mr. FRIEDMAN. Certainly, that is what we are trying to do.

Remember, you and Senator Ribicoff were on a recent chamber program with the president of the chamber talking about regulatory reform, and we intend to move forward with more programs and get out to the media with this kind of message.

That is our program for the next year.

Senator PERCY. I addressed the chamber of commerce at Woodstock, Illinois, on Friday. They were interested in regulatory reform. They wanted a program on it.

In the testimony that Senator Byrd and I gave, we developed a series of charts. I have now reduced those to slides, and they are available for showing at the U.S. Chamber of Commerce, or at any member chamber that wants them.

We will send you information on that and obviously, a script that goes right along with them and they could be adapted in any way you see fit.

A lot of it deals with the general prob'ems of regulation and we

Mr. KNOX. Senator, let me add one other point on this important will provide you as much information as we can.

subject of citizen participation in the regulatory process.

You will note that the touchstone of all of the testimony that we have offered this morning is that competition ought to be a vital part of every regulatory system.

In other words, unlike the proposed rules that Mr. Levitas described, they should not provide how many paper clips have to be used and that kind of detail.

A key part of every regulatory procedure should be the requirement, that we have suggested, that the manufacturer and the seller should have different ways of complying with the standards and procedures so that the consumer has a choice between manufacturers and sellers and the providers of services. The consumer should have a choice of the kinds of products with different features, rather than to have them narrowly defined. The consumer will take a very active part in the regulatory process because this kind of competition will provide the incentive for innovation, incentive for improvement, the incentive for providing effective and efficient distribution and marketing. Thus, the consumer can get price and competition for goods and services.

If there is anything that we have found in the present regulatory process that tends to deprive the consumer of a voice, it is the tendency in many of these statutes and mandatory procedures and their administration which denies the consumer his choice.

We think that in the short run, consumers make pretty good choices and in the long run they make very good choices. . . .

Senator PERCY. Do you support or oppose the notion of Congress reviewing all agency regulations before they become effective.

Could you explain briefly the reasons? I think possibly Mr. Egger and Mr. Knox might respond.

Mr. EGGER. I will say first as far as the Chamber is concerned, the Chamber did not take the position on those bills.

Senator Percy. That is why I am asking your personal opinion.

Mr. Egger. In our opinion, we all felt the problems of attempting to have Congress, in effect, duplicate the effort that is under our scheme intended to be carried out by the regulatory authorities is simply a duplication. The proper role of Congress ought to be simply to determine that the objectives which they sought in the original legislation are being carried out and not simply to carry each out and become the authority through which the objectives are carried out themselves.

I do not believe the Congress can do that.

Mr. Knox. Senator, while we did not address the bill specifically, I think the subject is what we are talking about in item 8 of the criteria we listed on page 4 of the testimony.

On balance, my own view is that the disadvantages of a one-House veto substantially outweigh the advantages. On the advantage side I think it is important to say that the Congress, through the number of these bills that have been introduced, shows a very commendable desire on the part of a lot of members of the Congress to assume a greater responsibility for the disappointing results of the regulatory process. It shows they want to more clearly involve themselves in giving the kind of direction to the agencies and the kind of establishing of priorities for the regulatory agencies that would make those results less dissapointing.

We are inclined to think that the application of the standards and the criteria that we suggested in our list would give the agencies the kind of direction that would decrease the need for the Congressional one-House veto. If it did not, then we would hope that it would provide the kind of a criterion as to what the basis should be for veto because those of us who have to take a position on proposed regulations or have to live with them will not quite know where we stand if there is a Congressional veto that does not really explain why the veto took place, or what the alternative should be or where do we go from there.

I am concerned about the problems that would be raised by it and on balance, would be inclined to oppose it, but certainly do feel very good about the interest of the Congress in taking a look at what happens to the regulatory experience.

All of us have had the disappointing feeling of talking to a member of the Congress or the Senate who is involved in drafting legislation and having the member shake his head and say, "well, that is not what we intended when we sent that bill downtown."

That does not help us a lot in living with the results.

Senator Percy. Congress undid through legislation one of the most unpopular regulations in recent years involving the interlocking seatbelts, but I am not sure that we should go through the whole legislative process in order to do something like that.

If you can in your deliberations come up with any easier way to do it, this record will be kept open so that you can make such suggestions to us.

Mr. Knox. One of our hopes is that it's the kind of criteria that we have suggested or other such criteria as the Congress determines are put in the bill, so that the agencies know what the Congress expects of them and we know what is expected of them. If they do not comply with that, there are options in the courts.

Senator Percy. I just have a few specific brief questions to find out whether you are in favor of having a periodic reevaluation of agency effectiveness in which the agency itself assumes the burden of proving the need of its continued existence and should the kind of procedure embodied in S. 2812 be repeated on a periodic basis so we do not have this as a one-shot deal?

Mr. EGGER. Our Task Force has not considered that point, but let me just offer something as a suggestion.

It seems to me imperative that there get built into each of the pieces of legislation authorizing regulatory action or directing regulatory action a fairly clearcut statement of the objectives to be achieved and these then could serve as the benchmark against which the agency's activities would be judged and the Congress has at its disposal several mechanisms through which that might be done.

One, of course, is the oversight of the appropriate committees having jurisdiction over that particular function.

Another might be the GAO in its expanded audit scope, undertaking a look and reporting back to the Congress as to the economy, efficiency and effectiveness under this new approach.

No. 1, we certainly agree, there has to be an ongoing look-see, whether or not it will take the form of going through this particular mechanism, I think is yet to be seen.

Surely, there has to be some continuing monitoring mechanism set up by the Congress so that the Congress cannot allow this kind of situation to develop again.

Mr. KNOX. I agree, Senator, and to use your phrase again about being part of the process of change, I think this is necessary.

If the economy changes, technology changes and consumer taste changes and even the wisest possible decisions could be looked at again at least every 5 years.

Senator PERCY. Finally, do you think that without the final so-called sunset provisions of S. 2812 the administration's bill would be a successful vehicle for overcoming opposition, and getting reform plans implementing rather than merely considered?

Mr. EGGER. We have seen time after time in which the Congress becomes effective in a sort of last-minute basis when they are up against a deadline and are up against a critical date of some sort. While we think that it would be nice if it would work some other way, our feeling is that by having this final sunset provision in here it becomes a means of assuring that some kind of action will take place before the critical date is reached.

We looked at this, of course, in connection with the proposal by the administration which does not include that, and we felt on balance, as our testimony indicates here, that we would like to see it stay in.

Senator PERCY. I have just a closing comment on your recommendation to allow the President to choose the order in which he will submit reform plans by having him select one of the areas each year.

In the administration's bill, they have already selected the order they want. They made that decision and that is why I would like to know whether you support their approach or the Percy-Byrd approach or if you can think of a third one which is even better. We are seeking the one that is the most effective and the one that is the most logical if it is at all possible to find logic in this situation.

I thank you once again for an absolutely magnificent job. You were right out in the forefront on this and moved before any other organization in the country on it, and I think that is why your testimony today has been so detailed and so very effective.

OPPOSITION AND PRESENTATION OF ALTERNATIVES BY PUBLIC CITIZENS' CONGRESS WATCH ([73], pp. 172–181)

During the Senate committee hearings, opposition to the Percy-Byrd bill was expressed in statements submitted by a public interest body known as Public Citizens' Congress Watch. Its objections to the bill included a lack of citizen participation and an anticipated flood of paperwork. The statements, which posed alternatives as well as registered objections, were not followed by questions or debate. The views of Congress Watch, or some variant of them, are applicable to much of the reform legislation and undoubtedly will be expressed again as future action-forcing reform legislation is considered.

Mr. Chairman, members of the Committee, my name is Joan Claybrook and I am director of Public Citizen's Congress Watch, a public interest organization concerned with the impact of government and corporate policies on citizens. With me is David Lenny, Congress Watch staff attorney. We appreciate the invitation to testify today on regulatory reform proposals before the Committee.

Regulatory reform, like just about everything else in a presidential election year, is all things to all people, a handy tool for impossible promises and symbolic gestures which alienate no one. President Ford promises to get the government off the back of business, which is code for a moritorium on health and safety protections ranging from clean air requirements to pesticide or drug clearances, while the massive subsidies and loan guarantees continue to flow from the public trough into corporate pocketbooks.

Former Governor Carter says he is going to reduce 1,900 agencies to 200. putting all consumer programs into one agency. Is he suggesting that we combine the Food and Drug Administration, the Federal Trade Commission, the Consumer Product Safety Commission, the National Highway Traffic Safety Administration and many others into one monstrous and probably useless one-stop shopping center for industry lobbyists?

And Governor Brown claims he is going to reduce government and lower our expectations—which means he will have to exclude the airline, railroad, trucking, agribusiness, nuclear, and many other industries from the breadline of tax-payer handouts where they have fed for too long.

The fact underlying all the rhetoric is that the politicians are responding, however simplistically, to voters dissatisfied with a national government which has grown ineffective and wasteful; has fallen captive to the special pleading economic interests, has bullied or ignored citizens and has become remote. secretive and unresponsive. At the same time, citizen disenchantment with corporate misfeasance has mushroomed in the face of corrupt business practices, illegal payoffs. concentrated market power, arrogant disregard for necessary safety precautions which deny consumer choice, and the vast distance between the producer and the aggrieved user.

The question before the Congress is whether this popular mandate to reform and repair wasteful or ill-conceived programs will spark government activities to serve the people or become an excuse to service the special interest lawyers and lobbyists who have laid siege to Washington, DC and set up camp in the White House.

Senator Percy and Senator Byrd have proposed—and President Ford has partially mimicked—a bill (S. 2812) with a specific timetable for review of federal regulatory agency activity. While the establishment of a firm deadline to combat legislature inertia is appealing, we see a number of deficiencies in the proposals, and a fundamental problem in treating all type of regulatory reassessment exactly alike.

1. DISTINCTION BETWEEN CARTEL AND SAFETY REGULATIONS

As has been mentioned in prior testimony before this committee and others, proposals for oversight of government regulations must distinguish between wasteful cartel regulation and life-saving consumer health and safety regulation. The distinction applies particularly to "sunset" proposals which wipe out an agency's authority unless it is reenacted. The powerful trucking industry, for example, obstructs attempts to remove Interstate Commerce regulations which coddle the industry. It maintains its preferential treatment by messaging Congress with campaign contributions, receptions, honoraria, and other goodies over a long period of years. In view of the slim likelihood that Congress will limit federal advantages for attentive industries, a time deadline for Congressional action can be useful.

But the constituency outside the Congress which favors continued regulation of the drug industry, for example, is a diverse and unorganized 200 million individuals whose interests are advocated, if at all, by a few citizens groups. If Congress considered narrowing the scope of a health or safety agency, the regulated industry would immediately lend a hand, but the consumers, the intended beneficiaries of health and safety programs, would lose what little influence and protection they have and government would become more fully than ever the captive of the greedy, the monied, and the powerful. The prompt removal of the mandatory seat belt interlock system (originally suggested by Henry Ford to avoid installation of passive restraints but systematically blamed on consumers) can be contrasted with the long delays in moving toward airline deregulation, for example.

Furthermore, logic dictates a distinction for consumers in the marketplace between economic regulation, and health and safety protections. Consumers can readily tell the difference between an airline ticket which costs $20 and one which costs $30 to the same destination. For this they don't need a CAB. But consumers cannot discern cancerous additives or pesticides in food, defects in cars, radiation in television sets, mutagens in drugs, flammability in apparel, and cannot avoid compulsory consumption such as pollution in the air or contaminants in water. For such products with hidden dangers which travel in interstate commerce, the only defense for consumers is the establishment and enforcement of minimum federal standards.

The Percy/Byrd bill appears to acknowledge this distinction by preserving rules which safeguard public safety, free and unregulated economic competition, or consumer interests where Congress disapproves a presidential reform plan but fails to enact its own. True to form, the White House bill does not make such a distinction. The aggressive efforts being made by the regulated industries to extract themselves from federal health and safety requirements, however make it questionable whether this provision will survive Congressional enactment, and if it is broadly construed, it could nullify the intent of the bill.

In view of the profound need for health and safety protection in the marketplace, the practical realities of an unorganized constituency, and the loquacious tendencies of Senator James Allen about consumer legislation, the health and safety agencies should clearly not be subject to the arbitrary deadlines set out in the bill. Enactment of such a law would crystallize Senator Allen's greatest dream—to filibuster all consumer health and safety programs into oblivion in one fell swoop.

Also to be considered as to the other programs is the question of whether a variety of remedies besides disappearance of all rules—such as a reduced budget, annual authorizations, zero-based budget, prohibition on any *new* regulations—should be available in the event there is a deadlock in the Congressional reform activity.

2. DEADLINES TOO SHORT

The deadlines for congressional action on the multitude of agencies to be considered each year are far too short. While specific deadlines allow for advance preparation, it cannot be ignored that all the President's proposals will have to be cleared by the Office of Management and Budget (which has numerous other responsibilities). For 1978, 1979, and 1980, most of the agencies slotted for review fall within the jurisdiction of the House and Senate Commerce Committees, imposing a mammoth workload, displacing virtually all other legislative activity, and requiring a tripling of the staff. The result will have to be a rubber stamping instead of detailed analysis of many of the President's proposals, this undermining the primary purpose of the bill—thorough Congressional review of executive branch agencies. Also, the bill's short deadlines gives those who would filibuster the upper hand by permitting them to scuttle the Congressional recommendations in favor of the Presidential plan with a filibuster which can be ended only by the votes of 60 Senators.

3. SIMULTANEOUS FLOOR CONSIDERATION EXCLUDES PUBLIC REPRESENTATIVES

The bill's requirement that the committee recommendations be sent to the House and Senate floors by the same date will exclude public interest representatives from adequate expression of their views; there are only a few lobbyists for the people and they cannot be in two places at once. The thoughtful "perrolation" time available in most legislative activity as a bill moves from one house to the other is eliminated.

4. FAILURE TO AFFECT REGULATORY POWER STRUCTURE

The bill does not attempt to deal with the power structure of the regulatory agencies. While directing that reform plans primarily consider organization deficiencies, the bill fails to require consideration of such problems as: the massive failure of government agencies to enforce present law and regulations; the concentration of market power resulting from regulatory agency protections; special exemptions for favored companies; the absence of citizen participation in the regulatory process; the interlock between business leaders and government regulators; the totally unnecessary secrecy in agency proceedings and information; insufficient funding of health and safety agencies; the appointment of ineffective administrators; administrators which promote a special interest.

5. NO PROVISION FOR CITIZEN PARTICIPATION

Another missing element in the legislation is any consideration of the need to assure citizen participation in the preparation and review of the reform plans. Whether citizens can effectively participate in such a process depends on whether there is money available to pay the expenses of such participation. Acknowledging the fundamental proposition that part of the cost of doing the business of government is the cost of assuring citizen participation, this bill should include an authorization for reimbursement to citizens for the cost of reviewing, studying and recommending proposals for reform of federal regulatory agencies which affect the daily lives of every Amercian citizen.

Regulatory reform must not be confined to a shuffling around of the boxes on an organizational chart. Any basic review of the responsiveness of federal regulatory agencies to the needs of the people must recognize the importance of citizen oversight as well as Congressional oversight. Increasingly, citizens have recognized that the survival of a humane and ethical society is dependent upon the ability of the citizenry to reassert its will in the marketplace and in the forum of government. Congressional delegation of authority to regulatory agencies to enforce and protect fundamental rights without citizen oversight is structurally flawed. The complexities spawned by multinational corporate entities and national government demand the fashioning of new tools to make government and business decision-makers accountable to the rights and legitimate needs of the people and to spark direct citizen action for enforcement of these rights. Mr. Lenny will describe some of these proposals which are an instrumental facet of regulatory reform.

STATEMENT OF DAVID M. LENNY, ATTORNEY, CONGRESS WATCH STAFF, A PUBLIC INTEREST ORGANIZATION

As this committee readily acknowledged, by its passage of S. 200, regulatory reform cannot be accomplished by cosmetic cure-alls parading as citizen involvement in government decision making. When we talk about new tools for government and business accountability, we are not referring to the cynical nod to consumer interests that is the sum total of President Ford's programs for consumers. The importance of citizen participation in government policymaking has been systematically ignored by this Administration, and its sole acknowledgement of the need to encourage citizens to present their interests to federal agencies was its so-called "consumer representation plans."

The bureaucratic, mumbo-jumbo ("input," "thruput," "output") of consumer representation plans reluctantly drafted by the 17 executive agencies were published in the Federal Register on November 26, 1975. If the few valuable proposals buried in these plans are implemented they will cost enormous amounts of money in spite of Presidential disclaimers. In the meantime they serve as a useful diversionary device behind which federal bureaucrats can yawn and continue their disregard for the interests of consumers.

Structurally, these plans are empty. They are hortatory at best. They do not create, acknowledge or even recommend any specific rights for consumers. They do not contain any independent authority to assure effective or forceful presentation and advocacy of consumer interests. They do not give any consumer representative the right to subpoena information if needed to carry out his/her authority. They do not assure consumers will have a voice in the multitude of agency decisions which affect their every day lives. They do not authorize consumer representatives to seek judicial review of an arbitrary agency decision adverse to consumers. Most importantly, they are not sufficient because they fail to alter the balance of power between the regulated industries and the general public. This imbalance of power will be altered only when regulatory agencies become accountable to the public interest they're designed to protect. We have identified several necessary changes in the structure of federal agencies which, if adopted, would sufficiently alter this balance of power in most agencies (more effectively than some of the more drastic reform bills) including:

CREATION OF AN AGENCY FOR CONSUMER ADVOCACY

Federal agencies daily make decisions affecting the interests of consumers in which consumers have no voice. This agency (created by S.200 and H.R. 7575, both of which have passed their respective houses) would be an independent advocate within the Executive Branch to represent the interests of consumers before the agencies and in the courts, and would be a central clearinghouse for consumers.

CITIZENS' ACCESS TO COURTS

Federal agencies too often disobey the law and take actions subservient to special interests. Yet, when citizens attempt to challenge such practices in court, they are rebuffed for lack of standing to sue. For example, agencies have given away valuable government patents to private industry although the Constitution clearly prohibits the practice as the lower found before the Court of Appeals dismissed for lack of standing. The Senate currently has before it two bills which would alter the rules in order to make illegal agency acts subject to citizens' challenge in the courts. S. 3295, introduced by Senator Kennedy, would allow any interested person to challenge an illegal agency action in court, and S. 495, already passed by this Committee, would have allowed Congressional standing to challenge such activities before the section permitting such suits was eliminated in full committee.

CIVIL SERVICE ACCOUNTABILITY

Initiatory rights for civil service accountability which allow aggrieved consumers, taxpayers and citizens to challenge the tenure of the civil servant or political appointee and to urge, in proper forum and with due process, the suspension, resignation, demotion or fine of employees who arbitrarily refuse to enforce the law or engage in waste or harassment.

REIMBURSEMENT FOR CITIZEN PARTICIPATION

Citizens are frequently unable to participate in federal agency decisions because of the cost involved. Bills such as S. 2715 provide compensation for costs of participation by citizen representatives in administrative and judicial proceedings where the participant would present meritorious views not otherwise represented.

Numerous other such reforms which would cover all federal agencies and which are already moving through the congressional process are detailed in the attached memorandum of April 1975, which was prepared for initial Congressional inquiries into reform proposals. It is presented here for the record.

In addition to these structural reforms of federal agencies currently in progress, there are several items now before Congress which would both add to citizen initiatory rights for assisting the government in regulating industry, rather than have all such initiatives come from the government itself, and which would give consumers needed tools to monitor corporate activities in the marketplace. These include: Authority to aggregate many small but identical claims in consumer class actions; authority to share in the penalties imposed on corporate law violators in return for bringing the action; creation of viable small claims courts; facilitating funding for development and expansion of local consumer cooperatives; and systematic methods for raising funds for citizens to oversee state-granted monopolies, such as through a voluntary check-off on periodic (monthly) bills.

These several items would lessen the need for government regulation, one of the most important reasons for the adoption of S. 2812 cited by the sponsors, by giving citizens the means through which they can "regulate" industry abuses themselves.

Even if the several reforms we have suggested, reforms which would alter the current state of affairs at all federal agencies, were not adopted, there are still other procedures Congress has at its disposal to alter harmful agency practices. With timely use of these procedures, Congress could enact limited but immediate changes pending completion of the various regulatory studies and allow time for thorough consideration of the scope and mandate of S. 2812.

As examples of these procedures, Congress has just recently refined several methods of controlling all federal agencies which are only now being implemented. The most important of these is the *appropriations process*. If Congress is displeased with a particular policy, it can merely amend the appropriation bill for that agency so that funds may not be used for a particular purpose. Two recent examples of this procedure illustrate its effectiveness. In one case, the House amended the Conference Report on HEW appropriations to forbid the Department from spending any money to enforce the sex integration of physical education classes which HEW had mandated by regulation. (See the *New York Times*, 4/17/75, p. 26, col. 1). In another case, Congress wrote into the Environmental Protection Agency's appropriation that they could not spend any money to enforce parking surcharges to discourage consumption of fuel by commuters driving to work. As EPA Administrator Russell Train said, "If you're not allowed to spend money on a program, legally you can't pursue the program." *Washington Post*, 4/21/76, p. 2-21, col. 6. Withdrawal of funding for agency actions Congress thinks are unjustified assures that such actions coincide with the will of Congress. The only obstacle preventing the use of this mechanism is Congress itself—an obstacle that will not be cured by "mandating" reform.

A second key method of controlling. thus reforming, federal agencies is through the *appointments process*. It is conceded by almost everyone that the effect a federal agency will have largely depends on the people who run it—that often the people count more than th details of the enacting statutes. As the Landis Report to the President-Elect suggested over 15 years ago. "The prime key to the improvement of the administration process is the selection of qualified personnel. Good men can make poor laws workable; poor men will wreak havoc with good laws."

To improve the method by which the Senate handles the nomination approval process, the Senate Commerce and Government Operations Committees and the House Oversight and Investigations Subcommittee participated in a November, 1975, symposium on the Quality of Regulatory Appointments. From this seminar, two distinct methods of improving the quality of appointees were developed. One proposal involved legislation incorporating criteria the President should use in making appointments, such as advance precautions against conflicts of interest, limits upon selection from a single part, provision for decision from a collegial body rather than a single party, provision for decision from a collegial body rather than a single administrator, and mandatory use of judicial standards. A second proposal involved procedures the committees approving appointments should use in evaluating presidential appointees, such as forcing public disclosure of financial statements of nominees, submitting detailed interrogatories to the nominees, increased advance notice of hearings on nominees to give outside organizations an opportunity to comment, and formulating criteria the nominees should meet before being accepted by the Senate. These would include expertise in the specific subject matter covered by the agency, administrative competency, demonstrated independence of various pressure groups the agency would be expected to encounter, sensitivity to consumer and minority needs, and the like. Together, these standards should in the future far greater competence in administrative appointees than has heretofore been the case.

Increased *congressional oversight* will also contribute greatly to reform of administrative agencies. Congress has just begun funding and encouraging oversight activities, and a first order of business for both House and Senate oversight committees has been regulatory reform, as evidenced by these very hearings. This process, taken seriously by Congress, done in a comprehensive fashion and conducted on a regular basis, with more available staff, could provide the regular review of federal agencies which has thus far not occurred and which has prompted the introduction of numerous regulatory reform bills.

The need for reform of regulatory agencies is widely recognized. The necessity for careful and thoughtful action in this area must also be recognized. The combination of increased use of the appropriations power, careful consideration of nominations, and oversight review, combined with the various structural reforms mentioned, would accomplish much of the regulatory reform envisioned by the sponsors of bills before this Committee.

Arguments Against a Statutory Power of Congressional Veto of Agency Rules

(By David M. Lenny)

The congressional veto is a product of the recent surge in efforts to reform federal agencies and to end unnecessary and counterproductive regulation. Yet it is clear from the mass of regulations Congress will have to consider as well as the confusion, delay, uncertainty and potential Constitutional problems that Congress would not reduce government, but increase its burden. The difficulties raised by a congressional veto over agency regulations will only add another layer of government between a problem and its solution, and could possibly slow other, more useful attempts to restructure and streamline federal agencies.

An even-handed, consistent evaluation of the regulations subject to a Congressional veto would require that each Committee have its staff review virtually every regulation, with the accompanying volumes of hearing records, which falls under its jurisdiction. But because of the large number of regulations issued every day, it is inevitable that only a few rules will receive Congressional attention. Because there are no criteria laid out for the selection of these few rules those private groups with the most political influence will bring enormous pressure to bear for a veto of rules they don't favor. With the multimillion dollar budget and other resources that the oil industry, banks, National Association of Manufacturers, Chamber of Commerce, and others have available to guide any legislation affecting them, these groups will have a considerable influence on Congress as it determines which regulations should be challenged. Thus, if Congress does not review all rules promulgated by Federal agencies, Congress will abdicate responsibility for choosing regulations which need consideration to private interests.

On the other hand, review of all regulations promulgated by agencies is also undesirable. Under the existing procedures for oversight of federal agencies, Congress has wisely focused its attention on questions of whether the agency has been tenacious and effective in carrying out its statutory mission. A comprehensive review of all the detailed regulations which each agency has promulgated would be extremely time consuming without comparable accompanying benefit. In the course of 10 working days, over 250 separate regulations adopted by administrative agencies are printed in the Federal Register, and each of these rules is supported by hearing records which include volumes of substantive materials. In a single FTC rulemaking proceeding, for example, these documents comprised a record of over 30,000 pages.

ALTERNATIVES TO THE CONGRESSIONAL VETO

Proponents of a Congressional veto imply it is the only way the policies of federal agencies can be adequately reviewed and controlled. This is simply not true, as the variety of alternative means for controlling agencies illustrate:

Congress should *amend, rewrite* or *revoke* legislation which is unworkable—not subject it to piecemeal scrapping by Congressional veto of individual regulations issued to implement the law. In fact, Congress has just done this with respect to motorcycle helmet requirements which the National Highway Traffic Safety Administration had sought to impose on the states, and which Congress has specifically prohibited the agency from putting into effect. See Section 208 (A) of Public Law 94-290.

Greater *Congressional oversight* is imperative. It should be comprehensive and conducted on a regular basis, with specific staff assigned to review agency actions. The importance and potential effectiveness of regular oversight was recognized by the Senate as its recent approval of a permanent committee to oversee intelligence activities illustrates. Energetic oversight, by itself, can provide Congress with the capacity to reign over a wayward or capricious bureaucracy.

Stricter standards for the *appointment process* must be developed. The present tone and format of many configuration proceedings suggest that the Senate can only reject the nominated appointee if the Senate can show that the nominee has acted illegally or immorally. Instead, the Senate should shift the burden to the nominees, requiring them to demonstrate that they are qualified for the particular office to which they have been nominated. Both the Senate and House should include in statutes creating appointive positions the particular qualifications which the nominee must satisfy, including relevant experience, full financial disclosures, the placing of assets in "blind" trusts, and the absence of any conflicting ties with the industries or groups to be regulated.

Expanding the opportunities for *judicial review* of agency actions would increase accountability of federal agency actions. Provisions for greater access to the courts for citizens to challenge illegal agency actions, and for a Congressional counsel to permit legislators to file suit to enjoin unlawful agency actions, would guarantee agency behavior that more closely follows Congressional mandates. Citizens should also be reimbursed through attorney and expert witness fees for participation in agency proceedings where they represent a small economic interest and in judicial review of agency actions where the citizen substantially prevails.

Through its control of the *authorizations* for the federal agencies, Congress has a potent tool for dealing with recalcitrant agencies which persist in circumventing Congressional policies. Wtihdrawal of funding authority for actions that Congress thinks are unjustified can ensure agency actions that coincide with the will of Congress.

Finally, Congress should place greater reliance on the *appropriations process*. A few examples suggest that this instrument can be quite effective in controlling agency actions. The House amended the Conference Report on HEW appropriations to forbid expenditure of money to enforce sex integration of physical education classes which HEW has mandated by regulation. Congress also prevented EPA from spending its appropriations to enforce parking surcharges to discourage consumption of fuel by commuters driving to work. As EPA Administrator Russell Train said, "If you're not allowed to spend money on a program, legally you can't pursue the program."

IT WOULD CREATE INCREDIBLE PROBLEMS IN IMPLEMENTING AGENCY RULES

The *effective date and substance* of the final, approved rule will remain totally *uncertain* for months after it has been promulgated:

It is *unclear which rules are subject to a veto.* Some Congressional veto statutes do not cover rules of "agency organization, practice, and procedure" or rules "granting or recognizing an exception or relieving a restriction." Neither Congress nor the courts have indicated or will know with greater specificity or certainty what kinds of rules would be vetoed.

It is *uncertain when the veto is to take effect.* The veto is effective after "90 days during which Congress is in session," but if 90 working days are not accumulated prior to the end of the session, the 90 day countdown must start anew. Delay and uncertainty are compounded because in counting "90 days," 3 day recesses, vacations, election and convention breaks further delay and confuse the process.

It is *unclear which provisions of the rule will take effect.* Since the rule can be sent back for agency reconsideration by either house instead of subjecting it to a veto, the individuals or groups affected by the regulation cannot even be sure that the substantive provisions of the regulation will remain unchanged.

The procedure adds substantial *delay* to the regulatory process. Any measure for regulatotry reform should reduce rather than increase the impediments that delay agency activities.

Agencies will *shift to case by case adjudication*, a time-consuming, duplicative and burdensome approach rather than formulate rules which would be subject to Congressional veto.

Those opposed to the rules *may no longer desire to participate at the agency level*, since it may be more productive to reserve their primary efforts to seeking a Congressional veto.

Because of the time limits found in most statutes authorizing judicial review, aggrieved parties will be forced to file for judicial review before Congressional veto activity is completed, thus *wasting the time of litigants and courts* concerning a rule eventually vetoed. To correct this deficiency it would be necessary to postpone judicial review, and the ultimate fate of the regulation, for as much as an additional year, thus adding delay, making an accurate effective date for a regulation impossible.

IT WILL COST AMERICAN BUSINESS MILLIONS

The incredible delay, uncertainty and confusion caused by this procedure will inevitably cost businesses money. If a business begins to comply with a regulation after it is promulgated, the expense may prove wasted if the rule is vetoed. Or, if they wait for completion of the veto process instead, the cost of complying rises during the delay. Informing Congress of industry views could become a potential nightmare to any business planner: first in Congress as the bill is passed, then at the agency level as a rule is considered during the veto process, then possibly back to the agency if Congress votes to force agency reconsideration, then back to Congress, then to the courts for judicial review.

IT VIOLATES THE CONSTITUTIONAL PRINCIPLE OF SEPARATION OF POWERS

Antonio Scalia, deputy attorney general, Department of Justice, has testified on behalf of the Administration that this bill is unconstitutional in two ways: it violates the doctrine of the separation of powers, and contravenes specific provisions of Article I of the Constitution (Section 7, clauses 2 and 3) which the Department believes specifically forbids Congressional review devices such as the veto. No additional questionably constitutional veto provisions should be adopted until this issue can be tested in the courts, as President Ford has said he intends to do.

IT WILL GIVE LOBBYISTS A "SECOND CHANCE" AT UNDERMINING FEDERAL LAWS WHEN THEY FAILED TO STOP THE LEGISLATION ON ORIGINAL PASSAGE

Once this procedure is adopted, the lobbying forces which actively fought to defeat strong health, safety, antitrust, credit discrimination, environmental and other socially desirable pieces of legislation, yet failed to weaken them on original passage, will march back to Capitol Hill to legislation already passed by Congress. The hearings on this legislation are continuously laced with claims that the Occupational Safety and Health Administration (OSHA) and the Environmental Protection Agency (EPA) regulations have a different effect than envisioned when Congress wrote the original acts. There is an abundance of handwriting over the constituency mail spawned by OSHA regulations being enforced in small business establishments. And yet the legislative history of OSHA shows that *all* legislative attempts to differentiate between small and large businesses were defeated by Congress; the legislation unequivocably expressed the legislative intent that *all employees deserved to be protected* against unsafe working conditions no matter how many employees the employer had hired. The remedy for legislators' unhappiness with OSHA or EPA regulations is to amend the act, not to veto the regulations.

IT WOULD SERIOUSLY HAMPER PUBLIC PARTICIPATION IN RULEMAKING

Under the current tax laws, many groups with expertise in certain areas who actively participate in agency-level proceedings are prohibited from lobbying because their funding comes from tax-deductible contributions. Thus, although they may participate at the agency proceedings, the views of these groups could not be made to legislators when a veto of a rule is being considered. By contrast, profit-making businesses may deduct their expenses for lobbying Congress as well as for participating in agency proceedings at an incalculable cost to the Treasury.

Members of the general public, including public interest organizations, operate on extremely limited budgets, which will have to be stretched twice as far if rules are considered by Congress as well as by the agencies. Because non-tax-deductible dollars are so difficult to raise, there are very few public interest lobby groups, and with their meager funds, they will be forced to choose between expending their resources on legislation or Congressional veto activity.

IT ACTUALLY MAY REDUCE ACCOUNTABILITY OF FEDERAL AGENCIES

In practical terms, the Congressional oversight resulting from this legislation constitutes an incomplete look at individual regulations, instead of a coordinated policy review of the agency's overall activities. Oversight on a case-by-case basis neglects the long-range policies and decisions with which Congress ought to concern itself. Use of the Congressional veto will result in a dilution of the effects of Congressional oversight, as committees become bogged down with reviewing a morass of particular regulations.

IT WILL CREATE ENORMOUS ADDITIONAL ADMINISTRATIVE BURDENS FOR CONGRESS

Having decided broad public policy issues, Congress has repeatedly and prudently delegated the day-to-day decisions for implementation to federal agencies. These agencies have the staff and technical expertise to develop comprehensive and specific regulations on matters which are often highly specialized and complex, including the safety standards of airplanes, health standards for drugs or the permissible language to be used on a limited warranty. Congress has neither the personnel nor the expertise to review these regulations: the amount of time required to read, let alone adequately evaluate, these regulations is beyond the capacity of a legislative body as presently staffed and structured.

IT CANNOT FORCE MORE OVERSIGHT FROM THE SAME STAFF RESOURCES

The Congressional veto bills imply that merely authorizing the Congressional veto will result in incraesed agency accountability and more effective Congressional oversight. This is a false promise: no greater oversight can ensue without provisions for additional staff positions. Only a perfunctory examination of the multitude of rules subject to the veto is likely to result, and even to accomplish this, many other issues will have to be given short shrift.

If the veto legislation remedied this deficiency providing for more staff members for oversight functions, it would also render the veto provision superfluous because the additional staff should be sufficient to remedy the failures attributed to the current efforts of the various committees which now oversee federal agencies.

IT WILL INVITE "WHOLESALE POLITICIZATION" OF FEDERAL AGENCIES

Federal agencies are formed for the technical expertise they lend to problems and solutions, and independent regulatory agencies are created primarily to provide such expertise and also some insulation from political influence on federal decision making. Both these benefits are lost when agency actions are subjected to the politically influenced and cursory examination likely to result from the hurried Congressional veto process. Agency rules will reflect the viewpoint of the most powerful lobbyists and pressure groups, since the agency will strive to avoid their opposition to a rule under the Congressional veto process and will weaken the rule to accommodate opposition. The regulations which will result from such politicization will reflect the lowest common denominator of all potential political objections, and will tend to result in innocuous half-steps toward problem-solving, disappointing all parties concerned.

THE CONGRESSIONAL VETO WILL ADD ANOTHER LAYER OF BUREAUCRACY TO CONGRESSIONAL OVERSIGHT

Under current procedures, final validation of agency regulations is completed at the agency level after comprehensive hearings, tests and extensive testimony by the public and government officials. The Congressional veto provisions would require a wasteful and redundant repetition of this information-gathering process at the Congressional level as well, since the whole show would shift to Congress when the rule comes up for review. Thus, instead of controlling the growth of bureaucracy, this procedure just adds to it.

THE PROBLEMS SOUGHT TO BE REMEDIED DO NOT JUSTIFY THIS PROCEDURE

The provisions of the proposed Congressional veto will result in wasteful redundancy, extensive time delays, additional burdens on oversight committees, and prolonged uncertainty. Such extraordinary procedures could only be justified by extraordinary needs and problems. Yet, a detailed reading of the hearing record on the Congressional veto produces few examples of the need for this procedure. Rather, one finds example after example of agency regulations with which various interests were displeased which currently-available means of challenging the rule could resolve. These include appropriations, amendments or judicial review which often were not even attempted or, when they were, were successful.

For further information on the Congressional veto, contact DAVE LENNY or JAMES HUMPHREYS, Congress Watch, 13 3C Street, SE, Washington, D.C., 20003, (202) 546-4936. 6/76.

NOTES AND REFERENCES

1. Zero-base budgeting requires a periodic review (e.g., every two years, every four years) of agency programs and activities to justify every dollar, from zero upward, sought in future appropriations for both existing and proposed programs. It is discussed in detail in Part III.

2. The Congressional Office of Regulatory Policy Oversight Act of 1976 (S. 2878) was introduced by Senators Jacob Javits and Edmund Muskie on January 27, 1976. It called for the creation of a congressional oversight office to analyze the impact of regulatory action and to develop recommendations for improving the effectiveness and efficiency of regulatory agency activities. Prior to this, on July 31, 1975, Senator William Brock introduced S. 2258, which provided for congressional review of agency rules and regulations during a 60-day period and which authorized veto over such regulations. Senator Sam Nunn's November 20, 1975 legislation of the Regulatory Limitation Act of 1975 (S. 2716) was similar to S. 2258. The texts of the three bills are available in [73], pp. 339 ff.

3. The *Yale Law Journal* article appears in the hearing transcript ([73], p. 16). The shorter summary reprinted here, "The Fallacy of Regulatory Independence," was submitted to the committee by Lloyd Cutler when he testified.

4. The federal agencies with primary responsibility for energy matters are the Energy Research and Development Administration, Federal Energy Administration, Federal Power Commission, Nuclear Regulatory Commission, and the Department of the Interior. A 1976 congressional study on reorganizing the energy agencies is partially reprinted in the appendix.

5. In his testimony, Lloyd Cutler cites the Congressional Office of the Budget; its official name is the Congressional Budget Office (CBO). The CBO was established in 1974 to provide Congress with basic budget data. Among its responsibilities are economic forecasting and fiscal policy analysis; preparation of an annual report on the budget; and special studies on budget-related areas, undertaken at the request of Congress.

6. The Administrative Conference of the United States was established in 1964 by Congress as a permanent, independent agency. Its purpose is to develop improvements in the legal procedures, by which federal agencies administer regulatory, benefit, and other government programs.

7. The sunset concept establishes an automatic termination date for government programs and/or agencies if their continuation is not justified within a periodic review process. It is discussed in Chapter 6. Senator Edmund Muskie's bill, the Government Economy and Spending Reform Act of 1976, which contains a sunset provision, is the subject of Chapter 8.

8. Senator Charles Percy is referring to the text of Roscoe Egger's prepared statement, submitted to the committee in advance. It is a common practice for witnesses to submit prepared statements prior to their appearance before a committee.

PART III

SUNSET CONCEPT AND ZERO-BASE REVIEW: REORGANIZATION THROUGH MANAGEMENT PROCESS

Introduction

Part III addresses the sunset concept and zero-base budget review procedures. They are the only sweeping, governmentwide federal reorganization concepts being widely discussed as President Jimmy Carter begins his new administration. They have dominated public debate on oversight and cost control of the federal bureaucracy. Because of their importance and applicability to both departmental reorganization and regulatory reform, they are being treated in a separate part in this volume. The sunset concept and zero-base review are management tools, representing reorganization through the management process. This process is a means by which government entities are periodically reviewed and reassessed through a set of management procedures; it is an ongoing process.

The sunset concept establishes an automatic termination date (sundown) for government programs and/or agencies if their continuation is not jusitfied within a periodic review procedure. This action-forcing mechanism was adopted first in Colorado in 1976. It quickly spread to other states and sparked bipartisan interest at the federal level. The responsible committees of the 94th Congress recommended sunset legislation that would apply to most congressionally authorized federal programs, but it was not enacted.

Zero-base budgeting is a system that requires each program expenditure to be reviewed from the ground up and allows examination of alternative funding increments, in comparison with anticipated program benefit increments. Each activity within an administrative structure is identified and described in terms of a "decision package," providing a programmatic administrative accounting system. The practice was first instituted in state government in 1971 by Jimmy Carter as governor of Georgia, and it was a significant element in the reorganization legislation considered by the 94th Congress.

Part III provides a documentary review of the background and status of proposals to install sunset and zero-base review at the federal level. The perception of the issues and the status of related legislation are reviewed, followed by chapters in which state level experience is recounted. The major pending legislative initiative is described and evaluated, and federal officials discuss the problems of implementation within the federal structure. Since there is no federal level experience with sunset–zero-base budgeting, the editors have selected documents on the state experience. Included also are the views of various experts as to how these reorganization tools might be adapted to the federal level. Most of the material in the chapters on sunset and zero-base budgeting assume congressional implementation of these action-forcing mechanisms. That is a presumption followed during the Ford administration, whose interest in reorganization was not great, judging from the few proposals presented.

The Carter administration could choose to have the Executive branch, most likely the Office of Management and Budget, assume or share in the task of administering sunset and zero-base budget procedures. The staffing and documentation implication of governmentwide use of these procedures is significant and Congress has not traditionally engaged in such detailed oversight. Any assumption of management responsibility by the Congress would require a major re-orientation. The recent entry of Congress into budget review represents a step in that direction, but the several million dollars and several hundred professionals involved in that effort are small compared to the requirements of a detailed zero-base budget examination of all government programs.[1] The management implications of these two approaches, as well as their effect on the balance of power between the Legislative and Executive branches, have yet to be discussed fully in the hearings on sunset and zero-base procedures. They will undoubtedly cause controversy in future debates.

1. The 1974 congressional decision to exercise close oversight on the budget resulted in the creation of new budgetary committees in the House and Senate, as well as the establishment of the Congressional Budget Office. The CBO is a service body related to both houses in much the same manner as the Library of Congress and the General Accounting Office. Its purpose is to provide Congress with basic budget data. A description of CBO appears in the appendix section of this volume.

OVERVIEW ([53], pp. 1–7)

Background and Analysis

In the continuing effort to fulfill Congress's oversight responsibilities, statutorily authorized in the Legislative Reorganization Act of 1946 and 1970, members are increasingly attentive to proposals which would set a time limit on the effective operation of Executive branch agencies, groups of related agencies, or programs. Following the passage of such a statute in Colorado, known as the "sunset" law, various proposals of this type have been introduced at the Federal level and are currently pending before Congress....

The sunset policy concept may be defined as the statutory specification of a time when the effective operation of Executive Branch agencies, groups of related agencies, or programs will terminate. The purpose of sunset is to establish a system for Congressional review of Executive instrumentalities on a periodic basis while simultaneously providing an incentive to the administrators of the entities to explain past performance.

On Apr. 22, 1976, Colorado enacted the first sunset law, which scheduled the periodic termination of various components of the Colorado Department of Regulatory Agencies. The effect of the Colorado law is to arrange for the "sun to set" on the agencies so as to provide for a mandatory review of their operations by the General Assembly. The review process was designed to be both an ongoing oversight arrangement and a method for possible reorganization of Colorado's 43 regulatory boards, divisions, and commissions, of which 36 are occupational licensing boards. The General Assembly's implementation of the sunset concept may be expressed simply: authorizations for one third of all the affected agencies are terminated every 2 years, hence giving an agency an authorization period of 6 years. Prior to the termination, continuation, or reestablishment of any such agency, a committee of reference in each house of the General Assembly must hold a public hearing to receive testimony from the public and parties administering the affected agencies. In such hearings, the affected agency must demonstrate a public need for its continued existence and the extent to which a change in or the transfer of the functions of the agency might increase the efficiency of administration or operation of the unit. If no action is taken to extend the authorization beyond the termination date, each affected entity would remain in existence for one full year to complete its activities prior to final termination and to allow time for legislative action if the General Assembly so desires.

The idea of a time limitation to facilitate the evaluation of the goals, objectives, and activities of Executive instrumentalities on the Federal level is not unprecedented. Legislation was proposed in the 92nd Congress to establish a 3-year limitation on nearly all authorizations in an effort to create a sunset-type oversight process.

Presently pending before Congress are a variety of proposals to establish "sunset" on executive instrumentalities in a variety of ways. Sunset legislation is typically structured to contain two basic components: an "action-forcing" mechanism designed to institutionalize the oversight process, and a provision for Congressional evaluation and review of the affected instrumentalities' past performance.

One type of action-forcing mechanism that has been proposed is to schedule the termination of an instrumentality's authorization, the basic legislation that facilitates the appropriation of funds for a Federal program or agency. Authorizations are of three types: annual, multi-year, and permanent. Some bills propose the institution of the sunset concept by requiring that almost all authorizations be on a multi-year basis (i.e., other than annual or permanent). One method of instituting multi-year authorizations would require the reauthorization of new budget authority every few years.

Another approach would require the periodic reenactment of an entity's organic statute if it contained a permanent authorization.

Another type of proposed action-forcing mechanism would focus upon the administrative rules of an agency or functional area. When established, many departments and agencies are delegated the quasi-legislative power of rule-making. Some would establish a system scheduling the periodic termination of these rules, thereby putting a time limit on the effective operation of affected agencies.

A fourth type of "action-forcing" sunset device would require the President to submit to Congress, on a periodic basis, a reorganization plan for specified agencies. Upon the submission of the President's plans, the Congress would be required to take legislative action. This sunset device is similar to the now expired delegated authority of the President to submit reorganization plans, the difference being that this proposal would require the submission of the plans by the President and the former reorganization authority could be used at the Chief Executive's discretion.

The second basic component of the sunset concept is the provision for mandatory review by the Congress of the affected instrumentality. Several sunset proposals seek to establish a "zero-base program review" process as a method of evaluation. The concepts of zero-base program review and zero-base budgeting are not the same and should not be confused. The term zero-base program review is a derivative of the appropriations management concept of zero-base budgeting (ZBB). ZBB is a way of organizing the Executive's budget preparation process so as to require that the appropriation level for each program be reviewed and justified from the ground up (zero base). First introduced in the public sector in 1971 by Georgia Gov. Jimmy Carter, ZBB is currently practiced in one form or another in eleven states. The concept of zero-base program review may be defined as a systematic evaluation by the legislative committees of the Congress, with assistance from Executive and Congressional support agencies, of government programs to determine if the existing authorized level for appropriation merits continuation, termination, or alteration. It is assumed such evaluations would be conducted from the ground up.

Proponents assert that sunset laws would create a process which Congress could use to manage uncontrollable growth in spending and duplicative governmental agencies and programs. Another frequently asserted advantage of sunset is that a core activity for the oversight process would be created. Presently, critics of the oversight process view it as somewhat nonsystematic, composed of such techniques as ad hoc investigations, the legislative veto, constituent casework, and such limited oversight as occurs in the existing appropriations and reauthorizations process....

Legislative Efforts in the 94th Congress

Summaries of significant sunset and zero-base budgeting bills introduced in the 94th Congress are reprinted here. None of the bills passed, but those studied in committees and hearings provide useful documentary antecedents in compiling legislative histories of measures that will eventually be enacted into law.

S. 2067 (Biden)/H.R. 11188 (Flowers)

Prohibits the authorization of budget authority for a period of more than 4 years for all laws passed after the effective date of the act and for all laws presently providing budget authority for a specified period of time for more than 4 years; requires Congressional committees to conduct a comprehensive review and study of existing programs in considering legislation extending budget authority for such programs. S. 2067 was introduced on July 6, 1975, and referred to the Senate Government Operations Committee. Hearings were held on Mar. 17-19, 24-25, and Apr. 6-7 by the Senate Subcommittee on Intergovernmental Relations. H.R. 11188 was introduced on Dec. 16, 1975, and referred to the House Committee on Government Operations.

S. 2812 (Percy)

Regulatory Reform Act of 1976. Requires the President to submit to Congress at least once a year a plan designed to establish more efficient organization and administration for the regulation of commerce; each plan submitted shall be reviewed by the Government Operations Committee of the Senate and of the House of Representatives. Subsequent to review, each affected committee shall report a bill approving or disapproving such plan in whole or part; directs that in the event no regulatory reform legislation has been enacted with respect to any area covered by the act, all rules of any agency described in the President's plan shall be of no force or effect after the last day of June in the calendar year following the calendar year in which the plan was submitted.... S. 2812 was introduced on Dec. 18, 1975, and referred to the Senate Committees on Government Operations and Rules.

S. 3318 (Hart of Colo.)

Federal Agency Pilot Termination and Review Act of 1975. Declares the purpose of establishing a pilot demonstration program of termination and review to cover all Federal agencies. Schedules the termination of the Civil Aeronautics Board, the Federal Aviation Administration, and the Occupational Safety and Health Administration Board by Oct. 1, 1979; and the Federal Energy Administration, the Interstate Commerce Commission, and the Federal Maritime Commission by Oct. 1, 1980. Allows the reestablishment by Congress of said agencies for up to 6 years after it has conducted public hearings to evaluate the agencies. Identical and companion bills include H.R. 13612 (Evans of Colo.), and H.R. 13764 (Keys). S. 3318 was introduced on Mar. 14, 1976, and was referred to the Senate Committee on Government Operations.

S. 2925 (Muskie)/H.R. 12055 (Neal)

Government Economy and Spending Reform Act of 1976. Title I: Terminates on specified dates budget authority for all Government programs except health care services, general retirement and disability insurance, and Federal employee retirement and disability programs which are funded by trust funds. Requires the Comptroller General, the Director of the Congressional Budget Office, and the Director of the Office of Management and Budget to identify the budget authority status of all Federal programs and activities. Title II: Requires the Comptroller General to conduct a study of all Government programs and activities to detect inactive and duplicative programs. Title III: Establishes a time table and procedure for quadrennial program review and evaluation. Title IV: Assigns additional functions to the General Accounting Office and requires the inclusion of specified program information in the President's budget. Title V: Amends the rules of the House and the Senate to allow for the implementation of the Act. S. 2925 was introduced on Feb. 3, 1976, and referred to the Committee on Government Operations. Hearings were held on Mar. 17-19, 24-25, and Apr. 6-7 by the Senate Subcommittee on Intergovernmental Relations. On May 13, 1976, markups were held and S. 2925 was referred to the full committee. Markups were held by the full Senate Government Operations Committee on Aug. 3 and 4, 1976, amendments were added, and the bill was reported to the Senate (S. Rept. 94-1137) by a vote of 9-0 as follows. Title I: Terminates on specified dates budget authority for all government programs except health care services, general retirement and disability insurance, and Federal employee retirement and disability on a 5-year cycle. Requires the Comptroller General, the Director of the Congressional Budget Office, and the Director of the Office of Management and Budget to identify the budget authority status of all Federal programs and activities. Title II: Establishes a procedure for zero-base program review to provide a systematic evaluation to determine if the merits of the program justify its continuation rather than termination, or its continuation at a level less than, equal to, or greater than the existing level. Title III: Amends the Legislative Reorganization Act of 1970 (31 U.S.C. 1176) and the Budget and Accounting Act of 1921 (31 U.S.C. 11) to provide for continuing program review and evaluation. Title IV: Provides for the establishment of a Citizens Bicentennial Commission on the Organization and Operation of Government. Title V: Provides for the termination and continuation of certain tax expenditure provisions and establishes a procedure for a zero-base review. Title VI: Directs the Office of Management and Budget to study the feasibility and advisability of establishing a zero-base budgeting system in the Federal government, establishes a sunset provision for titles I, II, and V, and amends the title of the bill. Identical and companion bills include H.R. 11734 (Blanchard), H.R. 12055 (Neal), H.R. 13305 (Flowers), H.R. 13370 (Mitchell of N.Y.), H.R. 13541 (Frenzel). S. 2925 was reported to the Senate, with amendments, by the Committee on Government Operations on Aug. 4, 1976.

H.R. 9125 (Mikva)

Regulatory Agency Self-Distruct Act. Schedules the termination of nine regulatory agencies on July 4, 1976, unless prior to such time (1) the President conducts both an impact and process evaluation of said agencies and recommends to the Congress that they should not be abolished and (2) the relevant committees of the House and the Senate conduct process and impact evaluations of said agencies and (3) the Congress adopts a concurrent resolution to disapprove such abolition. Provides that each regulatory agency not abolished by the stated procedure, or any successor agency established pursuant to this act, shall be abolished on July 4, 1983, except those agencies which have been in existence for 25 years or less shall be abolished on July 4, 1991. Further states that each regulatory agency established by the Congress on or after July 1, 1974, shall be abolished 15 years from the date on which it was created unless its abolition is disapproved by the above specified method. Identical and companion bills include H.R. 11278 (Mikva). H.R. 9125 was introduced on July 31, 1975, and was referred to the Committees on Government Operations and Rules.

H.R. 10655 (Lloyd of Calif.)

Regulatory Agency Abolition Act. Requires the automatic abolition of specified regulatory agencies every 3 years unless (1) the President recommends to Congress that any agency or agencies should not be abolished; (2) the relevant committee investigates and publishes a report on such agency; and (3) Congress adopts a concurrent resolution disapproving the abolition of such agency or agencies. Allows for the transfer of agency functions to the President or a successor agency with the continuation of the present rules and proceedings. Identical and companion bills include H.R. 10804 (Lloyd of Calif.), H.R. 10927 (Archer), H.R. 11165 (Lloyd of Calif.), H.R. 10655 was introduced and referred to the Committee on Nov. 10, 1975.

H.R. 12785 (Blouin)

Federal Agency Control and Review Act. Requires the Office of Management and Budget to conduct a study, lasting 1 to 2 years, of each Federal agency's efficiency and effectiveness. Authorizes the President to submit to Congress his recommendations with respect to such report. Requires that a report must be conducted on all existing agencies within 12 years, and that all studies must be repeated every 10 years. Subsequent to review, Congress would decide whether to continue, modify, or terminate the agency. Identical bills include H.R. 14660 (Blouin) and H.R. 14648 (Minish). H.R. 12785 was introduced on Mar. 25, 1976, and referred to the House Committee on Government Operations....

Chronology of Recent Events

This Congressional Research Service chronology was published in August 1976. In updating the chronology, the following items should be noted.

1/20/77   Jimmy Carter inaugurated as 39th president of the United States and pledges to undertake a major reorganization of the Executive branch.

10/1/76   94th Congress adjourns without taking action on any of several reorganization proposals or without extending the president's authority to submit reorganization plans.

08/04/76 -- Markups were held by the full Senate Government Operations Committee on S. 2925, amendments were added, and the bill was reported to the Senate by a vote of 9-0.

07/30/76 -- Governor Edwin Edwards signed into law Louisiana Senate Bill 28, Act 277, the nation's first comprehensive Sunset Law.

07/13/76 -- The Democratic National Convention adopted its 1976 platform containing an endorsement of the sunset concept.

06/28/76 -- Iowa Governor Richard Ray vetoed Iowa House File 1573, an Act designed to institute a comprehensive Sunset procedure.

06/17/76 -- Florida Governor Reubin Askew signed into law the "Regulatory Reform Act of 1976," the nation's second sunset law.

05/13/76 -- Markups on S. 2925 were held by the Senate Subcommittee on Intergovernmental Relations and the revised version of the bill was reported to the full Senate Committee on Government Operations.

04/22/76 -- The Governor of Colorado signed into law the nation's first "sunset" law, which established multi-year authorizations and a process for mandatory legislative review of the components of Colorado's Department of Regulatory Agencies.

04/07/76 -- Seven days of hearings by the Senate Subcommittee on Intergovernmental Relations were completed on S. 2925 and S. 2067.

07/09/75 -- Senator Joseph Biden introduced the first "sunset" bill in the 94th Congress in the form of S. 2067.

03/15/71 -- Governor Jimmy Carter announced that the State of Georgia would institute the appropriations management tool of zero-base budgeting for the first time in the public sector.

10/26/70 -- The Legislative Reorganization Act of 1970 (P.L. 91/510, 84 Stat. 1140) title II, Sec. 118(b), called on each standing committee to "review and study, on a continuous basis, the application, administration, and execution of the laws of those laws, or parts of laws, the subject matter of which is within the jurisdiction of that committee."

09/02/46 -- The Legislative Reorganization Act of 1946 (P.L. 74-601, 68 Stat. 812) Sec. 137 directed "continuous watchfulness" by recommending "Legislative oversight by standing Committees."

Chapter 6
Sunset Concept:
Colorado's Experience

THE COLORADO EXPERIENCE

Common Cause, the public affairs lobbying group, worked in concert with the governor of Colorado and reform advocates in the legislature to enact a sunset measure, and it is given substantial credit for successful passage of the first comprehensive sunset law at the state level. Reprinted here is Common Cause's brief exposition of the sunset concept, addressed to the Colorado situation, but applicable to any legislative body wishing to institute the process. It is followed by the testimony of several Colorado state officials: Sydney Brooks, chairman of the board, Colorado Common Cause; Raoul Rodriguez, executive director, Colorado Department of Regulatory Agencies; Senator Fred Anderson, president of the Colorado State Senate; and Representative Gerald Kopel, chairman of the House Judiciary Committee (Colorado). These officials testified in support of Senator Edmund Muskie's Government Economy and Spending Reform Act of 1976. Their statements summarize the sunset system at the state level.

Sydney Brooks ([83], pp. 77–85)

For two years Colorado Common Cause has studied the regulatory system of Colorado. As a result of this effort and in response to demonstrated regulatory weaknesses and shortcomings Common Cause has proposed to the Legislature its "Sunset Law". One columnist has observed that this effort may be "one of the most important legislative initiatives of our times."

Colorado Common Cause has designed and is now working to pass and implement its Sunset Law. Essentially the law is to address two related problems. First, we seek to establish an effective and continuing process of making government agencies and regulation responsive and accountable to the Legislature. Secondly, we want to design and implement a more streamlined system for trimming away ineffective or inefficient government regulation or those agencies which simply no longer serve a useful public purpose.

SUNSET PROCESS

The Colorado Sunset proposal provides that all boards and commissions in the Department of Regulatory Agencies be given a life span of six years. Upon the expiration of an agency's six year life, and only after holding public hearings, the Legislature could, by affirmative vote, re-establish that agency for another six year period. If, however, the Legislature did not affirmatively approve an agency's continuation, then that agency would, by operation of law, simply cease to exist.

The concept is simple: give an agency or program a terminable life and require it to justify its continuing existence prior to its automatic expiration.

The process which we are proposing is as follows:

1. Approximately one-third of all existing boards, divisions, commissions and agencies in the Department of Regulatory Agencies (43) would be scheduled to automatically terminate their activities, by process of dissolution, on July 1, 1977, July 1, 1979, and July 1, 1981, respectively. Boards and commissions with

similar functions or responsibilities are, where possible, grouped together for purposes of a more complete and coordinated review process.

2. Prior to the effective date of termination for each such agency, the Legislature is required to hold public hearings, the purpose of which is to review and evaluate the agency, its programs, performance and future. If the agency proves to the satisfaction of the Legislature that there is a present and continuing public need for the services rendered and that the particular agency is capable of delivering those services, then the Legislatur may, by affirmative vote, continue or re-establish that agency in such form as it deems proper.

3. If the Legislature fails to take this affirmative action—or "vote of confidence"—and decides to allow an agency to be terminated, then one year from its "termination date" that agency would cease all activities and expire.

During this one year period of time between the dates of termination and expiration the agency would function without diminished power or authority. However, the agency would, during this time, proceed to wind up its affairs in an orderly manner. This period could be used to transfer a "dying" agency's responsibilities or activities, if required by the Legislature.

4. All newly created agencies in the Department of Regulatory Agencies hall be subject to the review provisions of this law, and shall have a six year terminable life as do existing agencies.

5. Regardless of the provisions of this law the Legislature is in no manner precluded from engaging in regulatory agency review or modification at times and in ways not provided in this law. Sunset does not otherwise relieve the Legislature from its normal "oversight" responsibility.

PURPOSE

Government regulation is accelerating. There is a rush to increasing regulation. It is now greater in scope, intensity, cost and impact than ever before. Agencies proliferate, programs expand, rules and forms multiply at alarming rates, and there is no clear design to deter such growth. Indeed, there is no apparent program to control or guide this exploding process.

There is also an acknowledged dissatisfaction with the performance of government regulatory schemes and with the system itself. The purported effectiveness and achievements of much regulation is coming under increasing scrutiny . . . and doubt.

It is often found that the boards designed by the Legislature to regulate in the public interest tended to become self-serving and protective of the industry they were created to regulate. They often unnecessarily limited entry, discouraged competition, failed to follow up on complaints and in general showed greater allegiance to their colleagues than to the public interest.

In short, the public is distressed at what they see as unresponsive and unaccountable government largesse. Lewis Engman succinctly observed the problem to be that:

"Government cannot protect everything. There will always be bears in the woods. It is wiser to accept that fact and to proceed with appropriate caution than to employ a scorched earth regulatory policy which gets rid of the bears by getting rid of the woods and leaving everybody with a serious erosion problem."

The Sunset Law is intended to achieve several objectives. First, Sunset requires the Legislature to exercise its often neglected review and oversight responsibility. It imposes on the Legislature the continuing obligation to monitor, review and evaluate the agencies, their programs and the purposes for which they were originally designed.

Secondly, the Legislature must hold public hearings prior to the termination of any agency. The purpose of holding public hearings prior to the expiration of an agency is to require the agency to prove to the satisfaction of the Legislature:

That the agency was fulfilling the objectives for which it was originally intended, and,

That it is performing its task in an effective, responsible and positive manner, and

That there is a continuing and future need for the public service provided and that the particular agency is capable of fulfilling that need.

That the programs the agency administers are not duplicative of other programs unrelated but similar in nature.

The agency must justify its continuing existence. Each agency would have to support its position that there is a continuing and legitimate need for the services it provides and that those services can, in the future, best be met by that particular agency.

There is a third key feature to recognize. The Sunset system puts the burden of proof on the agency to demonstrate its worth rather than on those who question an agency's value. Sunset shifts the burden to those with whom it should rightfully rest—the proponents of regulation. Many government agencies perpetuate themselves by virtue only of their existence, not by demonstrated need. Sunset moderates this bureaucratic momentum and requires a showing of continuing public need.

The Sunset mechanism serves still another purpose. The Legislature spends a great deal of time creating, establishing, devising and implementing new programs and offices. It spends virtually no time reflecting back on its creations. The Sunset Law imposes a time for reflecting back on the initial purposes and the continuing need, if any, for a given agency.

It is just possible that if the Legislature spends more time perfecting its creations—in streamlining its programs and pruning away ineffective and inefficient bureaucratic largesse—it might "find" money available for new programs of genuine need and demonstrated utility. We might also redirect these newly found resources to existing, underfunded agencies whose programs are considered essential.

In short, the purpose of Sunset is to make the body of our regulatory system fit and trim to do the job its designed to do. To make the agencies responsive to the people, accountable to the Legislature and capable of more vigorous effective, efficient administration. Sunset, we believe, is a strong step in that direction. . . .

Raoul Rodriguez

My name is Raoul N. Rodriguez, and I am Executive Director of the Colorado Department of Regulatory Agencies. My purpose in testifying before this subcommittee is to share with you the Colorado approach to the issue of improving the operations of state programs. In my capacity as Executive Director of the Department of Regulatory Agencies, I have a particularly keen interest in Colorado's current effort to establish a system for periodic review of regulatory agencies.

In this, our Centennial-Bicentennial year, Governor Richard D. Lamm and I have taken the position that the Colorado Department of Regulatory Agencies has been in great need of review, and therefore, we support House Bill 1088—otherwise known as the "Sunset" proposal.

In 1968, the State of Colorado reorganized the executive branch creating the Department of Regulatory Agencies as an umbrella department to house thirty-three (33) boards and commissions. The purpose of this reorganization was to promote efficiency through "the grouping of state agencies into a limited number of principal departments primarily according to function . . ." and to increase accountability by strengthening "the powers of the Governor and provid[ing] a reasonable span of administrative and budgetary controls within an orderly organizational structure of state government. . . ." This was a change from the previous practice of each agency's reporting independently and directly to the Governor.

Since 1968, the number of boards and commissions has proliferated to forty-three (43). Given our past experience, this number is certain to increase after our present legislative session.

This Department affects the rights of most citizens by providing occupational licensure, through the promulgation of rules which have the effect of law and through the combined functions of investigation, prosecution, negotiation, settlement, informal action and other means of adjudication.

Presently there is no formalized state mechanism for review of the performance of these independent boards and commissions for the consideration of regulatory reform. Citizens are often adversely affected by the action or inaction of independent boards and commissions and the lack of recourse frequently results in a sense of frustration and apathy when dealing with state bureaucratic agencies.

Two hundred years ago this nation accepted the premise of unrestricted competition in a free-enterprise system. However, the proliferation of regulatory agencies has resulted in a conflict with that premise. The intention was to maintain competition while protecting consumers; yet, occupational licensing has often acted as a restraint on competition by limiting freedom of entry and is frequently used as a protection for those already admitted into the regulated occupation. "Sunset" proposes a method of constructive review to rectify this disparity between intent and effect. Practices which result in the restricting of entry lead to higher costs to the consumer. Obsolete and restrictive reciprocity laws further tend to raise costs and inhibit the right of relocation.

In Colorado, the management authority for testing, issuing licenses, and maintaining the professions and trades lies with the independent botrds who are not directly accountable to any branch of government. Once these board members are appointed, they serve for a definite term during which it is virtually impossible to remove them, even when there appears to be good cause. The board members, as a rule, come from the ranks of the same occupations which they are responsible for overseeing in an "unbiased" manner. This system is replete with conflicts of interest.

As a result of extensive testimony by consumers, board members, and members of the regulated professions, before a Joint Interim Study Committee, the abolishment of three boards and the consolidation of three others were recommended to the General Assembly. The testimony indicated that there were no substantial reasons to continue the existence of these boards in their present form—at least the harm that would befall the general public was not clearly identified.

I do not wish to imply by the foregoing that regulation is not at times valid, or that at the outset it was not the result of a good faith attempt to protect the consumer from abuses. I do, however, believe that the system should be continually reviewed and revised in response to the developing needs of the public.

One must recognize the fact that the whole institution of occupational licensing is embedded in a morass of federal, state, and local legislation suffused with tradition, custom, and jealously guarded "rights." The possibility of change, even relatively minor change, is likely to be perceived as a threat by those who gain not only prestige but also tangible economic benefits from the existing structure. In light of their history and the hidebound attitudes of many licensing boards, it is unrealistic to expect that they will all move quickly and vigorously to initiate necessary change.

Since the state has been instrumental in creating an increasing number of boards and commissions and has systematically receded from the notions of traditional private enterprise which have been the backbone of this country's economic well-being and growth, the state must develop a system for the meaningful review of its creations. It is my feeling that the "Sunset" bill is very timely in providing such a means of review.

This bill would provide a long needed system of public review and termination for agencies that have outlived their purpose "Sunset" appropriately places the burden on the proponents of regulation. The agencies will have to justify their perpetuation by demonstrating in a public forum their fulfillment of a public purpose. This review would also provide a positive method of allowing agencies an opportunity to address deficiencies in their organic statutes which may prevent them from fulfilling their statutory mandate. Other benefits of formal review will be an evaluation of the agency's record in achieving its original objectives and a reassessment of those objectives. Specific functions performed will be examined for effectiveness; indeed, the results may be the allocation of additional resources to increase their capability for better performance of necessary tasks.

This proposal is not a radical departure from procedures in other areas of government. We can look to the examples of our Congress and state legislatures comprised of elected officials who are made responsive to their constituency by virtue of the election process. The decisions of our courts are subject to review by higher courts, and our appointed officials may, in most instances, be removed at the pleasure of the appointing authority.

It has been argued that a beneficial board or commission may be allowed to die not because it was proven to be ineffective, but because it failed to demonstrate that it was effective, it became a political pawn, or because of some other inappropriate force. I do not dispute the theoretical possibility that this can happen, however, in its present state the Colorado proposal requires a hearing prior to termination and allows a winding down period sufficient to develop and implement alternative remedies where necessary. I believe, therefore, that with these due process protections, the benefits of "Sunset" far outweigh the postulated risks.

It is my contention that most agencies would welcome an opportunity to justify their continued existence. The legislative intent, certainly, is to protect the public through encouraging increased responsiveness and accountability. Providing the channels of communication through a public forum will benefit members of the regulated professions and occupations, the regulators, and consumers.

Fred Anderson

The State of Colorado joins the sponsors of S. 2925 in recognizing the need to control bureaucracy. It is like a dense forest which has overgrown its purpose. Just as pioneers once toppled trees and cleared brambles to make way for the controlled growth of crops and settlements, so contemporary Americans now admit to the need for taming governmental growth. The pioneers did not waste fallen trees, rather turned them to good use as fuel and shelter. We, too, recognize that each part of our vast system was founded in good faith as a specific answer to a specific want. We suggest that government respect the worth and the historical intent of each of its sub-bodies. We also suggest, though, that it is a worthy proposal which would help us to determine which programs and agencies have outlived their usefulness, which programh and agencies duplicate the functions of another, and which departments could be made to perform at the same efficiency with fewer funds.

Colorado has taken steps in this direction. Currently, our legislature is considering a "Sunset" bill which could eliminate state regulatory boards, if they are unable to justify their continuation. Our proposal, like S. 2925, calls for a regular review of agencies in order to determine if they should be continued. We have found that in some areas regulation which was once necessary, performs no function other than restraint of trade.

If they are unable to prove that they merit funds and staff, they will be terminated. Colorado's proposal parallels Senator Muskie's proposal as a call for greater accountability. We consider our Sunset bill a positive step towards making Colorado government 1976 match Colorado's needs, 1976.

We can endorse a measure which requires quadrennial review of government programs. Taking stock periodically makes good sense. Our only caution is that we should couple the desire to operate at top efficiency with the caution to sustain programs long enough for their effectiveness to reach a peak. It has been sain that we need new programs less than we need to make the ones we have efficient. We urge care in implementing and terminating the agencies, programs and grants upon which many hopes are hung. Abrupt starts and stops waste billions of dollars, and spread public disillusion that becomes hard to dispel.

In Colorado we are threatened by loss of General Revenue Sharing, undoubtedly one of the most successful state-federal programs ever initiated. It is essential to keep sight of the valuable things we have accomplished through these funds, now in jeopardy. This is only one instance of how federal decisions reverberate upon state planning. We have seen many programs begun with great optimsim, then tossed aside before they are nurtured to maturity of purpose.

I, therefore, would remind this Committee that the public welcomes reform, but the public despairs at the practice of heralding a program or agency's genesis and then slaying it before it can prove its worth. Mismanagement is a common cause, and political fortunes are sometimes to blame; each administration wants to level the reminders of the previous one. The public, though, is tired of paying for the remodeling effort especially when what is lost is more valuable than what can be gained.

It is to these problems that S. 2925 is addressed, for the periodic program review and justification will give you an oversight capacity which si badly needed.

This brings us to the issue of change. Many fear change, rightly we think—the known, however uncomfortable, has a certainty the future lacks. Many are apprehensive that a process such as S. 2925 suggests might deal destruction to a program which serves them well. This same fear is raised concerning our Colorado Sunset proposal. People fear an agency's fate may rest upon whim not rationale. To allay these fears I proposed an amendment to the bill which was adopted. It requires the legislative audit committee to cause to be conducted a performance audit of each division, board or agency scheduled for termination under this section. Said performance audit shall be completed at least three months prior to the date established by this section for termination. Upon completion of the audit report, the Legislative Audit Committee shall hold a public hearing for purposes of review of the report.

By using a performance audit report as the basic document for reviewing the reasons why an agency should or should not be terminated, there is factual evidence which precludes mere emotion becoming the deciding factor for an agency's continuance or termination. Anyone proposing or opposing an agency's continuance would have to back his demand with facts.

I have been critical in the past of Congress for not using the Government Accounting Office audit reports and evaluations to any greater degree in determining federal funding priorities.

It is my opinion that Congress should have a more structured procedure for audit review with the GAO.

From my perspective, the GAO is doing an admirable job. It tried to ease the Programing, Planning and Budgeting of the 1960's into the scheme of traditional appropriations. PPB failed, some say because it is impossible to link planning to budgeting. There are cases where this is true. Still, there is validity in the thought which sparked creation of PPB. It was to have given a scientific basis to the work of budgeting. Now, we have proposals to begin zero-based budgets. That sounds simple enough—pure accountability for dollars to be spent. But we have found in Colorado, that those dollars represent the desires, the needs, and the goals of a multitude of interest groups. Each sincerely wants funds for what he sees to be a critical need. Budgeting becomes the process of both objective and subjective judgment on whose needs can be met. Our joint Budget Committee, which just finished a long and tedious process of formulating the 1976-1977 fiscal state budget, can tell you that many lives are touched by the decisions they make.

While budget officers sympathize with the countless demands for government funds, their highest responsibility is to the common good. Everywhere we hear a plea for less government and more accountability from the government we have.

Government resembles patchwork—each piece tacked on from the material of a new era. We encourage panoramic vision of how each part works and contributes to the whole. One man cannot know all, but many coming together with intent to bring harmony to the entirety, can give the control we lack when operating piecemeal. We need decide together the nation's priorities. We need to accept, though, that even the federal budget is not limitless.

It is one thing to give a faction certainty that it will, at the least, receive as much as it did last year. If incrementalism is discarded, and each year there is the need to begin from a base of nothing—the justification process is even more difficult. Beginning zero-based budgeting in all facets of government will be a giant step. We suggest, though, that it is long overdue. America is proud to be the home of the world's most successful business and industrial endeavor. In the private sector we are the model for efficiency of production. The private sector voices frequent and substantial criticism of government's economic policy.

Should we continue to ignore those complaints, or shall we listen and learn from the wisdom of our critics? Business has what government often lacks—accountability. Business, generally, has the singular goal or profit. Government cannot always agree what its goals are. It too seeks profit, but often the product is not quantifiable. The product is fulfillment of human need. Nevertheless, there are devices to measure success. We wonder, then why is a program which is proven outmoded, ineffective or overlapping continued? We must admit that frequently those in a position to determine the lifespan of an agency or project, have a personal stake in its continuation. The decision to terminate rests with those who would suffer most from the loss.

This is less often the case in the private sector. What we can learn is greater objectivity, and a heightened awareness of what serves the general good rather than the specific want of one contingency. Perhaps the objectivity will always be lacking in the present structure. This is the value of Senator Muskie's bill. It brings to the public a process of: show results or be lost.

In summation, then we endorse the federal government's effort to chop away at the thicket which has evolved. Colorado's experience reenforces the conviction that removing some of the agencies, and programs will provide greater health and growth for what remains. Blending duplicative programs will avoid overlap of services, and forcing justification for each dollar spent will mean that we can finally tell the people of the United States that we are doing all we can to return the taxes they pay to our society in the wisest way. Actually, what S. 2925 should do is extend American economic knowledge to an area of our lives which we have unfortunately kept isolated from what some would call common sense.

Gerald Kopel

THE SUNSET PROPOSAL TO REVIEW LICENSING

In the last 25 years, the Colorado legislature has established twice as many regulatory agencies as the legislature had established in the previous 75 years.

In almost every instance, the addition of another licensing board was instigated by the persons to be licensed, and not by the consuming public.

Why- Three reasons:

Licensing restricts competition, and most people don't really want occupational competitors. Licensing gives the licensee something of "value," which didn't exist previously: a certificate indicating superiority over the unlicensed and approval by the State. Licensing increases business, since most of the Federal regulations governing payments for services emphasize payment to a licensed person.

In the typical licensing scenario, a trade association which includes many, but not *all*, of the persons in that business decide that the non-members are doing decidedly inferior work and should be stopped.

The association hires a lobbyist with good connections at the State legislature. Legislators are invited to group lunches or dinners where the association makes a presentation. Usually, they talk about *other* states which have licensed their business and how the crooks in those *other* states have fled to *our* state to carry on their rotten business.

By the time the legislature convenes, a bill has been prepared which attempts to recognize the trade association through standards to be applied in a testing system and through the process of *helping* the Governor choose the regulatory board members.

If the association is fortunate, the non-members won't appear to testify. If the *out* group appears or hires a lobbyist, that fact makes passage of the bill a little harder. But at no time will there be an appearance of consumers for whom the regulatory agency is supposedly being established as a protection. Well, that isn't exactly correct. The association will bring in a token consumer. If there is severe questioning, the consumer is usually found to have some relationship with a member of the association.

Too often, then, the Colorado legislature licenses for the wrong reason. It also fails to license for the wrong reasons, because licensing is an alternative which does have its place.

If there is a definite consumer rip-off occurring the best remedy is to define the activity and provide civil and criminal remedies. If that is not possible, the alternative is to license as a means of weeding out the crooks. This works best when *things* and not people, are licensed. The dance studio cheats were halted by licensing. The trade school swindles were halted by licensing. Owners of many of the dance studios and the trade schools vigorously fought against their licensing.

But when the rip-off which gave birth to the licensing ceases, so should, in a perfect world, the licensing.

Is there any solution to the continued expansion of licensing?

The bill we call "sunset" is the first of its kind in the United States. Under the sunset law, House Bill 1088, each of the seven regulatory divisions and 34 regulatory boards will have to prove to the legislature at six-year intervals why they should continue to exist. One division, the Public Utilities Commission, is protected by the constitution and can only be terminated if its regulatory activities are transferred to another agency. All of the others, no matter how widespread their powers or vast their numbers, are creatures of the legislature.

Under sunset, each agency will go through public hearings and introduction of a bill to continue its existence. The legislature will consider fourteen of the agencies every two years.

Theoretically, if an agency can't make a case, its renewal bill will be voted down in the legislative process, and the agency won't be renewed. Practically, enough pressure will be placed upon the legislature by lobbyists and licensees to insure the renewal of most of the agencies.

But any agency which has to travel the path of renewal through the legislature will not emerge in the same form as it started. The board's make-up of licensees will be diluted and its consumer representation will be strengthened. The testing system will be revamped to permit more of the "outs" to come "in." At least during the period before appearance at the legislature, complaints from consumers will be handled better, and, where deserving, licenses will be suspended or revoked. The regulatory board will have to produce in order to make its case for six more years of existence.

If a board is not successful in getting the legislature to pass a renewal bill, the agency will have one additional year of life to wind up its affairs and also to try the legislative process again.

The value of "sunset" then is in forcing the legislature and the agency to look again at why the agency was created, something both the legislature and the agency have successfully avoided in the past.

The sunset bill attempts to place agencies in review groupings which make sense, such as having most of the health-oriented boards considered at the same legislative year. This might well lead to a combination of some boards, such as one board for both registered and practical nurses.

This is not the first attempt at reform. In most prior cases, the agency to be reformed has successfully stifled the attempt. That is because it is so much easier to kill a bill than it is to pass one.

But if we look at just one board, the Shorthand Reporters, we can see what positive results occur when a board comes under the glare of investigation.

In the first two examinations given in 1975, for the certification of shorthand reporters (persons who transcribe proceedings in courts of law), 81 failed, and three passed, for a four percent passing average. After the Judiciary Committee began investigating the Board in October of 1975, the next examination in late November, 1975, 22 passed, and 21 failed, for a 55 percent passing average.

In the years to come, after sunset is adopted, every agency and division in the regulatory area will come under the glare of investigation. And the public will be the beneficiary.

Chapter 7
Zero-Base Budget Review: Carter's Georgia Experience

Zero-base budgeting is a reorganization tool that contains the basic elements of the sunset method, but explicitly sets forth the procedure by which an agency or program moving into sunset must justify its continuation. It does so through an elaborate accounting system in which all expense items begin with a budget of zero and are then systematically rejustified and rebuilt from the ground up, or from the base of zero. Like sunset, the idea is rather simple. Its significance lies in the discipline it affords and the detailed processes developed when it was implemented at the state level. President Jimmy Carter's native state of Georgia was the first state government to institute zero-base budgeting. In the late 1960s, Peter Pyhrr, an executive with Texas Instruments, created the system and was brought to Georgia by Governor Carter to consult on its application there.

As the zero-base approach is refined and adapted to the federal structure, the Georgia experience will serve as a significant guide. This chapter sets forth that experience and begins with President Carter's summary of the Georgia experience. Speaking to the National Governors Conference in 1974 as the governor of Georgia, he recounted how the zero-base system came to Georgia government and the benefits it brought. The text of that speech, as reprinted here, was used as a background paper in Carter's presidential campaign and illustrates his approach to reorganizing government.

PRESIDENT CARTER ON PLANNING A BUDGET FROM ZERO ([1], pp. 1–4)

On the campaign trail, a lot of promises are made by candidates for public office to improve economy and efficiency in government if they are elected. This pledge has a natural appeal to the financially overburdened taxpayer. But when the winning candidates take office, they too often find that it's easier to talk about economy and efficiency in government than to accomplish it. Entrenched bureaucracy is hard to move from its existing patterns.

Taxpayers, on the other hand, hear the promises but see few results. It seems to them that for every new program in government there must be a tax increase. Each government—whether federal, state or local— seems to have an insatiable financial need. No matter how much money is collected, it never seems to be enough.

When I campaigned for Governor, I promised that if elected there would be no general statewide tax increase during my four-year term in office. At the same time, I outlined a platform of eight general goals and 97 specific objectives that I wanted to accomplish. The twin promises, in my estimation, were not incompatible. I felt that this administration could reverse the past pattern of ignoring campaign promises.

Immediately upon election, I began planning a program to keep my commitments. I knew that simple appeals for greater productivity in government were not the answer. Economy and efficiency must come from basic, subtle changes that slice across the complete spectrum of a government's activity. The two areas that seemed to offer greatest possibilities of success were budgeting and planning. Through tight budgeting, more services can be squeezed out of every tax dollar spent. Through planning, the groundwork can be laid for implementing new programs and expanding existing ones in ways that will avoid possible pitfalls and launch the programs directly towards their goal from the beginning.

As a citizen interested in government and as a former legislator, I had long believed that too many governmental programs are botched because they are started in haste without adequate planning or establishment of goals. Too often they never really attack the targeted problems.

The services provided by Georgia's state government are now greatly improved, and every tax dollar is being stretched further than ever before. There has not been a general statewide tax increase during my term. In fact, there has been a substantial reduction in ad valorem tax. Neither will a tax increase be necessary when my successor takes office next year.

Reorganization Merges Planning and Budgeting

In budgeting, we initiated a new concept called zero-base budgeting to help us monitor state problems better and attain increased efficiency. In the area of planning, we merged the roles of planning and budgeting—which had previously operated completely independent of each other—so that they could work together in promoting more economy in government. At the same time, we clearly defined the various roles of planning and assigned the proper roles to the appropriate organizational unit.

The functions of planning and budgeting were merged in a broad reorganization program that completely streamlined the executive branch of Georgia's state government. Much of our success during the past three years in improving state programs is a direct result of reorganization.

We reduced the number of state agencies from about 300 to 22 major operating agencies and combined functions to eliminate duplication and overlapping of services. For instance, 33 agencies were combined to form the Department of Natural Resources. Reorganization is a separate story of government in action. My interest now is to stress how we changed our budgeting and planning procedures to help accomplish the previously stated goals.

Georgia was the first government to implement a program of zero-base budgeting. Under this novel concept, every dollar requested for expenditure during the next budget period must be justified, including current expenditures that are to continue. It also provides for examining the effectiveness of each activity at various funding levels. This is a dramatically different concept from that followed by most governments, which concentrate almost totally on proposed new expenditures when considering a new budget. Except for non-recurring programs or expenditures, the continuing expenditures in a current budget get little attention.

Take as an example a government with a budget of $1 billion. Projections are that the new budget will grow by $50 million during the next budget cycle because of growth in the economy, a tax increase or other factors. Department heads submit their budget requests with proposed increases to get a slice of the $50 million in new funds, either to expand existing programs, launch new programs, or to cover increases in costs through inflation. The governing officials rarely look at the existing expenditures to judge whether they are meeting their objective. The officials are concerned only with carving up the $50 million in new funds. If graded, a new program actually might become a greater priority than an existing program, but it doesn't get funded unless it can get a slice of the $50 million in new money.

Zero-base budgeting changed this practice in Georgia. Every program, existing and proposed, must now vie for funding in the new budget on an equal level. Every single dollar spent by a department in the current year must be justified if it is to be recommended by the governor for funding in the following year's budget.

Until the concept was implemented in Georgia, only one Texas corporation had ever used zero-base budgeting. The new technique was developed by that corporation as a means of reducing the costs of its overall operation. This was done by ranking every single function within the company's operations and abolishing the lowest-priority functions. Thus, the company was able to reduce expenses as required in a manner that retained the most-needed functions.

Decision Packages Establish Priorities

On a larger scale, zero-base budgeting in Georgia has peeled the veil of secrecy from around bureaucracy by opening up for inspection and scrutiny the activities of every single state employee. For the first time, a Governor, legislator, department head, or anyone else can study in detail what is being accomplished at the lowest level of state activity.

The heart of zero-base budgeting is decision packages, which are prepared by managers at each level of government, from the top to the bottom. These packages —10,000 in Georgia—cover every existing or proposed function or activity of each agency. The packages include analysis of the cost, purpose, alternative courses of action, measures of performance, consequences of not performing the activity, and benefits.

Merely compiling these packages would not accomplish any purpose other than to provide information. Therefore, they are ranked in order of importance against other current and new activities. This ranking forms the basis of determining what functions are recommended for funding in the new budget, depending, of course, upon the amount of money available. If less funds are appropriated than requested, the lowest-ranking functions and activities are cut out.

Planning Requirements

Besides placing priority on spending programs and revealing more information about actual governmental operations, zero-base budgeting achieves one more important action: it forces planning into levels of government where planning may never have existed. It forces all levels of government to find better ways of accomplishing their missions. It also gives a voice in governmental direction to the rank and file state employee who is responsible for delivering services. Besides making him a more integral part of the planning process, it elevates his own sense of importance of his position and prompts him to work harder and deliver more efficient services.

There are three ingredients necessary for successful implementation of zero-base budgeting: (1) unqualified support from top executives, (2) effective design of the system, and (3) effective management of the system.

Zero-base budgeting has been well received in Georgia. It has become an important planning tool to insure that we are placing our priorities on the proper programs and are constantly seeking the maximum services for every state dollar.

I don't want to mislead you and leave the impression that implementation of zero-based budgeting has created miracles in Georgia's state government. Obviously it has not. But it has been subtly at work for three years making basic changes in the operations of our government and will continue to pioneer further improvements in the years ahead.

The merging of budgeting and planning sevices into one cohesive organization has worked so well that one wonders why they were ever located in separate, non-cooperating agencies.

State planning was a function of the Bureau of State Planning and Community Affairs when I took office, while the Budget Bureau handled all budget matters. Although both agencies were under control of the Governor since he appointed both agency heads, they operated separately with no cooperation between them —a fact that minimized the probability of the planning output being implemented.

One of the most critical problems was that the Bureau of State Planning and Community Affairs, which had been created in 1967, had never really established its mission in Georgia's state government after four years of operation. Legislators didn't understand its functions and were skeptical of its entire operation. They felt that the planning bureau and the individual state departments were overlapping in their responsibilities. In some instances this was true. More importantly, the planning bureau was doing most of the program planning in state government without adequately synchronizing its efforts with the state agencies. When it came time to implement the planning efforts, department heads were skeptical and too often were reluctant to push for implementation of the proposed improvements. This created an impasse that made the work of state planners generally ineffective.

As soon as reorganization brought the budgeting and planning functions together into the same agency, the Office of Planning and Budget, changes began to occur. For the first time, planners and budget analysts worked side by side and began to coordinate their efforts.

Over a period of another year, further changes took place that changed completely the role of state planning. Through reorganization, most state agencies began to do their own functional program planning. This was made possible by creation of planning divisions within these departments for the first time, and also by the fact that the reduction in number of departments.made them large enough to justify their own program planning divisions.

A New Role for the Planning Division

Concurrently, planners in the Planning Division of the Office of Planning and Budget assumed a new role of policy planning rather than program planning. By restricting program planning to the agency level, there is now a greater chance that it will be implemented.

Georgia state law changes the OPB Planning Division with the responsibility for assessing accurately Georgia's physical, social and economic needs. On a periodic and timely basis throughout the year, these needs are identified, documented and analyzed.

One method that I have used to secure citizen participation in the state planning process was the Goals for Georgia program. This was a year-long program in 1971 in which Georgia citizens were given a chance to outline the types of programs they wanted their state government to emphasize in the years ahead. Since that time, state planning has been updating the results of this program continuously in the formulation of the state's goals and policies.

The role of OPB planners in preparation of the 1975 budget tells the story of how state planning is now done in Georgia.

Long before the state's budget analysts got deeply involved in preparation of the proposed fiscal year 1975 budget that would be submitted to the General Assembly, OPB planners started meeting with department heads to determine their program priorities for the following year. Detailed analyses were prepared and submitted to me for review. At the same time, I was meeting with the planners to outline my priorities. Later, I met with the planners and each department head to discuss both of our priorities. We reached a mutual agreement on many programs to be pursued and disagreed on others. Even though we didn't reach unanimity, we established a common ground of understanding about our conflicting goals. Later, when the budget analysts started putting together the actual budget proposals in dollars and cents, the spadework done by the planners proved to be an immense help.

OPB's Planning Division didn't stop at this point. Its staff continued to attend every budget meeting and provide assistance in ironing out details of the actual budget proposal to be made. Although planners had been involved in preparation of the proposed fiscal year 1974 budget, this was the first time they had actually been involved with a clear-cut role established for them. I can only say that I wish we had had this type of budgeting-planning relationship available when I became Governor. I am more than pleased with the working rapport that has been established. The relationship between me and all department heads concerning budgeting preparation has been improved considerably.

The work of the planners is reflected in our printed budget documents as well. One of the three budget documents we prepare in Georgia is an outline of proposed spendings on a program basis with a four-year projection of future needs for each program. This document is keyed by page number to the main financial display document for easy cross-reference.

One role of planners has been retained—program evaluation. This involves determining whether each program has attained its objective and making a thorough analysis of the strengths and weaknesses of each program.

OPB planners were left with this function because an objective, outside-the-agency evaluation is needed, and because many programs cross agency lines. It would not be fair for one line agency to evaluate the effectiveness of a related program in another line agency.

Along with the new objectives of OPB's Planning Division, one major change has taken place in our recruiting efforts. Instead of recruiting trained planners, we hire experts in the various areas of governmental activity such as education, law enforcement, mental health, etc. We provide them the in-house training necessary to work within the framework of our planning organization. This policy has been successful. By virtue of being experts in their activity of assignment, OPB planners can discuss programs on a level with department heads. They have an expertise that is creating more trust in state planning and is helping to establish better rapport between the Governor's office and the various state departments.

Georgia's state government still has a long way to go to achieve the quality of service that I would like to see. But we've come a long way since I took office in 1971.

The innovations involving zero-base budgeting and merging of the budgeting and planning staffs will be felt in Georgia for a long time. We are leaving a legacy to our next Governor that will allow him the flexibility and mechanism to move quickly into the decision-making process of a new administration that hasn't been available to Georgia's past governors.

FROM PRIVATE ENTERPRISE TO PUBLIC POLICY ([83], pp. 320-350)

Peter Pyhrr developed and implemented the zero-base budget system. An executive with Texas Instruments Corporation, he served as a consultant to the Georgia government and was charged with adapting the procedure to the state level. Pyhrr's book, *Zero-Base Budgeting: A Practical Management Tool for Evaluating Expenses* (Wiley, 1973), is regarded as the principal work on the subject. Testifying in favor of Senator Edmund Muskie's Government Economy and Spending Reform Act of 1976, he described the origins of the zero-base approach, discussed some of the management problems it poses at the federal level, and set forth its major elements in a brief memorandum. Pyhrr's testimony and supporting memorandum are reprinted here.

Mr. PYHRR. I was fortunate enough to work for Texas Instruments in the late 1960's where zero-base budgeting as the process has come to be known in the last 5 to 8 years, was initially developer into a workable process. I think that many of the concepts and ideas behind zero base have been in existence in both industry and government for quite a number of years, and what we succeeded in doing at Texas Instruments and then proceeded to do in other State and local governments and other industries was to develop a workable process, and a viable process that did not add tremendously to the burdens of budgetmaking and did not encumber itself with such a mass of paperwork and documentation that it ground to a halt.

I think many of those concerned about zero-base budgeting have very often stated their concern with masses of paperwork and documentation. However, my conclusion in taking a look at your bill and addressing the question of "Would zero-base budgeting work in the Federal Government," is that the answer must be "Yes."

However, I have to warn also that it is not merely enough to have good intentions of going into the process or to pass a law. I think that one of the comments I would like to repeat back to you, if I can take the liberty of repeating some of Senator Muskie's words, at the time of the introduction of this legislation, are most appropriate to such a massive change as I think zero-base budgeting would produce. Senator Muskie said:

* * * in too many cases we in Congress have satisfied ourselves with the rhetoric of legislation, leaving the hard work of implementation—from rulemaking to evaluation—to the executive branch. To put it another way, we in Congress have not paid enough attention to how well the programs we adopted were working—at least not beyond a cursory review every few years.

Some of the comments I would like to make address themselves to legislative responsibility. Zero-base budgeting has proven to be successful much beyond the area I thought it could be when I first worked in Georgia with Jimmy Carter. However, I have also seen it fail. In those successes and failures there are certain elements which I think in most cases make it succeed. There are certain common elements which also make it fail. I would like to address myself to a couple of those elements since I think I can give you some working knowledge and some examples that I think in your legislation, in your intent, should be addressed.

First, look at the users of the system. It was developed at Texas Instruments back in 1968, not by top management or the board of directors. It was developed by two operating divisions which had some severe problems, profit problems, changing situations, and we developed it for our own internal use.

Also, it has been adopted within other State agencies such as the Illinois Department of Corrections, again not at the direction of the Governor, but as an internal operating tool for that agency.

It is not a staff exercise that we should look at as adding to the bureaucracy of budget departments or facilities in State or local or Federal Government. We developed it as an operating procedure with the bulk of the analysis done by those best capable to do it. Those are the individuals responsible for the operations. A staff person could take many years to understand some of the specifics in the Department of Corrections or a prison or mental institution, and many of the places I have had an opportunity to work. But what we have done is taken the managers responsible for the operations, given them a mechanism whereby they are required to evaluate their operations and describe what they are doing, identify workload and performance measures, identify alternatives and evaluate them. What has happened is the staffs within the institutions, within the departments and State governments, have been able to review this information, which has been provided to them. They can then make some overall decisions and policy guidelines, or perhaps pick one good idea that surfaced in one institution and take it and spread it across institutions throughout the State.

Now, one of the things that we have found in defining zero base, basically, is that it is an operating tool for operating managers, but that it is also very powerful for top management, whether it be within an agency or the executive or the legislature.

The impetus for zero-base budgeting in Georgia was Jimmy Carter. In other States it has been the impetus of operating agencies. Once this zero-base information is developed on the operating areas within each agency, it can then either be given in the direct form that it was developed to top management, which is useful in smaller organizations, or it can be summarized or put into the program structure for larger organizations, which is the case done in Georgia. Now——

Senator GLENN. How was it done in Georgia? They started in departments and spread from department to department rather than going to the whole government ?

Mr. PYHRR. It was started 100 percent in agencies throughout all organizations in the executive branch of government. It was not done for the legislative or judicial budget. At that time, there were 65 major agencies having an expenditure probably in the neighborhood of $1.5 billion. The decision for 100 percent implementation was partially a political decision because Carter could not succeed himself after the 4 years, and since he was well aware that zero base is not a 1-year, one-shot kind of process. It is more of an evolutionary and developmental process, with the end result and the major result being the ability of program managers to evaluate their own programs.

Senator GLENN. Did you do it by setting up a separate group that came into the different agencies of government or you just told the agencies to rejustify themselves as they come through the budgeting process?

Mr. PYHRR. I believe there are a couple questions there. One, the only resource added to the State of Georgia was my time. We had no budget analysis at the State level or any departmental levels.

Senator GLENN. I trust the financial weight of your effort added not too substantially to the State budget ?

Mr. PYHRR. No, it did not.

If you take what we spent on my salary and what we spent as far as additional educational material, I think the total cost would not have exceeded $40,000 throughout the State.

So, at the central level we took a small pilot program in one of the agencies who was amenable to looking at the process; we then used that as an example to develop the forms and procedures to be used throughout the State, so there was a set of procedures from the State budget office that was used in all agencies.

Now, one of the problems that Georgia had when we first started is they did not have a well-developed program structure nor did they have a well-developed cost structure. The first year we gave the agencies a great deal of discretion on how far down in their organizations they would push the process.

In subsequent years, those who did not go too deep then continued to go deeper. In another agency which had better management or better cost structure, or had the desire to go there, it went down through all the institution the first year. In the prison system and mental health institutions we were looking at each of the operations within the institution. If you take mental health for example, you have all your maintenance, food, supplies, and your rehabilitation programs. What we tended to do is get the managers within each institution, try to familiarize them with the process, and start them in their evaluation of their own operations. Some of the things that happened as examples of what came out of this were: In one of the major institutions in Georgia which was woefully inadequate as far as its rehabilitative capabilities, they probably ended up with a budget which was 5 or 6 percent above the previous year and—that is what they would have gotten under any budgetary process.

In that institution though, we quadrupled the rehab services by taking those moneys from other maintenance types of programs.

Now, as an alternative, if we were looking for budget reductions we could have taken the options of cutting out maintenance and support costs, and rather than piling that back into rehab or changing the rehab programs, shown that as a cost-savings and hold back or reduce taxes or put those savings into other programs.

Senator GLENN. Are the figures in the lengthy statement that detail that area?

Mr. PYHRR. In this particular area, no.

Senator GLENN. I think those would be very interesting. We are interested in the dollar savings. It is one thing to say we did away with 20 departments of Government, but it doesn't mean anything if you just take those people and combine them in a conglomorate and they are doing the same thing in another agency. We are interested in the dollar and personnel savings. If you have any figures on that.

Mr. PYHRR. I think I can provide some.

Senator GLENN. We would appreciate it.

Mr. PYHRR. I would be happy to do so.

[The information follows:]

I'd like to give an example of the type of operational analysis and savings that a zero-base analysis can produce. The Georgia Highway Patrol, in their first year's implementation of zero-base budgeting, provides such an analysis. The Highway Patrol operated 45 patrol posts across the state. The sergeants managing each post did a detailed analysis of how much money was spent on each function and how the troopers spent their time. Their analysis produced the following types of cost savings:

Forty-seven trooper positions for administrative duties were replaced with clerk dispatchers or radio operators for a salary savings of $180,000.

Eight man-years ($100,000) were saved by having the Post Office deliver mail to the stations as part of the normal postal route rather than having 45 troopers spend one hour each day picking up mail from the post office.

More significant than these cost savings was the evaluation and realignment of patrol duties. After lengthy discussions, the sergeants decided that their main performance indicator should be the amount of preventive patrol time available. This analysis produced a minimum level decision package that would reduce the budget by 9% or $700,000, that would still produce a 14% increase in the amount of preventive patrol time available. The Highway Patrol proposed a total of 5 decision packages, identifying 5 increments of service and associated cost. If all 5 decision packages had been approved, preventive patrol time would have been increased 90% at a 16% cost increase (with inflation accounting for about 10% of the increase).

Mr. PYHRR. Part of the question when we look at funding decisions in Government is the question of whether the process of zero-base will actually reduce State or Federal expenditures, or will it retard the growth of expenditures?

Certainly from a purely business standpoint, if I could be king of the State of Georgia or supreme ruler of the United States, I could probably do a lot more things and make deeper cuts, and perhaps give the taxpayer back 10 to 20 percent of his taxes. I think from a more realistic political standpoint what we are looking at is two types of things. One, we are taking a look at reducing in those areas that cannot justify their expenditures. That is, either by finding programs that should not be in existence, or more commonly by taking a look at improving delivery systems and reducing administrative burdens, you look at reductions and streamlining—rather than wholesale elimination which is not as much in the political reality as elimination might be in industry.

We are also looking at trying to improve program delivery. Now, this can be done within the same money as the example I gave you with the institution which took moneys out of one pocket and put it into another pocket in order to perform better services in rehabilitative areas.

I think that with the result of these two types of changes, what we are looking at is retarding the increase in taxation and also at the same time trying to improve program services.

Those are two things we are trying to do.

I think if you take a look at what makes a process like zero-base budgeting succeed or what makes it fail, there are several very key elements.

No. 1 is the effective design of a mechanism which can be used by operating managers who must provide the basic data for us. If we come in with a system that is overburdening in what it requires or merely in a great generator of paper such as in PPSS, then I think we will fail. What we want is—you talked about a New Jersey example, what zero-base is, it is a decisionmaking process to be used within the agency. So we must have an effective design of the system. Several people that have tried this, New Mexico for one, probably ended up with a mechanical procedure which was very difficult to implement, and basically almost predetermined that the system would not be effective.

Second, that it must have the support of top management. If it is implemented by a director of an agency, that is top management.

If it is implemented by the President of the United States, that is top management. If it is implemented by the legislature, it must be supported both at the legislative level and the executive level.

So, the support of top management is essential, I think, to any major change whether it be zero-base budgeting or any other system.

Also it must be the sole budget procedure used within the agency. One of the failures I think of PPB is there was a traditional budget procedure that went along with PPB. Those managers who had been around government for a period tended to put their time and effort into that traditional budget process which would get them the funds, which I think we must assume most managers will do.

Now, some of the causes for failure—sort of the antithesis of what I just said—if there is an overburdensome procedure, with a lot of complicated mechanics to it, then there is no way that a large organization can succeed. If it has a great deal of opposition or infighting between the executive and legislature, that is another death knell for any process. There have been a couple of implementations in the public sector where you had the executive and legislature opposed to each other, and that is very difficult for an agency manager to step between.

Again, most of the areas that this has proved most effective did it as the only budget process. Unless you did zero-base budgeting in Georgia, you didn't get a budget. That adds incentive for the managers to use the process.

Senator GLENN. It gets their attention anyway.

Mr. PYHRR. Right. I think I learned from my experiences in government that you sort of have to get their attention and then give them a good swift kick in the rear and get them going.

I will leave for the record the summary paper that I prepared, that describes zero-base budgeting as an operating analysis which also ties into a budget.

[The information referred to follows:]

The Zero-Base Approach
To Government Budgeting
by Peter A. Pyhrr
3/15/76

Misdirection by Traditional Budget Procedures

The traditional budget procedure is based on "incremental budgeting." Most organizations start with the current operating and expenditure levels as an established base. They then analyze, in detail, only those desired increases (i.e., increments) from this established base -- thus looking at only a small fraction of the total dollars budgeted.

These traditional budget techniques reinforce, and are reinforced by, the psychology of governmental institution. This psychology was effectively explained by Peter F. Drucker in a recent article in The Public Interest on "Managing the Public

Service Institution." [1]   Mr. Drucker pointed out that service institutions were paid out of a budget allocation, whose revenues are normally allocated from a revenue base not directly tied to what the institution is doing. In addition, institutions usually have monopoly powers, and the intended beneficiary therefore has no choice in obtaining the desired services.

> "Being paid out of a budget allocation changes what is meant by 'performance' or 'results.' 'Results' in the budget-based institution means a larger budget. 'Performance' is the ability to maintain or to increase one's budget. The first test of a budget-based institution and the first requirement for its survival is to obtain the budget. And the budget is, by definition, related not to the achievement of any goals, but to the intention of achieving those goals.
> This means, first, that efficiency and cost control, however much they are being preached, are not really considered virtues in the budget-based institution. The importance of a budget-based institution is measured essentially by the size of its budget and the size of its staff. To achieve results with a smaller budget or a smaller staff is, therefore, not 'performance.' It might actually endanger the institution. Not to spend the budget to the hilt will only convince the budgetmaker - whether a legislature or a budget committee - that the budget for the next fiscal period can safely be cut." [2]

This psychology is often manifested in the fourth quarter rush to commit unspent funds. If all funds are not committed, not only is there the fear that others might consider the budget to be inflated, but the institution would loose these unspent funds from their "base" level of expenditure on which the next years increase is predicated. (Industry, in contrast, must satisfy the customer in order to retain business and has profit as a readily identifiable measure of performance.)

This traditional approach has often been described as "creeping incrementalism." Unfortunately, spurred by inflation and changing situations, the "creep" has turned into a "gallop" in many organizations.

Traditional budgeting is a static tool, weighted down by masses of detailed numbers for every conceivable type of expenditure. It does not provide management with a viable decision making tool to react to changing situations since the budget procedure does not ask:

---

1 Peter F. Drucker, "Managing the Public Sector Institution," *The Public Interest*, No. 33, fall 1973, pp. 43-60.

2 *Ibid.*, p. 50.

- Are the current activities efficient and effective?
- Should current activities be eliminated or reduced
  to fund higher priority new programs or to reduce
  the current budget?

The Zero-Base Approach

On December 2, 1969, at the Plaza Hotel in New York City,
Dr. Arthur F. Burns, then counselor to the President of the
United States, addressed the annual dinner meeting of the Tax
Foundation on the "Control of Government Expenditures." In this
speech, Dr. Burns identified the basic need for zero-base budgeting;
but he also expressed his concern that such a process would be
difficult if not impossible to implement:

> "Customarily, the officials in charge of an established
> program have to justify only the increase which they
> seek above last year's appropriation. In other words,
> what they are already spending is usually accepted as
> necessary without examination. Substantial savings
> could undoubtedly be realized if (it were required that)
> every agency . . . make a case for its entire
> appropriation request each year, just as if its program
> or programs were entirely new. Such budgeting
> procedure may be difficult to achieve, partly because
> it will add heavily to the burdens of budget-making,
> and partly also because it will be resisted by those
> who fear that their pet programs would be jeopardized
> by a system that subjects every . . . activity to
> annual scrutiny of its costs and results."

Dr. Burns was advocating that government agencies re-evaluate all
programs and present their requests for appropriation in such a
fashion that all funds can be allocated on the basis of cost/benefit
or some similar kind of evaluative analysis.

A methodology to implement zero-base budgeting was developed
and implemented at Texas Instruments during 1969. The process was
first adopted in Government at the direction of Governor Jimmy Carter
of Georgia. The state of Georgia adopted zero-base budgeting for
the development of its fiscal 1973 budget. The process was
successful and is still being used. Zero-base budgeting is an
emerging process which has been adopted by a variety of industrial
and governmental organizations, and is a process which is being
continually developed and modified to meet the needs of its users.

The fears of Dr. Burns that a zero-base approach "will add
heavily to the burdens of budget-making" have not proven to be the
case. None of the organizations that I am familiar with who have
implemented the approach have added additional time onto their
calendar for the preparation of a zero-base budget (other than
design and training prior to the budget preparation process which

is a normal start-up requirement of any new process). Although the zero-base process does not take more calendar time, it usually involves more managers and takes more management time than the traditional budget procedures. However, the zero-base approach includes objective setting, program evaluation, and operational decision making, as well as, budget making. Traditional budgeting procedures often separate these management aspects. In the worst case, the traditional budget process is merely a way to obtain an appropriation with the operational decision making and operating budgets determined after the appropriation has been determined. If we added the time requirements of these additional management elements to the time requirements of the traditional budgeting process, then the time requirements of zero-base budgeting do not add to management's burdens. In fact, after the initial year's implementation, the zero-base approach can actually reduce management's burden as the zero-base thought process and methodology become ingrained into management's normal way of problem solving and decision making.

Zero-Base Budgeting Procedures

The zero-base approach requires each organization to evaluate and review all programs and activities (current as well as new) systematically, to review activities on a basis of output or performance as well as cost, to emphasize manager decision making first, number-oriented budgets second, and increase analysis. However, I should stress that zero-base is an approach, not a fixed procedure or set of forms to be applied uniformly from one organization to the next. The mechanics and management approach has differed significantly among the organizations that have adopted zero-base, and the process must be adapted to fit the specific needs of each user.

Although the specifics differ among organizations, there are four basic steps to the zero-base approach that must be addressed by each organization:

- Identify "decision units."
- Analyze each decision unit in a "decision package."
- Evaluate and rank all decision packages to develop the appropriations request.
- Prepare the detailed operating budgets reflecting those decision packages approved in the budget appropriation.

Defining Decision Units

Zero-base budgeting attempts to focus management's attention on evaluating activities and making decisions. Therefore, the "meaningful elements" of each organization must be defined so that they can be isolated for analysis and decision making. For the sake of terminology, we have termed these meaningful elements "decision units." The definition of decision units in most organizations is straightforward, and the decision units may correspond to those budget units defined by traditional budget procedures.

For those organizations with a detailed budget unit or cost center structure, the decision unit may correspond to that budget unit. In some cases, the budget unit manager may wish to identify separately different functions or operations within his budget unit if they are significant in size and require separate analysis. He may therefore identify several "decision units" for a budget unit. If an organization has a well developed program structure, the decision unit may correspond to that lowest level of the program structure (program element, activity, function). Decision units may be defined at the sub-program level if there are separate organizational units within that program element. The resulting decision packages at the sub-program element level can then be grouped to evaluate the program element. In the same manner, decision packages for each program element (or sub-program element) can be grouped to evaluate each program.

The decision packages built around each decision unit are the building blocks of the budget and program analysis. These building blocks can be readily sorted either organizationally or programatically. For those organizations without a detailed program structure, the information and analysis provided by zero-base provides a readily usable data base from which a program structure can be developed.

Decision units can also be defined as major capital projects, special work assignments, or major projects. Each organization must determine for itself "what is meaningful." In practice, top management usually defines the organization or program level at which decision units must be defined, leaving it to the discretion of each manager to identify additional decision units if appropriate.

The Decision Package Concept

The "decision package" is the building block of the zero-base concept. It is a document that identifies and describes each decision unit in such a manner that management can (a) evaluate it and rank it against other decision units competing for funding and (b) decide whether to approve it or disapprove it.

The content and format of the decision package must provide management with the information it needs to evaluate each decision unit. This information might include:

1) Purpose/objective
3) Description of actions (What are we going to do, and how are we going to do it?)
6) Costs and benefits
5) Workload and performance measures
2) Alternative means of accomplishing objectives
4) Various levels of effort (What benefits do we get for various levels of funding?)

The key to developing decision packages is the formulation of meaningful alternatives. The types of alternatives that should be considered in developing decision packages are:

1) Alternative methods of accomplishing the objective or performing the operation: Managers should identify and evaluate all meaningful alternatives and choose the alternative they consider best. If an alternative to the current method of doing business is chosen, the recommended way should be shown in the decision package with the current way shown as the alternative not recommended.

2) Different levels of effort of performing the operation: Once the best method of accomplishing the operation has been chosen from among the various alternative methods evaluated, a manager must identify alternative levels of effort and funding to perform that operation. Managers must establish a minimum level of effort, which must be below the current level of operation, and then identify additional levels or increments as separate decision packages. These incremental levels above the minimum might bring the operation up to its current level and to several multiples of the current level of effort.

The identification and evaluation of different levels of effort is probably the most difficult aspect of the zero-base analysis, yet it is one of the key elements of the process. If only one level of effort were analyzed (probably reflecting the funding level desired by each manager), top management would be forced to make a yes or no decision on the funding request, thus funding at the requested level, eliminating the program, making arbitrary reductions, or recycling the budget process if requests exceeded funding availability.

A decision package is defined as one incremental level in a decision unit. Thus, there may be several decision packages for each decision unit. It is these incremental levels that get ranked. By identifying a minimum level of effort, plus additional increments as separate decision packages, each manager thus presents several alternatives for top management decision making:

Elimination:

Eliminate the operation if no decision packages are approved.

Reduced Level:

Reduce the level of funding if only the minimum level decision package is approved

Current Level:

Maintain the same level of effort if the minimum level, plus the one or two incremental levels (bringing the operation from the minimum level to the current level of effort) are approved (NOTE): The current level of effort refers only to the level of output or performance sometimes referred to as a "maintenance level." However, even at the current level of effort, managers may have changed their method of operation and made operating improvements, so that the current level of effort may be accomplished at a reduced cost.)

Increased Levels:

Increased levels of funding and performance if one or more increments above the current level is approved

The minimum level of effort is the most difficult level to identify since there is no magic number (i.e., 75 per cent of the current level) that would be meaningful to all operations. The minimum level must be identified by each manager for his operations. The minimum level must be below the current level of effort. The minimum level should attempt to identify "that critical level of effort, below which the operation would be discontinued because it loses its viability of effectiveness." There are several considerations which can aid managers in defining the minimum level of effort:

1) The minimum level may not completely achieve the total objective of the operation (even the additional levels of effort recommended may not completely achieve the objective because of realistic budget and/or achievement levels).

2) The minimum level should address itself to the most critical population being served or attack the most serious problem areas.

3) The minimum level may merely reduce the amount of service (or number or services) provided.

4) The minimum level may reflect operating improvements, organizational changes, or improvements in efficiency that result in cost reductions.

5) Combinations of 1 through 4.

By identifying the minimum level, each manger is not necessarily recommending his operation be funded at the minimum level but is merely identifying that alternative to top management. If a manager identifies several levels of effort, he is recommending that all levels be funded.

Example: Air Quality Laboratory

The following example of the Georgia Air Quality Laboratory (Air Quality Control) illustrates the type of analysis that each manager needs to make in order to prepare his decision packages. The Air Quality Laboratory tests air samples collected by field engineers throughout Georgia. It identifies and evaluates pollutants by type and volume, then provides reports and analyses to the field engineers. The manager involved made the typical two-part analysis; first, identifying different ways of performing the function; and secondly, identifying the different levels of effort.

1. Different ways of performing the same function:

(a) Recommended decision package: Use a centralized laborabory in Atlanta to conduct all tests (cost - $246,000). This expenditure would allow 75,000 tests and would determine the air quality for 90% of the population (leaving unsampled only rural areas with little of no population problem).

(b) Alternatives not recommended:

● Contract testing to Georgia Tech (cost-$450,000). The $6 per test charged by the University exceeds the $246,000 cost for doing the same work in the Air Quality Laboratory, and the quality of the testing is equal.

● Conduct all testing at regional locations (cost - $590,000). Cost $590,000 the first year due to setup cost and purchase of duplicate equipment, with a $425,000 running rate in subsequent years. Many labs would be staffed at a minimum level, with less than full utilization of people and equipment.

● Conduct tests in Central Laboratory for special pollutants only, which require special qualifications for people and equipment, and conduct routine tests in regional centers (cost - $400,000). This higher cost is created because regional centers have less than full workloads for people and equipment.

The recommended way of performing this laboratory function was chosen because the alternatives did not offer any additional advantages and were more expensive. The manager therefore recommended the level of 75,000 tests, at $246,000. Each manager has complete freedom to recommend either new way or the current way of doing business.

Once he had defined the basic alternatives and selected the one he considered best, he completed his analysis by describing different levels of effort for his chosen alternative. For the recommended Central Laboratory in Atlanta, the Air Quality Laboratory manager described and evaluated decision packages that called for different levels of effort for air quality tests. In this case, the manager believed that he could reduce the level of testing to 37,300 samples and still satisfy the minimum requirements of the field engineers who used his services. Therefore, he completed his analysis by identifying the minimum level and additional levels of effort for his recommended way of performing the testing as follows:

    2.   Different levels of effort of performing the function:

        (a) Air Quality Laboratory (1 of 3), cost- $140,000.
            Minimum package: Test 37,300 samples, determining
            air quality for only five urban areas with the
            worse pollution (covering 70% of the population).

        (b) Air Quality Laboratory (2 of 3), cost- $61,000.
            Test 17,700 additional samples (totaling 55,000,
            which is the current level), determining air
            quality for five additional problem urban areas
            plus eight counties chosen on the basis of worst
            pollution (covering 80% of the population).

        (c) Air Quality Laboratory (3 of 3), cost- $45,000.
            Test 20,000 additional samples (totaling 75,000),
            determining air quality for 90% of the population,
            and leaving only rural areas with little or no
            pollution problems unsampled.

The Air Quality Laboratory manager thus prepared three decision packages (1 of 3, 2 of 3, and 3 of 3).

Development of different levels as separate decision packages indicates that the functional manager thinks all levels deserve serious consideration within realistic funding expectations. He identifies three possible levels and leaves it to higher management to make tradeoffs among functions and level of effort within each function.

The Ranking Process

The ranking process provides management with a technique to allocate its limited resources by making management concentrate on these questions: "How much should we spend?" and "Where should we spend it?" Management constructs its answer to these questions by listing all the decision packages identified in order of decreasing benefit to the organization. It then identifies the benefits to be gained at each level of expenditure and studies the consequences of not approving additional decision packages ranked below that expenditure level.

The ranking process establishes priorities among the incremental levels of each decision unit (i.e., decision packages). The

rankings therefore display a marginal analysis. If the manager of
the Air Quality Program in Georgia developed decision packages for
the Air Quality Laboratory, Reviews and Permits, Source Evaluation,
Registration, and Research, his ranking might appear as follows:

Rank	Decision Package	Incremental Cost	Cumulative Program Cost
1	Reviews and Permits (1 of 2)	$ 116,000	$ 116,000
2	Source Evaluation (1 of 4)	103,000	219,000
* 3	Air Quality Laboratory (1 of 3)	140,000	359,000
4	Registration (1 of 3)	273,000	632,000
5	Source Evaluation (2 of 3)	53,000	685,000
* 6	Air Quality Laboratory (2 of 3)	61,000	746,000
7	Source Evaluation (3 of 3)	45,000	791,000
* 8	Air Quality Laboratory (3 of 3)	45,000	836,000
9	Reviews and Permits (2 of 2)	50,000	886,000
10	Research (1 of 2)	85,000	971,000

From a practical standpoint, the rankings of the minimum levels
for Reviews and Permits, Source Evaluation, Air Quality Laboratory,
and Registration may be requirements, so that the absolute ranking
of those decision packages (ranked 1 - 4) are not meaningful. However,
the priority of the packages with a lower ranking become significant
since management will ultimately make a decision on which packages
will be funded. If packages one through eight are funded, management
would approve a budget for Air Quality Control of $246,000.
Management would have funded all three levels of the Air Quality
Laboratory, thus increasing that budget; funded only the minimum
level of Registration, thus decreasing that budget; and not funded
any Research, thus eliminating that function. Discretionary programs
may have the minimum level ranked at a medium or low priority, while
increased levels for other programs may be given a high priority.
Therefore, the rankings can produce dramatic shifts in resource
allocations.

The key to an effective review and ranking process lies in
focusing top management's attention on key policy issues and discretionary expenditures. In a small organization such as the city
of Garland, Texas, all decision packages were reviewed by the City
Manager. The City Manager took the lower priority packages from
each organization that he thought were somewhat discretionary and
concentrated his ranking efforts on developing a consolidated ranking
across all city organizations for those discretionary decision
packages.

In large organizations, top management may be forced to rely
primarily on management summaries in lieu of concentrating on the

decision packages. In the state of Georgia, decision packages are ranked to the program level in each agency. The Budget Office prepares executive summaries based on the decision packages and program rankings submitted by each agency for the Governor's review.

It is also possible to prepare "activity decision packages" (an activity being the lowest element in the program structure). Activity decision packages would then be ranked for each program. "Program decision packages" could then be prepared based on the activity decision packages and the ranking at the program level. The program decision packages could have a similar format and content as the activity decision package, but provide a summary and program analysis for use by top agency management and the executive and legislative review process.

Regardless of organizational size and form of top management review, the decision packages and rankings form the backbone of analysis and decision making. The specific nature of each review process must be specifically designed to fit the size and personality of each organization.

Preparing the Detailed Operating Budget

The budget or appropriation requests prepared by each organization are usually subject to some form of legislative review and modification. If the legislative appropriation differs markedly from the budget request, many organizations who have used traditional bedgeting techniques are forced to recycle their entire budgeting effort to determine where the reductions should be made. Under the zero-base budgeting approach, the decision packages and rankings determine specifically the actions required to achieve any budget reductions. If the legislature defines reductions in specific program areas, we can readily identify the ocrresponding decision packages and reduce the appropriate program and organizational budgets. If the legislature identifies an arbitrary reduction (e.g., reduce budgets 5 per cent), each agency can use its rankings and eliminate those decision packages that it considers to be the lowest priority.

In the final analysis, each organization will have a number of approved decision packages which define the budget of each program and organizational unit. The decision packages also define the specific activities and performance anticipated from each program and organizational unit. This information can provide the basis for both budget and operational reviews during the year.

Practices and Problems

The term "zero-base" has many different connotations. To those who have merely heard the term, it tends to mean "the process of throwing everything out and starting all over again from scratch" or "reinventing the wheel." These connotations are incorrect and imply an effort of impractical magnitude and chaos.

In a more practical vein, "zero-base" means the evaluation of all programs. The evaluation of alternatives and program performance may occasionally lead us to completely rethink and redirect a program, in which case we do "throw everything out and start all over again." However, in the great majority of cases, programs will continue, incorporating modifications and improvement. For the majority of programs, we will concentrate our analysis on evaluating program efficiency and effectiveness and the evaluation and prioritization of different levels of effort.

This pragmatic approach offers us an extremely flexible tool. Managers can "reinvent the wheel" in those situations where preliminary investigation indicates the need and potential benefits of such an approach, and can concentrate their effort on improving programs that appear to be headed in the right direction.

The zero-base approach has led to major reallocation of resources. For example:

> The state of Georgia experienced a $57 million (5 per cent of general funds) revenue shortfall. Governor Jimmy Carter used the zero-base analysis to reduce budgets across 65 agencies, with reductions ranging from 1 per cent to 15 per cent. Program reductions within each agency ranged from no change to elimination.

In a political environment, the expectations for major shifts in resource allocations must be qualified. The major reallocations of resources will normally take place within major agencies such as shifting administrative and maintenance cost savings into direct program delivery. However, it is unrealistic to expect a 20 per cent decrease in the Department of Education to fund a 40 per cent increase in Mental Health. The political realities do not usually allow such shifts. It is also unrealistic to expect an automatic

tax reduction due to zero-base budgeting. When cost reductions
are achieved, the overriding political tendency is to plow the
money back into increased services in other programs.

"If we can't realistically expect major funding reallocations
among major agencies, and if we can't expect a tax decrease, then
why do zero-base budgeting?" I believe that there are four
overriding reasons that make the zero-base approach worthwhile:

1. Low priority programs can be eliminated or reduced.
   How the savings are used is a completely separate
   question.

2. Program effectiveness can be dramatically improved.
   Such improvements may or may not have a budgetary
   impact.

3. High impact programs can obtain increased funding by
   shifting resources within an agency, whereas the
   increased funding might not have been made available
   had the agency merely requested an increase in total
   funding.

4. Tax increases can be retarded. The first three benefits
   can significantly reduce the necessity for increased
   taxes by allowing agencies to do a more effective job
   with existing revenues. For the hard nosed executive
   or Legislature budgets can be reduced with a minimum
   of reduced services.

The zero-base approach is not without its problems. The
major problem is the threat that many bureaucrats feel towards
a process which evaluates the effectiveness of their programs.
The zero-base process also requires a great deal of effective
administration, communications, and training of managers who will
be involved in the analysis. Managers may also have problems in
identifying appropriate decision units, developing adequate data to
produce an effective analysis, determining the minimum level of
effort, ranking dissimilar programs, and handling large volumes of
packages. For many programs, workload and performance measures may
be lacking or the cause/effect and program impact may not be well
defined so that the analysis will be less than perfect. Therefore,
zero-base budgeting should be looked upon as a longer term
management development process rather than a one year cure-all.

Fortunately, the zero-base approach is not subject to the
gamesmanship one might anticipate. The traditional budget approach
offers maximum opportunity for gamesmanship because current operations
are seldom evaluated and many discreet decisions are never explicitly
identified and get "buried in the numbers." However, the zero-base
approach removes the umbrella from covering current operations and

requires mangers to clearly identify operating decisions. In zero-base, most obvious forms of gamesmanship would be to avoid identifying reasonable alternatives, to include the pet projects within the minimum level package, and to rank high priority programs low in the ranking in order to obtain additional funding. If the decision packages are formatted adequately to display the alternative's considered, workload and performance data, descriptions of actions, and enough cost data so that discretionary items cannot be built into the cost estimate, it become very obvious when such gamesmanship is attempted. Also, because the entire ranking of decision packages must be displayed, it is very easy to challenge a high priority item that received a low ranking or a low priority item which received a high ranking.

The problems in implementing zero-base budgeting are not to be minimized. The specific needs, problems, and capabilities of each organization must be considered in adapting the zero-base approach. Although most of the basic concepts of the zero-base approach have been maintained, the specifics of administration, formats, and procedures have been different for each organization that has adopted the approach. Zero-base can be applied on an intensive basis throughout all levels of an organization, applied only to selected programs, or applied only at major program levels rather than involving all operating managers. The strategy of implementing the zero-base approach must be developed for each organization depending on its specific needs and capabilities. It should be considered a management and budgetary improvement effort that may require several years to reach full utilization and effectiveness.

Zero-base budgeting challenges the security blanket and misdirection of traditional budget procedures. It is certainly not a cure-all to improve services and reduce taxes, but it offers a more rational approach to managing government.

Mr. PYHRR. All too often, the budgeting progress is the way to get money. Once you have the money, you turn around and say, "Now, what are we going to do with it?"

It is true in government and industry. What we are trying to do is get a management process. The reason zero base was developed was to produce a process that wrapped together: Management by objectives which is done in many organizations; identification of what you are doing and how you deliver the system; identification of costs, obviously; identification of workload and performance measures, which is obviously problematical in some areas. However, once we get into the operations I have a much easier time to understand caseload, workload, and the kind of people reached than I can by taking the whole social welfare program and trying to understand programs at that level. Then we are asking people in their zero-base analysis to identify alternatives. What we have built into the process in areas that it worked, is a manager-identified alternative for different means of program delivery or operations. If the manager incorporated the alternative into his decision package, it was automatic approval to change it; so he didn't have to get special approval to make changes after his decision packages were approved.

Ability to make change was built into the procedure, a very action and decision-oriented process. Managers had to identify what happened at different levels of funding, which obviously is——

Senator GLENN. Did you go through incremental funding as well as zero base?

Mr. PYHRR. Zero base the way I define it machanically requires a manager to identify what is called the minimum level of effort, which by definition must be below where he is right now. You can dictate it, say 75 or 50 percent, or you can allow managers to try to identify their own minimum level, which is the way we have done it in most cases.

You will start to see whether you should spend anything at all when a man has to say, "I am trying to justify—or this is what I am going to do for 50 or 75 percent of that money." Identifying that $100,000 or $1 million as minimum recommended spending, he adds incrementally on top of that, say, 25 percent to go from 75 to 100 percent: Here is what I spend and here is what I get for that increment.

In many cases you will fund only the minimum because you can eliminate some services, and you may end up cutting back in those programs because you will set new programs competing for the same funds at a higher priority.

The other thing we have done is require a ranking process, which is started down within the departments and can come up to program levels or agency levels.

Senator GLENN. In Georgia, did you go into tax expenditures—incentives—for zero-base analysis?

Mr. PYHRR. No, we did—the first year we did not go into that. I cannot comment on what happened in that specific area in the later years of the Carter administration. I was there for the first year. We took a look at the operating departments of the State which was the main focus.

Senator GLENN. With the complexities of the Federal Government and your experience in State government, do you think you can take this on as an across-the-government program all at one time?

Mr. PYHRR. No. I don't think you would get as effective a process as if it were done in a 2 or 3-year period. However, I am against phasing something in over a 5- or 10-year period; I think you lose a tremendous amount of momentum. What I would recommend would be to take a program area which may encompass more than one department, or may even be one large department, so that you can do it completely throughout that entire program area or throughout that entire department to get a very good operating feel for how the process works and see what kinds of benefits you could achieve. You can attempt to take selected operations or subprograms in each major agency in the Federal Government and attempt first implementation—do it there. Let each agency and——

Senator GLENN. If I understand, you start going downhill with some functional lines like manpower and that would overlap into quite a number of departments. On the other hand, you might start with spot programs at a much lower level perhaps out of individual board, commission or committee level and work up.

Mr. PYHRR. Yes. I think that what we found is that even within a State such as Georgia which did it uniformly throughout the State, that the mechanics of implementation and how it worked within the agency differed because of the nature of the people and the nature of the programs. We also allowed, within guidelines, each agency to modify some of the formats used to make it more meaningful for their programs.

Senator GLENN. We have had a lot of different thoughts on where to start at cross-the-board development level. I just reel off a few, it could be dollar value of expenditure, everything above $5 billion per program or $1 billion or whatever and work it down to lower levels later.

We could start with: (1) number of employees; (2) greatest geographical distribution; (3) greatest number of programs within the department; (4) greatest suborganization groups under them down to committees and subagencies or whatever the title might be.

Do you have any thoughts on that line? In other words, we are groping a bit for setting criteria of where to take this monster on.

Mr. PYHRR. I guess I only have a couple thoughts and, as you well can imagine from testimony, a lot of this is personal strategy. First of all, the money should be significant and the organization should be significant because what good is it testing a very small organization—it doesn't answer the question of how it works in such a massive bureaucracy as the Federal Government.

So, you have to get enough dollars involved to make it a worthwhile process.

That is one given, and from what I have heard you say, I don't think anybody suggested a very small pilot in a nonmajor area.

My personal approach has always been to try to identify the biggest problem area that we could identify in the State or in private industry and attack that. Because if it works in a big problem area, or an area that those say it won't work—if it will work there, it will work every place else.

That is why when I have been involved, I try to spend some time in maximum security prisions and mental health institutions, and places like that which are in ways very different to deal with, and tend to have a very hard-nosed type of management.

Senator GLENN. What do you think of Colorado's approach, taking the regulatory agencies as a place to start?

Mr. PYHRR. Well——

Senator GLENN. We are talking about a whole different magnitude of regulatory agencies when we get to the Federal agencies. It would be a major cut if we took them all on at once in the Federal Government.

Mr. PYHRR. I think if that were made one of the pilot programs and one area to attack I would say that it might have a very high priority. However, I would not make it the key area. I would get into a more operating area with a lot of Federal employees, with a lot of programmatic areas which are perhaps overlapping, spread throughout the country, where it is very difficult to sit here and see how this program is operating. It is certainly not only difficult for the legislature but I have found within agencies, even way down in agencies, that the information is not there to allow those managers to do an effective job. So, I would tend to pick more of an operating agency for the bulk of the test that involved more people, perhaps.

Senator GLENN. Did you say in Georgia you left judicial out of it?

Mr. PYHRR. Judicial was not in it the first year.

Senator GLENN. What was left out?

Mr. PYHRR. In the executive, nothing. It was 100 percent done for all executive agencies. The legislature and judicial did not use the process. I believe the judicial did in subsequent years.

Senator GLENN. How about the legislature, that would be a fertile field here. I think one of the first things here is to zero base Congress and see what happens here. I don't say that frivolously either. We have so many overlapping jurisdictions and duplicate functions that I think a zero-base analysis of Congress itself is in order.

Mr. PYHRR. I would agree.

Senator GLENN. They didn't do that in the Georgia legislature as far as you know?

Mr. PYHRR. I don't know. Let me put it that way.

Senator GLENN. We covered tax expenditures, I believe.

Mr. PYHRR. Yes.

Senator GLENN. In trying to analyze some of these things at the State government level, for instance did you ask for budgeting figures or require budgeting figures from the originator up through his review process, how it was changed and then on to final authority before it was put in the State budget?

Mr. PYHRR. The basic part of the process, the decision package I call it, basically remains unchanged throughout the entire cycle as you go up the organization unless succeeding levels of management go back and say you didn't do the analysis properly——

Senator GLENN. Did you have original figures available? This is what I am building up to. I am on the Interior Committee, and we have had experience with energy legislation and with trying to work through the budgets for instance from ERDA and FEA and some other people.

For instance, it is quite helpful to know what the original figures requested were for solar energy. Whatever the expert on solar energy has asked for gets submitted to ERDA, they massage the figures and determine priorities, and then they submit them of course to OMB. Then OMB makes their changes and they submit them over here and by the time it gets here it is a quite different set of figures than it was when it started out.

Congress in areas of particular importance such as energy right now may want to reweigh some of those evaluations to help set priorities apart from the OMB agency process.

We have had some tables put together by Chet Holifield which have become known in the energy business as the Holifield tables. He has taken the trouble to talk to enough people so that he was finally able to put together these things and put them together from the inception of the idea and what the ideal funding for solar would be. They traced what happened to those solar funds as they came up the process and came over to Congress. These have been helpful to us in committee trying to evaluate whether we should have that original amount for solar energy or the amount that got reduced uphill by somebody who may not have known beans about solar energy.

In establishing your priorities on zero-base budgeting, did you go through a process such as that?

Mr. Pyhrr. Yes; the identification starting at the lowest level of the organization where the analysis was developed would maintain its identity throughout the process going, both in Georgia for example and all other organizations that have done this, to the Governor and the legislature.

Now, in large organizations certain areas have been summarized.

Senator Glenn. Did you find that useful?

Mr. Pyhrr. I found it extremely useful because I could, within a reasonable period of time in a half a billion dillar operation like the Department of Human Resources, go through all the original documents, and in a cursory review identify where the basic problems were among institutions.

It was very easy to go back in from my standpoint, or the department administrators' standpoint, or the Governor's or legislature's standpoint, to go back into all the documents that as they initially were prepared in the institutions or in the bowels of each department.

Senator Glenn. We have found these extremely valuable here. As the figures come uphill, if you take the original figure and the final budget figure, either you obviously find some huge discrepancies here or find others that come through unscathed to follow the example of solar, they come through with the full amount as requested by the originator clear through the solar expert. If that comes through unscathed, obviously, he made his point properly. You will find some energy programs here getting only 10 percent of their request. Somebody made a judgment on priorities for energy that may or may not be correct. In our system of checks and balances it seems to me that it would be extremely valuable to have these figures available and I am glad to hear you say you have experience with that and it worked for you and that you found the figures valuable.

Mr. Pyhrr. Yes. One thing I should stress, we talk about figures and I interpret not only just dollar figures but programmatic figures, workload, et cetera.

Senator Glenn. Sure.

Mr. Pyhrr. One of the frustrations I know that many well intentioned people in the executive and large agencies have is to be able to get down into this data. Whereas, what I am sure you must find in your staff in looking at different areas of operation, 90 percent of the time is spent trying to find out what is happening and 10 percent spent doing something with that information. What zero-base budgeting should do is give you that information so you can spend the bulk of the time trying to look at programs, seeing whether you agree with the priorities, seeing whether you agree with the delivery mechanisms and making this available at all levels of government. And it is equally important to administrators in large departments as it is to you. They have the same problems.

Senator GLENN. I don't want to run too long but one other rather unique area at the Federal level is that we have a lot of programs of income transfer and entitlement programs and you are familiar with those. We have social security, all these things that eat up 72 percent of the Federal budget and we only have about a 28-percent discretionary funding option open to us in any one budget. I think that was the figure for 1974.

Now, in trying to establish a priority, obviously those areas are the most difficult to get into. Those areas of entitlement programs and so on.

Do you think we would be better advised to stay more in the operating end of the budget, the 28 percent in starting out? I am not trying to lead your thinking but what is your advice in that area?

Mr. PYHRR. I would suggest it be started in the operating departments, whether it be Defense, or HEW or whatever. I think the question you are asking is the same question faced at the State level because many of the State's dollars go out into local educational or grants to localities.

Of course, that gets into different political jurisdictions and becomes somewhat of a problem to say how can we now start evaluating what that money is used for. There is obviously the policy question of whether the Federal Government wants more or less strings attached to the local levels. Zero-based budgeting has been very effective at the local level and is in a way easier to install because of the smaller size. In cities such as Garland, Tex.; and Senator Roth isn't here, but I understand that Wilmington, Del., in his State, has also installed it and had very good success with it.

In Georgia, some of the localities, school districts and local administrations started picking up the process on their own, so the State started to get some visibility of where priorities should be and what the local needs were. Part of this is a policy consideration. Should you give the money out and let the localities do what they like? Or do you over a period of time get a better indication of how effective these moneys are being used.

Senator GLENN. Let me go to another area. What type department in State government did you see the largest benefits accrue from, if I am making myself clear?

In other words, you put this in across the State government.

Mr. PYHRR. Yes.

Senator GLENN. Where was it most effective first. Maybe that is the first area that would lead us to where we should go, or what bite we should take off first. Could you from your experience tell us where it was most effective earliest in State government?

Mr. PYHRR. I would say in the human resources area because that tended to be an area that was very emotional——

Senator GLENN. Was that a department?

Mr. PYHRR. HEW type of department.

Senator GLENN. That was a department in the State government; was it?

Mr. Pyhrr. No, it started out before the reorganization being a very fragmented organization. It was a welfare department, it was a health department, fragmented through several major agencies. After the reorganization they tended to get combined. As a matter of fact, one of——

Senator Glenn. As they combined was there a reduction of personnel and reduction of expenditure or more efficient operation?

Mr. Pyhrr. No, total costs were not reduced over the period of time of Carter's administration. From my evaluation of the State of Georgia, when I first got there, many of the programs were in very poor shape. Carter's priorities were twofold: No. 1, Don't increase taxes, which he did not do; second, was to plow the moneys that we saved in various areas back into program delivery. Now that was true over the 4-year period. An interesting thing happened the first year. He inherited a budget, and in the middle of the year there surfaced a $57 million shortfall. We had done zero-base budgeting looking at the next year, which was his first year that he impacted the budget directly.

He backed that analysis into the current year. It was a $57 million shortfall, 5 percent of State funds at that time in the agencies we were looking at. We made cuts in the agencies, and did it in about 2 weeks with the agencies since we had the material to do it with, which ranged from virtually nothing to 15 percent. Within agency cuts ranged from nothing to complete elimination of some areas. So in that period of time the budgets were reduced in a rational manner rather than let education maybe take a 3 percent cut and cut everybody else 7, which was the traditional way that kind of cut would have been made.

In the 4 years of administration, the budget, I believe, went up 20 to 25 percent, and that was a very high inflationary period, but no taxes were increased. There were major improvements in services, and especially in corrections and mental health.

Senator Glenn. We are going to have to end this I am afraid. I appreciate your coming in, Mr. Pyhrr. You have obviously had a lot of experience.

THE GEORGIA EXPERIENCE

Zero-base budgeting involves highly detailed program and management procedures that can best be illustrated by examining their actual application. The Senate Government Operations Committee, gathering background material on the Muskie proposal (S. 2925), utilized a number of explanatory documents supplied by the state of Georgia. The government of Georgia also provided the Senate committee with a summary of its experience and answers to specific questions; both are reprinted here. Sample forms used by the state are found in the appendix section of this volume. While the forms used for federal level zero-base budgeting will differ, the documentation of the decision packages undoubtedly will follow the logic of the Georgia system.

Summary of Zero-Base Budgeting in Georgia ([83], pp. 121–123)

Zero-base budgeting in Georgia is a program that requires every agency to justify every dollar sought in future appropriations—including existing programs as well as proposed new programs.

Zero-base budgeting, therefore, serves as a mechanism for monitoring State programs and encouraging greater efficiency in government. These goals are achieved by reducing *ALL* operations of State Government into functions and requiring budgets to be proposed on the basis of these functions.

Budgets for each function are analyzed in decision packages that become a part of the annual budget submission in the fall. Each function—those already funded and in operation, as well as new programs proposed for funding—must be rated according to each agency's priority for inclusion in the next year's budget.

Thus, under zero-base budgeting existing expenditures must battle with proposed new expenditures for the funds that are available in the upcoming budget cycle. This has the result of forcing existing programs to be compared against proposed new programs for funding purposes.

Most governmental budgets are now developed by assuming that all existing functions will be continued. New programs must vie with each other for funding based on the amount of new money available for appropriations. In Georgia, they clash head on.

Here is a hypothetical example (overly simplified, of course) of how the procedure works:

An agency identifies 19 existing functions and one new function, and ranks them according to priority. The new function gets a rating of 17, which means it is deemed more important than three existing functions.

When the Governor develops his budget for presentation to the General Assembly, projected funds available are adequate only to finance through the number 19 function. The result is that the new function is included in the proposed budget and function 20 is dropped from budget consideration. If the General Assembly goes along with this proposal, the existing function is abandoned because its priority is below the funding level.

Under the old budget procedure in Georgia, and under most budget procedures, there would not have been sufficient money for the new proposed program and it would not have been funded. But by giving it a higher rating than three existing programs in this example, it was funded.

Beginning for fiscal year 1977 Georgia is adding a new dimension to its zero-base procedures. This new concept will provide the first true evaluation of how well State programs are functioning by requiring performance measurements of every function of State Government.

For instance, if the Department of Public Safety is authorized to hire 25 State troopers to provide a specified number of additional hours of highway patrolling, the State of Georgia now has no official mechanism of requiring proof that the patrolmen were hired and that they were used for the purpose outlined in the budget request. Of course, this information can be obtained by budget analysts but it requires a special project and is not a part of budget procedures affecting every function of government.

Under the new evaluation procedures, the Department of Public Safety will be required to report to the Office of Planning and Budget on a regular basis exactly how many patrolmen have been hired and exactly how many hours they patrolled. In so doing, the department will be required to evaluate the effectiveness of the additional patrolling. The State can then determine whether the expenditure of the additonal patrolmen is justifiable in view of the results obtained.

Besides the departmental evaluation, each report will be evaluated by the budget analyst and the planner from the OPB staff assigned to that agency.

This procedure will apply to all functions of Georgia's State Government—old as well as new functions. For the first time, the State can truly evaluate whether its tax dollars are being spent wisely and, more importantly, whether they are being spent as the Governor and General Assembly believed they would be spent when the budget was passed.

Questions and Answers on the Georgia System

Question. Why is the State of Georgia involved in a new budget procedure?

Answer. Under the previous procedure we never examined in detail our current activities, and as a result never uncovered many inefficiencies that had developed throughout State Government.

Question. What will Zero-Base Budgeting do?

Answer. Zero-Base Budgeting requires each Agency to analyze and justify its entire appropriation request in detail—current activities as well as new activities.

Question. What is included in the Zero-Base Budgeting process?

Answer. The first step requires the preparation of a "decision package" for each function or activity. It includes an analysis of the cost, purpose, alternative courses of action, measures of performance, consequences of not performing the activity, and benefits. The second step requires that each decision package be ranked in order of importance against other current and new activities. This first year we are analyzing about 10,000 decision packages.

Question. Who is developing and ranking these decision packages?

Answer. Managers throughout all levels of State Government because they are the experts in their activities, and we want their recommendations and analyses. We also want them to become familiar with the budgeting and planning procedures, and to evaluate their own cost effectiveness.

Question. What alternatives are being identified in decision packages?

Answer. First, different ways of performing each activity are identified— such as centralized versus decentralized operations, or evaluating the economy of State-run print shops versus commercial printers. Second, alternatives for different levels of effort for performing each activity are identified. Managers must identify a minimum level of spending—often about 75 percent of their current operating level, and then identify in separate decision packages the costs and benefits of additional levels of spending for that activity.

Question. Why is the identification of different levels of spending for each activity required?

Answer. First, it forces every manager to consider and evaluate a level of spending lower than his current operating level. Second, it gives each manager the alternative of eliminating a function, or choosing from several levels of effort.

Question. Are current and new activities ranked together?

Answer. Yes. In order to fund some of the important new programs being proposed, we must eliminate or reduce some of the existing programs which are of lesser importance. Therefore, we must consider each decision package on its own merits, disregarding the fact that it is either a current or new activity.

Question. Will an activity that is eliminated or reduced cause lay-offs?

Answer. No. Normal turnover, plus shifting people into other activities should eliminate the need for any lay-offs even when the number of employees is reduced.

Question. Will the Legislature use this information in its review??

Answer. All the information will be available to the Legislature, and will aid the members in conducting their reviews and anayses.

Question. How does Zero-Base Budgeting relate to the Goals for Georgia and Reorganization programs?

Answer. All three programs fit together in a unified attempt to improve State Government. Reorganization is using the analysis provided by Zero-Base Budgeting in their study, and the decision packages will be used to develop a detailed budget that incorporates the reorganization effort. In the Goals for Georgia program, decision packages will be prepared to identify and evaluate specific methods and costs of implementing the goals.

Question. What impact will Zero-Base Budgeting have on State Government?

Answer. In the long run, the most significant impact will occur in the middle levels of agency management, where managers will have to evaluate in detail their planning, operations, efficiency, and cost effectiveness on a continuous basis. Duplication of effort will be identified, with duplication eliminated and similar functions considered for centralization. In addition, the taxpayer should benefit because high priority new programs will be funded in part by improved efficiency and elimination or reduction of current activities without significant reductions in service.

Chapter 8
Government Economy and
Spending Reform Act of 1976

BACKGROUND AND SCOPE OF THE LEGISLATION ([72], pp. 1–31)

Landmark legislation on sunset and zero-base budgeting was introduced in the 94th Congress as the Government Economy and Spending Reform Act of 1976. It was the most significant and extensive reorganization proposal put before Congress since President Richard Nixon's 1971 reorganization plan. Senator Edmund Muskie was the author of this bill, S. 2925, and he reintroduced it on the first day of the 95th Congress as S. 2 (meaning it was the second bill introduced in the Senate during that session). Senator Muskie's success in reforming congressional budget processes has established him as the authority in Congress on government reform and reorganization. In 1974, he sponsored the Congressional Budget Act, which resulted in Public Law 93-344, creating the Congressional Budget Office and thereby providing Congress with basic budget data. He is currently chairman of the Senate Budget Committee.

The Government Economy and Spending Reform Act, as proposed, would subject all federal government agencies and programs to periodic zero-base review through the budget authorization process. It contains several highly significant elements bearing on Executive branch reorganization. One is the far-reaching nature of the proposal. All agencies and programs would be affected, despite their assumed permanence. Another regards the functional grouping of agencies and programs into clusters for the review process. For instance, all health-related activities would be reviewed in the same time period, regardless of their location within the structure of government agencies and departments.

This bill (S. 2925) was subjected to detailed committee examination and laid the groundwork for governmentwide introduction of sunset and zero-base budgeting. While the procedures offered underwent modification in the course of deliberation, the analysis and debate concerning the 1976 act provide a valuable study of zero-base budgeting and sunset. The Senate Government Operations Committee submitted a report on S. 2925 to the Congress in August 1976, the summary of which appears here in abridged form.

Purpose of the Legislation

The purpose of S. 2925, as amended, is to close the gap between Congress and the results of its legislative work—the actual performance and accomplishments of Federal programs paid for out of the Federal budget.

The Committee proposes to accomplish this goal by establishing a process through which Congress can begin to exercise greater control over Federal programs it has enacted into law. The process which the Committee recommends—the termination and review provisions of S. 2925 as amended—is aimed at strengthening the congressional authorization process, one of the most important policy tools which the Congress has.

The process recommended in S. 2925 has two principal elements. The first requires that all authorizations of Federal programs and all tax expenditures—terminate over a five year period, unless they are reenacted. The second requires that all programs and all tax expenditures undergo a zero base review by the appropriate Congressional Committees with the assistance of executive branch departments or agencies, and congressional support agencies, before they are reauthorized or reenacted.

The Committee firmly believes that the termination and review of Federal programs should be a permanent feature of the authorization process in Congress. Nevertheless, the Committee is mindful that this is a new concept and that its operation cannot be fully envisioned at this time. S. 2925 as amended therefore, provides for the examination of the review process by the appropriate committees of Congress prior to the completion of the first five year cycle. At that time, Congress will be able to determine, on the basis of actual experience, the future course of this review process and redirect it in any manner that it deems appropriate.

Explanation of Committee Action

The Committee would like to state at the outset that S. 2925, as amended, does not require the reenactment of the entire U.S. Code. Rather, it only affects those provisions of law authorizing the expenditure of funds. Accordingly, substantive provisions of law—antitrust, civil rights, occupational safety laws, etc.—are not affected by the termination provision. If, however, an authorization is allowed to terminate, authority to enforce or issue new regulations would be suspended until a new authorization is enacted or new budget authority is provided.

While the Committee does not believe that such substantive provisions of law should be terminated during the five year period, the Committee does believe that the Congress should review, on a regular basis, the ways in which such laws, and the policies they reflect, are implemented by the Federal Government. And it believes that the best way for Congress to undertake that review is by forcing a regular reauthorization of the programs operated by those agencies.

Hence, the focal point of the termination and review process proposed in S. 2925, as amended, is intended to be those provisions of law which authorize or provide budget authority for the delivery of services or goods by the Federal Government.

Another section of this report documents in some detail the condition of the Federal Government which has led the Committee to conclude that this legislation is necessary. In summary, that condition is one in which the Congress finds itself increasingly removed from the results of its legislative work, because of several factors: (1) the vast number and complexity of Federal programs; (2) the dramatic increase in the percentage of Federal spending for so-called uncontrollable programs, comprising roughly 77 percent of the fiscal year 1977 Federal budget; and (3) the even more rapid growth in the cost of Federal programs with permanent appropriations, those which escape any systematic and thorough congressional review.

The Committee believes that these factors make it increasingly difficult for the Congress, under the business-as-usual approach, to make intelligent, rational decisions about Federal programs, be they new or old.

The Committee also believes that these factors threaten to seriously undermine the success of the most important congressional reform in recent years, the new budget process, by continually reducing the room in the budget for discretionary decisions which enable Congress to meet changing national priorities.

Finally, the Committee believes that the combined effect of these factors is the impression of a Federal Government where no one is in charge, and that this impression is in large part responsible for declining public confidence in the operations of Government.

In summary, the Committee believes that unless an effort is made to bring these factors under control, the Congress may not have the reserves it needs—either in the budget or the public trust—to pursue a legislative agenda that is changing with the nation.

The principal operative mechanism in S. 2925, as amended, is an automatic termination provision for Federal programs on a 5-year schedule. Any program, regardless of its size or importance, which is not reauthorized by the Congress, would be terminated. Programs are scheduled for termination and review on the basis of groupings by budget function, so that all programs within one function or subfunction will be considered and reauthorized during the same period of time. This process ensures not only that all programs will be subject to regular review, but also that the Congress will be forced to assess the Federal effort in an entire program area at one time. It is the Committee's hope that this procedure will lead to elimination of conflicts and duplication in programs.

N1   Title V of S. 2925, as amended, would require the termination over a 5-year period of all tax expenditures according to a schedule to be enacted by the Senate and House during the 95th Congress.

In order that the reauthorization process be more than a stepped up version of current authorization and appropriation process, S. 2925, as amended, requires that all programs scheduled for termination be subjected to a zero base review by the appropriate Congressional committees with the assistance of departments and agencies of the Executive Branch and the Congressional support agencies before they can be reauthorized. The Committee believes it is necessary to challenge the traditional assumption of budgeting—that because a program was funded last year, it deserves to be funded this year at the same or higher level. The zero base review concept included in S. 2925, as amended, has a very different assumption as its foundation—that programs are not entitled automatically to continued funding once they are created; rather that a case must be made for continued funding. Depending on how well that case is made, programs can be funded at the current level or at lower or higher levels, or revised to reflect the findings of the zero base review. If they fail to meet the test for reauthorization, they would be terminated.

The Committee recognizes that implementation of this process will require considerable groundwork. Therefore, S. 2925, as amended, provides for the creation of a temporary commission, to be modeled after the two previous Hoover Commissions, to provide information and recommendations needed by Congress and the executive branch for the reorganization and improved efficiency of the government.

The Committee believes that the termination provision, reinforced by the information provided Congress through the review process, will go far toward closing the gap between the authorizing committees and the operations of the programs within their jurisdiction. To the extent that this goal is achieved, the Committee believes that we will have made substantial progress toward the broader purpose of this reform—that of providing improved and more responsive services to the American people for the tax dollars they pay.

HISTORY OF THE LEGISLATION

The Intergovernmental Relations Subcommittee held 7 days of hearings on S. 2067 and S. 2925 in March and April of 1976.

In the course of these hearings, the subcommittee heard 34 witnesses, all of whom generally supported the goals of this legislation, though some raised questions and offered suggestions about its implementation. The following is a list of witnesses who testified at the hearings:

Senator Frank Moss of Utah; Senator Harry Byrd of Virginia; Senator Robert Dole of Kansas; Senator Patrick Leahy of Vermont; Congressman James Blanchard of Michigan; Congressman Norman Mineta of California; Congressman Elliott Levitas of Georgia; Congressman Stephen Neal of North Carolina; Congressman Martin Russo of Illinois, and Congressman Ralph Regula of Ohio.

Also, Elliot Richardson, Secretary of Commerce; James Lynn, Director, Office of Management and Budget; Dr. Alice Rivlin, Director, Congressional Budget Office; Don A. Paarlberg, Director of Agricultural Economics, Department of Agriculture; William Morrill, Assistant Secretary for Planning and Evaluation, Department of Health, Education, and Welfare; and Roy Ash, former Director, Office of Management and Budget.

Also, Allen Schick, Senior Specialist, Library of Congress; Arnold Weber, Dean of the Graduate School of Industrial Education, Carnegie Mellon Institute; Dwight Ink, former Deputy Administrator, General Services Administration; David Walker, Assistant Director, Advisory Commission on Intergovernmental Relations; and Bruce McDowell, Senior Analyst, Advisory Commission on Intergovernmental Relations.

Also, John Gardner, Chairman, Common Cause; Richard Leone, Treasurer of the State of New Jersey; Raoul Rodriguez, Executive Director, Colorado Department of State Regulatory Agencies; Fred Anderson, Colorado State Senior, Gerry Kopel, Colorado State Representative; Sidney Brooks, Board Chairman, Colorado Common Cause; Peter H. Pyhrr, Vice President Alpha Wire, Inc.; Donald Schwab, Legislative Director, Veterans of Foreign Wars; and Richard Lesher, President, U.S. Chamber of Commerce.

Following completion of these hearings, the subcommittee met on May 13 to consider this legislation. On May 13, the subcommittee voted favorably to refer S. 2925, as amended, to the full committee. The full committee met on August 3 and 4 and unanimously reported the bill with additional amendments.

PRINCIPAL COMMITTEE AMENDMENTS TO S. 2925

S. 2925 was introduced on February 3, 1976. Since its introduction the Committee has worked to improve the legislation so as to strengthen the role of Congress in authorizing Federal programs without imposing an unworkable burden. The scope of the legislation has been extended to require a review of Federal tax expenditures, and the bill, as amended, would create a Hoover-type commission to report on methods to improve the operation of Government.

The major changes which have been made in S. 2925 are as follows:

(1) The review and termination cycle for programs has been extended from four to five years to better distribute the workload for the Executive Branch and the Congress.

(2) The standards for conducting a zero-base review have been more clearly defined and broadened to assist the development of policy options in the authorization process. In addition. the Congress is given more flexibility in the application of these standards to each program in order to avoid needless paperwork and to permit reviews to be tailored to the nature of a particular program.

(3) The Congressional Committees of jurisdiction are now required to file tentative zero review plans for each of their programs by March 1 of the year before those programs are scheduled to terminate and to finalize those plans by April 1. This review plan should delineate the detail, scope, criteria and standards for each review as well as the priority the Committee gives the review and its elements, and the assistance the Committee expects to receive from the Executive Branch agencies and congressional support agencies in preparing it.

(4) The Director of the Office of Management and Budget is required to develop and submit to Congress by December 31, 1977, a study of the feasibility of applying zero base budgeting to all Federal agencies.

(5) A new Title V provides for the review within 5 years of all Federal tax expenditure provisions. Because tax expenditures are viewed as identical in many ways to direct expenditure programs and often are created to achieve similar purposes, they are to undergo a zero base review by the Ways and Means and Finance Committees before reenactment. Congress is required to enact a schedule for tax expenditure review in the first session of the 95th Congress.

(6) A new Title IV creates a Citizen's Bicentennial Commission on the Organization and Operation of Government. Similar to the previous two Federal Hoover Commissions, this 18-member commission would be given 33 months to examine the organization of the government and recommend program changes, consolidations and eliminations. Provisions from an earlier Title II for the identification of conflicting and overlapping programs have been included in this Title.

(7) The executive branch is required to give the Congress statements of agency budget requests and estimated fiscal year outlays on the day after the President submits his budget. In addition, authorizing committees would be able to request additional information regarding those requests and the requests of component units within Federal agencies.

(8) The review process itself would be sunset after completion of the first review cycle. This would provide the Congress with an opportunity to examine its experience under this new process and take steps to re-enact or redirect any of its features.

(9) When an authorization for a program terminates, the authority of the agency administering the program to issue and enforce rules, regulations, standards, decrees, citations, and orders, to issue licenses, to establish rates, or to impose civil penalties under the program is suspended until such time as the authorization is reenacted.

THE SCOPE OF THE LEGISLATION

INTRODUCTION

The Congressional Budget Act of 1974, provides, for the first time, a mechanism with which the Congress can set spending levels for the Federal budget as a whole. Under that new law, Congressional attention is now focused on total spending levels for the entire Government, as well as on broad categories—or budget functions—which, taken together, constitute a comprehensive but general statement of national priorities.

S. 2925, as amended, has been proposed in recognition of the fact that no matter how successful the new budget process is, Congress will not have truly effective control over budgetary decisions and policymaking unless it moves to strengthen its control over the individual parts—the thousands of programs which are the building blocks of national priorities. As one witness at the hearing put it, "In any battle between the whole and its parts, the parts will always win out."

The focus of S. 2925, as amended, is on these building blocks. The mechanism for ensuring greater congressional control over them is the termination provision set out in Title I of the legislation in combination with the zero base review provisions of Title II. Through this two-pronged mechanism, the Congress will not only have better information with which to make more informed decisions about program continuation, but will also be forced to take affirmative action if any or all programs are to be continued.

APPLICATION OF TERMINATION PROVISION TO THE AUTHORIZATION PROCESS

(1) The legislation requires the scheduled termination of provisions of law which authorize budget authority for Federal programs and activities, including those which authorize permanent budget authority as well as those provisions of law which provide permanent budget authority.

While the legislation does require the termination and reauthorization process over a five-year cycle, it does not preclude the authorizing committees of the Congress from reauthorizing a program for a shorter period of time, as long as the zero base review is performed according to the schedule in Title I.

In delineating the scope of the termination provision, the Committee clearly intends that it applies solely to authorizations and permanent budget authority, not to any other provisions of law. In other words, the legislation defines the scope of the termination provisions by distinguishing between authorizations which provide budget authority and those substantive provisions of law which do not. This distinction is described more fully below:

(a) *Authorizations to be included under termination provision*

(1) All authorizations for a government program in effect on the effective date of the legislation. This category is to include provisions of law which authorize for limited periods of time or which provide permanent budget authority.

(2) All provisions of law which provide new budget authority (or permanent budget authority) for a program for a fiscal year beginning after the termination date applicable to such program.

(3) Some programs have non-specific authorizations. This is the case with agencies and departments which derive their authority from some organic legislation which does not provide a specific authorization. The Committee found several examples of such laws, and believes there are many more. For the purpose of House and Senate rules, such laws are deemed to be authorizations, even though the authorization itself is nonspecific. While no such provisions of law would be terminated under S. 2925. as amended, such provisions no longer would be deemed to satisfy the requirements as authorizations for budget authority under the rules of the House and Senate.

The legislation further requires that all authorizations be made specific. Accordingly, after the completion of the five year cycle, all programs will have specific authorizations for budget authority, and these would terminate in accord with the schedule.

No substantive provisions of law other than authorizations would be terminated. For example, civil rights laws, antitrust laws, occupational safety standards and the Federal criminal code would not be terminated under Title I of S. 2925, as amended.

(1) Procedures relating to tax expenditures

Although S. 2925, as amended, does not propose to terminate substantive provisions of law in general, there is one exception to this limitation. Title V of the bill, as amended, would terminate tax expenditures, on the basis of a schedule which must be approved by the Senate and House during the first session of the 95th Congress.

The Committee has recommended this special case because of the unique nature of tax expenditures. The Committee believes that tax expenditures are in many respects the equivalent to direct Federal expenditures in that they attempt to accomplish the same goals through a different mechanism. Thus, they should be subject to the same kind of regular review as are direct expenditures, through programs, under the provisions of S. 2925, as amended.

(2) In order to provide assistance in the implementation of the first termination and review cycle, S. 2925, as amended, requires the Appropriations Committees and the Budget Committees of the House and Senate with the cooperation of GAO to submit to the Congress by April 1, 1977—before the beginning of the review cycle—a report including the following information.

An identification of each program carried on under provision of law authorizing the enactment of new budget authority;

An identification of each program carried on under provision of law which permanently authorizes the enactment of new budget authority;

An identification of each program carried on under provision of law which acts as a non-specific authorization;

An identification of each program carried on under a provision of law which provides permanent budget authority.

And, in the case of regulatory programs, the provisions of law which provide regulatory authority for those programs and the nature of that authority.

The information provided in this report shall also include references to appropriations bills for each program, and the authority under which each is carried on. The information is to be cross-referenced so as to provide the authorizing committees of the Congress with information pertaining to the programs within their jurisdiction.

N3   In addition, the Comptroller General is instructed, in compiling this report, to identify programs in a manner which:

Assures that all provisions of law which serve as authorizations of budget authority or which provide regulatory authority are included in the identification of programs;

Classifies each program in only one functional and subfunctional category;

Provides that each program is administered by only one government agency;

Is consistent with the structure of national needs, agency missions, and basic programs required by the Budget and Accounting Act of 1921, as amended by the 1974 Congressional Budget Act;

To the maximum extent feasible is consistent with the appropriations account structure of the Federal Government;

To the extent appropriate, groups related authorizations into a single program.

TERMINATION SCHEDULE

The Committee has given considerable consideration to the order of the termination schedule in Title I of the legislation, in order to assure that the workload is as evenly balanced as possible, both on individual committees and from year to year in the review process.

The termination schedule that appeared in S. 2925, as introduced, was designed to insure that similar Federal activities would be considered during the same year by the Congress. The schedule also reflected the best assumptions of the bill's sponsors about the number of programs in each function and subfunction and how the termination of these programs each year in the schedule would affect all committee workloads.

While the original schedule was generally balanced in its effects on committee workload, it was possible to fine tune the schedule as more information was made available by the General Accounting Office. The termination schedule in the reported bill is the product of that refinement.

The committee staff was, unfortunately, unable to precisely count the number of programs terminated each year by the schedule since such information is not currently available. A program count combined with committee assignments will be conducted and formalized under other provisions of S. 2925. The committee staff was, however, able to estimate, on the basis of the data supplied, the approximate number of programs to be terminated each year for each committee.

A glance at the revised schedule shows three major changes—functions 300 (natural resources, environment and energy), 750 (law enforcement), and 350 (agriculture) have been broken down into subfunctions for the purposes of termination. This breakdown was made to more evenly balance the workload over the five year schedule for four committees: Interior and Insular Affairs, Judiciary, Agriculture, and Commerce.

For example, under the termination schedule as introduced, the Interior and Insular Affairs Committee's projected workload looked like this—

Programs terminated

Year:
1979 _____ 4
1980 _____ 9
1981 _____ 130
1982 _____ 1
1983 _____ 14

Obviously, in terms of workload mandated by the schedule, 1981 presented a problem.

An examination by the committee staff of the Interior Committee programs terminated in 1981 revealed that 134 of the 153 were in function 300, Natural Resources, Environment and Energy. By breaking function 300 down to its six subfunctional categories and distributing them among the five years of the schedule, the Interior Committee's workload picture was balanced to—

Programs terminated

Year:
1979 _____ 13
1980 _____ 55
1981 _____ 1
1982 _____ 58
1983 _____ 31

The committee was not able to achieve a perfect balance by the subfunctional division because there are simply more programs in some subfunctions than in others. For example, for Interior, subfunction 301 has 58 programs while subfunction 304 has only two.

The workload for the other three committees principally affected by the schedule change is shown below, with the workload under the original schedule contrasted with that under the schedule in the bill as reported:

Year	Number of programs	
	Schedule as introduced	Schedule as reported
Judiciary:		
1979	66	37
1980		29
1981	3	3
1982	2	2
1983	5	5
Commerce:		
1979		30
1980	3	3
1981	115	48
1982	46	48
1983	13	48
Agriculture:		
1979	3	12
1980	95	45
1981	55	14
1982		71
1983	12	23

The Committee believes that these changes in the termination schedule will alleviate the workload problems substantially.

Although the Committee notes that there is no particular magic to the actual order set out in the schedule, the Committee does note that there are definite and sound reasons for certain parts of the order.

For example, national defense is first on the list for a specific reason: Under existing practice, much of the military budget is authorized and appropriated annually. Thus it should be easier to accommodate the national defense function under the termination provision than it will be for many other programs which have long-range or permanent authorizations.

Furthermore, the defense function is divided into far fewer individual program parts than are many of the other functions, such as natural resources. In the case of defense, only a handful of major authorization bills are involved. The same is true, though to a lesser degree, for other functions scheduled at the beginning of the five-year cycle. But for other functions, the number of individual authorizations which must be renewed is much greater.

In general, the particular order for termination in Title I was structured to proceed from the "easier" functions to the more difficult—with difficulty measured by the degree of fragmentation of the function between programs, agencies and congressional committees.

In the case of tax expenditures (Title V), the Committee has not recommended a specific schedule in the language of the legislation. The Committee does intend that they be terminated on a staggered schedule, as are programs under Title I. However, the Committee recognizes that a specialized perspective must be used in determining a schedule for tax expenditures and so recommends that such schedule be developed by the Joint Committee on Internal Revenue Taxation, after consultation with the Treasury Department and the House and Senate Budget Committees, and referred to the Committees on Ways and Means and Finance. A termination schedule is to be enacted by the 95th Congress.

MAJOR ELEMENTS OF THE PROCESS

Congressional commitment

The Committee recommends the legislative initiative embodied in S. 2925, as amended, rather than reliance solely upon administrative action, because it believes there is a real need for congressional approval of and commitment to such a new process. We have seen with the early success of the new budget process that a congressional commitment to this kind of reform is an essential ingredient in making the reform work. Budget reform addressed a fundamental congressional problem. S. 2925, as amended, does the same. The Committee believes that the enactment of this legislation, in and of itself, will be a powerful incentive for the Congress to take the process seriously.

Linkage to the authorization process

Under the rules of the House and the Senate, both an authorization and an appropriation are generally needed to finance Federal programs. In S. 2925, as amended, the termination and zero base review provisions have been tied to the congressional authorization process, for two principal reasons.

In the first place, the authorization process provides Congress with a handle on questions of Federal policy. Since a fundamental purpose of S. 2925, as amended, is to force the regular review of congressionally determined policies as implemented through federal programs,

it is both appropriate and logical that the process be tied to authorizations, which are the responsibility of the legislative committees of
Congress.

Second, the Committee believes that certain current trends in Federal spending patterns have weakened the authorization process and
are thus undermining recent congressional efforts to reassert control
over Federal budget and spending policies.

These trends include the dramatic growth in programs with
permanent authorizations and appropriations—funds spent with
essentially no review by Congress. This is now the fastest growing
component of the Federal budget.

The Committee believes that these trends bode ill, not only for the
new congressional budget process, but for the all-important role of
Congress as the policy-developing arm of the Federal government as
well. Therefore, the Committee has proposed, in S. 2925, as amended,
a mechanism for strengthening the authorization process and thereby
bringing Congress closer to the results of its legislative work.

Automatic termination provision

The fact that individual programs must justify their existence or
else be terminated is the strongest incentive in the legislation for the
new process to be taken seriously—one which operates on both program managers in the Executive Branch and on congressional supporters of particular programs.

S. 2925, as amended, requires that the authorization for a program
will terminate unless reenacted. It further states that a reauthorization measure will be out of order unless the required review by the
authorizing committee has been completed. The Committee believes
that these two provisions taken together are very strong incentives for
all participants in the process to do the job well.

Termination by budget function

Under the termination schedule set out in title I of S. 2925, as
amended, programs are grouped by budget function or subfunction.
The purpose of this approach is to encourage the Congress to examine
the Federal effort in an entire policy area—across the jurisdictional
boundaries of agencies and committees—rather than in an unrelated
program-by-program fashion in order to avoid conflicts or duplication
between programs.

The Committee recognizes that any classification of budget functions
may need to be changed from time to time, and it therefore provides
in the legislation for changes in the termination schedule to conform
to improvements and revisions in the categories of budget functions
as they occur.

The Committee believes that in reviewing programs by function or
subfunction Congress will be taking a more comprehensive look at the
broad policy area than it now does.

Neutrality of the process

The Committee believes that one of the major strengths in S. 2925,
as amended, lies in the absolute neutrality of the proposed process.
That process does not attempt to judge the merits of any one program,
or of the priorities for Federal spending as a whole. It only suggests
that Congress should arrive at the decision to have every Federal program—military, foreign or domestic—through positive action.

And hopefully, through the process proposed in S. 2925, as amended, Congress will have better information with which to make the important policy decisions which go into determining those priorities.

Incentives to make the process work

The Committee believes that over and above the incentive provided by the termination provision, there are unstated incentives in S. 2925, as amended which will contribute substantially to the success of the overall process.

From the perspective of the authorizing committees, insuring that they receive useful information is half the battle, of course. Beyond that, there is the fact that the Congress will be looking at the reauthorization of an entire budget function or subfunction at one time. The process cannot prevent Congress from simply re-enacting all programs currently on the books in a particular function, without asking any questions. But should the Congress go this route, it will be publicly acknowledging that it either cannot, or does not choose to, exercise greater control over what it has created. Furthermore, the competition between committees with jurisdiction over different parts of the same budget function should help ensure that there will be substantive debate on reauthorization proposals.

Finally, the Committee believes that there will be enormous pressure for rationalizing program structures when the Congress reviews an entire function at one time and sees the degree of overlap and confusion, both between executive agencies and departments, and between the congressional committees themselves.

HOW THE PROCESS WOULD WORK

The review and termination process set out in Titles I and II of S. 2925, as amended, would be as follows:

Assume that Program X is scheduled to terminate on September 30, 1981, according to the termination schedule set out in Title I.

(1) The first step toward meeting this deadline would come on or before March 1, 1980—the year before termination is scheduled—at which time the Congressional committee with jurisdiction over Program X would file a tentative plan for the zero base review of the program. During the next month, the affected Executive agencies and the Congressional support agencies would have an opportunity to comment on the tentative plan. The plan becomes effective on April 1. (The Committee's plans would encompass all programs within the Committee's jurisdiction scheduled to terminate in 1981, including Program X). In this plan, the Committee would set out its intentions as to the scope of the review of Program X, the priority to be assigned to this review relative to that of other programs within the Committee's jurisdiction scheduled for termination, and the criteria to be used in conducting the review of the program. The criteria and priorities set out in this review plan are to serve as guidelines for the report to be submitted by the Executive Branch agencies and departments to the standing committees of Congress.

(2) On or before October 1, the GAO is to submit to the committee of jurisdiction the results of any prior audits or studies it has conducted of Program X.

(3) On or before December 1, 1980, the affected Executive Branch agencies or departments responsible for administering Program X are to submit to the committee of jurisdiction a report on Program X prepared pursuant to the request of that committee and in accordance wih the guidelines set out in the Committee's review plan. In addition to this required report, executive agencies are required to submit such information and assistance as is requested.

(4) During the course of the year in which the review occurs, the Congressional committees will receive assistance from the four Congressional support agencies, as requested in the review plan. These support agencies (General Accounting Office, Congressional Budget Office, Congressional Research Service, and Office of Technology Assessment) are to provide the principal technical assistance for the committees in their review of terminating programs and of the reports submitted by executive agencies and departments.

(5) On or before May 15, 1981, the Committee with jurisdiction over Program X must file the report of its zero base review of Program X, along with its legislative recommendations for the program. It will be out of order for Congress to consider the reauthorization of Program X unless this zero base review report has been submitted to the House or the Senate, as the case may be.

(6) The Congress has from May 15, 1981 to September 30, 1981, to act upon the Committee's recommendations concerning Program X. If no action is taken, then the authorization for Program X will terminate.

The Workload Question

S. 2925, as introduced would have required the authorizing committees of the House and Senate to reauthorize each year those programs which would be terminated under title I of the Act, according to the functional categories set out in the termination schedule. The bill as introduced would further have required that before any program be reauthorized, it would have to be subjected to a zero base review by the executive branch and the legislative committees of Congress.

Many of the witnesses who testified before the subcommittee on S. 2925 as introduced cautioned that the potential workload of this process could be staggering, and that if the process were not implemented with great care it could fall of its own weight.

Proposed remedies to the workload problem were numerous and varied. Among the suggestions were: (1) a pilot testing of certain programs within functional categories or agencies; (2) a more gradual phase-in of the termination and review process than the four year schedule in the bill; (3) broadening the category of programs exempted from termination and review; (4) a shifting of more of the review responsibility to the Executive Branch, rather than relying so heavily upon the Congressional committees.

In view of the frequency with which this issue was raised, the Committee and its staff gave very careful consideration to the workload question. It was unanimously agreed that the Members did not wish to kill an important and promising new idea by making it unworkable from the outset.

In amending the legislation, the Committee took the following actions in response to the workload issue:

(1) S. 2925, as introduced, would have required termination of all programs on a four year schedule. The Committee has extended this period to five years. This change ease should substantially ease the workload, and if the sunset process is continued beyond the first cycle it also has the additional virtue of ensuring that the same programs are not always scheduled for termination during an election year.

(2) S. 2925, as introduced, would have placed equal—and somewhat duplicative—burdens on the Executive Branch and the authorizing committees of Congress. Both would have had the responsibility for conducting a zero base review for each program scheduled for termination, but their reviews would have been conducted separately and independently. S. 2925, as amended, eliminates that duplication by requiring that only the Congressional committees be responsible for the zero base reviews. Further, because the Committee recognizes that undertaking a zero base review of all programs may strain the current capacity of most Committees, S. 2925, as amended, includes statutory requirements that the Executive Branch and the Congressional support agencies provide the Committees with necessary help in completing the zero base reviews. The result is that while the authorizing Committees retain responsibility for producing the zero base reviews, they are given the authority to request substantial assistance from the Executive Branch agencies and the Congressional support agencies.

(3) S. 2925, as introduced, would have required that the same priority be given to all zero base reviews of programs within a committee's jurisdiction, regardless of whether that committee believed that the review of some programs should have a higher priority than the review of others. It also required that the scope and depth of all zero base reviews be the same. The committee realized that these two requirements would place an inflexible and backbreaking burden on the legislative committees. As a result, S. 2925, as amended is more flexible on both counts. First, it allows the legislative committees to determine the priority the zero base review of each program should be given in relation to the reviews of other programs they are reviewing that same year. Second, it allows these committees to determine the depth, detail and scope of each zero base review within their jurisdiction. There is no single formula for review. The legislation sets out important questions which a committee might decide to address in the review process. But ultimately, the formulation of the review plan is left to the legislative committee. Thus, under S. 2925, as amended, the legislative committees will have substantial control over their workload under the zero base review process.

(4) The termination schedule set out in S. 2925, as introduced, has been amended by the Committee in order to distribute more evenly the workload of the standing committees during each year of the five year termination cycle. The revised schedule, which is discussed in more detail in another section of this report, includes greater breakdown by budget subfunction, rather than by total function, thereby reducing the possibility that any one committee will face an insurmountable workload for any one year of the review cycle. For example, under S. 2925 as introduced, all of Budget Function 750—Law Enforcement and Justice—was scheduled to terminate in 1979. Under S. 2925, as amended, Function 750 has been broken down into Subfunction 751—Federal Law Enforcement and Prosecution, Subfunction 752—Federal judicial activities, Subfunction 753—Federal Correctional Rehabilitation Activities; and Subfunction 754—Law En-

forcement Assistance. Instead of all terminating in the same year, each individual subfunction will terminate at different times during the five-year cycle.

Even though the Committee believes that the steps it has taken to ease the workload problem are substantial, it recognizes that the imposition of the "sunset" and zero base review processes will necessarily result in more work for the legislative committees. That is in large part because these committees will now have to review and take periodic action on heretofore permanent programs.

However, exercising greater control of permanent programs is a fundamental objective of the legislation, and thus the resultant increased workload should not deter the Congress from pursuing that objective.

As a result, the Committee decided that the best way to deal with potential workload problems is to provide the legislative committees with the flexibility to manage their work in the zero base review process.

In taking these steps to meet the workload problem, the Committee rejected proposals to pilot test the proposed process before implementing it government-wide.

In the first place, pilot testing of this process would undercut the impact of the "sunset" concept. Pilot testing has been suggested because of the difficulty of coming up with an evaluation mechanism suitable for all government programs. However, the Committee has responded to this criticism by increasing the flexibility of the evaluation process. The focal point of the legislation is the termination provision and pilot testing has little to offer by way of strengthening this fundamental provision. If anything, it would weaken the termination concept substantially.

Second, the Committee believes that the chances for success of this new process are closely tied to its neutrality. Pilot testing would inevitably require selecting out certain programs or agencies for the initial trial runs. The Committee believes that this would jeopardize the principal of neutrality, thereby conceivably making the process politically unworkable.

THE TERMINATION SCHEDULE AND COMMITTEE WORKLOAD

One of the Committee's major concerns in its consideration of S. 2925 was the impact of the process on the workload of congressional committees. Therefore, since S. 2925 was introduced, the Government Operations Committee has sought to determine the degree to which committees might expect their workload to increase.

The increase in committee workload could be fairly accurately estimated if a comprehensive list of Federal programs and appropriate committee jurisdictions were available. Unfortunately, however, no such compilation currently exists.

As a result, the Committee used three other measures to estimate committee workloads. First, using data provided by the General Accounting Office, the committee staff was able to estimate the number of programs to be terminated each year for each committee.

The other two measures, developed by the Congressional Budget Office, utilize a count of budget accounts and a count of public laws, broken down according to the schedule and by committee.

Committee staff estimates

The committee staff, using data provided by GAO made the following estimates for the number of programs to be terminated each year of the schedule for each of the following Senate committees:

Agriculture and Forestry:
1979	12
1980	45
1981	14
1982	71
1983	23

Commerce:
1977	30
1980	3
1981	48
1982	48
1983	48

Finance:
1979	8
1980	
1981	9
1982	5
1983	12

Government Operations:
1979	
1980	
1981	
1982	5
1983	35

Judiciary:
1979	37
1980	29
1981	3
1982	2
1983	5

Veterans' Affairs:
1979	
1980	
1981	
1982	27
1983	

Banking, Housing and Urban Affairs:
1977	1
1980	29
1981	9
1982	10
1983	6

District of Columbia:
1979	
1980	2
1981	2
1982	
1983	2

Foreign Relations:
1979	26
1980	1
1981	1
1982	4
1983	1

Interior and Insular Affairs:
1979	13
1980	55
1981	5
1982	54
1983	32

Labor and Public Welfare:
1979	14
1980	15
1981	38
1982	36
1983	7

NOTE.—The Committee did not provide a breakdown for all committees because the GAO was not able to provide the Committee with complete data regarding program counts and committee jurisdiction.

Also with the information provided by GAO, the committee staff was able to develop a measure of *increased* workload by breaking out the number of permanently authorized programs and those with implied permanent authorizations from those authorized for a specific number of years. (Implied authorizations are similar to permanent authorizations for the purpose of determining increased workload since they provide authorization for an indefinite period.)

Increased workload can be estimated by combining permanent and implied permanent authorizations since these programs normally do not come up for cyclical consideration by their committees of jurisdiction after they are enacted. Further, most—if not all—of the programs with specific termination dates would come up for reconsideration by the appropriate committees at some point during the five year schedule. As a result the zero base review of these programs wil not substantially increase the workload of the committees.

For example, one could roughly estimate the increased workload of the Commerce Committee with the following breakdown—

| | Number of programs | | | |
	Permanently authorized	With implied permanent authorizations	With specific termination dates	Total
1979	11	14	5	30
1980		1	2	3
1981	31	6	11	48
1982	23	1	24	48
1983	33	6	9	48

The following table shows the breakdown by number of programs permanently authorized, number of programs with implied permanent authorizations and the number of programs with specific termination dates for several committees—

| | Number of programs | | | |
	Permanently authorized	With implied permanent authorizations	With specific termination dates	Total
Agriculture and Forestry:				
1979		1	11	12
1980	42	2	1	45
1981	6	4	4	14
1982	65	3	3	71
1983	18	4	1	23
Banking, Housing and Urban Affairs:				
1979	1			1
1980	16	4	9	29
1981	7		2	9
1982	7	1	2	10
1983	1	4	1	6
Commerce:				
1979	11	14	5	30
1980		1	2	3
1981	31	6	11	48
1982	23	1	24	48
1983	33	6	9	48
District of Columbia:				
1979				
1980		2		2
1981	2			2
1982				
1983		2		2
Finance:				
1979	1	1	6	8
1980				
1981	3	4	2	9
1982	3		2	5
1983	3	8	1	12
Foreign Relations:				
1979	8		18	26
1980			1	1
1981			1	1
1982	1		3	4
1983			1	1
Government Operations:				
1979				
1980				
1981				
1982	3		2	5
1983			35	35
Interior and Insular Affairs:				
1979	8		5	13
1980	48	5	2	55
1981	1	4		5
1982	52		2	54
1983	25	2	5	32
Judiciary:				
1979	24	16		37
1980	26	3		29
1981		2		3
1982	3			2
1983	2	2	1	5

	Number of programs			
	Permanently authorized	With implied permanent authorizations	With specific termination dates	Total
Labor and Public Welfare:				
1979	13	1	-------------	14
1980	4	1	10	15
1981	18	12	8	38
1982	17	-------------	19	36
1983	2	-------------	5	7
Veterans' Affairs:				
1979				-------------
1980				-------------
1981		25	2	27
1982	-------------			
1983				

Note: Programs which GAO did not list as permanent programs and for which there is no termination date, were considered as implied permanent authorizations for purposes of this compilation.

Congressional Budget Office estimates

The CBO has developed its own method of estimating workload, based on (1) number of budget accounts for each committee for each year of the schedule and (2) the number of public laws under each committee's jurisdiction for each year of the schedule.

(1) Budget accounts

CBO noted that the budget accounts method is imperfect since in some cases a single budget account may fund many different program authorizations as in the case of the National Cancer Institute, the National Institute of Allergy and Infectious Diseases, and the National Eye Institute. On the other hand, some accounts fit the requirements of S. 2925, as amended, by identifying specific programs as in the case of the National Institute of Education.

Imperfect as it may be, the program account method does provide another estimate of workload. The following table shows the number of budget accounts by committee of jurisdiction for each year of the schedule.

Aeronautical and Space Sciences:
1979 --------------------------- 1
1980 --------------------------- --
1981 --------------------------- --
1982 --------------------------- --
1983 --------------------------- --
Armed Services:
1979 --------------------------- 86
1980 --------------------------- --
1981 --------------------------- 4
1982 --------------------------- 8
1983 --------------------------- 7
Commerce:
1979 --------------------------- 7
1980 --------------------------- 8
1981 --------------------------- 59
1982 --------------------------- 12
1983 --------------------------- 30
Finance:
1979 --------------------------- 3
1980 --------------------------- 4
1981 --------------------------- 12
1982 --------------------------- 10
1983 --------------------------- 10

Government Operations:
1979 --------------------------- --
1980 --------------------------- --
1981 --------------------------- 1
1982 --------------------------- 1
1983 --------------------------- 38
Judiciary:
1979 --------------------------- 21
1980 --------------------------- 18
1981 --------------------------- 3
1982 --------------------------- 9
1983 --------------------------- 16
Post Office and Civil Service:
1979 --------------------------- 1
1980 --------------------------- 2
1981 --------------------------- 6
1982 --------------------------- 5
1983 --------------------------- 17
Rules:
1979 --------------------------- 3
1980 --------------------------- 19
1981 --------------------------- 1
1982 --------------------------- 1
1983 --------------------------- 19

Agriculture and Forestry:

1979	7
1980	27
1981	9
1982	52
1983	11

Banking, Housing and Urban Affairs:

1979	9
1980	43
1981	10
1982	12
1983	30

District of Columbia:

1979	--
1980	5
1981	2
1982	--
1983	12

Foreign Relations:

1979	66
1980	1
1981	4
1982	9
1983	--

Interior and Insular Affairs:

1979	16
1980	21
1981	5
1982	32
1983	31

Labor and Public Welfare:

1979	5
1980	24
1981	42
1982	27
1983	6

Public Works:

1979	5
1980	17
1981	31
1982	15
1983	35

Veterans' Affairs:

1979	--
1980	--
1981	--
1982	31
1983	--

(2) *The public laws method*

The Committee realizes that a count of public laws by legislative committee broken-down by each year of the schedule does not represent a true measure of the committee workload under the provisions of S. 2925. It does, however, add to the understanding of the workload which committees might anticipate under the operation of the legislation.

The following tables show the number of public laws authorized by each committee broken down for each year of the schedule.

Aeronautical and Space Sciences:

1979	4
1980	--
1981	--
1982	--
1983	--

Armed Services:

1979	52
1980	--
1981	7
1982	7
1983	7

Commerce:

1979	13
1980	9
1981	46
1982	28
1983	24

Finance:

1979	14
1980	1
1981	9
1982	12
1983	21

Government Operations:

1979	--
1980	2
1981	1
1982	2
1983	29

Judiciary:

1979	20
1980	10
1981	3
1982	8
1983	13

Post Office and Civil Service:

1979	1
1980	3
1981	6
1982	5
1983	19

Rules:

1979	3
1980	19
1981	--
1982	1
1983	20

Agriculture and Forestry:

1979	24
1980	33
1981	4
1982	21
1983	12

Banking, Housing and Urban Affairs:

1979	7
1980	37
1981	8
1982	9
1983	28

District of Columbia:

1979 _____ --
1980 _____ 5
1981 _____ 2
1982 _____ 1
1983 _____ 5

Foreign Relations:

1979 _____ 47
1980 _____ 2
1981 _____ 1
1982 _____ 10
1983 _____ 3

Interior and Insular Affairs:

1979 _____ 22
1980 _____ 27
1981 _____ 6
1982 _____ 29
1983 _____ 42

Labor and Public Welfare:

1979 _____ 5
1980 _____ 39
1981 _____ 67
1982 _____ 52
1983 _____ 10

Public Works:

1979 _____ 5
1980 _____ 13
1981 _____ 18
1982 _____ 31
1983 _____ 36

Veterans' Affairs:

1979 _____ --
1980 _____ --
1981 _____ --
1982 _____ 21
1983 _____ --

AN ILLUSTRATION OF THE TERMINATION AND REVIEW PROVISIONS

S. 2925 provides for the periodic termination and review of all but a few federal programs. The manner in which this process will work will depend on the particular program. Review techniques must be tailored to the characteristics of the program being evaluated. Inevitably, a somewhat different set of techniques will be applied to a program which disburses periodic payments to eligible individuals than to one which involves a one-time contract for the acquisitions of facilities.

Nevertheless, it is worthwhile to illustrate how S. 2925 might work for an existing federal program, so as to clarify both the intent and the workability of the new process.

The Occupational Safety and Health Act of 1970 (29 U.S.C. 651–678) directs the Secretary of Labor to promulgate and enforce standards to protect the safety and health of American workers. This responsibility is carried out by the Occupational Safety and Health Administration (OSHA) in the Department of Labor. Pursuant to its statutory authority, OSHA has issued a number of regulations and it inspects factories and other workplaces to assure that proper safety and health conditions are maintained. OSHA also is authorized to bring suit to restrain dangerous work conditions and to issue citations when standards have been violated. OSHA operates under a permanent authorization without limit of time or money, in accord with 15 U.S.C. 678: "There are authorized to be appropriated . . . for each fiscal year such sums as the Congress may deem necessary." The financial and program levels for OSHA are determined each year through the congressional appropriations process.

OSHA programs and activities are part of the Health function, although administratively they are under the Department of Labor, which is in another function (Other Labor Services) to be reviewed in another year. Under the review schedule prescribed in section 101 of S. 2925, as amended, the authorization for OSHA will expire on September 30, 1981, and each fifth year thereafter. The only provision of law that will terminate will be the specific section that authorizes the enactment of appropriations, section 678 which was cited above. Every other provision of the Occupational Safety and Health Act will remain in law, although the provisions of that Act providing regulatory authority for the program would be suspended until such time that new budget authority is again authorized or provided, as the case may be, for OSHA. During a period when budget authority is not authorized and regulatory authority suspended, OSHA will continue as an administrative unit of the Department of Labor, and all regulations issued pursuant to the 1970 law will continue in effect. Civil and criminal proceedings begun prior to the termination date will continue. The courts will continue to be empowered to restrain injurious work practices. A citizen would also continue to be entitled to initiate or pursue any private right of action provided under the law. However, the Secretary of Labor will not have authority to issue and enforce new safety and health standards under the Occupational Safety and Health Act as long as funding is not authorized or provided for OSHA. Should Congress fund OSHA by a continuing resolution, that resolution would serve to reauthorize as well as actually fund the program, and regulatory authority would continue in effect.

In accord with section 205 of S. 2925, the Congressional Committees of jurisdiction—the Committee on Labor and Public Welfare in the Senate—would conduct a zero base review of OSHA with the assistance of the Department of Labor and the Congressional support agencies and employing evaluation techniques appropriate for this type of program.

The process would work as follows:

By April 1, 1980, the Committee on Labor and Public Welfare would submit to the Senate its plan for a zero base review of OSHA. In its plan the Committee would indicate the priority it gives to the review of OSHA as compared to the reviews of other programs within its jurisdiction which come up for reauthorization at the same time; the criteria and standards it will apply to the review of OSHA; the elements of a zero base review that it feels are appropriate for the OSHA review; the information, reports, and analyses it wants from the Congressional support agencies; and the scope and detail of the report on the OSHA program it will receive from the Department of Labor by December 1, 1980.

The next step would be for the Committee on Labor and Public Welfare to complete its zero base review of OSHA in accordance with the zero base review plan it has filed with the Senate. The deadline for the Committee's report on its zero base review would be May 15, 1981, the same as the deadline that already applies to authorizing legislation. (And assuming the Committee recommended reauthorization of OSHA, its zero base review report or a summary thereof would be included as part of the report accompanying the reauthorization bill.)

At this point, Congress would have a number of options with regard to OSHA and its programs:

(1) It could simply reenact section 678, thereby reauthorizing appropriations for OSHA. This would continue the present arrangement under which funding levels are determined solely through the appropriations process. However, the new authorization would have effect for no more than 5 years, when the authorization would expire.

(2) It could decide to reauthorize OSHA for a period of less than 5 years, thereby providing for more frequent congressional review.

(3) It could place a limitation on the amount authorized. In lieu of the "such sums as the Congress shall deem necessary" clause, the new section 678 could specify the amount authorized. Such amount would also be the maximum amount that could be appropriated.

(4) It could use the zero base review as an opportunity to examine various provisions of law relating to OSHA and the standards and regulations pursuant thereto. Congress could decide to expand or contract OSHA's authority to promulgate safety and health standards, or it could recast any other provision of the OSHA law. The important thing, however, is that such changes could be made only by a new enactment of law. If no new law is enacted, all the provisions of the Occupational Safety and Health Act of 1970 would remain in effect.

(5) Congress might not reauthorize section 678, thereby removing the provision of law which authorizes the appropriation of funds for OSHA. If this were to occur, OSHA would remain in existence, although funding would be lacking to carry out its functions and its regulatory authority would be suspended.

(6) Should Congress fail to reauthorize section 678, it still might be possible under special circumstances to appropriate funds for OSHA, since the requirement that a program be authorized before an appropriation is made is not a statutory provision but derives from the rules of the Senate and House.

The foregoing case, as indicated, applies only to OSHA, but the basic circumstances apply to other Federal agencies and programs.

REVIEW OF TAX EXPENDITURE PROVISIONS

S. 2925 as amended would provide for a zero base review of Federal tax expenditure provisions much in the same way it requires a review of direct expenditures under programs and activities. Tax expenditures are revenue losses which result from Federal tax provisions that grant special tax relief designed to encourage certain kinds of behavior by taxpayers or to aid taxpyares in special circumstances. These provisions are, in effect, the equivalent of a simultaneous revenue collection and a direct budget outlay of an equal amount to the beneficiary taxpayer.

Over the past ten years the growth of tax expenditures has in fact occurred at a faster rate than the growth of direct expenditures. The Joint Committee on Internal Revenue Taxation has recently estimated that in the decade from 1967 to 1977, Federal spending will climb by 161 percent, from $158 billion to the $413 billion as proposed in the first concurrent budget resolution for fiscal year 1977. In the same period, tax expenditures will grow by 176 percent to an estimated $100 billion in fiscal year 1977 from a level of $36 billion in fiscal year 1967.

Shielding tax expenditures from periodic review is the fact that they operate much like entitlement programs with no systematic review by the Congress after their initial adoption. This legislation would require a zero base review of these provisions over a five year period.

The Committee did not attempt in this legislation to establish a schedule for termination and revision of those provisions of law or regulation considered to be tax expenditures or their proper grouping for review. Title V requires the Joint Committee on Internal Revenue Taxation to develop a proposed schedule for review and termination of these provisions, after consultation with the Treasury Department and the Budget Committees of the House and Senate. The Joint Committee is required to present this schedule to the Ways and Means and Finance Committees by April 1, 1977, so that those committees can report legislation and Congress can complete action on the schedule by the end of the first session of the 95th Congress.

In developing the schedule, the Congress should consider reviewing tax expenditures in the same year as similar programs and activities which attempt to achieve similar purposes. To assist in achieving this goal, the Budget Committees of both Houses are required to report by February 1, 1977 to the Joint Committee and to the Congress on the relationship between tax expenditures and programs and activities in the same function and subfunctional categories.

The guidelines for executive and congressional review of these tax expenditure provisions are very similar to those prescribed for programs and activities.

THE EVALUATION PROCESS

The Committee recognizes that, as a number of witnesses emphasized, evaluation is both art and science, and that one evaluation mechanism may not be applicable to all Federal programs. A program authorizing the construction of a dam or missile system clearly cannot be evaluated in the same fashion as a program intended to alleviate poverty or restore urban neighborhoods.

Therefore, S. 2925, as amended, provides for substantial flexibility in the evaluation procedures to be used. Instead of proposing a single, rigid evaluation model for all Federal programs and activities, S. 2925, as amended, contains only broad guidelines as to the kind of information whch may be included in the zero base reviews prepared by the authorizing committees.

While allowing the evaluation process to remain relatively flexible, the Committee does have a clear purpose it wishes to achieve through this process—a purpose which is reflected by the use of the term "zero base review." The Committee believes it is essential for the Congress to begin to challenge the traditional assumption about program funding which holds that a program or activity deserves to be continued with the same or increased funding one year simply because it was funded the previous year. The essence of zero base review is its assumption that it is possible to cut into the base of a program's funding level—that the program must be justified from the ground up. It is that assumption which S. 2925, as amended, seeks to establish as the framework or foundation for the entire Congressional authorization process.

The Committee believes that the injection of the zero base concept into the reauthorization process will give Congress an expanded range of options to consider when contemplating program continuation, termination, or consolidation. Thus, the Committee regards the zero base review concept as an important policy tool for the Congress to use in developing a broad overview of program activities in a particular budget function, and in shifting the parts of the whole in order to better serve program purposes.

RESPECTIVE ROLES OF CONGRESS AND THE EXECUTIVE BRANCH UNDER S. 2925

Under S. 2925, as introduced, Congress and the Executive Branch would have shared more or less equally in the responsibility for the zero base review of programs scheduled for termination.

In response to concern about the effect of the evaluation requirements on the workload of the standing committees of Congress, the Committee, in amending the legislation, has refined the distribution of responsibility in the following way: Under S. 2925, as amended, the committees of jurisdiction retain full responsibility for initiating, guiding and preparing the zero base review reports submitted to Congress on all programs scheduled for termination. The Executive Branch agencies and departments are responsible for submitting reports to these committees—on programs scheduled for termination— to assist these committees in their preparation of the zero base reviews.

The Committee believes that this distribution of responsibilities between Congress and the Executive Branch is well balanced and in keeping with the constitutionally mandated responsibilities of the two branches of government.

Under the process set out in the legislation, Congress retains clear authority over policy decisions involving all Federal programs. In addition, by putting all programs on a regular review cycle and thus eliminating indefinite authorizations, the process in the bill actually strengthens Congressional control over financial and program policy.

The legislation leaves to the Executive Branch the responsibility of preparing information for the zero base reviews sought by the legislative committees. In S. 2925, as amended, the Committee has sought to minimize the possibility that the information provided by the Executive Branch will be "tilted" in favor of a particular administration policy by authorizing the standing committees to require the Executive Branch to provide specified quantitative information. In addition, the information provided by the Executive Branch must still be subject to both Committee and Public scrutiny during the Committee's own review process. Further, the legislation permits the legislative committees to seek information from the General Accounting Office, Office of Technology Assessment, Congressional Research Service and Congressional Budget Office so as to enable them to make an independent assessment of programs under review.

The Committee believes that under this distribution of responsibility, the principal policy tool of the Congress—the authorization process—will be strengthened substantially.

COMMITTEE STATEMENT ON BEHALF OF S. 2925

INTRODUCTION

In laying out the case for S. 2925, as amended, the Committee begins with the premise that the findings of the Harris surveys of American attitudes toward their government are substantially correct: a majority of Americans think that government officials don't care what they think, that government is not responsive to their needs, and that even the simplest day-to-day tasks are beyond the capability of government. The only government worker who gets high marks from the American public is the local trash collector—because at least people know whether or not he is doing his job.

In summary, people think government is not accountable to anyone, least of all to the public.

In recent years, Congress has begun to move toward making the operations of the Federal Government more accountable. Campaign spending reform and open government meetings are just two examples of that movement.

Perhaps the most significant reform taken by the Congress, however, has been budget reform.

But if by implementing budget reform, Congress is beginning to exercise control over the priorities for spending Federal dollars, it has not yet taken control of the delivery of services which Federal dollars are intended to buy. Federal programs are too often funded one year because they were funded the year before. Levels of funding usually reflect overall spending priorities, but seldom do they reflect consideration of which programs are actually producing results and which are not.

In this context, the reforms proposed in S. 2925, as amended, are a logical follow-up to budget reform. Hopefully, S. 2925, as amended, will accomplish for Federal programs individually what budget reform has begun to do for the Federal budget as a whole—that is, lend a new element of discipline and control to the way the Federal government handles the American taxpayers' money.

The proliferation of Federal programs

The 1976 Catalog of Federal Domestic Assistance lists 1030 programs administered by 52 Federal agencies. In Fiscal Year 1976, these programs provided an estimated $59.8 billion to the 50 states and nearly 80,000 units of local government, for a total of almost 25 percent of Federal domestic outlays and an estimated 25.2 percent of all State and local government expenditures.

In the health field alone, there are 302 different programs, administered by 11 separate Federal agencies. Under the broad category of community development, there are 259.

NOTE.—The numbers in this section are taken from the Catalog of Federal Domestic Assistance and, therefore, are based on different assumptions than the numbers used elsewhere in the report that were compiled from GAO or CBO data.

As the program category is narrowed, the number of programs is no less bewildering. The 1976 Federal Catalog lists 39 different programs under the Veterans category, with another 28 under the heading Veterans Medical Facilities and Services. Under the category of Vocational Education, there are 27 different programs listed. The reader is referred to the Job Training Subcategory of the Employment, Labor and Training Category for other programs in this area. Under the heading of Transportation, there are 45 separate entries.

A GAO study on health services in outpatient health centers in the District of Columbia, found seven different programs—administered by HEW and OEO. Coordination was so lacking, the GAO found, that one neighborhood had eight clinics, several of which were badly underutilized.

Another GAO study of the use of military maintenance facilities found extensive duplication and underutilization of these facilities because of the emphasis each service placed on developing its own facilities rather than sharing existing facilities of other services. The study concluded that substantial long-range savings could be realized through greater inter-service maintenance, but that despite repeated encouragement from the Department of Defense, the individual services had continued to circumvent both the spirit and intent of such policy.

An HEW study found over 50 Federal programs providing some type of service to handicapped youth. Most of these programs were administered by HEW—by 14 separate units within that department.

A GAO study of the HEW study found no point within HEW at which all these efforts were coordinated.

Finally, a study by the Joint Economic Committee found 62 separate programs involved in providing aid to the needy and social insurance, at a projected cost in fiscal year 1975 of $142 billion.

Note: Since 1966 the importance of categorical programs in the total Federal aid picture has lessened. In 1966, categoricals comprised 98 percent of total Federal aid. By 1975, they comprised about 75 percent, with block grants and general support aid (revenue sharing, e.g.) accounting for the difference.

The growth of permanent programs

Side-by-side with the growth in the number of Federal programs over the last 10 years has been a dramatic increase in the amount of Federal funds spent on programs with permanent appropriations—funds spent without any review by Congress. From 1966 to 1976, these programs have become the fastest growing component of the Federal budget, tripling from $55 billion in 1966 to $165 billion in 1976.

In a different category, but representing a similar problem are the very large number of programs with permanent authorizations—programs enacted with authorizations stating "such sums as may be necessary" and containing no termination date.

A review of programs under the jurisdiction of the Senate Agricultural Committee (chosen because such a list had been prepared by the GAO at that Committee's request), showed 277 programs operating under permanent legislative authority. Only 65 programs were based on legislation which provided fixed termination dates. The 277 permanent programs represented a total year 1977. The 65 programs subject to periodic reauthorization compromised $6.8 billion in fiscal year 1977 budget requests.

What these two examples point out is that there is a significant segment of the Federal budget which escapes congressional review on a regular cycle.

The growth in uncontrollable spending

The cost of continuing all 1976 programs in the 1977 budget was estimated at approximately $45–$50 billion higher than last year's spending level. Thus, despite targeted program cutbacks, the first budget resolution for fiscal year 1977 set spending at $413 billion, about $40 billion above the final budget figure for FY 1976.

Most of this growth is attributable to the increase in "uncontrollable" spending, which in 1967 accounted for about 59 percent of that year's budget but which in 1977 will take up roughly 77 percent of all Federal spending. Thus, uncontrollable spending is, in the words of one witness, "bleeding" the controllables. This witness, Dr. Allen Schick of the Congressional Research Service, testified further, that: "If we compared the 1966 and 1976 budgets, we would find dozens of major programs which were funded then, but not now. We would find dozens more which have grown less than inflation. And we would find dozens in which there is a significant and growing gap between the amount authorized and the amount actually appropriated."

Thus every year the uncontrollables are reducing the policy options open to the Congress in determining priorities for Federal spending.

The growth in governmental agencies

In addition to the proliferation of programs administered by the Federal government, there has also been an extraordinary growth in the number of Federal agencies, commissions, bureaus and the like. According to the Library of Congress, from 1960 to 1974, 329 such governmental bodies were created, while only 126 were abolished. Of the 329 themselves, only 63 had been abolished by 1974. In 1974 alone, 85 separate governmental bodies were created.

The growth of federally-mandated layers of Government

The last decade has seen not only a rapid growth in the activities of the Federal government, but also a mushrooming of new layers of government mandated or spawned by Federal programs.

At the highest level, there are 10 Federal Regional Councils, promoted by the Nixon administration as part of its New Federalism efforts to decentralize Federal activities.

Far more significant in terms of numbers and confusion are the single and multipurpose districts required or spawned by various Federal grant-in-aid programs.

According to a study by the Advisory Commission on Intergovernmental Relations on substate regionalism, released in 1974, over 4,000 geographic program areas had been recognized under 24 different Federal programs involving 11 Federal agencies. These included 481 Law Enforcement Planning regions, 957 Community Action agencies, 419 Cooperative Area Manpower Planning System Councils, 247 Air Quality Regions, 195 Comprehensive Areawide Health Planning agencies, and 165 Resources Conservation and Development districts, among others.

CONCLUSION

It cannot be emphasized too often that it is not the intent of the Committee to pass judgment on any of the programs mentioned in this discussion or on any Federal programs for that matter. The sole purpose of this discussion is to illustrate that because of the growing number of Federal programs, because of the growing number of uncontrollable and permanent programs, and because of the growth in the number of Federal agencies and even layers of government, the Congress is becoming increasingly removed from the results of its legislative work. The Committee believes that this is an unhealthy trend and that it is time for the Congress to respond.

The Committee further believes S. 2925, as amended, is a vehicle for this Congressional response through which Congress can begin to reassert control over the delivery of services to the American taxpayer.

SELECTED COMMENTS OF COMMITTEE WITNESSES ON S. 2925

I. NEED FOR THE LEGISLATION

Norm Mineta, Congressman from the State of California:

As a former mayor, I would hold that the implementation of this program review process by the Congress has the potential to greatly improve direct Federal-local relations under the grant-in-aid system.

By focusing our attention on the whole—the entire functional area—rather than its programmatic parts, S. 2925 should provide us with a mechanism for resolving the competing and often-time contradictory objectives of individual programs—the cross-purposes, if you will, that manifest themselves so clearly at the local level.

*   *   *   *   *   *   *

As projected by the Congressional Budget Office, Federal outlays will reach $564 billion by FY 1981, an increase of $140 billion in four years, if existing programs are continued and no new initiatives are taken.

I would hope that we would all agree that this is a frightening prospect; and that it is, by no means, a satisfactory alternative, not when severe needs are unaddressed, present program deficiencies and inequities uncorrected, and spending levels seemingly out of control.

Elliot Richardson, Secretary of Commerce:

In the course of my government service, I have developed the strong belief that we must continually review government programs to assure that they are effective and that they are appropriatey meeting the changing needs of society. While large amounts of Federal resources are often provided to solve a national problem, we sometimes seem reluctant to review whether the use of these resources actually contributed to the solution. We continue to see too may cases of national problems stubbornly resisting major programs. We find ourselves wondering if there are not better solutions. We see too many programs that are outmoded or too costly for the benefits achieved—programs that continue indefinitely because we do not take action to repeal or alter the legislation that initiated them. If we want to pursue new national goals and solve existing programs faster, we are going to have to make choices—choices between new and old purposes and choices between alternative solutions to existing problems.

Roy Ash, Former Director, Office of Management and Budget:

Management is simply a process of effectively closing the loop from objectives to results. Senate Bill 2925, as I see it, then, is intended to add an important link to what should essentially be a managed circle of perfect performance, not a too often open-ended circle of uncontrolled happenings.

Authorizing programs and appropriating money is not enough. Claiming performance on the basis of the amount of money is worse than not enough . . . For each program the simple questions to be kept in front of us are what we are trying to accomplish, how much it will cost, is it worth it, are we actually accomplishing something, should we change something in order to achieve a better match between objecttives and results. This is the closed circle model of program management in its essence.

John Gardner, Chairman of Common Cause:

The popular impression is that Executive Branch flaws stem mainly from the unimaginative species known as bureaucrats—little people with green eyeshades whose only concern is to collect their pay and protect their turf. The indictment is unfair ... The problem lies not with the much-maligned bureaucrats but with organizational arrangements that make for inertia, duplication of effort and all the other familiar ills. That is too big a subject to be examined here. But S. 2925 addresses itself to a central piece of the subject: The need for tough periodic re-examination of programs.

*   *   *   *   *   *   *

In strictly budgetary terms, we can no longer afford government programs that have outworn their usefulness, that duplicate other programs, that have proven unworkable.

Even if we could afford the expense, we can't afford the erosion of public confidence that stems from government programs so ill-designed that they would not withstand searching scrutiny.

The time has finally come when Congress must look squarely at the elusive problem of oversight ... honest legislators know that most oversight as now practiced is a farce. I have made no secret of the fact that I think the sunset provision will entail a lot of enormously hard work. But if for the first time, it establishes congressional oversight as a rigorous, continuing process, it will be well worth the effort.

*   *   *   *   *   *   *

The Netsilik Eskimos, if I may quote from an exotic source, Mr. Chairman, defend their traditional beliefs with the maxim: "It is so because it is said it is so." Executive Branch programs tend to develop the same self-validating quality: they go on because they've been going on. But if you look behind what seems to be inertia, you will find more earthy reasons for continuity. The beneficiaries of government programs organize to lobby for continuity and ultimately weave a network for allies in both Congress and the Executive Branch.

Add to these forces the sheer convenience and comfort of incremental budgeting. It's God's gift to the harried department or agency head who has to review and defend dozens, even hundreds, of programs.

Allen Schick, Senior Specialist, American National Government Library of Congress:

From 1967 to 1977, uncontrollable spending has risen from 59 percent to 77 percent of the budget. Thus we have a situation where the uncontrollables are "bleeding" the controllables. If we compare the 1966 and 1976 budgets, we would find dozens of major programs which were funded then but not now. We would find dozens more which have grown less than inflation. And we would find dozens in which there is a significant and growing gap between the amount authorized and the amount actually appropriated. One purpose of S. 2925 is to insure that the putting in and the driving out of programs is done by Congress rather than by the uncontrollable forces of the budget.

The fastest growing component of the Federal budget, from 1966 to 1976, is in permanent appropriations—those which escape any review by Congress whatsoever.

Arnold Weber, Dean, Graduate School of Industrial Education, Carnegie Mellon Institute:

When I was at OMB, (we) always used to say the budget process was a fight of the parts against the whole, and the parts always won. To some extent that describes the current situation. It seems to me that your earlier Budget Reform Act tried to deal with the notion of the whole having priority over the parts, and this (legislation) logically is an effort to deal with the parts to make them consistent with the whole.

Gerry Kopel, State Representative from Colorado:

One of the major factors in sunset and why it is such a beautiful concept is that it does put the burden on the agency to come forth. If all they had to do, which is what they have to do now, were to kill an attempt to repeal their continuation, that is very easy to do.

Sidney Brooks, Chairman, Colorado Common Cause: (Quotation from a statement by the Colorado General Assembly):

The General Assembly in Colorado finds the State Government has produced an inexorable increase in numbers of agencies, growth of programs and proliferation of rules and regulations, and that the whole process developed without legislative oversight, regulatory accountability, or a system of checks and balances. The General Assembly further finds that by establishing a system for determination, continuation of reestablishment of such agencies, it will be in a better position to evaluate the needs for the continued existence of regulatory bodies.

I submit that that is a remarkable statement, that a legislature has in effect admitted that it has created a fourth branch of government and has virtually lost control of it . . . .

*   *   *   *   *   *   *

Many agencies perpetuate their existence simply by virtue of their existence, rather than by demonstrated need. We want a program whereby they have to demonstrate the need.

Finally, we want the legislature reflecting back on that which they have created. We think it is important that they spend time reflecting on it. If they do a good job at that, they can trim away some regulatory obesity, and they might find money to apply to other programs of demonstrated need, or programs that we consider essential, but which are already underfunded.

II. ZERO BASE REVIEW

Elliot Levitas, Congressman from the State of Georgia:

From a legislator's point of view, the biggest boon of zero base budgeting is that it gives legislators options on which to make decisions. They can look at different increments of funding and compare them against different increments of program benefit.

Richard Leone, State Treasurer of New Jersey:

The principal advantage of zero base budgeting is that it forces decisions out into the open. It forces consideration of what lies behind a program, what its justification is, what is its constituency. If a program has no constituency, it is not worth having.

*　　　*　　　*　　　*　　　*　　　*　　　*

These budgeting procedures (zero base budgeting) also helped us to deal with the question of equity in spending public dollars. We frequently look at equity in terms of how money is raised—that is, who pays how much . . . but there are also arguments of equity in terms of how tax dollars are spent.

In New Jersey, for example, it costs us about $500 in state money to provide the rail subsidy for each rail commuter. Most of the latter group do not think of themselves as equivalent to "people on welfare" but they cost us about as much. This sort of analysis is new to our state. . . . It has helped us to determine who gets hurt and who gets helped by budget decisions.

NOTES AND REFERENCES

1. Senator John Glenn cosponsored the Muskie bill, S. 2925, and was the author of this particular provision (Title V). He and Senator William Roth, who also cosponsored the Muskie bill, are advocates of zero-base budgeting in the Senate.

2. Transcriptions of the hearings of the Intergovernmental Relations Subcommittee on S. 2067 and S. 2925 are found in [72], [73], and [83].

3. The Comptroller General of the United States is the head of the General Accounting Office, which is an oversight and investigatory unit of the Congress. Among GAO's responsibilities, as allocated by Congress, are those related to accounting, auditing, claims settlements, and legal functions concerning programs and operations of the federal government. It also makes recommendations to provide for more effective government operations.

Chapter 9
Implementation at the Federal Level

The Senate Committee on Government Operations held hearings from March to May 1976 on Senator Edmund Muskie's Government Economy and Spending Reform Act, during which a variety of expert witnesses testified. Abridged transcripts of their testimony are included in this chapter. The testimony of these witnesses offers general support to the concepts of sunset and zero-base budgeting, but it does raise some practical questions on how such implementation procedures would work within an established bureaucracy. The full text of the hearings is available in [72], [73], and [83].

BUREAUCRATIC CONCERNS: ERNEST FITZGERALD ([83], pp. 193–204)

When Ernest Fitzgerald testified before the Senate Committee on Government Operations, he was the deputy assistant secretary for productivity management, Department of the Air Force. He has become somewhat of a folk hero among those who are critics of excessive Defense Department spending and has himself been an inside critic at the Pentagon for a number of years— transferred into obscure positions, then turning up again; once dismissed, but then reinstated. He is always a favorite witness before congressional committees examining defense spending and government efficiency. As an accomplished bureaucratic in-fighter, Fitzgerald speaks with authority in the following testimony and warns of some political impediments to the use of new management techniques in reorganizing and reforming the defense establishment.

Senator MUSKIE. It is a pleasure to welcome this morning our second and last witness of the day, Deputy Assistant Secretary Ernest Fitzgerald of the Air Force.

It should be noted that he is the author of the "High Priests of of Waste." That is a good title. I wish I had thought of it myself. And it is from that perspective that he will undertake to make his presentation this morning.

I understand you have no prepared statement, but that you will proceed in your own way, Mr. Secretary.

Mr. FITZGERALD. Thank you, Mr. Chairman.

I favor the objectives of S. 2925 and in general endorse the summary and explanation of the act that was furnished me. Without the types of controls that you are proposing, individual programs and, indeed, the entire Federal budget is likely to continue to run out of control without actually delivering the goods and services the taxpayers are told they are paying for.

Traditional Government budgeting methods simply must be improved. Extrapolating the trends of past year costs and similar mindless approaches to budgeting produce a climate in which justifying and defending statistical projections themselves are major goals of powerful spending coalitions, both in and out of Government.

Too little thought is given to real achievement of the stated, ostensible purposes of the spending. As a rule, if ostensible goals are not met, for particularly politically popular programs, the bureaucratic managers as a rule suffer no personal penalty so long as they continue to obtain ever-increasing sums from the taxpayers.

The projections, especially increased projections, acquire constituencies and lives of their own. If they promise sufficient patronage, they tend to become self-fulfilling prophecies.

A good example is the current military budget. Back in 1972, late 1972, during the time I was temporarily fired from the Pentagon, I got hold of some of the internal budget trends that were being examined in the Pentagon at that time, a time in which our spending for military purposes was in the neighborhood of $80 billion for the Department of Defense.

I took these figures, extrapolated the trends, added up the pieces and arrived at a figure, total obligational figure, of $141 billion for fiscal year 1980.

Now, this was quite a shock to people who were watchers of the budget, because at that time it was assumed that with the winding down of the Southeast Asia war there would be a huge peace dividend, as it was called. It seemed incredible that anyone could suggest that we would have this enormous increase. However, I had enough confidence to use the figure in an article I wrote at the time for World Magazine, an article which was published in early 1973.

Each year since that time the rationalizations for the increases have changed, but the overall figures track very closely the extrapolation of the trend of actual costs. These became organizational goals and that is not unique to the Defense Department, of course. It just happened that I had their figures and was interested in it.

Business plans are made based on these projections, people are hired in anticipation of getting the money projected for them. And so, as I say, given sufficient patronage support, the statistical projections in and of themselves tend to become self-fulfilling prophecies.

Now, having said how much I think we need your proposal, Mr. Chairman, I would like to now inject a few words of caution.

The political environment I have touched on briefly will make success very doubtful unless the climate can be changed. I want to illustrate this with an example of a similar approach which proved extremely disappointing both to me personally and in terms of not realizing its potential for saving money and improving services to the taxpayers. It had to do with pricing of military hardware.

Traditionally, we have priced military hardware using what are called historical costs, a very similar approach to what we use in overall budgeting. We extrapolate the trends of elements of costs from the same company or make a comparison of the program under examination to past or similar programs, and, using statistical inference or extrapolations, arrive at the prices for the new programs.

Quite obviously this approach is heavily dependent on the validity of the data which you use as a base. If these data include fat, inefficiency, bribes, corruption, or just plain foulups, well, that is all built in and used as a base for extrapolation or analogy. So it became obvious, as I think it would to anyone who examined it, that this is an expensive and wasteful approach to pricing hardware.

As is typical in almost all governmental activity, once the money has been obtained, there is enormous pressure to spend it whether it is needed or not.

The stated goals of government agencies very often include flat statements that the organization must achieve a zero balance of funds at the end of the year, and if there is one thing we are good at, it is that. Those goals are almost always achieved.

Well, starting in the midfifties I and a number of my associates and people in the same field that I was working in—in industrial engineering, cost accounting and budgeting and that sort of thing—began developing the approach which eventually became called the "should-cost" approach. The old historical costing system was called "will cost" in that it projected what the cost would probably be with continuation of business as usual.

The "should-cost" approach was aimed at identifying fat in the programs, avoidable activities, savings that might be made to get the same product for less money, which in terms of approach is exactly what you are thinking of in zero-base budgeting.

Well, no one could argue with this. You couldn't politically endorse opposing "should-cost" pricing, so it became popular. There was testimony on the Hill before the Joint Economic Committee—I gave some of it before the House Government Operations Committee, the House Armed Services Committee—and in every case the approach was endorsed.

So there was great momentum behind using "should cost" to price out military hardware. But now what happened?

Obviously the people who benefit from these outlays like that sort of thing, the old way of doing business, even though I think personally improvements in efficiency would be good for the big contractors—and this is what we are talking about, the giants—that is where the money is. It is also true that in the short run it costs them sales, costs jobs, to be honest, in areas where you can't use additional quantities of hardware such as ICBM's. It is simply not reasonable to say we will reapply the savings to buy more of them, because we don't need them.

So what happened was the expected. The entire spending coalition—and I am sorry to say, including some of the arms of Congress—rallied around the name "should cost" but changed the system.

The approach as used in the beginning had been refined and we got to where we could actually do these incisive, productive analyses more quickly and more cheaply than the statistical projections. I did one on a major program shortly before I joined the Pentagon for less than $9,000, which is, as you know, unheard of now. You couldn't write a proposal for that.

But in the evolution of the bureaucratic approach, lacking the proper motivation and drive toward actual reduction of the cost of the products, the thing we were generating, in place of the incisive, quick quantitative approach that was originally developed, became long, drawn out, nonspecific, qualitative work employing literally droves of analysts, who in the end woodenly marched through those fat operations and announced solemnly that they found no fat.

So the result of the pseudo—"should cost" became a counterproductive thing. We had a false certification that this contract is fat free when in reality it was not. This tends to discourage further inquiry.

You find yourself having to contradict established and respected institutions and organizations if you want to challenge that sort of false certification. So the upshot of it is that I finally testified in 1973, before Senator Proxmire's Subcommittee on Priorities and Economy in Government of the Joint Economic Committee on November 15, 1973, giving the whole and history of this example.

I finally recommended to Senator Proxmire that he and his committee withdraw the endorsement of the approach because I thought it was doing more harm than good. I think the same fate could befall zero-based budgeting if you don't take care in the way it is applied and make certain that it—make certain that the motivations and the objectives are clearly enough stated and enforced, that the people doing the work don't lose sight of what they are trying to do.

As a matter of fact, I think the bill might be strengthened by reemphasizing the objective of minimizing the cost to the taxpayers of the necessary goods and services that we choose to buy.

I don't think you can say that too often or reinforce it by your actions too often.

The other problem is in the nature of a political problem, I think. The ostensible, stated objectives, the official purposes of many programs, are not the real ones that motivate people to support them. Occasionally these subterranean or unstated purposes which, as I say, are often more real than publicly stated ones, emerge publicly.

I wanted to read you an excerpt from the hearings on the Lockheed loan guarantee. It was dialog between—a colloquy, I guess—between Senator Proxmire and the then Secretary of Treasury, John Connally. I will quote from the hearing records:

Senator PROXMIRE. I think you are absolutely right in saying this might be something that can have a profound effect on our economy. What bothers me so much about this, Mr. Secretary, is that Lockheed's bailout, I would agree with Senator Tower, is not a subsidy. It is different from the subsidy. It is the beginning of a welfare program for large corporations.

I would remind you that in a subsidy program it is different. There is a quid pro quo. You make a payment to a railroad and, in turn, they build trackage. You make a payment to an airline, and they provide a certain amount of service for it.

In welfare, of course, you make a payment and there is no return. In this case the Government gives the guarantee and there is no requirement on the part of Lockheed to perform under the guarantee. The guarantee of $250 million and no benefit, no quid for the quo.

Secretary CONNALLY. What do you mean, no benefit?

Senator PROXMIRE. Well, they don't have to perform.

Departing from the quote, here is the astounding part in that it is so candid——

Secretary CONNALLY. What do we care whether they perform? What we are guaranteeing them basically is a $250 million loan. Why for? Basically so that they can hopefully minimize their losses so they can provide employment for 31,000 people throughout the country * * *

Mr. FITZGERALD [continuing]. And on in that vein.

As I say, this is an unusually candid expression of the subterranean purposes of many expenditures. If we can get at those, I think it is healthy in itself. On the other hand, if the subterranean purpose is to give welfare to a big corporation or to provide a certain number of jobs without caring what the outcome is, then activities such as "should cost" and "zero-based budgeting" become problems in themselves. They are the problem and will attract opposition and will likely be defeated if these subterranean objectives can't be dealt with.

As a matter of fact, the beginning of the downfall, the highwater mark actually, of the "should cost" approach was on the F-111 program, a program I had many adventures with before I got fired at the Pentagon.

In 1967 the program was obviously deathly ill, and we had considerable support within the Pentagon from the Office of the Secretary of Defense to do something about the ever-increasing costs.

Senator MUSKIE. What year was that?

Mr. FITZGERALD. 1967. Secretary McNamara was Secretary of Defense at that time. We set out to try to do a "should cost" just as many of us had done on a smaller program, very successfully.

Well, the program was moving well, so well in fact that we scared the opposition just as you, Mr. Chairman, said that once it became clear your bill is going to be effective, then the opposition would rise.

We had no opposition until it became clear that we meant business. We were going to cut out the fat. We were going to find the true technical status.

The upshot of it was the general in charge of the program, the system program director, Major General Zoeckler, simply countermanded the direction that had come from the Secretary of Defenuse's Office through people like me and told his people they were not to do that. His exact words were: "Inefficiency is national policy." [Laughter.]

Now, I was very angry at General Zoeckler, I was furious as a matter of fact, for a number of weeks. But then it dawned on me, as the months and years went on, General Zoeckler was right, at least as regarded the F-111 program and similar things. He was right because the subterranean purposes, if not the primary purpose, at least the secondary and tertiary purposes were making work. This is what you have to deal with in making the zero-based budgeting work effectively.

If you can solve the intent problem, the objectives problem, I think that the sooner this kind of activity can proceed, the better.

I would like to suggest to you, Mr. Chairman, some things to be on guard against, perhaps to consider incorporating or changing in the legislation, that I think will make it more effective.

In the first place, I think some of the areas excluded could be very usefully included in coverage. One that occurs to me in particular is health care. I mean all health care, including that financed by trust funds. From my work with former Congressman Waldie on the Federal employee program over in the House of Representatives during the time I was consulting on the Hill, I became convinced that some of the language in the original medicare legislation was a root cause of the runaway unit cost and total cost of health care.

And it could be examined very profitably. Even though the Federal Government does not finance all of the Nation's health care, I think it leads the way. It sets the pattern for practices, for procedures, for pricing out, paying for it and all that sort of thing. It could be very usefully examined and I think as a related matter the very fact that the costs of health care is escalating so dramatically, particularly since 1966 when the medicare legislation was passed, that it almost guarantees that sooner or later the Government is going to have to undertake support of it.

I saw this both from my work with Congressman Waldie and my own personal experience with my family. I think it is clear that the ordinary family today can no more afford a serious illness such as a drawnout cancer case than they can afford their own B–52. They simply can't bear the expense.

While I think this is not necessarily a good thing, I think it is a fact of life we have to face, that for whatever reason the price has gotten so high people cannot afford it on their own. With this in mind, I think it would be useful to consider taking the whole health care industry as an area of study.

I think some of the other things that are omitted from the bill might be looked at, too, even such things as debt service. I notice in looking over the new budget that it either passed or threatens to pass—my recollection is it has passed very slightly—the appropriations for HEW. I believe it is the second largest item in the Federal funds schedule.

Senator MUSKIE. I think it comes pretty close to that; yes.

Mr. FITZGERALD. Second only to national security outlays.

So this makes it an item of prime concern. There are alternatives, at least medium- and long-term, to this enormous burden. There are things that can be considered such as financing some of the things now financed out of trust funds out of current receipts or general revenues. I am not sure that is a good thing, but I am suggesting it is an alternative.

The alternatives that are available to support programs more from the tax system than from the money and banking system could be considered and would have an impact on this. So these are things that I think could be considered.

While not very large in terms of comparison to other activities, the executive branch activities, I think the activity of the Congress itself could be considered, the various committees that oversee executive branch activities. I think that will point out something to you that may surprise you. You may conclude that parallel activities are not always bad. I think it is quite clear that many of the things that have been revealed as being wrong with the executive branch would not have been revealed had there not been more than one congressional committee looking at it.

Simarily I think there are instances in which the approach engineers call "parallel development," particularly in the early stages of development activities, are very useful. You get some intense competition to see which one survives. The trick in making this thing pay off is killing the ones that don't work out. It takes considerable courage to do that.

N1   The activities of the General Accounting Office, I think, could bear a lot of scrutiny. I think you should go back historically and look at what the Congress did to the General Accounting Office in 1965. You can see ways to improve it. There was terrible damage done to the GAO at that time by a House Government Operations Committee inquiry.

So I think you could add certain things to the list profitably, at least consider them.

There is another matter that I suppose is implicit—but to make certain I would like to add, and that is the notion of technical evaluation. This is one of the most difficult things that Congress has to do in connection with some of the programs.

This is especially true, I think, in health care, in national security affairs, in military spending, NASA, ERDA, things that have usually gone beyond the expertise of Congressmen and Senators.

I want to take another example, again from Lockheed, since I know a lot about that, to illustrate.

Mr. Chairman, you no doubt remember the problems which we still have with us with regard to the wings on the C–5. As you know, they threaten to fall off and we are going to pay Lockheed or whoever finally gets the business $1.5 billion, more or less, to fix them.

Senator MUSKIE. You talked about having your own B–52. How about having your own C–5A?

Mr. FITZGERALD. I don't know, it would be a hard choice. I couldn't afford either, so it is a moot question. Let me quote from a floor speech made by a Senator who was favoring the C–5 project at the time some others were criticizing it:

"There has been one criticism of the wing. As I said earlier, I think Lockheed should be congratulated for having come up with that kind of trouble. It is really too strong, but it is too strong just in the upper part of the aileron. That is giving it some trouble in maintaining the flexibility needed in that type of wing, but that can be easily corrected.

In fact, the Secretary of the Air Force has received the results of the analysis made by a study group appointed for the purpose—and I quote just one part of it: "Flight performance of the C–5A meets the guarantees of the contract within the accuracy limitation of good flight test measurements."

Now, in hindsight everybody knows that is a lot of nonsense. You know it is now perfectly clear. Even at the time, most people who examined it closely knew it was a lot of nonsense. But the point I wanted to make is that the Senator was undoubtedly depending completely on the assertion, a self-serving assertion, as it turned out, of the advocates of that program. He had no independent capability to assess what he was being told or if he did, he didn't avail himself of it. But I think it is fair to say he didn't have it.

So that is something else it would be wise to consider carefully, particularly in programs with high technical content.

Another point implicit but not stated—at least I didn't find it stated as clearly as it might be—is that when programs are being considered, we consider the life cycle cost of the program as well as the projected known costs that are contained in appropriation requests.

I think a problem that is inevitable that you must overcome is the extreme shortage of good people who have experience and skill in doing the kinds of things that have to be done to do good zero-base budgeting.

Finally, to reiterate a point I touched on earlier, why wait? I think that it is possible that a literal interpretation of the legislation as written could even delay the realization of some of the benefits that could be gotten. I think that, given the limitations of people and problems of intent and assumptions you can overcome those, you can start now doing some of these things, and that we should concentrate on the big accounts, not get bogged down in small items just because it is time to do them on the schedule. Concentrate on the big accounts as any good businessman does when he is confronted with budget problems. Continually monitor the big accounts. Don't allow them to proceed certified fat-free for 4 years without examination.

We can do much better in getting reports on current status, problems and outlook for major programs than we do now.

I thank you, Mr. Chairman, and I am prepared to answer questions.

Senator MUSKIE. Well, thank you very much for your testimony, Mr. Secretary.

You offer a very refreshing as well as a very useful insight and you have a way or articulating it that I think arrests one's attention.

With respect to the defense program—first of all, if we were to apply to the defense budget this year the kind of analysis that you have been fighting for, would the requested increases in defense be required in your judgment, or have you had a chance to look at that?

Mr. FITZGERALD. I have not had a chance to look at it as I would like because I am somewhat limited in what I am allowed to look at in the Pentagon at the moment. I would further have to say, and I should have said this at the outset, that my opinions here today, particularly on this subject, are my own and I'm not expressing the policy of the Pentagon.

Senator MUSKIE. I thank you for that.

Mr. FITZGERALD. I think you have to consider two things: One.— you spell this out very well in the bill—the need for the programs in the first place. And then, secondly, having established that, how much of the program you need, which is also covered, and how much they should cost if you buy them.

Now, I don't really have as much knowledge of the threat that we are confronted with as I did while I was working on the Hill, because I have been, as I say, restricted pretty much to in-house activities since my return to the Pentagon over the objections of some of my colleagues.

But I think it is quite clear that, given the programs that are projected, we could save a lot of money by squeezing out the fat. We have proposals to do so in-house. Whether we will succeed is another matter, but I think the important thing to realize about the military budget is that the figures that are now being talked about were not made up recently. These were figures that were made up a long time ago.

The budget cycle is very long in the Pentagon and the long-range planning cycle is even longer. As I mentioned to you, the track that is being followed is one that I detected being set up 3½ years ago. Each year after that you have different rationalizations for need of these things.

I think you could look at such things as what the weapons program ought to cost. That can be determined with a sort of a rough justice without the hordes of analysts that I cited. As I said, I will furnish the committee. the staff at least, the story of this approach which I think might be helpful.

We could look at excessive layering. We have layer on layer of organizations and intermediate layers of doubtful utility. Every Secretary of Defense. it seems to me, comes to the department and is immediately appalled by the number of layers that he finds, organizational layers he has to go through to communicate and give directions and receive responses.

It also seems that every one adds a layer or two before he leaves. That could be corrected.

One of the reasons that we have too many layers, particularly in the military organizations, in my opinion, is that we have too many generals.

Senator MUSKIE. Every general has to have his own layer?

Mr. FITZGERALD. Why, of course. The general must be at the peak of the pyramid of organization. One of the main defenses for questionable organizations is that they provide what are called "general officer slots".

Now, if you could do away with those, you would strip away much of the political protection. It is then much easier to combine or even reduce the numbers of ordinary civil servants and lower ranking military people. Once stripped of this protection, you can do something about it. So even though it seems like the cart before the horse, I think simply reducing the number of generals would help a lot.

In the support activities—that is, accounting and procurement and areas like that—we in most cases employ what is called "dual staffing". That is to say, the senior military person has a civilian deputy. The military people rotate in and out of those jobs, the civilian deputies stay there through many changes of military commanders as a rule, and in fact in most cases are the real technical directors of the activity.

Now, it is clear to me that we don't need dual staffing. The civilian equivalents are cheaper and cost us less both on a current basis and much less on a life-cycle basis, so we could easily absorb reduction of generals through attrition.

I have made this proposal by the way. It is not something that would be new to my bosses. As a matter of fact, I made it in testimony before the Defense Manpower Commission. At that time we were expecting retirement of some 168 generals and flag officers, the year before last I believe, and I suggested that the vacancies in administrative and support area general officer slots simply not be filled and that vacancies in operating commands, where you do really need military people, be filled by transfer of general officers from operating and support activities to those operating commands. Put them back to what they really know best for the most part.

Military science today is a very complicated and exacting thing and for one thing it is unfair to expect a person who spent his life to be a good soldier or airman to almost instantly become a competitor with the president of a giant corporation negotiating a contract, even if he were so inclined.

So that is another thing that can be done. The list is almost endless for opportunities for saving.

Senator MUSKIE. I was going to ask whether the defense programs should be authorized for more than a year at the time. That question seems to be irrelevant from what you have said.

Mr. FITZGERALD. Well, authorize or appropriate?

Senator MUSKIE. They are authorized each year like many other programs.

Mr. FITZGERALD. That is true.

Senator MUSKIE. We have both functions performed each year. Does it make any difference?

Mr. FITZGERALD. Yes, I think it does. I think that there should be at least a tentative plan in most cases for the life of a program and we do have that. Those are available at least to some of the committees. I don't think the whole Congress gets them, the 5-year defense plan and entire program projections, for particularly long, drawn-out acquisition programs. The research and development are, of course, pieces of the acquisition program.

I think it is useful to know what the long-range plan is, and I think that the annual budget should be a piece of the total plan. Now, right now, it is not necessarily true. The budget very often is whatever you can get. Whereas you could very well authorize and appropriate a year at a time, there should be some visibility of what the total program is.

I know I have dodged your question a little bit, but I think that is the kind of information that I would want to have available to me if I were looking at it. I would like to know what the plans were whether or not I authorized it. I think the practice of feeding the Congress a piece at a time is a very bad practice. As a matter of fact, though it is greatly favored by some of the old-timers in military budgeting. It is called the "come on theory" you know, just get them accustomed to it a little at a time and then feed it to them a little more each year. And then at the time you come to question it, you are confronted with the "sunk cost" argument.

Senator MUSKIE. Yes, it is a very familiar scheme.

Mr. FITZGERALD. It is either too early, you can't question this program because it is too early, or all of a sudden it is too late. I am sure you have suspected there must be some small window in time at which it is just right to address it, but you never hear about it.

One of the classics among non-military programs, a program that I call the "underground C–5A, is Metro—[Laughter.]

[Continuing] I happen to live in a District where we are going to have to pay the bills and they are crushing. It is a very serious thing to us. That is what happened on that program.

I had a friend, Colonel Smith, I worked with years ago in the Pentagon, who was a consultant on the program. In 1971 or so he sort of blew the whistle on the program, saying it would cost several billion dollars more than the public figures showed. And, of course, he got fired as you always do, I guess. [Laughter.]

He riled up all the principals in the program, from General Graham on down. They stoutly denied his story; "No problem in any way, too early to tell."

Well, Colonel Smith could tell. So, either he was right and the others were wrong, or he was simply telling the truth and the others weren't. It turned out he was telling the truth. He didn't make up figures himself, he just got hold of the pieces of the estimate and added them up.

So we are going to pay the bill for that now, all of us, I suppose. The Congress will be asked to bail out Virginia and suburban Maryland and the rest of us. So it is not restricted to military programs. The "come on theory" is with us everywhere.

Senator MUSKIE. I have never heard the label before, but it certainly fits.

How much of the defense budget programs escape periodic review that would be required by our bill?

Mr. FITZGERALD. I would say most of it.

Senator MUSKIE. Most of it.

Mr. FITZGERALD. Yes. Again, let me say I don't think that is peculiar to the Defense Department. As a matter of fact, in some areas they may have gotten more reviews than some other areas in the past, not that it has been all that effective. I think that is the problem.

There has been a lot of talk and debate and hearing activity that is not really effective. Concern is often focused on things that are immaterial, and there is a current example of that. It has to do with the use of the dollar model budget on the Soviet Union force structure.

I don't see how that has a bearing on the threat we are confronted with. You see, if you follow that practice to its most ludicrous extreme, you really end up attributing our own inefficiencies, to the extent we have them—and we have them in increasing degree—to the Soviets, and assuming that each time we have another overrun on the B-1 the Soviet military budget goes up.

It is an almost Catch 22 sort of rationalization. What we ought to be looking at is what genuine threats we face and how to counter them.

The arguments about how much they pay for different pieces of hardware, it seems, is immaterial to me. Yet, much of the discussion in the newspapers and what I have heard from Capitol Hill is focused on that. Often you get off on sidetracks that don't really matter.

Senator MUSKIE. It is a different rationalization every year, as you put it.

Mr. FITZGERALD. That's right.

Senator MUSKIE. Different selling scheme every year.

Mr. FITZGERALD. Oh, sure. And the difficulty that all of us face and, of course, Congressmen and Senators more acutely than others, because they have to vote on it, is knowing when the cries of wolf are real and when they are just to get more budget.

That makes it a tough decision.

Senator MUSKIE. Are we getting closer to the real wolf?

Mr. FITZGERALD. I don't know. I wish I did.

Senator MUSKIE. Well——

Mr. FITZGERALD. I think certainly, Mr. Chairman, that wasteful expenditures don't help us at all. As a matter of fact, I have written many times and it is my honest conviction that the first casualty of the big military boondoggling, to put it bluntly, that really got out of hand in the early 1960's was true military capability. As the costs of these programs have gone out of control, just to keep some semblance of fiscal order, we have been forced to cut back on programs and accept substandard hardware and all that sort of thing.

So, I think the injection of good discipline and contract enforcement, which is the simplest thing in the world, would both save money and increase our military capability. It has the potential of doing so.

You know, it is going to be very difficult after the depredations of Mr. Packard to enforce big contracts. The Lockheed precedent was a devastating one. Most people think Lockheed was bailed out with a loan, and that was indeed part of it. But, in fact, the major portion of the bailout was action technically known as an "amendment without consideration" under Public Law 85–804, which means exactly what it says. It is an amendment where you increase the price of the contract and don't get anything in return. In this case, in the case of the C–5 and the Cheyenne and perhaps some others that they picked up in the same action, we actually got less than the old contract called for.

It amounted to an outright grant of more than $1 billion in the case of the C–5.

Now, you know, if I were a competitor of Lockheed, I would scream bloody murder if the Defense Department came along and wanted to enforce my contract having let my competitor off the hook. So I think we have severe problems in that area.

Senator MUSKIE. Are they under control?

Mr. FITZGERALD. No, sir.

Senator MUSKIE. Mr. Secretary, thank you very much for your testimony.

Mr. FITZGERALD. Thank you, Mr. Chairman.

Senator MUSKIE. I find it sufficiently refreshing so that I probably will invite you back sometime.

Mr. FITZGERALD. Thank you. I hope I will survive to return.

OVERSIGHT AND UTILIZATION: ELMER STAATS ([83], pp. 125–130, 155–173, 175–192)

The General Accounting Office, as an official investigatory arm of Congress, has vast experience in examining and evaluating the structure and efficiency of government. Its head, Comptroller General Elmer Staats, testified in support of S. 2925 and was joined by several key aides in answering questions on zero-base budgeting and sunset procedures before the Senate Government Operations Committee. The aides testifying were Harry Havens, Albert Hair, Phillip Hughes, Bill Thurman, and Robert Derkits. Their testimony, especially regarding the workload problem in zero-base budgeting, raised some serious questions as to how a governmentwide reorganization program could be speedily implemented.

Mr. STAATS. ....We are pleased to be here this morning to present our views on Senate bill 2925, the "Government Economy and Spending Reform Act of 1976." The bill would require authorizations of new budget authority for Government programs and activities at least every 4 years. It would also establish a procedure for zero-base review and evaluation of Government programs and activities every 4 years—with the ultimate objective of expanding the budgetary options available to the Congress by redefining or eliminating ineffective and duplicative programs and with the objective of more creative and flexible planning of Federal efforts.

Our rough calculations indicate that of the total outlays proposed by the fiscal year 1977 budget, the reauthorization or termination provision of the bill would apply to about $135 billion in domestic assistance and $115 billion in direct Federal operations, mainly, national defense. Outlays excluded from the provision—interest payments on the public debt, Medicare, and retirement and other trust funds payments—total about $144 billion.

We have studied S. 2925 with a great deal of interest and we certainly agree with its purpose of strengthening congressional control over Federal programs. I am particularly encouraged by the sections of this bill which are designed to concentrate congressional attention on what the Federal Government is doing in an entire policy area.

Through the new budget process the Congress has begun to regain control over the Federal budget—the most important statement of national priorities that we have. Important as getting better control of the budget may be—we should not lose sight of the importance of getting our money's worth from old and established programs. From our vantage point, it appears that both the executive and legislative branches have been more concerned with starting new programs than with making certain that those we already have are working satisfactorily or could be improved. All too frequently, in any organization, the tendency is to look at the increases—the add-ons—rather than whether economies can be achieved by making present programs work better, by making them less costly, or by eliminating them entirely.

In any event, it will be important to properly relate activities undertaken under the terms of S. 2925 to the work of the Congress, and particularly, of the Budget Committees and the Congressional Budget Office, under the terms of the Congressional Budget and Impoundment Control Act. One of the most effective means of reflecting the conclusions from reviews of ongoing programs would be to integrate them into the congressional review of the Federal budget. Doing this smoothly will require careful scheduling and coordination.

I understand that the subcommittee is primarily interested in information on GAO's past studies and reviews which have identified problems resulting from duplicative Federal programs and activities. Before proceeding into this subject, I would like to offer a few impressions and comments for the subcommittee's consideration. Obviously, the bill has many significant implications for the Congress, the executive branch, and GAO.

The 4-year cycle under title I of the bill for reauthorizing legislation will place a heavy workload on the authorizing committees. The extent and nature of the impact on the working arrangements and workloads of committees is hard to predict with accuracy since it is not posible to develop an accurate count of the total number of programs and activities which would require attention under the bill. One of the problems which clearly needs to be addressed is the development of workable definitions of the terms "program" and "activity." The terms are used throughout the bill and the interpretation of them is crucial in carrying out its provisions.

We have defined both terms in the "Budgetary Definitions" glossary published under requirements of title VII of the Congressional Budget and Impoundment Control Act of 1974. Our definitions of these terms were intentionally somewhat general, because we found there was a wide variance within the Government as well as the general public as to the concept of an "activity" or a "program."

Over the past few months, we have been working with 25 authorizing committees and over 70 departments and agencies to get the fiscal year 1977 budget data reported to the committees in terms of "programs" as created in authorizing legislation. The committees are using this information in their review of the President's proposed funding levels and in preparing their views and estimates reports to the Budget Committees. This work is a continuing part of our assistance to committees under title VIII of the Congressional Budget Act of 1974. As soon as we complete our current work on the fiscal year 1977 budget information we will begin identifying ways of improving the reporting for the fiscal year 1978 budget, especially the classification of programs in terms of the authorizing legislation with the cross references to committee jurisdiction and appropriation account. We feel this work will provide a useful informational aid for relating the Congress' budgetary process with its legislative and oversight activities, as well as beginning to establish for congressional use and reporting the entities that are to be called "programs."

Consideration should be given to the question of whether a fixed frequency of review and reauthorization is appropriate for all programs. A valid argument can be made that some programs ought to be reviewed more frequently than every 4 years, because of rapidly changing circumstances, while others do not need the same frequency of review. The reauthorization workload and its impact on the congressional budget cycle should also be considered. The legislative deadlines mandated by the 1974 Budget Act could be more easily met if the trend toward more frequent authorizations were reversed.

We have previously taken the position favoring longer periods for authorization for some programs. We have also recommended advance authorizations for certain others, coupled with periodic comprehensive reviews of major programs. We feel the emphasis should be on strengthening procedures for committee oversight through more thorough and frequent reviews and evaluations of programs or groups of programs impacting on major national needs. We would therefore suggest that alternatives for increasing flexibility and decreasing workload through screening and variable cycles of reauthorization be considered by the subcommittee.

Title II of the bill would require GAO to conduct a study of all Federal programs and activities to identify those programs and activities for which no outlays have been made for the last 2 completed fiscal years and those programs and activities which have duplicative objectives. Interim reports to the Congress on the results of the study would be required with a final report due on or before July 1, 1977.

I fully endorse and support the objectives of this title. The way in which the bill is drafted, however, raises the exceptionally difficult technical problem of distinguishing between those programs which are similar in important respects and those which are duplicative. To illustrate, in a recent report to the Congress, we noted that 228 programs—programs as defined by the Catalog of Federal Domestic Assistance—could provide funds to State and local governments for health-related activities. Of these programs:

24 were for facility planning and construction; 22 were for health services planning and technical assistance; 22 were for mental health; and 24 were for narcotic addiction and drug abuse. At the broadest level, the 228 programs could be considered to have duplicative objectives in that all related to health. At a lower level one could look for duplication among the 22 mental health programs.

Our experience with Federal domestic assistance programs indicates that each program is claimed to have unique characteristics which distinguish it from other programs. However, in practice, many programs serve very similar purposes and we agree with the basic thrust of the bill that there are opportunities to improve effectiveness of Federal efforts by consolidating programs serving similar objectives. The identification, of these opportunities is certainly no easy task, but we do not believe it is necessary to demonstrate total overlap or duplication in order to provide a basis for recommending consolidation.

Over the past few years we have performed studies documenting the problems that arise from having many Federal programs serving closely related objectives, particularly when responsibility for implementing the programs is fragmented among different Federal agencies and operating organizations. We have found that such studies are quite complex and time consuming, requiring a comprehensive understanding of multiple Federal programs and activities, relationships among Federal agencies, agencies' relationships with clientele groups, and the operations of grantee organizations. These complexities mean that even with a major reorientation of GAO's overall work program, we would not be able, within the time frame allowed, to accomplish the study envisioned by title II.

I recommend that this title be amended to require that during its reviews GAO give special priority to the identification of problems resulting from Federal programs and activities having similar objectives and report its findings and recommendations to the Congress and cognizant committees as promptly as possible.

The job of identifying programs and activities for which there have been no outlays for 2 fiscal years could be more readily accomplished by the agencies responsible for the programs than by GAO. Accordingly, I would suggest that title II be amended to assign this responsibility to the executive branch, with coordination responsibilities in OMB.

I also strongly support the objectives of title III, to provide periodic congressional review and zero-based evaluation of Federal programs. I believe a procedure for systematic review and evaluation will strengthen congressional control over Federal programs as well as provide information needed for exercising congressional oversight.

I am concerned, however, about the massive amount of data and analysis which would be necessary to implement this approach effectively. Accordingly, I have some reservations about undertaking such a task across the board without some prior experience in actually conducting zero-base reviews and evaluations. I would suggest, as one possible alternative, some type of pilot test of this legislation which could perhaps help the Congress uncover and resolve some of the complexities associated with the zero-based approach. Perhaps the test might consist of pilot programs to take place over the next 6 months, in which each standing committee considers one program for zero-based review and evaluation. The Congress could call on the President and the agencies for cooperation in developing their zero-base review and evaluation of each program considered in the pilot project. Useful knowledge could be gained from such a test by both the Congress and the executive branch as to problems encountered, issues which need to be resolved, and possible solutions.

Title IV of the bill would require us to perform followup audits and report at least once every 6 months on any program or activity which GAO has audited and found to be substantially deficient in achieving its objectives. Followup audits would be required until we are satisfied that the deficiencies have been eliminated.

It is normal GAO policy to followup on its recommendations. However, the requirement to make followup audits and reports every 6 months would place an unnecessary strain on our limited staff resources. As an alternative, I would suggest that within 60 days of the date of a GAO report which makes recommendations to the head of a Federal agency, and not less often than once every 6 months thereafter, the agency be required to report to the appropriate committees, and to us on actions taken and progress made in implementing GAO recommendations. Reports would be continued until in our judgment all reasonable actions have been completed on the recommendations, and no purpose would be served by further reports.

You know now, Mr. Chairman, that the statute requires that agencies report to the Appropriations and the Government Operations Committees within 60 days of any report made by the GAO which makes recommendations to them. And what this would do would simply have a followup series of reports from the agency that would be in line with that procedure.

Section 236 or the Legislative Reorganization Act of 1970, which places a more limited reporting requirement on Federal agencies, would need to be rescinded if this provision were adopted. That is the one I just referred to.

Our staff has spent considerable time reviewing the various provisions of the bill and we do have other comments and suggestions, which are attached to this statement. We would appreciate the opportunity to work with the subcommittee sttaff and to provide whatever assistance we can.

In the broad sense, the bill goes to the essence of GAO's present role in Government. Starting in 1921, GAO was primarily concerned with assuring the Congress as to the legality and fiscal integrity of Federal expenditures. Later on, we became increasingly involved in identifying ways that Federal programs could be carried out more economically and efficiently. More recently GAO has become deeply concerned with basic questions of whether programs are working as they should, whether they need modification to make them work better, and whether they should be expanded, cut back, or discontinued.

As you know, we are constantly trying to identify opportunities to improve the economy and effectiveness of Government programs and operations. Where possible, we make estimates of savings which are directly attributable to GAO recommendations, which are acted upon by the agency. Such measurable savings amounted to $503 million in fiscal year 1975. Of this $147 million will continue to be saved annually in future years. Over the past 2 years, measurable savings resulting from our work totals nearly $1.1 billion.

In addition, numerous actions resulted in financial savings which could not be fully or readily measured. Examples include reducing grant aid for the Korean Security Assistance program, substantial savings possible through increased agency purchases through the General Services Administration, and eliminating duplication between DOD and Energy Research and Development Administration in the development of nuclear weapons.

Even more important is the large number of recommendations we make which, while not resulting in immediate dollar savings, point to ways to improve program effectiveness. For example, our work helped to expedite disability compensation payments, change the military body armor program to further emphasize reduction in casualties, increase control and consumer awareness of salmonella in raw meat and poultry, improve control over suspected fraud and abuse in medicaid, strengthen energy conservation standards for new homes, and provide better job placement assistance to displaced Federal civilian employees. . . .

...............Currently, either at our own initiative or at the request of Congress, we have underway approximately 1,400 studies or reviews covering a wide range of Federal activities. In fiscal year 1975, we issued 1,043 reports. In fiscal year 1976, through December 31, we issued 423 reports. A number of these reports and assignments deal with similar, overlapping or redundant programs which Title II of the bill seeks to address.

Prior GAO reviews of the management of the operations of the Department of Defense and the military services indicate possible economies from elimination of overlapping activities. In recent years we have reported on such activities as the management of ammunition, service maintenance workloads, equipment development, and training programs. In each of these reports, we concluded that more interservice cooperation and joint undertakings would void unnecessary duplication and result in budgetary savings.

A report we issued in July 1973, points out the problems that arise, mainly unnecessary costs, when an individual military service approach is used to accomplish an objective which is really defensewide. The report cited potential for greater consolidation of the maintenance workloads in the military services. While the Secretary of Defense required each military service to use the maintenance capability of another service to avoid duplication, we found that each service overemphasized developing its own maintenance capability. The services extensively duplicated maintenance facilities; some were underused. Only 2 percent of the $3 billion worth of depot maintenance done in the United States was interservice in nature.

Responsibility for maintenance within the Defense Department was fragmented, but we concluded that it was feasible to consolidate workloads. We recommended that a single manager be responsible for specific maintenance items. The Defense Department agreed that the dollar volume of interservice agreements was not large and that the single manager concept had merit. DOD advised us that some progress in this direction has been made and was hopeful that further studies would result in additional progress.

While our studies of Defense activities will no doubt continue to reveal the kind of situation just described, we are of the opinion that the problem of program overlap is even more severe in Federal domestic assistance programs, mainly because of the greater variety and sheer numbers of domestic assistance programs and activities, and the many Federal agencies, State and local governments and other organizations involved.

Domestic assistance has been provided by the Federal Government for over a century to accomplish specified national objectives and priorities in partnership with State and local governments and other organizations. In 1862 the Congress enacted the Morrill Act to help the States establish and maintain land-grant colleges. The act carefully specified the grant's objectives, placed conditions on the use of revenue derived from the sale of granted lands, and required annual reports. This established the pattern of categorical grants—providing needed resources for specific purposes.

This pattern continued with the enactment of the Federal Aid Road Act of 1916, which authorized construction of public roads over which U.S. mail would be transported. Under that act, each State was required to create a highway department and match Federal funds dollar for dollar. Furthermore, provision was made for advance Federal approval of projects and for continuing Federal supervision. These types of provisions continued under the wide range of welfare and economic security programs enacted during the 1930's.

In the 1960's the number and dollar amount of Federal assistance programs grew substantially. Major steps were taken to broaden elementary, secondary, and higher educational opportunities; to promote development in economically depressed areas; to help finance health services and medical care for the indigent; to launch a war on poverty; and to attempt a comprehensive physical, social, and economic program to transform slum and blight-ridden cities into model neighborhoods.

During the late 1960's and into the 1970's, the Federal Government began new approaches to providing assistance to State and local governments. The pattern of increasing assistance through narrowly defined categorical programs was altered with the enactment of broader purpose block grants and general revenue sharing. Fundamental to both approaches was the intent to provide State and local government with greater discretion in deciding how Federal funds would be used.

The number of programs established during the 1960's is difficult to quantify because of varying definitions. For example, the Office of Management and Budget in its 1970 edition of the Catalog of Federal Domestic Assistance, listed 1,019 programs. Using the number of separate authorizations as a definition, the Advisory Commission on Intergovernmental Relations estimated a 1970 total of 530 grant-in-aid programs, four-fifths of which were enacted after 1960.

In the early 1970's, the establishment of new grant programs slowed considerably. In fact, the number of programs decreased slightly due to legislation consolidating certain categorical programs into broader purpose block grant programs. In the last year or 2, however, the trend has reversed. The 1975 Catalog of Federal Domestic Assistance lists 1,030 assistance programs administered by 55 Federal agencies.

The rapid growth in the number and variety of Federal assistance programs has been accompanied by increasing criticism and demands for reform. Since the mid-1960's numerous attempts have been made by both the legislative and executive branches to improve the delivery of domestic assistance, particularly at the State and local level.

Actions have been taken to promote intergovernmental cooperation, to simplify administrative requirements associated with Federal aid, to facilitate the funding of projects that require funds from two or more Federal agencies, to place greater reliance on State and local governments, and to move some Federal decisionmaking out of Washington, D.C.

We have concluded that despite the actions taken, basic problems continue. In August 1975 we issued a report to the Congress entitled "Fundamental Changes Are Needed in Federal Assistance to State and Local Governments." In conducting the study which led to this report we attempted to take a broad look at the Federal assistance system, its impact on States and localities, and the various attempts to improve it.

The report calls attention to the multiplicity of domestic assistance programs which provide funds for closely related purposes. In our view, many of the problems associated with our domestic assistance efforts are directly attributable to the large number of programs and the fragmentation of responsibility among different Federal departments and agencies.

Our overall conclusions were that the present delivery system lacks an adequate means for disseminating grant information needed by State and local governments, creates a high degree of funding uncertainty due to late congressional authorizations and appropriations and executive impoundment of appropriate funds, fosters complex and varying application and administrative processes, and is fragmented, with similar programs being administered by different Federal agencies or agency components and with programs too restrictive to meet State and local needs.

These problems, individually and collectively, cause the planning and implementation of State and local projects to be greatly impeded.

We found that State and local governments must devote considerable time and effort to simply keep informed of available Federal assistance. Because of funding uncertainties associated with many of the programs, available assistance is often learned of too late or offered under time constraints which sometimes preclude States and localities from taking advantage of the assistance.

On the basis of this study we recommended that the Congress consolidate separate programs serving similar objectives into broader purpose programs and assign programs with similar goals to the same Federal agency. We suggested as an approach to achieving these objectives, the enactment of previously proposed amendments to Intergovernmental Cooperation Act of 1968, which would direct the President to periodically examine the various assistance programs and recommend to the Congress program consolidations deemed necessary or desirable.

We also recommended that the Congress, in order to reduce funding uncertainties associated with Federal assistance, consider greater use of both advanced and forward funding and authorization and appropriations for longer than 1 fiscal year.

In previous reports to the Congress we have addressed the multiplicity of Federal programs and the complex and confusing delivery system. For example: 17 Federal programs provided funds for manpower services for the disadvantaged; seven Federal and one local program provided funds for health services in outpatient health centers; and 11 Federal programs provided funds for childcare activities. Members of our staff are prepared to brief the subcommittee on each of these three studies, and these charts are available for the presentation.

As you know, Mr. Chairman, section 602 of the Intergovernmental Cooperation Act of 1968 requires that upon request of any committee having jurisdiction over a grant-in-aid program, GAO will undertake a study to determine among other things the extent to which "such program conflicts with or duplicates other grants-in-aid programs." Quite frankly we are a bit surprised that this provision has attracted little interest.

We find your subcommittee's interest in this whole subject most gratifying. We wish to cooperate in any feasible manner.

Mr. Chairman, if I may, I would like to add one thing to this statement which occurred to me after it was finished, which would be useful in this connection. On August 11, 1972, I addressed a letter to the chairman of each of the legislative committees of the Congress and to the Director of OMB in which I suggested that—maybe I should perhaps read it, it is one paragraph.

I urge that the Congress give careful consideration in authorizing new programs or in reauthorizing existing programs to including in the authorizing legislation specific statutory requirements for a systematic evaluation by the department or agency involved of the results of programs in operation. In line with this thought, I am directing our staff in developing comments on draft bills and pending legislation submitted to this office for review, to suggest wherever appropriate language which we believe could most usefully accomplish this objective. In addition, we will be glad to work with the committees and committee staffs in developing suitable language tailored to meet specific cases.

Then I go ahead and say:

I hope that the OMB in clearing legislation submitted by the executive agencies would similarly include provisions for this type of evaluation. We feel that it is a fundamental responsibility of the agency administering the program to provide evaluations to the Congress.

One of the difficulties in the past has been that reports are required, annual reports or other periodic reports, but the specifications of what is to be included in those reports are missing.

It seems to us that in the language of the statute or in the language of the Committee report there could be specifics on alternatives, answers to questions which arise during the development of legislation, and evaluation of end results in a manner which would enable the Congress to do a better oversight job.

We could help formulate the specifics for such evaluations at the time the committee reports are written and we could also criticize those evaluations as they come forward and give the committees the benefit of our judgment about them.

We have had some favorable response to this suggestion, not as much as we frankly would have liked, so we are going to renew this suggestion. I am renewing it here this morning; and we have been working also with Senator Leahy, from Vermont, who has had a lot of interest in developing what might be called "models" or specifics for evaluations as they could be written into legislation.

I think it is his intent to develop legislation for consideration in this committee, in fact.

Mr. Havens, to my right, in our Office of Program Analysis has been working with Senator Leahy and his staff to do some pilot testing along this line. I wanted to add this to our statement because it seems very much on point and it is possible you might want to consider something along this line as an addition to your bill.

Senator MUSKIE. It sounds like a very constructive suggestion and I will ask the staff to explore its inclusion in the bill.

All of this included in the bill itself, as you pointed out, involves a massive amount of data. Is there any way—I assume there must be with our computer technology—of making access to that data, along the lines of your suggestions, more readily available to the committees of Congress. What have you done about that?

Mr. STAATS. Well, we have given a good deal of thought to that, and we have a booklet in preparation which we are going to distribute to all the members and to the staff; I am going to renew in personal communication to each of the legislative committees what I have read. We have attempted to incorporate language or specific suggestions and comments that we have made on legislation which is referred to the GAO for comment. These are some of the things that we have done or have in our plans. In summary, we believe that there are a number of different avenues to try to encompass a system for program evaluation and we like your bill. We think there are some changes that can be made to make it perhaps less burdensome for us, and still accomplish your objective, but the whole concept here of zero-based budgeting and program evaluation are inseparably linked. They are simply two different approaches to the same end objective.

It is in this area that we think we can make a pretty good contribution to the Congress' oversight and the judgments that it must make on budgetary allowances and on authorizations of programs

About 40 percent of our total manpower today is devoted to work which we describe as "program evaluation." Now, this has increased very substantially over the last 5, 6, 7 years, and since the 1970 Reorganization Legislative Act and the Budget Act, it has gained impetus. We find the requests coming to us from the committees of Congress are emphasizing program evaluation more and more.

We don't want to reach the stage where so much of our effort is concerned with strictly program evaluation, important as that is, to the point where we cannot also cover responsibilities we have in the area of fiscal integrity and fiscal audit and in economy and efficiency. I should add here, when we make a review of program effectiveness, we also have to look at the management of that program. You cannot, in our opinion, make a good program evaluation without looking at the adequacy of the administration of that program.

You can do a great deal in looking at programs from a strictly economy and efficiency standpoint such as procurement and lease versus purchase and many, many things can be looked at. But without focusing on the end objective of that program, you can't really do the reverse very well.

You have to look at the management program in order to be able to reach good conclusions as to effectiveness.

Senator MUSKIE. My impression, which was fortified by a discussion Senator Bellmon and I had with you and Mr. Lynn, is that neither OMB nor GAO really is equipped at this point to inaugurate a comprehensive program of program evaluation.

Mr. STAATS. Not on every program across the board.

Senator MUSKIE. There is not now in place any such——

Mr. STAATS. There is not now in place a complete capability to do that on a cyclical basis. We can do it on a program by program basis. And I assume—and Mr. Lynn would best speak for himself— I assume OMB is trying through their process to do zero-based budgeting but zero-based budgeting is a kind of uncertain term, depending on how intensive an evaluation you do.

And this is what I think your bill is trying to get at, a more comprehensive and more detailed evaluation of the effectiveness of these programs.

Senator MUSKIE. Well, before I put the question to you, to be sure we understand, let me make an observation. I think the GAO has a high credibility and confidence base in the Congress based upon its performance. So what I am about to ask you is not intended to suggest that you are not doing your job. I think you are doing your job. But it seems to me we are putting in place a system for looking at the effectiveness of a program or its relevance to its statutory objective, or its relevance to the public interest. We have failed so far to put in place anything which enables us to look at a program like this.

The President, the Director of OMB, or committee chairmen, want to have evaluation of program performance, and today you find it almost impossibly time consuming to get the data. Is that correct?

Mr. STAATS. I think that is a fair statement. What would help, I believe, would be a comprehensive system—and I think your bill moves in that direction—so that it is understood what the various elements are that feed into a total system of budget review and program evaluation.

I think that that would be a major contribution.

Senator MUSKIE. Now the problem is trying to avoid biting off so much that it would fall of its own weight before we were able to make any progress at all.

Mr. STAATS. But, Mr. Chairman, I would like to add here that you are raising the question of feasibility and building up expectations beyond what could be realized. I think that is a very important point. But if you add the element in it, which I added to my statement, of getting the agencies involved here. then you have got a whole lot more manpower that can be brought into the picture.

Our responsibilities are growing all the time in the GAO as every new statute goes on the books it automatically increases our responsibility for monitoring, auditing, and evaluation of them. So we see here a very important point of trying to get the agencies involved in terms of the specifications which the legislative committees can set forth. We need a lot more manpower and we are putting the focus on where responsibility rests for carrying it out and that is the agency that heads it. We have a staff that currently is concerned with looking at the adequacy of the central staff facilities in each of the agencies from the standpoint of program evaluation, auditing, and budgeting. We are doing this because we think we can get a lot more maybe for our money, for our manpower effort if we can put the spotlight there and see whether or not they are doing the job the way they should be doing the job.

We tried to develop some standards pursuant to the title VII of the Congressional Budget Act; we will be issuing very soon some standards and guidelines for program evaluation in the public sector which we think will be applicable and useful in the Congress, to the agencies and to State and local government.

We have issued and have had outstanding now for about 3 years, a booklet, guidelines which we formulated for the State and local government people, and the public accounting profession, describing what constitutes an adequate oversight of governmental programs. We define it as including fiscal audit; compliance with rules and regulations such as equal opportunity and so forth; economy and efficiency; and program evaluation.

We have established in each of the 10 regional centers now what we call an intergovernmental audit form, and we have the national form, where this is all being brought together in an effort to try to upgrade the quality of State and local government auditing and relying more and more on State and local governments to conduct these evaluations in the Federal assistance area.

This is a long answer to your question I am afraid, but we do see as a part of this what might be called the comprehensive system, the need to put in some additional language in the bill which would spell out the agency's role and how the congressional review can be related to it.

Senator MUSKIE. I suspect a lot of these agencies have an instinct for anonymity and would rather not have the question of their justification exposed to public review or congressional review. We have to have something, though, to be sure they don't take refuge in anonymity, don't you think?

Mr. STAATS. Oh, I guess so.

Senator MUSKIE. On page 15 of your statement you referred to three studies that members of your staff are prepared to present to us so that we may get a more detailed picture of some of the problems?

Mr. STAATS. Yes, Mr. Hair and Mr. Thurman are here to make that presentation, Mr. Chairman, and if you would like to turn to that point now——

Senator MUSKIE. Yes.

Mr. STAATS [continuing]. We are prepared to proceed.

Senator MUSKIE. Before they do, I do understand you have to leave at 11 o'clock, right?

Mr. STAATS. Yes.

Senator MUSKIE. The staff tells me we could use some specific help from GAO with respect to two matters: The data on Federal programs by functional categories, a list of all Federal programs by functional categories; and a separate list of all Federal programs with permanent budget authority. Is that something within your competence, within your bailiwick?

Mr. HAVENS. We have been discussing this with your staff, Mr. Chairman. We have compiled some data which was acquired in connection with the efforts that we went through for the authorizing committees in which we attempted with intensive cooperation from the agencies to identify the programs under the jurisdiction of each authorizing committee and associate those programs with the dollars in the budget for that committee.

I would have to say that the results of this at this point are rather spotty. They are very good in some areas. They are less good in others.

Some committees specifically asked only for a piece of their committee jurisdiction to be covered this year because that is all they were really interested in obtaining details on. In no sense do we have a comprehensive data base of programs by committee jurisdiction and by function.

We have something which we will be more than happy to share with your committee staff and we are in the process of putting that material together at this time.

Senator MUSKIE. What would we have to do to improve upon it?

Mr. HAVENS. I guess I would say that we would have to go back to the agencies again and make sure we have it all, do a doublecheck between the data we have and the budget to make sure we have in fact covered everything. That would be a very time consuming task, it would be time consuming and manpower intensive.

Senator MUSKIE. Is it a job worth doing? It strikes me that once it is done and it establishes a baseline it can be useful.

Mr. HAVENS. You are correct. It is useful data and we have put a substantial amount of manpower into getting as far as we have. It is more a question of the timing within which we try to do it rather than whether or not we try to do it. We are committed to doing it in a matter of time.

Senator MUSKIE. If there is anything we can do that would be helpful that would help you proceed more expeditiously, we will.

Mr. HAVENS The fact that you are interested enough to ask the question is enough to give it priority.

Mr. STAATS. We may have to ask for some more money in next year's budget.

Senator MUSKIE. Senator Hollings is briefed on this.

Mr. STAATS. Mr. Havens is quite right, it is a technical and detailed job and it needs to be done and accurately and precisely and it takes manpower to do that.

Senator MUSKIE. I understand that.

Mr. STAATS. We are, of course, asking for an additional amount in that area.

Senator MUSKIE. I think it could be a very useful part of this committee's consideration of the bill. I don't know how fast we are going to be able to move on this bill. We have not yet appeared to be sufficiently credible to stir the kinds of fears on the part of those affected, so that we have not yet ran up against the obstacles that I am sure we will encounter at some point. I guess they don't think we really mean business with this bill, or that we will be able to really move it.

I hope that we can establish that so that affected interests will begin to come in and pick holes in it. You can't really put together a piece of legislation unless and until those are impacted by it are sufficiently stirred up to pick holes in it. We have not gotten to that process yet but when we do I think the basic data that I just requested will be very useful.

[The information referred to is available in subcommittee files.]

Mr. STAATS. It might well be, Mr. Chairman, that some of the reaction you were referring to here may be because it is such an overwhelming job and if we could—if we could develop the system, as I call it, and the objective down the road, even though we can't accomplish all of it next year or even 3 or 4 years from now, still it would give us a roadmap to which we could all be working against. I think it would be very helpful.

Senator MUSKIE. A number of our witnesses, Mr. Ash, for example, Dean Weber, Mr. Schick and yourself have focused on the problem of trying to break down the workload in some kind of rational orderly way so that we can move without being blocked by the sheer weight of the total job.

Mr. STAATS. Perhaps different timetables could be developed with respect to different parts of the legislation.

Senator MUSKIE. We would welcome your assistance in trying to define the job in that respect and again I apologize to you for having been so late this morning.

Mr. STAATS. That's all right.

Senator MUSKIE. And we will continue with your staff presentation.

Mr. HAIR. Mr. Chairman, the presentation we will make this morning is designed to demonstrate the problems of conflicting and overlapping programs. All of that which you have been discussing this morning, whether it be evaluating Federal programs, whether it be getting the list of them, no matter what it is would all be simplified by fewer programs. The mechanisms designed to gain this effectiveness all would be simplified. This demonstration attempts to reinforce one of the sections of the bill, something that would result in fewer programs, without the necessity of fundamentally changing the thrust of the programs, but simply to recognize that the administrative load of this enormous number of programs is getting to the point where developing systems to review them, budget for them or anything else, even now, just to get a list of them, is quite out of hand.

Mr. Thurman and several of his staff people are ready to show you our show.

Mr. THURMAN. Mr. Chairman, back in 1970, we decided to review selected domestic assistance programs from the perspective of the local government. Our objective was to determine what the impact of similar purpose grants from different Federal agencies would be on accomplishing the objectives of the programs within the local government. A task force was formed and the District of Columbia was selected for study because our audit authority extended not only over Federal programs, but also over city operations.

Although two of the three studies which we will discuss this morning were performed exclusively in the District, it was our view that our findings would have applicability in most major urban areas of the Nation. To test this hypothesis, our first study in the District was followed by a similar study in two other cities, Chicago and St. Louis, and the results were similar to those found in the District.

We have several charts with us this morning which depict, chronologically, the growth of Federal programs serving similar objectives, the funding flow of each program, and the organizations involved. The top rows of the charts show the Federal agencies and programs. The middle row shows the local administering organizations and the bottom row, the providers of the services.

Our first chart—appendix III —depicts the results of our study of programs which provided educational and day care services for preschool children, generally children of 3 and 4 years of age. We found 11 Federal programs operating in the District which funded for such child-care services. The first program, aid to families with dependent children—AFDC—color red on the chart, was established in 1935. In 1964, four new programs, shown in blue, were created under which funds were provided for childcare services. In 1965, three additional programs, shown in green, were funding child-care services and by 1971, an additional three programs, shown in yellow, began providing these services.

Senator MUSKIE. I think if you turn that chart a little so that the members of the audience can see it, I think I will still be able to see it.

Mr. THURMAN. Each program——

Senator MUSKIE. That is four different layers then.

Mr. THURMAN. Four different layers, yes, sir.

Each program was specifically designed to serve seemingly different client groups. For example, the work incentive child-care program—WIN—provided for child-care services to enable welfare clients to obtain training and employment. The manpower training programs, the blue boxes on the right, provided child-care services for children of program enrollees to enable them to undertake training and employment. The Headstart program was for poor and underprivileged children while the Elementary and Secondary Education Act, Title I program—ESEA I— was for educationally deprived children from low-income families.

The services provided to these seemingly different client groups, however, were the same. One child-care operator included in our review, which is noted on the chart as box A, had enrolled children from four different programs—AFDC, WIN, Headstart, and model cities. The children sat side by side in the child-care center, receiving the same services and distinguished only by color dots in the center's records. WIN children were coded one color, AFDC, another, and so.

A point brought out by the funding chart is that no one organization had control of the funding or operations at either the Federal or local level—at the Federal level five agencies were involved and at the local level, three district agencies, the Community Action Agency, and several private organizations were involved. With no single responsible organization, the goals of these programs—getting adequate child-care services to those in need—were not fully met.

Some of the shortcomings, which we found, included these: Centers were not located geographically in proportion to the number and residences of children in need because of little coordinated planning among the local agencies in locating child-care centers; some children of working parents received only half-day services while other children received full-day, requiring the former to make other arrangements for the remainder of the day.

In summary, no one knew: How many children needed services; how many centers existed; the number of children receiving services; and the unmet need.

Our next chart—appendix I —depicts the results of our study of manpower training services provided to unemployed and underemployed persons under federally assisted programs. Job training as a federally sponsored program goes back to the vocational education program authorized by the Smith-Hughes Act of 1917 and, later the Vocational Education Act of 1963. The very familiar Federal-State employment services program was established in 1935, authorized by the Wagner-Peyser Act of 1933 and the Social Security Act of 1935.

The 1960's saw a tremendous growth in manpower training programs, increasing in number in the District of Columbia from 2 to 12 programs. These additions consisted of two programs in the early 1960's—shown in blue on the chart—authorized by the Economic Opportunity Act of 1964, the Adult Basic Education Act, and the Manpower Development and Training Act of 1962.

In 1965, three additional programs, shown in purple, began operating—authorized by the Economic Opportunity Act of 1964 and the Manpower Development and Training Act of 1962.

Senator MUSKIE. Could I ask a question here? You refer to three additional programs but the purple blocks number several times that number. What do the number of blocks represent?

Mr. HUGHES. If I understand your question, Senator, I think the answer is that the new agencies are reflected up at the upper level, on the left, the NYC program and the OIC program and the CAP program, the blocks below reflect organizations in some sense responsive to or funded by the three new agencies, like UPO, the District of Columbia personnel office, the Washington OIC organization, and multiple agencies down below that in turn the funds go through from them.

Mr. THURMAN. In 1967, and 1968, five new programs shown in green, were started. These programs were authorized by the Economic Opportunity Act, the Manpower Development and Training Act, and the National Defense Act of 1916.

I might mention with respect to that date, Mr. Chairman, that the charts indicate when the programs began operating within the District.

The early 1970's and the final flip of the chart adds the five most recent programs, shown in yellow, authorized the Economic Opportunity Act of 1964, the Manpower Development and Training Act of 1962, the Social Security Act of 1935, as amended in 1967, and the Demonstration Cities and Metropolitan Development Act of 1966.

Organizationally, five Federal agencies and nine local administering agencies were involved, spending about $23 million annually in Federal assistance in the District of Columbia.

The manpower programs were enacted for different client groups. The work incentive program enabled welfare recipients to get job training. There were training programs for young people and training programs for older people. There were training programs that involved on-the-job learning and in-the-classroom learning. And there were training programs for those who lived in certain geographic areas of the city. All of these programs, however, had the same general objective—prepare people for jobs.

We found, for instance, that a youth, who lived in the model cities area and was part of a welfare family was eligible for all but one or two of the programs on the chart, and he most likely registered for several of the programs to insure himself a training slot. Multiple registrations resulted in the appearance that more people wanted training than in fact did. For instance, the manpower planning agency for the District estimated that 140,000 persons needed some form of manpower training services. The individual manpower service operators, however, individually estimated that they would serve over 300,000 persons.

The individual program approach and the resulting individual delivery systems meant that no single organization coordinated this service on a citywide basis. The broad objective of the manpower training programs—to prepare people for jobs—was not fully met because each of the operators had: His own outreach and intake centers; his own training programs and facilities; and his own placement services.

People were waiting for training from one operator while other operators had underused training facilities.

In summary, no one knew how many persons were being trained, where they were being trained, for what occupations they were being trained, or the impact of the training on the demand for skilled workers. We should point out that with the enactment of the Comprehensive Employment and Training Act of 1973, the 13 Labor Department manpower programs which are shown on the chart were reduced to 6.

Our third and final study of overlapping programs—appendix II —in the District involved health services provided in outpatient health centers. This study focused on the issue of who was providing health care for the poor. Our study identified seven Federal programs and one District program providing about $11 million annually for outpatient health services.

The Federal Government's involvement to financially assist State governments in support of their public health responsibilities dates back to the Social Security Act of 1935. Since then, many health programs have come into being. Most of the programs included in our review, however, began in the 1960's and are embodied in either the Social Security Act or the Public Health Services Act.

The client groups for some of the health programs were narrowly defined. For instance, programs were established to provide prenatal and postnatal care to mothers and their infants, to promote health care and services for children and youth of school and preschool ages, and to provide comprehensive health care to low-income persons residing in certain geographic areas. The District Government and three private, nonprofit organizations provided the services.

Unlike the federally assisted child care and manpower programs which generally used a target group approach, that is, the only criteria for participating in the program was being in the eligible client group—the federally assisted health programs used both a target group approach and, in several cases, a target area approach. In some of the health programs residents of only certain geographic areas of the city could participate in the program. Generally, the health services provided were restricted to only those services authorized by each program.

The narrowness of some of the programs prevented the District from attaining its goal of providing comprehensive health services to an entire family. A 1970 District report characterized the situation with the following question, "Why are services planned and implemented in a fragmented way—separating one service from another—as if part of the human body—and the family, for that matter—can be separated and treated in isolation?"

With the multiplicity of programs and the existence of many separately funded organizations, no mechanism existed to oversee the provision of outpatient health services. The individual agency and program approach was used rather than a District-wide coordinated program approach and the results were not conducive to providing adequate and efficient health services. We found that: Health centers were located disproportionately in relation to areas where the health needs were greatest. We have, before you, a map of the District showing the location of health centers and the obvious overconcentration in one area of the city.

Second, facilities, equipment, and personnel were underused on one hand and overburdened or lacking on the other. A second chart is on display showing patient visits per day per physician for four health services for each of the outpatient health centers. The vertical red lines show AMA and American Dental Association data indicating the average number of patient visits a physician should be able to handle. So the bars to the left of the lines indicate underutilization using that standard, the bars to the right represent an overburdening situation.

And finally, our conclusion was that less than comprehensive health care was provided.

To summarize the results of these three studies, it was our view that the categorical approach in the delivery of child care, manpower training, and health services lessened the opportunity for, or even precluded, the comprehensive, effective, and efficint delivery of the services.

Mr. Chairman, that concludes our briefing.

Thank you very much.

[Charts accompanying the briefing follow:]

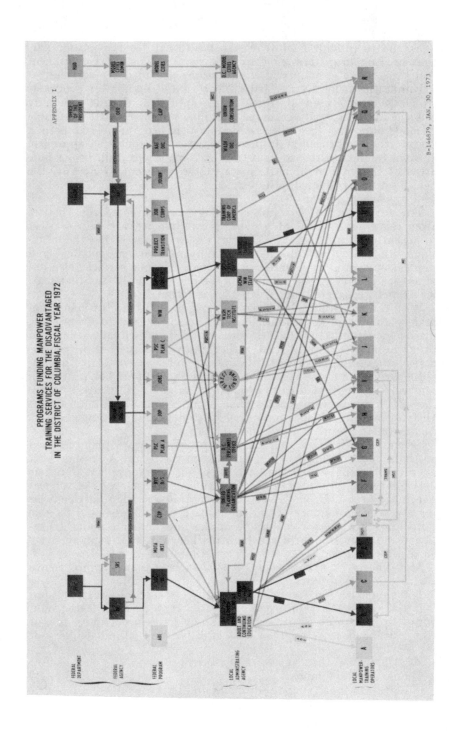

PROGRAMS FUNDING MANPOWER
TRAINING SERVICES FOR THE DISADVANTAGED
IN THE DISTRICT OF COLUMBIA, FISCAL YEAR 1972

APPENDIX I

B-146879, JAN. 30, 1973

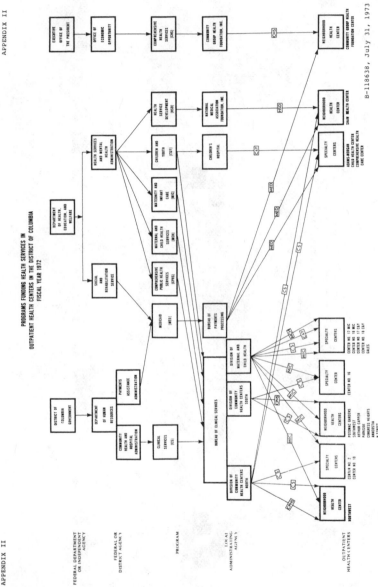

APPENDIX II

PROGRAMS FUNDING HEALTH SERVICES IN
OUTPATIENT HEALTH CENTERS IN THE DISTRICT OF COLUMBIA
FISCAL YEAR 1972

B-118638, July 31, 1973

CHILD-CARE ACTIVITIES IN THE DISTRICT OF COLUMBIA

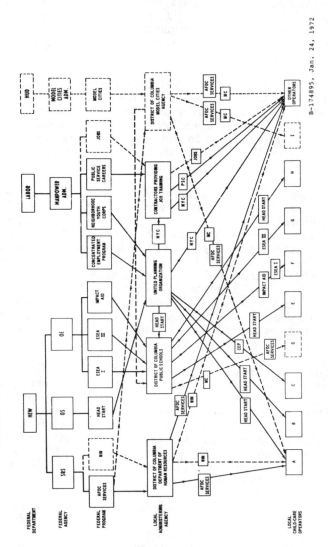

B-174895, Jan. 24, 1972

Senator MUSKIE. Well, if S. 2925 needs a visual demonstration of the condition it seeks to treat I guess that is about as good as you can get.

You say that condition could be duplicated in most of the urban areas of the country?

Mr. THURMAN. Yes, sir. That was our hypothesis and we did test it in one of the studies, the child care study, and found similar situations existed in two other communities.

Senator MUSKIE. The fact that the District is so called the Federal city doesn't make it a special case.

Mr. THURMAN. That is correct.

Senator MUSKIE. We have already discussed somewhat with Mr. Staats the need of a more precise approach to the problem of screening Federal programs in order to reduce the intial scope of the bill.

Mr. Hughes, I know, has a long background in all of this and I wonder if you might wish to add to that presentation?

Mr. HUGHES. Well, Mr. Chairman, please stop me if I duplicate territory you have covered. I was meeting elsewhere and couldn't get here earlier.

But it seems to me the message of the charts and the objective of the bill are, as you suggest, pretty much in synchronization with one another.

The question really both with the program situation as reflected in the charts and with the bill itself, is how best and most effectively to get there.

The administration and the Congress have done some experimenting in this area with respect to revenue sharing. It is an approach which moves toward the other end of the spectrum with respect to detail and control. That has also presented problems of a sort, raising questions whether national objectives are adequately achieved. I think those questions can only be answered in time.

Our own suggestion—and some of the legislation that the administration is apparently considering and has already offered—deal with in a problem in a "block grant" fashion, attempting to reduce the detail, confusion and burden by consolidating programs into broader units and simplifying requirements, and thereby simplifying the administrative structure that is necessary to carry it out.

S. 2925 would have as its objective, as I read it, assuring, that programs are achieving the purposes for which they were enacted and providing a more or less automatic vehicle for examination and modification of the program, if the examination revealed the desirability of modification.

We in GAO are concerned whether the bill might bite off more than we can chew in terms of the formality and the frequency of the review process. We have raised some of the same questions with respect to the 4-year program review and reauthorization schedule. The objectives of the periodic review on a systematic basis, and of some sort of zero-based review selectively, are beyond question. We would encourage both and would be pleased to work with the committee to try and develop the kinds of criteria which would assure the achievement of the objectives of the bill while at the same time not overcoming us.

Senator MUSKIE. Would the program review required by the bill help to force a reduction of the kinds of duplication that these charts represent?

Mr. HUGHES. It seems to me it would be helpful in doing that. Your recent comments, I think, suggest as much, Senator. Looking at the chart we showed is in itself an incentive to do something about the problem confronting the situation is certain to be helpful. I don't think though that the process is automatic, however.

Those programs weren't enacted in their present form by accident. Each of them represents an area of public concern, each of them has a clientele, if you will, and one or more interest groups which support it. For example, I noticed in the paper recently some expressions of concern with respect to the community mental health program, whether it would be lost, modified, swallowed up, whatever, in a broader block grant dealing with health programs.

I don't think there are any guarantees of success in these sorts of things, but the first step in reform is certainly a careful examination of the problem that we have gotten ourselves into. The bill would certainly facilitate and really make imperative that kind of review.

Senator MUSKIE. To what extent is the creation of duplicative programs the result of a lack of information as to the existence of such programs when new legislative initiatives are started? I mean these ideas are constantly being generated. Do we have an effective way of searching out assistance programs in order to bring pressure to tie new initiatives to what has already been enacted and to consolidate at time of birth?

Mr. HUGHES. My perception, Senator, would be that the answer to that question is somewhat mixed. As you know, I was in the executive branch when we did some of that—

Senator MUSKIE. A lot of that. [Laughter.]

Mr. HUGHES. I think we were generally aware of the existence of other programs somewhat differently targeted, somewhat differently structured. We knew enough to know that and were rather attentive to it. We were *not* I think fully cognizant, nor were the States or the localities cognizant of the ramifications of program proliferation as action down through the structure. You saw on the chart that three new programs made a whole lot more than three new blocks on the chart. Those were the phenomena that we didn't fully recognize as we were trying to target new programs to meet what were perceived as national needs.

The cure, it seems to me, is in better appreciation of what goes on in the States and localities and in somewhat broader program structure to accommodate to that so that the localities don't need to break their backs to administer a new narrowly targeted program.

Senator MUSKIE. To an extent then, the problem is both legislative and administrative. Could more have been done administratively to moderate this duplicating picture that we see here?

Mr. HUGHES. Well, I think, Mr. Chairman——

Senator MUSKIE. In other words, as new laws come along, could more have been done to rationalize them together?

Mr. HUGHES. You say "could it have," Senator, and I think the answer is yes. Again, my familiarity with executive branch efforts goes back a few years. There is some legislation, 1972 legislation, I believe, specifically designed to permit the blocking up of programs into broader units. However, for some of the same reasons that it has been difficult to do that legislatively it has been difficult to do it administratively also. The reasons are structural and political and in terms of statutory requirements and so forth. But I think the short answer is yes, I think it is true we could have done more then and probably still could do a good deal more administratively in such areas as simplifying application requirements, consolidating application forms, and, thereby, achieving something of a consolidation of programs without necessarily modifying the legislation. But it is difficult to do.

Senator MUSKIE. Do we need something like S. 2925 to achieve its objectives or can we do it administratively?

Mr. HUGHES. It seems to me that legislation which expressed— which gives direction to administrative efforts and which expresses the position or philosophy of the Congress would be very helpful and would provide useful incentive.

Senator MUSKIE. Well, gentlemen, I appreciate very much your testimony and the help you have been giving us and which you will give us as we proceed to develop this legislation. I am rather eager to get into the controversial phase of the hearings. I am sure there is going to be a lot of controversy if there appears to be any chance that this legislation will move. Then at that time we will have to focus more precisely on some of the problems raised.

I appreciate your testimony. I think we have one more witness this morning and I better let you go so we can get to him.

Mr. HUGHES. Thank you very much, Mr. Chairman.

[Additional information submitted by Mr. Staats follows:]

TITLE I: AUTHORIZATION OF NEW BUDGET AUTHORITY

Reauthorization of legislation on a 4 year cycle

N3   Section 101 of the proposed Bill provides for termination of all provisions of law which authorize the enactment of new budget authority or which provide new budget authority beginning after the termination date established in a schedule ranging from September 30, 1979, to September 30, 1982. The schedule of termination dates is based on functional or subfunctional categories. This termination schedule is not applicable to programs in subfunctional categories 551, 601, 602, and which are funded through trust funds. It should be noted that although the legislation does provide for more control over the budget, over one third of the estimated FY 1977 outlays are for programs that would be exempted. Also exempted is new budget authority, initially provided for in a fiscal year beginning before the subfunction termination date, but is available for obligation or expenditure in a fiscal year after that date.

The four year expiration term for authorizing legislation will place a heavy workload on the authorizing committees during the final

portion of the reauthorization cycle. In general the impact of the
Bill on the working arrangements and workloads of committees is hard
to predict with accuracy since it is difficult at this time to develop
an accurate count of the total number of programs and activities which
would require attention under this Bill. However, since the laws to
be reauthorized and programs and activities to be reviewed and evaluated on a zero base premise probably number well over a thousand,
using the "Catalog of Federal Domestic Assistance" alone, the impact on the
Congress, Executive Branch, States and localities will probably be
considerable. Because of the large number of laws to be examined,
one method for reducing the number of laws to be examined would be
the development of screening criteria for the reauthorization, review
and evaluation provisions of the Bill. The screening criteria could,
for example, provide for reauthorizations of laws resulting in new budget authority or including permanent budget authority if the amount
to be authorized exceeds a given dollar limit. It should be noted
that legislation, such as for regulatory programs require special
attention since their budget authority may be low but their costs to
the consumer and the economy in general may be high.

Consideration should also be given to the question of whether a
fixed frequency of review and reauthorization is appropriate for all
programs. A case could be made that some programs ought to be reviewed more frequently than every four years because of rapidly changing
circumstances, while others do not need the same frequency of review.
Consideration should also be given to the reauthorization workload
and its impact on the congressional budget cycle. For example, legislative deadlines mandated by the 1974 Budget Act could be more easily
met if authorizations were for longer periods.

We have previously taken the position favoring longer periods
for authorization for some programs or advance authorizations for others,
coupled with periodic comprehensive reviews of major programs. We
feel the emphasis should be on strengthening procedure for committee
oversight through more thorough and frequent reviews and evaluations

of programs or groups of programs impacting on major national policy areas. We would therefore suggest that alternatives for increasing flexibility and decreasing workload through screening and variable cycles of reauthorization be considered by the subcommittee.

Changes in functional and subfunctional categories

Section 2(b) specifies that for purposes of this Bill the functional and subfunctional categories are those submitted in the President's budget for Fiscal Year 1977. It is quite possible that the functional and subfunctional categories will be changed in the future and, although we expect them to remain relatively constant, changes will continue to be made from time to time. Therefore, we do not feel it is advisable to include any specific list in the Bill. In addition, we would prefer that the reference to the categories be to those approved by the Comptroller General under Section 202(a)(1) of the Legislative Reorganization Act of 1970, as amended, rather than those submitted in the President's budget. This would avoid any confusion over our responsibilities and authority.

For budgeting purposes it is necessary to identify each program with one budget function based on its primary objective. For the purpose of program evaluation, however, there is a need to identify programs in functions which have closely related secondary objectives. For instance, a drug abuse program may be primarily recorded under category 751-Federal law enforcement and prosecution, but it may have a component of 552-health research and education. If we limit a program to one budget functional code, we may be losing some valuable supporting information. We, therefore, favor adopting a method of supplemental coding for these secondary objectives.

Definition of Terms

Section 101(a) of Title I refers to the termination of authorizing legislation that provides budget authority for a government "program" or "activity." Those terms are used throughout the Bill and the interpretation of them is crucial in carrying out its provisions.

Working definitions of the terms are not included in the Bill and it is difficult to ascertain precisely what is intended to be included under those terms.

GAO has defined both terms in its "Budgetary Definitions" glossary published under requirements of Title VIII of the Congressional Budget and Impoundment Control Act of 1974. The terms were defined as follows:

> Activity - any project, task or process required to carry out a program. A combination of several activities such as research and development, training of personnel, and distribution of information may be elements in a particular program. Activities constituting a program vary with the nature and purpose of the program.

> Program - an organized set of activities directed toward a common purpose, objective, or goal undertaken or proposed by an agency in order to carry out responsibilities assigned to it.

Our definitions of these terms were intentionally left general at the time, because there is such a wide variance within the Government as well as by the general public as to the concept of an "activity" or a "program." We feel, however that these definitions provide the framework for the development of detailed working definitions in the future.

Over the past few months, we have been working with 25 authorizing committees and 70 departments and agencies to get the FY 1977 budget data reported to the committees in terms of "programs" as created in authorizing legislation. The committees are using this information in their review of the President's proposed funding levels and in preparing their Views and Estimates reports to the Budget Committees. We feel this work will provide a useful informational aid for relating the Congress' budgetary process with its legislative and oversight activities, and begin to establish for congressional use and reporting the entities that are to be called "programs."

Identification of programs and activities by functional and subfunctional categories

Section 103 requires House and Senate Appropriations and Budget Committees to submit reports on or before July 1, 1977, providing the functional or subfunctional category and the committee or committees with legislative jurisdiction for each program or activity. The Comptroller General is to provide such assistance as necessary.

Based on experience, we believe we could comply with requests anticipated from the Committee on Appropriations or the Committee on the Budget of the Senate and House of Representatives as a result of this section of the proposed legislation.

Section 104 requires a report from the Comptroller General on or before April 1, 1977, on each program or activity which permanently authorizes the enactment of new budget authority or provides permanent budget authority for a program or activity. The report is to include: (1) the law or laws under which the program is carried on, (2) the committee with legislative jurisdiction, (3) the annual appropriation bill where applicable, and (4) the amount of new budget authority provided for the last four fiscal years. An update of this report is required on or before April 1, 1978, and each year thereafter.

The Comptroller General's April 1, 1977, report will precede the House and Senate Appropriations and Budget Committees' July 1, 1977, reports discussed in the previous section. Information on legislative jurisdiction for each program or activity will be required for both reports. Our comments on identifying programs as created in authorizing legislation are equally applicable to this section.

As discussed previously, we believe a sound data base can and should be developed and that the work we are doing is leading to the establishment of the cross-references required by th_s section. Assignment of this responsibility to GAO is consistent with our broad responsibilities under Title VIII of the Congressional Budget Act. The subcommittee may wish to consider revising the reporting dates in view of the progress already being made and to better coincide with the reporting we are already making under Title VIII on these subjects.

TITLE II: EARLY ELIMINATION OF INACTIVE AND DUPLICATE PROGRAMS

Title II would require the Comptroller General to conduct a study of all Federal programs and activities to identify (1) those programs

and activities for which no outlays have been made for the last two
completed fiscal years and (2) those programs and activities which have
duplicative objectives. Interim reports to the Congress on the results
of the study would be required with a final report due on or before
July 1, 1977.

The legislative committees of the House and Senate would, to the
extent possible, eliminate or consolidate duplicative programs by
March 15, 1978.

Duplicative programs

We fully endorse and support the objectives of eliminating those
programs and activities which have duplicative objectives. The way
in which the Bill is drafted, however, raises the exceptionally difficult technical problem of distinguishing between those programs which
are similar in important reports and those which are duplicative. Our experience with Federal domestic assistance programs indicates that each
program ostensibly has unique characteristics which distinguish it from
other programs. However, in practice, many programs serve similar
purposes and we agree with the basic thrust of the Bill that there
are opportunities to improve effectiveness of Federal programs by
consolidating programs serving similar objectives. This is certainly
no easy task, but we do not believe it is necessary to demonstrate
total overlap or duplication before recommending consolidation.

To illustrate, in a recent report to the Congress, we noted that
228 programs (programs as defined by the Catalog of Federal Domestic
Assistance) could provide funds to State and local governments for
health-related activities. Of these programs 22 were for mental health.
At the broadest level, the 228 programs could be considered to have
duplicative objectives in that all relate to health. At a lower level,
one could look for duplication among the 22 mental health programs.

Over the past few years GAO has performed several reviews which
document the coordination problems that arise from having many Federal
domestic assistance programs serving similar objectives particularily
when responsibility for implementing the programs is fragmented among

different Federal agencies and operating organizations. We have found, however, that such reviews are quite complex and time consuming, requireing comprehensive understanding of multiple Federal programs and activities, relationships among Federal agencies, agencies's relationships with their clientele, and the operations of grantee organizations. These complexities mean that even with a major reorientation of GAO's overall work program, we would not be able, within the time frame allowed, to accomplish the study envisioned by Title II.

We recommend that this title be amended to require that during its reviews GAO give special priority to the identification of problems resulting from Federal programs and activities having similar objectives and report its findings and recommendations to the Congress and cognizant committees as promptly as possible.

Inactive programs

We feel that the job of identifying programs and activities for which there have been no outlays for two fiscal years could be more readily accomplished by the agencies responsible for the programs than by GAO. Accordingly, we would suggest that Title II be amended to assign this responsibility to the Executive Branch, with coordination responsibilities in OMB.

TITLE III: QUADRENNIAL REVIEW AND EVALUATION

Program evaluation and zero base evaluation

We also strongly support the objectives of Title III, to provide periodic Congressional review and evaluation of Federal programs. We believe a procedure for systematic review and evaluation will strengthen Congressional control over Federal programs as well as provide information needed for exercising Congressional oversight.

Various provisions in the Legislative Reorganization of 1970, as amended by the Budget Control Act of 1974, indicate the desire of Congress for increased efforts in reviewing and evaluating government programs. S.2925 would mandate the performance of such analyses by establishing a systematic quadrennial review procedure.

S.2925 is a logical complement to the Congressional Budget Control Act. The Budget Act focuses on the macro-aspects of policy, while S.2925 will focus on the micro-component parts of policy.

Program evaluation is a process of assessing the contribution that programs make toward achieving intended goals. Zero base evaluation focuses on the question - What would happen if we did nothing (or zero)? as well as looking at alternative ways of accomplishing intended results. Though zero base evaluation is consistent with our concepts of the scope and nature of program evaluation, examining alternative approaches in addition to evaluating the current program is a much more complex and time consuming task.

From our experience in evaluating government programs, we have noted that techniques for measuring program results are usually less adequate than desired and that absolute agreement on the precise goals of a program is usually lacking.

The quadrennial review procedure may stimulate efforts toward addressing and resolving these problems, but we believe that it is to early to tell whether   accepted standards for measuring program achievement can be developed for most programs. The 4 year review cycle may not be long enough to observe the results of certain programs of a long term investment nature. And as long as there are disagreements over program objectives, no evaluation can show a program to be a "success" or "failure" to everyone's satisfaction.

Focusing evaluations on national needs

As required by Title III, evaluations and reviews of the many programs which address a particular need or national policy may overwhelm Congress with detailed program information and in doing so, fog the main issue of specific national needs. If Congress is to confront reviews and evaluations of the literally thousands of programs and activities put forward by the Federal Government it may get bogged down and lose sight and control of national policy needs. We would

therefore encourage that the emphasis on periodic review and evaluation
be placed on evaluations of groups of similar programs to determine
how they together are addressing the national needs for which they
were intended.

Definition of zero base evaluation

Part I of Title III covers the timetable and the definition
of a zero base review and evaluation of all Federal programs. The
term "zero base review and evaluation" is defined as

> "a comprehensive review and evaluation to determine if the merits
> of the program or activity support its continuation rather than
> termination and to reach findings as to what incremental amounts
> of new budget authority for the program or activity should be
> authorized to produce correspondingly larger levels of service
> output."

To maintain consistency with the concept of zero base, we would
recommend a change in the wording of this definition. Zero base
budgeting usually entails submitting alternative budgets detailing
program outputs and alternative approaches to achieve these outputs
at various levels of funding above and below current levels.

On the point of alternatives, we have long felt that Congress
needs to know what alternative approaches might be considered with
respect to a particular program. The definition of zero base review
and evaluation should allow for this interpretation so that Congress
can consider different approaches to accomplishing an objective and
can ask, "Why was this approach used and why was this other approach
discarded?"

The zero base review and evaluation from the President should
provide Congress with valuable information as to what would be gained
or lost if funds were reallocated, expanded, or contracted and provide
descriptions of the quality and quanity of outputs for alternative
approaches. This information should help Congress in its decision
making.

The President must also provide a specification of the objectives
of a program over the next four years. This method of tying back

performance to the expectations of the programs will be extremely useful to Congress in its oversight of Federal programs.

GAO's reports of prior reviews

GAO's role under Title III is two-fold. Under section 312 GAO is required to report results of prior audits, reviews, and evaluations to the committees responsible for zero base reviews. This is something that the GAO currently does for appropriations committees regarding civil programs. In the defense area we have, in the past, reported on the cost growth of major weapon systems for the House Committee on Armed Services. We feel that reports of this nature, tailored to the desires of the committees, could be produced with a moderate effort on our part. We would be happy to assist the standing committees by reporting on any studies we have made of programs which are subjects of their review.

Additional Congressional request work

Section 312 requires that GAO provide information and analyses at the request of standing committees. We now make many audits or studies at the specific request of congressional committees. In addition, we respond to requests of individual Members when feasible. Some of these requests can be answered with little effort, while others require a great deal of work. Members' requests, if of sufficient importance from a Government-wide standpoint, may result in reports to the Congress. In addition, we provide responses to Members on requests relating to claims by and against the United States. While this section of Title III does not grant any authority or impose any new requirements on the GAO, we would anticipate a much increased workload by virtue of increased Congressional requests for assistance if a full-scale zero base review and evaluation were undertaken for all Federal programs.

In addition, we should recognize that the scope and nature of this review is such that all programs within a function will be reviewed in the same time period. Reviewing all Federal programs and activities included in a particular function or subfunction, is complicated by the series of questions Congress must address involving the mix of programs, the trade-off of outputs, and the cross-impact among programs. Other complications, as we see it, will arise in how to handle cross-committee, cross-agency, cross-mission, and primary-secondary relationships.

Some possible alternatives

While we strongly concur with the objectives of Title III, we have some reservations about undertaking such a zero base review and evaluation without prior experience. We would suggest, as one alternative, some type of test of this process which could perhaps help the Congress uncover and resolve some of the complexities associated with the zero base approach. Perhaps the test might consist of pilot programs in which each standing committee considers one program for zero base review and evaluation. The Congress could call on the President and the agencies for cooperation in developing their zero base review and evaluation of each program considered in the pilot project. Useful knowledge could be gained from such a test by both the Congress and the President as to problems encountered, issues which need to be resolved, and possible solutions.

Consideration should also be given to the fact that zero base reviews and evaluations are called for by both the standing committees in section 311, and the Executive Branch in section 321. Both performing the same analysis may result in a duplication of effort. It has been our longstanding feeling that the responsibility for program evaluations rests with the responsible agencies because we feel that program evaluation is a fundamental part of effective program administration. Therefore, an alternative for this section of the Bill might be to have the Executive Branch provide the evaluations to the committees for review. The committees would then have a chance to review the information and decide which programs need emphasis in the congressional reviews and evaluations. To do this, the Executive Branch should submit their evaluations in advance of the date called for in section 301 to allow for sufficient congressional review and further evaluation if necessary.

<u>TITLE IV: CONTINUING REVIEW AND EVALUATION</u>

Functions of GAO

Section 401(a) would require the Comptroller General to perform follow-up audits at least once every six months on any program or activity which GAO has audited and found to be substantially deficient in achieving its objectives. Follow-up audits would be required until the Comptroller General is satisfied that the deficiencies have been eliminated. GAO would be required to report the results of follow-up audits to the Appropriations Committees of both Houses and to the cognizant legislative committees.

It is normal GAO policy to follow-up on its recommendations. However, the requirement to make follow-up audits and reports every 6 months would place an unnecessary strain on our limited staff resources. As an alternative, we suggest that within 60 days of the date of a GAO report which makes recommendations to the Head of a Federal agency, and not less often than once every six months thereafter, the agency be required to report to the appropriate committees the actions taken and progress made in implementing GAO recommendations. Reports would be continued until, in our judgement, all reasonable actions have been completed on the recommendations, and no purpose would be served by further reports.

Section 236 of the Legislative Reorganization Act of 1970, which places a more limited reporting requirement on Federal agencies, would need to be rescinded if this provision was adopted.

Program information in the President's Budget

Section 402 of the Bill requires that the Executive Budget include annual objectives for each program or activity and an annual analysis of how programs are achieving previously set annual objectives. This is to apply to the fiscal year 1979 and subsequent years.

Annual program objectives set by the Executive Branch may differ from objectives or goals included in authorizing legislation as understood by the responsible congressional committees. Although the Management by Objectives (MBO) system currently used by the Executive Branch attempts to make program objectives explicit and quantifiable, and identifies multiple and conflicting objectives, it is primarily a management control system which is designed to provide feedback and measurement of annual accomplishments. Though this information is useful for congressional oversight, emphasis may be placed on identifying process variables as program objectives. We feel that impact variables which link agency missions to the national needs addressed in the authorizing legislation should also be considered by relating them to annual accomplishments.

Title VI of the Budget Act of 1974, amends the Budget and Accounting Act of 1921 to require that the Executive Budget (starting in the fiscal year ending September 30, 1979) include descriptive information in terms of --

(1) a detailed structure of agency needs which shall be used to reference all agency missions and programs;

(2) agency missions; and

(3) basic programs.

We feel that the requirements in Section 402 of S.2925 should be linked to Title VI of the Budget Act by considering national needs and agency missions (as agreed to by the cognizant congressional committee and the Executive Branch) when setting annual objectives and assessing annual progress.

Because of the large volume of new information that will be produced by this section of the Bill we feel that its inclusion in the Executive Budget may make that document too voluminous. Consideration should be given to publishing this information in separate documents for interested committees.

IMPLEMENTATION MECHANISM: JAMES LYNN ([83], pp. 379–406)

Insofar as the federal government has a continuing concern with reorganization and reform of its structure and purposes, that concern tends to find expression through the Office of Management and Budget. The OMB is the main representative for the Executive branch in reorganization and reform measures. Its director under President Gerald Ford was James Lynn, who testified as an administration spokesman on S. 2925 before the Senate Government Operations Committee.

Lynn appeared before the committee prior to a presidential election and subsequent to the impact of the Watergate crisis. The political climate of the times undoubtedly tempered the dialogue and perhaps his testimony. Lynn endorsed the objective of programmed, scheduled evaluation of plans, but called for flexibility in the scheduling of reviews. He did not fully embrace the concepts of sunset and zero-base budgeting, but his comments on practical implementation difficulties, such as the paperwork implications, provide some useful insights and warnings.

First, I want to add my voice to the chorus supporting the general purpose of the bill—to foster periodic quality assessment of the various activities of the Federal Government and full use of such assessments in decisionmaking as to the future of such activities. The question is not whether to do it. We must do it.

It is no secret that virtually from the time I knew the President wanted me to take this job I have targeted improvement of the evaluation processes of the Government as a top, essential priority. Although we still have a substantial way to go, there has been some progress. Here are some of the things we have been working on:

The development of priorities and schedules for evaluation of various kinds. Increasingly, this is linked to the budget process.

The establishment of a unit within each agency, responsible only to the agency head, which can assist the various operational units of the agency in identifying evaluation priorities and in designing and conducting such evaluations.

Improving the design of evaluations. Over the years we have learned a good deal. But in many respects evaluation is still a very imperfect art requiring constant experimentation and demonstration with a variety of techniques.

Building evaluation requirements and the necessary program information systems into statutes and regulations for new or modified activities, whether national in scope or demonstration efforts.

Better coordination of the evaluation effort where, as is increasingly the case, a multiple agency approach is necessary.

Developing better communication with both the Congress and the public at various stages of the evaluation process.

Seeking out for evaluation not just those programs that look weak but also those that seem to work. In this way, we may learn more about why some work and others do not. We may discover ways to make good programs even better and, very importantly, verify their worth both to ourselves and to the American people.

Determining whether we can codify the do's and don't's of evaluation systems in an OMB circular that will do more good than harm.

In some respects, Mr. Chairman, we share the same kind of a problem. Perhaps our problem will be easier to solve since it is easier to modify an OMB circular than to modify a statute.

This last point brings me to an overriding problem that I have with the legislative approach before us. It is far too mechanical and inflexible. Some activities should be evaluated more frequently than once every 4 years. Some evaluations need not be conducted in a comprehensive way every 4 years. Some evaluations can and should be accomplished in only 3 or 4 months. Some can take substantially more than a year.

As other witnesses have testified, there is a need for more selectivity and a need for assessing priorities. There is no need every year to grind out paper that struggles to identify the increase or decrease in benefits derived from each program of the Federal Government if more or less resources were devoted to it.

It may be that there is some way that new legislation can further our common objectives and yet avoid being mired down in unneeded paperwork and wasted effort. However, given the need for flexibility, it will be difficult. If discretion and flexibility are to be incorporated in the legislative approach, the perspective of committees that have Government-wide jurisdiction, such as the Government Operations, Budget and/or Appropriations Committees is highly desirable in determining priorities and in exercising appropriate discretion. On the other hand, the other committees of the Congress have the detailed knowledge and resources, activity by activity, to examine program effectiveness. In considering whether new legislation is needed, I think a very important fact should be recognized: if a committee or committees of the Congress desire an evaluation of a particular activity by the executive branch or by the GAO, that evaluation will be conducted. It does not take a new law for Congress to bring this about.

We welcome and applaud the interest of a growing number of Members of Congress in expressing the review of existing Federal activity. The question now, as I stated at the outset, is how we can make this management tool substantially more effective in both executive branch and legislative branch decisionmaking. At least thus far I have very substantial doubts as to whether any new legislative rules will further the purposes sought. However, whether or not you—or even I—ultimately conclude that these fears are justified, please be assured we wish to work with you constructively. To this end I am providing illustrations of the effect of the provisions of this bill, as currently written, on the executive branch.

[Supplement to written views follows:]

EFFECT OF PROVISIONS OF S. 2925

Some of the specific provisions of S. 2925 could work at cross-purposes with the basic intent of the bill. A discussion of some of these problems follows:

LIMITING AUTHORIZING LEGISLATION TO FOUR YEARS

Title I imposes a 4-year limit on authorizing legislation for most Federal programs and activities. This means that these programs must be reauthorized every four years or be terminated. The Senate and House Budget Committee would have jurisdiction over deviations from that schedule.

The bill covers virtually all Federal programs, except interest payments on the national debt. While it exempts Medicare, social security and other retirement and disability trust funds, these programs could not be changed unless a zero-base review and evaluation had been conducted and the results reported by the legislative committee to the House and Senate.

The provision ignores some realities. The functions of some agencies (as opposed to the efficiency with which these functions are carried out) are not subject to dispute. For example, there seems to be no disagreement that Justice must enforce Federal laws, Defense must maintain the national security and the Bureau of Census must count the population.

Tying the mandatory reauthorizations to the functional classification will insure that the programs in each category will be reviewed simultaneously. However, this does not provide for focusing review and reauthorization on government-wide issues that may cut across functions or subfunctions. In addition, it is unlikely that any fixed classification could provide for such focus. Use of the functional classification would also make restructuring of that classification more difficult to accomplish.

The processing and paper work that would be required *each* year for those Federal programs being reauthorized would be mountainous. The end result of this provision would be to divert time from focusing on those programs or activities for which changes should be made. The necessity to prepare detailed justifications and evaluations for all reauthorizations would impose an unnecessary workload and paperwork burden on those agencies whose functions are not subject to dispute and those agencies whose efficiency is not questioned.

The means already exist for concentrating evaluation efforts on those areas for which they are most needed. The legislative committees of the Congress clearly have it within their power to specify that evaluation studies will be made in conjunction with new authorizing legislation or amendments and extensions of existing law. Moreover, the Government Operations Committees and Budget Committees would appear to have both the authority and the interest to suggest areas of study. Of course, the Appropriations Committees have a strong interest in program evaluation, too, but the horizon of the appropriations process is generally too short to encompass a complete evaluation cycle. This is not to say that progress reports to Appropriations Committees are not appropriate. Finally, the Executive Branch, particularly OMB, has ideas on where program evaluation is most needed.

ZERO-BASE REVIEW AND EVALUATION BY THE EXECUTIVE BRANCH

Section 321 of the bill requires the Executive Branch to conduct zero-base review and evaluation every year for about a fourth of the Federal programs. A very complex and technical evaluation would have to be conducted to assess the level of program quality and quantity that could be purchased at various expenditure levels. The results of the reviews conducted by the Executive Branch would be required to be transmitted to the Congress at the same time as the President's annual budget. To accomplish this each year in connection with the annual budget would either very seriously degrade the quality of the regular budget review of the programs not subject to zero-base evaluation or require significantly greater resources and more time than is now available for the budget review process.

If the type of zero-base review and evaluation defined in section 302 of the bill is to be made, program impact levels must be measured accurately—in terms of service output—and be related to resource inputs in terms of incremental amounts of budget authority. The initial program analysis and evaluation of this bill coupled with the reauthorization process will suffer the same data and paperwork problems experienced for the Program, Planning, and Budgeting Systems in the late 1960's. It proved impossible to use effectively the considerable amount of information provided by that system.

The magnitude of this task for most, if not all, programs can be illustrated by the following example of a two-step process.

Step 1—Measurement of Effort. Determination of the program impact of a specific level of budget authority is frequently so difficult that it is virtually impossible to anticipate how much time it will take to have useful results.

An excellent, though not extraordinary, example of these problems is provided by an elaborate evaluation of Title I of the Elementary and Secondary Education Act (ESEA). The measurement instruments for this evaluation are now undergoing tests. Title I of the ESEA is aimed at meeting the special needs of educationally disadvantaged children. The evaluation study is expected to take 7 years—at a cost of approximately $7 million for the first 2 years. Design and measurement techniques in such an evaluation present a formidable task due to the diversity of projects that have been undertaken under Title I. State and local educational jurisdictions have taken highly varied and individualized approaches in designing corrective programs for the educationally disadvantaged. Moreover, the measurement of educational attainment is clouded by the absence of standard tests for which there is agreement among educators as to their validity, and by the unavailability of adequate comparison groups. All of these uncertainties about the success of this long-term, expensive evaluation project are set against a background of previous efforts that frequently have been unable to demonstrate conclusive evidence concerning the effect of such special educational programs. The difficulty and expense of measuring program effects is not to be taken lightly.

Step 2—Production Functions. Even if these vexing measurement problems can be solved—and we are constantly seeking solutions—true zero-base review and evaluation as outlined in the bill, requires a good deal more. It requires relating such efforts to varying dollar and employment levels.

Even with more program impact than it is reasonable to expect, the development of such production functions would be a challenging analytical task in itself. It is likely that sophisticated mathematical models will be required. We are not aware that such techniques have been successfully developed for any significant social programs, not because of a lack of will on the part of those who have attempted to develop them but because of the great methodological difficulties inherent in them and excessive costs alluded to previously.

At this point, it is not more evaluations, but better evaluations, that are needed.

There are also reservations to the indiscriminate use of the zero-base technique. This technique may be inappropriate to many Federal programs and in such cases less complex, less detailed techniques may better serve the purpose while at the same time requiring fewer resources.

It is doubtful that the basic purpose of this bill is best served by requiring in law that across-the-board zero-based evaluations be performed every four years. The resultant lack of flexibility, may not be worth the added emphasis that a statute would provide. It may be that despite its noble intent, enactment of the bill as presently written, would cause more harm than good. It would so systematize a very complex and sensitive process and so diffuse our current efforts to encourage quality evaluations that it might cause a net loss of useable data to evaluate and manage Federal programs.

The Congress should allow the heads of agencies to work with the authorizing committees to determine where evaluations are needed as well as their frequency. It should be possible to impose a discipline without the rigidities and inefficiencies involved in taking the across-the-board statutory requirement approach.

ANNUAL OBJECTIVES INCLUDED IN THE PRESIDENT'S BUDGET

Section 402 requires that the President's Budget include specific annual objectives for *each* Federal program or activity and an analysis of how the objectives set forth in previous budgets were met. In addition, sections 321 and 311(b) require that the President and the Congress specify—in quantitative terms—the objectives of the programs and activities as part of the four-year reauthorization process.

Considerable care must be taken in the proper development of performance measures. Otherwise, these measures often show how busy people are rather than the cost-benefit of their activity. The development of a meaningful performance measurement requires significant managerial effort and reorientation. In addition, the maintenance of the process requires that Congressional and Executive decisions be based on these analyses or the process will be discredited.

This effort would be staggering. There are more than 1,000 Federal domestic assistance programs alone. The amount of information to be included in the President's budget would be so great that detailed analysis by the OMB and agency staff would—necessarily—give way to "pro forma" examination. OMB policy officials could not possibly do an adequate job of reviewing such a large mass of material and devote the time and effort required during the already overloaded budget review process. Agency accounting systems, many of which are computer based, would have to be redesigned and reprogrammed. These crushing data requirements would be superimposed on those added by the Congressional Budget and Impoundment Control Act, which have stretched the abilities of OMB considerably. The requirements of S. 2925 are more—much more—than the system should be expected to meet.

OVERLAPPING WORK BY THE LEGISLATIVE AND THE EXECUTIVE BRANCHES

The bill requires evaluations to be conducted by Congressional Committees, the GAO, the CBO, and the Executive Branch (Sections 311, 312, and 321). A great deal of overlap would be inevitable. An alternative is to reach an understanding on the design of the evaluation—which should be fully coordinated at the start—then have either the Executive or the Legislative Branches conduct the evaluation and avoid duplication of effort.

SUMMARY

The development of an effective process that provides a systematic mechanism for periodic, full-scale review and evaluation of Federal programs is complex and difficult.

Legislation that provides the flexibility that is needed to make the process work could well be too broad to be meaningful. On the other hand, specificity in the legislation could result in an unduly restrictive and inflexible approach. Rather, it would appear that legislation is not necessary to accomplish needed evaluations.

A more fruitful approach would be to reach agreement with the appropriate legislative committees on a limited number of major program areas that should be evaluated, develop cooperatively a study design for evaluating the programs included in those areas, and then work closely together to make certain that the studies are completed on schedule. It would also make a great deal of sense if the legislative committees were to impose evaluation requirements whenever new programs are instituted or the authorizations for old ones are extended.

This approach differs considerably from the plan outlined in the bill. But it should be possible to find a more appropriate way to accomplish the objectives of this bill without a legislated mechanical, and inflexible approach.

Director LYNN. Mr. Chairman, I would be happy to answer your questions.

Senator MUSKIE. Thank you very much. May I say at the outset that as far as I am concerned it is immaterial whether this process is triggered administratively or legislatively.

I have heard so much rhetoric about the need for program evaluation around here for 18 years that it strikes me that unless some kind of a prod, whether by way of legislative requirements or whatever, is established we will not get the kind of evaluation we need. As a matter of fact I think the Intergovernmental Cooperation Act has a requirement for periodic review of programs.

Director LYNN. I think that is right, Mr. Chairman.

Senator MUSKIE. That has been honored in the breach more than it has actually. I think it was 15 or 16 years ago that I first introduced legislation to limit the life of programs for the purpose of mandating review. I think President Nixon picked that idea up from some source in 1969 and sent up legislation to that effect.

And here we are still talking about the desirability of it.

So I am interested in exploring any approach, administrative or legislative, that would advance the objectives that we speak of.

It seems to me, speaking for the Congress more than for the executive branch because I know the Congress better, that requiring reauthorization keyed to a mandate for zero-base review is one way of forcing the Congress to do something that the Congress has not really done at all.

Director LYNN. I must say, Mr. Chairman, I am intrigued with the idea of having a cutoff date, whether it is for 3, 4, 5 or 6 years, at least for a good many of the programs that do not have them now. It might be helpful. I have to say, though, that in my 6 years before coming to OMB I have lived through numerous reauthorizations of legislation that were about to expire. But required reauthorization, in and of itself, even with an evaluation, will not necessarily assure that the kind of review that we both want will occur.

Senator MUSKIE. So often——

Director LYNN. This does not mean we should not try to do more evaluation but I do not think the kind of review that we both want to see can be accomplished unless there is a general acceptance both in the executive branch and in the Congress that these issues and activities must be looked at broadly—broader than a particular program in most cases. I know how difficult it is to do this in the executive branch and I have some sympathy for what kind of a problem it may be on the Hill.

As I was thinking about the testimony today I remembered a chart I had prepared earlier in the year. I found no use for it in the budget process, but now I found at least one use for it. It is somewhat incomplete, depending on how you want to view programs. But having been in the Commerce Department and HUD I was particularly interested in programs impacting on economic development in the United States. This is only a partial chart. [Laughter.]

Director LYNN. This chart does not include regular highway programs, one of the main purposes of which is certainly economic, not entirely by any means, but part of it; or aviation programs; or many other programs such as those that Elliot talked about relating to job development.

This chart, if I may take a moment——

Senator MUSKIE. Yes.

Director LYNN. [continuing] Covers the following programs.

Senator MUSKIE. If you can put that chart into words——

[Laughter.]

Director LYNN. I cannot totally.

Senator MUSKIE. It would be a miracle.

Director LYNN. You must admit if I were to frame it from here down, somebody would believe it to be a Jackson Pollock early edition.

Senator MUSKIE. Do not get into the primary elections now. [Laughter.]

Director LYNN. As the chart shows, there are Farmers' Home Administration business and industrial development loans; Farmers' Home industrial development grants; and community facility loans and waste water disposal programs.

HUD has community development grants. As you know, 20 percent of that money goes for rural areas, 80 percent goes to urban programs, and a good part of that money is used for economic development activity.

Under the HUD New Communities Administration, there are new communities grants and new communities guarantees. The Small Business Administration has State and local development company loans. The Economic Development Administration assists with public works; business development, including procurement; technical assistance planning grants, State grants, economic adjustment assistance, and supplemental grants, and regional action planning commissions are in that same business.

The Appalachian Regional Commission has a whole set of programs for the same purpose.

In the Federal Highway Administration—the only program we showed was one that was specifically directed at economic development. The Tennessee Valley Region General Resources Development Fund is from TVA.

The Bureau of Indian Affairs has its own set of programs; the Community Services Administration has its community economic development program; and so on.

Now, I looked at our problem, when we tried, through the Domestic Council and OMB, to coordinate evaluations in this area. We asked ourselves: Are we doing a good job of economic development? Are we in the things as a Federal Government that we should be in?

Should we be in them to the extent it is called for through tax expenditures or through explicit subsidies? Are we canceling ourselves out trying to get the same Xerox plant in a rural area while a large city needing new development is trying to work on the same problem?

When I look at committee structure up here, even when we use functional categories, it cuts across functions.

We have Senate Agriculture and Forestry, Senate Appropriations, Agriculture and Related Agencies; we have Senate Banking; Housing and Urban Affairs; House Small Business, Senate Appropriations Subcommittee on HUD and Independent Agencies, Senate Public Works, Senate Appropriations Subcommittees on Public Works and on Transportation; Senate Labor and Public Welfare; Senate Interior; et cetera.

Now, we have to do a better job in the executive branch. I think the Domestic Council task forces are a useful concept, but it needs still more development than we have now. OMB and the budget processes in the Congress are also very helpful. But I think both the executive branch and the Congress have to realize that if we are going to have real evaluations and do something with them, we are going to have to have some way to cut across jurisdications.

Senator MUSKIE. Would you put in words the function of the lines in this chart to the lower level?

Director LYNN. This line shows the people that benefit—that is the groups that receive the moneys.

There are so-called hold-harmless areas, local or State development companies, individuals, corporations, and other private profit-making entities, counties, municipalities, States, multi-State commissions areawide districts, Indian tribes, nonprofit organizations, nonprofit community development corporations, and territories.

Then this portion of the chart is divided geographically in a given set of cuts. Here is shown all areas, SMSA populations not over 10,000, SMSA under 50,000, SMSA over 50,000, EDA redevelopment, EDA development districts, urban counties, Appalachia New England, Tennessee Valley, Old West, coastal, Pacific Northwest, Ozarks, Indian reservations, and communities of more than 100,000, only three areas per State. That one I must admit I do not remember exactly how it developed.

Senator MUSKIE. Can this chart be reduced to a size to still fit our record and be legible?

Director LYNN. We could try, sir. Let us see whether we can.

Senator MUSKIE. That would be very useful. Is there another chart under that one?

Director LYNN. No; I think that is all there is. That is enough I think.

[Laughter.]

Senator MUSKIE. Well, pictures are better than a thousand words, they say.

Director LYNN. Yes; and I found, sir, from watching carefully and learning from many people in the executive branch, the Congress and other places that communications is a very important part of one's job.

[The chart referred to and subsequently supplied follows:]

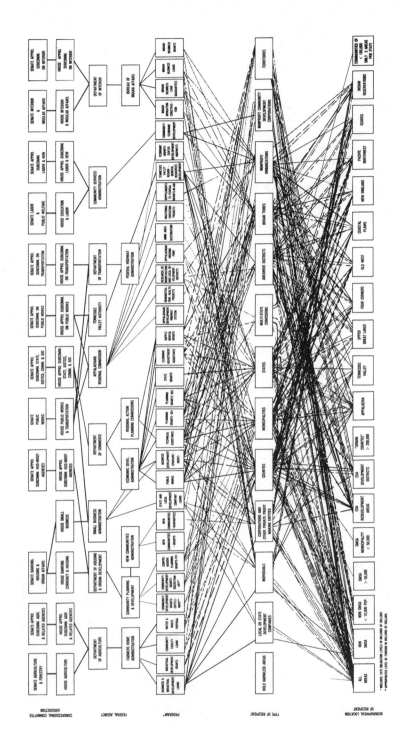

ECONOMIC DEVELOPMENT PROGRAMS OF THE FEDERAL GOVERNMENT

Senator MUSKIE. I agree with you that the formula of the bill could become very mechanical and inflexible. It is a quick first impression one gets from it and it is essential that we try to avoid that result.

Director LYNN. I bear in mind, sir, the words you used—and I know they are concurred with by Senator Roth—that the purpose of introducing the bill was to have a focal point to get the discussion process and, if you will, debate going. As I said in my testimony, perhaps there is some way of solving that problem. I must say it does raise some very interesting problems of committee jurisdication and the like.

Senator MUSKIE. We may have to deal with that.

Director LYNN. I will add that I sense there is an awareness now of these kinds of problems and the desire to work on them. To the extent we could capitalize on that, as the OMB Director, I welcome that. I do not want to end up with an OMB circular or with legislation that looks good on paper but, if anything, results in a process so weighted down that people become discouraged and do not do what both you and I would like them to do.

Senator MUSKIE. I think the committee jurisdiction problem is a very serious one. I understand how it developed, of course. There were a number of motivations, one of them to divide up the work into smaller pieces so that it could be done better. But the result has been to create more work, I think, for individual Members of the Senate than they can handle efficiently.

It is sort of counterproductive in that respect.

As far as I am concerned I would be willing to throw all my committee assignments into the pot on the assumption that when we reorganize I would be given something useful to do. I do not have any hangups about hanging on to what I have gotten including, I might add, the chairmanship of the Senate Budget Committee. But I really think that it is so serious that in effect every Senator ought to be willing to do that. Throw every committee assignment into the pot and come up with a rational way of reorganizing our responsibilities so that we can do it more efficiently, and clearly. This chart is clearly the result as much of the committee fragmentation on the Hill as it is problems with organization in the executive branch.

Director LYNN. If I might, sir, on that, some further bad news but maybe a helpful suggestion.

I asked my people to advise me as to the legislative process on the energy situation, and my figures show a total of over 500 days of energy-related hearings were held in the first 9 months of the 94th Congress, involving 12 Senate committees and 25 subcommittees, 17 House committees and 35 subcommittees. FEA alone, in calendar 1975, appeared in 46 Senate hearings, 58 House hearings, and 8 joint committee hearings; and during the first 3 months of 1976, FEA has already testified 31 times.

From my standpoint, I want to free as much time for management of the departments as we can for those departmental heads so that there cannot be the excuse, "Well, I was too busy testifying on the Hill." It would be helpful to me if there could be some way to develop a consolidated approach.

Now, I am breaking with a long-standing rule of mine of leaving unto Caesar what is Caesar's, but I might give you an observation on what I found in looking at executive branch reorganization. Certainly we have room for improvement over the months ahead, and in the next budget I would think we will have some initiatives in that area. But the more I look at functions of a budget or at executive branch organization, there is no set of organizations that will allow any real, important problem to be assessed and evaluated within that one department.

More and more as Pat Moynihan always used to say, "Everything is related to everything else." No matter what we do with executive branch reorganization or what Congress does with any kind of reorganization of the committee structure on the Hill, there will still need to be a coordinating mechanism. Now, the Domestic Council is useful in that regard, but standing committees of the Domestic Council really do not work very well. When dealing with any particular problem you find, just like advisory committees to the executive branch, any standing committee will include some people that really should not be into that area and yet it does not have as participants some people whose views you would like to have.

So what we have gone to more and more in the executive branch is a task force concept. A task force may last only 2 or 3 weeks, or it may go on literally for years, fashioned around a particular set of problems. Now there has been some effort at that in the Congress. If I recall correctly on superport legislation, there was an effort made to approach that legislation with a jointly appointed task force subcommittee that had markup authority given to it by the three or four committees that had jurisdiction. The task force reported the bill up to the full committee structure. I do not know whether that is the right way to do it, but all I am saying is it may not be as important to have standing committee and subcommittee changes as it is to have a process whereby you can put together a customized ad hoc committee to consider a group of problems.

This is what we are struggling with in the executive branch and I really believe there is no organizational set up to address that problem. You must have the coordinating mechanism.

Senator MUSKIE. Well, in the Budget Committee we have gotten away from the subcommittee approach and we have started with the task force approach. I am not sure that it works effectively because the members of those task forces have got so many other committee responsibilities including those outside the Budget Committee that they do not function effectively as a task force.

The concentration of effort and attention is an important ingredient, of course, but we do not seem to get it.

I would like to get into another subject, the sorting out approach to the legislation. Secretary Richardson this morning had some suggestions and we have received others. . . .

I wondered whether you are in a position to identify activities that could be sorted out along those lines. For instance you say some activities should be evaluated more frequently than once every 4 years. Could you identify those?

Director LYNN. First of all I ought to say at the outset I have glossed over, deliberately, in the interest of brevity and in the knowledge that we would get into it in the question and answer period, the distinction between different kinds of evaluations. There is a zero-based evaluation that goes to whether or not a program is adequately and effectively carrying out its objectives to improve this country and the lives of the people in one way or another. Many times that gets you into "compared with what" question.

That kind of an evaluation often takes a long time, because you are crosscutting with other areas.

When I was at HUD, the first assignment I was given, there being no money—not literally but figuratively—for lower income housing and community development-type programs, was that of doing a study of housing with particular emphasis on housing problems of lower income families. We completed that study in about 7 months. It was a massive effort, but I believe there were a number of things in that study that could have been improved given more time. There are studies of CETA that are going on now that will take much more than a year to get to the ultimate result.

But on the other hand, there may be an evaluation of a segment of a program, which seeks to determine how to make it work more effectively. The issue is not whether or not that program should stay on the books or whether it is a good program: you have concluded that it is. But that there will be one part of it—paperwork processing, for example, or a section of its regulations—that you want to go back and evaluate, to find out whether there is a more efficient way of doing it to save administrative costs or to carry out its objectives in a way that does not hassle the people you are trying to help. Many times, that evaluation can be done in 3 months, but it is very important. It is not zero-base but it is very important from the standpoint of the taxpayer's dollars and from the standpoint of the burden we may be imposing on people.

So the purpose of evaluation is not always to determine whether the program is the best way of achieving a national objective. I think we must constantly find evaluations that take smaller slices, as well.

Many can be done in a very short period of time but they are extremely important.

Senator MUSKIE. Would you describe those as management evaluations?

Director LYNN. Yes, but——

Senator MUSKIE. Or program evaluations?

Director LYNN. Let me give you an example of how they blend. As OMB Director, I was struck in my first spring review with the variety of enforcement techniques that we use on various regulatory-type statutes.

In the SEC the reliance is on self-enforcement. When I was a lawyer in private practice you would give the prospectus to the SEC and the SEC would look carefully up to see if there was something suspicious in it and follow up with suggestions on more detail and so on.

But they did not go out and count the number of oil wells or the number of factories or what was made in them and so on. But they had the tools that they knew were very effective out there. One was the rule that said if the stock issue was based on misleading statements the whole thing could be rescinded. In effect the person who bought the stock had a put on the corporation because there were misleading statements. That is a very powerful tool.

There also was the tool that the whole board of directors is liable and, with more recent decisions, so are the lawyers in some circumstances.

And the accountants, too.

Believe me, when there is personal liability involved it is amazing how careful you are.

Now, take an opposite extreme. In FHA we do it just the opposite way. There is a whole cadre of people in FHA who are architectural or engineering experts; so that when a plan comes in for a multifamily project or a subdivision of small houses, FHA's own architects and engineers go over all those plans and it becomes more of a game of "catch me if you can" than an emphasis on the liability side.

On poultry inspection we inspect every one of those birds going through the line.

In the antitrust laws we rely on a sample audit by Justice, and by the FTC taking a long hard look as to where there may be troubles and bringing suits where they believe there should be, with a lot of reliance on the penalties built in in the way of treble damage suits, injunctive relief in the private sector and so on. I want to see whether we have rational explanations for these differences in approach, but this is inextricably linked to good program management: maybe you do not need as many employees in some of these shops as you have; or conversely, maybe the self-enforcement approach is not as good as we thought it was and more employees are needed over there.

You get into very poor policy decisions, so it is hard to say they are strictly management's fault. Yet, that kind of a study does not take a prolonged period of time to at least let you know what you do not know, to go to the next step and design a management information system to allow you to do a more detailed study later.

Senator MUSKIE. Have you pretty much illustrated all of the points in the paragraph on page 3?

N6

Director LYNN. No. I also mentioned the idea of alternative resource levels. I believe that one of the prior witnesses said that what ought to be tried is a pilot system using, for example, some social programs that are difficult to evaluate and then I am sure he didn't mean a pun, but he said "more concrete programs that are easier".

I am sure he didn't mean the concrete and highways together, but the thought occurred to me it is not that easy to evaluate the highway program. If you want to evaluate it from an economic development standpoint for use in the budget process, that is, whether another dollar in this program today will mean more to where our country is going than the same dollar in aviation or in maritime or in a tax expenditure by way of some further incentive for capital investment, such an evaluation is very difficult.

It is all too easy just to say that if you put in another billion dollars, you can get this much more asphalt and concrete in the country.

Therefore, I am fearful of a process that requires that we take massive numbers of programs each year and show how much more you could get for that program, even on the ones that appear to be easy. It is deceptively easy.

Now the natural instinct in many of the offices in the Government in the operating agencies will be to do it the first way. If you gave me a billion dollars more, and I am just using the highway program example of what could happen in any program, I can build this many more ribbons and these cities will be benefited by it and that will help them economically more than it was before.

Now, picture the top management getting 20, 50, 80 of those— usually at the last minute unless the systems are pretty good, because many times you don't want the top management of the Department to have too long to look at them—trying to cope with all of those and wrestle annually with putting them in proper focus. Picture, too, the need for coordination across the Government in looking at that kind of an issue.

This was what I meant when I said we have begun to crawl in this area. We may be even approaching a very slow walk. Progress is being made, very unevenly across the executive branch, but we have to speed up the tempo.

How can we choose those priorities of things that can be done in three months, within a year, and those that should be done over a period of 4 or 5 years?

I will give you an example of a longer one. We estimated that although we would have some useful data in 2 years on the housing allowances—I preferred to call it "direct cash assistance"—the total to do the evaluation is a 5-year run.

Senator MUSKIE. Senator Percy has one or two questions.

Senator PERCY. Yes; Mr. Chairman, I am sorry I could not be here at the outset of the hearings today, but we had our own S. 400 up before the Foreign Relations Committee this morning, so we had to work on the intelligence community and also a colleague of Mr. Lynn to be confirmed this morning, Mr. Secretary Robinson.

I have just three brief questions, Mr. Lynn.

When Roy Ash testified earlier on this legislation, he urged Congress to work with the executive branch of Government in devising a zero-budget system and to include the executive as an integral part in the final process. What role do you believe the Office of Management and Budget could play in such a process?

Director LYNN. Well, first of all, Senator, I would say we already are a player in the process. We do have many evaluations going on— some quite well designed. Some of great importance which coincide with my sense of priorities; others to which I would give lesser priority. We are trying in the budget system starting this year to give some further direction to get that priority arrangement into better balance.

But our function now is to assist the departments and agencies in any way that we can to help them carry out effective evaluation activities, either individually or on a coordinated basis. I think that Mr. Peter Phyrr testified that it is essential that the primary work be done in the agencies and deparements. I would add that it is absolutely essential within that Department, as I said in my testimony, that there be a group responsible only to the Secretary and the Under Secretary which looks over the shoulders, so to speak, of the operational units in the design and implementation of evaluations. This group should see that the natural tendency of people to justify what they have is overcome and that they follow at least a straight-up approach.

I think our role is similar to that of the Congress. Where we can be helpful on evaluations, like giving advice, we give it—whether it is to the Congress itself or to the GAO.

I think we can also provide a function of keeping track of evaluation activities in better ways than we have in the past, so that we are not reinventing the wheel in various areas, and so that we can cross-fertilize design techniques used in one area or department into others.

Senator PERCY. Thank you very much.

Second, during our first hearings on this legislation Roy Ash and Dean Weber, both formerly of OMB, differed on the need to state program objectives specifically. Roy Ash believed that they should be "stated clearly and precisely"—and if I remembered his own words—"and effectively examined and evaluated."

Dean Weber believed that too precise a definition robbed programs of necessary flexibility. Where do you stand on this issue, Mr. Lynn?

Director LYNN. Where OMB directors usually stand, right in the middle. I think they are both right and I really do mean that. I think if there had been a debate—I did skim-read that part of the testimony—you wouldn't have found them terribly far apart.

To the extent a program lends itself to explicit objectives, stating such objectives is very useful. However, there are a number of programs that currently do not lend themselves to specificity—and we should explore every way that there is to find a way of doing that without becoming mechanical.

I have to say, and I know there is disagreement in the Congress on this, that setting a goal as to an explicit number of housing units in a given 5- or 10-year period, I believe can be counterproductive in examining the total effect of a program on our economy.

But what Dean Weber is saying on the other side is, we have missions, broader goals that we want to and should state. There isn't anybody that disagrees with the overall mission of a decent home and suitable living environment for every American family.

Now that has got to be the mission of people who are interested in housing and interested in community development.

I think Roy Ash is saying that there may be programs which will lend themselves to more specific objectives and where—to the extent they do—we should examine ways of doing that. The Dean is saying on the other side, that there may be some programs where that is not productive.

I think they are both right.

Senator PERCY. Lastly, I would like to just put into the record a few figures to indicate the kind of problem that we face.

In 1975, 47 agencies were established, 27 agencies continued, 6 abolished, 4 transferred, and 2 names were changed. The moral of the story: It is easy to create new programs and agencies, it is very hard to abolish.

I think that is what we are talking about. As Senator Muskie sits with the awesome responsibility of being chairman of our

Senate Budget Committee, and as you sit in what I consider to be the most difficut job in the Federal Government, even more difficult than the President, because——

Director LYNN. Oh, I don't believe that.

Senator PERCY. They are honored to have him say "no" to them. But when you say "no"——

Director LYNN. Do you mean, Senator, that I provide a very useful political function of being in a place where lightning can strike and leave room for negotiations and communication with the President? I think I would have to agree with you, but it goes with the territory.

Senator PERCY. It must tear your heart out to see new programs that can be created and are adaptable and are needed; or existing programs that are vital and necessary, and yet we have got so much that we are carrying on, never having really evaluated and reviewed them. that the new priorities we just get squeezed out.

Now, next week I am addressing the UAW. Once again I am going to tell them, and I was booed a little last year when I told them there would be no national health insurance program in this Congress. But I think they are now going to realize a year later that I was right last year. There is no possibility of our doing that. We are not going to do that out of deficit financing and add to the debt.

We don't have a delivery system for it anyway.

The luncheon I have today just happens to be with Dean Simpson and Dr. Goldman of the Boston Dental School—Graduate School of Dentistry, Boston University. They are desperately concerned about our inability to keep dental students in school or only find that young men and women with wealthy parents would be able to afford the school, because we have a gradual disintegration of programs to train dentists.

Now, how are we going to move toward a goal of better health in this country if the number of doctors—we have a third of our doctors now every year come trained from developing countries. We don't have the medical schools for them here. Here we have good people turned down every year, even when they are eligible to get it.

The cost is absolutely astronomical. Cutbacks in financial aid to many medical schools resulted in tuition rates increasing between 36 and over 150 percent, depending upon Federal assistance levels. The cost per student is just skyrocketing and loans available are going down, scholarships are going down. It is getting worse because among competing priorities these just get squeezed out.

This kind of a program is where we, I think, can get a handle on our priorities and keep our eyes on an objective. I am not—I don't want to lobby you for a particular program, but I am just presenting to you the problems that we are facing and the pressures that we are under. How do we justify talking national health insurance and squeezing out the number of dentists and doctors we are going to have in this country.

I applaud, therefore, your statement saying that you support the general purpose of the bill. We are aiming in the right direction. Whether it is exactly the way to do it, that is something else again.

But I would appreciate any comments you would care to make on why we can't afford in this country, with the $400 billion budget, to adequately train dental and medical students, how do we justify that?

Director LYNN. Well, Senator, we only have limited time, but you have all seen my other charts on health services. Here is a chart of the health services of the United States. This is why the President said in October, let's hold down expenditures and give a further tax cut, we have to get rid of programs that don't work and make room for those that do.

New programs must be substituted for programs that don't work. Many times these things are evolutionary. When I was trying to assist the Congress in getting through the Community Development Act, I pointed out that if we never had urban renewal and model cities and so on, we wouldn't have had the cadre of people or the knowledge it took to build the bloc grants.

But the time is here on something like this. The time is here in my judgment to take action on child nutrition programs. There are 16 programs, annually funded at $2.9 billion; and yet there are 700,000 kids in America that live at or below the poverty line, we estimate, that are not getting a nickel of the $2.9 billion. And my kids that go to a Montgomery County school get a 23.5-cent Federal subsidy toward their lunch.

Well now, that is wrong. Or take education, which is a bloc grant program that we really need.

We see a kind of split personality. We are not yet willing to go all the way apparently as a government to helping the student and letting that student choose the educational institution he will go to. We still fund older programs where you give the money to institutions which, in turn, go out and seek the lower income student.

We have got to make up our minds. There isn't room in this budget for both approaches.

Senator PERCY. What I am impressed with, Mr. Lynn, both you and I are organization-minded, when you hold up a chart and show that superstructure, it is unbelievable. The overhead is unbelievable. But what we are interested in is the bottom line.

How much gets through? How much trickles down? You have all this money going into the top and how much gets down to the people that really need it?

Director LYN. There are 2,300 people in the 26 programs the President wants to consolidate into——

Senator PERCY. How many employees does HEW have? I will tell you, 157,000.

Director LYNN. 129,000.

Senator MUSKIE. Now we have had three figures.

[Laughter.]

Senator MUSKIE. Mr. Richardson——

Senator PERCY. Plus or minus 30,000 then.

Director LYNN. We are all correct. This is full-time positions that we have given you. The other figure you were given is total employees, which includes part-time people.

Senator PERCY. Whatever it is, it is a huge army. But here we are down below here, here is what is happening. The health professions' scholarship and loan program expired June 30, 1974, going on a year-to-year basis, but there are no funds available for students who entered after June 30, 1974, and 1974 to 1975, 47 percent of the dental students at Boston University, for instance, received either a loan or scholarship, but the scholarship was $705, the loan average $2,456. That won't even make a downpayment on what that education is going to cost, and I just point that out to show that we have got to have something here——

Director LYNN. Again, Senator——

Senator PERCY. [continuing.] To evaluate, to set priorities and keep our eye on the objective.

Director LYNN. That is a good area. Suppose you came up with a study of that area, taking the number of people going to medical schools in the country or to the dental schools, and looking at the requirements for those health services over the foreseeable future.

Suppose you find you already have enough people going to the schools. Now, if that is so, you have got a lovely policy conflict. On the other hand you do not want to use Federal dollars to end up with more people in an area than you need. There has been some indication at least from some of the teachers that I have heard that have said we may have done that in that area.

We may have done it with the engineers, may or may not. I am not sure we have the final answer.

On the one hand, I want to see any kid qualified if, knowing the facts, go to dental school; but on the other hand, you have the policy issue of using the Federal taxpayers' dollars wisely, especially you consider that other kids are going to go to school anyway and consider that you may well end up with more people than there are available jobs.

Now, I am not saying which of those answers is necessarily right, but what I am saying goes to your point. Let's get an evaluation. Let's get a design of an evaluation on which everybody had a chance to make his comments, whether it is Hill people, the general public, whatever. Then when we get the results of the study, let's use it rather than putting it on the shelf and everybody continuing to engage in the rhetoric as if there isn't any study. We need it desperately.

If I might, sir, one of the things that struck me as I was thinking about my testimony today is what we are all grasping for is better ways of management generally. Back in 1974 as Secretary of HUD I had an obligation that is repeated every 2 years for the Secretary, of coming up with something called the "national growth and development report". It comes out of the Banking, Housing, and Urban Affairs Committee in the Senate and what used to be the Banking and Currency Committee in the House.

It is a requirement this was assigned by the President in, I believe, December 1974, shortly after he took office, and we used it as an occasion to put together a thing called "Toward Guidelines for Federal Decisionmaking." It is a little like the checklist of a pilot on a good airplane of the things to keep in mind when considering new legislation, new regulations, or the like.

When you read this checklist, which is relatively short, and if I might, I would like to give some copies of this to the members of the committee.

[The checklist referred to follows:]

Excerpt From:

National Growth And Development

**Second Biennial Report
to the Congress
Submitted pursuant
to Section 703(a)
of Title VII,
Housing and Urban
Development Act
of 1970**

Prepared Under Direction of

**The Committee on
Community Development**

The Domestic Council

December 1974

- 2 -

TOWARD GUIDELINES FOR FEDERAL DECISION-MAKING

Whatever the mechanisms for bringing people together to achieve coordination in policy and program development and implementation, the likelihood that **approach issues with similar perceptions** sound policies and programs will result would be considerably enhanced if each participant were to approach the issue or bundle of issues, with at least similar perceptions about **how** such issue or issues should be analyzed and about the **technique** of determining what constitutes the "public interest."

But the government decision-maker rarely pays systematic attention to the effects of his actions except as they relate to his own mission. This myopic tendency is not easily cured.

Existing laws and regulations do not require and may not permit the consideration of Federal actions on the attainment of goals outside of individual mission areas. Further, the effects of Federal actions are often difficult to ascertain; and they are doubly difficult to predict in advance. The data necessary to measure impacts are often unavailable. The methodologies for analysis of that data often do not exist. The effects may be remote or may occur sometime in the future.

Yet it is increasingly necessary to take into account multiple impacts of a single Federal action on national goals. Consider the large number and variety of national goals. Most are well defined and long established; some have been more recently emphasized and raised in priority. All relate to "national growth policy." To name only a few: **assess multiple impacts program**

national goals related to growth

- maintenance of national security and defense of the country,
- preservation and enhancement of a private-enterprise (investment, risk, profit) society,
- economic freedom and efficiency through competition,
- full employment without harmful inflation,
- equal opportunity,
- for regulated industries, quality services at reasonable rates,
- safe and liveable communities, in both urban and rural areas,
- preservation of important natural resources, and clean air and water,
- secure and reasonably priced energy sources,
- decent, safe and sanitary housing, preferably owner-occupied, and
- health, education, and public safety services adequate for individual self-fulfillment.

Thus the policy-makers' task is to understand, as well as possible, how and whether present and proposed actions affect these goals. This requires: **the policy-makers' task**

- Systematic review in the course of decision-making of the possible effects, not just on the mission goal of each decision-maker, but on other national goals as well.
- Improved evaluation of existing activities with emphasis on both attainment of the mission goal and effects on other goals.

- 3 -

Much easier said than done. A very useful step in this direction would be efforts toward developing, refining and using an agreed upon set of guidelines for the Federal decision-making process. Such guidelines might well be in the form of sets of questions that should be answered, insofar as feasible, in assessing, on a one time or periodic basis, existing policies and programs and in considering new proposals. Such an effort toward a "decision-maker's checklist" will require extensive participation and indeed debate among many parties. For purposes of illustration, the following list is offered:

a "decision-maker's checklist"

- **What is the public problem being addressed?**
  Is the problem real or apparent, or merely a symptom of a larger problem?
  Can the problem be quantified? How large is it?
  Are other forces at work that are either solving the problem or making it worse?
  Does the public perceive a problem?
  Are those who perceive the problem among the intended beneficiaries?

- **Are the means proposed to solve the problem well suited to attain the desired ends?**
  Are other means available that are less expensive either to taxpayers, to consumers, or to the economy generally?
  Are there other means that would be more efficient?

- **Does the problem, the approach selected to solve it, or the effect intersect with other public programs or goals?**
  Should other agencies be consulted?

- **What methods of evaluation can be designed at the outset to determine at a later time the direct consequences and the effectiveness of the proposed action?**

- **What are possible inadvertent and second order effects of the proposed solution? Do the potential adverse effects outweigh the desirability of taking action on the immediate problem?**

- **What institution is best equipped to resolve the problem?**
  Can the private sector resolve the problem effectively?
  If not, what public sector response is suitable and feasible?
  - Is a Federal response appropriate, and if so, should it be uniformly applicable or flexible?

Such guidelines reflect the creed of modern management, that good policy-making results from the discipline of well-thought out approaches to each major policy decision. Procedurally, such discipline, self-imposed, most surely leads to increased demand for better methods of collecting and analyzing data and stronger interest in obtaining the viewpoints of others with different mission goals. Substantively, such discipline also helps to ensure that public policy-making—whether by executives or legislators—will lead to programs that are consistent with long term national goals and the values we hold important in our democracy, including goals and values relating to national growth.

policy-making consistent with national goals

Director Lynn. You will see, underlying it all—as an essential tool—is evaluation.

I wonder whether or not there might be some way in legislation, with key words like "to the maximum extent feasible"—words that give you time to experiment and that do not impose the evaluation requirement massively across the Federal Government—that would make it possible to address this more broadly? I am on the Paperwork Commission, and we are broaching this problem of management from that standpoint. The Procurement Commission approached it from a different viewpoint; environmental impact statements approach it from still another standpoint. Our inflation impact statements approach it from still another way.

The budget review process does it in a somewhat different way. It seems to me we have to bring it all together with a list of the kinds of considerations that are taken into account to the maximum extent possible before any important policy or programmatic decision is made.

I don't know whether there is a way of weaving that into legislation while avoiding the problems that I foresee if the bill before us were adopted as is; but I believe we have come to a time where there ought to be a comprehensive group of rules.

When you have hearings up here, you can ask whether the means proposed to solve the problems are well-suited. Are there less expensive means available? Are there any other means that are more efficient? Is this something that Government should be in at all? If so, should it be the Federal Government, the State or local government? And so on.

Senator Percy. Mr. Lynn, I presume that that evaluation process is being undertaken now by OMB with the Federal Energy Administration. That dies June 30. There is no budget for fiscal 1977 up before the Congress yet. Are you going to——

Director Lynn. There will be very shortly.

Senator Percy. Are you going to resolve that difference on the evaluation?

Director Lynn. We are close, sir. I would hope that those papers would be up here, if not this week, early next week. But I am struggling to make it this week.

Senator Percy. Because I think we have an evaluation process to go through——

Director Lynn. Absolutely.

Senator Percy [continuing]. As to whether or not FEA should stay, in fact, or whether you start now with phasing it out over 37 months or whether we ought to peel off some of those things that can be put in other agencies and departments.

Thank you very much indeed.

Director Lynn. Thank you, Senator.

Senator Percy. Thank you, Mr. Chairman.

Senator Muskie. Thank you.

Mr. Lynn, I think I have run out of time myself and I suspect you have, too.

I think your testimony is very useful in suggesting some of the complexity of the problem of evaluations and the need for flexibility. But at the same time, I would say that, perhaps without intending to, you have impressed me with the urgent need for some kind of mandated process. I recognize the risk that that will result in a mechanistic, even unrealistic kind of a process; one that would even be counterproductive.

Let me ask you a question that I think Senator Roth would ask if he were present. Is there a need, in order to achieve some momentum in the direction in which we all want to move, for something like a Hoover Commission to study this?

Director LYNN. I am presently helping to prepare papers in this area for the President. Let me express my own view that the most important use of that kind of a commission.

That would be to get increased awareness of the problems. I have found in the few years that I have been in Washington that the key in the democratic process is for people to understand why you think certain things should have priority and to get a consensus, which is sometimes hard to do, of both an understanding of the problem and what ought to be done.

A broadly based commission with representatives from various segments, if done right, could do that. It would be useful. I would have to say again, Mr. Chairman, with some fear and trepidation that I hope it wouldn't be limited to problems of the executive branch in organization, in technique and so on.

I would want to see precisely what the charter was, I think, Mr. Chairman, before I recommended to the President endorsement or nonendorsement of a particular form. But I have to say to you, my thinking at the moment is that it would do some real good; that a charter, properly conceived, can get the public to understand the issues.

I would only hope if there were such a commission, that it would not be used as a vehicle to put off needed reforms, whether it is in the executive branch or in the Congress, that we already have identified as something that are worthwhile steps.

My own views on block grants is that while what we do 10 or 15 years from now may be entirely different, right now we have seen areas where we think block grants will be better than what we presently have. Will it be perfect? Heavens no; but will they do a better job than what we are doing now? Yes.

With that caveat, I wouldn't like to see a commission used to put off an action on important issues identified now. My tentative feeling is that it would be something we ought to welcome.

Senator MUSKIE. Yes, I think it would be very helpful at the point that you first raised it.

Let me ask what I think is the key question, to get your general feel from this. Do you believe that zero-base review should be applied periodically to all Federal programs at some point?

Director LYNN. The word "all" is very encompassing, and so is "zero-base budgeting." I do believe every program of the Federal Government needs periodic review. But the review may assume that you need the function.

Let me give an example. At least for the foreseeable future we need a defense function, and the idea of providing defense is necessary. You also need U.S. attorneys in a judicial system provided by the Constitution.

So, therefore, an evaluation in that area could be one that moves on the spectrum toward efficiency, better ways of doing business, a careful analysis as to how various programs impact on the need for U.S. attorneys, say, for example rather than the need for the function itself.

I would think that this would mean that in the course of 4 to 5 years, an activity in the Federal Government has had some kind of an evaluation that is appropriate to that particular function at that time.

Senator MUSKIE. Could you have some of your people prepare an analysis of zero-base budgeting from that point of view, describing the different approaches? We have had witnesses that have given us suggestions and hints of how different functions and programs should be handled in zero-base budgeting. Could you have someone knowledgeable prepare a comprehensive analysis of that?

I think that would be helpful in developing the sorting-out kind of mechanism.

Director LYNN. Let us give that a good try, sir. I think we can be helpful.

Senator MUSKIE. That strikes me as one of the more sensible approaches to the problem, rather than the automatic process we are talking about.

[The information referred to follows:]

AN OUTLINE OF A MECHANISM FOR ACCOMPLISHING

ZERO BASE REVIEWS

Introduction

There is a clear need to establish and maintain a process for the systematic review and evaluation of government programs and activities. The process requires the involvement of both the executive and legislative branches, and must be tied to the principal decisionmaking processes of both branches. The approach adopted must be systematic but it must not be mechanical. That is, it must be flexible enough to allow for selectivity, prioritizing of efforts, broad coordination, and to permit periodic evaluations -- which are appropriate in scope and kind at that time -- of programs, activities, or program groups.

Principles

Past experience and sound management practice suggest that the process should reflect the following considerations:

- The process should foster a cooperative relationship between the President and the Congress, but should not compromise the constitutional prerogatives of either branch.

- The process should provide for the setting of evaluation priorities by the President, and for informing the Congress of intended evaluations.

- The Congress should retain the right to mandate additional specific evaluations, to be conducted by either branch.

- The process should not require that all programs be evaluated in any fixed period, nor according to any standard technique; rather all programs should be <u>regularly</u> considered for evaluation using some agreed-upon criteria; and should be subject to some "sunset" provision to be determined on a case-by-case basis (perhaps with a maximum life set in law).

- The process should link evaluation results to the congressional authorization process, including the development of new programs. Some positive "finding of fact" should be required in any committee report on a proposed new or reauthorized program; and by the Administration in recommending new or reauthorized programs.

- The process should enable the President to utilize evaluation results in his budget and other policy development processes. Priority evaluations conducted by the executive agencies should be reported first to the President, for his review and comment prior to their release to Congress.

- Where possible, evaluations should focus on groups of related programs; however, it is not possible to specify in legislation what groups are appreciated.

Specific Statutory Provisions

The flexibility necessary to maintain available, productive process minimizes the amount of detail to be mandated by legislation. The following provisions are essential, however:

A separate title of the bill should require consideration of evaluation components in all new or reauthorized legislation and the inclusion, where appropriate, of measurable objectives, structure, and resources for later evaluation.

- The bill should provide for variable authorization periods dependent upon the reasonable necessity for a given function. The maximum authorization periods for functions whose necessity may be commonly assumed, e.g., defense, should be greater than the present five years. This would not preclude authorizations of individual programs and activities for lesser periods. Similarly, specific priority evaluations of programs and activities within a function could be conducted more frequently if deemed appropriate.

- The bill should require congressional acknowledgement of the findings of reviews and evaluations conducted by the executive branch even if such data is rejected in final congressional actions.

Director LYNN. I have to say that I certainly agree with that. As I said, testifying yesterday before Senator Chiles on another matter, I have come to learn that a statute does set a certain priority and, therefore, I find myself torn, frankly, as OMB Director between having that additional tool to go to the Departments and agencies and say in a particular Department, "Your priority on evaluation efforts isn't high enough, and now the Congress as well as the President says you are going to do it, and we are going to get a little more action here."

I am attracted to that approach, but am also trying to find a way to construct a legislative mandate that is not going to use up the time of more than a few good people. In every agency and department you have people that are superb and dedicated—there are more of those than most Americans think—but we must use their time in the most effective way.

Let me give you an example I used in discussing this with your staff the other day. One of the problems is something we in OMB call the "Washington Monument syndrome." It is a historic term used to describe what used to go on in the Interior Department. I won't say in what time frame, so we leave that alone and get politics out of it. When anyone went to the Interior Department and said we want you to slow down on rate of expenditures or cut back on rate of expenditures, the response was always: "The first thing we will have to do is cut down the number of hours that the Washington Monument is open."

NOTES AND REFERENCES

1. The General Accounting Office is an oversight and investigatory unit of the Congress. Its functions are designated by Congress and include such areas as accounting, auditing, claims settlements, and legal procedures regarding programs and operations of the federal government. It also makes recommendations for more effective government operations. The GAO is headed by the comptroller general of the United States.

2. The charts referred to in the text are reprinted on succeeding pages. They indicate the number of overlapping federal programs that provide similar services.

3. This commentary on bill S. 2925 was attached to the statement of Comptroller General Elmer Staats, which he submitted to the Senate Subcommittee on Intergovernmental Relations, Committee on Government Operations. The full text of this bill, the Government Economy and Spending Reform Act of 1976, and a section-by-section analysis of it appear in [72]. Neither is reprinted here because of space limitations.

4. In his testimony before the Senate Committee on Government Operations, OMB Director James Lynn is referring to the Domestic Council Review Group for Regulatory Reform. President Gerald Ford established the DCRG on June 17, 1975. Its function is to coordinate the Executive branch's review of regulatory policies. Based largely on the efforts and findings of DCRG, President Ford submitted to Congress his legislation S. 3428, Agenda for Government Reform, on May 13, 1976.

5. The chart, supplied by OMB and titled "Economic Development Programs of the Federal Government," is reprinted here in substantially reduced size. During the 1970s, OMB frequently used charts of this kind to support arguments about structural problems in Executive branch organization and congressional committee jurisdictions, which, in many instances, adhere closely to the structural pattern of the Executive branch. This chart, like many submitted to Congress, provides no explanation of the lines moving from box to box; the use of multiple linking and crisscrossing lines helps to create the impression of a confusing bureaucratic maze.

6. Senator Edmund Muskie is referring to the text of OMB Director James Lynn's statement, which was distributed to the committee members before he testified. It is not unusual for witnesses to submit prepared statements to the committee prior to their appearance in a hearing.

Bibliography

PUBLIC DOCUMENTS

The bibliography of public documents comprises the body of documentary material examined for this compilation. The list represents the significant, publicly available government documents pertaining to the scope of this book. The time period covered is from 1970 through late 1976, with a few exceptions, such as the Hoover Commission material. Many of the documents in this bibliography are out of print, but almost all those cited should be available in government depository libraries in hard copy and in some libraries in microform. Since few libraries carry government documents in their general catalog, it may be necessary to request assistance from a reference librarian to locate them. A private firm, Congressional Information Service (CIS, 7101 Wisconsin Ave., Bethesda, Md. 20015), publishes microfiche editions of the congressional committee documents and produces abstracts of them in hard copy through SDC.

The *Congressional Record* and the *Federal Register* contain frequent references to reorganization matters, some of which are cited in the text. For exhaustive references to those publications, the reader should refer to the indexes of the *Record* and *Register*, published by the Government Printing Office and available in most libraries. During the 93rd and 94th Congresses, detailed annotated indexes and abstracts of the *Record* were published by *CSI Reports* (Capitol Services, Inc.) and *Congressional Record Abstracts*. Coverage of the *Federal Register* by CSI began in 1976. The publications *CSI Reports* and *Congressional Record Abstracts* have merged and are available in some libraries in hard copy or through Systems Development Corporation's (SDC) automated data base. They can also be ordered from Capitol Services, Inc., 511 Second St. N.E., Washington, D.C. 20002.

1. Carter, Jimmy. "Planning a Budget from Zero." Unpublished transcript of speech to the National Governors Conference. June 1974.
2. *Commission on the Organization of the Government for the Conduct of Foreign Policy* (Murphy Commission). Report. Washington, D.C.: GPO, 1975. 8 vols.
3. Executive Office of the President (Nixon). Office of Management and Budget. *Papers Relating to the President's Departmental Reorganization Program: A Reference Compilation*. Revised February 1972. Washington, D.C.: GPO, 1972.
4. ____. *Statement of Paul H. O'Neill, Deputy Director of Management and Budget, before the House Budget Committee, Task Force on the Budget Process*. July 27, 1976.
5. General Services Administration. National Archives and Records Service. Office of the Federal Register. *1976/77 United States Government Manual*. Revised May 1, 1976. Washington, D.C.: GPO, 1976.
6. President's Commission on CIA Activities within the United States (Rockefeller Commission). *Report of the Commission*. Washington, D.C.: GPO, 1975.

7. President's Committee on Administrative Management (Brownlow Commission). *Report of the President's Committee: Administrative Management in the Government of the United States*. Washington, D.C.: GPO, 1937.

8. Presidential Message (Nixon). *Reorganization Plan No. 2 of 1970*. House document no. 91-275. March 12, 1970. Washington, D.C.: GPO, 1970.

9. _____. *Reorganization Plan No. 4 of 1970*. House document no. 91-365. July 9, 1970. Washington, D.C.: GPO, 1970.

10. _____. *Reorganization Plan No. 2 of 1973. Establishing a Drug Enforcement Administration*. House document no. 93-69. March 28, 1973. Washington, D.C.: GPO, 1973.

11. *Task Force on Government Organization (1964)*, chaired by Don K. Price. Unpublished document available in Lyndon Baines Johnson Library, Austin, Tex.

12. *Task Force on Government Organization (1966)*, chaired by Ben W. Heineman. Unpublished document available in Lyndon Baines Johnson Library, Austin, Tex.

13. U.S. Commission on the Organization of the Executive Branch of the Government (Hoover Commission). *Hoover Commission Report on the Organization of the Executive Branch of the Government*. Reprint of 1949 edition. Westport, Conn.: Greenwood. 1971. 540 pp.

14. U.S. Congress. General Accounting Office. *Congressional Oversight–Methods and Techniques*. Prepared jointly with Library of Congress, Congressional Research Service, for the Subcommittee on Oversight Procedures of the Senate Committee on Government Operations. July 1976. Washington, D.C.: GPO, 1976.

15. U.S. Congress. Congressional Budget Office. *Budget Options for Fiscal Year 1977: A Report to the Senate and House Committees on the Budget*. March 15, 1976. Washington, D.C.: GPO, 1976.

16. _____. *Responsibilities and Organization*. May 1976. Washington, D.C.: GPO, 1976.

17. U.S. Congress. House. Committee on Government Operations. *Amending Reorganization Plan No. 2 of 1973*. Hearing on H.Res. 8245. June 14, 1973. Washington, D.C.: GPO, 1973.

18. _____. *Amending Reorganization Plan No. 2 of 1973*. Report on H.Res. 8245. Report no. 93-303. June 21, 1973. Washington, D.C.: GPO, 1973.

19. _____. *Approving Reorganization Plan No. 1 of 1970* (Telecommunications). Report on H.Res. 841. Report no. 91-930. March 19, 1970. Washington, D.C.: GPO, 1970.

20. _____. *Approving Reorganization Plan No. 3 of 1970*. Report on H.Res. 1209. Report no. 91-1464. September 23, 1970. Washington, D.C.: GPO, 1970.

21. _____. *Department of Community Development Act*. Report to accompany H.Res. 6962. Report no. 92-106. Washington, D.C.: GPO, 1972.

22. _____. *Energy Reorganization Act of 1973*. Report on H.Res. 11510. Report no. 93-707. December 7, 1973. Washington, D.C.: GPO, 1973.

23. _____. *Executive Reorganization: A Summary Analysis*. Report no. 92-922. March 15, 1972. Washington, D.C.: GPO, 1972.

24. _____. *Government in the Sunshine*. Hearings on H.Res. 10315 and H.Res. 9868. November 6 & 12, 1975. Washington, D.C.: GPO, 1975.

25. _____. *Reorganization of Executive Departments (Part 1–Overview)*. Hearings on H.Res. 6959, H.Res. 6960, H.Res. 6961, and H.Res. 6962. June 2, 3, 7, 8, 14, & 16; July 7, 8, 22, & 27, 1971. Washington, D.C.: GPO, 1971.

26. _____. *Reorganization of Executive Departments (Part 2–Department of Community Development)*. Hearings on H.Res. 6962. November 3, 9, & 11, 1971; January 25 & 27; February 7, 8, & 29; March 1, 2, 9, 13, 14, 21, & 27; and April 11, 1972. Washington, D.C.: GPO, 1972.

27. _____. *Reorganization Plan No. 1 of 1970* (Office of Telecommunications Policy). Hearings. March 9 & 10, 1970. Washington, D.C.: GPO, 1970.

28. _____. *Reorganization Plan No. 2 of 1970* (Office of Management and Budget; Domestic Council). Hearings. April 28, 30; May 5, 1970. Washington, D.C.: GPO, 1970.

29. _____. *Reorganization Plan No. 3 of 1970* (Environmental Protection Agency). Hearings. July 22, 23; August 4, 1970. Washington, D.C.: GPO, 1970.

30. _____. *Reorganization Plan No. 4 of 1970* (National Oceanic and Atmospheric Administration). Hearings. July 28 & 29, 1970. Washington, D.C.: GPO, 1970.

31. _____. *Reorganization Plan No. 1 of 1973* (Office of Emergency Preparedness; Office of Science and Technology; and National Aeronautics and Space Council). Hearing. February 26, 1973. Washington, D.C.: GPO, 1973.

32. _____. *Reorganization Plan No. 1 of 1973* (Office of Emergency Preparedness; Office of Science and Technology; and National Aeronautics and Space Council). Second report. Report no. 93-106. April 4, 1973. Washington, D.C.: GPO, 1973.

33. _____. *Reorganization Plan No. 2 of 1973* (Drug Enforcement Administration). Hearings. April 4; May 3, 1973. Washington, D.C.: GPO, 1973.

34. _____. *Disapproving Reorganization Plan No. 2 of 1973* (Drug Enforcement Administration). Report on H.Res. 382. Report no. 93-228. May 25, 1973. Washington, D.C.: GPO, 1973.

35. U.S. Congress. House. Committee on Interstate and Foreign Commerce. Subcommittee on Oversight and Investigations. *Regulatory Reform–Vol. I: Quality of Regulators.* Joint hearings with Senate Committees on Commerce and Government Operations. November 6 & 7, 1975. Serial no. 94-80. Washington, D.C.: GPO, 1976.

36. _____. *Regulatory Reform–Vol. II: Federal Power Commission; Food and Drug Administration.* Hearings. November 21 & 24, 1975; March 15 & 19, 1976; April 12, 1976. Serial no. 94-81. Washington, D.C.: GPO, 1976.

37. _____. *Regulatory Reform–Vol. III: Interstate Commerce Commission.* Hearings. February 22 & March 5, 1976. Serial no. 94-82. Washington, D.C.: GPO, 1976.

38. _____. *Regulatory Reform–Vol. IV: Consumer Product Safety Commission; National Highway Traffic Safety Administration; Federal Trade Commission.* Hearings. January 30; February 19 & 27; March 29; April 24, 1976. Serial no. 94-83. Washington, D.C.: GPO, 1976.

39. U.S. Congress. Library of Congress. Congressional Research Service. *Analysis of Senate Bill 2925 and Discussion of Zero-Based Budgeting,* by Robert Keith. Washington, D.C., February 27, 1976.

40. _____. *Budget Concepts and Terminology: The Appropriations Phase,* by Louis Fisher. Multilith 74-210 GGR. Washington, D.C., November 21, 1974.

41. _____. *Congressional Oversight–Methods and Techniques.* Prepared jointly with the General Accounting Office for the Subcommittee on Oversight Procedures of the Senate Committee on Government Operations. July 1976. Washington, D.C.: GPO, 1976.

42. _____. *Emerging Issues of Possible Legislative Concern Relating to the Conduct and Use of Evaluation in the Congress and the Executive Branch,* by Genevieve J. Kenzo. Multilith 75-39 SP. Washington, D.C., November 16, 1974.

43. _____. *Executive Reorganization,* by Ronald C. Moe. Issue brief no. 75014. August 23, 1976.

44. _____. *Federal Energy Reorganization–Issues and Options.* Report to the Senate Committee on Government Operations for Senator Charles H. Percy. September 1976. Washington, D.C.: GPO, 1976.

45. _____. *Federal Financial Regulatory Agency Reform: Monetary Policy Operations,* by Roger S. White. January 12, 1976.

46. _____. *Federal Regulatory Agencies: Congress Studies Their Future,* by Ronald C. Moe. August 23, 1976.

47. _____. *Financial System Reform Proposals,* by F. Jean Wells and H. Curtiss Martin. August 24, 1976.

48. _____. *Independent Department of Justice/Special Prosecutor,* by Richard C. Ehlke. July 23, 1976.

49. _____. *"Legislative Oversight and Program Evaluation: A Seminar Sponsored by Congressional Research Service Prepared for the Subcommittee on Oversight Procedures of the Senate Government Operations Committee."* May 1976. Washington, D.C.: GPO, 1976.

50. _____. *Postal Service,* by Bernevia McCalip. August 4, 1976.

51. _____. *The Role of Congress in the Department of Defense Reorganization Act of 1958,* by Nathaniel Gregory. June 2, 1975.

52. _____. *Status of Rules and Regulations Issued by an Abolished Agency,* by Jay R. Shampansky. Washington, D.C., February 11, 1976.

53. _____. *Sunset Laws: Establishing Systematic Oversight Procedure,* by John P. Ridley. August 17, 1976.

54. _____. *Watergate Reorganization and Reform Act of 1976,* by Joseph E. Cantor. August 2, 1976.

55. U.S. Congress. House. Committee on Post Office and Civil Service. Subcommittee on Postal Facilities, Mail, and Labor Management. *New Criteria for Small Post Office Closings and New Regulations to Control Personnel Costs.* Hearings. December 3 & 5, 1975. Serial no. 94-60. Washington, D.C.: GPO, 1976.

56. _____. *Subcommittee on Postal Service. Abolish the Postal Rate Commission and Index Postal Rate Increases with the Consumer Price Index.* Hearings on H.Res. 10109. March 30 & 31; April 6 & 7, 1976. Serial no. 94-70. Washington, D.C.: GPO, 1976.

57. _____. *Cutbacks in Postal Service.* Hearings. May 4 & 5, 1976. Serial no. 94-74. Washington, D.C.: GPO, 1976.

58. _____. *Postal Reorganization Act Amendments of 1975.* Hearings on H.Res. 2445. February 18, 21, & 28; March 11 & 13, 1975. Serial no. 94-4. Washington, D.C.: GPO, 1975.

59. _____. *Postal Service Finance.* Hearing. December 10, 1975. Serial no. 94-61. Washington, D.C.: GPO, 1976.

60. _____. *Subcommittees on Postal Service; and Postal Facilities, Mail, and Labor Management. GAO's Recommendation that 12,000 Small Post Offices Be Closed.* Joint hearings. September 23 & 24; October 8, 1975. Serial no. 94-45. Washington D.C.: GPO, 1975.

61. U.S. Congress. Senate. Committee on Banking, Housing, and Urban Affairs. *Compendium of Major Issues in Bank Regulation.* August 1975. Washington, D.C.: GPO, 1975.

62. _____. *Federal Reserve Reform Act.* Report on H.Res. 12934. Report no. 94-1151. August 20, 1976. Washington, D.C.: GPO, 1976.

63. _____. *Financial Institutions Supervisory Act Amendments of 1976.* Report on S. 2304. Report no. 94-843. May 13, 1976. Washington, D.C.: GPO, 1976.

64. _____. Subcommittee on Financial Institutions. *Financial Institutions Act of 1975.* Hearings on S. 1267, S. 1475, S. 1540. May 14, 15, & 16; June 11, 1975. Washington, D.C.: GPO, 1975.

65. U.S. Congress. Senate. Committee on Commerce. *Regulatory Reform–Vol. I: Quality of Regulators.* Joint hearings with House Committee on Interstate and Foreign Commerce; Subcommittee on Oversight and Investigations; and Senate Committee on Government Operations. November 6 & 7, 1975. Serial no. 94-80. Washington, D.C.: GPO, 1976.

66. _____. Subcommittees for Consumers and on the Environment. *Symposium–Regulatory Myths.* Hearing. June 23, 1975. Serial No. 94-26. Washington, D.C.: GPO, 1975.

67. U.S. Congress. Senate. Committee on Government Operations. *Congressional Oversight–Methods and Techniques.* Prepared jointly by Library of Congress, Congressional Research Service, and General Accounting Office. July 1976. Washington, D.C.: GPO, 1976.

68. _____. *Establish a Department of Community Development.* Hearings on S. 1430. Part 4. April 11 & 12, 1972. Washington, D.C.: GPO, 1972.

69. _____. *Establish a Department of Energy and Natural Resources.* Hearings on S. 2135. July 31; August 1; September 13, 1973. Washington, D.C.: GPO, 1974.

70. _____. *Executive Reorganization Proposals.* Hearings on S. 1430, S. 1431, S. 1432, S. 1433. Part 1. May 25 & 26; June 22, 1971. Washington, D.C. GPO: 1971.

71. _____. *Federal Energy Reorganization–Issues and Options.* Report for Senator Charles H. Percy by Library of Congress, Congressional Research Service. September 1976. Washington, D.C.: GPO, 1976.

72. _____. *Government Economy and Spending Reform Act of 1976.* Report on S. 2925. Report no. 94-1137. August 6, 1976. Washington, D.C.: GPO, 1976.

73. _____. *Improving Congressional Oversight of Federal Regulatory Agencies.* Hearings on S. 2258, S. 2716, S. 2812, S. 2878, S. 2903, S. 2925, S. 3318, and S. 3428. May 18, 20, 24, & 25, 1976. Washington, D.C.: GPO, 1976.

74. _____. *Regulatory Reform–1974.* Hearings on S. 704, S. 770, S. 3604, S. 4155, S. 4167, and S.J.Res. 256. Part 1. November 21, 22, & 24, 1974. Washington, D.C.: GPO, 1974.

75. _____. *Regulatory Reform–1974.* Hearings on S. 704, S. 770, S. 3604, S. 4145, S. 4167, and S.J.Res. 256. Part 2. November 26, 1974. Washington, D.C.: GPO, 1975.

76. _____. *Regulatory Reform–1975.* Hearings on S.Res. 71. October 29 & 30; December 5 & 19, 1975. Washington, D.C.: GPO, 1976.

77. _____. *Regulatory Reform–Vol. I: Quality of Regulators.* Joint Hearings with House Committee on Interstate and Foreign Commerce; Subcommittee on Oversight and Investigations; and Senate Committee on Commerce. November 6 & 7, 1975. Serial no. 94-80. Washington, D.C.: GPO, 1976.

78. _____. *Watergate Reorganization and Reform Act of 1975*. Hearings on S. 495 and S. 2036. Part 1. July 29, 30, & 31, 1975. Washington, D.C.: GPO, 1975.

79. _____. *Watergate Reorganization and Reform Act of 1975*. Hearings on S. 495 and S. 2036. Part 2. December 3, 4, & 8, 1975; March 11, 1976. Washington, D.C.: GPO, 1976.

80. _____. *Watergate Reorganization and Reform Act of 1976*. Report on S. 495. Report no. 94-823. May 12, 1976. Washington, D.C.: GPO, 1976.

81. _____. Subcommittee on Executive Reorganization and Government Research. *Reorganization Plan No. 2 of 1970*. Hearing. May 8, 1970. Washington, D.C.: GPO, 1970.

82. _____. *Reorganization Plan Nos. 3 and 4 of 1970*. Hearings. July 28 & 29; September 1, 1970. Washington, D.C.: GPO, 1970.

83. _____. Subcommittee on Intergovernmental Relations. *Government Economy and Spending Reform Act of 1976*. Hearings on S. 2925 and S. 2067. March 17, 18, 19, 24, & 25; April 6 & 7, 1976. Washington, D.C.: GPO, 1976.

84. _____. Subcommittee on Oversight Procedures. "Legislative Oversight and Program Evaluation: A Seminar Sponsored by Congressional Research Service." May 1976. Washington, D.C.: GPO, 1976.

85. _____. Subcommittee on Reorganization, Research, and International Organizations. *Reorganization Plan No. 1 of 1973*. Hearing. February 22, 1973. Washington, D.C.: GPO, 1973.

86. _____. *Reorganization Plan No. 2 of 1973*. Hearings. Part 1. April 12, 13, & 26, 1973. Washington, D.C.: GPO, 1974.

87. _____. *Reorganization Plan No. 2 of 1973*. Hearings. Part 2. May 14, 1973. Washington, D.C.: GPO, 1974.

88. _____. *Reorganization Plan No. 2 of 1973*. Hearings. Part 3. May 18, 1973. Washington, D.C.: GPO, 1974.

89. _____. *Reorganization Plan No. 2 of 1973*. Hearings. Part 4. May 25, 1973. Washington, D.C.: GPO, 1974.

90. _____. *Reorganization Plan No. 2 of 1973*. Hearings. Part 5. May 29, 1973. Washington, D.C.: GPO, 1974.

91. _____. *Reorganization Plan No. 2 of 1973*. Hearings. Part 6. May 31; June 1, 1973. Washington, D.C.: GPO, 1974.

92. _____. *Reorganization Plan No. 2 of 1973*. Hearings. Part 7. June 1 & 4, 1973. Washington, D.C.: GPO, 1974.

93. _____. *Reorganization Plan No. 2 of 1973. Establishing a Drug Enforcement Administration in the Department of Justice*. Report no. 93-469. October 16, 1973. Washington, D.C.: GPO, 1973.

94. U.S. Congress. Senate. Committee on Interior and Insular Affairs. *Establishing a Department of Natural Resources*. Hearings pursuant to S. Res. 45: A National Fuels and Energy Policy Study. January 28, 1972. Washington, D.C.: GPO, 1972.

95. U.S. Congress. Senate. Committee on the Judiciary. Subcommittee on Separation of Powers. *Removing Politics from the Administration of Justice*. Hearings on S. 2803 and S. 2978. March 26, 27, & 28; April 2, 1974. Washington, D.C.: GPO, 1974.

96. U.S. Congress. Senate. Committee on Post Office and Civil Service. *Explanation of the Postal Reorganization Act and Selected Background Material*. Revised July 1975. Washington, D.C.: GPO, 1975.

97. _____. *Postal Reorganization*. Hearings on S. 2844. Part 1. January 27 & 28, 1976. Washington, D.C.: GPO, 1976.

98. _____. *Postal Reorganization*. Hearings on S. 2844. Part 2. February 16 & 20, 1976. Washington, D.C.: GPO, 1976.

99. _____. *Postal Reorganization*. Hearings on S. 2844. Part 3. March 29, 1976. Washington, D.C.: GPO, 1976.

100. _____. *Postal Reorganization*. Hearings on S. 2844. Part 4. April 19 & 20, 1976. Washington, D.C.: GPO, 1976.

101. _____. *Postal Reorganization Act Amendments of 1976*. Report on H.Res. 8603. Report no. 94-966. June 21, 1976. Washington, D.C.: GPO, 1976.

102. _____. *Problems of the U.S. Postal Service: A Compendium of Studies, Attitudes, and Statements on the U.S. Postal Service*. March 1976. Washington, D.C.: GPO, 1976.

103. U.S. President's Advisory Council on Executive Organization (Ash Council). *Establishment of a Department of Natural Resources. Organization for Social and Economic Programs.* Memoranda for the President of the United States. Washington, D.C.: GPO, 1971.

104. _____. *A New Regulatory Framework: Report on Selected Independent Regulatory Agencies.* Washington, D.C.: GPO, 1971.

105. White House. Office of the White House Press Secretary. "Agenda for Government Reform." Fact Sheet. May 13, 1976.

ADDITIONAL REFERENCE SOURCES

This list was compiled from bibliographies in Library of Congress, Congressional Research Service documents ([39–54]).

Adams, Bruce. "Sunset: A Proposal for Accountable Government." *Administrative Law Review* article, inserted in the *Congressional Record* of October 26, 1976, p. 18219.

American Academy of Political and Social Sciences Annals. "Government as Regulator." Vol. 400. Philadelphia: American Academy of Political and Social Sciences, 1972. 237 pp.

Appleby, Paul H. "The Significance of the Hoover Commission Report." *Yale Review* 39 (September 1949): 1–22.

Arnold, Peri E. "The First Hoover Commission and the Managerial Presidency." *Journal of Politics* 38 (February 1976): 46–70.

Bernstein, Marver H. *Regulating Business by Independent Commissions.* Princeton, N.J.: Princeton University Press, 1955, 306 pp.

Bonafede, Dom. "Bureaucracy, Congress, and Interests See Threat in Nixon Reorganization Plan." *National Journal,* May 8, 1971, pp. 977–986.

Cary, William L. *Politics and the Regulatory Commissions.* New York: McGraw-Hill, 1967. 149 pp.

Cohen, Richard E. "Regulatory Reform—535 Different Meanings for Members of Congress." *National Journal,* April 10, 1976, pp. 476–481.

Cushman, Robert E. *The Independent Regulatory Commissions.* New York: Oxford University Press, 1941. 780 pp.

Cutler, Lloyd N., and David R. Johnson. "Regulation and Political Process." *Yale Law Journal* 84 (June 1975): 1395–1418.

Dean, Alan L. "The Goals of Departmental Reorganization." *Bureaucrat* 1 (Spring 1972): 23–30.

Dixon, Robert G., Jr. "The Independent Commissions and Political Responsibility." *Administrative Law Review* 27 (Winter 1975): 1–16.

Emmerich, Herbert. *Federal Organization and Administrative Management.* University: University of Alabama Press, 1971. 304 pp.

Fesler, James W. "Administrative Literature and the Second Hoover Commission Reports." *American Political Science Review* 51 (March 1955): 135–157.

Gardner, Judy. " 'Sunset' Bills: An Eye on Big Government?" *Congressional Quarterly,* April 24, 1976, pp. 955–956.

Hector, Louis J. "Problems of the CAB and the Independent Regulatory Commissions." *Yale Law Journal* 69 (May 1960): 931–964.

Kaufman, Herbert. *Are Government Organizations Immortal?* Washington, D.C. Brookings Institution, 1976. 79 pp.

Krislov, Samuel, and Lloyd D. Musolf, eds. *The Politics of Regulation.* Boston: Houghton Mifflin, 1964. 261 pp.

Mansfield, Harvey C. "Federal Executive Reorganization: Thirty Years of Experience." *Public Administration Review* 29 (July/August 1969): 332–345.

Nathan, Richard P. *The Plot That Failed: Nixon and the Administrative Presidency.* New York: Wiley, 1975. 193 pp.

National Academy of Public Administration. "A Proposal by an Ad Hoc Citizens' Committee for Study of the U.S. Government: A Bicentennial Commission on American Goverment." August 26, 1975.

————"Watergate: Its Implications for Responsible Government: A Report Prepared by a Panel of the National Academy of Public Administration at the Request of the Senate Select Committee on Presidential Campaign Activities." March 1974. 143 pp.

Neustadt, Richard E. "The Constraining of the President: The Presidency after Watergate." *British Journal of Political Science* 4 (October 1974): 383–397.

Noll, Roger. *Reforming Regulation: An Evaluation of the Ash Council Proposals.* Washington, D.C.: Brookings Institution, 1971. 116 pp.

Oqul, Morris S. *Congress Oversees the Bureaucracy: Studies in Legislative Supervision.* Pittsburgh: University of Pittsburgh Press, 1976. 231 pp.

Phillips, Almarin, ed. *Promoting Competition in Regulated Markets.* Washington, D.C.: Brookings Institution, 1975. 397 pp.

Pyhrr, Peter A. *Zero-Base Budgeting: A Practical Management Tool for Evaluating Expenses.* New York: Wiley, 1973. 231 pp.

Reagan, Michael D., ed. "Regulatory Administration: Are We Getting Anywhere? A Symposium." *Public Administration Review* 32 (July–August 1972): 283–310.

"Removing Politics from the Justice Department: Constitutional Problems with Institutional Reform." *New York University Law Review* 50 (May 1975): 366–435.

"Return of the Invisible Hand: The New View of Economic Regulation: A Symposium." *Columbia Journal of Law and Social Problems* 9 (Fall 1972): 1–27.

Seidman, Harold. *Politics, Position, and Power: The Dynamics of Federal Organization.* New York: Oxford University Press, 1975. 354 pp.

"Symposium on Federal Regulatory Agencies: A Response to the Ash Report." *Virginia Law Review* 57 (September 1971): 925–1108.

U.S. Civil Aeronautics Board. "Report on Procedural Reform." Advisory Committee on Procedural Reform. December 31, 1975. 52 pp.

"Watergate, Politics, and the Legal Process." Washington, D.C.: American Enterprise Institute for Public Policy Research, 1974. 89 pp.

Weidenbaum, Murray L. "Government-Mandated Price Increases: A Neglected Aspect of Inflation." Washington, D.C.: American Institute for Public Policy Research, 1975. 112 pp.

Willougby, William F. *The Reorganization of the Administrative Branch of the National Government.* Baltimore: John Hopkins Press, 1923. 298 pp.

Wilson, James C. "The Dead Hand of Regulation." *Public Interest,* no. 24, Fall 1971, pp. 39–58.

Wolanin, Thomas B. *Presidential Advisory Commissions: Truman to Nixon.* Madison: University of Wisconsin Press, 1975. 298 pp.

Appendix 1
List of Acronyms

This list was compiled from the National Archives and Record Service of the General Services Administration ([5], pp. 792–796). The editors of this volume have added acronyms which did not appear in the original list.

ABMC: American Battle Monuments Commission.
ACA: Agency for Consumer Advocacy.
ACDA: Arms Control and Disarmament Agency.
ACE: Active Corps of Executives.
ACP: Agriculture Conservation Program.
ACUS: Administration Conference of the United States.
AD: Airworthiness Directive.
ADAMHA: Alcohol, Drug Abuse, and Mental Health Administration.
ADP: Automatic Data Processing.
ADTS: Automated Data and Telecommunications Service.
AEC: Atomic Energy Commission.
AFDC: Aid to Families with Dependent Children.
AID: Agency for International Development.
ALR: Authority Lease Rentals.
AMA: American Medical Association.
AMS: Agricultural Marketing Service.
Amtrak: National Railroad Passenger Corporation.
AOA: Administration on Aging.
APA: Assistance Payments Administration.
APHIS: Animal and Plant Health Inspection Service.
ARBA: American Revolution Bicentennial Administration.
ARC: American Red Cross.
ARS: Agricultural Research Service; Advanced Record System.
ASCS: Agricultural Stabilization and Conservation Service.

BDC: Bureau of Domestic Commerce.
BEWT: Bureau of East-West Trade.
BIA: Bureau of Indian Affairs.
BIB: Board of International Broadcasting.
BIC: Bureau of International Commerce.
BIEPR: Bureau of International Economic Policy and Research.
BLM: Bureau of Land Management.
BLS: Bureau of Labor Statistics.
BPA: Bonneville Power Administration.
BRTA: Bureau of Resources and Trade Assistance.

CAB: Civil Aeronautics Board.
CAP: Civil Air Patrol.
CBO: Congressional Budget Office.
CC: Common Cause.
CCC: Commodity Credit Corporation.
CDC: Center for Disease Control.
CEA: Council of Economic Advisers.
CENTO: Central Treaty Organization.
CEP: Concentrated Employment Program.
CEQ: Council on Environmental Quality.
CETA: Comprehensive Employment and Training Act.
CFR: Code of Federal Regulations.
CFTC: Commodity Futures Trading Commission.
CIA: Central Intelligence Agency.
CIEP: Council on International Economic Policy.
CIS: Congressional Information Service.
CNO: Chief of Naval Operations.
CONUS: Continental United States.
CPSC: Consumer Product Safety Commission.

CRS: Community Relations Service.
CSA: Community Services Administration.
CSC: Civil Service Commission.
CSRS: Cooperative State Research Service.

DARPA: Defense Advanced Research
Projects Agency.
DCA: Defense Communications Agency.
DCAA: Defense Contract Audit Agency.
DCD: Department of Community
Development.
DCMA: District of Columbia Manpower
Administration.
DCPA: Defense Civil Preparedness
Agency.
DCRG: Domestic Council Review Group
for Regulatory Reform.
DEA: Drug Enforcement Administration.
DENR: Department of Energy and Natural
Resources.
DEPA: Defense Electric Power
Administration.
DHR: Department of Human Resources.
DIA: Defense Intelligence Agency.
DIBA: Domestic and International Business
Administration.
DIS: Defense Investigative Service.
DMA: Defense Mapping Agency.
DNA: Defense Nuclear Agency.
DNR: Department of Natural Resources.
DOD: Department of Defense.
DOT:Department of Transportation.
DSA: Defense Supply Agency.
DSAA: Defense Security Assistance
Agency.
DSARC: Defense Systems Acquisition
Review Council.

EDA: Economic Development
Administration.
EEC: European Economic Community.
EEO: Equal employment opportunity.
EEOC: Equal Employment Opportunity
Commission.
EHS: Environmental Health Services.
EMS: Export Marketing Service.
EPA: Environmental Protection Agency.
EPGA: Emergency Petroleum and Gas
Administration.
ERDA: Energy Research and Development
Administration.
EROS: Earth Resources Observation
Systems.

ERS: Economic Research Service.
ESA: Employment Standards
Administration.
ESARS: Employment Service Automated
Reporting System.
ESEA: Elementary and Secondary
Education Act.
ETA: Employment and Training
Administration.
EXIMBANK: Export-Import Bank of the
United States.

FAA: Federal Aviation Administration.
FAIR: Fair Access to Insurance
Requirements.
FAO: Food and Agriculture Organization of
the United Nations.
FAS: Foreign Agricultural Service.
FBI: Federal Bureau of Investigation.
FCA: Farm Credit Administration.
FCC: Federal Communications
Commission.
FCIA: Foreign Credit Insurance
Association.
FCIC: Federal Crop Insurance
Corporation.
FCS: Farmer Cooperative Service.
FDA: Food and Drug Administration.
FDAA: Federal Disaster Assistance
Administration.
FDAC: Federal Domestic Assistance
Catalog.
FDIC: Federal Deposit Insurance
Corporation.
FDPC: Federal Data Processing Centers.
FEA: Federal Energy Administration.
FEBs: Federal Executive Boards.
FEO: Federal Energy Office.
FHA: Federal Housing Administration.
FHLBB: Federal Home Loan Bank Board.
FHWA: Federal Highway Administration.
FIA: Federal Insurance Administration.
FIC: Federal Information Centers.
FICA: Federal Insurance Contribution Act.
FIP: Forestry Incentive Program.
FLETC: Federal Law Enforcement
Training Center.
FMC: Federal Maritime Commission.
FMCS: Federal Mediation and Conciliation
Service.
FmHA: Farmers Home Administration.
FNMA[1]: Federal National Mortgage
Association.
FNS: Food and Nutrition Service.

[1]Referred to as "Fannie Mae."

FPA: Federal Preparedness Agency.
FPC: Federal Power Commission.
FRA: Federal Railroad Administration.
FRCs: Federal Regional Councils.
FRS: Federal Reserve System.
FSLIC: Federal Savings and Loan Insurance Corporation.
FSS: Federal Supply Service.
FTC: Federal Trade Commission.
FTS: Federal Telecommunications System.
FWS: Fish and Wildlife Service.

GAO: General Accounting Office.
GATT: General Agreement on Tariffs and Trade.
GNMA: Government National Mortgage Association.
GNP: Gross national product.
GPO: Government Printing Office.
GSA: General Services Administration.

HEW: Department of Health, Education, and Welfare.
HRA: Health Resources Administration.
HSA: Health Services Administration.
HUD: Department of Housing and Urban Development.

IADB: Inter-American Defense Board.
IAEA: International Atomic Energy Agency.
IATA: International Air Transport Association.
ICAF: Industrial College of the Armed Forces.
ICAO: International Civil Aviation Organization.
ICC: Indian Claims Commission; Interstate Commerce Commission.
ICEM: Intergovernmental Committee on European Migration.
IDA: International Development Association.
IEA: International Energy Agency.
IFC: International Finance Corporation.
ILO: International Labor Organization.
IMF: International Monetary Fund.
INS: Immigration and Naturalization Service.
INTERPOL: International Criminal Police Organization.
IRS: Internal Revenue Service.
ITU: International Telecommunications Union.

JAG: Judge Advocate General.
JCS: Joint Chiefs of Staff.
JFMIP: Joint Financial Management Improvement Program.
JOBS: Job Opportunities in the Business Sector.

LEAA: Law Enforcement Assistance Administration.
LMSA: Labor Management Services Administration.
LORAN: Long-range navigation.

MA: Maritime Administration.
MAC: Military Airlift Command.
MEDLARS: Medical literature analysis and retrieval system.
MESA: Mining Enforcement and Safety Administration.
MESBIC: Minority Enterprise Small Business Investment Companies.
MSC: Military Sealift Command.
MSSD: Model Secondary School for the Deaf.
MTB: Materials Transportation Bureau.
MTMTS: Military Traffic Management and Terminal Service.

NAB: National Alliance of Businessmen.
NAE: National Academy of Engineering.
NARS: National Archives and Records Service.
NAS: National Academy of Science.
NASA: National Aeronautics and Space Administration.
NATO: North Atlantic Treaty Organization.
NBS: National Bureau of Standards.
NCA: New Communities Administration.
NCUA: National Credit Union Administration.
NDU: National Defense University.
NEA: Noncareer Executive Appointments.
NFPCA: National Fire Prevention and Control Administration.
NHTSA: National Highway Transportation Safety Administration.
NIE: National Institute of Education.
NIER: National Industrial Equipment Reserve.
NIH: National Institutes of Health.
NLM: National Library of Medicine.
NLRB: National Labor Relations Board.
NMB: National Mediation Board.

NMC: Naval Material Command.

NOAA: National Oceanic and Atmospheric Administration.

NRC: Nuclear Regulatory Commission; National Research Council.

NSA: National Security Agency.

NSC: National Security Council.

NSF: National Science Foundation.

NSVP: National Student Volunteer Program.

NTIS: National Technical Information Service.

NTSB: National Transportation Safety Board.

NWC: National War College.

NYC: Neighborhood Youth Corps.

OAS: Organization of American States.

OCD: Office of Child Development.

OCR: Office of Coal Research.

OCSE: Office of Child Support Enforcement.

OECD: Organization for Economic Cooperation and Development.

OEDP: Office of Employment Development Programs.

OEO: Office of Economic Opportunity.

OEP: Office of Emergency Preparedness.

OFCC: Office of Federal Contract Compliance.

OFDI: Office of Foreign Direct Investments.

OFR: Office of the Federal Register.

OGSM: Office of the General Sales Manager.

OHD: Office of Human Development.

OHI: Office for Handicapped Individuals.

OHMO: Office of Hazardous Materials Operations.

OIC: Opportunities Industrialization Center.

OIGR: Office of Intergovernmental Regulations.

OJT: On-the-Job Training.

OMB: Office of Management and Budget.

OMBE: Office of Minority Business Enterprise.

ONAP: Office of Native American Programs.

ONR: Office of Naval Research.

OOG: Office of Oil and Gas.

OPB: Office of Planning and Budget (State of Georgia).

OPEC: Organization of Petroleum Exporting Countries.

OPIC: Overseas Private Investment Corporation.

OPSO: Office of Pipeline Safety Operations.

ORD: Office of Rural Development.

OSHA: Occupational Safety and Health Administration.

OT: Office of Telecommunications.

OTA: Office of Technology Assessment.

OTP: Office of Telecommunications Policy.

OYD: Office of Youth Development.

OWRT: Office of Water Research and Technology.

PAGGO: President's Advisory Committee on Government Organization.

PAHO: Pan American Health Organization.

PBGC: Pension Benefit Guaranty Corporation.

PBS: Public Buildings Service.

PEP: Public Employment Program.

PHS: Public Health Service.

PMA: Pharmaceutical Manufacturers Association.

PMDS: Property Management and Disposal Service.

PPB: Programing, Planning and Budgeting.

PRC: Postal Rate Commission.

PSC: Public Service Careers Program.

PTO: Patent and Trademark Office.

R & D: Research and Development.

RDS: Rural Development Service.

REA: Rural Electrification Administration.

REAP: Rural Environmental Assistance Program.

RECP: Rural Environmental Conservation Program.

RIS: Regulatory Information System.

RRB: Railroad Retirement Board.

RSA: Rehabilitation Services Administration.

RSVP: Retired Senior Volunteer Program.

RTB: Rural Telephone Bank.

SALT: Strategic arms limitation talks.

SAO: Smithsonian Astrophysical Observatory.

SBA: Small Business Administration.

SBIC: Small Business Investment Companies.

SCORE: Service Corps of Retired Executives.

SCS: Soil Conservation Service.

SDC: Systems Development Corporation.

SEATO: Southeast Asia Treaty Organization.

SEC: Securities and Exchange Commission.

SESA: Social and Economic Statistics Administration.

SITES: Smithsonian Institution Traveling Exhibition Service.

SLS: Saint Lawrence Seaway Development Corporation.

SMSA: Standard Metropolitan Statistical Area.

SPARS: Women's Coast Guard Reserves (from Coast Guard motto "Semper Paratus—Always Ready").

SRS: Statistical Reporting Service; Social and Rehabilitation Service.

SSA: Social Security Administration.

SSIE: Smithsonian Science Information Exchange, Inc.

SSS: Selective Service System.

TNEC: Temporary National Economic Committee.

TVA: Tennessee Valley Authority.

UAW: United Auto Workers.

UIS: Unemployment Insurance Service.

UMTA: Urban Mass Transportation Administration.

UN: United Nations.

UNESCO: United Nations Educational, Scientific and Cultural Organization.

UNICEF: United Nations International Children's Emergency Fund (now United Nations Children's Fund).

UPO: United Planning Organization.

USA: United States Army.

USAF: United States Air Force.

USCG: United States Coast Guard.

USDA: United States Department of Agriculture.

USES: United States Employment Service.

USGS: United States Geological Survey.

USIA: United States Information Agency.

USIS: United States Information Service.

USMC: United States Marine Corps.

USN: United States Navy.

USPS: United States Postal Service.

USRA: United States Railway Association.

USTS: United States Travel Service.

UYA: University Year for Action.

VA: Veterans Administration.

VISTA: Volunteers in Service to America.

VITA: Volunteers in Technical Assistance.

VOA: Voice of America.

WAC: Women's Army Corps.

WAVES: Women Accepted for Volunteer Emergency Service.

WHO: World Health Organization.

WIN: Work Incentive Program.

WMO: World Meteorological Organization.

YCP: Youth Challenge Program.

ZBB: Zero-Base Budgeting.

Appendix 2
The Congressional
Budget Office

The material in Appendixes 2–8 is of two types. The first type includes documents that bear directly on the text, but that are technical or highly detailed. They are a description of the Congressional Budget Office, the Ford administration's Fact Sheet ("Agenda for Government Reform Act"), and replicas of the management accounting forms used in Georgia's zero-base budgeting system. The second type includes documents pertaining to important reorganization activities falling outside the focus of the book. Summary information is reprinted on three different reorganization proposals pertaining to specific functions of the federal government, which are the postal service, the financial regulatory agencies, and the energy agencies. Finally, a proposal on a permanent structure apparatus (e.g., a special prosecutor) to oversee and enforce ethical standards is included under the heading of Watergate Reorganization and Reform. The placement of this material in the appendix is not intended to suggest it is less significant than that in the main body of the text. Each of the matters treated is very significant—within the specific area of government it addresses; however, the bulk of the material in the volume tends to address more comprehensive and far-reaching issues.

The Congressional Budget Office (CBO), established pursuant to Public Law 93–344, the Congressional Budget Act of 1974, is a nonpartisan organization which provides the U.S. Congress with information and analyses it needs to make decisions about budget and fiscal policies and national priorities. This report discusses CBO's responsibilities and outlines how it is organized and staffed to assist the U.S. Congress.

Responsibilities of the Congressional Budget Office

The Congressional Budget Act of 1974 established a new procedure by which the U.S. Congress considers and acts upon the annual federal budget. The act reorganizes the budget cycle and creates three new institutions: House and Senate Committees on the Budget and the Congressional Budget Office. CBO's mission is to provide the Congress with detailed budget information and studies of the budget impact of alternative policies. The law makes clear that the CBO is to have a nonpartisan, highly professional staff and that it is to provide a wide range of fiscal and budget information and analyses. CBO does not make recommendations on policy matters but provides Congress with options and alternatives for its consideration.

Note: This appendix is reprinted from [16], pp. 1–5, 7–9.

The act spells out some general and specific responsibilities of CBO (listed in Attachment A) that fall into the following general categories:

Economic Forecasting and Fiscal Policy Analysis

The federal budget both affects and is affected by the national economy. The Congress, therefore, considers the federal budget in the context of the current and projected state of the national economy. CBO provides periodic forecasts and analyses of economic trends and alternative fiscal policies.

Scorekeeping

Under the new budget process, each spring the Congress adopts a concurrent resolution setting expenditure and revenue targets for the fiscal year beginning October 1st. In September the Congress reviews the detailed spending and taxing decisions it has made during the summer, and then adopts a second concurrent resolution, affirming or changing the totals in the spring resolution. While the first resolution sets targets, the second establishes actual ceilings for spending and a floor for revenues. CBO keeps score of Congressional action on individual authorization, appropriation and revenue bills against the targets (or ceilings) in the concurrent resolutions.

Cost Estimates and Projections

CBO is required to develop five-year cost estimates for implementing any public bill or resolution reported by Congressional committees. At the start of each fiscal year, CBO provides five-year projections on the costs of continuing current federal spending and taxation policies.

An Annual Report on the Budget

By April 1 of each year, CBO is responsible for furnishing the House and Senate Budget Committees a fiscal policy report which includes a discussion of alternative spending and revenue levels, levels of tax expenditures under existing law, and alternative allocations among major programs and functional categories, all in the light of major national needs and their effects on balanced growth and development of the United States.

Additional Studies

CBO undertakes specific studies requested by committees and subcommittees of the Congress on budget-related issues.

Organization and Staffing

CBO's authorized staffing level is established by the Congress. The professional staff represents a mix of analytical expertise and practical budget experience.

As the attached organization chart indicates, CBO is organized to accomplish the tasks specified in the law. Brief descriptions of each staff and its responsibilities are given below.

Office of the Director and Deputy Director

The Director bears full responsibility for seeing that all the duties of the organization specified in the Congressional Budget Act are performed effectively and in a manner most useful to the Congress. The Deputy Director assists the Director in the overall management of the organization and acts in the absence of the Director. Both positions are specified by the statute.

Director:

Alice M. Rivlin is an economist. She was formerly a Senior Fellow at the Brookings Institution and an Assistant Secretary of the Department of Health, Education, and Welfare.

Deputy Director:

Robert A. Levine, also an economist, is a former President of the New York City Rand Institute and Assistant Director of the Office of Economic Opportunity for Research, Plans, Programs, and Evaluation.

Office of the General Counsel

The General Counsel performs legal work for CBO, interpreting applicable statutes, analyzing proposed legislation, overseeing procurement actions, etc. The General Counsel also serves as a senior adviser on policy issues.

Assistant Director-General Counsel:

Alfred B. Fitt is an attorney; former Legal Advisor to the Governor of Michigan; General Counsel of the Army; Assistant Secretary of Defense (Manpower); and most recently, the Special Adviser to the President, Yale University.

Office of Intergovernmental Relations

The Office of Intergovernmental Relations (OIGR) serves as the communications center and the point of contact with the Congress, external organizations, and the news media.

One of the most important functions of the office is to provide Members of the Congress with timely and substantive responses to inquiries concerning general budget issues and CBO reports and studies.

OIGR coordinates requests from state and local governments, national organizations, educational institutions and interest groups. In that regard, OIGR is establishing a dialogue with state and local government officials to assist them in understanding the Congressional budget process and receiving federal budget data.

OIGR also provides the editorial support to assist the other divisions of CBO with preparation of reports and other manuscripts for publication.

Director, Office of Intergovernmental Relations:

Stanley L. Greigg is a former Member of Congress from Iowa; Mayor of Sioux City, Iowa; and Dean, Morningside College.

Budget Analysis Division

The Budget Analysis Division is the focal point for providing CBO's routine support of the budget process. The Division's primary responsibility is ensuring that accurate and comprehensive budget information is available to the Congress on a timely basis.

The Division has two subunits. The larger of these two units is responsible for:

Budget scorekeeping—The provision of periodic reports comparing Congressional actions affecting the budget with the limits set in the concurrent resolution, the President's budget, and other indices of government activity.

Cost analysis of pending public legislation—The development of cost estimates for public bills and resolutions reported by committees in the House of Representatives and the Senate.

Five-year projections—Preparation of five-year projections of Congressional budget action.

The other subunit of the Budget Analysis Division is concerned with the budget process, budget concepts, and an automated budget information system. It assumes CBO's statutory responsibilities in the areas of budget terminology, studying the feasibility of advance appropriations and support to the House and Senate Budget Committees in their continuing studies of additional budget reform proposals. In addition, this unit is responsible for development of an automated system which meets the budget information needs of the Congress and for undertaking the legislative classification work relating the budget to authorizing statutes.

Assistant Director for Budget Analysis:

James L. Blum, economist and budget analyst, is a former Deputy Director of the Council on Wage and Price Stability, Acting Deputy Assistant Secretary of Labor for Planning and Evaluation, and Assistant Division Chief of the Office of Management and Budget for education and labor programs.

Fiscal Analysis Division

The Fiscal Analysis Division provides forecasts of economic trends and analyses of alternative economic policies. These analyses focus on production, inflation, employment, and the impact of the federal budget on them.

In developing these reports and analyses, the staff draws on at least four kinds of information:

- Current information about the economy,
- Current information about fiscal and monetary actions,
- Forecasts from econometric models and other sources, and
- Policy "multipliers" modifying these forecasts on the basis of alternative economic policies.

Assistant Director for Fiscal Analysis:

Frank de Leeuw is an economist. He was formerly Chief of the Special Studies section at the Federal Reserve Board and Senior Fellow at the Urban Institute.

Tax Analysis Division

The Tax Analysis Division is responsible for revenue estimation, analysis of tax expenditures, and related studies and evaluations. The Division consists of two subunits. The receipt and distribution unit prepares the revenue and receipts estimates required in the CBO annual report and the five-year projection reports.

The tax expenditure unit evaluates and analyzes existing and proposed tax expenditures. Both units work closely with the House Ways and Means Committee, the Senate Finance Committee, the task forces of the Budget Committees, the Joint Committee on Internal Revenue Taxation, other Committees interested in tax expenditure programs, and the Treasury Department.

Assistant Director for Tax Analysis:

Charles Davenport, an attorney, formerly served on the legal staff of the Assistant Secretary of the Treasury for Tax Policy; taught at the University of California; and recently served as Project Director for the Internal Revenue Service Project, Administrative Conference of the United States.

Division of Natural Resources and Commerce

The Natural Resources and Commerce Division prepares analyses of program and budget issues in the areas of energy, environment, natural resources, science, agriculture and rural development, commerce, transportation, and communications.

Assistant Director, Natural Resources and Commerce:

Douglas M. Costle, an attorney, is a former Connecticut Commissioner of Environmental Protection and Senior Staff Associate of the President's Advisory Council on Executive Organization.

Human Resources and Community Development Division

The Human Resources and Community Development Division provides analyses of program and budget issues in the areas of income assistance, education, employment, health, veterans' affairs, and community development and housing.

Assistant Director for Human Resources and Community Development:

C. William Fischer, budget and program analyst, is a former Assistant Chief, International Division; Deputy Assistant Director for Legislative Reference; and Deputy Associate Director for Human Resources, Office of Management and Budget.

National Security and International Affairs Division

The National Security and International Affairs Division prepares studies and analyses of budget matters relating to the defense establishment and international economic programs.

The Division consists of two subunits, the first of which concerns itself with national defense budget issues.

The second group examines the impact on the economy and on the federal budget of foreign programs, such as commodity agreements, foreign aid, tariff and subsidy programs, and international monetary agreements.

Assistant Director for National Security and International Affairs:

John E. Koehler is a former senior economist with the Rand Corporation where he worked on National Security Council information systems, the impact on force planning of limited nuclear option capabilities, and economic assistance programs.

Management Programs Division

The Management Programs Division fulfills a dual role in CBO. First, the Division provides internal administrative and management support services for all other components of CBO. These activities include personnel management, financial services, library services for the professional staff, contracting, computer support, and office services. The Division also prepares the CBO annual budget, and establishes and manages an internal budget control system.

The Management Programs Division exercises its other major responsibility as one of the program analysis divisions. It provides information and analyses of general government programs—those managed by the Civil Service Commission, General Services Administration, Postal Service, Treasury Department, and other similar agencies, and conducts studies of the budget issues involved in government-wide organization, manpower utilization, executive branch reorganizations, regulatory program management, and other broad management areas.

Assistant Director for Management Programs:

Howard M. Messner, public administrator and management analyst, is a former Deputy Assistant Administrator for Administration, U.S. Environmental Protection Agency, and Senior Management Analyst, Office of Management and Budget.

ATTACHMENT A

STATUTORY TASKS ASSIGNED TO CBO

Listed in the order in which they appear in the Congressional Budget Act of 1974 (PL 93-344). Citations are to the US Code and, in parentheses, to section numbers of PL 93-344.

(1) In general, provide information to the two Budget Committees on all matters within their jurisdictions, *2 USC 602(a), (202(a))*.

(2) On request, provide information to the appropriating and taxing committees, *2 USC 602(b), (202(b))*.

(3) On request of any other committee, provide information compiled under 1) and 2) plus "to the extent practicable," additional information which may be requested, *2 USC 602(c)(1), (202(c)(1))*.

(4) On request of a Member, provide information compiled under 1) and 2) plus "to the extent available," additional information which may be requested, *2 USC 602(c)(2), (202(c)(2))*.

(5) Perform the duties and functions formerly performed by the Joint Committee on Reduction of Federal Expenditures, *2 USC 602(e), (202(e)), see also 31 USC 571*.

(6) Annually on or before April 1, furnish to the Budget Committees a report on fiscal policy for the next fiscal year, to include a discussion of alternative levels of revenues, budget authority, outlays and tax expenditures, plus alternative allocations among major programs and functional categories, all in the light of major national needs and the effect on "balanced growth and development of the United States," *2 USC 602(f)(1), (202(f)(1))*.

(7) From time to time, furnish the Budget Committees such further reports as "may be necessary or appropriate," *2 USC 602(f)(2), (202(f)(2))*.

(8) Develop and maintain filing, coding and indexing systems for all information obtained by CBO from the Executive Branch or from other agencies of the Congress, *2 USC 603(b), (203(b))*.

(9) With respect to each committee bill providing new budget authority, furnish to the reporting committee for its consideration: (a) a comparison of the bill to the most recent concurrent resolution on the budget, (b) a 5-year projection of outlays associated with the bill, and (c) the amount of new budget authority and resulting outlays provided by the bill for State and local governments, *31 USC 1329(a)(1), (308(a)(1))*.

(10) With respect to each committee bill providing new or increased tax expenditures, furnish to the reporting committee for its consideration: (a) a report on how the bill will affect the levels of tax expenditures most recently detailed in a concurrent resolution on the budget, and (b) a 5-year projection of the tax expenditures resulting from the bill, *31 USC 1329(a)(2), (308(a)(2))*.

(11) Periodically, issue a scorekeeping report on the results of Congressional actions compared to the most recently adopted concurrent resolution on the budget, plus status reports on all bills providing new budget authority or changing revenues or the public debt limit, plus up-to-date estimates of revenues and the public debt, *31 USC 1329(b), (308(b))*.

(12) Annually, "as soon as practicable after the beginning of each fiscal year," issue a 5-year projection of budget authority and outlays, revenues and tax expenditures, plus the projected surplus or deficit, year by year, *31 USC 1329(c), (308(c))*.

(13) Prepare "to the extent practicable," a 5-year cost estimate for carrying out any public bill or resolution reported by any committee (except the two appropriating committees), *31 USC 1353, (403)*.

(14) Jointly study with OMB, but separately report, on the feasibility and advisability of year-ahead budgeting and appropriating, the report to be made by February 24, 1977, *31 USC 1020 note, (502(c))*.

(15) Cooperate with the Comptroller General in the development of standard fiscal terminology, *31 USC 1152(a)(1), (801(a)), (Sec 202(a)(1) of the Legislative Reorganization Act of 1970)*.

(16) Cooperate with the Comptroller General in developing an inventory of fiscal information sources, providing assistance to Congress in obtaining information from those sources and furnishing, on request, assistance in appraising and analyzing information so obtained, *31 USC 1153(b), (801(a)), (Sec 203(b) of the Legislative Reorganization Act of 1970)*.

(17) With the Comptroller General, establish a central file or files "of the data and information required to carry out the purposes of this title," *31 USC 1153(c), (801(a)), (Sec 203(c) of the Legislative Reorganization Act of 1970)*.

(18) Cooperate with OMB in providing useful federal fiscal information to State and local governments, *31 USC 1153(d), (801(a)), (Sec 203(d) of the Legislative Reorganization Act of 1970)*.

CONGRESSIONAL BUDGET OFFICE

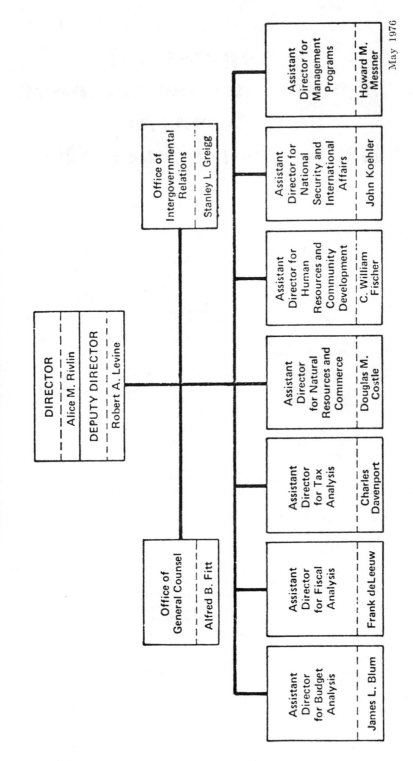

May 1976

DIRECTOR
Alice M. Rivlin

DEPUTY DIRECTOR
Robert A. Levine

Office of General Counsel
Alfred B. Fitt

Office of Intergovernmental Relations
Stanley L. Greigg

Assistant Director for Budget Analysis
James L. Blum

Assistant Director for Fiscal Analysis
Frank deLeeuw

Assistant Director for Tax Analysis
Charles Davenport

Assistant Director for Natural Resources and Commerce
Douglas M. Costle

Assistant Director for Human Resources and Community Development
C. William Fischer

Assistant Director for National Security and International Affairs
John Koehler

Assistant Director for Management Programs
Howard M. Messner

Appendix 3
Agenda for Government
Reform Act
(White House Fact Sheet)

The President is sending to Congress today the proposed "Agenda for
Government Reform Act" which would establish a timetable for the Pres-
ident and Congress to make comprehensive and fundamental changes in
Government regulatory activities which affect the American economy.
The legislation would:

-- Require consideration of the views of the American people who
   want solutions to our regulatory problems.

-- Require an analysis of the costs and benefits of Government
   regulatory activities.

-- Commit the President to develop and submit major reform
   proposals to Congress no later than the end of January in
   each of the next four years.

-- Encourage more effective Congressional oversight of the
   operations of Government and commit Congress to act on
   needed reforms each year.

The purposes of this legislation are to: eliminate excessive regulatory
constraints on the economy; develop better, less costly ways to protect
public health and safety; reduce federal paperwork requirements; eliminate excessive delay; and streamline the costly regulatory bureaucracy.

BACKGROUND

In October of 1974, President Ford launched a major program of regulatory reform. Since that time, significant administrative improvements
have been achieved. A reduction in Government-imposed paperwork requirements has been accomplished. Major regulatory agencies have been
asked to reduce delays, increase reliance on market competition, and
improve consumer access to regulatory decisions.

In addition, legislation has been enacted to repeal fair trade laws,
increase competition in the securities industry, and eliminate outdated railroad regulation. The President has also submitted legislative proposals to improve regulation of our airlines, motor carriers,
and financial institutions.

Note: This appendix is from [105], pp. 1-6.

The President will continue to stress the need for administrative improvements and to request Congressional action on pending reform proposals. The legislation he is submitting today builds upon and com-
plements his earlier efforts and charts a specific course for the
second phase of regulatory reform over the next four years.

PRINCIPAL OBJECTIVES OF THE LEGISLATION

1. To encourage broad scale public participation in seeking practical
    solutions to complex regulatory problems. A fundamental re-exami-
    nation of regulatory practices will foster increased public under-
    standing of how the system works and how it affects individual
    Americans. And it will provide an opportunity for individuals in
    all walks of life to voice their concerns and register their ideas
    and suggestions for realistic reform.

2. To focus attention on the cumulative effect Government actions have
    on individual sectors of the economy. The results of this legisla-
    tion would be to provide a better understanding of both the objec-
    tives and effects of regulatory actions -- thereby laying the foun-
    dation for lasting, commonsense solutions to our regulatory prob-
    lems. Also, this legislation would permit the American people to
    make more informed trade-offs between desirable regulatory goals
    such as environmental protection and energy conservation.

3. To minimize the costs which Government programs impose on tax-
    payers and the general economy. Paperwork requirements, unneces-
    sary program duplication, costly delay and burdensome compliance
    requirements multiply the cost of Government intervention -- often
    without providing commensurate benefits in return. The legislation
    would help identify the cumulative costs of Government activities
    which must be borne by all Americans.

4. To require the President and Congress to act on concrete reforms
    according to a specific schedule. This legislation would commit
    both the President and Congress to cooperate in the development and
    implementation of needed reforms according to a systematic agreed-
    upon schedule. Close cooperation between Congress and the Execu-
    tive will encourage the public to work in concert with their Gov-
    ernment to build a more rational regulatory system.

NEED FOR OVERALL REFORM

In general, each time a new national problem is identified, a new Federal program or agency is established to address it. Often, because
solutions must be found quickly, new policies or organizations are
created without sufficient attention to their indirect economic effects,
or to the overlap and duplication which may result.

Once established, these programs and agencies strongly resist change.
Even where regulations are having a negative effect or are competing
with other national objectives, the "status quo" tends to prevail.
Generally, regulatory problems are caused not by a single regulation
but by the cumulative effect of many Government regulations. Business,
labor, and consumers find it difficult to become actively involved in
changing a system that is confusing, overlapping, and complex.

The American economy is divided into many sectors. Government regulatory activities affect these sectors in different ways and to varying
degrees. For example, environmental regulations have a greater impact
on the transportation industry than they do on the financial community
and small businesses often feel the effects of Government proportion-
ately more than large corporations do. Each industry faces its own
unique regulatory problems. And presently, the cumulative effects of
Government regulatory activities on any given industrial sector are
unknown.

TIMETABLE FOR REFORM

The Agenda for Government Reform Act would establish a four-year program of fundamental reform. Each year, the President would assess the
cumulative effects of Government regulatory activities on major economic
sectors and develop legislative proposals for change along the following agency lines (example only):

Year	Sectors of the Economy	Agencies Considered for Legislative/ Administrative Action
1977	Transportation & Agriculture - transportation industry including water carriers and pipelines - crop and livestock production - forestry - fishing	National Highway Traffic Safety Administration, DOT Federal Maritime Commission Animal and Plant Health Inspection Service, USDA Agricultural Marketing Service, USDA U.S. Forest Service, USDA Interstate Commerce Commission Civil Aeronautics Board
1978	Mining, Heavy Manufacturing and Public Utilities - pulp and paper industries - chemicals - petroleum refining - rubber/plastics - stone/glass/concrete - automobiles - primary metals - fabricated metal - machinery - electric, gas, sanitary services	Mine Enforcement and Safety Administration, Department of the Interior Environmental Protection Agency Federal Energy Administration Federal Power Commission Nuclear Regulatory Commission
1979	Light Manufacturing and Construction - housing and other construction - general contractors - special trade contractors - food processing	Occupational Safety and Health Administration, Department of Labor Food and Drug Administration, Department of Health, Education, and Welfare Department of Housing and Urban Development

- textiles	Equal Employment Opportunity
- lumber & wood products	Commission
- printing & publishing	Consumer Product Safety Commission

1980   Communication, Finance,   Securities and Exchange Commission
Insurance, Real Estate,   Department of the Treasury
Trade, Services   Federal Trade Commission
- banking, credit &   Federal Communications Commission
   insurance
- real estate
- broadcasting
- wholesale & retail
   trade
- business & personal
   services

ORGANIZATION OF THE REFORM EFFORT

The agenda begins with areas where significant analysis has already been done so that recommendations can be developed quickly.

The White House will coordinate the efforts in each of the four areas. Once the President's proposal is passed:

- Basic research and public participation in developing major issues will begin simultaneously in each of the areas.

- Public hearings will be held in all parts of the country to assure that the President has the best thinking available.

- Each year, the President will submit specific legislative proposals to Congress for action and provide a report to the Congress and the American people on the nature and extent of Government intervention in the economy, including an analysis of the costs and benefits of regulatory activities.

- The President will direct agencies to make administrative improvements where necessary.

Where regulatory activities affect a wide range of industries -- environmental regulations or occupational health and safety standards, for example -- it may be desirable to defer recommendations for any fundamental changes until a number of different sectors have been examined. The agenda identified in this legislation takes this into account and postpones major recommendations on cross-cutting regulations until sufficient data is available. Thus, although analysis of the effects of OSHA regulations on the transportation and agricultural industries will begin in the first year, major recommendations for any fundamental changes in these areas may not be made until after the President has considered their impact on mining, construction, and manufacturing.

Each year, the President is required to submit reform recommendations to Congress by the end of January. These recommendations are then reviewed by the appropriate Congressional committees. If the House and Senate have not acted on reform legislation by November 15, the President's proposals become the pending business on the floor and remain so until acted on by each House.

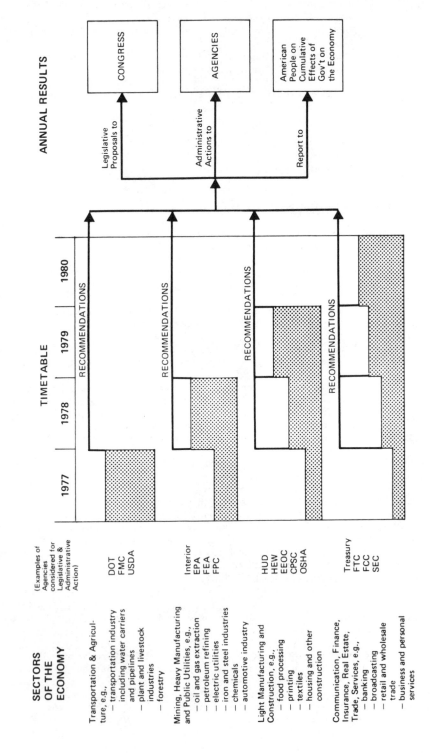

AGENDA FOR GOVERNMENT REFORM

ANNUAL RESULTS

CONGRESS

AGENCIES

American People on Cumulative Effects of Gov't on the Economy

Legislative Proposals to

Administrative Actions to

Report to

TIMETABLE

1977   1978   1979   1980

RECOMMENDATIONS

RECOMMENDATIONS

RECOMMENDATIONS

RECOMMENDATIONS

SECTORS OF THE ECONOMY

(Examples of Agencies considered for Legislative & Administrative Action)

Transportation & Agriculture, e.g.,
– transportation industry including water carriers and pipelines
– plant and livestock industries
– forestry

DOT
FMC
USDA

Mining, Heavy Manufacturing and Public Utilities, e.g.,
– oil and gas extraction
– petroleum refining
– electric utilities
– iron and steel industries
– chemicals
– automotive industry

Interior
EPA
FEA
FPC

Light Manufacturing and Construction, e.g.,
– food processing
– printing
– textiles
– housing and other construction

HUD
HEW
EEOC
CPSC
OSHA

Communication, Finance, Insurance, Real Estate, Trade, Services, e.g.,
– banking
– broadcasting
– retail and wholesale trade
– business and personal services

Treasury
FTC
FCC
SEC

SECTION-BY-SECTION ANALYSIS

Section 2 sets forth the findings of the Congress and the purposes of
the Act. It points out that although the American economic system was
founded on the principles of market competition and minimal Government
intervention in the private sector, the Government's role in the economy has grown over the years. In many cases, its regulatory responsibilities have become confusing, overlapping and contradictory. The
direct and indirect costs and benefits of regulatory activities are
not clear.

Accordingly, the purpose of the legislation is to achieve positive and
lasting reform of Federal regulatory activities with increased public
participation, more effective Congressional oversight and systematic
Presidential action.

The bill would require the President to develop legislative reforms
every year for the next four years. It would require Congress to act
on these reforms without delay.

Section 3 defines the specific terms used in the legislation including
agency and Federal regulatory activity.

Section 4 specifies the sequence in which reform proposals are to be
developed. The timetable is described in detail above in this fact
sheet. This section requires that each Presidential proposal include
among other things an identification of the original purposes of the
regulatory activity under review, an assessment of the effectiveness
of the regulation, and specific recommendations for reform, elimination, or continuation of the particular regulatory activity.

Section 5 explains Congressional responsibilities under the Act. It
specifies that reform proposals be referred to appropriate committees
in the House and Senate and would require Congress to act on reform
legislation by November 15th of each year. If the two Houses of Congress should fail to do so, the President's reform proposals would
become the pending business of the House and Senate and remain so
until acted on by each House.

Appendix 4
Zero-Base Budget Procedures in Georgia: Fiscal Year 1977 Budget Development

F. Y. 1977 ZERO-BASE BUDGET

Procedures and Instructions

TABLE OF CONTENTS

i

Note: This appendix is from [83], pp. 88–120.

ZERO·BASE BUDGET
Procedures & Instructions

EXECUTIVE DEPARTMENT	
OFFICE OF PLANNING AND BUDGET – Budget Division	
SECTION	
F. Y. 1977 ZERO-BASE BUDGET INFORMATION	
SUBJECT	
A. BUDGET ACT PROVISIONS, B. CONCEPT AND PURPOSE, C. SIGNIFICANT MODIFICATIONS, D. SUBMISSION DATA	

A.   Budget Act Provisions

Code Section 40-4 of Georgia Laws (Budget Act) provides for estimates of financial needs to be submitted to the Office of Planning and Budget (OPB) each year by the Head of each Budget Unit by September 1.

The Budget Division of OPB has developed the Budget Procedures for the estimation of F. Y. 1977 financial requirements by State Departments of Georgia State Government.

A lot of work has gone into the revision of forms and procedures for the F. Y. 1977 Zero-Base process. The Governor feels that the changes will be useful to the Department as well as to OPB. No standard set of forms can be devised which will meet everyone's needs. OPB is prepared to review any form changes necessary.

B.   Concept and Purpose

The State of Georgia finds its budgeting responsibilities and needs best met by the budgetary process known as "Zero-Base Budgeting."

The concept of Zero-Base Budgeting is that all the financial requirements for a budget unit are justified and analyzed by decision makers and not just the increased or additional requirements. Managers are to assess benefits from ongoing operations, as well as needs for additional funds. The process identifies, to all levels of management, the cost, benefits and suggested operational improvements associated to reach their objectives. The objectives, as established by management, are communicated to the functional managers before the preparation of the budget begins.

The Zero-Base Budget process begins by identifying functions in the organization where cost data are maintained. The budget request for each function is developed in a series of "Decision Packages." Each Decision Package represents the fund requirement to support particular levels of the operations. The first package of a series of packages is developed at a Minimum Level of operations for the function. Additional levels of effort are Base Level, Workload, and New or Improved. See instructions for definitions of these levels.

The ranking of Decision Packages is completed by each Activity Manager and submitted to higher management. The final ranking is completed at the Department level. The ranking process offers each manager the opportunity to express service priorities at different funding levels. Refinements and modifications to the system are made from time to time, but the basic concept and purpose of Zero-Base remains intact.

C.   Significant Modifications

Significant modifications have been made to the Zero-Base Budget Preparation System. The more significant changes are as follows:

- 1.   Previously, one form was designed for use as a Decision Package. The levels of effort for each function were determined by each agency and the same basic form was used for each level of effort. The Zero-Base System as modified for this year defines each level of effort through the design of four (4) kinds of Decision Packages - Minimum Level Decision Package, Base Level Decision Package, Workload Decision Package, and New or Improved Decision Package. Definitions of each are included in the instructions for the use of the forms.

- 2.   Functions, organizational cost units within an Activity, were previously defined exclusively by each agency. This year, OPB will request that each agency submit a list of functions at which a series of decision packages will be developed. The list will be reviewed and approved by OPB in order that planning and budget analysis can begin at an earlier date. Many budget functions in State Government have been defined as units much too large or much too small in the past. Our cooperative efforts in defining function units will be beneficial to both OPB and the Departments in insuring reasonable budget levels.

DATE Rev. 6/75	PAGE 1	OPB · Budget · General

ZERO·BASE BUDGET Procedures & Instructions

EXECUTIVE DEPARTMENT	
OFFICE OF PLANNING AND BUDGET — Budget Division	
SECTION	
F. Y. 1977 ZERO-BASE BUDGET INFORMATION	
SUBJECT	
C. SIGNIFICANT MODIFICATIONS, D. SUBMISSION DATA (Continued)	

— 3. Reporting of performance measures for functional units have been informal and inadequate in previous years. This year, OPB will request that each agency submit a list of Effectiveness, Workload, and Efficiency Measures for each function prior to preparation of the budget. Budget Analysts and Planners will work with each agency to formalize the performance measures during the months of July and August. This effort will be of vital importance to you in the Fall budget hearings with the Governor and during the Legislative Session.

— 4. The Decision Package previously allowed only total amounts for each sub-object and object of expenditure. This year, detailed schedules of Rents, Motor Vehicle Equipment Purchases, Equipment Purchases, Per Diem and Fees, Computer Charges, Other Contractual Expense, and Capital Outlay are required at each level of effort requested for a function except for the Minimum Level Package. A schedule of Personal Services and a Detail of Fund Sources are required at the Activity Level as a summary of Base Level functional packages while a separate Personal Services Schedule and Detail of Fund Sources are required as attachments to Workload and New or Improved Packages where positions are requested. The instructions and sample forms explain and display the use of the schedules.

D.   Submission Data

The new forms to be used in the F. Y. 1977 Budget Preparation are listed as follows:

OPB-Budget-30	—	Decision Package – Minimum Level
OPB-Budget-31	—	Decision Package – Base Level
OPB-Budget-32	—	Decision Package – Workload
OPB-Budget-33	—	Decision Package – New or Improved
OPB-Budget-40	—	Schedule of Rents
OPB-Budget-41	—	Schedule of Motor Vehicle Equipment Purchases
OPB-Budget-42	—	Schedule of Equipment Purchases
OPB-Budget-43	··	Schedule of Per Diem and Fees
OPB-Budget-44	··	Schedule of Computer Charges
OPB-Budget-45	—	Schedule of Other Contractual Expense
OPB-Budget-46	··	Capital Outlay Detail
OPB-Budget-47	··	Personal Services Schedule
OPB-Budget-48	—	Detail of Fund Sources
OPB-Budget-50	—	Decision Package Ranking
OPB-Planning-51	—	Activity Information Summary
OPB-Budget-52	—	Activity Financial Summary
OPB-Budget-60	—	Budget Unit or Department Summary

Submission procedures for the F. Y. 1977 Budget are as follows:

— 1. Submit the F. Y. 1977 Budget Request to OPB on or before September 1, 1975, as required by law.

— 2. Submit (4) four copies of the Budget in a looseleaf notebook and tab each Activity.

— 3. Arrange the forms as shown in the assembly diagram (see next page) and place the Department Summary at the front of the notebook. The Department Head is required to sign the summary.

DATE Rev. 6/75	PAGE 2	OPB - Budget - General

ZERO-BASE BUDGET
Procedures & Instructions

EXECUTIVE DEPARTMENT

OFFICE OF PLANNING AND BUDGET — Budget Division

SECTION

ZERO-BASE ASSEMBLY FORMAT

SUBJECT

ASSEMBLY OF FORMS FOR SUBMISSION TO OPB

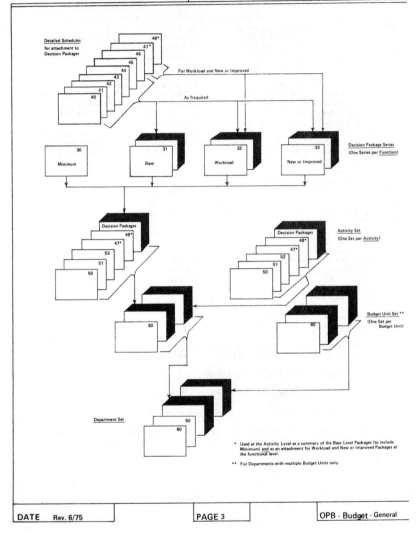

* Used at the Activity Level as a summary of the Base Level Packages (to include Minimum) and as an attachment for Workload and New or Improved Packages at the functional level.

** For Departments with multiple Budget Units only.

DATE   Rev. 6/75

PAGE 3

OPB · Budget · General

DECISION PACKAGE — MINIMUM LEVEL

OPB-BUDGET-30

OPB- Budget -30
(Rev. 6-75)

F. Y. 1977

ZERO-BASE BUDGET REQUEST
DECISION PACKAGE — MINIMUM LEVEL

Human Resources
Department

Community Injury Control
Activity

Emergency Medical Health
Function

	Positions This Package 2	Function F.Y.76	This Pkg. F.Y. 77	Cum%
Describe the Function in terms of its objective County and City Medical Centers are charged to meet emergency situations such as sudden illness, injury, natural or man-made disasters, and poison cases. The centers do not coordinate their efforts across county and city lines nor do they have exposure to the latest techniques and equipment in the emergency medical field. Some centers are highly successful due to a special innovation that other centers do not share.	A. TOTAL PERSONAL SERVICES	25,624	17,686	69
	1. Motor Vehicle Expenses and Repairs	900	600	
	2. Supplies and Materials	1,900	1,200	
	3. Repairs and Maintenance	500	300	
	4. Communications	400	280	
	5. Power, Water, Natural Gas	250	200	
Describe the Function in terms of service provided in F. Y. 1976 Utilize a central staff to conduct medical emergency courses around the State to monitor the operations of the Injury Control Program. The courses will provide instruction to the centers on the latest medical emergency techniques and methods. The Base Level provides service for the 100 most populated counties by conducting one medical emergency course at each.	6. Rents	273	273	
	7. Insurance and Bonding			
	8. Workmen's Comp. and Indemnities			
	9. Direct Benefits			
	10. Tuition and Scholarships			
	11. Grants to Counties or Cities			
Explain the Minimum Level of Service this Package provides Two positions and expenses to coordinate, develop, and conduct a medical emergency course in the 75 largest medical centers in the State. Two persons are required to conduct a course in each center and two persons can cover 75 medical centers annually.	12. Assessments by Merit System	132	88	
	13. Other Operating Expenses	450	206	
	14. Extraordinary Expenses			
	B.REG. OPERATING EXPENSES(Add 1-14)	4,805	3,147	65
	C. TRAVEL	800	550	69
	D. MOTOR VEHICLE EQUIP. PURCH.	4,680		
Explain the Impact of terminating the Service now provided that this Minimum Level Excludes	E. PUBLICATIONS AND PRINTING	1,350	1,000	74
One position and related expenses are deleted in the minimum level package. Approximately 25 medical centers will not have a medical emergency course in F.Y. 1977 that did have one in F.Y. 1976. Each excluded center would have to develop its own medical emergency plan. Some excluded centers would not choose to do so and an emergency situation in the area served by the center would not be met with the same efficiency as before.	F. EQUIPMENT PURCHASES	750		
	G. PER DIEM AND FEES	2,000	1,500	75
	H. COMPUTER CHARGES	2,900	2,000	69
	I. OTHER CONTRACTUAL EXPENSE	1,600	550	34
	J. AUTHORITY LEASE RENTALS			

Quantitative Measures (Effectiveness, Workload, Efficiency)	F. Y. 1976 Function	F. Y. 1977 Minimum Level				
			K. GENERAL OBLIGATION BONDS			
			L. CAPITAL OUTLAY			
Different Medical Centers Aided	100	75	M. LIST OTHER OBJECTS:			
Medical Emergency Courses conducted	100	75				
Cost Per Course/Total funds	$445	$352				
Cost Per Course/State funds	$245	$165	TOTAL EXPENDITURES (Add A-M)	44,509	26,433	59
			FEDERAL FUNDS	16,000	10,000	63
			OTHER FUNDS	4,000	4,000	100
			STATE GENERAL FUNDS	24,509	12,433	51

Package Name: Emergency Medical Health   Package 1 of 4

Prepared By: John Smith   Activity Rank 4

4

ZERO·BASE BUDGET Procedures & Instructions

EXECUTIVE DEPARTMENT	
OFFICE OF PLANNING AND BUDGET — Budget Division	
SECTION	
DECISION PACKAGE PREPARATION – MINIMUM LEVEL	
SUBJECT	
INSTRUCTIONS FOR FORM OPB-BUDGET- 30	

Form Purpose

A Decision Package Series identifies a function below the Activity Level where costs are recorded. You should generate a package or series of packages at the functional level approved by O. P. B. Each function you want to continue should have one or more Decision Packages, depending on how many levels of funding are requested for the function. The form OPB-Budget-30 is a Minimum Level Decision Package. For every function you will develop at least one minimum level below the F. Y. 1976 Budget for that function. The Minimum Level is a level of effort, expressed in terms of service and cost, below which it is not realistic or feasible to operate the function at all. For example, the Minimum Level in the sample shows two positions for conducting courses since one person could not efficiently conduct the particular coursework involved.

1.   Describe the Function in Terms of its Objective

   — Explain the function by describing the need for the existence of the function in terms of a problem area or target group the function serves. The decision will be whether to fund the minimum level or not to fund the function at all.

2.   Describe the Function in Terms of Service Provided in F. Y. 1976

   — Outline and explain the service provided by the function during F. Y. 1976. The service outlined should be explained in terms of solving the problem outlined in the objectives box. All services provided by the function in F. Y. 1976 should be outlined.

3.   Explain the Minimum Level of Service This Package Provides

   — The Minimum Level Package represents a level of service below the level of service provided in F. Y. 1976 by the function. Explain the service provided by this level of effort in terms of which services can be provided at the minimum level.

4.   Explain the Impact of Terminating the Service Now Provided That This Minimum Level Excludes

   — Outline and explain the services provided in F. Y. 1976 that the Minimum Level does not provide for. Item 3 and 4 together should total to Item 2 in terms of service provided.

Quantitative Measures (Quantitative Measures are required on the Decision Packages)

— Effectiveness data measures how well the services provided solve the problem and meet the objectives of the function both for F. Y. 1976 and for the Minimum Level for F. Y. 1977.
— Workload data measures the effort required to deliver the services both for F. Y. 1976 and for the Minimum Level for F. Y. 1977.
— Efficiency data measures the cost per unit of workload both for F. Y. 1976 and for the Minimum Level for F. Y. 1977.

Financial Information

— Enter amounts budgeted for the function in F. Y. 1976
— Enter amounts requested for the Minimum Level under "This Pkg. F. Y. 1977".
— The Cum % is calculated by dividing the "This Pkg. F. Y. 1977" amount by the "Function F. Y. 1976" amount.   Do not show Cum % for sub-classes of expenditure.

NOTE: Detailed forms 40-48 are not required on the Minimum Level Package.

DATE Rev. 6/75	PAGE 5	OPB - Budget - 30

DECISION PACKAGE – BASE LEVEL

OPB-BUDGET-31

		OPB- Budget-31
F. Y. 1977	ZERO-BASE BUDGET REQUEST	(Rev. 6-75)
	DECISION PACKAGE – BASE LEVEL	
Human Resources	Community Injury Control	Emergency Medical Health
Department	Activity	Function

Describe the Function in terms of its objective County and City Medical Centers are		Positions This Package____1____	**	Function F.Y.76	This Pkg. F.Y. 77	Cum%
charged to meet emergency situations such as sudden illness, injury, natural or		A. TOTAL PERSONAL SERVICES		25,624	9,276	105
man-made disasters, and poison cases. The centers do not coordinate their efforts		1. Motor Vehicle Expenses and Repairs		900	326	
across county and city lines nor do they have exposure to the latest techniques and		2. Supplies and Materials		1,900	700	
equipment in the emergency medical field. Some centers are highly successful due		3. Repairs and Maintenance		500	200	
to a special innovation that other centers do not share.		4. Communications		400	176	
		5. Power, Water, Natural Gas		250	98	
Describe the Function in terms of service provided in F. Y. 1976 (Base Level)		6. Rents	*	273	77	
Utilize a central staff to conduct medical emergency courses around the State to		7. Insurance and Bonding				
monitor the operations of the Injury Control Program. The courses will provide		8. Workmen's Comp. and Indemnities				
instruction to the centers on the latest medical emergency techniques and methods.		9. Direct Benefits				
The Base Level provides service for the 100 most populated counties by conducting		10. Tuition and Scholarships				
one medical emergency course at each.		11. Grants to Counties or Cities				
		12. Assessments by Merit System		132	44	
Explain the Cost Increase or Decrease in the Base Level over F. Y. 1976		13. Other Operating Expenses		450	244	
Personal Services – Within-grade increases and annualization of a part-year position.		14. Extraordinary Expenses				
Regular Operating Expenses – Primarily due to rental contract increase for office		B.REG. OPERATING EXPENSES(Add 1-14)		4,805	1,865	104
space.		C. TRAVEL		800	350	112
Travel – Increase in rate from 10 cents to 12 cents per mile.		D. MOTOR VEHICLE EQUIP. PURCH.	*	4,680	5,112	109
M. V. Equipment Purchases – Replacement vehicle.		E. PUBLICATIONS AND PRINTING		1,350	500	111
Equipment Purchases – 3 pocket calculators in addition to replacement of office		F. EQUIPMENT PURCHASES	*	750	1,550	206
equipment.		G. PER DIEM AND FEES	*	2,000	750	112
		H. COMPUTER CHARGES	*	2,900	900	100
		I. OTHER CONTRACTUAL EXPENSE	*	1,600	1,050	100
		J. AUTHORITY LEASE RENTALS				

Quantitative Measures (Effectiveness, Workload, Efficiency)	F. Y. 1976 Function	F. Y. 1977 Base Level	K. GENERAL OBLIGATION BONDS			
			L. CAPITAL OUTLAY			
Different Medical Centers Aided	100	100	M. LIST OTHER OBJECTS:			
Medical Emergency Courses conducted	100	100				
Cost Per Course/Total funds	$445	$478				
Cost Per Course/State funds	$245	$278				
			TOTAL EXPENDITURES (Add A - M)		44,509	21,353	107
			FEDERAL FUNDS **		16,000	6,000	100
			OTHER FUNDS **		4,000		100
			STATE GENERAL FUNDS		24,509	15,353	113

Package Name: Emergency Medical Health	Package 2 of 4	* Attach detailed schedule for F. Y. 1977 Base Level (Including Minimum Level) funds requested.
Prepared By: John Smith	Activity Rank 7	** Detailed schedule for the Base Level is to be developed at the Activity Level.

6

ZERO·BASE BUDGET Procedures & Instructions	EXECUTIVE DEPARTMENT
	OFFICE OF PLANNING AND BUDGET – Budget Division
	SECTION
	DECISION PACKAGE PREPARATION – BASE LEVEL
	SUBJECT
	INSTRUCTIONS FOR FORM OPB-BUDGET-31

Form Purpose

The Base Level Decision Package is the next package developed after the Minimum Level Decision Package for a function below the Activity. The Base Level is a level of effort, expressed in terms of service and cost, that represents a <u>continuance of services or a reduction of services provided in F. Y. 1976 and no more.</u> Funds for additional service needs should be requested only on a Workload Decision Package or a New or Improved Decision Package. The Base Level Package costs will vary by function. Non-recurring expenditures should be excluded from cost as well as other funds budgeted in F. Y. 1976 but not needed in F. Y. 1977 to deliver the same level of <u>service.</u> Include increased costs for F. Y. 1977 (to deliver the same level of service delivered in F. Y. 1976) such as within-grade increases, postage increases, etc. The Base Level Package, then, will express only cost increases and decreases associated with the same level of services provided for in F. Y. 1976. Decreased service and corresponding decreased cost can be outlined in this package but not increased services.

1.   Describe the Function in Terms of Its Objective

  – Repeat information displayed on the Minimum Level Package.

2.   Describe the Function in Terms of Service Provided in F. Y. 1976

  – Repeat information displayed on the Minimum Level Package.

3.   Explain the Cost Increase or Decrease in the Base Level Over F. Y. 1976

  – Assuming the same level of service (same or less, but not more) as provided in F.Y. 1976, outline the financial reasons why this package added to the Minimum Level Package costs less or more than was budgeted for the function in F. Y. 1976. Increases or decreases for the various object classes should be explained. Attach additional pages if more space is needed.

Quantitative Measures (Quantitative Measures are Required on the Decision Packages)

– Effectiveness data measures how well the services provided solve the problem and meet the objectives of the function both for F. Y. 1976 and for the Base Level for F. Y. 1977.
– Workload data measures the effort required to deliver the services both for F. Y. 1976 and the Base Level for F. Y. 1977.
– Efficiency data measures the cost per unit of workload both for F. Y. 1976 and for the Base Level for F. Y. 1977.

Financial Information

– Enter amounts budgeted for the function in F. Y. 1976.
– In the column headed "This Pkg. F. Y. 1977" enter incremental amounts requested above the Minimum Level and <u>not</u> the total requested for the Base Level.
– The Cum % is calculated by dividing "This Pkg. F. Y. 1977" amounts from both the Minimum Level and the Base Level by "Function F. Y. 1976" amounts. Do not show Cum % for sub-classes of expenditures.

NOTE: Detailed form 47 and 48 are not required at the functional Base Level but are required at the Activity Level by summarizing the functional Base Level Packages.
Detailed forms 40-46 are required to be attached to the Base Level Package for amounts requested in F. Y. 1977 where an asterisk appears on the Base Level Decision Package Form.

DATE Rev. 6/75	PAGE 7	OPB · Budget · 31

DECISION PACKAGE — WORKLOAD

OPB-BUDGET-32

F. Y. 1977

OPB-Budget · 32
(Rev. 6-75)

ZERO-BASE BUDGET REQUEST
DECISION PACKAGE — WORKLOAD

Human Resources	Community Injury Control	Emergency Medical Health
Department	Activity	Function

		Positions This Package 2	Function F.Y. 76	This Pkg. F.Y. 77	Cum%
Describe the Function in terms of its objective County and City Medical Centers are charged to meet emergency situations such as sudden illness, injury, natural or man-made disasters, and poison cases. The centers do not coordinate their efforts across county and city lines nor do they have exposure to the latest techniques and equipment in the emergency medical field. Some centers are highly successful due to a special innovation that other centers do not share.		A. TOTAL PERSONAL SERVICES	25,624	15,810	166
		1. Motor Vehicle Expenses and Repairs	900	150	
		2. Supplies and Materials	1,900	600	
		3. Repairs and Maintenance	500	100	
		4. Communications	400	50	
Describe the Function in terms of service provided in F. Y. 1976 Utilize a central staff to conduct medical emergency courses around the State to monitor the operations of the Injury Control Program. The courses will provide instruction to the centers on the latest medical emergency techniques and methods. The Base-Level provides service for the 100 most populated counties by conducting one medical emergency course at each.		5. Power, Water, Natural Gas	250		
		6. Rents	273		
		7. Insurance and Bonding			
		8. Workmen's Comp. and Indemnities			
		9. Direct Benefits			
		10. Tuition and Scholarships			
Explain the Workload Increase in terms of service provided above the Base Level Conduct a medical emergency course in each of the 63 centers not covered in the State. Every center in the State would receive one course annually. This additional workload is demanded by the centers not now being served.		11. Grants to Counties or Cities			
		12. Assessments by Merit System	132	88	
		13. Other Operating Expenses	450		
		14. Extraordinary Expenses			
		B. REG. OPERATING EXPENSES(Add 1-14)	4,805	988	124
		C. TRAVEL	800	300	150
Explain the Workload Cost Over the Base Level Personal Services — Two new positions, including fringes, less one month delayed hiring factor. Related Expenses — To cover 63 additional centers, the new positions will need additional expenses and office space renovations. Computer Charges — Expansion of the system to add 63 centers. Federal funds are available to help cover the additional centers.		D. MOTOR VEHICLE EQUIP. PURCH.	4,680		109
		E. PUBLICATIONS AND PRINTING	1,350	250	129
		F. EQUIPMENT PURCHASES	750	100	220
		G. PER DIEM AND FEES	2,000		112
		H. COMPUTER CHARGES	2,900	300	110
		I. OTHER CONTRACTUAL EXPENSES	1,600	200	112
		J. AUTHORITY LEASE RENTALS			
		K. GENERAL OBLIGATION BONDS			

Quantitative Measures (Effectiveness, Workload, Efficiency)	F. Y. 1976 Function	F. Y. 1977 Base-Level	F. Y. 1977 Cumulative		L. CAPITAL OUTLAY		2,000	
Different Medical Centers Aided	100	100	163		M. LIST OTHER OBJECTS:			
Medical Emergency Courses conduc.	100	100	163					
Cost per Course/Total funds	$445	$478	$415					
Cost per Course/State funds	$245	$278	$250		TOTAL EXPENDITURES (Add A-M)	44,509	19,948	152
					FEDERAL FUNDS	16,000	7,000	144
					OTHER FUNDS	4,000		100
					STATE GENERAL FUNDS	24,509	12,948	166

Package Name: Emergency Medical Health   Package 3 of 4

Prepared By: John Smith   Activity Rank 10

* Attach detailed schedule for F. Y. 1977 Workload funds requested in this package.

8

ZERO·BASE BUDGET Procedures & Instructions

EXECUTIVE DEPARTMENT

OFFICE OF PLANNING AND BUDGET – Budget Division
SECTION

DECISION PACKAGE PREPARATION – WORKLOAD
SUBJECT

INSTRUCTIONS FOR FORM OPB-BUDGET-32

Form Purpose

The Workload Decision Package is developed only where funds are needed to meet increased workload at the functional level. Additional workload must be quantified and explained fully in terms of service and cost. A Workload Package must be documented in terms of additional funds needed above the Base Level. Additional workload which can be met without the need for additional funds should be included in the Base Level Package for the function.

1. **Describe the Function in Terms of Its Objectives**
   - Repeat information displayed on the Minimum Level Package.

2. **Describe the Function in Terms of Service Provided in F. Y. 1976**
   - Repeat information displayed on the Minimum Level Package.

3. **Explain the Workload Increase in Terms of Service Provided above the Base Level**
   - Explain additional workload which requires additional funds not provided for in the Base Level. The additional workload which can be met without the need for additional funds should be explained in the Base Level Package and not in the Workload Package. Workload must be quantified.

4. **Explain the Workload Cost Over the Base Level**
   - Point out the reasons why the additional workload will require more funds. The explanation should be expressed in terms of what the funds will be expended for to accommodate the additional workload above the Base Level.

Quantitative Measures (Quantitative measures are required on the Decision Packages)

- Show Quantitative Measures for "F. Y. 1976 Function." The "F. Y. 1977 Base Level" column will be repeated from the Base Level Package. The "F. Y. 1977 Cumulative" column will include the Minimum, Base, and Workload quantitative measures as a running total.
- Effectiveness data measures how well the services provided solve the problem and meet the objectives of the function.
- Workload data measures the effort required to deliver the services.
- Efficiency data measures the cost per unit of workload.

Financial Information

- Enter amounts budgeted for the function in F. Y. 1976.
- "This Pkg. F. Y. 1977" enter incremental amounts requested above the Base Level and _not_ the total requested through the Workload Package Level.
- The Cum % is calculated by dividing "This Pkg. F. Y. 1977" amounts summed from the Minimum, Base and Workload Packages by "Function F. Y. 1976" amounts. Do not show Cum % for sub-classes of expenditure.

NOTE: Detailed Forms 40-48 are required to be attached to the Workload Package for amounts requested in F. Y. 1977 where an asterisk appears on the Workload Decision Package Form.

DECISION PACKAGE — NEW OR IMPROVED

OPB-BUDGET-33

F. Y. 1977

OPB-Budget - 33
(Rev. 6-75)

ZERO-BASE BUDGET REQUEST
DECISION PACKAGE — NEW OR IMPROVED

Human Resources	Community Injury Control	Emergency Medical Health
Department	Activity	Function

	Positions This Package 2	Function F.Y.76	This Pkg. F.Y.77	Cum%
Describe the Function in terms of its objective County and City Medical Centers are charged to meet emergency situations such as sudden illness, injury, natural or man-made disasters, and poison cases. The centers do not coordinate their efforts across county and city lines nor do they have exposure to the latest techniques and equipment in the emergency medical field. Some centers are highly successful due to a special innovation that other centers do not share.	A. TOTAL PERSONAL SERVICES *	25,624	15,810	229
	1. Motor Vehicle Expenses and Repairs	900		
	2. Supplies and Materials	1,900	500	
	3. Repairs and Maintenance	500		
	4. Communications	400	50	
Describe the Function in terms of service provided in F. Y. 1976 Utilize a central staff to conduct medical emergency courses around the State to monitor the operations of the Injury Control Program. The courses will provide instruction to the cneters on the latest medical emergency techniques and methods. The Base Level provides services for the 100 most populated counties by conducting one medical emergency course at each.	5. Power, Water, Natural Gas	250		
	6. Rents *	273	150	
	7. Insurance and Bonding			
	8. Workmen's Comp. and Indemnities			
	9. Direct Benefits			
	10. Tuition and Scholarships			
Explain the New or Improved in terms of service Conduct an additional 37 medical emergency courses. This improvement will provide 37 centers with at least 2 courses. The centers serving the greatest population will receive more intensive instruction and more specialized courses. Improved coordination for local services will mean better emergency medical health statewide.	11. Grants to Counties or Cities			
	12. Assessments by Merit System	132	88	
	13. Other Operating Expenses	450		
	14. Extraordinary Expenses			
	B. REG. OPERATING EXPENSES(Add 1-14)	4,805	788	141
Explain the New or Improved in terms of Cost Personal Services — Two new positions, including fringes, less one month delayed hiring factor. Related Expenses — To conduct 37 additional courses, the new positions will need additional expenses and office space rental. No additional Federal funds are available for expansion.	C. TRAVEL	800	200	175
	D. MOTOR VEHICLE EQUIP. PURCH. *	4,680		109
	E. PUBLICATIONS AND PRINTING	1,350	100	137
	F. EQUIPMENT PURCHASES *	750	100	233
	G. PER DIEM AND FEES *	2,000		112
	H. COMPUTER CHARGES *	2,900		110

Quantitative Measures (Effectiveness, Workload, Efficiency)	F. Y. 1976 Function	F. Y. 1977 Cumulative			
			I. OTHER CONTRACTUAL EXPENSE *	1,600	112
			J. AUTHORITY LEASE RENTALS		
Different Medical Centers Aided	100	163	K. GENERAL OBLIGATION BONDS		
Medical Emergency Courses Conducted	100	200	L. CAPITAL OUTLAY *		
Cost Per Course/Total funds	$445	$423	M. LIST OTHER OBJECTS:		
Cost Per Course/State funds	$245	$289			

			TOTAL EXPENDITURES (Add A-M)	44,509	16,998	190
			FEDERAL FUNDS *	16,000		144
			OTHER FUNDS *	4,000		100
Package Name: Emergency Medical Health	Package 4 of 4		STATE GENERAL FUNDS	24,509	16,998	236
Prepared By: John Smith	Activity Rank 14		* Attach detailed schedule for F. Y. 1977 New or Improved funds requested in this package.			

10

ZERO·BASE BUDGET Procedures & Instructions

EXECUTIVE DEPARTMENT	
OFFICE OF PLANNING AND BUDGET — Budget Division	
SECTION	
DECISION PACKAGE PREPARATION – NEW OR IMPROVED	
SUBJECT	
INSTRUCTIONS FOR FORM OPB-BUDGET-33	

Form Purpose

The New or Improved Decision Package is developed for a requested improvement of an ongoing operation of the function or for a requested new operation in a function. The New or Improved operation within an existing Activity must be quantified and explained fully in term of service and cost. Any complete new function under an Activity would be requested on a separate series of Decision Packages and not on the New or Improved Decision Package.

1. **Describe the Function in Terms of Its Objective**
   - Repeat information displayed on the Minimum Level Package.

2. **Describe the Function in Terms of Service Provided in F. Y. 1976**
   - Repeat information displayed on the Minimum Level Package.

3. **Explain the New or Improved in Terms of Service**
   - Explain the additional service provided which helps the function to better meet its objectives. An Improvement is an expansion of an ongoing operation of the function while a New operation is, by definition, an operation not conducted in the function for F. Y. 1976.

4. **Explain the New or Improved in Terms of Cost**
   - Point out reasons why the New or Improved service will require additional funds. The explanation should be expressed in terms of what the funds will be expended for to accommodate the New or Improved service.

Quantitative Measures (Quantitative measures are required on the Decision Packages)

- Show Quantitative Measures for "F. Y. 1976 Function." The "F. Y. 1977 Cumulative" column will include the Minimum, Base, Workload, and New or Improved Package quantitative measures as a running total.
- Effectiveness data measures how well the services provided solve the problem and meet the objectives of the function.
- Workload data measures the effort required to deliver the services.
- Efficiency data measures the cost per unit of workload.

Financial Information

- Enter amounts budgeted for the function in F. Y. 1976.
- "This Pkg. F. Y. 1977" enter incremental amounts requested above the previous level for function and not the total requested through the New or Improved Package Level.
- The Cum % is calculated by dividing "This Pkg. F. Y. 1977" amounts summed from the Minimum, Base, Workload, and New or Improved Packages by "Function F. Y. 1976" amounts. Do not show Cum % for sub-classes of expenditure.

NOTE: Detailed forms 40-48 are required to be attached to the Workload Package for amounts requested in F. Y. 1977 where an asterisk appears on the New or Improved Package Form.

DATE Rev. 6/75		PAGE 11		OPB - Budget - 33

SUPPLEMENTAL SCHEDULES

On the following pages are Supplemental Schedules to substantiate your request for funds in the following objects:

Object	Form Schedule Number
Rents	OPB-Budget-40
Motor Vehicle Equipment Purchases	OPB-Budget-41
Equipment Purchases	OPB-Budget-42
Per Diem and Fees	OPB-Budget-43
Computer Charges	OPB-Budget-44
Other Contractual Expenses	OPB-Budget-45
Capital Outlay	OPB-Budget-46
Personal Services	OPB-Budget-47
Detail of Fund Sources	OPB-Budget-48

Forms 40 through 46 are to be prepared as needed and attached to each decision package for a function. Forms 47 and 48 are to be prepared for the entire Activity as a summary of the Base Level Packages (to include Minimum), however, forms 47 and 48 should be prepared as needed and attached to each Workload and New or Improved Package for a function.

12

ZERO·BASE BUDGET Procedures & Instructions

EXECUTIVE DEPARTMENT	
OFFICE OF PLANNING AND BUDGET — Budget Division	
SECTION	
SCHEDULE OF RENTS	
SUBJECT	
INSTRUCTIONS FOR FORM OPB-BUDGET-40	

Form Purpose

This form is a detailed schedule of Rents for the function which will be attached to each decision package, except for a Minimum Level Package, where an amount is requested for Rents in F. Y. 1977. The schedule, upon completion, should be copied and attached to each decision package, except Minimum, as a fully completed display.

— List type of Rents.

Examples — Xerox Rental, Postage Machine Rental, Office Equipment Rental, Office Space Rental, Post Office Box Rental.

— Identify the need for the Rents.

— Show funds budgeted for each type of Rents for F. Y. 1976.

— Show funds requested for rents for F. Y. 1977 divided into the three funding levels as requested on the decision packages.

— The F. Y. 1977 Rents requests will be listed on this form from the individual Decision Packages where funds are requested for this particular object, with the exception of the Minimum Level which will be included in the Base Level for schedule purposes.

F. Y. 1977   ZERO-BASE BUDGET REQUEST / SCHEDULE OF RENTS   Page 1 of 1   OPB-Budget-40 (Rev. 6-75)

Human Resources — Department   Community Injury Control — Activity   Emergency Medical Health — Function

Type of Rent	Reason Service Needed	F. Y. 1976 Budgeted	Minimum and Base Level	Workload	New or Improved
			F.Y. 1977 REQUESTED		
Office Machine Rent	Rental of Postage Machine for mailings to medical centers	153	230		
Post Office Rent	Rental of Post Office Box for the Atlanta Office	120	120		
Office Space Rent	Rental of Office Space for Regional Seminar to be conducted semi-annually in Atlanta for course work				100
Total Rents		273	350		100

DATE Rev. 6/75	PAGE 13	OPB - Budget- 40

ZERO-BASE BUDGET Procedures & Instructions

EXECUTIVE DEPARTMENT	
OFFICE OF PLANNING AND BUDGET — Budget Division	
SECTION	
SCHEDULE OF MOTOR VEHICLE EQUIPMENT PURCHASES	
SUBJECT	
INSTRUCTIONS FOR FORM OPB-BUDGET-41	

Form Purpose

This form is a detailed schedule of Motor Vehicle Equipment for the function which will be attached to each decision package, except for a Minimum Level Package, where an amount is requested for Motor Vehicle Equipment in F. Y. 1977. The schedule, upon completion, should be copied and attached to each decision package, except Minimum, as a fully completed display.

— List type of Motor Vehicle Equipment.

— List, first, the Motor Vehicle Equipment requested to replace existing equipment.

— List second, Motor Vehicle Equipment additions to your present equipment fleet.

— Describe the purpose for which the Motor Vehicle Equipment is needed.

— Show funds requested for Motor Vehicle Equipment for F. Y. 1977 divided into the three funding levels as requested on the decision packages.

— The F. Y. 1977 Motor Vehicle Equipment requests will be listed on this form from the individual decision packages where funds are requested for this particular object with the exception of the Minimum Level which will be included in the Base Level for schedule purposes.

F. Y. 1977

ZERO-BASE BUDGET REQUEST
SCHEDULE OF MOTOR VEHICLE EQUIPMENT PURCHASES

Page 1 of 1

OPB-Budget-41
(Rev. 6-75)

Human Resources	Community Injury Control	Emergency Medical Health
Department	Activity	Function

Type of Motor Vehicle (List Replacement then Additional)	Use of Vehicle	F.Y. 1977 REQUESTED		
		Minimum and Base Level	Workload	New or Improved
Replacement:				
1 Van Truck (mileage on old truck — 98,000)	Used to Transport demonstration Medical Supplies to County Health Offices	5,112		
Total Motor Vehicle Equipment Purchases		5,112		

DATE Rev. 6/75	PAGE 14	OPB - Budget - 41

ZERO·BASE BUDGET Procedures & Instructions	EXECUTIVE DEPARTMENT
	OFFICE OF PLANNING AND BUDGET — Budget Division
	SECTION
	SCHEDULE OF EQUIPMENT PURCHASES
	SUBJECT
	INSTRUCTIONS FOR FORM OPB-BUDGET-42

Form Purpose

This form is a detailed schedule of Equipment for the function which will be attached to each decision package, except for a Minimum Level Package, where an amount is requested for Equipment in F. Y. 1977. The schedule, upon completion, should be copied and attached to each decision package, except Minimum, as a fully completed display.

— List the type of Equipment.

Example: Office Equipment — Typewriters
                 Office Equipment — Adding Machines and Calculators
                 Office Equipment — Furniture
                 Lab and Medical Equipment
                 General Equipment Furnishings

NOTE: Any one piece of equipment which costs over $500 must be listed separately.

— Show funds requested for Equipment Purchases for F. Y. 1977 divided into the three funding levels as requested on the decision packages.

— The F. Y. 1977 Equipment requests will be listed on this form from the individual decision packages where funds are requested for this particular object, with the exception of the Minimum Level which will be included in the Base Level for schedule purposes.

F. Y. 1977

ZERO-BASE BUDGET REQUEST
SCHEDULE OF EQUIPMENT PURCHASES

Page 1 of 1

OPB-Budget - 42
(Rev. 6-75)

Human Resources	Community Injury Control	Emergency Medical Health
Department	Activity	Function

Type of Equipment (List Replacement then Additional)	F.Y. 1977 REQUESTED		
	Minimum and Base Level	Workload	New or Improved
Replacement:			
Office Equipment — Typewriters	450		
Office Equipment — Adding Machine	175		
Additional:			
Portable EKG Unit*	925		
Office Equipment — Adding Machine		100	100
Any individual equipment item over $500 is to be listed separately.			
Total Equipment Purchases	1,550	100	100

DATE Rev. 6/75	PAGE 15	OPB - Budget - 42

ZERO·BASE BUDGET Procedures & Instructions

EXECUTIVE DEPARTMENT	
OFFICE OF PLANNING AND BUDGET — Budget Division	
SECTION	
SCHEDULE OF PER DIEM AND FEES	
SUBJECT	
INSTRUCTIONS FOR FORM OPB-BUDGET-43	

Form Purpose

This form is a detailed schedule of Per Diem and Fees for the function which will be attached to each decision package, except for a Minimum Level Package, where an amount is requested for Per Diem and Fees in F. Y. 1977. The schedule, upon completion, should be copied and attached to each decision package, except Minimum, as a fully completed display.

— Categories for type of Per Diem is provided. List per diem not categorized under the caption "List Other."

— Identify the need for the Per Diem and Fee Categorized.

— Show funds budgeted for each type of Per Diem or Fee for F. Y. 1976.

— Show funds requested for Per Diem or Fees for F. Y. 1977 divided into the three funding levels as requested on the decision packages.

— The F. Y. 1977 Per Diem and Fees requests will be listed on this form from the individual decision packages where funds are requested for this particular object, with the exception of the Minimum Level which will be included in the Base Level for schedule purposes.

F. Y. 1977

ZERO-BASE BUDGET REQUEST
SCHEDULE OF PER DIEM AND FEES

Page 1 of 1

OPB - Budget - 43
(Rev. 6-75)

Department: Human Resources
Activity: Community Injury Control
Function: Emergency Medical Health

Type of Per Diem	Reason Service Needed	F.Y. 1976 Budgeted	F.Y. 1977 REQUESTED Minimum and Base Level	Workload	New or Improved	TOTAL
Board/Commission Membs.	Local Board Members Per Diem	1,000	1,350			
Accounting/Audit						
Management Consulting	Study for Improving Special Medical Emergency Care	750	600			
Engineer/Architect						
Legal						
Educational	Medical Emergency Training Class at G. S. U.	250	300			
Medical						
Research						
List Other:						
Total Per Diem and Fees		2,000	2,250			

DATE Rev. 6/75	PAGE 16	OPB - Budget· 43

ZERO-BASE BUDGET

Procedures & Instructions

EXECUTIVE DEPARTMENT	
OFFICE OF PLANNING AND BUDGET — Budget Division	
SECTION	
SCHEDULE OF COMPUTER CHARGES	
SUBJECT	
INSTRUCTIONS FOR FORM OPB-BUDGET-44	

Form Purpose

This form is a detailed schedule of Computer Charges for the function which will be attached to each decision package, except for a Minimum Level Package, where an amount is requested for Computer Charges in F. Y. 1977. The schedule, upon completion, should be copied and attached to each decision package, except Minimum, as a fully completed display.

— Show the account number of the system (assigned by DOAS).

— Show the narrative description of the system.

— Show the funds budgeted, by function, for F. Y. 1976 for each system and the funds requested for F. Y. 1977 as divided into the three funding levels.

— List new system development separately.

— The F. Y. 1977 Computer Charges requests will be listed on this form from the individual decision packages where funds are requested for this particular object, with the exception of the Minimum Level which will be included in the Base Level for schedule purposes.

NOTE: DOAS can help provide the information you need to prepare this form.

F. Y. 1977

ZERO-BASE BUDGET REQUEST
SCHEDULE OF COMPUTER CHARGES

OPB-Budget - 44
(Rev. 6-75)

Human Resources	Community Injury Control	Emergency Medical Health
Department	Activity	Function

		F. Y. 1976	F.Y. 1977 REQUESTED		
Account Number	SYSTEM DESCRIPTION	Budgeted	Minimum and Base Level	Workload	New or Improved
82121	Statistical system for county injury control	1,800	1,800		
92181	Payroll System	1,100	1,100	300	
	Total Computer Charges	2,900	2,900	300	

DATE Rev. 6/75	PAGE 17	OPB - Budget - 44	

ZERO-BASE BUDGET
Procedures
&
Instructions

EXECUTIVE DEPARTMENT	
OFFICE OF PLANNING AND BUDGET – Budget Division	
SECTION	
SCHEDULE OF OTHER CONTRACTUAL EXPENSE	
SUBJECT	
INSTRUCTIONS FOR FORM OPB-BUDGET-45	

Form Purpose

This form is a detailed schedule of Other Contractual Expense for the function which will be attached to each decision package, except for a Minimum Level Package, where an amount is requested for Other Contractual Expense in F. Y. 1977. The schedule, upon completion, should be copied and attached to each decision package, except Minimum, as a fully completed display.

— List type of contract.

— Identify the need for the contract

— For each contract, show the amount budgeted for F. Y. 1976.

— Show funds requested for F. Y. 1977 for each contract, divided into the three levels of funding as taken from the decision packages.

— The F. Y. 1977 Other Contractual Expense requests will be listed on this form from the individual decison packages where funds are requested for this particular object, with the exception of the Minimum Level which will be included in the Base Level for schedule purposes.

F. Y. 1977

ZERO-BASE BUDGET REQUEST
SCHEDULE OF OTHER CONTRACTUAL EXPENSES

OPB-Budget-45
(Rev. 6-75)

Human Resources	Community Injury Control	Emergency Medical Health
Department	Activity	Function

Type of Contract	Reason Service Needed	F. Y. 1976 Budgeted	Minimum and Base Level	Workload	New or Improved
			F.Y. 1977 REQUESTED		
Ambulance Service	Emergency Ambulance Service for counties with no statewide system	1,600	1,600	200	
Total Other Contractual Expenses		1,600	1,600	200	

DATE Rev. 6/75	PAGE 18	OPB - Budget- 45

ZERO-BASE BUDGET
Procedures & Instructions

EXECUTIVE DEPARTMENT	
OFFICE OF PLANNING AND BUDGET — Budget Division	
SECTION	
CAPITAL OUTLAY DETAIL	
SUBJECT	
INSTRUCTIONS FOR FORM OPB-BUDGET-46	

Form Purpose

This form is a detailed explanation of Capital Outlay for the function which will be attached to each decision package where an amount is requested for Capital Outlay in F. Y. 1977. Any additional information needed to explain the request should be attached.

— All sections of the form (A through G) should be completed for each project requested for each kind of decision package where applicable.

— All construction or project funds should be requested as Capital Outlay and not as General Obligation Bonds or Authority Lease Rentals.

F. Y. 1977

OPB-Budget-46
(Rev. 6-75)

ZERO-BASE BUDGET REQUEST
CAPITAL OUTLAY DETAIL

Human Resources	Community Injury Control	Emergency Medical Health
Department	Activity	Function

A. THIS PROJECT: (Check One)

___ Is an Original Facility   _x_ Renovates an Existing Facility
___ Is an Addition to an Existing Facility ___ Replaces an Existing Facility
___ Is part of a Master Plan (Previously Authorized) (Proposed)

B. LOCATION: Atlanta, Georgia

Size of Site Required _____

(Check where appropriate)

_x_ Site on Currently Owned Property   _x_ Utilities Already Available
___ Site to be Selected   _x_ Access Already Available
___ Site Already Selected

C. DESCRIPTION OF FACILITY:

General Description: (Attach Basic Layout, if possible)
Renovation of Offices in Atlanta, Labor Building, by adding partitions.

Functional Space Requirements: (in square feet) No additional square
feet needed
Special Standards or Requirements: Glass and metal partitioning bolted
to existing walls

D. JUSTIFICATION OF NEED:
This Renovation is needed to accommodate new positions requested in the Workload Decision Package. Present office space can be utilized if partitioned.

Number to be served by Facility ___2___

If new Facility, Indicate Alternatives Considered:

___ Leasing   ___ Renovation

E. ESTIMATED COST OF PROJECT:

Source of Estimate: _____ J. M. Bennett, Building Supervisor

1. Design and Planning:	$	100
2. Land Acquisition:	$	
3. Construction: ___ sq. feet @ ___ per sq. foot	$	
4. Architectual Fees and Contingencies:	$	200
5. Utilities:	$	
6. Air Conditioning/Heating:	$	
7. Equipment:	$	
8. Other: Renovation Cost	$	1,700
TOTAL COST	$	
Less Other Funds Available		
Source	$	
STATE FUNDS REQUIRED	$	2,000

F. ESTIMATED OPERATIONAL COST AT COMPLETION:

Expected Completion Date: January, 1977
Number of Additional Personnel Required None
Additional Funds Required when Project is in Full Operation $ None
Personal Services and Operating Expenses $ None

G. STATE FUNDS REQUESTED FOR ADDITIONAL YEARS:

If Funding will be extended over more than one year, explain and indicate the amount required for each year: N/A

DATE Rev. 6/75	PAGE 19	OPB - Budget - 46

ZERO·BASE BUDGET Procedures & Instructions

EXECUTIVE DEPARTMENT	
OFFICE OF PLANNING AND BUDGET — Budget Division	
SECTION	
ACTIVITY PERSONAL SERVICES SCHEDULE PREPARATION	
SUBJECT	
INSTRUCTIONS FOR FORM OPB-BUDGET-47	

Form Purpose

This form serves two purposes: 1) Summarizes and details Personal Services from the Minimum and Base Level functional packages for an entire Activity, 2) Details Personal Services for either a function Workload Package or a functional New or Improved Package and is attached to the package.

Column 1 — Number of Budgeted Positions

— Enter the number of positions for each position title on the same grade and step and anniversary date.

Column 2 — Position Title

— Enter position titles alphabetically per Merit System Classification.

Column 3 — Grade, Step, Anniversary

— Use Merit System pay grade assigned to the position title and pay step as it applies to each position.
— ANNIV. (Month and Year) are listed to facilitate the calculations across the form for each position.

Column 4 — Payroll June 30, 1975, Annual Rate

— Enter position cost from the payroll listing at the annualized rate of gross pay as of June 30, 1975. Do not include salary increases effective July 1, 1975.

Column 5 — F. Y. 1976 September 1 Raise and Within-grade Increases at Annual Rate

— Enter combined amounts for full-year costs of any F. Y. 1976 within-grade increases and the 12-month cost associated with the September 1 pay adjustment.

Column 6 — Annual Salary Rate June 30, 1976

— Enter the sum of column 4 and 5. These gross salary amounts should represent the gross F. Y. 1976 ending salary for each position. Do not include salary increases requested to be effective July 1, 1976.

Column 7 — All or Part-year Within-grade Increases F. Y. 1977

— Enter the amounts for within-grade increases which will occur in F. Y. 1977. This amount will vary, depending on the number of months the raise is in effect.

Column 8 — Personal Services Budget

— Enter the sum of columns 6 and 7. These amounts represent the cost of the position for F. Y. 1977 and not the annual salary rate.

A.   F. Y. 1977 Current Positions

  — List positions alphabetically and group by filled or vacant positions.
  — Group positions with same position title, grade and step, and anniversary date.
  — Position titles listed should be taken from the Annual Operating Budget (Form OPB-Budget-3).
  — Enter correct position cost in column 4 from the June 30 payroll.
  — Show beside position title the percentage of Federal funds which apply to the funding of a particular position. Example: 1 50% Federal funded position would be — Clerk II (50% Federal).
  — Show additional positions appropriated in F. Y. 1976 separate under both filled and vacant positions.
  — Enter Total Current Positions by adding items under A. See sample.

DATE Rev. 6/75	PAGE 20	OPB - Budget· 47

ZERO-BASE BUDGET Procedures & Instructions

EXECUTIVE DEPARTMENT	
OFFICE OF PLANNING AND BUDGET — Budget Division	
SECTION	
ACTIVITY PERSONAL SERVICES SCHEDULE PREPARATION	
SUBJECT	
INSTRUCTIONS FOR FORM OPB-BUDGET-47 (Continued)	

B. **F. Y. 1977 Requested Position Changes**

  – List positions which have been <u>deleted</u> or <u>added</u> in the entire activity for the Minimum and Base Level functional packages.
  – Delete positions on the grade and step they currently are on.
  – List any new positions on step 1.
  – Enter Total Position Changes by adding items under B. See sample.

C. **F. Y. 1977 Other Salary Cost**

  – Enter amounts in column 8 for Other Salary Cost:

  NOTE: Separate Decision Packages are made for upgrading a class of personnel. Do not list here.
  – Stipends
  – Overtime
  – Night Pay Differential
  – Enter Total Other Salary Cost by adding items under C. See sample.
  – Enter Total Salaries, after item C, by adding A, B, and C. See sample.

D. **F. Y. 1977 Requested Fringe Benefits**

  – Enter amounts for fringe benefits in column 8.
  – F. Y. 1977 Rates:
    – <u>F.I.C.A.</u> rate is 5.85% on a base of $14,100.
    – <u>Retirement</u> rate is 8% on Total Salaries.
    – <u>Health Insurance</u> rate is 3% on Total Salaries.
  – Enter Total Fringe Benefits by adding items under D. See sample.

E. **F. Y. 1977 Temporary Help**

  – Enter amounts for temporary help in column 8.
  – Include fringe benefits for temporary help.

F. **F. Y. 1977 Requested Lapse Factors**

  – Enter negative amounts for Delayed Hiring and Turnover in column 8 as applicable.
  – Delayed Hiring can only exist where new positions are requested or where new institutions are phasing into operation.
  – Enter Total Lapse Factors by adding items under F. See sample.

G. **F. Y. 1977 Total Personal Services**

  – Add amounts in column 8 to get Personal Services Total for F. Y. 977.

  NOTE: An upgrading should be detailed on a New or Improved Decision Package for each classification for which an upgrading is requested and is not shown on this form.

DATE Rev. 6/75	PAGE 21	OPB - Budget - 47

PERSONAL SERVICES SCHEDULE — MINIMUM AND BASE LEVELS   OPB-BUDGET-47

F. Y. 1977

ZERO-BASE BUDGET REQUEST
PERSONAL SERVICES SCHEDULE

Page 1 of 1

OPB-Budget - 47 (Rev. 6-75)

Human Resources — Department
Community Injury Control — Activity (Base Level to include Minimum Level)
Function (Only for Workload and New or Improved)

Positions (1)	Position Title (2)	G R A D E	S T E P (3)	A N N I V.	Payroll June 30, 1975 Annual Rate (4)	F.Y. 1976 Sept. 1 Raise & Within-grade Increases at Annual Rate (5)	Annual Salary Rate June 30, 1976 (6)	All or Part Year Within-Grade Increases F.Y. 1977 (7)	Personal Services Budgeted F.Y. 1977 (8)
	(A) F.Y. 1976 CURRENT POSITIONS (Minimum and Base Levels for the Entire Activity)								
	Filled Positions								
1	Accountant II	17	4	5-76	12,252	1,080	13,332	104	13,436
2	Caseworker II	14	2	1-76	17,112	1,592	18,704	396	19,100
2	Clerk II	10	3	9-75	12,624	1,352	13,976	480	14,456
1	Clerk III	11	2	8-75	6,588	688	7,276	286	7,562
1	Director of Community Health	N/M			21,360	800	22,160		22,160
1	Steno II	11	5	3-76	7,500	736	8,236	120	8,356
	Vacant Positions								
1	Caseworker II	14	1	7-76	8,196	400	8,596	360	8,956
	Additional Positions Appropriated F. Y. 1976								
1	Clerk II	10	1	7-76	5,796	400	6,196	252	6,448
10	TOTAL CURRENT POSITIONS				91,428	7,048	98,476	1,998	100,474
	(B) F.Y. 1977 REQUESTED POSITION CHANGES								
	None								
-0-	TOTAL POSITION CHANGES								-0-
	(C) F.Y. 1977 REQUESTED OTHER SALARY COST								
	Stipends								-0-
	Overtime								4,000
	Night Pay Differential								
	TOTAL OTHER SALARY COST								4,000
10	TOTAL SALARIES								104,474
	(D) F.Y. 1977 REQUESTED FRINGE BENEFITS								
	F.I.C.A. (5.85% x 96,414)								5,640
	Retirement (8% x 104,474)								8,358
	Health Insurance (3% x 104,474)								3,134
	TOTAL FRINGE BENEFITS								17,132
	(E) TEMPORARY HELP (Include Associated Fringe Benefits)								1,500
	(F) F.Y. 1977 REQUESTED LAPSE FACTORS								
	Delayed Hiring								-0-
	Turnover								(3,462)
	TOTAL LAPSE FACTORS								(3,462)
10	(G) F.Y. 1977 TOTAL PERSONAL SERVICES (Minimum and Base Levels for the entire Activity)								119,644

PERSONAL SERVICES SCHEDULE — WORKLOAD   OPB-BUDGET-47

F. Y. 1977

ZERO-BASE BUDGET REQUEST
PERSONAL SERVICES SCHEDULE

Page 1 of 1

OPB-Budget - 47 (Rev. 6-75)

Human Resources — Department
Community Injury Control — Activity (Base Level to include Minimum Level)
Emergency Medical Health — Workload
Function (Only for Workload and New or Improved)

Positions (1)	Position Title (2)	G R A D E	S T E P (3)	A N N I V.	Payroll June 30, 1975 Annual Rate (4)	F.Y. 1976 Sept. 1 Raise & Within-grade Increases at Annual Rate (5)	Annual Salary Rate June 30, 1976 (6)	All or Part Year Within-Grade Increases F.Y. 1977 (7)	Personal Services Budgeted F.Y. 1977 (8)
	(A) NEW POSITIONS REQUESTED F. Y. 1977 (This Package)								
1	Health Program Coordinator	15	1	1-77			9,352	198	9,550
1	Health Program Aide	7	1	1-77			4,924	96	5,020
2	TOTAL NEW POSITIONS (This Package)						14,276	294	14,570
	(B) REQUESTED FRINGE BENEFITS								
	F.I.C.A. (5.85% x $14,470)								852
	Retirement (8% x $14,570)								1,166
	Health Insurance (3% x $14,570)								437
	TOTAL FRINGE BENEFITS								2,455
	(C) REQUESTED LAPSE FACTOR								
	Delayed Hiring								(1,215)
	Turnover								-0-
	TOTAL LAPSE FACTOR								(1,215)
2	TOTAL PERSONAL SERVICES (This Package)								15,810

ATTACH TO WORKLOAD PACKAGE

22

PERSONAL SERVICES SCHEDULE — NEW OR IMPROVED

OPB-BUDGET-47

F. Y. 1977

OPB-Budget . 47
(Rev. 6-75)

ZERO-BASE BUDGET REQUEST
PERSONAL SERVICES SCHEDULE

Page 1 of 1

Human Resources
Department

Community Injury Control
Activity (Base Level to include Minimum Level)

Emergency Medical Health — New or Imp.
Function (Only for Workload and New or Improved)

Positions (1)	Position Title (2)	G R A D E	S T E P (3)	A N N I V.	Payroll June 30, 1975 Annual Rate (4)	F. Y. 1976 Sept. 1 Raise & Within-grade Increases at Annual Rate (5)	Annual Salary Rate June 30, 1976 (6)	All or Part Year Within-Grade Increases F. Y. 1977 (7)	Personal Services Budgeted F. Y. 1977 (8)
	(A) NEW POSITIONS REQUESTED F. Y. 1977 (This Package)								
1	Health Program Instructor	15	1	1-77			9,352	198	9,550
1	Health Program Aide	7	1	1-77			4,924	96	5,020
2	TOTAL NEW POSITIONS (This Package)						14,276	294	14,570
	(B) REQUESTED FRINGE BENEFITS								
	F.I.C.A. (5.85% x $14,570)								852
	Retirement (8% x $14,570)								1,166
	Health Insurance (3% x $14,570)								437
	TOTAL FRINGE BENEFITS								2,455
	(C) REQUESTED LAPSE FACTOR								
	Delayed Hiring								(1,215)
	Turnover								-0-
	TOTAL LAPSE FACTOR								(1,215)
2	TOTAL PERSONAL SERVICES (This Package)								15,810

ATTACH TO NEW OR IMPROVED PACKAGE

23

ZERO·BASE BUDGET Procedures & Instructions

EXECUTIVE DEPARTMENT	
OFFICE OF PLANNING AND BUDGET — Budget Division	
SECTION	
SCHEDULE OF FUND SOURCES	
SUBJECT	
INSTRUCTIONS FOR FORM OPB-BUDGET-48	

Form Purpose

This form is a detailed schedule of Federal and Other Funds by itemized source of the funds.

— List Federal funds by Federal Domestic Assistance Catalog (F.D.A.C.) number and the Federal Agency granting the funds.

— List Other funds by source identification. Example: Student Fees, Park Receipts, Patient Fees.

-- Show funds budgeted for each source of funds for F. Y. 1975 Actual and F. Y. 1976 budgeted per the latest approved amendment to the Annual Operating Budget.

— Show funds requested for F. Y. 1977 divided into the three funding levels as requested on the decision packages.

NOTE: This form is prepared at the Activity Level as a summary of the function Base Level Packages (to include Minimum Levels) except that for Workload and New or Improved functional packages, attach a separate schedule to each package where increases in fund sources occur in them. Do not include Workload and New or Improved amounts in the Base Level summary for the Activity.

F. Y. 1977

OPB - Budget - 48
(Rev. 6-75)

ZERO-BASE BUDGET REQUEST
SCHEDULE OF FUND SOURCES

Human Resources	Community Injury Control	
Department	Activity (Base Level to include Minimum Level)	Function (Only for Workload and New or Improved)

DETAIL OF FEDERAL AND OTHER FUNDS	F.Y. 1975 Actual	F.Y. 1976 Budgeted	Minimum and Base Level	Workload	New or Improved	TOTAL
Federal Funds:						
H.E.W., F.D.A.C. No. 17.121, Title 16	10,000	16,000	16,000			
TOTAL FEDERAL FUNDS	10,000	16,000	16,000			
Other Funds:						
Charges collected for Demonstration Equipment		4,000	4,000			
TOTAL OTHER FUNDS		4,000	4,000			

DATE Rev. 6/75	PAGE 24	OPB - Budget - 48

SCHEDULE OF FUND SOURCES – WORKLOAD

OPB-BUDGET-48

F. Y. 1977

OPB - Budget - 48
(Rev. 6-75)

ZERO-BASE BUDGET REQUEST
SCHEDULE OF FUND SOURCES

Human Resources		Community Injury Control		Emergency Medical Health --Workload		
Department		Activity (Base Level to include Minimum Level)		Function (Only for Workload and New or Improved)		
	F. Y. 1975	F. Y. 1976	F . Y . 1 9 7 7 R E Q U E S T E D			
DETAIL OF FEDERAL AND OTHER FUNDS	Actual	Budgeted	Minimum and Base Level	Workload	New or Improved	TOTAL
Federal Funds:						
H.U.D., F.D.A.C. No. 26.148, Title 20				7,000		7,000
TOTAL FEDERAL FUNDS				7,000		7,000
Other Funds:						
ATTACH TO WORKLOAD PACKAGE						
TOTAL OTHER FUNDS						

25

ZERO-BASE BUDGET Procedures & Instructions

EXECUTIVE DEPARTMENT	
OFFICE OF PLANNING AND BUDGET — Budget Division	
SECTION ACTIVITY OR DEPARTMENT	
DECISION PACKAGE RANKING PREPARATION	
SUBJECT	
INSTRUCTIONS FOR FORM OPB-BUDGET-50	

Form Purpose

This form displays the Activity or the Departmental State Fund priorities for F. Y. 1977 for each decision package and the functional State fund cost for F. Y. 1976 for each first package in a series.

Rank

— Enter priority number of each package, starting with number 1 as the highest priority and ending with a number which equals the total number of packages. In any functional series of packages; e.g., 1 of 3, 2 of 3, and 3 of 3, Package 1 of 3 is always ranked higher than 2 of 3 or 3 of 3. However, Package 1 of 3 or 2 of 3 or 3 of 3 in one functional series can be ranked higher or lower than Packages in another functional series.

Package Name

— Enter package name of each Decision Package ranked and note the series number by it. Names of Decision Packages should be as descriptive of the function as possible, preferably the name of the function.

F. Y. 1976 Amount

— Enter the F. Y. 1976 Amount for State funds budgeted for the function and number of positions for each first package of a series; i.e., Package 1 of — will always have the F. Y. 1976 State funds and positions for the entire function shown. Package 2 of — or 3 of —, etc., will show a blank in the F. Y. 1976 amount column since the F. Y. 1976 amount was already shown by the first package of the series.

F. Y. 1977 Amount

— Enter the F. Y. 1977 amount for State funds requested and number of positions for each Decision Package ranked.

Cumulative Level

— Enter the Cumulative State funds, the percentage the cumulative amount represents to the Total F. Y. 1976 State fund total, and the cumulative number of positions.

Ranking Packages

— All Decision Packages are ranked even if Federal or Other funds finance the package.
— State fund amounts will be the only funds listed on the ranking sheet even if package is funded partially or fully by Federal or Other funds.
— Show positions for all ranked packages.
— Rank Decision Packages as to how effectively and efficiently each one contributes to the Departmental goals and objectives in terms of service.
— Decision Packages are ranked for each Activity and for the Department as well.

Debt Service Ranking

— Existing Authority Lease Rentals (A.L.R.'s) and General Obligation Bond (G. O. Bond) payments should be ranked with a high priority.
— DO NOT request new A.L.R.'s or G. O. Bond payments for construction in F. Y. 1977.
— Any request for construction in F. Y. 1977 shall be requested as Capital Outlay.

DATE Rev. 6/75	PAGE 26	OPB - Budget - 50

ACTIVITY RANKING

OPB-BUDGET-50

F. Y. 1977

ZERO-BASE BUDGET REQUEST
DECISION PACKAGE RANKING

OPB-Budget - 50
(Rev. 6-75)

Human Resources — Department | Community Injury Control — Activity

RANK	PACKAGE NAME	F. Y. 1976 BUDGETED		F. Y. 1977 REQUESTED		CUMULATIVE LEVEL		
		State Funds	Positions	State Funds	Positions	State Funds	% 77/76	Positions
1	Executive Admn. (1 of 2)	32,420	1	24,200	1	24,200	14.9	1
2	Planning (1 of 1)	34,121	2	30,200	2	54,400	33.5	3
3	Patient Appraisals (1 of 2)	24,946	2	11,748	1	66,148	40.7	4
*4	Emergency Medical Health (1 of 4)	24,509	2	12,433	2	78,581	48.3	6
5	Food Service (1 of 2)	20,000	3	16,200	3	94,781	58.3	9
6	Housekeeping (1 of 3)	26,593	4	14,000	2	108,781	66.9	11
*7	Emergency Medical Health (2 of 4)			15,353	1	124,134	76.3	12
8	Executive Admn. (2 of 2)			15,200	1	139,334	85.7	13
9	Patient Appraisals (2 of 2)			17,000	1	156,334	96.2	14
*10	Emergency Medical Health (3 of 4)			12,948	2	169,282	104.1	16
11	Capital Outlay (1 of 1)			2,000		171,282	105.3	
12	Food Service (2 of 2)			19,000		190,282	117.0	
13	Housekeeping (2 of 3)			11,000	2	201,282	123.8	18
*14	Emergency Medical Health (4 of 4)			16,998	2	218,280	134.3	20
15	Housekeeping (3 of 3)			15,000		233,280	143.5	20
	Activity Totals	162,589	14	233,280	20			
	* Decision Packages in Sample			233,280 / 162,589 = 143.5%				

Frank Doe / Approved By | Activity Manager / Title | August 18, 1975 / Date | Page 1 of 1

DEPARTMENT RANKING

OPB-BUDGET-50

F. Y. 1977

ZERO-BASE BUDGET REQUEST
DECISION PACKAGE RANKING

OPB-Budget - 50
(Rev. 6-75)

Human Resources — Department | Department Ranking — Activity

RANK	PACKAGE NAME	F. Y. 1976 BUDGETED		F. Y. 1977 REQUESTED		CUMULATIVE LEVEL		
		State Funds	Positions	State Funds	Positions	State Funds	% 77/76	Positions
1	Executive Adm. (1 of 2)	32,420	1	24,200	1	24,200	3.3	1
2	Administrative (1 of 2)	44,200	4	32,000	3	56,200	7.7	4
3	General Obligation Bond (1 of 1)	200,000		200,000		256,200	35.1	
4	Authority Lease Rentals (1 of 1)	100,000		100,000		356,200	48.8	
5	Planning (1 of 1)	34,121	2	30,200	2	386,400	52.9	6
6	Emergency Facilities (1 of 3)	156,004	20	65,000	6	451,400	61.8	12
7	Housekeeping (1 of 3)	26,593	4	14,000	2	465,400	63.8	14
8	Administrative (2 of 2)			15,100	1	480,500	65.8	15
9	Patient Appraisals (1 of 2)	24,946	2	11,748	1	492,248	67.4	16
10	Emergency Facilities (2 of 3)			29,000	5	521,248	71.4	21
11	Food Services (1 of 2)	20,000	3	16,200	3	537,448	75.6	24
12	Staff Training (1 of 4)	62,200	6	7,000	1	544,448	74.6	25
13	Capital Outlay (1 of 1)	5,000		25,000		569,448	78.0	
*14	Emergency Medical Health (1 of 4)	24,509	2	12,433	2	581,881	79.7	27
15	Emergency Facilities (3 of 3)			110,721	9	692,602	94.9	36
16	Staff Training (2 of 4)			16,900	2	709,502	97.2	38
17	Housekeeping (2 of 3)			11,000	2	720,502	98.7	40
*18	Emergency Medical Health (2 of 4)			15,353	1	735,855	100.8	41
19	Executive Admin. (2 of 2)			15,200	1	751,055	102.9	42
20	Capital Outlay (1 of 1)			2,000		753,055	103.2	
*21	Emergency Medical Health (3 of 4)			12,948	2	766,003	104.9	44
22	Staff Training (3 of 4)			27,000	2	793,003	108.6	46
23	Housekeeping (3 of 3)			15,000		808,003	110.7	
*24	Emergency Medical Health (4 of 4)			16,998	1	825,001	113.0	47
25	Staff Training (4 of 4)			22,000		847,001	116.0	48
26	Food Services (2 of 2)			19,000		866,001	118.6	
27	Patient Appraisals (2 of 2)			17,000	1	883,001	121.0	49
	TOTALS	729,993	44	883,001	49			

Sam Doe / Approved By / * Decision Packages in Sample | Department Director / Title | August 26, 1975 / Date | Page 1 of 1

ZERO·BASE BUDGET Procedures & Instructions

EXECUTIVE DEPARTMENT	
OFFICE OF PLANNING AND BUDGET — Planning Division	
SECTION	
ACTIVITY INFORMATION SUMMARY	
SUBJECT	
INSTRUCTIONS FOR FORM OPB-PLANNING-51	

Form Purpose

This form displays descriptive information about an Activity and shows specific.data which indicates effectiveness of the Activity.

1. Activity Purpose

—Review and revise, if necessary, the statement of purpose for this activity found in Volume II, Program Display, of the Governor's Recommended Budget for FY 1976. Assure that the statement is consistent with expressed intent of pertinent enabling legislation or other source of authority. If at all possible, this statement should be expressed in terms that suggest measures of accomplishment.

2. Activity Description

—Review and revise, if necessary, the functional description of this activity found in Volume II of the Governor's Recommended Budget for FY 1976. Identify the service(s) being provided and categorize the recipients by service need. Indicate quantitatively the type and volume of service provided to each category of recipients.

3. Degree of Accomplishment of Activity Purpose

—Indicate quantitatively and qualitatively (where possible) the degree to which the activity is accomplishing its stated purpose. Use the measure(s) of accomplishment previously submitted to the Office of Planning and Budget.

4. Forecast of Substantive Changes in Scope of Activity

—Identify any expected (within the next five years) changes in the scope of activity purpose or in the functions performed. Identify the expected source of initiative for these changes and explain the expected effects of these changes on services being provided and on categories of recipients (examples: objectives accomplished thereby ending the need for that program; changing Federal program regulations).

DATE Rev. 6/75	PAGE 28	OPB - Planning - 51

ACTIVITY INFORMATION SUMMARY

OPB-PLANNING-51

F. Y. 1977	ZERO-BASE BUDGET REQUEST ACTIVITY INFORMATION SUMMARY	OPB - Planning - 51 (Rev.6/75)

Human Resources	Community Injury Control
Department	Activity

1. Activity Purpose

Plan and support the provision of emergency medical services to individuals in emergency situations such as sudden illness, injury, and natural or man-made disaster. Support and monitor the county operated medical emergency centers.

2. Activity Description

Conducts medical self-help courses and monitors operation of the injury control program. Plans for new EMS programs such as hospital disasters plans and exercises. Conduct medical emergency courses for county medical centers. The following is an indication of the types of services provided, categorized according to need:

	F. Y. 1975
Persons treated in injury control centers	32,000
Persons treated in poison control centers	1,200
Persons who have ready access to this service	2,500,000

3. Degree of Accomplishment of Activity Purpose

Of the estimated 70,000 individuals who needed emergency medical services during this program year, 68,000 received prompt and effective service through certified county EMS programs. One EMS training course was conducted in all 159 counties and 40 counties received 2 training courses thereby completing the total EMS instructional program. An estimated 90 percent of all poisonings were treated through poison control centers. Fatal injury/accident rates decreased by 1.2 percent.

4. Forecast of Substantive Changes in Scope of Activity

New Federal Health Planning legislation will bring about administrative and functional changes in the organization of EMS. These changes will affect the planning and funding of EMS in Georgia over the next 3 years.

ACTIVITY FUND SOURCES	Budgeted F. Y. 1976	Requested F. Y. 1977	DEPARTMENTAL ACTIVITY PROJECTIONS				
			F. Y. 1978	F. Y. 1979	F. Y. 1980	F. Y. 1981	F. Y. 1982
Federal Funds	16,000	23,000	50,000				
Other Funds	4,000	4,000					
State Funds	162,589	190,724	215,420	231,462	257,587	283,345	311,679
TOTAL FUNDS	182,589	217,724	265,420	231,462	257,587	283,345	311,679

ZERO·BASE BUDGET Procedures & Instructions

EXECUTIVE DEPARTMENT	
OFFICE OF PLANNING AND BUDGET — Budget Division	
SECTION	
ACTIVITY FINANCIAL SUMMARY	
SUBJECT	
INSTRUCTIONS FOR FORM OPB-BUDGET-52	

Form Purpose

This form is a summary of sub-objects, objects, and fund sources of the Decision Package Ranking Forms, supported by the decision packages, for a entire Activity.

— Show amounts by categories listed for F. Y. 1975 Actual, F. Y. 1976 Budget, and F. Y. 1977 requested. F. Y. 1977 requested is divided into four funding levels summarized from the functional decision packages submitted.

— Amounts for F. Y. 1976 should represent the Annual Operating Budget to include amendments thereto approved by OPB since the beginning of the Fiscal Year.

F. Y. 1977

ZERO-BASE BUDGET REQUEST
ACTIVITY FINANCIAL SUMMARY

OPB-Budget-52
(Rev. 6-75)

Human Resources — Department

Human Resources — Budget Unit

Community Injury Control — Activity

OBJECTS/FUNDS	F. Y. 1975 Actual	F. Y. 1976 Budgeted	F. Y. 1977 REQUESTED				
			Minimum Level Packages	Base Level Packages	Workload Packages	New or Improved Packages	TOTAL All Packages
Number of Budgeted Positions	10	14	10	4	4	2	20
A. TOTAL PERSONAL SERVICES	110,024	148,200	92,100	27,544	27,200	21,400	168,244
1. Motor Vehicle Expenses and Repairs	900	1,500	1,000	600	250		1,850
2. Supplies and Materials	3,000	3,600	2,900	1,200	800	1,000	5,900
3. Repairs and Maintenance	700	900	600	500	200		1,300
4. Communications	600	750	490	600	100	100	1,290
5. Power, Water, Natural Gas	375	500	300	300			600
6. Rents	1,500	2,600	2,100	1,000		300	3,400
7. Insurance and Bonding	180	215	200	110		100	410
8. Workmen's Comp. and Indemnities							
9. Direct Benefits							
10. Tuition and Scholarships							
11. Grants to Counties or Cities							
12. Assessments by Merit System	360	574	440	176	176	88	880
13. Other Operating Expenses	1,000	1,200	900	400	100		1,400
14. Extraordinary Expenses	500	750	500	300			800
B. REG. OPERATING EXPENSES(Add1-14)	9,115	12,589	9,430	5,186	1,626	1,588	17,830
C. TRAVEL	1,200	1,400	700	800	400	200	2,100
D. MOTOR VEHICLE EQUIP. PURCHASES	4,600	8,200	10,000				10,000
E. PUBLICATIONS AND PRINTING	2,000	3,900	2,000	2,200	400	200	4,800
F. EQUIPMENT PURCHASES	900	1,200		2,400	275	200	2,875
G. PER DIEM AND FEES	600	2,500	2,000	1,000			3,000
H. COMPUTER CHARGES	2,651	3,200	2,500	1,200	400		4,100
I. OTHER CONTRACTUAL EXPENSE	900	1,400	900	1,500	375		2,775
J. AUTHORITY LEASE RENTALS							
K. GENERAL OBLIGATION BONDS							
L. CAPITAL OUTLAY				2,000			2,000
M. LIST OTHER OBJECTS:							
TOTAL EXPENDITURES (Add A - M)	131,990	182,589	119,630	41,830	32,676	23,588	217,724
FEDERAL FUNDS	10,000	16,000	10,000	6,000	7,000		23,000
OTHER FUNDS		4,000	4,000				4,000
STATE GENERAL FUNDS	121,990	162,589	105,630	35,830	25,676	23,588	190,724

DATE Rev. 6/75	PAGE 30	OPB · Budget · 52

ZERO·BASE BUDGET
Procedures & Instructions

EXECUTIVE DEPARTMENT
OFFICE OF PLANNING AND BUDGET – Budget Division
SECTION
BUDGET UNIT OR DEPARTMENT SUMMARY
SUBJECT
INSTRUCTIONS FOR FORM OPB-BUDGET-60

Form Purpose

This form is a summary of objects and fund sources of the Activity Financial Summaries for each Budget Unit, if an agency has more than one Budget Unit, and for the entire Department. The F. Y. 1974 Actual Column should be per the Audit Report.

— Show amounts by categories listed for F. Y. 1974 Actual, F. Y. 1975 Actual, F. Y. 1976 Budget, and F. Y. 1977 requested. F. Y. 1977 Requested is divided into four funding levels summarized from the Activity Financial Summaries.

— Amounts for F. Y. 1976 should represent the Annual Operating Budget to include amendments thereto approved by OPB since the beginning of the Fiscal Year.

F. Y. 1977

ZERO-BASE BUDGET REQUEST
BUDGET UNIT OR DEPARTMENT SUMMARY

OPB-Budget - 60
(Rev. 6-75)

Human Resources — Department

Human Resources — Budget Unit

OBJECTS/FUNDS	F. Y. 1974 Actual	F. Y. 1975 Actual	F. Y. 1976 Budgeted	F.Y. 1977 REQUESTED Minimum Level Packages	Base Level Packages	Workload Packages	New or Improved Packages	TOTAL All Packages
Number of Positions	33	35	44	25	15	6	3	49
A. TOTAL PERSONAL SERVICES	315,786	330,124	430,493	306,171	151,126	42,126	32,126	531,549
B. REG. OPERATING EXPENSES	110,100	135,000	150,000	95,110	65,210	18,100	7,200	185,620
C. TRAVEL	7,048	8,100	8,900	7,210	2,010	1,000	500	10,720
D. MOTOR VEHICLE EQUIP. PURCH.	10,500	11,600	16,300	15,100	5,112			20,212
E. PUBLICATIONS AND PRINTING	1,530	3,686	4,200	4,100	900	400	200	5,600
F. EQUIPMENT PURCHASES	600	900	3,100	2,100	2,000	300	200	4,600
G. PER DIEM AND FEES	1,200	2,181	3,600	2,800	800			3,600
H. COMPUTER CHARGES	2,500	5,281	7,000	4,900	2,000	1,800		8,700
I. OTHER CONTRACTUAL EXPENSE	500	900	1,400	900	1,100	400		2,400
J. AUTHORITY LEASE RENTALS	75,000	75,000	75,000	75,000				75,000
K. GENERAL OBLIGATION BONDS	50,000	50,000	50,000	50,000				50,000
L. CAPITAL OUTLAY						2,000		2,000
M. LIST OTHER OBJECTS:								
H.E.W.-County Health Grants	800,000	875,000	1,000,000	1,010,000				1,010,000
TOTAL EXPENDITURES (Add A - M)	1,374,764	1,497,772	1,749,993	1,573,391	230,258	66,126	40,226	1,910,001
FEDERAL FUNDS	800,000	875,000	1,016,000	1,010,000	6,000	7,000		1,023,000
OTHER FUNDS			4,000	4,000				4,000
STATE GENERAL FUNDS	574,764	622,772	729,993	559,391	224,258	59,126	40,226	883,001

Official Signature
(Signature required only on Department Summary)

Commissioner
Title

August 29, 1975
Date

Appendix 5
Reorganizing
The Postal Service

ISSUE DEFINITION

On July 1, 1971, the U.S. Postal Service was established as an independent agency to process the mail. This new agency, set up along
lines of a modern business corporation, promised to improve on the
heavily criticized ways of its predecessor, the U.S. Post Office. In
creating the new agency, Congress prohibited political appointments and
had the Postmaster General report to a board of governors rather than to
the President. Congress hoped that the board of governors would bring
their expertise in business to bear on the problems of processing mail.
Although some success has been achieved during the past four years,
there have been many disappointments and public dissatisfaction has become widespread. According to the 1975 Annual Report of the Postmaster
General costs are up and estimated to go higher, service now is not at
its best, mail volume declining, and private mail services are becoming
more competitive with the Service. Because of the mounting complaints
from dissatisfied postal customers, both House and Senate Subcommittees
on Postal Service have considered legislation aimed at tightening up
postal operations and relieving the financial pressures on the independent Postal Service.

BACKGROUND AND POLICY ANALYSIS

Since the Postal Reorganization Act, which became effective on July
1, 1971, Congress' role regarding the U.S. Postal Service has been
limited. Appointments of postal officials are made by the Board of
Governors and the Postmaster General: independently of Congressional
approval and postal rates are set up by the Postal Rate Commission.

Although Congress' role has been mainly reduced to one of oversight responsibility, this does not mean that Congress is no longer
expressing an active interest in postal affairs. Complaints about
poor service began on July 2, 1971, and are quite widespread today.
The House Post Office and Civil Service Subcommittee on Postal Service
began studying the performance of the U.S. Postal Service in April 1972.
It held extensive hearings with witnesses representing the service,
unions, large mailers, and the general public, as well as other Congressional members. This investigation continued into 1975. In 1973
the Senate Committee on Post Office and Civil Service began its hearings on the performance of the Postal Service which continued into 1975.

Note: This appendix is from [50], pp. 1-7.

PROBLEM OF SELF-SUFFICIENCY (The Breakeven Principle)

The Postal Reorganization Act was intended to put the newly reorganized Postal Service on a break-even basis by 1984 and to improve mail service at the same time. So far these two objectives have not been fulfilled.

The Postal Service reported to Congress a deficit of $989 million for FY75. Postmaster General Benjamin Bailar estimates that the service will lose about $1.5 billion in FY76 unless costs can be cut. The FY75 loss was $161 million more than the $828 million deficit the Postal Service had previously expected. Much of the unexpected increase in the deficit was due to a greater than expected rise in the costs of doing business during FY75.

The Postal Service's inability to become self-sufficient, or to achieve a balancing of its revenues and costs, is essentially attributable to the following factors: (1) lengthy delays in the rate making process, and (2) unexpected sharp increases in labor and operational costs. The Postal Service asserts that the rate setting process is too slow.

Since reorganization of the Postal Service, three rate proposals have been considered by the Postal Rate Commission. The first rate case, filed in February 1971 before reorganization of the Post Office Department, took 17 months to complete, and the second, filed in September 1973, was completed in 1975. The third rate case, filed in September 1975, is presently awaiting approval from the Postal Rate Commission.

Labor costs, which account for 85% of the Postal Service's total budget have risen sharply in recent years. Since reorganization of the Post Office in 1971, three labor agreements have been reached between the Postal Service and the four postal unions. The labor agreement reached on July 21, 1975 was the first to cover three years. The previous two contracts each covered two years. Under the July 21, 1975 contract's provisions, employees are to receive pay increases totalling $1,500 over a three-year period as well as cost-of-living adjustments tied to percentage increases in the Consumer Price Index (CPI). In 1975 the CPI rose nearly 10%. This added $400 million to the postal deficit. In addition, the sharp increases in the cost of the fuel needed to operate the processing facilities and motor vehicle fleet also increased the deficit.

The Postal Service has made several efforts in modernizing its operations. In doing so, a substantial amount of money has been committed. Since the inception of the Postal Service, a total of $2.73 billion has been committed to new facilities and inside machinery. Nearly $1 billion of this total has been invested in the new National Bulk Mail System which handles about one-third of all mail. It has been asserted by some users of the mail system, however, that so far mechanization has failed to produce the cost saving that was expected. Postal officials, on the other hand, assert that mail service now is better than it has been in five years.

Within the Postal Service, cost-cutting programs are underway to curb rising costs. Such measures include: jobs cut through attrition, transferring of employees from overstaffed offices to understaffed ones, and curbing of overtime pay and parttime help. The Service estimates that these efforts should result in savings of about $1 billion over the next

3 years. On June 30, 1976, the Postal Service announced that it has suspended plans to close and consolidate 231 post offices while Congress considers legislation to authorize increased postal appropriations.

POSTAL COMPETITION

Postal rate increases and poor service have caused many companies to turn to private mail services that promise reliable and relatively inexpensive delivery of third-class bulk mail. Some utility companies and magazine publishers are delivering their own mail. Many private mail delivery firms now accept relatively small parcels for delivery. Among them are Greyhound Package Service, American Airlines, and over 80,000 local and short-haul truckers, specialized carriers, and retail store delivery services. In the general handling and delivery of parcels, though, the Postal Service has but one major competitor, United Parcel Service, which makes 600 million deliveries of packages weighing one to 50 pounds annually.

In the face of mounting deficits and increased competition from privately owned mail services, the Postal Service is taking a new tack. The Postmaster General has said that "we should revive support for the public service function." He proposes federally subsidized postal services in those areas and operations that cannot be made competitive. The other postal services could then operate in competition with private industry.

This public service strategy was incorporated in H.R. 8603--Postal Reorganization Act of 1975. The bill would increase the annual Postal Service subsidy to $2.6 billion from its present public service subsidy of $920 million. During consideration of H.R. 8603, the House adopted an amendment offered by Congressman Alexander which completely altered H.R. 8603. The amendment would require the Postal Service to go to Congress each year for its authorization and appropriations and to deposit its revenues in the U.S. Treasury. For all intents and purposes, the Alexander amendment would take away a large proportion of the Postal Service's financial independence given them by Congress in 1970.

Senate action so far has not supported the House's proposal to sharply reduce the financial independence of the Postal Service. On June 11, 1976, the Senate Committee on Post Office and Civil Service amended and reported H.R. 8603 for consideration by the full Senate. H.R. 8603, as passed by the House, was amended by the Senate committee by deleting the original text and substituting the language of S. 2844. The Senate version of H.R. 8603 would limit Federal subsidies to $500 million a year for the next 2 fiscal years. In addition, the bill prohibits the closing of any post office serving 35 families or more on a regular basis, any smaller post office without first the approval of at least 60% of regular patrons of such an office. H.R. 8603 further provides for a moratorium on rate increases and service cuts during the period beginning with the first Federal subsidy payment. [See Note 1.]

POLICY ISSUES

Policy issues that have evolved around problems of the Postal Service include:

(1) Whether to abolish the Postal Service and repeal the Postal Reorganization Act. The real question here is whether the Post Office is a business or service.

(2) Should the "break-even" principle of the Postal Service be delayed? Under present law, the Postal Service is expected to attain self-sufficiency by 1984 except for continuing appropriations to subsidize second- and third-class non-profit mails and other preferential mail.

(3) Should Congress through its appropriation ease the burden of sharply increasing postage rates for first-class mailers as well?

(4) Should Congress exercise more control over the operations of the Postal Service?

LEGISLATION

- H.R. 8603 (Hanley et al.)

- Authorizes the appropriation of $500 million for FY76 and FY77 to be applied against the accumulated operating indebtedness of the Postal Service as of Sept. 30, 1976 and Sept. 30, 1977. Provides that during the period from the appropriation of the first $500 million until Feb. 15, 1977, the Service shall not effect rate or fee increases, shall not provide lesser types of postal service, and shall not close any post office where 35 or more families regularly receive mail. Requires door delivery or curbline delivery during such period to all permanent residential addresses. Requires the Postal Service to present to Congress information on plans designed to comply with the policies of the Postal Reorganization Act of 1970, and on the speed and reliability of the Postal Service upon request for appropriations. Limits any decrease in the rates for zone-rated parcels. Changes the appointment process of all Postal Rate Commission commissioners from direct Presidential appointment to Presidential nomination subject to Senate confirmation. Establishes a 10-month time limit within which the Commission must issue a recommended decision following a request for a rate increase. Requires the Service to wait 10 months (instead of the currently required 90 days) after a rate request is filled before imposing temporary rates. Limits temporary rates to the permanent rate proposal, and, when combined with all other funds, to the total costs of the Service. Allows temporary rates to continue in effect for 150 days following submission of the Commission's recommended decision. Establishes a Commission on Postal Service which shall report by Feb. 15, 1977, to the President and the Congress on the problems facing the Service, and shall 60 days thereafter cease to exist. Authorizes necessary appropriations for such purpose.

- S. 2844 (McGee) [See Note 2]

- To provide authorization for appropriation through FY79 in amounts not exceeding 10% of the total estimated operating expenses of the Postal Service. Establishes a study commission to study the public service functions of the Postal Service. Requires that the President appoint members of the Postal Rate Commission with the advice and consent of the Senate.

• H.R. 2559

• To provide for the application to the United States Postal Service of provisions of law providing for Federal agency safety programs and responsibilities pursuant to the Occupational Safety and Health Act of 1970. Approved Aug. 9, 1975; P.L. 94-82.

HEARINGS

U.S. Congress. House. Committee on Post Office and Civil Service. Briefing by Postal Rate Commission. Hearings, 94th Congress, 1st session. Mar. 6, 1975. Washington, U.S. Govt. Print. Off., 1975. 46 p.

----- Briefing by the Postmaster General. Hearings, 94th Congress, 1st session. Feb. 20, 1975. Washington, U.S. Govt. Print. Off., 1975. 74 p.

----- Postal reorganization. Hearings, on S. 2844 94th Congress, 2d session. Washington, U.S. Govt. Print. Off., 1976. 3 pts. Hearings held Jan. 21-28; Feb. 16, 20; Mar. 29, 1976.

U.S. Congress. House. Committee on Post Office and Civil Service. Subcommittee on Postal Service. Postal Reorganization Act Amendments of 1975. Hearings on H.R. 2455, 94th Congress, 1st session. Washington, U.S. Govt. Print. Off., 1975. 368 p. Hearings held Feb. 18, 21, 28; Mar. 11, 13, 1975.

----- Cutbacks in postal service. Hearings, 94th Congress, 2d session. May 4 and 5, 1976. Washington, U.S. Govt. Print. Off., 1976. 163 p.

----- Abolish the Postal Rate Commission and Index Postal Rate Increase with the Consumer Price Index. Hearings on H.R. 10109, 94th Congress, 2d session. Washington, U.S. Govt. Print. Off., 1976. 243 p. Hearings held Mar. 30, 31; Apr. 6, 7, 1976.

----- Postal Service finance. Hearing, 94th Congress, 1st session. Dec. 10, 1975. Washington, U.S. Govt. Print. Off., 1975. 37 p.

U.S. Congress. House. Committee on Post Office and Civil Service. Subcommittees on Postal Service and Postal Facilities, Mail, and Labor Management. GAO's recommendation that 12,000 small post offices be closed. Hearings, 94th Congress, 1st session. Sept. 23, 1975. Washington, U.S. Govt. Print. Off., 1975. 170 p.

----- Postal Inspection Service's monitoring and control of mail surveillance and mail cover programs. Hearings, 94th Congress, 1st session. May 6, 1975. Washington, U.S. Govt. Print. Off., 1975. 238 p.

----- New criteria for small post office closings and new regulations to control personnel costs. Hearings, 94th Congress, 1st session. Dec. 3 and 5, 1975. Washington, U.S. Govt. Print. Off., 1975. 120 p.

REPORTS AND CONGRESSIONAL DOCUMENTS

U.S. Congress. House. Committee on Post Office and Civil Service. Postal Reorganization Act Amendments of 1975: report together with individual views to accompany H.R. 8603. Washington, U.S. Govt. Print. Off., 1975. 46 p. (94th Congress, 1st session. House. Report no. 94-391)

U.S. Congress. House. Committee on Post Office and Civil Service. Subcommittee on Postal Facilities, Mail, and Labor Management. Subcommittee Staff Report on the United States Postal Service's National Bulk Mail System. Washington, U.S. Govt. Print. Off., 1976. 12 p.
    At head of title: 94th Congress, 2d session. Committee print.

U.S. Congress. Senate. Committee on Post Office and Civil Service. Explanation of the Postal Reorganization Act and selected background material. Washington, U.S. Govt. Print. Off., 1975. 314 p.
    At head of title: 94th Congress, 1st session. Committee print.

----- Postal Reorganization Act Amendments of 1976: report together with supplemental views to accompany H.R. 8603. Washington, U.S. Govt. Print. Off., 1976. 46 p. (94th Congress, 2d session. Senate. Report no. 94-966)

----- Problems of the U.S. Postal Service. Washington, U.S. Govt. Print. Off., 1976. 183 p.
    At head of title: 94th Congress, 2d session. Committee print.

CHRONOLOGY OF EVENTS

07/18/76 -- New rates became effective.

06/30/76 -- Postal Rate Commission endorsed the Postal Service's request to make temporary rate increases permanent.

06/21/76 -- Reported to Senate with amendment. S.Rept. 94-966.

03/30/76 -- Hearings held by Committee on Post Office and Civil Service on H.R. 10109.

03/29/76 -- Hearing held by Committee on Post Office and Civil Service on S. 2844.

02/26/76 -- Suit filed in U.S. District Court, Washington, D.C., by 51 members of Congress.

01/27/76 -- Two hearings held, the last on Feb. 20, by the Senate Committee on Post Office and Civil Service on S. 2844.

12/31/75 -- New postal rates became effective.

11/03/75 -- H.R. 8603 was referred to the Senate Committee on Post Office and Civil Service.

10/30/75 -- House passed H.R. 8603, as amended, 267-113.

09/29/75 -- The Alexander amendment was adopted, 267-123.

09/18/75 -- U.S. Postal Service filed request for new postal rate increase.

09/14/75 -- U.S. Postal Service Board of Governors approved U.S. Postal Rate Commission's decision making current postal rates permanent.

08/09/75 -- H.R. 2559 approved P.L. 94-82.

07/24/75 -- House Post Office and Civil Service report on H.R. 8603, Postal Reorganization Act Amendments of 1975. House Report no. 94-391, approved: unanimous.

02/18/75 -- Five hearings held, the last on March 13 by Subcommittee on Postal Service of House Committee on Post Office and Civil Service on Postal Reorganization Act Amendments of 1975: H.R. 2445.

ADDITIONAL REFERENCE SOURCES

Boorstin, David. Postal Reevaluation, p. 88-904. Washington, D.C.: Editorial Research Reports, 1975.

Congressional Budget Office. Financing Postal Operations: Alternative Approaches and Their Budgetary Implications. Report. 1976. 13 p.

Kessler, Ronald. "The Great Mail Bungle." Washington Post, 2 part series, June 9-15, 1974.

----- "Our Messed-Up Mail: A Case of Mismanagement." Washington Post, April 11, 1976, p. C1, C4.

President's Commission on Postal Organization. Towards Postal Excellence. Report. Washington, D.C.: GPO, 1968. 212 p.

U.S. Postal Service. Government Executive. October 1974, p. 13-14, 17, 21, 24, 26-28, 33-35.

----- Annual Report of the Postmaster General, 1974-1975. Washington, D.C., 55p.

"Why the Post Office Can't Break Even." Business Week, March 29, 1976, p. 63, 66, 70.

EDITORS' NOTES

1. H.Res. 8603 became Public Law 94-421 on September 24, 1976. Debate and passage in the Senate can be examined in the Congressional Record, August 24, 1976, p. S14454.

2. S. 2844 and H.Res. 2559 were not passed by the 94th Congress.

Appendix 6
Financial System
Reform Proposals

ISSUE DEFINITION

Interest in financial system reform has been building in Congress during the past several years. This results in large part from experiences dating from the mid-1960s which indicate that current financial institution structural arrangements are inadequate to assure institutional stability and efficiency and stable flows of funds to various sectors of the economy under the pressure of changing economic conditions. In addition, there is concern about the effectiveness of Federal regulation following the difficulties identified within the banking system over the past few years. During this session, both Houses are considering specific legislative proposals dealing with financial institutions and regulatory agency reform.

BACKGROUND AND POLICY ANALYSIS

Financial institutions have historically served as barometers of the economy. In turn, they exert their own influence on it. The experience of the nation's financial system during the latter part of the 1960s led to the recognition in many quarters of the need to consider possible measures of financial reform if financial institutions are to serve the economy's needs with maximum effectiveness in the years ahead.

Of particular significance, during the mid-1960s, general economic and monetary conditions have resulted in several periods of tight money and high interest rates. This in turn has reduced the availability of funds in the financial system and threatened the stability of some of the nation's financial institutions. The reduced availability of funds has also led to restricted financing for some classes of borrowers, especially in the housing sector.

Following the difficulties identified in the past few years in the commercial banking system, including the failures of a few large banks in 1973-1974, there has been increasing interest both in restructuring the Federal financial regulatory agencies and in providing additional regulatory authority to supervise specific bank practices. Other factors influencing the interest in financial reform include technological developments and legislative initiatives on the state level.

Note: This appendix is from [47], pp. 1-12.

As a result of interest in financial reform, a number of measures dealing with the functions of financial institutions and their regulation by the Federal Government are being considered in the 94th Congress. Legislative measures pending in the House and in the Senate in their current form cover many similar issues but vary considerably in terms of specific proposals to deal with these problems. In addition general interest in regulatory reform may lead to formalized systematic procedures for the review of regulatory agencies. If such procedures are adopted, it is expected that Federal bank regulatory agencies would be included in the reviewing process.

SENATE ACTIVITIES

On Dec. 11, 1975, the Senate passed the Financial Institutions Act of 1975 (FIA 75), which deals with financial institution reform. FIA 75 incorporates Administration proposals based on the recommendations of the President's Commission on Financial Structure and Regulation (the Hunt Commission), issued as a report in December 1971, and related bills and proposals.

In general, the Senate-passed bill reflects the Hunt Commission's philosophy that the most efficient way to allocate scarce funds is to provide for more competition among financial institutions and to encourage free market activities. Specifically, FIA 75 would provide for a restructuring of the nation's depository institutions--commercial banks, thrift institutions (savings and loan associations and mutual savings banks), and credit unions, for the purpose of improving the stability of these institutions, increasing service to consumers, and improving flows of credit to the housing sector. As a general rule, the legislation provides for uniform regulatory treatment of similar types of activities by competing institutions.

At the same time, a major objective is to increase the flexibility of thrift institutions in responding to changing economic conditions while preserving their role as the primary supplier of residential mortgage credit in the private sector. This would be accomplished by improving their ability to compete for funds while maintaining quantitative restrictions on the portion of their portfolio that must be invested in primarily residential mortgage loans and liquidity investments. Recognizing, too, that housing is an area of high social priority which does not always receive sufficient funds through the operation of competitive forces, FIA 75 would provide an incentive for mortgage investment by establishing a mortgage investment tax credit, available to all mortgage lenders.

Specific titles of the bill deal with the payment of interest on deposits or accounts, reserves and expanded deposit liability powers, lending and investment powers, charters for thrift institutions, credit unions, Government insured and guaranteed mortgage loans, and the effective date.

The title of the bill dealing with tax laws provides that the special bad-debt reserve provisions for thrift institutions would be phased out by 1979. Instead, as a special aid to housing, a sliding tax credit on residential mortgage income would be available to all lenders, based on the percentage of assets invested in residential mortgages. S. 1267 as passed by the Senate would not be effective until enactment of the

tax provisions which were separated out of the original bill at the
time it was considered on the Senate floor and referred to the Senate
Finance Committee.

The Committee is also considering a number of proposals dealing
with regulatory issues including structural changes in the National
Credit Union Administration and changes in the regulatory powers of the
Federal banking agencies, including the Federal Reserve, and provisions
to control bank holding company activities and bank concentration.
Hearings have also been held on a bill proposed by the Federal Reserve
to provide for Federal regulation of foreign bank activities in the
United States.

HOUSE ACTIVITIES

In April 1975 the House Banking Committee decided to undertake an
independent study before considering legislation. This study led the
Committee to hold hearings on a number of far-reaching proposals which
were originally intended to incorporate into a general omnibus bill.
However, since these wide-ranging proposals did not receive broad support from various interest groups, the Committee narrowed its focus and
the legislation was split into three bills dealing with the Federal
Reserve, depository institutions, and foreign banking. At the time
these bills were introduced it was announced that mark-up would proceed
at the earliest possible date. An amended version of H.R. 12934, the
Federal Reserve Reform Act of 1976, passed the House on May 10. The
original International Banking Act of 1976, H.R. 13211, was amended in
subcommittee and a clean bill, H.R. 13876, was considered by the full
committee and reported on May 26. However, planned mark-up of the
depository institutions bill, H.R. 13077, did not proceed as intended
and the bill has been referred to the Subcommittee on Financial
Institutions.

H.R. 13077, the Financial Reform Act of 1976 (FRA 76), is the most
complex and possibly the most controversial of the three bills. It
contains provisions dealing with the powers of depository institutions,
a number of housing aids, and various regulatory provisions. Thrifts
and credit unions generally support the bill; however, the commercial
banking industry is opposed primarily because it feels the bill gives
advantages to non-bank institutions without any compensating conces-
sions for banks, and labor and the home building industry are afraid
that the provisions will allow a more or less serious shift from
housing loans by thrift institutions.

Like the Senate bill, FRA 76 would provide for broader powers for
thrift institutions and credit unions. However these increased powers
are generally more restrictive than the Senate-passed provisions. For
example, Federally-chartered savings and loan associations would be
permitted to invest a smaller portion of their assets in primarily non-
housing related investments and there is no provision for investment in
commercial paper and other corporate debt securities. Savings and loan
associations would also not be permitted personal trust services. Third
party payment accounts could be offered by Federally-chartered thrift
institutions and credit unions only to the extent that state law allows
similar state-chartered institutions to offer such accounts. Additional

interest-bearing third party payment accounts would not be permitted
until after Jan. 1, 1978. Commercial banks have been particularly
critical of the deposit power provisions since these would have the effect of lifting the statutory ban on the payment of interest by banks
as of Jan. 1, 1978, whatever the competitive conditions prevailing at
that time. Unlike earlier versions of the proposed legislation, the
bill in its current form does not contain provisions dealing with reserve requirements.

Title III of the bill would establish a Deposit Interest Rate Control Committee to set interest rate ceilings on depository accounts.
As an aid to housing finance, the Committee would be required to allow
thrifts at least a quarter point differential over commercial banks on
interest payments on time and savings deposits. The concern for housing is emphasized by the statutory differential requirement, the provision that the Chairman of the Federal Home Loan Bank Board would be
the chairman of the Committee, and the provision requiring that the
Committee report annually on its activities, including information on
the housing-related asset composition of financial institutions. As
in the Senate bill, the interest ceiling authority would expire after
five and one-half years. Prior to that date the Committee would be
required to report to Congress its findings and recommendations regarding ceilings.

Recognizing that these institutional arrangements alone may not
assure adequate mortgage credit during periods of tight money, there
is a provision for a countercyclical Federal Home Loan Bank Board
advance program to make funds available to financial institutions for
loans on non-luxury housing. This approach differs from the Senate
bill which relies on a mortgage interest tax credit as a housing finance incentive. Although it has been reported that Representative
Reuss, chairman of the House Banking Committee, favors tax equity between thrift institutions and commercial banks, the House bill does not
propose changes in the tax laws governing thrift institutions.

Major proposals to consolidate Federal financial regulatory activities, including the transfer of bank regulatory powers of the Federal
Reserve, were dropped before the reform measures took bill form. Nonetheless, the bill contains a wide range of regulatory changes within
the existing regulatory structure. Provisions include the modification of the organization of several of the Federal financial regulatory
agencies and increased budgetary control, increased disclosure and reporting requirements for financial institutions, additional restrictions on "non-banking" activities of bank holding companies, and increased statutory and regulatory powers to deal with certain financial
institution practices. The bill also creates a National Credit Union
Administration Discount Fund to meet temporary liquidity needs of
credit unions.

The Federal Reserve Reform Act as passed by the House on May 10,
1976, would make the terms of the chairman and the vice chairman of the
Board of Governors of the Federal Reserve System coincident with that
of the President of the United States, would add three public interest
members to the board of each of the regional Federal Reserve banks, and
would make permanent the provisions of a Congressional resolution passed
in 1975 which requires the Federal Reserve to consult quarterly with
Congress on monetary policy. On Aug. 20, 1976 H.R. 12934 was favorably

reported by the Senate Committee on Banking, Housing and Urban Affairs.
A full description of this bill and its implications is found in CRS
Issue Brief 75058, Federal Reserve System: Congressional Oversight.

The International Banking Act of 1976 would provide for increased
Federal regulation and supervision of foreign bank activities in the
United States. This bill seeks to achieve the same purposes as a bill
drawn up by the Federal Reserve although the specific provisions of the
two bills differ. The International Banking Act was passed by the
House on July 30, 1976.

The Subcommittee on Commerce, Consumer and Monetary Affairs of the
House Committee on Government Operations is also holding a series of
hearings on the efficiency and adequacy of the Federal bank regulatory
system.

LEGISLATION CONSIDERED BY THE 94TH CONGRESS

Editors' Note: None of the following measures were enacted into law. A
listing of bills passed during the 94th Congress is found in the Congressional Record, October 26, 1976, p. D1399.

S. 958 (Proxmire by request)/H.R. 5617 (St. Germain, by request)

A bill drawn up by the Federal Reserve Board to be known as the
Foreign Bank Act of 1975. This bill seeks to establish a comprehensive system of Federal regulation and supervision of foreign bank activities in the United States consistent with the principles of national
treatment or non-discrimination. It seeks to achieve the same purposes
as H.R. 13876 although the specific provisions of the two bills differ.
The Senate Banking Committee began hearings on the bill Jan. 28, 1976.

S. 1267 (Proxmire, by request)

An Administration bill entitled "The Financial Institutions Act of
1975" (FIA 75). FIA 75 is a revised version of an Administration bill
introduced in the 93d Congress and incorporates recommendations issued
in December 1971 by the President's Commission on Financial Structure
and Regulation (the Hunt Commission). The bill deals specifically with
the structure of commercial banks, thrift institutions (savings and loan
associations and mutual savings banks), and credit unions. It contains
a wide range of recommendations to be considered as a package, the general thrust of which would be to allow for more competition among financial institutions and to encourage free market activities as the most
efficient way to allocate scarce funds. An amended version of S. 1267
passed by the Senate 79-14, Dec. 11, 1975; referred to House Committee
on Banking, Currency, and Housing on Dec. 15, 1975.

S. 1267 (Proxmire, by request)

An amendment (Senate Amendment No. 927) proposed by the Federal
Home Loan Bank Board concerning lending and investment powers of Federally chartered savings and loan associations. This proposal was a
complete substitute for the original proposals in FIA 75 regarding the
lending and investment powers of Federal thrift institutions and was
incorporated into the bill reported by the Senate Banking Committee.

S. 1475 (Proxmire)/H.R. 6074 (St. Germain, by request)

A credit union bill to amend the Federal Credit Union Act in order to improve the efficiency and flexibility of the financial system of the U.S. by permitting Federal credit unions to operate more efficiently and to better serve the family financial needs of their members; by reorganizing the National Credit Union Administration; by establishing a Central Liquidity Facility for Federal and State credit unions, and for other purposes. The Senate Banking Committee considered certain provisions of this bill at hearings on FIA 75. Although the House Banking Committee has taken no formal action on this bill, many similar provisions are included in H.R. 13077.

S. 1540 (Sparkman, by request)/H.R. 9134 (St. Germain, by request)

A bill by the National Savings and Loan League entitled "Family Financial Centers Act of 1975." This bill would provide for mutual or stock Federal Savings and Loan Associations which would have broadened lending, investment, deposit, and consumer service powers, including trust powers. Other provisions deal with variable interest rate mortgages and flexible payment schedules, the retention of "regulation Q" interest rate ceilings on time and savings deposits, and changes in the structure and operations of the Federal Home Loan Bank Board. The Senate Banking Committee considered certain provisions of this bill at hearings on FIA 75. Although the House Banking Committee has taken no formal action on this bill, many similar provisions are included in H.R. 13077.

S. 2209 (McIntyre)

A bill to amend the Bank Holding Company Act of 1956, as amended, to provide special procedures for the acquisition of failing banks or bank holding companies and for the acquisition of banks or bank holding companies in emergencies. This bill represents an amended version of a bill drafted by the Federal Reserve Board. Passed by the Senate, July 30, 1975. Similar provisions appear in H.R. 13077.

S. 2298 (Proxmire)

A bill to establish a Federal Bank Commission to administer all Federal laws relating to the conduct of banking business. The Senate Banking Committee began hearings on S. 2298, Oct. 31, 1975.

S. 2304 (Proxmire)/H.R. 9743 (St. Germain, by request)

A bill drafted by the 3 Federal bank regulatory agencies to strengthen the supervisory authority of the Federal banking agencies over financial institutions and their affiliates with regard to the power of regulatory agencies to prohibit insider loans, assess civil penalties, issue cease and desist orders applicable to banks and/or officers of banks, remove officers, and take other remedial actions. Ordered reported as amended by the Senate Banking Committee, Apr. 29, 1976. S. Rept. 94-843.

S. 2721 (Proxmire)

A bill to amend the Bank Holding Company Act and the Bank Merger Act to restrict the activities in which registered bank holding companies may engage and to control the acquisition of banks by bank holding com-

panies and by other banks. The Senate Banking Committee began hearings
on the bill, Mar. 4, 1976.

S. 2772 (McIntyre)

Contains the tax provisions of S. 1267 which were separated out of
the bill at the time it was considered on the Senate floor, December 11,
1975. Referred to the Senate Finance Committee.

S. 3312 (McIntyre)

A bill to reorganize the National Credit Union Administration. This
bill represents an amended version of Title II of S. 1475 and was ordered reported by the Senate Banking Committee, Apr. 14, 1976. S. Rept.
94-751.

H.R. 5618/H.R. 5619 (St. Germain, by request)

Identical to S. 1267 except that the tax portion of the Administration's proposed legislation is omitted. The tax provisions are contained in H.R. 5619. Referred to Committee on Banking, Currency, and
Housing.

H.R. 12934 (Reuss)

The Federal Reserve Reform Act of 1976, would make permanent the
provisions of H.Con.Res. 133 and would change the terms and manner of
appointment of some Federal Reserve Officials. Passed by the House, as
amended, on May 10, 1976.

H.R. 13077 (St. Germain)

The Financial Reform Act of 1976, deals with the powers of depository institutions, a number of housing aids, and various regulatory
provisions. Its stated purpose is "to expand competition, provide for
the flow of funds for mortgage credit, provide improved financial services, and strengthen financial institutions and regulatory agencies;
"and for other purposes." At the time the bill was introduced, Apr. 7,
1976, it was announced that a mark-up would be held at the earliest
possible date. At a mark up session on May 3, Mr. Reuss, Chairman of
the Committee on Banking, Currency and Housing noted that there was not
"a clear majority in favor of the bill" and referred H.R. 13077 to the
Subcommittee on Financial Institutions, Committee on Banking, Currency,
and Housing.

H.R. 13876 (Rees)

A clean bill in lieu of H.R. 13211, The International Banking Act of
1976, would require that the activities of foreign banks operating in
the United States more closely conform to those permitted American
banks. Reported by the Committee on Banking, Currency and Housing, on
May 26.

HEARINGS

U.S. Congress. House. Committee on Banking, Currency, and Housing.
     To promote the independence and responsibility of the Federal

Reserve System. Hearings, 94th Congress, 2d session. Washington, U.S. Govt. Print. Off., 1976. 64 p.
"H.R. 12934, a bill to promote the independence and responsibility of the Federal Reserve System."
Hearing held Apr. 9, 1976.

U.S. Congress. House. Committee on Banking, Currency, and Housing. Subcommittee on Financial Institutions Supervision, Regulation and Insurance. Financial institutions and the nation's economy (FINE) "discussion principles." Hearings. 94th Congress, 1st and 2d session.ss Parts 1-3. Washington, U.S. Govt. Print. Off., 1976. 3 v. 2495 p.
Hearings held Dec. 2, 1975-Jan. 29, 1976.

----- Financial Reform Act of 1976. Hearings. 94th Congress, 2d session. Parts 1&2 Washington. U.S. Govt. Print. Off., 1976. 2v. 1302 p.
Hearings held Mar. 4, 9, 11, 16, 17, 18, and 23, 1976.

U.S. Congress. House. Committee on the Budget. Mortgage Interest Tax Credit. Hearings 94th Congress, Second Session. Washington. U.S. Govt. Print. Off., 1976. 107 p.
Hearing held Feb. 25, 1976.

U.S. Congress. Senate. Committee on Banking, Housing, and Urban Affairs. Federal Bank Commission Act. Hearings, 94th Congress, 1st session. Washington, U.S. Govt. Print. Off., 1976. 301 p.
"S. 2298, to establish a Federal Bank Commission to administer all Federal laws relating to the conduct of the banking business both foreign and domestic including all such laws relating to the chartering of banking institutions and their branching activities, bank holding companies and their activities, Edge Act corporations and their activities, and the examination, supervision, and regulation of all banking institutions under Federal law."
Hearings held Oct. 31, and Dec. 1, 8, 1975.

----- Problem banks. Hearing, 94th Congress, 2d session. Washington, U.S. Govt. Print. Off., 1976. 410 p.
Hearings on how well the regulatory agencies are managing their supervisory and regulatory authority to assure a safe and sound banking system.
Hearing held Feb. 5, 1976.

U.S. Congress. Senate. Committee on Banking, Housing, and Urban Affairs. Subcommittee on Financial Institutions. Emergency Acquisition of Banks or Bank Holding Companies. Hearings, 94th Congress, 1st session. Washington, U.S. Govt. Print. Off., 1975. 120 p.
"S. 890, to amend the Bank Holding Company Act of 1956, as amended, to provide special procedures for the acquisition of failing banks or bank holding companies and for the acquisition of banks or bank holding companies in emergencies and to provide for the acquisition by bank holding companies of banks outside their state of principal banking operations in emergency situations and situations involving a failing bank or bank holding company."
Hearings held July 22 and 28, 1975.

----- Financial Institutions Act of 1975. Hearings, 94th Congress, first session. Washington, U.S. Govt. Print. Off., 1975. 835 p.

"S. 1267, to expand competition, provide improved consumer services, strengthen the ability of financial institutions to adjust to changing economic conditions, and improve the flows of funds for mortgage credit: S. 1475, to amend the Federal Credit Union Act in order to improve the efficiency and flexibility of the financial system of the United States by permitting Federal credit unions to operate more efficiently and to better serve the family financial needs of their members; by reorganizing the National Credit Union Administration; by establishing a central liquidity facility for Federal and State credit unions; and for other purposes; S. 1540, to provide for family financial centers and for other purposes."

Hearings held May 14-16, June 11, 1975.

----- Financial Institutions Supervisory Powers. Hearings. 94th Congress, 2d session. Washington. U.S. Govt. Print. Off., 1976. 90 p.

Hearing held Mar. 26, 1976.

----- Financial Institutions Act - 1973. Hearings, 93d Congress, second session. Washington, U.S. Govt. Print. Off., 1974. 1094 p.

"S. 2591, to improve the efficiency and flexibility of the financial system of the United States in order to promote sound economic growth, including the provision of adequate funds for housing."

Hearings held May 13-17, 1974.

----- Financial structure and regulation. Hearings, 93d Congress, 1st session. Washington, U.S. Govt. Print. Off., 1973. 670 p.

Hearings on recommended changes in the structure of the nation's financial system.

Hearings held Nov. 6, 7 [and] 8, 1973.

----- Housing and financial reform. Hearings, 93d Congress, 2d session, Washington, U.S. Govt. Print. Off., 1974. 51 p.

Hearings on the impact of the proposed Financial Institutions Act on the future of housing in America.

Hearings held Dec. 11, 1974.

----- Reform of financial institutions - 1973. Hearings, 93d Congress, 2d session, Washington, U.S. Govt. Print. Off., 1974. 747 p.

Hearings on the views of members of the academic community and public interest groups on S. 2591, the Financial Institutions Act of 1973.

Hearings held Sept. 11, 12 and 25, 1974.

----- Restructuring the National Credit Union Administration. Hearing, 94th Congress, 2d session. Washington, U.S. Govt. Print. Off., 1976. 49 p.

Hearing on Title II of S. 1475 to reorganize the National Credit Union Administration.

Hearing held Mar. 10, 1976.

----- Variable rate securities and disintermediation. Hearings, 93d Congress, 2d Session, Washington, U.S. Govt. Print. Off., 1974. 250 p.

  Hearings on the ability of financial institutions to attract and retain deposits at a time of particularly high interest rates when tremendous competition for funds is in the capital markets.

  Hearings held July 24 [and] 25, 1974.

----- Competition in Banking Act of 1976. Hearings. 94th Congress, 2d session, on S. 2721. Washington. U.S. Govt. Print. Off., 1976, 327 p.

  Hearings held Mar. 4 and 5, 1976.

U.S. Congress. Senate. Committee on Banking, Housing, and Urban Affairs. Subcommittee on Housing and Urban Affairs. Housing goals and mortgage credit: 1975-80. Hearings, 94th Congress, 1st session. Washington, U.S. Govt. Print. Off., 1975. 450 p.

  "To receive testimony on residential mortgage credit needs of the nation for the period 1975-1980: whether our existing financial system is adequate to meet these needs, and what changes need to be made in Federal law or regulations to insure adequate mortgage flows for the future."

  Hearings held Sept. 22, 23 [and] 25, 1975.

REPORTS AND CONGRESSIONAL DOCUMENTS

U.S. Congress. House. Committee on Banking, Currency and Housing. Explanation of proposed Financial Institutions Act of 1976. 94th Congress, 2d session. Washington, U.S. Govt. Print. Off., 1976. 9 p.

  At head of title: Committee print.

----- Compendium of Papers prepared for the FINE Study. 94th Congress, 2d session. Books 1 and 2. U.S. Govt. Print. Off., 1976. 1111 p.

----- Financial Institutions and the Nation's Economy (FINE): a compendium of papers prepared for the FINE study. 94th Congress, 1st Session. Washington, U.S. Govt. Print. Off., 1975. 370 p.

  At head of title: Committee print.

----- Financial Institutions and the Nation's Economy (FINE) Discussion Principles. 94th Congress, 1st session. Washington, U.S. Govt. Print. Off., Nov. 1975. 21 p.

  At head of title: Committee print.

----- Financial Reform Act of 1976. 94th Congress, 2d session. Washington. U.S. Govt. Print. Off., Feb. 25, 1976. 217 p.

  At head of title: Committee print.

----- House Banking Committee will launch major review of Nation's financial institutions. News release. Washington. Apr. 24, 1975. 4 leaves.

----- International Banking; A Supplement to a Compendium of Papers
Prepared for the Fine Study. Staff Report. Washington. U.S.
Govt. Print. Off., 1976. 447 p.
       At head of title: Committee Print.

----- Report to accompany H.R. 12934, the Federal Reserve Reform Act
of 1976. Washington, U.S. Govt. Print. Off., 1975. 16 p.
(94th Congress, 2d session. Report no. 94-1073)

----- Report to accompany H.R. 13876, The International Banking Act
of 1976. Washington. U.S. Govt. Print. Off., 1976. 31 p.
(94th Congress, 2d session. Report no. 94-1193)

U.S. Congress. Senate. Committee on Banking, Housing and Urban
Affairs. Compendium of major issues in bank regulation. 94th
Congress, 1st session. Washington, U.S. Govt. Print. Off.,
1975. 957 p.
       At head of title: Committee print.

----- Report to accompany H.R. 12934. The Federal Reserve Reform
Act. Washington, U.S. Govt. Print. Off., 1976 (94th Congress,
2d session. Senate report 94-1151)

----- The Emergency Bank Holding Company Acquisition Act. Report to
accompany S. 2209. Washington, U.S. Govt. Print. Off., 1975.
2 p. (94th Congress, 1st session. Senate Report no. 94-338).

----- Financial Institutions Act of 1975; report to accompany
S. 1267 together with additional views. Washington, U.S. Govt.
Print. Off., 1975. 65 p. (94th Congress, 1st session. Senate
Report no. 94-487).

----- Report to accompany S. 2304, Financial Institutions Supervisory
Act Amendments of 1976. Senate Report 94-843. Washington.
U.S. Govt. Print. Off., 1976. 21 p.

----- Reorganization of National Credit Union Administration; report
to accompany S. 3312. Washington, U.S. Govt. Print. Off., 1976.
6 p. (94th Congress, 2d session. Senate Report no. 94-751).

----- The report of the President's Commission on Financial Structure
and Regulation (Dec. 1971) including recommendations of Department of the Treasury. Washington, U.S. Govt. Print. Off., 1973.
213 p.
       At head of title: Committee print.
       Reproduces the report of the President's Commission on
Financial Structure and Regulation (The Hunt Commission Report),
the original edition of which is no longer available.

CHRONOLOGY OF EVENTS

08/20/76 -- H.R. 12934, the Federal Reserve Reform Act favorably re-
            ported from the Senate Committee on Banking, Housing and
            Urban Affairs. Rept. no. 94-1151.

07/30/76 -- H.R. 13876 the International Banking Act passed the
            House.

05/20/76 -- H.R. 13876 reported by House Committee on Banking, Currency, and Housing.

05/17/76 -- House Subcommittee on Financial Institutions considered H.R. 13211. A clean bill, H.R. 13876 was introduced for consideration of the full Banking Committee.

05/10/76 -- H.R. 12934, the Federal Reserve Reform Act of 1976, passed House by a vote of 279-85.

05/03/76 -- H.R. 13077 referred to Subcommittee on Financial Institutions.

04/27/76 -- The House Banking Committee marked-up H.R. 12934, the Federal Reserve Reform Act of 1976, the first of three pending financial reform bills. (House Report no. 94-1073)

03/30/76 -- Representative Reuss announced that the proposed financial reform legislation in the House would be split into three bills dealing with the Federal Reserve, depository institutions, and foreign banking, respectively, and that the Committee would mark up these bills at the earliest possible date. The bills are inclusive of Senate-passed legislation (The Financial Institutions Act of 1975) and deal with several additional areas which are being considered as separate bills in the Senate during this Congress. While legislative measures pending in the House and in the Senate in their current form cover many similar issues, they vary considerably in terms of specific proposals to deal with these problems.

03/04/76 - 04/09/76 -- The Subcommittee on Financial Institutions of the House Banking Committee held a second series of hearings and the full Committee also held a hearing on provisions for financial reform contained in a Committee Print setting forth specific legislative language which was issued in February.

12/11/75 -- The Senate passed The Financial Institution Act of 1975 (FIA 75) which deals with financial institution reform. FIA 75 incorporates Administration proposals based on the Hunt Commission and related bills and proposals. The Administration first introduced legislation in 1973 and in 1975 the Administration introduced a second version of the bill, taking into account findings of hearings held by the Senate Banking Committee in 1973-1974. The Senate Banking Committee held additional hearings in the 94th Congress on the Administration bill as well as legislative proposals for various interest groups before taking final action.

12/02/75 - 01/29/76 -- The Subcommittee on Financial Institutions of the House Banking Committee held hearings on the FINE "Discussion Principles."

11/00/75 -- The House Banking Committee issued "Discussion Principles" in connection with the Financial Institutions and the Nation's Economy (FINE) study.

04/24/75 -- Representative Reuss, chairman of the House Banking Committee, and Representative St. Germain, chairman of the Subcommittee on Financial Institutions, announced that the Committee would undertake a major review of the nation's financial institutions and their regulation by the Federal government [the Financial Institutions and the Nation's Economy (FINE) study], leading to implementing legislation.

12/00/71 -- Report of the President's Commission on Financial Structure and Regulation (the Hunt Commission) released.

ADDITIONAL REFERENCE SOURCES

U.S. Department of the Treasury. The Financial Institutions Act of 1975. Washington, D.C. March 19, 1975. 35 p.
    Includes President Ford's message to the Congress, March 19, 1975; a summary of the Financial Institutions Act of 1975; and descriptive material.

U.S. Federal Home Loan Bank Board. Office of Economic Research. A Financial Institution for the Future: Savings, Housing Finance, Consumer Services. Washington, D.C. 1975. 73 p.
    "An examination of the restructuring of the savings and loan industry."

U.S. League of Savings Associations. Committee on the Study of Alternatives for Future Development. Future Alternatives Report. November 1974. 67 p.
    Includes as Appendum A a draft of revised Section 5 (c) of the Home Owners Loan Act by the Rand Committee, a special ad-hoc committee of the United States League of Savings Associations, October 2, 1974.

U.S. Library of Congress. Congressional Research Service. Changing Financial Institution Structures: Savings and Loan Associations, by Susan H. Dovell and F. Jean Wells. Washington, D.C. May 2, 1976. 28 p.

----- The Credit Union Industry: Major Legislative Proposals in the 94th Congress, by Pauline Smale. Washington, D.C. February 26, 1976. 15 p.

----- U.S. President's Commission on Financial Structure and Regulation: Selected References, by Felix Chin. Washington, D.C. January 2, 1974. 5 p. (See also IB75058 Federal Reserve System: Congressional Oversight.)

Appendix 7
Federal Energy
Reorganization

ISSUES AND OPTIONS

This paper summerizes the principal observations on the government
organization for energy affairs raised in the course of a June 22-23, 1976
workshop in the Whittall Pavilion at the Library of Congress. The workshop
was arranged by the National Academy of Public Administration Foundation for
the Congressional Research Service in response to a request by Senator Charles
Percy of the Senate Committee on Government Operations. Its timing and
content were designed to assist that Committee in its consideration of legislation extending or revising the authority of the Federal Energy Administration
and other Executive energy bodies.

In addition to the transcript of the discussions, this summary draws
upon written statements submitted by a number of participants and other authorities, and discussions with a few persons who were unable to attend.

PARTICIPANTS

Charles F. Bingman, Deputy Administrator, Urban Mass Transportation
    Administration; former energy specialist, Office of Management
    and Budget

Lynn Alan Brooks, Commissioner, Connectucut State Department of Planning
    and Energy Affairs

Monte Canfield, Jr., Director, Energy and Minerals Division, General
    Accounting Office; former Deputy Director, Energy Policy Project,
    Ford Foundation

Chester L. Cooper, Institute for Energy Analysis, Oak Ridge Associated
    Universities; former Director, International and Social Studies,
    Institute for Defense Analyses

Note: This appendix is from [71], pp. 36-37, 39-61, 205-219.

Alan L. Dean, Vice President, U.S. Railway Association; former Senior Analyst, Bureau of the Budget; Assistant Secretary, Department of Transportation

William O. Doub, Attorney; former Commissioner, Atomic Energy Commission; Chairman, Federal Energy Regulation Study Team

George C. Eads, Executive Director, National Commission on Supplies and Shortages

Harold B. Finger, Manager, Center for Energy Systems, General Electric Company; former Director, nuclear systems and propulsion, National Aeronautics and Space Administration and Atomic Energy Commission

Bernard L. Gladieux, Consultant; former Partner, Booz, Allen and Hamilton; Director, Knight, Gladieux and Smith

Charles J. Hitch, President, Resources for the Future; former President, University of California; Assistant Secretary, Department of Defense

Frank Pollara, Special Assistant to the Officers, American Federation of Labor-Congress of Industrial Organizations

Clem Rastatter, Director, Energy Conservation Project, The Conservation Foundation

Cecily Cannan Selby, President, Americans for Energy Independence; former Executive Director, Girl Scouts

Robert F. Steadman, Consultant; former Director of Government Studies, Committee for Economic Development

William E. Warne, Consultant; former Assistant Secretary, Department of Interior

National Academy of Public Administration

Roy W. Crawley, Executive Director (workshop chairman)

Erasmus Kloman, Harold Orlans (staff)

Contributors

James E. Akins, former Ambassador, Saudi Arabia; former Director, Office of Fuels and Energy, Department of State; Energy Adviser, White House

Harold P. Green, Attorney; Professor, National Law Center, George Washington University

William A. Johnson, Director, Energy Policy Research Project, George Washington University; former Assistant Administrator, Federal Energy Office

Hans H. Landsberg, Co-Director, Energy and Materials Division, Resources for the Future

John C. Sawhill, President, New York University; former Administrator, Federal Energy Office

Chauncey Starr, President, Electric Power Research Institute; former Dean, School of Engineering, University of California at Los Angeles; former president, Atomics International

Mason Willrich, Professor, Law School, University of Virginia

A Central Energy Agency or Department?

The arguments for and against concentrating important energy programs in a major new agency or department were extensively discussed.

Against a Central Agency: Reorganization is costly in the time it takes a new agency and new officials to settle in and function effectively. There has been too much energy reorganization already and too frequent changes in leadership and direction--"The United States has had at least nine energy czars in three years."[*] ERDA was established only in January 1975 and should be given a chance to prove itself. It could be hurt by inclusion in a new agency, especially a department in which old line agencies of the Department of the Interior would have a major voice. Large bureaucracies are often inefficient and have difficulty attracting good people to serve in subsidiary positions; ERDA is already "a giant" and FEA, "a jungle." There is a tendency to expect too much from a new organization--that it formulate and implement a consistent national energy policy, whereas the inconsistency of government policies reflects the diversity of domestic interests that is likely to persist despite any reorganization.

A large agency can lead to an excessive concentration of power and the reduction of public debate, the subduing of rejected viewpoints that can find expression in one of many independent agencies. This viewpoint was stressed especially by Clem Rastatter, who feared that conservationist efforts might lose out in a centralized organization, and by Chauncey Starr, who was concerned to maintain a maximum number of policy options. In a fragmented structure, policy conflicts are more likely to be aired in public before they are resolved in the Executive Office of the President and the Congress.

All of the programs and powers important to the formulation and achievement of the nation's energy goals could be concentrated in a single department only if the entire government were put into one department. The Treasury, State, Defense, Housing, and Transportation depart-

---

[*] William A. Johnson, "Why U.S. Energy Has Failed" (April 1976), in Robert Kalter and William Vogely, eds., Energy Supply and Government Policy, Cornell University Press (forthcoming).

ments, for example, all have major responsibilities that effect the supply
or use of energy and therefore will remain powerful independent forces in
energy affairs. Nonetheless, many programs are candidates for inclusion
in a centralized department.

A major centralization of energy programs and controls
assumes that we know, or can resolve upon, a concerted course of action
to deal with the nation's complex and difficult energy problems. "Since
we don't know the right answers, it is very dangerous to assume one direction to the detriment of all others....With an uncertain future and
uncertain outcomes of any action the wisest path is one of multiple
programs, each of which has potential merit either as an investment in
our energy future or as an insurance against negative outcomes. The
answer...is judicious diversity" (Chauncey Starr).

For a Central Agency: The present dispersion and fragmentation
of agencies and programs produces waste, confusion, duplication of effort,
and needless bureaucratic conflicts. The nation has accomplished too little
for its energy efforts and expenditures -- "we're not getting very far very
fast." Though the amalgamation or agglomeration of independent agencies
into a large organization provides no assurance that their independent
programs will be coordinated, duplicated activities eliminated, and conflicting policies reconciled, it makes these goals more feasible. To be
sure, all energy programs and powers cannot be concentrated in one department, but the secretary of a modern department has the power and resources
to forge and administer meaningful national policies and to defend them
in Executive and Congressional councils more forcefully than can the
heads of numerous minor agencies. And the assignment to one secretary
of responsibility for fractionated energy functions can promote more
balanced programs, as the formation of ERDA has promoted a better
balance between research on nuclear and other fuels and the Department
of Transportation has helped to provide a better balance between automotive and other modes of transportation.

The key to the effectiveness of a modern department is the
assignment to it of major related functions; the removal of encrusted
legislative restrictions; the transference to the secretary of power
to realign functions and to delegate responsibilities as he sees fit;
and the provision, in the secretary's office, of sufficient, high-

quality staff to monitor, evaluate, and coordinate the previously
independent functions and to propose general policies. It is not size
but the failure to clarify and delegate responsibility that creates
inefficiency and makes the recruitment of able staff difficult. The
fear that a department will inhibit public debate is unwarranted--
"The Cabinet Secretaries are not going to take over the country."
Secretaries and their line officials are accountable to the Congress;
close communication with, and promotion of, their special constituencies
is characteristic of departmental units, which leak like sieves. Con-
trariwise, the dispersion of functions among independent agencies
frustrates public accountability and participation in policy development,
as agency conflicts are resolved by nameless presidential aides protected
by Executive privilege, operating in a highly politicized situation, and
unaccountable to the Congress or the public. A major reorganization of
energy affairs would be opportune and advisable early in 1977, when a
fresh administration should enjoy the customary period of grace extended
to a newly elected president.

The Composition of a New Energy Agency

Few would perpetuate the present Federal Energy Administration,
a stopgap agency with inadequate and temporary authority and accomplishments. A reconstituted FEA, given stronger powers and data-gathering functions, together with ERDA, and a new public body to finance energy facilities,
such as the proposed Energy Independence Authority, would constitute the
core of any new agency. The distinction between an energy "agency" or
"authority" and a "department" hinges largely on the Department of Interior natural resource responsibilities that might be incorporated in
the latter, particularly the Bureaus of Mines, Land Management, and
Reclamation; its five Power Administrations; and the Geological Survey.
Opponents of a Department of Energy and Natural Resources fear that it
will be nothing more than "a retreaded Interior," a stultified bureaucracy that is a "captive" of Western interests. They might favor such
a department were it possible, by waving a wand, to make existing
statutes and staff vanish and reappear in fresh forms suited to current
realities.

In an independent ERDA, Senator Percy suggests, "researchers
tend to select...technical approaches which do not completely meet the

needs of the users of new technology...." The inclusion of ERDA in an

agency with broader energy functions should link research more closely

to application and, hence, promote the early adoption by industry and

the public of new modes of energy production, transmission, and con-

servation. It would also, Charles Hitch observes, be more likely to

provide incentives for private energy research and demonstration:

> A technology oriented agency like ERDA, with the best of
> intentions (which it has), is always likely to "tilt" to-
> ward government sponsored R and D. In a Department of Energy
> and Natural Resources, an Assistant Secretary for Fossil Fuels,
> for example, exercising what are now FEA and ERDA and perhaps
> other functions, might be expected to ask: wouldn't it be
> better if industry built this demonstration plant...and isn't
> there some way--other than a government R and D contract--
> to induce them to do it? Or an Assistant Secretary for Conser-
> vation might well decide that the most effective thing he
> could do in the residential area would be to provide help to
> homeowners to finance the purchase of insulation, heat pumps,
> and (hopefully before long) solar heating and cooling units.

However, some consider the resultant emphasis upon the early commercial-

ization of new technology as grounds for opposing the inclusion of ERDA

in a larger agency, because they regard commercialization as a proper

function of industry, not government, or because they are concerned

lest attention to short-term technological improvements draw attention and

funds from such long-term developments as fusion, the breeder reactor, or

solar energy, And Chauncey Starr is so much in favor of the dispersion of

power that he would break up ERDA into three agencies devoted, respectively,

to nuclear energy, fossil fuel, and advanced technical systems.[*]

Even if all of Interior, including the National Park Service

and the Bureau of Indian Affairs, were absorbed into a new department,

significant energy-related programs such as those of the Forest Service,

the Army Corps of Engineers, and the National Oceanic and Atmospheric

Administration would remain in other departments. The location of the

independent Environmental Protection Agency and the Council on Environ-

mental Quality in the Executive Office of the President would also have

----

[*] "...it is clear from the structure of ERDA that this agency has segregated itself into several major areas. The current experience with
that agency would indicate that it could probably be operated more
effectively if the nuclear sector, the fossil fuel sector, and the
advanced technical systems each had the national status which was
originally that of the five-man AEC. The overlap of technical programs between such groups is so small that coordination of their
activities could well take place at a coordinating level rather than
at an operating level."

to be determined. Some favor and others oppose the addition of EPA to
a department, but even those who favor it would retain the CEQ as an
independent voice for environmental concerns at the highest levels of
government.[*]

The location of regulatory and data-gathering functions will
be discussed subsequently.

In sum: A minority of workshop participants favored a continuation of the present proliferation of energy agencies; the majority
favored the union of FEA and ERDA into a new agency or the establishment of a new department including FEA, ERDA, most of Interior, and
perhaps EPA and portions of other departments. The support for such a
Department of Energy and Natural Resources was more evident in the
workshop than it has been in much recent public discussion. William
Warne conceives of DENR as an interim ("25-year") step toward the eventual
creation of a mammoth Department of Civil Resources Management embracing
but retaining DENR, Commerce, and Labor as separate departments, much as
the Department of Defense embraces the separate services. Similarly,
those who deem the early creation of a Department of Energy and Natural
Resources inadvisable or impracticable may accept the formation of a
more modest energy agency as a reasonable compromise or interim step.[**]

National Policy Formation and Coordination

The executive organization for formulating and coordinating
energy policies is disorderly and inadequate or adequate only for
formulating disorderly policies. Few will openly defend this situation

---

[*]
This was also the view of the Committee for Economic Development in its
December 1974 report Achieving Energy Independence, which recommended
the transfer of EPA to a department of energy and natural resources:
"...the Council on Environmental Quality [should] be retained in the
Executive Office of the President as an independent monitor of environmental impact..."

[**]
That is the position, among others, of John Sawhill and the General
Accounting Office. GAO has "proposed combining FEA's permanent
energy policy responsibilities with ERDA's energy research and development policy responsibilities into a new National Energy Administration. The most critical need in solving the Nation's energy problems
is to have a unified and concentrated effort for developing national
energy policies, plans, and programs....this new agency can bring
about this effort, and its creation is a logical first step toward
the longer term creation of a Department of Energy and Natural Resources" (Monte Canfield, Jr.).

except those who contend it is better than a tidy organization which
produces consistent policies that can be disastrous. Thus Chauncey
Starr states, "...we have only a primitive knowledge of the real role
of energy in our society....legislative and administrative actions taken
under these circumstances are apt to be at best superficial and palliative,
and at worst may be dangerously destructive." However, the dispersion
of power limits the damage even a powerful government executive can wreak.
"...an energy 'czar' in government would not be given the tools and the
full responsibility to perform, but would likely become at best an ex-
pediter, usually a coordinator, and at worst a bottleneck."

Does the nation have an energy policy? "It's a happening, not
a policy." Or, it is a policy but "a bad one: to do nothing"; "to import
regardless of price"; to provide "an abundance of clean, secure energy"
with some attention to conservation. Evident conflicts exist between
energy policies (such as attaining energy independence and depleting
national fuel reserves or letting market forces operate freely and
yet regulating their operation) and between energy and other public
policies (such as increasing energy supply and improving the environment or raising energy prices to increase supply and yet fighting
inflation). If a reduction of oil imports is a fair test of energy
independence, that policy is failing.

A clear organizational focus for energy policy formulation
is now lacking. No single organization is shaping national policy for
oil, for coal, or, since the Atomic Energy Commission was bifurcated, for
nuclear power. "No one has an overview of any one fuel or of all the
fuels," Mason Willrich remarks. FEA lacks "clout"; the Energy Resources
Council lacks independent staff and, as a council of equals, has difficulty imposing consistent policies upon its members.

This situation can be improved by 1) assigning to a new
energy agency or department responsibility for developing Executive
energy policies, and by 2) strengthening ERC with independent staff
and statutory authority, or replacing it with an Energy Policy Council
in the Executive Office of the President. The council should monitor
and coordinate all Executive programs and policies with major effects
upon the supply and use of energy, and attempt to concert the nation's

energy policies with its economic, social, environmental, foreign, and
security policies.

Some see an energy unit as part of the Office of Management and
Budget. James Akins believes that, if a Department of Energy and Natural
Resources is established, no independent unit is needed and that existing
bodies in the Executive Office of the President such as the National Security
Council, the Economic Policy Board, and the Office of Management and Budget can
undertake any government-wide policy responsibilities that a DENR Secretary
cannot discharge. However, the predominant view is that energy affairs
are sufficiently important and pervasive to merit the exclusive attention of a special independent Energy Council and staff in the Executive
Office. It should take the lead in formulating and coordinating national
policy for new and conventional fuels; give policy guidance to independent
regulatory agencies; help to coordinate federal and state, domestic and foreign energy policy; and concert energy policy with other economic and social
policy.

On Data Gathering and Policy Analysis

Many agencies are collecting data on energy and fuel supplies,
demand, reserves, stocks, and prices, notably the Federal Energy Administration, ERDA, the Bureau of Mines, Geological Survey, Federal Trade Commission, and Federal Power Commission. As new energy functions are added, so
are new data requirements and much duplication results; industry complaints about duplication "are largely valid." The government is said
to operate "98 separate computerized data bases or major files...of
energy-related data."[*] Denied access to industry data gathered by the
Census, on grounds of confidentiality, FEA proposes to collect the same
data independently; four agencies have conducted natural gas reserves
studies, yet the data base of each is incompatible with the others.[**]
On the whole, data on fuel production and exports are good; data on oil,
gas, coal, and uranium resources are poorer. In one ten-day period,
estimates of the oil reserves in the Atlantic Outer Continental Shelf

---

[*] Improvement Still Needed in Federal Energy Data Collection, Analysis
and Reporting, Report to the Congress by the Comptroller General of
the United States, June 15, 1976, p. 22.

[**] Ibid., pp. 34-35.

dropped from 132 to 2-4 billion barrels. "The federal government knows
next to nothing about the quality and types of coal that it owns." There
is a limit to what can be learned from additional paper studies; to improve
our knowledge of the nation's fuel reserves, direct investigation is needed:
dip-stick verification of oil stocks; government field exploration for oil,
gas, and uranium.

Different projections of future national energy requirements
have been issued by ERDA, FEA, and the Bureau of Mines and no effort has
been made to rectify or explain the differences. Different data and
forecasts lend weight to different policies and undermine public confidence
in the reliability of each data series and the objectivity of their analysis.
Rightly or wrongly, the credibility of FEA data continues to be questioned
because of the agency's reliance on industry sources. The General Accounting
Office can do "a mediocre job" and have credibility, Monte Canfield remarks;
FEA cannot. The widespread suspicion of industry and government energy data
has led to the assignment to GAO, in the 1975 Energy Policy and Conservation
Act, of responsibility for verifying energy data submitted to federal agencies.

The dilemma of data collection and analysis is that, if they are
to be relevant to policy issues--to inform and clarify public debate and
promote rational policy decisions--they should be undertaken in close
proximity to the agencies and officials responsible for energy policies.
Yet that very closeness endangers their credibility, since it is assumed
that data are collected, selected, and--especially--published to support the
interests and policies of those who collect and analyze them. The solution
recommended by the General Accounting Office and generally accepted by the
workshop is to locate primary responsibility for energy data collection and
analysis in a unit that is part of the FEA or whatever new energy agency or
department may succeed it, and to protect the unit's independence and
professional integrity by measures that would give it a status akin to
that of the Census or the Bureau of Labor Statistics. Some measures
suggested by the GAO[*] are:

--Appointment of the director by the President for a term
of 5 to 9 years and his confirmation by the Senate.

--The director and deputy director should be professionally
qualified and chosen on a merit basis.

---

[*] In a statement prepared for the workshop by Monte Canfield, Jr.

--The director should report directly to the administrator
of FEA or its successor agency.

--The independence of the agency should be stipulated by
statute and its director authorized and instructed to
testify directly before Congress.

George Eads advances a comparable proposal for an independent staff in
the Executive Office of the President to analyze not only energy issues
but a broad range of government-wide economic and resource questions."[*]

The credibility of industry data is also related to its confidentiality. Industry asks for confidentiality to protect itself from competitors
and, no doubt, from adverse government action. However, a GAO report contends that "the terms confidential and proprietary...have been overused
and...steps should be taken to restrict confidential data to the absolute
minimum."[**]   The good record of the Census in obtaining public
and industry cooperation is founded in part upon its special legislative
authority to maintain confidentiality, and some experts believe that
similar authority is a key to obtaining reliable energy data from
industry.

The Relation of Public Regulation to Public Policy

Over 40 federal bodies exercise regulatory powers over the supply
or use of energy. Although a recent Presidential commission noted "remarkably
little duplication of statutory authority"[***] among them, the number,
independence, and frequent inconsistency of their objectives and standards
present serious obstacles to the implementation of consistent national
energy policies. The regulatory scene is further complicated by the power
of the states to regulate plant siting and safety, power transmission,
utility prices, gasoline taxes, etc. (The role of the states will be
discussed subsequently.)

---

[*] "...one option I find intriguing involves the creation, either within
or closely attached to OMB or the Council of Economic Advisers, of a
small group of Senior Specialists who would serve the needs of all
Executive Office agencies for advice on and evaluation of the current
status and long-run prospects of key industries and other important
segments of the economy, who would initiate and coordinate cross-
agency and cross-industry analyses of the impact of current and proposed governmental actions..., and who would serve to bring emerging
longer run problems to the attention of senior decision-makers."

[**] Improvement Still Needed..., p. 36.

[***] William Doub, citing a finding of the Presidential Study Commission
on Federal Energy Regulation, which he chaired (cf. Federal Energy
Regulation: An Organizational Study, April 1974, p. 11).

Regulatory bodies tend to operate on an individual case basis, a "piecemeal approach...leading to inconsistent and incompatible decisions which could be counterproductive to national needs and priorities." As the number of agencies and interests involved in a particular case has increased, "regulation by consensus" has developed in which the regulatory body attempts to hear and to compromise the views of conflicting interests.

> What results are a group of decisions being made from the vantage point of each agency's own narrow perspective. While this may accommodate the desires of a particular interest group, it is merely myopic decision-making which often does not serve the broader "public interest". Indeed, unable to meet the demands of each group, some regulatory agencies take the extreme reverse position that no action is the best action (William Doub).

There are many forms of _de facto_ regulation in addition to the formal type in which an order is made or a license issued after an extensive, formal hearing process. Administrative rule-making and compliance procedures, the rules accompanying government grants and contracts, rules setting forth health and safety standards and the inspection systems enforcing them can have the same force and effect as regulatory decrees. Thus, government regulation of the supply and use of energy is widespread and growing. The extent to which it should grow and the degree to which extensive and often inconsistent regulation can prove effective is much debated.

Chauncey Starr cites government regulation of the energy industry as laying the basis of bad management, since regulatory agencies constrain the operations of industry without being responsible or accountable for the effects of their constraint upon the industry's subsequent performance. He suggests that regulation should concentrate mainly on "the large and obviously undesirable effects" of energy plants on the public health and safety and that excessive attention has been devoted to "marginal and hypothetically-projected" dangers. Harold Finger asks the government to let the free market work: but also recognizes the need for government intervention in that market to provide financial incentives to stimulate greater energy supply, to restrain or equalize the competition of foreign firms subsidized by their governments, and in the interests of social equity.

William Doub offers several administrative suggestions to speed up and improve the cumbersome and protracted process by which federal and state agencies now make decisions governing the siting, planning, construction, and operation of energy facilities. These include the creation of

an office to coordinate and schedule the licensing functions of federal
and, if possible, state agencies; and the exchange and standardization
of data among regulatory agencies, to be facilitated by a central energy
data organization such as the GAO has proposed.

However, the fundamental problem posed by regulatory agencies
is not that of reconciling their schedules and data, but of reconciling
their independence of judgment with the government's energy policies.
Regulation is a fourth branch of government that occupies a politically
awkward position betwixt and between the three principal independent
branches. "Every Executive report on reorganization from that of the
Brownlow Commission of 1937 to the Ash Council of 1970 has severely
criticized the independent commissions."[*] That is understandable,
because independent judgment is necessary to even-handed justice, and
yet observance of designated governmental policy is necessary to effective
administration.

The workshop grappled with this problem but did not resolve it.
The general opinion was that there is too much regulation and the scope of
regulation should be narrowed.[**] The growth of regulation often represents
a temporizing measure, a failure of the Congress to make up its collective
mind and to legislate public policy clearly. "...the independent regulatory
commission was an expression of the Congress saying, 'We would have legislated if we had the time, but we didn't'", Charles Bingman observes. Unfortunately, there is no agreement on what functions are "truly" regulatory and
thus require independent adjudication. William Doub suggests that the main
emphasis in the last 20 years, exemplified by the Nuclear Regulatory Commission
and the Environmental Protection Agency, has been upon the regulation of new

---

[*] Federal Energy Organization, A Staff Analysis, Committee on Interior and
Insular Affairs, United States Senate, 1973, p. 23. (Actually, it was
the Brownlow Committee or The President's Committee on Administrative
Management, chaired by Louis Brownlow.)

[**] William Johnson describes "the regulatory morass that the FEA has now
become....On January 2, 1974 the government first published 27 pages of
allocation regulations for comment in the Federal Register. By January
1976 it had published over 5,000 additional pages....The Commerce Clearing
House tabulation of the FEA's regulations...is now a three volume compendium,
seven inches thick, of turgid, legalistic prose unintelligible even to many
of the FEA officials who must administer the controls. The Commerce Clearing
House has also published two additional volumes containing decisions by FEA's
Office of Exceptions and Appeals. Most recent regulations are intended to
plug loopholes and modify or otherwise correct errors in earlier regulations"
("Why U.S. Energy Policy Has Failed," op. cit.).

technology to protect the public health and safety and that much economic
regulation in the energy arena can and should be absorbed into the normal
process of Executive policy-making and administration. However, economic regu-
lation--the adjudication of the prices and profits of monopolistic public
utilities and services--remains the philosophical basis of much government
regulation and even heavily technological regulation retains a strong economic
element, since varying degrees of technological safety or reliability cost
varying amounts of money.

Whatever may be the proper definition and scope of the regulatory
function, it should be segregated from policy promotion to ensure the integrity of regulatory actions. For this reason, the regulation of nuclear
plants and materials was separated from that of promoting their development,
and the General Accounting Office recommends that the regulatory functions
of FEA be separated from its policy functions and assigned to a new independent agency or to the Federal Power Commission. The eventual affiliation of
two or more regulatory bodies--FPC, NRC, and the regulatory functions of FEA
are most frequently cited--into a federated energy regulatory agency can also
be envisaged.[*]

How can energy regulation be both insulated from and yet influenced
by national energy policies? William Doub suggests that a National Energy
Council (designated earlier in this summary as "an Energy Policy Council in
the Executive Office of the President") give policy guidance openly.

> Conveying policy guidance openly might include the submission of
> position papers on the formal record or appearances by the National
> Energy Council at public hearings. Policy information would not
> substitute for every regulator's obligation to consider each case
> on its merits, and whenever policy guidance was linked to a specific
> case or rule-making proceeding, the guidance would have to relate
> exclusively to effects on national energy objectives. With these
> ground rules, the result should not be a less independent regulatory
> process but a better informed one--with an enhancement of public
> understanding.

Mason Willrich futher suggests that regulatory agencies, particularly the
Nuclear Regulatory Commission and the Federal Power Commission, be confined
to domestic regulation and be governed by Presidential policy in foreign
affairs such as the export of fuels and nuclear materials.

---

[*] "In the [1974] Energy Reorganization Act, Congress invites the President to
submit further recommendations concerning energy organization, including the
option of 'consolidation in whole or part of regulatory functions concerning
energy.' We are convinced that national regulatory policies would benefit from
the perspective provided by a comprehensive agency embracing all energy forms
in a single, unified structure" (Achieving Energy Independence, Committee for
Economic Development, December 1974, p. 61)

Concerting Federal and State Policy

State and local governments can facilitate or obstruct federal
energy policies and programs, and there is much recent evidence of obstruction due to the failure to concert federal and state policies and powers.
As Senator Percy observes, there are no federal police to enforce the federal
law setting a 55 mile per hour speed limit--"the one mandatory law that we
were able to pass ever since the oil embargo"--and state enforcement is often
weak or nonexistent. William Warne finds state and local energy officials
"increasingly resentful and suspicious of federal agency collaboration. The
federal agencies...are accused of cooperating only on their own terms....
Initiatives in California have indicated...that many millions of voters are
even more suspicious of big brother in Washington than are the state and
local governments." Federal agencies may have the final authority to license
nuclear facilities or to issue leases for coal mines on federal land and oil
drilling on the Outer Continental Shelf, but states can delay or stop the
operation, as the imposition by the state of a heavy use tax led to the closing
of a nuclear waste burial site in Kentucky.

Opposition to energy plants can stem from their noxious character,
producing what Charles Hitch terms "the 'not in my backyard' syndrome." Or,
it can reflect a concern about the financial impact of major facilities upon
taxpayers and governments, which must build roads, schools, and playgrounds
and provide police, fire, and other services for the influx of workers and
their families. The National Governors' Conference has accepted as policy
that states should neither lose nor gain financially from the impact of new
energy facilities: enough lead time should be allowed for the necessary public
construction and the federal government should advance any sums needed for
capital and cash flow purposes.

Greater recognition of state interests and powers, greater coordination of federal and state plans and policies, and the fuller participation
of state representatives in the development of federal policies is plainly
needed. Though many state governments lack adequate energy staffs, others,
like California and New York, have exercised leadership in certain technical
areas (e.g., dam inspection) and those with major universities and energy
laboratories have ready access to expert advice. Lynn Brooks cites the participation of state representatives in the Energy Resources Council's development

of coal policy and Interior's development of policy for the Northeast Outer
Continental Shelf as examples which should (and the Nuclear Regulatory
Commission, which "wants to exclude the states," as an example which should
not) be emulated by other federal agencies. According to one authority,
ERDA appears to be developing a good cooperative approach toward the states,
while FEA "leaves a lot to be desired."

The Federal Energy Regulation Study Team recommended

> ...that information exchanges and policy decisions take place
> regularly between two new groups that would represent the
> Federal and state levels respectively in all matters related
> to energy. The first would be a Federal office devoted exclu-
> sively to interchanges with the states and localities; the
> second would be a permanent representative body consisting of
> state-designated officials, who should be of sufficient stature
> to reflect promptly and accurately the policies and intentions
> of their governments (William Doub).

Informed decisions on the Alaska pipeline or Western oil shales cannot all
be taken in Washington and, as one state spokesman notes, "The Governors
cannot run to Washington for everything." Federal regional offices with
real authority would afford a good compromise between the concentration of
decision-making in Washington and individual negotiations with 50 states,
providing convenient sites where state and federal agencies can work out
policies adapted to the needs of each region. The Ford Energy Project also
recommended the development of regional energy planning[*] (and one Project
study recommended that state regulatory commissions be replaced by a
federally chartered regional regulatory agency).

The Congress

Fifteen of 18 committees and 33 subcommittees of the Senate have
jurisdiction over energy affairs; a similar situation exists in the House,

---

[*] "...planning at the state level is very limited. The states of Montana,
Wyoming and North Dakota are dotted with proposed projects on the drawing
boards of dozens of companies...Some plans would export coal from the
region, some would burn it there for electricity, others would convert
it to gas or liquids. Still others would do nothing with it for some
time, but hold it to speculate on its increasing value....
"No mechanism exists at the federal level to comprehensively examine
regional problems....The energy planning that does take place is highly
fragmented. It is usually done by local offices of federal agencies,
or by state agencies which have limited ability to enforce their decisions
on federally owned resource areas" (A Time To Choose, Energy Policy Project
of the Ford Foundation, Ballinger, Cambridge, 1974, p. 284).

which rejected a 1974 recommendation of the Bolling Committee that responsibility for legislation on the environment and energy conservation, regulation, and power administration be concentrated in one committee. The 1,001 energy bills that were introduced in 1974 were referred to over 35 committees and subcommittees. "The president's omnibus energy program was split up and referred to four different committees in the House and nine in the Senate."*

This situation leads some observers to despair of attaining any rationality or consistency in national energy policies and programs; the value of any Executive energy reorganization will, they believe, be diminished until the Congress rationalizes and simplifies its committee structure. Others are more hopeful. "The Congress is a collegial body...and usually disposes rather than proposes," Alan Dean observes. So long as the Executive knows what it wants, the fractionation of committee authority is no overwhelming obstacle to obtaining it. "Energy" is, in any event, an all-pervasive subject that can no more be assigned to a single committee than to a single Executive department. That has not stopped energy legislation. In fact, "there has been an amazing legislative response to a whole range of energy issues...[due] in part to the President's initiative, but a good deal on their own initiative" (Charles Bingman).

Senator Percy points to the organization of Congress and the Executive to handle the space program as an indication that the government can organize to do some things

> extraordinarily well....It is straightforward. It is relatively simple, and the way we organized at the federal level and inter-related the private sector in establishing a goal and setting out to accomplish it really is a miracle of organization and accomplishment and a national will backed up by a national sense of purpose and a clearly enunciated policy.

Granted, energy policy is a more complicated matter than a moon landing but some improvement in energy organization should be possible, in the Congress as well as the Executive. The Congress responded to the creation of the Office of Management and Budget with the introduction of its new budgetary system--"and it is working remarkably well"; it may respond in similar fashion to a reorganization of Executive energy affairs.

---

* Andrew S. Carron, "Congress and Energy," Policy Analysis, Spring 1976, p. 292.

Staff agencies that serve the entire Congress can help to
provide common information and analyses to all committees, and thereby
to overcome the splintering effects of multiple committees. But these
agencies have themselves multiplied and, together with committee staffs,
have grown so greatly as to constitute a growing bureaucracy of their
own. The General Accounting Office now has a budget of $140 million and
a staff of 5,000; the Congressional Research Service has a staff of
750; the Congressional Budget Office and the Office of Technology
Assessment, staffs of about 185 and 95, respectively.* In addition,
perhaps 5,000 of the 17,000 persons on the staffs of individual Congressmen and Congressional committees are engaged in legislative and policy
work (as against service to constituents). "Congress should be aware...
that it is establishing a system of bureaucracies in the legislative
branch, and that these bureaucracies will have all the same bureaucratic
problems that the executive agencies have and...they don't have the same
policing supervision that the Congress gives the Executive agencies"
(William Warne).

The growth of Congressional staff in the last seven years,
Alan Dean suggests, is at least partly a consequence of the division
in party control of the Executive and the Congress, of "rather tremendous Congressional majorities...aligned against the President," and
"mistrust between the Executive and Legislative branch..." Congressional
mistrust was aggravated by the anonymity and unaccountability of Presidential aides and the massive Presidential impoundment of Congressional
appropriations. Staff growth may abate when one party gains control of
both branches and a good working relation is restored between them.

A reorganization of Congressional committees to parallel the
reorganization of the Executive is necessary, Chester Cooper insists, if
energy reorganization is to work. "If...Seamans has to talk to 37 parts
of Congress, how many hunks of Congress would the new secretary of this
new department...have to report to...?" "...no more than he started
with," is the reply. Under the best of circumstances, any agency head

* See "A Look at the 19,467 People Who Keep Congress Running," National
Journal, July 10, 1976, p. 960-1.

has to deal with at least three or four committees in each house.   "It
is never going to get down to one, it is always going to be a minimum
of eight."   One voice was raised for a joint committee on energy,
natural resources, and the environment, and a second voice for a select
committee on energy in each new congress; but most participants seemed
to expect the Congress and the country to go on with only moderate
concentration of Congressional energy authority, if any.

Three Basic Legislative Alternatives

Three immediate alternatives for the organization of Executive
energy functions may be summarily identified:

1. High Decentralization: The Status Quo

A continuation of current programs and functions among existing
agencies: extension of FEA with its limited powers; ERDA; the natural
resource agencies in the Department of Interior; the independent regulatory functions of the Federal Power Commission, the Nuclear Regulatory
Commission, and FEA; and the coordinative functions of the Energy Resources Council. Additional decentralization could be achieved by
dividing ERDA into three independent agencies devoted to nuclear energy,
fossil fuel, and advanced technical systems; an independent agency to
promote energy conservation might be established; and the regulatory
functions of FEA could be assigned to a new independent agency.

2. Moderate Centralization: A National Energy Organization

The scope of a moderately centralized energy organization has
been outlined by the General Accounting Office. It would consist of
ERDA; the non-regulatory functions of FEA; a data gathering agency with
special statutory powers and independence, whose head would report
directly to the Congress; and an agency to finance major new energy
supply and conservation undertakings. An energy conservation authority
might also be included. A staff in the administrator's office would
help to formulate and coordinate policies within the agency and to assist
a strengthened Energy Policy Council in the Executive Office of the
President, which would replace the present Energy Resources Council.
The new Council would have a staff of its own and primary responsibility

for developing and coordinating federal-state and government-wide energy

policies and for reconciling them with domestic and foreign policies.

3. Major Centralization: A Department of Energy and Natural

Resources

A Department of Energy and Natural Resources would incorporate

all of the agencies and functions noted in paragraph 2, as well as most

of the present Department of Interior and possibly the Environmental

Protection Agency. An effort would also be made to narrow the regulatory

functions of FPC and NRC and to attach the excised administrative func-

tions to the Department. The central regulatory functions of FPC, NRC,

and FEA might be regrouped into a federated energy regulatory agency

which would receive open policy guidance from the Energy Policy Council

in the Executive Office of the President. The other functions of the

Council would be similar to those noted in 2. As a member of the cabi-

net, the DENR Secretary would have more power and authority than the ad-

ministrator of the moderately centralized National Energy Organization;

hence, the strong central policy staff attached to his office, working

closely with the Energy Policy Council, would play an important role in

the formulation and coordination of government-wide energy policies.

SELECTED LIST OF READINGS PERTAINING TO ENERGY POLICY AND ENERGY ORGANIZATION

Prepared by the Environment and Natural Resources Policy Division
of the Congressional Research Service of the Library of Congress

Part I consists of selected readings: journal articles and books, published since January 1974.

Part II is a list of Federal publications selected from the approximately 300 issued on the general subject of energy policy since January 1974.

These citations were annotated by the Library Services Division of
the Congressional Research Service and collated by A. C. Grenfell,
Environment and Natural Resources Policy Division. June 1976.

SELECTED READINGS: PART I

Adelman, Morris A, and others. Energy self-sufficiency: an economic evaluation.
Technology review, v. 76, May 1974: 23–58.
"... a summary of U.S. energy policy alternatives to 1980, the result of an
intensive study of energy technology and economics by members of the
M.I.T. Energy Laboratory, colleagues, and consultants."
No time to confuse: a critique of the final report of the Energy Policy
Project of the Ford Foundation A Time to Choose America's Energy Future.
San Francisco, Calif., Institute for Contemporary Studies [c 1975] 156 p.
Partial contents.—U.S. energy policy, by M. A. Adelman.—On energy,
poverty, and the environment, by M. B. Johnson.—Private enterprise and

energy, by W. J. Mead.—"U.S. energy policy in the world context" by A. B. Moore.—Energy research and development, by J. C. DeHaven.

Aron, Joan. Epitaph for a super superagency. New York affairs, v. 2, spring 1975: 80–89.

Discusses the former Interdepartmental Committee on Public Utilities which under Mayor Lindsay "made an effort to have the city government speak with one voice on increasingly difficult energy problems . . ."

Bailey, Gil. The contest for leadership in energy policy: Congress or the White House? Cry California, v. 10, summer 1975: 13–17.

Barfield, Claude E. Compromise is expected on reorganization plans. National journal reports, v. 6, Mar. 23, 1974: 439–444.

"The Administration is ready to drop its effort persuade Congress to create one big department to deal with energy as well as other natural resources policy and settle for a compromise reorganization. Sen. Henry M. Jackson, D–Wash., has reached a similar conclusion."

Barnea, Joseph. The energy crisis and the future. New York, UNITAR, 1975. 117 p.

"The study of the medium and long-term aspects of the energy crisis has been written during the first few months of 1974 and is designed to analyze problems and possible future action on various institutional levels. It is by intention both an analytical and idea paper. It is not crammed with statistics, nor is it designed to have a definite answer to every problem. On the contrary, it often suggests that detailed studies of problems and proposals."

Brannon, Gerard Marion, 1922–. Energy taxes and subsidies; a report to the energy policy project of the Ford Foundation [by] Gerard M. Brannon, Cambridge, Mass., Ballinger Pub. Co. [1974] xvi, 177 p. 24 cm. Includes bibliographical references.

1. Energy policy—United States. 2. Power resources—Taxation—United States. 3. Subsidies—United States. 4. Public utilities—Rates I. Ford Foundation. Energy Policy Project. II. Title HD9502.U52 B68.

Breeder reactor: questions on cost, safety. Congressional quarterly weekly report, v. 33, Feb. 1, 1975: 231–236.

A technical and political analysis of the prospects for the development of liquid metal fast breeder reactors in the U.S.

Breyer, Stephen G., 1938–. Energy regulation by the Federal Power Commission [by] Stephen G. Breyer [and] Paul W. MacAvoy, Washington, Brookings Institution [1974]. x. 163 p. illus. 24 cm. (Studies in the regulation of economic activity). Includes bibliographical references.

1. United States. Federal Power Commission. 2. Energy policy—United States. I. MacAvoy, Paul W., Joint author, II. Title. Services). HD9502. U52 B7.

Burg, Nan C. Energy crisis in the United States: a selected bibliography of nontechnical materials. Monticello, Ill., 1974. 67 p. (Council of Planning Librarians. Exchange bibliography 550).

Commission of the European Communities.

Problems, resources and necessary progress in Community energy policy 1975–1985 / Commission of the European Communities. [Luxembourg]: The Commission.]1975?[54 p.: 25 cm. Includes bibliographical references.

1. Energy policy—European Economic Community countries. 2. Power resources—European Economic Community countries. I. Title. HD9502.E862 C65 1975.

Towards a new energy policy strategy for the Community: communication presented to the Council by the Commission on 5 June 1974. [Luxembourg]: European Communities Commission. [1974]. 35 p.: 25 cm. (Bulletin of the European Communities: Supplement: 4/74. Includes bibliographical references.

1. Energy policy—European Economic Community countries. I. Council of the European Communities. II. Title. (Series). HD9502.E862 C65 1974a. Domestic affairs study 45).

Conference on Regulatory Reform, Washington, D.C. 1975.

Regulatory reform: highlights of a conference on government regulation. Washington, American Enterprise Institute for Public Policy Research [c1976] 65 p. (American Enterprise Institute for Public Policy Research. Domestic affairs study 45)

Contents.—Power-energy regulation.—Health care regulation.—Transportation regulation.—Agency for Consumer Advocacy.—Government regulation: What kind of reform?

Corrigan, Richard. Ford position strengthened by lack of consensus in Congress. National journal reports, v. 7, June 7, 1975: 837–841.

"Democratic congressional leaders who promised early in the year that they would have an alternative to President Ford's energy plans now are combating a President who is in a considerably stronger position to do what he wants than he was a few months ago."

Doub, William O. Federal energy regulation—toward a better way. American Bar Association journal, v. 60, Aug. 1974: 920–923.

"There must be a better way of exercising governmental oversight of the generation and distribution of energy. That's the one thread of continuity that ran through presentations to the Federal Energy Regulation Study Team, whose report is now under consideration."

Drinan, Robert. Nuclear power and the role of Congress. Environmental affairs, v. 4, fall 1975: 595–627.

"There is a growing debate within Congress over the risks and benefits of nuclear power, a debate sustained more by rhetoric and assertion than by reliable, unbiased, valid information and analysis. This article addresses the problem of improving the quality of the ultimate decision, together with a brief discussion of the status of this debate."

The Energy crisis and U.S. foreign policy, edited by Joseph S. Szyliowicz, Bard E. O'Neill; foreword by John A. Love, New York: Praeger, 1975. xv, 258 p.: ill.; 24 cm. (Praeger special studies in international politics and government) Includes index. Bibliography: p. 233–254.

1. Energy policy—United States—Addresses, essays, lectures. 2. Petroleum industry and trade—United States—Addresses, essays, lectures. 3. United States—Foreign relations—Addresses, essays, lectures. I. Szyliowicz, Joseph S., ed. II. O'Neill, Bard, ed. HD9502, U52 E484.

Energy emergency—exploring the maze. American federalionist, v. 82, Mar. 1975: 1–10.

"The record demonstrates that the major U.S.-based international oil companies failed to provide for the long-run energy needs of the U.S. and its citizens. Moreover, these companies, which largely dominate the American energy picture, are also a dominant influence on the government's agencies involved in the oil and related industries."

Executive energy messages. Printed at the request of Henry M. Jackson, chairman, Committee on Interior and Insular Affairs, United States Senate pursuant to S. Res. 45: a National Fuels and Energy Policy Study. Washington, U.S. Govt. Print. Off., 1975. 329 p.

At head of title: 94th Cong., 1st sess. Committee print. "Serial no. 94–22 (92–112)"

Ford Foundation, Energy Policy Project. A time to choose: America's energy future; final report. Cambridge, Mass., Ballinger Pub. Co. [1974] xii, 511 p. illus. 23 cm. Includes bibliographical references.

1. Energy policy—United States. I. Title. HD9502.U52 F67 1974a.

Franssen, Herman T. Federal energy planning: scenarios for disaster. World oil, v. 182, Apr. 1976: 45–49.

Analysis of the U.S. energy budget between now and 1985; concludes that the U.S. will become increasingly dependent on Arab oil imports.

The Free market and the energy crisis: MacAvoy, Proxmire, Buckley and Friedman. Business and society review/innovation, no. 9, spring 1974: 82–88.

Excerpts from a seminar on short- and long-term solutions to the energy crisis held in January 1974 by the Schuchman Foundation Center for the Public Interest. Professor Paul MacAvoy discusses the manner in which price controls have inhibited the production of natural gas. Senator William Proxmire and Senator James Buckley debate on the proper role, or non-role, of the Federal Government in providing for adequate supplies of energy. Professor Milton Friedman defends the concept of excess profits made by energy firms.

Gilliland, Martha W. Energy analysis and public policy. Science, v. 189, Sept. 26, 1975: 1051–1056.

"The energy unit measures environmental consequences, economic costs, material needs, and resource availability."

Gordon, Richard L. Mythology and reality in energy policy. Energy policy, v. 2, Sept. 1974: 189–203.

Argues that current problems in worldwide energy supply arise from conflicting energy policies in both consuming and producing nations.

Hagel, John. Alternative energy strategies: constraints and opportunities, by John Hagel III. New York: Petroleum Information Foundation, c1974. 2 v.; 23 cm.

Includes bibliography and index. Contents: pt. 1. Alternatives to petroleum. pt. 2. Options in energy policy.

1. Energy policy—United States—Collected works. 2. Energy policy—Collected works. 3. Power resources—United States—Collected works. 4. Power resources—Collected works. I. Title. HD9502.U52 H33.

Havemann, Joel. Crisis tightens control of U.S. energy production. National journal reports, v. 7, Apr. 26, 1975 : 619–634.

Comprehensive analysis of government regulation of energy in the U.S. excluding coal. Includes desire of industry and Ford administration to end regulation versus Congress' fear of higher prices and no competition.

Barfield, Claude E. Simon's efforts take effect, order emerges from chaos. National journal reports, v. 6, Feb. 2, 1974 : 153–158; Feb. 16 : 229–237.

Two articles on the way the executive branch has reorganized itself to meet the energy crisis. The second part examines Administration proposals to Congress to establish a Federal Energy Administration (FEA), an Energy Research and Development Administration (ERDA) and a Department of Energy and Natural Resources (DENR).

Holdren, John P. The nuclear controversy and the limitations of decision-making by experts. Bulletin of the atomic scientists, v. 32, Mar. 1976 : 20–22.

"Policy-makers must stop waiting for technical consensus where none is possible, and concentrate instead on how to minimize the social costs of uncertainty; the California initiative presents such an opportunity."

Jones, Douglas N., and others. The energy industry : organization and public policy ; background papers prepared pursuant to S. Res. 45, a national fuels and energy policy study. Washington, U.S. Govt. Print. Off., 1974. 106 p.

At head of title : 93d Cong., 2d sess. Committee [on Interior and Insular Affairs] print. "Serial No. 93–28 (92–63)"

Kissinger, Henry A. Energy : the necessity of decision. Atlantic community quarterly, v. 13, spring 1975 : 7–22.

An address by the Sec. of State before the National Press Club, Feb. 3, 1975, in which he discussed proposals of U.S. to be presented at a Conference of Members of the International Energy Agency over the problem of the dependency of consuming countries on oil imports.

Klausner, Samuel Z. Energy rationing and energy conservation : foundations for a social policy. Energy systems and policy, v. 1, No. 2, 1975 : 119–141.

Promotes "a program for managing energy consumption which would regulate the social behavior in which energy is implicated rather than directing regulation of the flow of the commodities."

Knorr, Klaus Bugen, 1911–. Toward a U.S. energy policy/Klaus Knorr. New York : National Strategy Information Center, [1975] vii, 48 p. ; 22 cm. (Agenda paper—National Strategy Information Center ; No. 2) Includes bibliographical references.

1. Energy policy—United States. I. Title. II. Series : National Strategy Information Center. Agenda paper—National Strategy Information Center ; No. 2. HD9502.U52 K54.

Leonard, William N. How economic policies provoked the energy crisis. Challenge, v. 17. Mar.–Apr. 1974 : 56–58.

"Central to understanding the energy crisis is the realization that governmental policies have tended to depress the price of energy, especially of oil and natural gas. In the resulting paradise of cheap energy, prodigality has been the order of the day."

Leshy, John D.

Lash, Terry R. A black mark : failure of the Federal coal-leasing policy. Environment, v. 17, Dec. 1975 : 6–13.

Advocates involving states and localities in Interior Dept. coal-leasing policy formulation.

Levine, Richard O. The congressional role in formulating national policy : some observations on the first session of the Ninety-third Congress. Harvard journal on legislation, v. 11, Feb. 1974 : 161–180.

Describes the challenge perceived by Congress "precipitated by Presidential assertions of power, to the legislature's role as a coordinate branch of government." Analyzes congressional actions re : the War Powers resolution, impoundment, energy policy and the Rules of Evidence and discusses congressional sources of information.

Louis Harris and Associates. A survey of public and leadership attitudes toward nuclear power development in the United States. [New York, Ebasco Services Incorporated] 1975. 131 p.

"Study No. 2515."

"This report presents the findings of a major survey conducted by Louis Harris and Associates for Ebasco Services Incorporated. The study was designed as a measure of attitudes of the public and their leaders—political leaders, business leaders, officials of regulatory agencies, and environmentalists—toward the development of nuclear energy in the United States."

Lovins, Amory Block. The energy problems in our future. Atlas world press review, v. 22, Mar. 1975 : 15–16, 18.

"The major prolems that face us today are ipso facto insoluble, for it takes time to solve problems and all we have time for now is Band-Aids; but the problems of the mid–1980s and beyond might be soluble if attacked now. Therefore, my focus is on how to solve the problems that we shall face after immediate uncertainties have been resolved."

MacAvoy, Paul W.

Stangle, Bruce E. Tepper, Jonathan B. The Federal Energy Office as regulator of the energy crisis. Technology review, v. 77, May 1975 : 38–45.

"Faced with the crisis of 1974, the F.E.O. acted in the tradition of the established regulatory agencies. Its policies appear to have created the oil shortages."

MacDonald, Scot. Fuel, New Federalism and the OMB. Government executive, v. 6, Feb. 1974 : 24–25, 28.

Reviews OMB's role in structuring government operations, especially with respect to the Federal Energy Office, procurement and assistance to state and local government. Article is in large part an interview of Frank G. Zarb, an associate director of OMB.

Mancke, Richard B., 1943–. The failure of U.S. energy policy [by] Richard B. Mancke. New York, Columbia University Press, 1974. vi, 189 p. illus. 23 cm. Bibliography: p. [183]–186.

1. Energy policy—United States. 2. Environmental policy—United States. 3. Petroleum—Taxation—United States. I. Title. HD9502. U52 M35.

Mancke, Richard B., 1943–. Performance of the Federal Energy Office/Richard B. Mancke. Washington: American Enterprise Institute for Public Policy Research, 1975. 25 p.; 23 cm. (National energy study ; 6)

On cover: National Energy Project. Includes bibliographical references.

1. United States. Federal Energy Office. 2. Energy policy—United States. I. AEI National Energy Project. II. Title. (Series) HD9502.U52 M353.

Miller, William H. Energy : the hotest show in Washington. Industry week, v. 182, Sept. 23, 1974 : 38–40, 42, 44, 46.

"Although last winter's crisis has eased, concern over long-term energy problems is bringing a reshuffling of the federal energy bureaucracy. The creation of the FEA has centralized some functions, but other energy- related offices continue to sprout."

Mitchell, Edward J. U.S. energy policy : a primer. Washington, American Enterprise Institute for Public Policy Research [1974] 103 p. (American Enterprise Institute for Public Policy Research. National energy study 1.)

Argues that Americans are suffering from a seesawing policy of government intervention in the energy market. Focuses on the petroleum and natural gas industries.

Muntzing, L. Manning. The new NRC: its mandate and challenge. Public utilities fortnightly, v. 95, Mar. 13, 1975 : 19–23.

Discusses the role and function of the new Nuclear Regulatory Commission in the light of new demands on the administration and Congress.

Nader, Ralph. Who benefits? Center magazine, v. 7, Mar.–Apr. 1975 : 32–37.

"Without information about the facts of the energy situation, with a great deal of secrecy, and with inherent conflicts of interest, it is not hard to predict that the policy of the government will be as it has been in the past, one that parallels that of the oil industry itself."

National Economic Research Associates. Electric utility policy issues. Printed at the request of Henry M. Jackson, Chairman, Committee on Interior and Insular Affairs, United States Senate, pursuant to S. Res. 45, the National Fuels and Energy Policy Study. Washington, U.S. Govt. Print. Off., 1974. 155 p.

Paper prepared by National Economic Research Associates, Inc., and the law firms of Debevoise & Liberman, of Washington, D.C., and Hunton, Williams, Gay & Gibson, of Washington, D.C., and Richmond, Virginia. Describes the development and structure of the electric utility industry and the impact of government policies thereon.

Post, R. F. Ribe, P. L. Fusion reactors as future energy sources. Science, v. 186, Nov. 1, 1974 : 397–407.

Purposes that fusion power should be considered as the ultimate source of energy, and other sources of power. inclduing conventional nuclear, should be considered as interim sources.

Reese, Thomas J. The energy bill: lessons for tax reformers. Tax notes, v. 3, June 30, 1975 : 3–9, 23.

"The House passage of a substantially weakened Energy Conservation and Conversion Act (H.R. 6860) has been widely cited as an example of the inability of democratic institutions to take harsh steps to head off a potential crisis that is not currently felt by the electorate. While that sweeping indictment may be true, there are some more specific conclusions that can be supported from an analysis of the debate and voting patterns, conclusions that may serve as lessons for supporters of tax reform."

Reports of the Atlantic Council's Energy Policy Committee. Atlantic community quarterly, v. 13, spring 1975 : 23–93.

Contents.—World energy and U.S. leadership, by H. Cleveland.—An approach toward resolution of energy problems through international coordination and cooperation, by E. Thomson and R. Harbert.—Financing Free World energy supply and use, by J. Gray.

Ridgeway, James. Energy : steps toward an alternative. Working papers, v. 3, fall 1975 : 61–64.

Discusses "what can be done to control the energy companies, conserve fuel, and still make low-cost power widely available."

Conner, Bettina. Public energy : notes toward a new system. Working papers for a new society, v. 2. winter 1975 : 45–50.

Urges the establishment of public energy districts that would have jurisdiction over production and distribution of energy within their areas. Regional authorities would allocate resources among districts, and the Federal agency would regulate interregional commerce.

Ridgeway, James, 1936—New energy : understanding the crisis and a guide to an alternative energy system/James Ridgeway and Bettina Conner. Boston : Beacon Press, [1975] xiii, 224 p. : 21 cn.

"An Institute for Policy Studies book." Includes bibliographical references and index.

1. Energy policy—United States. 2. Petroleum industry and trade—United States. 3. Power resources—United States. I. Conner, Bettina, joint author. II. Title.

HD9502.U52 R53.

Rose, David J. Energy policy in the U.S. Scientific American, v. 230, Jan. 1974 : 20–29.

"The President's appeal for U.S. energy self-sufficiency by 1980 cannot be regarded as realistic.

The long-range options that are open to the nation are here considered in a 'taxonomic' approach."

Roseman, Herman G. Utility financing problems and national energy policy. Public utilities fortnightly, v. 94, Sept. 12, 1974 : 19–30.

"The consequences of continued financial problems of the electric utility industry are certain to have a severe impact on national energy policies."

Samuelson, Robert. The oil policy we needed but didn't get : too little too late. New republic, v. 174, Jan. 3 & 10, 1976 : 12–19.

Presents a political analysis of how current enegy policy developed. Emphasizing petroleum facts, author discusses future prospects resulting from U.S. energy policy or the lack thereof.

Schmidt, Herman J. The government's role in energy. Conference Board record, v. 11, May 1974 : 20–22.

Author is skeptical of proposals to establish a government oil company and to impose price controls on domestically produced crude oil and natural gas moving in interstate commerce the same as now imposed on gas destined for interstate commerce.

Seaborg, Glenn T. Opportunities in todays energy milien. Futurist, v. 9, Feb. 1975 : 22–24, 37.

"A world-renowned chemist suggests ways in which we can come to terms with our energy problems. He sees a transition to a less energy-intensive, more conservation-oriented society and an accompanying change in public attitudes toward consumption and waste."

Seamans, Robert C., Jr. What are the future sources of power? Public utilities fortnightly, v. 96, Sept. 25, 1975 : 24–26.

"A discussion of the alternatives described in a plan developed by ERDA for meeting future national energy goals."

Goodwin, Irwin. U.S. energy prospects. Strategic review, v. 3, winter 1975 : 6–15.

Due to the Arab oil embargo and price increase the country faces the necessity of adapting to changed conditions. "A special Task Force on Energy of the National Academy of Engineering has evaluated national needs and

charted options to reduce dependence on imported oil in the next decade."
A concise summary of its findings is included.

Shinnar, Reuel. Energy in perspective. Chemical technology, v. 5, Feb. 1975 : 225–231.

"We don't have a crisis in energy, we have a crisis in our ability to manage and understand a complex technological society."

Sirkin, Abraham M. Living with interdependence : the decades ahead in America. Futurist, v. 10, Feb. 1976 : 4–14.

Discusses the growing interdependence of nations and segments of the national economy and what impact this will have on individual Americans over the next 25 years. The areas of energy, environment, and food are discussed in particular.

Smith, A. Robert. No shortage of energying lobbying. Bulletin of the atomic scientists, v. 30, May 1974 : 11–13.

Discusses the activities of industrial lobbyists in the field of energy policy.

Spain, Ora. Forecast : doubled coal production in Appalachia. Appalachia, v. 8, June–July 1975 : 1–10.

Describes an Appalachian Regional Commission study to determine "what effect various national energy policies would have on the Appalachian energy industry and its markets outside the Region, and to see what impact changes in energy production or consumption would have on the people, economy and environment of the Region."

Sporn, Philip. Multiple failures of public and private institutions. Science, v. 184, Apr. 19, 1974 : 284–286.

Points to both public and private sectors as being responsible, through inaction, for the energy crisis. Presents suggestions for achieving a more efficient and more effective energy use.

Stang, David P. Is the U.S. running out of gas? National review, v. 27, Aug. 1, 1975 : 818–827.

A political discussion of the energy policy differences between President Ford and the U.S. Congress.

Starratt, Patricia E. The natural gas shortage and the Congress. Washington, American Enterprise Institute for Public Policy Research (1974) 68 p. (American Enterprise Institute for Public Policy Research. National energy study 5).

Symposium: administrative law and environment problems. Administrative law review, v. 26, spring 1974 : 141–198.

Contents.—Agency functions in light of environmental problems, by M. Wilkey.—Environmental problems and the agency process : an English view, by Sir H. Forbes.—Energy, the environment and the administrative process, by J. Nassikas.—Technological regulation and environmental law, by W. Doub.

Teller, Edward. Energy : a plan for action : a report * * * to the Energy Panel of the Commission on Critical Choices for Americans. [New York, Commission on Critical Choices for Americans, 1975] 80 p.

Panel I of the Commission on Critical Choices for Americans is concerned with "Energy and its Relationship to Ecology, Economics and World Stability." "Dr. Teller was asked to set forth an action plan with as much specificity as possible including additional U.S. Energy production, conservation measures, national security and financial considerations."

Tilton, John E. U.S. energy R. & D. Policy : The role of economics. John E. Tilton. Washington : Resources for the Future, 1974. vii, 134 p. ; 26 cm. (RFF Working paper ; EN–4) Includes bibliographical references.

1. Energy policy—United States. I. Title. II. series : Resources for the Future. Working paper ; EN–4. HD9502.U52 T54.

Tussing, Arlon R. Cooper, Benjamin S.

Economic analysis of President Ford's energy program : a staff analysis prepared at the request of Henry M. Jackson, chairman, Committee on Interior and Insular Affairs, United States Senate pursuant to S. Res. 45, the National Fuels and Energy Policy Study. Washington, U.S. Govt. Print. Off., 1975. 173 p.

At head of title : 94th Cong., 1st sess. Committee print. "Serial no. 94–4 (92–94)"

Udall, Stewart L. The energy balloon [by] Stewart Udall, Charles Conconi [and] David Osterhout, New York, McGraw-Hill [1974] 288 p. 22 cm.

Bibliography : p. [285]–288.

1. Energy policy—United States. 2. Technology and civilization. 3. United States—Civilization—1945–1. Conconi, Charles, joint author. II, Osterhout, David, joint author. III. Title.
HD9502.U52 U4

Vogely, William A. Energy options for today and tomorrow. In National Public Policy Conference, 25th, Clymer, N.Y., 1975. Increasing understanding of public problems and policies—1975. Chicago, Farm Foundation [1975] p. 43–54.

Reviews U.S. reaction to the OPEC embargo and oil price increases; examines energy policies proposed by the President and those that are emerging from Congress; and discusses related major policy areas.

Wagner, Craig A. National energy goals and FEA's mandatory crude oil allocation program. Virginia law review, v. 61, May 1975: 904–937.

Note discusses the origins of the U.S. petroleum supply problem, traces the history of the FEA's regulatory programs, and analyzes how the FEA's Mandatory Crude Oil Allocation Program contributes to the achievement of national energy goals.

Warne, William E., ed. The energy crunch of the late 20th century: a symposium. Public administration review, v. 35, July–Aug. 1975: 315–354.

Contains 7 articles offering glances "at the problems of organizing to meet energy problems—at national, state, and local levels—at conservation and environmental interfaces, at what may be meant by a change in life style enforced by energy stringencies, and at what the 93rd Congress did and did not do about the whole matter of energy supplies."

Willrich, Mason. Energy and world politics/by Mason Willrich, with Joel Darmstadter . . . [et al.]. New York: Free Press, [1975] xiv, 234 p.; 22 cm.

"Published under the auspices of the American Society of International Law." Includes index. Bibliography: p. 213–221.

1. Energy policy. 2. Power resources. 3. Petroleum industry and trade. I. American Society of International Law. II. Title. HD9502.A2 W54

Administration of energy shortages: Natural gas and petroleum/by Mason Willrich. Cambridge. Mass.: Ballinger 1976

Energy independence for America. International affairs (London), v. 52, Jan. 1976: 53–66.

Analyzes "the basic issues underlying energy independence from an American viewpoint." Maintains that "the energy path America chooses, whether consciously or by default, will have major ramifications for international stability and security, the world economy and the global environment."

Wigner, Eugene P. Weighing our energy options. Prism, v. 3, Jan. 1976: 51–54.

"If we want to keep all our machines running, says this Nobel physicist, we can't afford to rely on any single source of power."

Power resources—[U.S.]/Energy policy—[U.S.] TP 360 LRS 76–963

Witt, Elder. Arrandale, Tom. Energy policy: "overestimating the capability of Congress?" Congressional quarterly weekly report, v. 33, June 28, 1975: 1343–1346.

"Some say the delay has been caused by the nature of the problem, but other members of Congress are sharing the Ford administration's doubts that congressional Democrats can ever formulate a comprehensive national energy policy."

Zumwalt, Elmo R., Jr. Public understanding—an answer to the energy impasse. Public utilities fortnightly, v. 96, Sept. 25, 1975: 38–41.

"Outlines a program to be undertaken by a new organization in the public interest to awaken Americans to risks which they face and urging a positive response to the challenge."

Annual Review of Energy, vol. I Edited by Jack M. Hollander and Melvin K. Simmons. Palo Alto: Annual Reviews 1976.

Includes: "Energy Self-Sufficiency" by Peter L. Auer 685–713; "Energy Regulation: A Quagmire for Energy Policy" by William O. Doub 713–725; "International Energy Issues and Options" by Mason Willrich 743–772.

SELECTED READINGS: PART II—GOVERNMENT PUBLICATIONS

U.S. Congress. Conference Committees, 1974.

Federal Energy Administration Act of 1974; conference report to accompany H.R. 11793. [Washington, U.S. Govt. Print. Off.] 1974. 34 p. (93d Cong., 2d sess. House Report No. 93–999.)

Federal Nonnuclear Energy Research and Development Act of 1974; conference report to accompany S. 1283. [Washington, U.S. Govt. Print. Off.] 1974. 31 p. (93d Cong., 2d sess. House Report No. 93–1563.)

U.S. Congress. Conference Committees, 1975.

Energy Policy and Conservation Act; conference report to accompany S. 622. [Washington, U.S. Govt. Print. Off.] 1975. 218 p. (94th Cong., 1st sess. Senate. Report No. 94–516.)

U.S. Congress. House. Committee on Banking and Currency. Ad Hoc Committee on the Domestic and International Monetary Effect of Energy and Other Natural Resource Pricing.

Oil imports and energy security: an analysis of the current situation and future prospects; report. Washington, U.S. Govt. Print. Off., 1974. 228 p.

At head of title: Committee print.

U.S. Congress. House. Committees on Banking, Currency and Housing. Subcommittee on International Trade, Investment and Monetary Policy.

Briefing on Operation Independence. Hearing, 94th Cong., 1st sess. Mar. 12, 1975. Washington, U.S. Govt. Print. Off., 1975, 37 p.

U.S. Congress, House. Committee on Government Operations. Conservation, Energy, and Natural Resources Subcommittee.

Investigative hearings on energy and environmental activities of Federal agencies during 1975 (part 1). Hearings, 94th Cong., 1st sess. Washington, U.S. Govt. Print. Off., 1975. 668 p.

Hearings held April 10 . . . June 17, 1975.

U.S. Congress. House. Committee on Interior and Insular Affairs.

Establishing a national program for research and development in non-nuclear energy sources; report to accompany H.R. 13565. Washington, U.S. Govt. Print. Off., 1974. 42 p. (93d Cong., 2d sess. House Report No. 93–1157.)

Providing for a national fuels and energy conservation policy, establishing an Office of Energy Conservation in the Department of the Interior, and for other purposes; report to accompany H.R. 11343. [Washington, U.S. Govt. Print. Off.] 1974. 12 p. (93d Cong., 2d sess. House. Report No. 93–1546.)

U.S. Congress. House. Committee on Interior and Insular Affairs. Subcommittee on Energy and the Environment.

Oversight hearings on nuclear energy—overview of the major issues. Hearings, 94th Cong., 1st sess. Part 1. Washington, U.S. Govt. Print. Off., 1975. 901 p.

Hearings held Apr. 28–29, and May 1–2, 1975. "Serial No. 94–16".

Surface mining veto justification briefing. Hearing before the Subcommittee on Energy and the Environment and the Subcommittee on Mines and Mining of the Committee on Interior and Insular Affairs, House of Representatives, 94th Cong., 1st sess., on the President's veto of H.R. 25. June 3, 1975. Washington, U.S. Govt. Print. Off., 1975. 342 p.

U.S. Congress. House. Committee on International Relations. Subcommittee on International Economic Policy.

Authorization legislation for and the operations of the Council on International Economic Policy. Hearing. 94th Cong., 1st sess. Apr. 15, 1975. Washington, U.S. Govt. Print. Off., 1975. 81 p., Foreign economic relations—[U.S.]—Law and legislation.

U.S. Congress. House. Committee on International Relations. Subcommittee on International Organizations.

Legislation on the International Energy Agency. Hearing before the Subcommittees on International Organizations and on International Resources. Food, and Energy of the Committee on International Relations, House of Representatives, 94th Cong., 1st sess. Mar. 26, 1975. Washington, U.S. Govt. Print. Off., 1975. 79 p.

U.S. Congress. House. Committee on International Relations. Subcommittee on International Resources, Food, and Energy.

U.S. international energy policy. Hearing, 94th Cong., 1st sess. May 1, 1975. Washington, U.S. Govt. Print. Off., 1975. 189 p.

U.S. Congress. House. Committee on Interstate and Foreign Commerce. Subcommittee on Energy and Power.

Energy conservation and oil policy. Hearings, 94th Cong., 1st sess., on titles II, III, IV, XII, and XIII of H.R. 2633, identical bill H.R. 2650, and H.R. 2151. Washington, U.S. Govt. Print. Off., 1975. 2 v.

Hearings held Mar. 10. . . . May 7, 1975. "Serial No. 94–17 and 94–18".

U.S. Congress. House. Committee on Interstate and Foreign Commerce. Subcommittee on Oversight and Investigations.

FEA enforcement policies. Hearings. 94th Cong., 1st sess. Apr. 9, 11; May 6, 7, and 8, 1975. Washington, U.S. Govt. Print. Off., 1975. 459 p.

U.S. Congress. House. Committee on Science and Technology.

Comprehensive plan for energy research, development and demonstration. Hearing, 94th Cong., 1st sess. July 21, 1975. Washington, U.S. Govt. Print. Off., 1975. 674 p. "No. 28".

U.S. Congress. House. Committee on Ways and Means.

Background readings on energy policy: selected materials complied by the staff of the Committee on Ways and Means with the assistance of the

Congressional Research Service. Washington, U.S. Govt. Print. Off., 1975. 883 p.

At head of title: 94th Cong., 1st sess. Committee print.

"Robert W. Anderson, George N. Chatham, Jane Gravelle, Frances A. Gulick, David E. Gushee and David M. Lindahl of the Congressional Research Service" assisted in the preparation of materials.

Energy Conservation and Conversion Act of 1975: report on H.R. 6860. Washington, U.S. Govt. Print. Off., 1975. 242 p. (94th Cong., 1st sess. House. Report No. 94–221.)

Summary of the major provisions of H.R. 6860 the Energy Conservation and Conversion Act of 1975 as passed by the House of Representatives on June 19, 1975. Washington, U.S. Govt. Print. Off., 1975. 7 p.

At held of title: 94th Cong., 1st sess. Committee print.

U.S. Congress. House. Committee on Ways and Means.

Alternatives for consideration in an energy program: based upon work done by eight task forces of the majority Members of the Committee on Ways and Means, U.S. House of Representatives/Committee on Ways and Means, U.S. House of Representatives. Washington: U.S. Govt. Print. Off., 1975. iii, 15 p.; 24 cm.

At head of title: 94th Cong., 1st sess. Committee print.

1. Energy policy—United States I. Title. HD9502. U5, 1975a.

The energy crisis and proposed solutions. Panel discussions, 94th Cong., 1st sess. Washington. U.S. Govt. Print. Off., 1975, 4 v. Hearings held Mar. 3–17, 1975. Parts 1, 2, 3, and 4.

The energy crisis and proposed solutions; prepared statements presented in panel discussions by administration officials. Washington, U.S. Govt. Print. Off., 1975. 85 p. At head of title: 94th Cong., 1st session. Committee print.

The energy crisis and proposed solutions: prepared statements presented in panel discussions on the subject of general economic discussion of the effect of administration and other energy programs. Washington. U.S. Govt. Print. Off., 1975. 55 p. At head of title: 94th Cong., 1st sess. Committee print.

The energy crisis and proposed solutions. Prepared statements presented in panel discussions on the subject of tax policy in the energy sector. Washington, U.S. Govt. Print. Off., 1975. 121 p. At head of title: 94th Cong., 1st sess. Committee print.

The energy crisis and proposed solutions; prepared statements presented in panel discussions on the subjects of international financial aspects of the energy problem and other issues. Washington, U.S. Govt. Print. Off., 1975. 88 p. At head of title: 94th Cong., 1st sess. Committee print.

The energy crisis and proposed solutions: prepared statements presented in panel discussions of the subject of petroleum supply. Washington, U.S. Govt. Print. Off., 1975. 74 p. At head of title: 94th Cong., 1st sess. Committee print.

The energy crisis and proposed solutions; prepared statements presented in panel discussions on the subject of gas and other energy sources. Washington, U.S. Govt. Print. Off., 1975. 120 p. At head of title: 94th Cong., 1st sess. Committee print.

Summary of testimony presented by panelists on the subject of energy crisis and proposed solutions. Mar. 3–14, 1975. Washington, U.S. Govt. Print. Off., 1975. 51 p.

Partial contents.—Increasing oil and gas prices (import fees on tariffs and excise taxes on domestic oil and gas; deregulation of oil and gas).—Limiting oil supplies (import quotas; allocation; rationing).—Energy conservation incentives.—Capital incentives.—Alternative energy sources.—Utility rate structure changes.—Macroeconomic impact of alternative energy programs.

U.S. Congress. Joint Committee on Atomic Energy. (Cont.)

Development, growth, and state of the nuclear industry. Hearings, 93d Cong., 2d sess. Feb. 5–6, 1974. Washington, U.S. Govt. Print. Off., 1974. 606 p.

"Developments in the energy industry in general and the nuclear power industry in particular, pursuant to section 202 of the Atomic Energy Act of 1954, as amended."

Future structure of the uranium enrichment industry. Hearings, 93d Cong., 2d sess. Washington, U.S. Govt. Print. Off., 1975. 2 v.

Hearings held June 25–Dec. 3, 1974.

Part 3—Vol. I—Hearings: Vol. II—Appendixes and exhibits; Phase III AEC, industry, and finance witnesses.

U.S. Congress. Joint Committee on Internal Revenue Taxation
   Summary of Testimony on the Energy Conservation and Conversion Act
of 1975 on July 10–11 and 14–18, 1975. Washington, U.S. Govt. Print. Off.,
1975. 35 p. At head of title: 94th Cong., 1st sess. Committee print.
U.S. Congress. Joint Economic Committee. Subcommittee on Consumer
Economics.
   The FEA competition in the oil industry, Hearing, 93d Cong., 2d sess.
June 13, 1974. Washington, U.S. Govt. Print. Off., 1974. 58 p.
   A reappraisal of U.S. energy policy; report together with supplementary
views. Washington. U.S. Govt. Print. Off., (1974. 47 p. At head of title: 93d
Cong., 2d sess. Joint committee print.
U.S. Congress. Joint Economic Committee. Subcommittee on Energy.
   U.S. foreign energy policy. Hearings, 94th Cong., 1st sess. Sept. 17 and
19, 1975. Washington, U.S. Govt. Print. Off., 1976, 75 p.
U.S. Congress. Joint Economic Committee. Subcommittee on International
Economics.
   The State Department's oil floor price proposal: should Congress endorse
it? Report together with supplementary and other views. Washington, U.S.
Govt. Print. Off., 1975. 14 p. At head of title: 94th Cong., 1st sess. Joint com-
mittee print.
U.S. Congress. Office of Technology Assessment.
   An analysis of the ERDA plan and program. [Washington, For sale by the
Supt. of Docs., U.S. Govt. Print. Off.] 1975. 318 p.
   "The ERDA Plan [volume I] is a significant milestone in the evolution
of a long-term national energy policy. However, the ERDA Program [volume
II], to implement this plan does not appear adequate to achieve the stated
goals."
U.S. Congress. Senate. Committee on the Budget.
   The 1976 first concurrent resolution on the budget. Hearings, 94th Cong.,
1st sess. Vol. 1. Washington. U.S. Govt. Print. Off., 1975, 552 p. Hearings
held Mar. 4 . . . Mar. 10, 1975.
   Seminars: macroeconomic issues and the fiscal year 1976 budget. Washing-
ton, U.S. Govt. Print. Off., 1975. 214 p. At head of title: 94th Cong., 1st sess.
Committee print.
   Vol. I: Feb. 3, 1975—Economic considerations and the FY 1976 budget;
Feb. 4, 1975—Program priorities in the FY 1976 budget; Feb. 1975—
Revenues.
   Vol. II—Feb. 18, 1975—Critical choices in physical resources; Feb. 19,
1975—Critical choices in human resources; Feb. 20, 1975—Critical choices
in national defense; Feb. 25, 1975—Energy policy and the 1976 budget; Feb.
26, 1975—Monetary policy and the credit markets in 1975.
U.S. Congress. Senate. Committee on Finance. Subcommittee on Energy.
   Capital requirements of energy independence. Joint hearings before the
Subcommittee on Energy and the Subcommittee on Financial Markets of
the Committee on Finance, United States Senate. 94th Cong., 1st sess. May 7
and 8, 1975, Washington, U.S. Govt. Print. Off., 1975, 184 p.
U.S. Congress. Senate. Committee on Foreign Relations.
   Energy and foreign policy. Hearings, 93d Cong., 1st sess. May 30 and 31,
1973. Washington, U.S. Govt. Print. Off., 1974. 239 p.
   Presents the state of policy as of May 1973.
U.S. Congress. Senate. Committee on Foreign Relations. Subcommittee on Multi-
national Corporations.
   The international petroleum cartel, the Iranian Consortium and U.S. na-
tional security. Washington, U.S. Govt. Print. Off., 1974. 158 p. At head of
title: 93d Cong., 2d sess. Committee print.
   Presents copies of formerly secret government documents from the 1950s.
"These documents explain and relate two conflicting policies of the United
States Government in the field of international oil. These policies were 1)
prosecution of the International Petroleum Cartel Case, and 2) creation
of the Iranian Consortium. The first of these actions accused the five major
American oil companies of illegally combining and contracting in the production, refining, transportation, and marketing of oil; the second encouraged the same companies to combine and contract in the first three of these
areas. The decisions taken to resolve this conflict have shaped our national
energy policy for the past twenty years."
U.S. Congress. Senate. Committee on Government Operations.
   Establish a Department of Energy and Natural Resources. Hearings,
93d Cong., 1st sess., on S. 2135. July 31, Aug. 1 and Sept. 13, 1973. Washington, U.S. Govt. Print. Off., 1974. 233 p.

U.S. Congress. Senate. Committee on Government Operations. Permanent Subcommittee on Investigations.

Materials shortages: workshop on resource management. Washington, U.S. Govt. Print. Off., 1975. 76 p. At head of title: 94th Cong., 1st sess. Committee print.

Contains proceedings of a recent workshop on resource management held by the National Academy of Public Administration under contract to the Congressional Research Service (Warren H. Donnelly and Frances Gulick assisted in the workshop).

Partial contents.—Current context of resource allocation: a fundamentally changed world.—Government intervention and market efficiency.—Appendix 3, Resource allocation experience 1939–48 and its application to 1975–85 energy program management.—Appendix 4, Role of government in the distribution of materials to support the energy program.

U.S. Congress. Senate. Committee on Government Operations. Subcommittee on Reorganization, Research, and International Organizations.

To establish a Department of Energy and Natural Resources, Energy Research and Development Administration, and a Nuclear Safety and Licensing Commission. Hearings, 93d Cong., 2d sess., on S. 2135 [and] S. 2744. Feb. 26–27 and Mar. 12–13, 1974. Washington, U.S. Govt. Print. Off., 1974. 583 p.

U.S. Congress. Senate. Committee on Government Operations. Subcommittee on Reports, Accounting, and Management.

Energy advisory committees. Hearing, 94th Cong., 1st sess. Aug. 1, 1975. Washington, U.S. Govt. Print. Off., 1975. 401 p.

U.S. Congress. Senate. Committee on Interior and Insular Affairs.

Energy information needs—study by the General Accounting Office; pursuant to S. Res. 45, a national fuels and energy policy study. Washington, U.S. Govt. Print. Off., 1974. 76 p.

"Ser. no. 93–33 (92–68)".

Reprints GAO report B–178205 (Feb. 6, 1974). Actions needed to improve Federal efforts in collecting, analyzing, and reporting energy data, together with the Comptroller General's summary of that report.

Greater coal utilization. Joint hearings, pursuant to S. Res. 45, the national fuels and energy policy study, 94th Cong., 1st sess., on S. 1777. Parts 1, 2, and 3. Washington, U.S. Govt. Print. Off., 1975. 3 v.

Hearings held June 10 . . . June 23, 1975. "Serial no. 94–18 (92–108)".

National Energy Production Board. Hearings, 94th Cong., 1st sess., on S. 740. Washington, U.S. Govt. Print. Office., 1975. 2 v.

Oil price decontrol. Hearings, pursuant to S. Res. 45; the National Fuels and Energy Policy Study, 94th Cong., 1st sess. Sept. 4 and 5, 1975. Washington, U.S. Govt. Print. Off., 1975. 399 p. "Serial no. 94–23 (92–113)".

Standby Energy Authorities Act; report together with minority and additional views to accompany S. 622. Washington, U.S. Govt. Print. Off., 1975. 90 p. (94th Cong., 1st sess. Senate. Report no. 94–26)

Strategic Energy Reserves Act of 1975; report to accompany S. 677. [Washington, U.S. Govt. Print. Off.] 1975. 53 p. (94th Cong., 1st sess. Senate. Report no. 94–260)

U.S. Congress. Technology Assessment Board.

An analysis identifying issues in the fiscal year 1976 ERDA budget; report prepared for the Committee on Science and Technology, U.S. House of Representatives; Committee on Interior and Insular Affairs, U.S. Senate and the Joint Committee on Atomic Energy, Ninety-fourth Congress, first session. Washington, U.S. Govt. Print. Off., 1975. 84 p. "Serial D". At head of title: Joint committee print.

OTA's assessment of the energy issues implicit in 1976 ERDA budget.

U.S. Dept. of Housing and Urban Development. Office of Policy Development and Research.

Modular integrated utility system. Washington [For sale by the Supt. of Docs., U.S. Govt. Print. Off., 1974] 20 p.

U.S. Dept. of Labor.

Labor report. [Washington] Federal Energy Administration [for sale by the Supt. of Docs., U.S. Govt. Print. Off.] 1974. 187 p. At head of title: Project Independence blueprint; final task force report.

". . . analyzes the future supply of labor with specific occupational skills and compares the availability to labor requirements for increased energy production."

U.S. Energy Research and Development Administration.

A national plan for energy research, development and demonstration; creating energy choices for the future. [Washington, For sale by the Supt. of Docs., U.S. Govt. Print Off., 1975] 1 v. (various pagings). "ERDA–48". Volume 1 : The plan.

According to the Federal Nonnuclear Energy Research and Development Act of 1974, the plan "is to be designed to achieve solutions to energy supply system and associated environmental problems in (a) the immediate and short-term (to the early 1980's) ; (b) the middle term (the early 1980's to 2000) ; and (c) the long-term (beyond 2000)."

Second public meeting on a national plan for energy research, development and demonstration; synopsis of proceedings. Seattle, 1975. 51 p. "ERDA–48 (H–2)".

"The Seattle public meeting on 'A National Plan for Energy Research, Development and Demonstration' was held at the Seattle Center on December 2 and 3, 1975. This meeting was the second in a continuing series of scheduled meetings which the Energy Research and Development Administration (ERDA) will conduct throughout the country to create a dialogue with the public and interested regional groups to assure their viewpoints are represented in ERDA's planning process."

A national plan for energy research, development & demonstration ; creating energy choices for the future summary. [Washington, 1975] 8 l.

Eight page summary outlines specific conclusions and recommendations of the full report which projects plan in three stages (A) short-term to early 1980's ; (B) mid-term, to 2000; (C) beyond 2000.

U.S. Energy Research and Development Administration. Office of Conservation.

The International Energy Agency with emphasis on the Subgroup on Energy Research and Development and the Energy Conservation Working Party. [Washington] 1975. 34 p. "ERDA 76–13".

As a result of the 1973 oil embargo and rising oil prices the United States and other members of the Organization for Economic Cooperation and Development (OECD) created an International Energy Agency (IEA) to administer an International Energy Program. The program's objectives are: to insure that all participating countries will be able to satisfy their minimum oil requirements; to promote cooperation between oil producing and oil-consuming countries; and to reduce dependence on imported oil through research and development, energy conservation, use of alternative energy sources, and uranium enrichment."

U.S. Federal Energy Administration.

Financing Project Independence, financing requirements of the energy industries, and capital needs and policy choices in the energy industries. [Washington, For sale by the Supt. of Docs., U.S. Govt Print. Off.] 1974. 1 v. (various pagings) At head of title: Project Independence blueprint; final task force report.

An historical perspective. [Washington, For sale by the Supt. of Docs., U.S. Govt. Print. Off.] 1974. 47 p.

At head of title: Project Independence blueprint; final task force report. ". . . traces the history of the various major energy sources, concentrating on the period from the end of World War II to the eve of the Arab oil embargo. The reserves, consumption, technology, economics and government policy toward oil, coal, natural gas, nuclear energy, electric power, and energy sources are examined."

Project Independence: a summary. Washington, For sale by the Supt. of Docs., U.S. Govt. Print. Off., 1974. 65, 50 p.

Highlights of energy legislation in the 93d Congress, 1st session ; a background paper prepared at the request of Henry M. Jackson, chairman, Committee on Interior and Insular Affairs, United States Senate, pursuant to S. Res. 45, a national fuels and energy policy study. Washington, U.S. Govt. Print. Off., 1974. 116 p. "Serial no. 93–38 (92–73)". At head of title: 93d Cong., 2d sess. Committee print.

U.S. Federal Energy Administration. Office of Intergovernment, Regional and Special Programs.

Directory of Federal agencies engaged in energy related activities/Office of Intergovernmental, Regional and Special Programs. Washington: Federal Energy Administration: for sale by the Supt. of Docs., U.S. Govt. Print. Off., 1975. ix, 80 p. ; 26 cm.

1. Energy policy—United States—Directories. 2. United States—Executive departments—Directories. I. Title. HD9502.U52 U52 1975.

U.S. Federal Energy Regulation Study Team.

Federal energy regulation : an organizational study. Washington, For sale by the Supt. of Docs., U.S. Govt. Print. Off. 1974. 1 v. (various pagings) ". . . the most pressing need of the Federal energy regulation system at

U.S. Library of Congress. Environmental Policy Division.

The 94th Congress and the energy record: a progress report. Prepared at the request of Henry M. Jackson, Chairman, Committee on Interior and Insular Affairs, United States Senate pursuant to S. Res. 45, a national fuels and energy policy study. Washington, U.S. Govt. Print. Off., 1976. 78 p. "Serial no. 94–30 (92–120)". At head of title: 94th Cong., 2d sess. Committee print.

Congress and the Nation's environment; environmental and natural resources affairs of the 93d Congress. Prepared . . . at the request of Henry M. Jackson, Chairman, Committee on Interior and Insular Affairs, United States Senate. Washington, U.S. Govt. Print Off., 1975. 940 p. At head of title: 94th Cong., 1st sess. Committee print.

Contents.—Energy and fuels, by F. Gulick, W. Donnelly, D. Lindahl, D. Beard, G. Pagliano, G. Siehl, B. Rather, S. Abbasi, R. Anderson, D. Thompson, and W. Fletcher—Mines and minerals, by D. Thompson and L. Lindahl.—Land use policy and planing, by W. Fletcher.—Public lands, by R. Wolf.—Water resources, by H. Brown.—Parks, recreation and wilderness, by G. Siehl.—Forestry, by R. Wolf.—Fisheries and wildlife conservation, by W. Jolly.—Appraisal of natural resources supply and demand, by H. Hughes.—Urban environment, by S. Abbasi.—Government reorganization for energy, environment and natural resources, by S. Abbasi.—Natural hazards, by H. Brown.

Materials shortages: selected readings on energy self-sufficiency and the Controlled Materials Plan. Prepared for the Permanent Subcommittee on Investigations of the Committee on Government Operations, U.S. Senate. Washington, U.S. Govt. Print. Off., 1974. 256 p. At head of title: 93d Cong., 2d sess. Committee print.

U.S. Library of Congress. Science Policy Research Division.

Energy facts II. Prepared for the Subcommittee on Energy Research, Development, and Demonstration of the Committee on Science and Technology, U.S. House of Representatives, 94th Cong., 1st sess. Washington, U.S. Govt. Print. Off., 1975. 536 p. At head of title: Committee print.

Energy policy and resource management. Report prepared for the Subcommittee on Energy of the Committee on Science and Astronautics, U.S. House of Representatives, 93d Cong., 2d sess. Washington, U.S. Govt. Print. Off., 1974. 100 p. At head of title: Committee print. "Serial R".

A collection of policy analyses, with background material, of various aspects of the energy crisis. Includes bibliographies.

U.S. Panel on Project Independence Blueprint.

CTAB recommendations for a national energy program. [Washington. For sale by the Supt. of Docs., U.S. Govt. Print. Off., 1975] 70 p.

Final report and recommendations of the Commerce Advisory Board's Panel on Project Independence Blueprint. The Panel's "purpose was to make an independent review and assessment of the actions and policies resulting from the Project Independence study which was then under preparation by the Federal Energy Administration (FEA)".

this time is for mechanisms that coordinate, rather than consolidate, diver, agencies and their functions."

U.S. Federal Power Commission. Task Force on Energy Sources Research.

National power survey: energy sources research; the report and recom mendations. Washington. For sale by the Supt. of Docs., U.S. Govt. Print. Off,. 1974. 125 p.

Covers all forms of energy and recommends an order of priority ranking on research and development for the various energy sources.

U.S. Federal Power Commission. Technical Advisory Committee on Conservation of Energy.

National power survey: energy conservation; the report and recommendations. Washington. For sale by the Sutp. of Docs., U.S. Govt. Print. Off., 1974. 177 p.

"The Technical Advisory Committee on Conservation of Energy was established by the Federal Power Commission in September 1972. The Committee was given the responsibility to study and report on activities and issues in energy conservation, and to make recommendations as to desirable related policies and actions."

U.S. General Accounting Office.

Actions needed to improve Federal efforts in collecting, analyzing, and reporting energy data; study requested by chairman, Senate Committee on Interior and Insular Affairs. [Washington] 1974. 35 p. "B–178205, Feb. 6, 1974".

"We need to start now to establish a fully integrated comprehensive energy data system building, where possible, on existing data collection systems and programs. . . . General responsibility for developing the comprehensive system should be placed in an organization within the executive branch which has the opportunity to establish itself as a professional, objective, independent gatherer of energy information. The organization should be responsible for data collection and technical analysis, without any responsibility for an involvement in energy policy analysis or formulation."

Domestic crude oil pricing policy and related production, Federal Energy Administration. [Washington] 1974. 19 p. "B–178205, Aug. 19, 1974".

Issues related to foreign sources of oil for the United States, Department of State; report to the Congress by the Comptroller General of the United States. [Washington] 1974. 65 p.

"This report discusses (1) the State Department's role before eruption of hostilities in the Middle East in October and Arab curtailment of petroleum exports and (2) the critical problems facing the Department in resolving the issues connected with the current and future availability of this vital raw material from sources outside the United States."

Outlook for Federal goals to accelerate leasing of oil and gas resources on the Outer Continental Shelf, Department of the Interior, Federal Energy Administration; report to the Congress by the Comptroller General of the United States. [Washington] 1975. 40 p. "B–118678, Mar. 19, 1975".

"This report, first of a series on Federal leasing policies and practices, focuses on how Interior determined its goal for accelerating leasing of oil and gas resources on the Shelf, how this goal is related to project Independence, and constraints which may hinder its accomplishment."

Problems in the Federal Energy Administration's compliance and enforcement effort, Federal Energy Administration; report to the Subcommittee on Reorganization, Research and International Organizations, Committee on Government Operations, United States Senate. [Washington] 1974. 22 l. "B–178205, Dec. 6, 1974".

U.S. Library of Congress. Congressional Research Service.

Energy facility siting in coastal areas, prepared at the request of Hon. Warren G. Magnuson, Chairman, Committee on Commerce and Hon. Ernest F. Hollings, Chairman, National Ocean Policy Study for the use of the Committee on Commerce and the National Ocean Policy Study pursuant to S. Res. 222. Washington, U.S. Govt. Print. Off., 1975. 126 p. At head of title: 94th Cong., 1st sess. Committee print.

Highlights of energy legislation in the 94th Congress (through June 30, 1975): a background paper. Prepared . . . at the request of Henry M. Jackson, Chairman, Committee on Interior and Insular Affairs, United States Senate, pursuant to S. Res. 45, a national fuels and energy policy study. Washington, U.S. Govt. Print. Off., 1975. 98 p. At head of title: 94th Cong., 1st sess. Committee print.

Prepared by Frances Gulick, EPD. Appendix III contains "Nuclear power and the 94th Congress: a mid-term report," by Warren H. Donnelly and Barbara L. Rather.

Appendix 8
Watergate Reorganization
and Reform Act of 1976

This 1976 Congressional Research Service issue brief explains efforts to reorganize certain federal activities to prevent a recurrence of some of the abuses associated with Watergate. If there had not been structural deficiencies in the organization of government oversight, it is possible that Watergate and related abuses might not have happened at all. The bills referred to as pending in this document did not pass in the 94th Congress, but are likely to be reintroduced, in modified form, in the 95th Congress. The chronology of events and bibliography of reference sources offer particularly useful research tools on the subject of Watergate; and the document itself is a significant case study in federal reorganization.

ISSUE DEFINITION

The Senate Select Committee on Presidential Campaign Activities, established by S.Res. 60 on Feb. 7, 1973, investigated alleged illegal, improper, and unethical activities connected with the 1972 Presidential campaign. Subsequent to extensive hearings, the Committee issued on June 27, 1974, its report and recommendations, most of which were embodied in S. 4227, introduced in the 93d Congress by Senator Ervin, chairman of the Select Committee, on Dec. 11, 1974. The bill was reintroduced in the 94th Congress as S. 495, the Watergate Reorganization and Reform Act, by Senator Ribicoff on Jan. 30, 1975. Many of the Committee's recommendations regarding campaign financing were included in P.L. 93-443, the Federal Elections Campaign Act Amendments of 1974.

BACKGROUND AND POLICY ANALYSIS

S. Res. 60 specifically authorized the Select Committee on Presidential Campaign Activities to investigate the Watergate break-in, the misuse of campaign funds, and "dirty tricks" in the 1972 Presidential campaign. It also directed the Committee to make legislative recommendations designed to prevent the recurrence of such activities in the future. A total of $2 million was appropriated for the Committee's functions.

After hearing testimony from 62 witnesses in 53 days of public session, and from 68 witnesses in 71 days of executive session, the Committee issued its final report on June 27, 1974, with 35 recommendations. Many of the Select Committee's recommendations were in-

Note: This appendix is from [54], pp. 1-14.

corporated into the Watergate Reorganization and Reform Act introduced
by Senator Ervin as S. 4227 in December 1974 and reintroduced as S. 495
by Senator Ribicoff in January 1975.   Between July 1975 and March 1976,
the Senate Government Operations Committee held 7 days of hearings with
testimony from 20 witnesses on S. 495 and related bills.   On April 9,
following two days of markup, the Committee ordered reported an amended
version of S. 495 which incorporated recommendations from the Select
Committee, Members of Congress, and concerned organizations.   According
to Senator Ribicoff, the bill goes beyond the Watergate scandals and
generally "is directed at ensuring accountability of government officials."   The bill was reported on May 12 and referred to the Senate
Judiciary Committee with instructions to report it out in 30 days.
Hearings were held on May 26 by the Judiciary Committee.   The 30-day
limit was extended 5 days, and the bill was automatically discharged
on June 15, without any committee recommendation.

As reported by the committee, the bill focuses on four major proposals: a Division of Government Crimes within the Department of Justice,
a triggering mechanism for the appointment of a temporary special prosecutor, a Congressional Legal Counsel, and financial disclosure requirements for government officials.

On July 19, the Senate began consideration of S. 495.   President Ford
announced that the Administration was willing to abandon its opposition
to the bill, provided that certain changes were made particularly in the
title I provisions on the special prosecutor.   As debate continued in
the Senate on July 20, Government Operations Committee Members and staff
met with Administration officials to arrange a compromise version of
title I.   The substitute version was submitted and approved on July 21,
one of twenty amendments added to the bill, and the bill itself was
shortly thereafter ratified by a vote of 91-5.   A summary of the major
provisions of the Senate-approved bill follows.

TITLE I: Office of Special Prosecutor, Office of Government Crimes, and
           Office of Professional Responsibility

This section establishes a permanent, independent Office of Special
Prosecutor in the Justice Department headed by a Special Prosecutor
appointed by the President for a three-year term and subject to Senate
confirmation.   No one could be appointed to the position if at any
time during the preceding five years he held a high position in the
campaign of a candidate for Federal elective office.   The Prosecutor
could only be removed by the President for extraordinary improprieties,
malfeasance in office, willful neglect of duty, permanent incapacita-
tion, or conduct constituting a felony.   Any removal action could be
challenged in U.S. District Court.   The Special Prosecutor would have
the authority to investigate and prosecute violations of Federal criminal law by individuals who hold or held the positions of: President,
Vice President, Attorney General, FBI Director, any Cabinet member, any
high-level Government officials compensated at a rate at least equal to
level II of the Executive Schedule, all Members of Congress, and all
members of the Federal judiciary.   The section sets forth the authority
of the Prosecutor, making it clear that he is almost totally independent
of the Attorney General.

Title I also creates in the Justice Department an Office of Government Crimes to handle criminal violations of Federal law by lower-level
Federal employees and officers, past or present, as it affected their

Federal employment. The Office would also be responsible for investigating violations of lobbying and election laws and conflicts of interest. It would be headed by a Director appointed by the President with Senate approval and who, like the Special Prosecutor, may not have held a high campaign position for a candidate for Federal elective office during the preceding five years. The Office of Government Crimes would perform much the same function as the Public Integrity Section established in January 1976 in the Criminal Division of the Justice Department to handle Federal corruption charges.

Title I also codifies the Office of Professional Responsibility established by Attorney General Levi on Dec. 9, 1975. The Office, which is headed by a Counsel appointed by the Attorney General, has and would continue to have responsibility for conducting preliminary investigations of charges of wrongdoing against Justice Department employees.

Finally, Title I includes a provision prohibiting a person who has played a leading partisan role in the election of a President from being appointed Attorney General or Deputy Attorney General.

The proposals in Title I are a composite of ones made by the Watergate Special Prosecution Force in its final report in October 1975, the American Bar Association in February 1976, President Ford, Senate Members, and other academicians and commentators.

Title II: Congressional Legal Counsel

This section establishes an Office of Congressional Legal Counsel to represent Congress in court actions involving the constitutional powers of Congress or of its Members, employees, or committees in civil actions arising from the performance of official duties. The Office is to be headed by a Congressional Legal Counsel, appointed for a 4-year term by the President pro tempore of the Senate and the Speaker of the House with the approval of both chambers. Congress may authorize the Congressional Legal Counsel to act in the following types of cases: (1) when a Member, officer, employee, agency or committee of Congress is a defendant in a civil action; (2) when a House of Congress authorizes the Counsel to bring a civil action to enforce a subpoena; and (3) where Congress' point of view needs to be represented in cases involving the constitutionality of a statute or Congress' powers. This proposal is seen as alleviating the need for Congress to rely on the Justice Department to represent it in civil actions and as generally strengthening Congress' capabilities in protecting its own constitutional powers.

TITLE III: Financial Disclosure

This section requires full and complete public disclosure by all government employees earning a salary comparable to that of a GS-16 or above (approximately $36,000). This would apply to the President, Vice President, each Member of Congress, all Federal judges, all Federal employees and officers compensated at a rate equal to or greater than GS-16, all members of the armed services compensated at a rate equal to or greater than 0-7, and all candidates for Federal elective office. The annual statements by the approximately 15,000 individuals covered shall be filed with the Comptroller General and will be available to the public for inspection. The information to be reported is to include the identity of any business asset, liability, or transaction in real prop-

erty or securities over $1,000 (the exact value of which is not re-
quired), items of income valued in excess of $100, gifts received valued
in excess of $500 or the aggregate from any one source in excess of
$500, and a listing of any agreements for future employment. Non-
elected Federal employees must report the name of any employer in the
private sector who paid them more than $5,000 in any of the previous 5
years. This section of S. 495 is intended to extend uniform coverage
and requirements to all important Federal officials, in all branches of
the government, in order to enable a greater degree of accountability to
the public.

LEGISLATION

H.R. 970 (Rooney)

Establishes an Office of General Counsel to the Congress to provide
legal advice and opinions to Members, committees, and legislative employees and, in certain situations, to represent such in legal proceedings involving official actions. The bill was introduced on Jan.
14, 1975, and was referred to the Committee on House Administration.

H.R. 3249 (Kastenmeier)

Requires candidates for Federal office, Members of Congress, and
officers and employees of the United States to file statements with
the Comptroller General with respect to their income and financial
transactions. The bill was introduced on Feb. 19, 1975, and was referred to the House Committees on the Judiciary and Standards of Official Conduct.

H.R. 6279 (Spellman)

Establishes in the legislative branch the Office of General Counsel
to render legal opinions; assist in legislative review of executive
actions; argue in behalf of Congress' powers in court; represent Congress, or its members, or committees in legal actions; and other functions. The bill was introduced on Apr. 22, 1975, and referred to the
House Administration Committee.

H.R. 14476 (Hungate)

Establishes a Division of Government Crimes in the Justice Department and sets up a triggering device for the temporary appointment of a
special prosecutor. The bill was introduced on June 21, 1976, and was
referred to the House Judiciary Committee.

H.R. 14795 (Hutchinson)

President Ford's substitute version of S. 495. The bill was introduced on July 21, 1976, and was referred to the Committees on the
Judiciary, Rules, and Standards of Official Conduct.

S. 243 (Proxmire)

Establishes an independent Special Prosecutor's Office. The bill was
introduced on Jan. 17, 1975, and was referred to the Senate Committee on
the Judiciary.

S. 181 (Case)

Requires the President, Vice-President, Members of Congress, certain officers and employees of the Government, and candidates for Federal office to file annual financial disclosure statements with the Comptroller General. The bill was introduced on Jan. 16, 1975, and was referred to the Senate Committee on Rules and Administration.

S. 563 (Humphrey)

Includes a provision to establish an Office of Congressional Counsel General to provide legal opinions and perform specified duties with respect to legislative review of executive actions. The bill was introduced on Feb. 5, 1975, and was referred to the Government Operations Committee.

S. 1682 (Bentsen)

Prohibits appointment of Presidential campaign officials to high Department of Justice positions, and provides for Hatch Act coverage of all Department of Justice officers. The bill was introduced on May 7, 1975, and was referred to the Senate Committee on the Judiciary.

S. 2036 (Javits)

Promotes accountability in the executive branch of the Government, requires the disclosure of the financial status of public officials, and establishes an Office of Legal Counsel to the Congress. The bill was introduced on June 26, 1975, and was referred to the Senate Committee on Government Operations.

S. 2731 (Abourezk)

A bill to establish an Office of Congressional Legal Counsel to revitalize the Constitutional separation of powers by enabling the legislative branch of the government to represent its interest in litigation before the judicial branch of the Government. The bill was introduced on Dec. 2, 1975, and was referred to the Government Operations Committee.

HEARINGS

U.S. Congress. House. Committee on the Judiciary. Subcommittee on Criminal Justice. Special Prosecutor and Watergate Grand Jury Legislation. Hearings, 93d Congress, 1st session. Oct. 29 & 31; Nov. 1, 5, 7 & 8, 1973. Washington, U.S. Govt. Print. Off., 1973. 496 p.

U.S. Congress. Senate. Committee on Government Operations. Watergate Reorganization and Reform Act of 1975. Hearings, 94th Congress, 1st session. July 29-31, 1975. Washington, U.S. Govt. Print. Off., 1975. 453 p.

----- Watergate Reorganization and Reform Act of 1975. Hearings, 94th Congress, 1st session. Dec. 3, 4, 8, 1975; Mar. 11, 1976. Washington, U.S. Govt. Print. Off., 1976. 745 p. Pt. 2.

U.S. Congress. Senate. Committee on the Judiciary. Special
Prosecutor. Hearings, 93d Congress, 1st session. Oct. 29-31;
Nov. 1, 5-8, 14-15, 20, 1973. Washington, U.S. Govt. Print.
Off., 1973. 382 p. Pt. 1.

----- Hearings, 93d Congress, 1st session. Oct. 29-31; Nov. 1, 5-6,
14-15, 20, 1973. Washington, U.S. Govt. Print. Off., 1973.
232 p. Pt. 2.

U.S. Congress. Senate. Committee on the Judiciary. Subcommittee
on Separation of Powers. Removing Politics From the Administration of Justice. Hearings. 93d Congress, 2d session. Mar.
26-28; Apr. 2, 1974. Washington, U.S. Govt. Print. Off., 1974.
529 p.

U.S. Congress. Senate. Select Committee on Presidential Campaign
Activities. Campaign financing. Hearings, 93d Congress, 1st
session. Nov. 7, 8, 13, 14, and 15, 1973. 1 book. Washington,
U.S. Govt. Print. Off., 1974. p. 5273-5858.

----- Campaign practices. Hearings, 93d Congress. 1st session.
3 books. Washington, U.S. Govt. Print. Off., 1974. p. 3899-
5272.
    Hearings held Sept. 26; Oct. 3, 4, 9-11, 31; Nov. 1, and 6,
1973.

----- The Hughes-Reboso investigation and related matters. Hearings,
93d Congress, 1st and 2d sessions. 7 books. Washington, U.S.
Govt. Print. Off., 1974. p. 9345-12966.
    Hearings held July 24; Sept. 11-13; Dec. 4, 14, 18-20, 1973;
Feb. 8; Mar. 16, 20-23, 28; Apr. 1, 10, 11, 15, 16, 29; May 2,
5, 7, 10, 13, 15, 17, 22, 28, 29; June 6, 10-12, and 14, 1974.

----- Milk fund investigation. Hearings, 93d Congress, 1st and 2d
Congress. 4 books. Washington, U.S. Govt. Print. Off., 1974.
p. 5859-8173.
    Hearings held Nov. 12-16; Dec. 4, 11, 14, 18, 19-21, 1973;
Jan. 9, 10, 25, 28, 31; Feb. 5, 7, 8, 20, 21; Mar. 11-13, 20,
22, 25, 26; Apr. 2, 11, 26; May 21, 31; June 13, 1974.

----- Use of incumbency responsiveness program. Hearings, 93d
Congress, 2d session. 2 books. Washington, U.S. Govt. Print.
Off., 1974. p. 8175-9343.
    Hearings held Jan. 31; Feb. 9; Apr. 8; and May 28, 1974.

----- Watergate investigation. Hearings, 93d Congress, 1st session.
9 books. Washington, U.S. Govt. Print. Off., 1974. p. 1-3898.
    Hearings held May 17, 18, 22-24; June 5-7, 12-14, 25-29;
July 10-13, 16-20; 23-27; 30, 31; Aug. 1-3, 6, and 7, 1973.

REPORTS AND CONGRESSIONAL DOCUMENTS

Ervin, Sam J., Jr. Some personal observations of Senator Sam J.
Ervin, Jr. respecting Watergate. Congressional record [daily
ed,] v. 120, July 16, 1974: S12552-12555.

Hungate, William L. Preventing improper influence of Federal law
enforcement agencies. Congressional record [daily ed.] v. 122,
June 21, 1976: E3493–3494.

U.S. Congress. Senate. Committee on Government Operations.
Watergate Reorganization and Reform Act of 1976; report to
accompany S. 495. Washington, U.S. Govt. Print. Off., 1976.
117 p. (94th Congress, 2d session. Senate. Report no. 94-823)

U.S. Congress. Senate. Select Committee on Presidential Campaign
Activities. Appendix to the Hearings of the Select Committee on
Presidential Campaign Activities of the United States Senate.
93d Congress, 1st and 2d sessions. 2 v. Washington, U.S. Govt.
Print. Off., June 28, 1974. 2157 p.
At head of title: Presidential Campaign Activities of 1972.
Senate Resolution 60.

----- Election reform: Basic references. Washington, U.S. Govt.
Print. Off., November 1973. 719 p.
At head of title: 93d Congress, 1st session. Committee
print.

----- The Final Report of the Select Committee on Presidential
Campaign Activities, United States Senate. Washington, U.S.
Govt. Print. Off., June 1974. 1250 p.
At head of title: 93d Congress, 2d session. Senate.
Report no. 93-981.

U.S. President, 1974-1976 (Ford). Watergate Reforms. Communication
from the President of the United States transmitting proposed
substitute language to correct constitutional and practical
problems contained in S. 495, the Watergate Reorganization and
Reform Act of 1976, currently pending before the Senate. Washington, U.S. Govt. Print. Off., 1976. (94th Congress, 2d session. House. Document no. 94-550).
Message dated July 19, 1976.

Watergate Reorganization and Reform Act of 1976. Debate in the
Senate. Congressional record [daily ed.] v. 122, July 19,
1976: S11852-S11875; July 20, 1976: S11952-S11972; July 21,
1976: S12076-S12118.

CHRONOLOGY OF EVENTS

07/28/76 -- The House Judiciary Subcommittee on Administrative Law
and Governmental Relations began hearings on H.R. 3249,
a financial disclosure bill, and related bills.

07/23/76 -- The House Judiciary Subcommittee on Criminal Justice held
hearings on H.R. 14476, the Special Prosecutor Act of
1976.

07/21/76 -- Senate passed S. 495 by a vote of 91-5. The House Democratic Caucus approved a resolution calling for a strict
financial disclosure law this year.

07/19/76 -- Senate began consideration of S. 495. President Ford
submitted suggestions for changes in the form of a substitute amendment.

06/15/76 -- S. 495 discharged from Senate Judiciary Committee without
a committee recommendation.

05/26/76 -- Senate Judiciary Committee held hearings on S. 495.

05/12/76 -- Senate Government Operations Committee reported out
S. 495 (S.Rept. 94-823). It was referred to the Judiciary Committee with instructions to report not later
than June 11, 1976 (later extended 5 days).

02/16/76 -- The American Bar Association adopted recommendations designed to insulate Federal law enforcement from political
considerations, including a special prosecutor when
Watergate-type situations occur, the prohibition of Presidents from appointing top campaign aides as Attorney
General, and a requirement for Justice Department attorneys to log outside contacts on pending cases.

01/14/76 -- A Public Integrity Section was established in the Justice
Department's Criminal Division to handle Federal corruption charges involving public officials or institutions.

12/22/75 -- The Maryland Court of Appeals ruled unconstitutional an
office of special prosecutor created in 1975, on the
grounds that it usurped constitutional powers granted to
the attorney general and states' attorneys (Murphy v.
Yates, No. 68).

12/03/75 -- The Senate Committee on Government Operations resumed its
hearings on S. 495 and other bills dealing with financial
disclosure and a Congressional Legal Counsel.

10/16/75 -- The Watergate Special Prosecution Force released the
final report on its activities.

07/29/75 -- The Senate Committee on Government Operations began a
series of hearings on S. 495.

01/30/75 -- S. 495, the Watergate Reorganization and Reform Act of
1975, was introduced by Senator Ribicoff.

01/01/75 -- H. R. Haldeman, John D. Ehrlichman, John N. Mitchell, and
Robert C. Mardian were found guilty of involvement in the
Watergate coverup. Kenneth W. Parkinson was acquitted.

12/11/74 -- S. 4227, the Watergate Reorganization and Reform Act of
1974, was introduced by Senator Ervin.

12/04/74 -- The Federal grand jury empaneled June 5, 1972, which
brought the original Watergate indictments and coverup
indictments, was dismissed.

10/25/74 -- Leon Jaworski stepped down as Special Prosecutor and was
succeeded by Henry Ruth, former Deputy Special Prosecutor.

10/01/74 -- Watergate cover-up trial began.

09/30/74 -- Senate Select Committee on Presidential Campaign Activities formally ended.

09/19/74 -- Richard Nixon was subpoenaed by Leon Jaworski as a witness in the Watergate cover-up trial.

09/08/74 -- President Ford pardoned former President Nixon for any and all crimes that he may have committed while in office 1969-1974.

08/29/74 -- Richard Nixon was subpoenaed as a defense witness in the Watergate cover-up trial.

08/08/74 -- President Nixon announced his resignation.

07/27/74 -- The first impeachment article was passed by the House Judiciary Committee.

07/24/74 -- The U.S. Supreme Court ruled 8-0 that President Nixon must turn over the tapes of Presidential conversations to Judge Sirica.

06/27/74 -- The final report of the Select Committee on Presidential Campaign Activities was submitted to the Senate.

05/28/74 -- S. Res. 328, allocating additional funds to the Select Committee, was adopted.

05/21/74 -- S. Res. 327, extending the time period for the Select Committee's report, was adopted.

05/09/74 -- The House Judiciary Committee formally opened impeachment hearings.

04/30/74 -- President Nixon released 1,308 pages of edited transcripts to the House Judiciary Committee and to the public.

04/28/74 -- Mitchell and Stans were acquitted in criminal conspiracy case.

04/03/74 -- The Internal Revenue Service disclosed that President and Mrs. Nixon owe $432,787 in back taxes, plus $33,000 in interest.

03/01/74 -- S. Res. 286, allocating additional funding to the Select Committee, was adopted.

02/19/74 -- Public hearings by the Select Committee on Presidential Campaign Activities ended. S. Res. 287, requiring the Select Committee to report by May 28, 1974, was adopted.

02/08/74 -- Judge Gesell ruled that President Nixon did not have to comply with the Select Committee's subpoenas.

01/04/74 -- In a letter to Senator Ervin, President Nixon refused to honor the Select Committee's subpoenas.

12/19/73 -- The Select Committee issued three subpoenas for nearly 500 Presidential tapes and documents.

12/04/73 -- S. Res. 209, allocating additional funding to the Select Committee, was adopted.

11/21/72 -- Judge Sirica disclosed a 18.5-minute gap in a Presidential tape.

11/07/73 -- S. Res. 194, stating the sense of the Senate that the Select Committee has authority to subpoena Presidential tapes and papers, was adopted.

10/20/73 -- Special Prosecutor Archibald Cox was fired; Attorney General Richardson resigned.

10/10/73 -- Vice-President Agnew resigned.

09/24/73 -- Select Committee hearings were resumed.

08/13/73 -- Second Watergate grand jury was convened on ITT, obstruction of justice, and illegal campaign financing.

08/09/73 -- Select Committee filed suit for Presidential tapes.

08/07/73 -- Select Committee hearings recessed after 37 daily sessions, sworn testimony from 35 witnesses and 7,537 pages of testimony.

08/01/73 -- Select Committee released Colson memo linking President Nixon and Attorney General Mitchell to the ITT settlement.

07/31/73 -- First impeachment resolution against Richard Nixon was introduced in the House.

07/26/73 -- Select Committee voted to file suit for Presidential tapes.

07/23/73 -- President Nixon refused Senator Ervin's request for Presidential tapes. Select Committee adopted resolution authorizing subpoena of the tapes.

07/16/73 -- Alexander Butterfield revealed the existence of the Presidential tapes under questioning by the Select Committee.

07/06/73 -- President Nixon refused to testify or give papers to the Select Committee.

06/27/73 -- The existence of the enemies list was revealed.

06/25/73 -- S. Res. 132, allocating additional funding for the Select Committee, was adopted.

06/12/73 -- Federal district court rejected Special Prosecutor Cox's plea to halt broadcasting of the Select Committee's hearings.

06/05/73 -- The Select Committee rejected Special Prosecutor Cox's request to suspend its hearings for one to three months.

05/18/73 -- Archibald Cox was named Special Prosecutor.

05/17/73 -- Televised Select Committee hearings began.

05/11/73 -- Pentagon papers trial was dismissed on grounds of government misconduct.

05/10/73 -- Former Attorney General Mitchell and Former Secretary of Commerce Maurice Stans were indicted by a New York grand jury on 3 counts of conspiracy to obstruct justice and 6 counts of perjury related to Robert Vesco's $200,000 campaign contribution.

04/30/73 -- President Nixon announced the resignations of H. R. Haldeman, John Erlichman, and John Dean.

04/27/73 -- Patrick Gray resigned as acting FBI Director following the disclosure that he destroyed Howard Hunt's files.

04/18/73 -- Guidelines for the Select Committee's hearings were released; sworn testimony will be required of all witnesses in open session.

04/17/73 -- President Nixon announced a new Watergate investigation because of serious charges brought to his attention on Mar. 21, 1973.

03/30/73 -- The White House announced that its staff will testify only in closed session before the Select Committee or grand jury.

03/28/73 -- The Select Committee heard testimony from James McCord in closed session.

03/23/73 -- Judge Sirica disclosed McCord's letter stating that "higher-ups" were involved in the Watergate break in.

02/21/73 -- Senator Ervin was elected Chairman and Senator Baker Vice-Chairman of the Select Committee on Presidential Campaign Activities.

02/07/73 -- S. Res. 60, establishing the Select Committee on Presidential Campaign Activities, was adopted unanimously.

01/30/73 -- A jury found Gordon Liddy and James McCord et al. guilty.

01/26/73 -- The Committee to Re-elect the President pleaded nolo contendere to campaign financing law violations and is fined $8,000.

01/11/73 -- The Justice Department filed suit against the Committee to Re-elect the President for eight violations of campaign financing laws, including the Hugh Sloan payment to G. Gordon Liddy.

12/07/72 -- The existence of the White House "plumbers" unit, involving David Young, G. Gordon Liddy, Howard Hunt, and
Egil Krogh, was disclosed.

09/15/72 -- A Federal grand jury indicted James McCord, Bernard
Barker, Frank Sturgis, Virgilio Gonzalez, G. Gordon
Liddy, and Howard Hunt.

08/26/72 -- The General Accounting Office reported five apparent, and
four possible, violations of the Federal Election Campaign Act of 1971 by the Committee to Re-elect the President.

06/22/72 -- President Nixon denied White House involvement in the
Watergate break in.

06/19/72 -- The Justice Department announced that it will make a
full investigation of the Watergate break in.

06/19/72 -- Howard Hunt's name was found in address books belonging
to Bernard Barker and Eugenio Martinez.

06/18/72 -- James McCord's association with the Committee to Re-elect
the President and the White House was disclosed.

06/17/72 -- James McCord, Bernard Barker, Frank Sturgis, Eugenio
Martinez, and Virgilio Gonzalez were apprehended in the
Democratic National Committee's headquarters and were
charged with burglary.

ADDITIONAL REFERENCE SOURCES

Angle, Martha. "Congress Lags on Laws that Might Prevent Future
Watergates." Washington Star, June 15, 1975, p. A-1.

----- "Ford Bows, Senate Votes Watergate Bill." Washington Star,
July 21, 1976, p. A-1.

----- "Levi Lobbies to Block Watergate Reform Bill." Washington
Star, June 28, 1976, p. A-1.

----- "Panel Ok's 'Watergate' Action Plan." Washington Star, April
8, 1976, p. A-3.

----- "Senate Panel Weighs 'Watchman in the night'." Washington
Star, July 29, 1975, p. A-3.

Baker, Howard H., Jr. "The Proposed Judicially Appointed Independent
Office of Public Attorney: Some Constitutional Objections and an
Alternative." Southwestern Law Review Journal 29 (Fall 1975):
671-683.

Brown, Clifford W., Jr. "Watergate." Ripon Quarterly 1 (Summer
1974): 3-18.

Brown, Warren. "Ford Urges Changes in Watergate Reform Bill."
Washington Post, July 20, 1976, p. A-10.

Caraley, Demetrios, and others. "American Political Institutions after Watergate—A Discussion." Political Science Quarterly 89 (Winter 1974-75): 713-749.

Cohen, Richard E. "Watergate May Alter Style but Not Substance of Power." National Journal Reports, September 7, 1973, p 1340-1349.

----- "Watergate Reform Isn't Over Yet." National Journal Reports, November 11, 1975, p. 1581.

Cox, Archibald. "Ends." New York Times Magazine, May 20, 1974, p 27-29, 66-69, 72, 79-80, 92, 94, 97.

Gardner, John W. Rebirth of a Nation. Washington, D.C.: Common Cause, 1974. 20 p.

Hendel, Samuel. "Separation of Powers Revisited in Light of 'Watergate.'" Western Political Quarterly 27 (December 1974): 575-588.

Link, Mary. "Senate Passes Watergate Reform Measure with Administration Changes." Congressional Quarterly Weekly Report 34 (July 24, 1976): 1953-1954.

----- "Senate Prepares To Debate Watergate Reform Measure." Congressional Quarterly Weekly Report 34 (July 17, 1976): 1903-1904.

Madden, Richard. "Senate Approves Prosecutor Post." New York Times, July 22, 1976, p. 11.

Miller, Arthur Selwyn. "Implications of Watergate: Some Proposals for Cutting the Presidency Down to Size." Hastings Constitutional Law Quarterly 2 (Winter 1975): 33-74.

National Academy of Public Administration. Watergate: Its Implications for Responsible Government: A Report Prepared by a Panel of the National Academy of Public Administration at the Request of the Senate Select Committee on Presidential Campaign Activities. March 1974. 143 p.

Neustadt, Richard E. "The Constraining of the President: the Presidency after Watergate." British Journal of Political Science 4 (October 1974): 383-397.

"Removing Politics from the Justice Department: Constitutional Problems with Institutional Reform." New York University Law Review 50 (May 1975): 366-435.

Rich, Spencer. "Senate Votes a Permanent Prosecutor." Washington Post, July 22, 1976, p. A-1.

----- "Watergate Reform Bill Advances." Washington Post, July 21, 1976, p. A-16.

Shabecoff, Philip. "President Calls for a Prosecutor of U.S. Officials." New York Times, July 20, 1976, p. 1.

Stuart, Peter. "Future 'Watergate' Bill Causes Lawyers Clash."
    Christian Science Monitor, May 27, 1976, p. 7.

Sundquist, James L. "Checking the Presidency." Washington Post,
    November 11, 1973, p. C-1.

Thompson, Fred D. "One Lawyer's Perspective on Watergate."
    Oklahoma Law Review 27 (Spring 1974): 226-234

Watergate, Politics, and the Legal Process. Washington, D.C.:
    American Enterprise Institute for Public Policy Research,
    1974. 89 p.

Watergate Special Prosecution Force: Report. Washington, D.C.:
    GPO, October 1975. 277 p.

Wicker, Tom. "Possible Precautions against a New Watergate."
    Washington Star, June 18, 1975, p. A-15.

Winter, Ralph K., Jr. Watergate and the Law, Political Campaigns
    and Presidential Power. Washington, D.C.: American Enter-
    prise Institute for Public Policy Research, 1974. 85 p.

"Witnesses Disagree on Watergate Reform Bill." Congressional
    Quarterly Weekly Report 33 (August 9, 1975): 1786-1787.

Index of Included Documents

Arranged by Source

663

Index of Subjects and Names

Federal reorganization : the executive
branch / compiled and edited by
Tyrus G. Fain, in collaboration with
Katharine C. Plant and Ross Milloy ;
with a foreword by Bert Lance. --
New York : Bowker, 1977.
    xxxiii, 671 p. : ill. ; 24 cm. --
(Public documents series)

    Includes bibliographies and index-
es.
    ISBN 0-8352-0981-4

                    (Cont. on next card)
                              77-23444